REVOLUTIONARY SOCIAL CHANGE IN COLOMBIA

Revolutionary Social Change in Colombia

The Origin and Direction of the FARC-EP

James J. Brittain

Foreword by James Petras

PlutoPress
www.plutobooks.com

First published 2010 by Pluto Press
345 Archway Road, London N6 5AA and
175 Fifth Avenue, New York, NY 10010

Distributed in the United States of America exclusively by
Palgrave Macmillan, a division of St. Martin's Press LLC,
175 Fifth Avenue, New York, NY 10010

www.plutobooks.com

British Library Cataloguing in Publication Data
A catalogue record for this book is available from the British Library

ISBN   978 0 7453 2876 8   Hardback
ISBN   978 0 7453 2875 1   Paperback

Library of Congress Cataloging in Publication Data applied for

This book is printed on paper suitable for recycling and made from fully managed and sustained
forest sources. Logging, pulping and manufacturing processes are expected to conform to the
environmental standards of the country of origin. The paper may contain up to 70% post
consumer waste.

10 9 8 7 6 5 4 3 2 1

Designed and produced for Pluto Press by
Curran Publishing Services, Norwich
Printed and bound in the European Union by
CPI Antony Rowe, Chippenham and Eastbourne

To Sarah: my best friend, my confidant, and, most of all, the love of my life

CONTENTS

FIGURES, TABLES, AND MAPS

FIGURES

TABLES

MAPS

ACRONYMS

ACCU	Peasant Self-Defence Units of Córdoba and Urabá
ACDEGAM	Association of Peasants and Ranchers of the Middle Magdalena
AED	accelerated economic development
ANUC	National Association of Peasants
ARENA	National Republican Alliance
ATPA	Andean Trade Preference Act
ATPDEA	Andean Trade Promotion and Drug Eradication Act
AUC	United Self-Defence Forces of Colombia
BP	British Petroleum
BPO	business process outsourcing
CDN	Canadian dollars
CERI	Canadian Energy Research Institute
CI	counterinsurgency
CIA	(US) Central Intelligence Agency
CIDA	Canadian International Development Agency
CODHES	Consultancy for Human Rights and Displacement
CONVIVIR	Community Security Associations/Private Security and Vigilance Cooperatives
CP	Communist Party
CPSU	Communist Party of the Soviet Union
CRB	Bolivarian Chain Radio – Voice of the Resistance
CTC	Confederation of Colombian Workers
CUT	Central Trade Union Federation of Colombia
DANE	National Administrative Department of Statistics
DAS	Department of Administrative Security
DEA	Drug Enforcement Agency
DIA	Defence Intelligence Agency
DMZ	Demilitarized Zone
ELN	National Liberation Army
ETB	Bogotá Telecommunications Company
EU	European Union
EZLN	Zapatista Army of National Liberation
FARC-EP (FARC)	Revolutionary Armed Forces of Colombia-People's Army
FDI	foreign direct investment
FEDECAFE	National Federation of Coffee Growers of Colombia
FENSUAGRO	National Federation of United Agricultural Farming Unions
FMLN	Farabundo Martí National Liberation Front
FSLN	Sandinista National Liberation Front
FTA (TLC)	Free Trade Agreement
FTAA	Free Trade Area of the Americas
GATT	General Agreement on Tariffs and Trade
GDP	Gross Domestic Product
IBRD	International Bank for Reconstruction and Development
ICA	International Coffee Agreement
ICRC	International Committee of the Red Cross

IDMC	Internal Displacement Monitoring Centre
IDP	internally displaced persons
IFI	international financial institution
ILI	international lending institution
ILO	International Labour Organization
IMF	International Monetary Fund
INCORA	Colombian Institute for Agrarian Reform
ISA	Interconexion Eléctrica
IUCN	World Conservation Union
JAC	Juntas Accíon Comunal
JICA	Japan International Cooperation Agency
LAZO (LASO)	Latin American Security Operation
M-19	19th of April Movement
MAS	Death to Kidnappers
MAS	Movement for Socialism
MBNC	Bolivarian Movement for a New Colombia
MNC	multinational corporation
MORENA	Movement of National Restoration
MOVICE	National Movement of Victims of State-Sponsored Crimes
NGO	Nongovernmental Organization
NSDD 221	National Security Decision Directive Number 221
OAS	Organization of American States
ONDCP	Office of National Drug Control Policy
OPEC	Organization of Petroleum Exporting Countries
PCC (CPP)	Colombian Communist Party
PCCC	Clandestine Colombian Communist Party
PLANTE	National Alternative Development Plan
POLO	Alternative Democratic Pole
PSC	Colombian Socialist Party
PSR	Revolutionary Socialist Party
PST-CITO	Workers Socialist Party
SAP	Structural Adjustment Program
SIDA	Swedish International Development Cooperation Agency
SOA	School of the Americas
UN	United Nations
UNCHR	United Nations Commission on Human Rights
UNDCP	United Nations Drug Control Programme
UNDP	United Nations Development Programme
UNEP	United Nations Environment Programme
UNODC	United Nations Office on Drugs and Crime
UP	Unión Patriótica
URNG	Guatemalan National Revolutionary Unity
USAID	United States Agency for International Development
USD	United States of America currency
VAT	Value-Added Tax
WB	World Bank
WHINSEC	Western Hemisphere Institute for Security Cooperation
WTO	World Trade Organization

ACKNOWLEDGMENTS

Society cannot and does not exist without the collective and cooperative nature of humanity. In lieu of this reality, the following book is not a work of one but the vigilant accomplishment made real through the support and encouragement of many. Although I am unable to recognize all the persons who have made this possible, it is necessary to highlight a few of the important people related to its realization.

Fittingly, the first two people that must be acknowledged, and to whom I owe my life and passion for social justice, are Mary Louise and Robert Finley Brittain. If not for these two unconditionally loving parents, courageous workers, and personal heroes, my life and dreams would have gone unfulfilled. To you both I express my love and appreciation for all you have done for me (and my family). Jim Sacouman, beside me throughout the inception and completion of this book, has been a true friend and whose commitment to the struggle for consequential social change remains an inspiration. I am mutually indebted to Jennie Hornosty whose time, ear, and ideas were a constant throughout the research of this work. James Petras and Garry Leech are also thanked as their insight broadened my understanding of the necessity and implications of change in Colombia.

As disturbing as it may be a space must be left blank for all those that cannot be mentioned in light of the reactionary period in which our society finds itself. During the process of this work, unknown numbers of people seeking an equitable, fair, and at peace Colombia were slaughtered. Over the past few years, I was fortunate enough to meet and listen to but a handful of these champions. Unfortunately, because of their murder, torture, and/or disappearance they can never be thanked. The space below is for those who have and continue to fight for social justice and an egalitarian Colombia. While life may be taken from their bodies their memory shall be carried on in the living (struggle).

As stated, the preceding highlights just a few of the essential people involved in the completion of this work. There is, however, one person who, above all, is responsible for this accomplishment. Sarah, it was truly through your understanding, sacrifice, and fearless love that this work was able to take place. It was through your patience and commitment, and the tolerance of our beautiful children, Grace, Emma, and Andrew, that I was continually inspired and capable to complete this work. Fittingly, the acknowledgement began with those that gave me life and ends with the woman who sustains it. I love you, Sarah, with all my heart – forever, and ever.

James J. Brittain

FOREWORD

The political practice of demonology, where politicians, journalists, mass media pundits, and academics attribute derogative labels and heinous behaviour to political regimes, leaders, and movements on the basis of unsubstantiated claims, has become common practice. What is worse, demonizing the the Revolutionary Armed Forces of Colombia-People's Army (FARC-EP) has spread from the top downward, from the right to the center-left, from the mass media to the progressive websites.

In recent years, no other mass social-political movement in Latin America has been demonized more than FARC-EP. Perhaps that is vice's tribute to virtue – as the FARC-EP, as Brittain's account thoroughly documents is the largest, longest-standing and most effective popular insurgency in the past quarter of a century. In contrast to the highly charged, poorly informed, ideologically driven diatribes emanating from the mass media, Brittain presents a detailed historical and empirically based survey of FARC's origins, organizational and political trajectory, as well as a rigorous account of the socioeconomic matrix out of which it grows and thrives. Brittain has written the definitive study of the FARC, one that will be a basic reference for years to come.

The most sustained and serious charges come from Washington and the current President of Colombia, who denounce the FARC-EP as a "criminal terrorist" and "narco-terrorist" organization. Washington has placed the FARC-EP on its list of "terrorist organizations," a policy which was subsequently followed by the European Union – but not by the majority of Latin American governments.

Brittain's historical account challenges these claims by demonstrating that the FARC originated in the early 1960s as a rebellious peasant movement, that expanded its territorial and social support over the next 40 years – particularly in the countryside – by defending peasant interests and communities from the depredations of landlord financed death squads and military repression.

The spread of the "terrorist" label took hold after September 11, 2001 as part of President Bush's global military-ideological offensive dubbed the "War on Terrorism." The specious basis of this campaign is evident in the preceding period (1999–2001) when the FARC-EP was recognized as a belligerent force, a legitimate interlocutor in peace negotiations by all the major European and Latin American regimes. During this period FARC-EP was invited to France, Spain, Scandinavia, the Low Countries, Mexico, and elsewhere to discuss the peace process. During the same period top US leaders and businesspeople, along with dozens of trade unionists and electoral politicians from across the spectrum, engaged the FARC-EP in a demilitarized zone in Colombia, where the United Nations mediated peace negotiations between the FARC and then President Pastrana. While Washington opposed the entire peace process and President Bill Clinton secured passage of a huge multi-billion dollar military package (Plan Colombia), the United States was not able to scuttle the process, or to pin the narco-terrorist label on the FARC-EP.

It was only after Washington went to war against Iraq and Afghanistan, and the US-dominated mass media launched a massive and sustained propaganda blitz labeling all critics and adversaries of US global militarism, that the "terrorist" label was pinned on the FARC. Under intense pressure from the elite media and under the scrutiny of the US security apparatus, many otherwise progressive intellectuals and writers caved in and joined the chorus labeling the FARC as "terrorist." What is astonishing in the progressive opinions' unseemly haste in slandering the FARC is the absolute and total ignorance of any facet of its history, social practice, political support, and its failed efforts to secure a political settlement. Between 1984 and 1988, the FARC agreed to a ceasefire with the Betancur regime and many of its militants opted for electoral politics by forming a mass-based political party, the Union Patriotica or Patriotic Union. Before, during, and after scoring substantial electoral victories in local, state, and national elections, the military-backed death squads murdered three of the Patriotic Union's (Unión Patriótica) presidential candidates. Over 5,000 legal electoral activists were killed. The FARC-EP was forced to return to armed opposition because of US and Colombian regime-sponsored mass terrorism. Between 1985 and 2008, tens of thousands of peasant leaders, trade unionists, human rights activists, and neighborhood leaders as well as journalists, lawyers, and congresspeople were killed, jailed, or driven into exile.

As Brittain demonstrates, the US-backed regime's campaign of rural terror and dispossession of 3 million peasants is the driving force accounting for the growth of the FARC-EP, and not "forced recruitment" and "narco-trafficking."

This book is based on extensive interviewing of FARC supporters, leaders, and local farmers covering several years, and provides a precise account of the relationship between coca production, the drug trade, money laundering, the military, the political system, and the FARC. What his findings reveal is that 95 percent of the earnings from the narcotic chain accrue to US-backed political parties, military officials, members of the Colombian Congress, and US and European banks. The FARC charges a transport and carry tax on the coca leaf buyers in exchange for safe passage through FARC-controlled territory.

Brittain's book posits a fundamental question for all democratic political practitioners and writers: How does one pursue equitable social policies and the defense of human rights under a terrorist state aligned with death squads and financed and advised by a foreign power, which has a public policy of physically eliminating their adversaries? Even as legal trade unions, Indian and peasant movements and political opposition members operate, they suffer high rates of attrition; not a week goes by without reported assassinations, disappearances, and forced flights abroad. Courageous judges and prosecutors receive daily death threats and have 24-hour bodyguards; some rarely sleep in their own homes. Parliamentary politics under the all pervasive threats of personal danger does not and cannot reform the terrorist apparatus, let alone do justice to the 4 million peasants forcibly displaced from their communities. Without institutional recourse and facing long-term, large-scale injustice, Brittain's thesis that the FARC-EP represents a legitimate force for political democracy and social change is plausible, even highly convincing.

James Petras

PREFACE

Throughout the past decade the Revolutionary Armed Forces of Colombia-People's Army (*Fuerzas Armadas Revolucionarias Colombianas-Ejército del Pueblo*, FARC-EP) has been cited as "the most powerful and successful guerrilla army in the world" (Petras and Brescia, 2000: 134; see also Petras and Veltmeyer, 2003a: 32). The FARC-EP is the largest and longest-established insurgency in Latin American history and unlike most twentieth-century guerrilla movements has sustained its revolutionary struggle (Veltmeyer and Petras, 2002: 82). While it can be described as "the most important military and political force in South America opposing imperialism" (Escribano, 2003: 299), Washington has preferred to classify the FARC-EP as the hemisphere's most dangerous terrorist organization. Uniquely Marxist-Leninist, the insurgency adheres to a structure viewed by many as no longer applicable within existing geopolitics.[1] In a period that has largely seen the demise, or cooptation, of ideologically motivated attempts at procuring social change via revolution, the FARC-EP promotes a radical transformation of Colombia's capitalist system through collective action and armed struggle. Yet amidst being a significant force in the global context the guerrilla group is oddly one of the world's least researched politico military organizations. As no in-depth scholarship has been conducted on the FARC-EP's ideological or practical relation to contemporary social change, there is much need for such a study.[2] The purpose of this book is to highlight the FARC-EP's revolutionary theory and practice, and show through what tangible mechanisms – if any – the guerrillas are supporting the creation of a new Colombia.

Many scholars, journalists, and governments have subjectively categorized today's FARC-EP as a movement void of ideological position, seeking individualistic economic power through violent means (Sweig and McCarthy, 2005: 18; LeGrand, 2003: 179; Collier, 2000; Collier and Hoeffler, 2000). Perplexingly, these critics have failed to carry out any first-hand analysis of the insurgency or its regions of influence. Testing the accuracy of such claims I examined existing works, public documents, and other material related to the FARC-EP and carried out five years' worth of field studies in guerrilla territory. Rather than blindly following the rhetoric of "experts," the mass media, or state-based reports, the research related to this book investigated the insurgency directly.

It would be impossible to study, detail, and comment on the FARC-EP's activities in every enclave of Colombia. Therefore, to conduct a realistic examination of the insurgency I specifically analyzed rural southwestern Colombia. The birthplace and continued stronghold of the FARC-EP, this region was perceived to be the best location to gauge the movement's true intentions. Methodologically, I employed naturalistic and participant observation alongside semi-structured in-depth interviews with members of the guerrilla group and civilians. The people interviewed belonged to various ethnic groups,[3] lived in a variety of locales, came from a range of occupational backgrounds, and were of both sexes. During observational research I took note of the socioeconomic, cultural, and political circumstances and conditions that existed throughout insurgent territory. I was also able to travel with the guerrillas on routine patrols to areas beyond FARC-EP encampments. This entailed trekking through jungles or whisking through river systems to visit other guerrillas, check on facilities and infrastructure projects, and attend meetings or everyday exchanges with general inhabitants. Throughout these excursions I was able to assess an array of issues. Did the FARC-EP appear to be superior to the rural population, or did the two interact as equals? In areas of governance, did the insurgency dominate policy or accept debate? Were the guerrillas offering services – such as education, health, justice, environmental protection – to the most exploited, or only for those within the FARC-EP itself? Attention was dually paid to the FARC-EP's ties to the rural political economy, especially important when trying to understand and measure the insurgency's revolutionary program.

While allowing me to observe their activities and internal relations, the FARC-EP was in no way connected to the choosing of those involved in the interview process. I made special arrangements guaranteeing that all interviewees and responses would be kept in strictest confidence. I eliminated all chances of anyone, including the guerrillas, knowing who was involved, what time the interview took place, and where the talks occurred. I also made a point of asking whether any respondents had been contacted by the FARC-EP concerning my activities. I was made aware of only one account where the FARC-EP had discussed the possibility of a *norteamericano* doing research with the local populace. At the end of a weekly educational class put on by the insurgency, an instructor (a FARC-EP member) informed the class of roughly two dozen peasants that a Canadian studying Colombia's civil war would be travelling through the department. The guerrilla stated a *sociólogo* would be asking questions pertaining to the area's social and political conditions, coca, and the economy, and most likely the people's feelings toward the FARC-EP. The respondent told me the instructor did not try to influence or "plant ideas in our heads" about what to say, but rather asked those in attendance to be as open as possible. At a later date another respondent conveyed how few have ever taken the time to hear what *campesinos* in today's Colombia have to say, and "knowing that this information will finally get to the public is all our community has wanted."

Divided into several chapters, this book offers a glimpse into where and why the FARC-EP came into existence, and what attempts have been made to alter Colombia's rural socioeconomic, cultural, and political conditions. The following chronicles the insurgency's formation, contextualizes Colombia's rural political economy, details methods employed by the dominant class to suppress the guerrillas' support, and analyzes the insurgency's revolutionary vigor and capacity to create social change. There has never before been a thoroughly conducted examination and revue of the FARC-EP's contemporary praxis and approach toward supporting an emancipatory transformation of Colombia. At the very least, this work will provide an in-depth examination of the FARC-EP's place within modern society, while situating its importance alongside other influential social movements and important struggles in Latin American history.

AN OVERVIEW OF THE REVOLUTIONARY ARMED FORCES OF COLOMBIA-PEOPLE'S ARMY (FARC-EP): A HISTORY OF RADICALISM IN THE COUNTRYSIDE

The FARC-EP's distinct history is but one of the reasons why a study of the insurgency is important. The FARC-EP demonstrate a breach from orthodox Marxist-Leninist claims that the peasantry will and can only be successful in the short term of a revolutionary struggle, eventually subsiding to industrial working-class movements. Over the past half century, the FARC-EP has proven itself capable of achieving power throughout various sectors of Colombia, as those from the countryside have played a very real role in organizing, sustaining, and leading the entire period of revolutionary activity. Amidst this reality it is still common to hear that peasants are too weak, simple, or disorganized to act as a consequential class body. If such assumptions are true, how did the FARC-EP come to be such a formidable force? An attempt to answer this question is found partially through an examination of the peasantry's prominent association with the Colombian Communist Party (*Partido Comunista Colombiano*, PCC).

THE PCC'S UNIQUE ORGANIC HISTORY AND RESPONSE TO A DUAL ECONOMY: PARTY AND SUPPORT BUILDING IN THE COUNTRYSIDE

According to renowned Latin Americanist Jorge Castañeda (1994: 19, 24–5), many communist parties (CPs) of Central and South America were both foreign-guided political organizations, based around an alien socioeconomic theory, and formally arranged in a way that excluded the majority of those living in the countryside. An examination of the PCC therefore plays an important role in understanding the historic relevance and atypical approach that emerged and continues in Colombia.

As with many communist organizations in Latin America during the twentieth century, the FARC-EP has not only a historic link to the national CP (that is, the PCC) but also internationalist connections to the Communist Party of the Soviet Union (CPSU) (Safford and Palacios, 2003: 356; Richani, 2002a: 64). While many important works have been devoted to examining the development of communism in Latin America, there has been a significant lapse in understanding the idiosyncratic construction of the Colombian left.[1] Although a handful have effectively examined Colombia's social-democratic left-of-center, many falter in their limited depiction of the relevant history of anti-capitalistic struggle via the PCC's promotion toward radical social change (see Green, 2004; Braun, 1986; Sharpless, 1978). Others have taken a different direction and over-generalize the Latin American left as being unified in its structural subservience to the interests of the USSR during the Cold War (Castañeda, 1994; Alexander, 1973, 1957). Such broad generalizations misrepresent the PCC's historic and contextual development, which, unlike most Latin American CPs, established itself beyond mere metropolitan populated centers, while openly (or clandestinely, depending on the time period) supporting a revolution against the Colombian capitalist class and state.[2]

It has often been claimed that Latin American CPs failed to functionally organize the rural populace as a revolutionary force (see Fairbairn, 1974: 30–1). Positions such as these demonstrate a lack of knowledge or underestimation of the PCC's programmatic formula, and strategic understanding of Colombia's dual economy.[3] Following the PCC's formal accreditation in 1930, the Party immediately called for "social transformation, unionism, and the education of the working class" and quickly established programs "for the improvement of *both urban and rural workers'* rights and labour conditions" (Osterling, 1989: 184, 185 , italics added).[4] The intelligence of the PCC was in understanding that the "improvements in conditions" for rural and urban workers were, like the dual economy, different in social, economic, cultural, and political scope, thus differing responses needed to be employed.

Jorge P. Osterling (1989: 83) wrote how the PCC at this time enacted a practice of mobilizing "peasant leagues in rural regions" while simultaneously organizing "popular fronts in urban areas," thereby establishing a cross-cultural and geographical class-linkage between city and countryside (see also Brittain, 2005f). Hence, in Colombia's dual economy there would need to be varying forms of organization in relation to the national struggle (Maullin, 1973: 22). Acknowledging the rural membership, the PCC noted the need to create liberating conditions specific to regional class conditions.[5] For those in the countryside this meant supporting organic defensive structures against (state-supported) large landholder-based violence. Hence,

> the policy known as mass self-defence is not an invention of the Colombian Communists. This form of struggle was evolved by the peasants themselves. By supporting it and incorporating it in its own line – not as an aim in itself but as a means of advance towards higher forms of struggle – our Party showed that it had its finger on the pulse of Colombian life and took cognizance of all its aspects.
>
> (Gomez, 1972: 248)

Although it was ratified in the 1930s, accounts show the Party supported rural militancy from the 1920s onward.[6] Members organized seizures of land, strikes, protests, and established several enclaves and self-defense groups in areas of southern Colombia that not only remained communist-based socio-politically controlled regions, but were materially able to withstand – and in some cases intimidate – state forces while maintaining the subsistence needs of the local populace (Green, 2004: 60–1; Osterling, 1989: 296; Henderson, 1985: 318n.38; Gott, 1973: 280–1; 1970: 231–2; Alexander, 1973: 46; 1957: 252; Poppino, 1964: 5; Hobsbawm, 1963: 17). By the 1940s, the Party had "established a strong rural influence" in specific regions of the countryside (Wickham-Crowley, 1992: 145).

> Unlike most areas of Latin America, where communism gained strength in urban and labor-export enclaves, in Colombia the Communist Party developed its greatest influence in rural areas, particularly the coffee regions, and among landless peasants and small farmers.
>
> (Chernick, 2007: 432n.10)

In 1958, the Colombian peasantry made up 40 percent of the members who attended the PCC Party Conference (Wickham-Crowley, 1992: 145-6).[7] Less than a decade later, at the Tenth Congress of the Party (January 1966), the proportion of peasants had grown to 48 percent (Gott, 1970: 27). Historian Catherine LeGrand, demonstrating the uniqueness of the PCC and its relation to the countryside, noted that the formation of the Party occurred during

> a period of agrarian unrest in coffee regions in the eastern and central mountain ranges. Although numerically small, the PCC involved itself almost immediately in these struggles over Indian communal lands, the rights of tenant farmers, and public land claims. This early rural orientation of the Communist Party in Colombia and particularly its success in putting down roots in several areas of the countryside, some not far from Bogotá, is unusual in the Latin American context.
>
> (LeGrand, 2003: 175)

The PCC illustrated an exceptional approach in relation to other CPs. Its uniqueness was in its method of organizing not only the industrial and margin-alized urban working class, but also the growing mass of semi-proletarianized workers in the countryside.[8] Colombian historian Gonzalo G. Sánchez (1985: 795) documented that the late 1940s and 1950s saw the PCC become the primary instrument for organizing peoples into politically motivated collectives (see also Marulanda, 2000; Gomez, 1972). Even critical scholars, bombarded by proof, acknowledged that "during the 1950s the Colombian Communist Party achieved what countless groups throughout the hemisphere would fail to do later: it created a mass base, with a significant peasant following" (Casta-ñeda, 1994: 75). One leading scholar on Latin American communist influence and formation during the twentieth century highlighted the power of this strategy by commenting how the "renewed Communist activity in the rural parts of Colombia is even more important than growing Communist influence in the ranks of organized labour" (Alexander, 1963: xiv). Even Régis Debray

(1969: 511), who criticized much of the left's methods in Colombia, applauded this "atypical" approach toward Marxism (see also Aguilar, 1968: 44n.2). Colombia had proven to be the "most successful example of communist influence among peasants" (Hennessey, 1972: 15n.12).

Apart from demonstrating how rural inroads were made by the PCC, it is important to put into context the Party's pre-accreditation period. Prior to the formal establishment of the PCC, peasants had been organized beside communists in the central mountain ranges and Magdalena River since 1918 (Urrutia, 1969: 55). In fact, communists were active throughout much of Colombia's urban and rural territories during the entire post-Great War period (Decker and Duran, 1982: 80-1). Some sources have dated the roots of the PCC even earlier, as left-wing workers' collectives began to mobilize around Marxist ideals during the 1910s (Osterling, 1989: 184–5).[9] Interestingly, Colombians were rallying behind Marxism well before the Russian Revolution of 1917 or the landing of any external communist (Decker and Duran, 1982: 80–1; Urrutia, 1969: 55, 81–3; Comisión del Comité Central, 1960). This is important as it contradicts claims that Marxism was a foreign-delivered ideology. Some suggested communist sympathies arrived to Colombia in 1924 through Russian Silvestre Savisky or by way of Joseph Zack in the late 1920s (Alexander, 1973: 36; 1957: 243). Such accounts undermine the activities of domestic Marxists.[10] The accreditation of communist formation in Colombia must be ascribed to those who had been organizing long before foreign influence. It was these individuals who founded the Party's roots in the early 1920s.[11] Then, alongside various groups with leftist sympathies, a group of Colombians created the Revolutionary Socialist Party in 1926 (Partido Socialista Revolucionario, PSR). Within two years the PSR became affiliated with the Third International (Comintern), and by 1930 evolved into the PCC (Osterling, 1989: 185). In 1935, official internationalist relations between the USSR and the PCC were solidified (Aguilar, 1968: 264; Poppino, 1964: 194).

Some have tried to make the case that Latin American Marxist activity only came to fruition in a post-1917 Soviet context. In other words, communism in Central and South America is not an organic product of the intellectual and political capacity of the working class, but rather a theoretical political import (see Castañeda, 1994; Munck, 1984b). The outline above should serve to counter such claims, and the next section further clarifies the intimate links between the PCC and the early formation of the FARC-EP, while highlighting how much scholarship related to the subject has been misleading.

AN EXAMINATION OF THE PCC AND FARC-EP'S FORMATION: A RESPONSE TO A LIMITED ANALYSIS

Many have claimed the FARC-EP "emerged directly out of the Colombian Communist Party and radical Liberalism" (see LeGrand, 2003: 175).

In southern Tolima the guerrillas were drawn from members of the Communist

Party and Liberal Party. The Communists were led by Isauro Yosa (alias Major Lister) and Jacobo Pias Alape (alias Charro Negro), all of whom were peasants. Among the latter group, the current legendary leader of the FARC, Manuel Marulanda Velez (Tiro Fijo) started his revolutionary career.

(Richani, 2002a: 60)[12]

While partially correct, such depictions over-simplify the programmatic history and strategic formation of the PCC and the evolution of armed struggle in Colombia.[13] For example, of those listed above, none were of a Liberal persuasion during the 1950s but were all members of the PCC. In fact, Yosa, Alape, and Marulanda were representatives of the Party's Central Committee (Cala, 2000: 57–8; Pomeroy, 1968: 312). In response to long-made assertions that the FARC-EP has extensive roots in a bilateral Communist–Liberal alliance, the insurgency's beginnings are systemically aligned with the PCC while Liberals remained an insignificant factor in its formative history (Avilés, 2006: 36; Safford and Palacios, 2003: 355; Kline, 1999: 18; de la Peña, 1998: 331, 353; Osterling, 1989: 187).[14] To state otherwise negates the breadth of chronological information outlining the structure of the PCC in relation to the FARC-EP's pre-inception via the self-defense groups of southern Colombia during the mid-twentieth century (Arenas, 1972; Gomez, 1972).

For decades the Liberal Party proved to do very little to change Colombian political policy, while the PCC mobilized sectors of the populace into specific defensive networks (Sánchez, 1985: 795).[15] The Party deeply supported the development of political enclaves outside the vicious power struggle of Colombia's two dominant parties. Timothy P. Wickham-Crowley (1994: 556) affirmed that "there is no doubt that those regions that became safe havens from the violence – the 'peasant republics' – historically were mainly rural islands of Communist Party influence in a sea of Liberals and Conservatives."

It is apparent when examining those connected to the PCC and Liberal parties that clear material differences existed. Unlike the Liberal "guerrillas," who stole and laundered for individual profit and revenge, the PCC organized a class-conscious movement that rallied against the state and the ruling class therein (Chavez, 2007; Gomez, 1972; Williamson, 1965). During the 1950s it was the communists that made Liberals aware of the exploitive social relations surrounding the means of production in the countryside, the coercive responsibility of the state to maintain such processes, and encouraged them to leave behind their "sectarian vision of struggle" (Chavez, 2007: 93).

In time, "the Liberal Party disowned those members who aligned themselves with the PCC and its support of 'class struggle'" (de la Peña, 1998: 331). Certain regions saw the Liberal Party commit violence towards the Party, as the PCC continued to organize persons into the self-defense collectives. In the department of Tolima, Liberal cadres joined divisions of the Colombian military and carried out aggressive actions against the communist communities (Chavez, 2007: 94). Hence, the self-defense groups that would later form the FARC-EP were never constructs of social-democratic elements of Liberal leftist factions, but solely from the PCC (Gomez, 1972; see also Marulanda, 2000:

34, 37; de la Peña, 1998: 331; 353; Wickham-Crowley, 1992: 331; Hobday, 1986: 363; Pomeroy, 1968: 312). According to political scientist William Avilés (2006: 36), it is unquestionable that the FARC-EP "emerged under the leadership of the Communist Party and operated with the support of peasants who sought refuge from the repression of La Violencia."

The PCC's rural self-defense strategy and the FARC-EP

The preceding section talked of violent turmoil during the mid-twentieth century. Between 1948 and 1958 a period known as *la Violencia* swept across much of Colombia.[16] Under the pretence of ending this decade of politically and economically motivated violence, the leadership of the Liberal and Conservative parties constructed a truce known as the National Front agreement (1958), which, according to some, ushered in a period of "liberal–bourgeois order" (Fals Borda, 1969: 150–1). The "agreement" called for a sharing of political office between the two principal parties, with all legislative bodies being divided equally regardless of electoral results (Kline, 1983: 54). International relations scholar Doug Stokes (2005: 68) argued that the National Front "served to alternate power between ... aligned sections of the Colombian Conservative and Liberal elite while strengthening the Colombian armed forces to suppress popular reforms" (see also Chernick, 2007: 53; Avilés, 2006: 25, 152n.1; Hylton, 2003: 55–6; LeGrand, 2003: 173; Dix, 1967: 404; Lieuwen, 1961: 87, 89). Others examined how the National Front specifically targeted the PCC's momentum during the 1950s by structurally eliminating "the legitimacy of a multiparty system and electoral competition" (Ferreyra and Segura, 2000: 24).

We must remember that the PCC was increasingly consolidating both rural and urban workers, thereby becoming a small but significant political force – or potential threat and economic liability from the view of Colombia's dominant class (Shugart, 1992; Alexander, 1957).[17] The PCC was quickly barred from the conventional political process (Chernick, 2007: 53).[18] Avilés (2006: 32) claimed that the "pact was not only an agreement to mitigate the history of violent conflict over the spoils of the state between the two parties, but it was also a pact within Colombia's establishment to co-opt and marginalize more radical alternatives" (see also Stokes, 2005: 68; Ferreyra and Segura, 2000: 24, 34n.7; Peeler, 1985: 97–9).[19] Criminologist Alfredo Schulte-Bockholt (2006: 102–3) asserted that it "further cemented oligarchic rule by excluding other groups from the political process, particularly those representative of the urban poor and the peasants," the very groups the PCC mobilized (see also Berry, Hellman and Solaún, 1980; Dix, 1967: 129-168).[20] It:

> continued the trend that had existed since the turn of the century, facilitating the development of the country in the direction that political and economic elites saw fit. The input from representatives of peasants, independent unions, and leftist political forces in policymaking would be limited and/or excluded.
>
> (Avilés, 2006: 32)

The growing political momentum of the communists had been stopped in its tracks, especially in the countryside, as the PCC was subsequently made illegal (Rochlin, 2003: 97; Ferreyra and Segura, 2000: 34n.7; Ratliff, 1976: 57; Poppino, 1964: 7–8; see also Brittain, 2005f).[21] Essentially the National Front enabled the dominant political parties, which shared a unified programmatic structure, to centralize political power among the elite (Avilés, 2006: 25, 152n1; Stokes, 2005: 68; Hylton, 2003: 55–6; Maullin, 1973: 125n2; Dix, 1967: 404; Payne, 1968).[22] However, the monopoly of power would not stay within the confines of politics.

Beyond the political restriction of the National Front once mobilized peasants were further destabilized through a newly adopted economic model entitled accelerated economic development (AED). Developed by Nova Scotia-born economist Lauchlin Currie, AED depicted campesino production methods as perpetuating the "mal-use, misuse and under-use of human resources," coupled with the "underutilization of the county's best lands" (Currie, 1971: 887; Dix, 1967: 26; see also Ross, 2006; Currie, 1981, 1967, 1966, 1950; INCORA, 1963: 17). The rationale behind AED was to maximize capital through the concentration of agriculture, with industrialization by large landowners.[23] Consecutive administrations supported the "development of larger capitalist-operated farms that received extensive state support and assistance," going so far as to use violent repression, as opposed to socioeconomic policies of reform, to perpetuate efficiency (Avilés, 2006: 27, 37, 40; see also Cruz and Ramírez, 1994: 101). Some argued that expanding agro-industry in Colombia was "as important in some ways as the continuing industrial expansion" (Hagen, 1971: 202).

According to Jenny Pearce (1990a: 92), "large-scale commercial farms expanded dramatically in the 1960s" throughout the southwest. Legislation was soon aimed at assisting capitalist interests of diversification, market expansion, and expanded profits through export-based production, which structurally disenfranchised an immense small-scale rural-producing population. Land concentration policies soon saw a decrease in lots for the majority of small producers, a massive rise in displacement, and an influx in landlessness amongst the rural population.

> Between 1960 and 1970 large commercial farms of 200–500 hectares increased their area by 21 percent; by 1970 the latifundio (farms over 50 hectares) held approximately 77.7 percent of the arable land, a slight increase over 1960. The minifundio (less than 10 hectares) decreased in number from 926,000 in 1969 to 860,000 in 1970; the landless, estimated to be about 190,000 in 1973, were increasing.
>
> (Fernández, 1979: 56)

There was a threefold effect during this period. First, there was an increased reserve army of labor in the urban centers, reducing the cost of labor while increasing surplus profits for industrial capitalists.[24] Second, there was further monopolization of rural land in the hands of urban-based capitalists, already large landowners, and cattle ranchers (the class to which Currie belonged[25]).

Last was an attempt to delink an increasingly mobilized peasantry from political change (Brittain, 2005b). Recognizing the democratic closing of society via the National Front agreement, and the violent suppression of primitive accumulation during the pre-and-post-AED period, antagonistic elements connected to the PCC strategically furthered subsistence-level self-defense collectives across southern Colombia (Gomez, 1972: 250–3). Rather than succumbing to political-economic repression, these communities soon challenged Colombian class interests and their imperialist alliance.[26]

The militant sociopolitical construction of the self-defense groups: negating passive interpretations

Virtually all scholars of Colombian politics and history have documented the infamous "independent republics" of the 1950s and 1960s as autonomous enclaves of radical peasants.[27] Many, however, minimize or altogether ignore the ideological and material connection of these communities to the PCC, and their subsequent relation to the guerrillas.[28] The FARC-EP was formed on May 27, 1964. This constitutes the "official date of origin of the FARC-EP," as it witnessed a series of significant US-supported military operations carried out against peoples nestled in the Marquetalia region of southern Tolima, Huila, and Cauca (FARC-EP, 1999: 143; see Map 1.1).[29] Two years later, the insurgency became officially recognized as a guerrilla movement during the Tenth Congress of the PCC (Gott, 1970: 518–21, 255–6; Pomeroy, 1968: 308–10). Prior to Congress the guerrilla movement established itself as a goal-oriented defense-based peasant collective[30] in the face of extreme political and militaristic coercion.[31] Working with several thousand rural civilians, the PCC organized networks of cooperation and security in response to expanding capitalist interests which sought the elimination of primitive accumulation through state-induced repression (Livingstone, 2003: 180; FARC-EP, 1999: 15; Pearce, 1990a: 60; Gilhodés, 1970: 433, 445).

Attempts were made to establish an uncorrupted stable society based on local control and a new approach to counter repressive centralized state power through the construction of self-defense communities in various rural areas of the southwest (Simons, 2004: 43; LeGrand, 1986: 163; Petras, 1968: 335).[32] "A real peasant movement, a response to official violence and military repression," such groups were the basis on which the FARC-EP was constructed (LeGrand, 2003: 176).[33]

> In their areas of influence they [the guerrilla/PCC leadership] encouraged the peasant communities to share the land among the residents and created mechanisms for collective work and assistance to the individual exploitation of parcels of land and applied the movement's justice by collective decision of assemblies of the populace. These became areas with a new mentality and social and political proposals different from those offered by the regime. The decisive factor was the presence in power of the people themselves.
> (FARC-EP, 1999: 15; see also Ramírez Tobón, 1981)

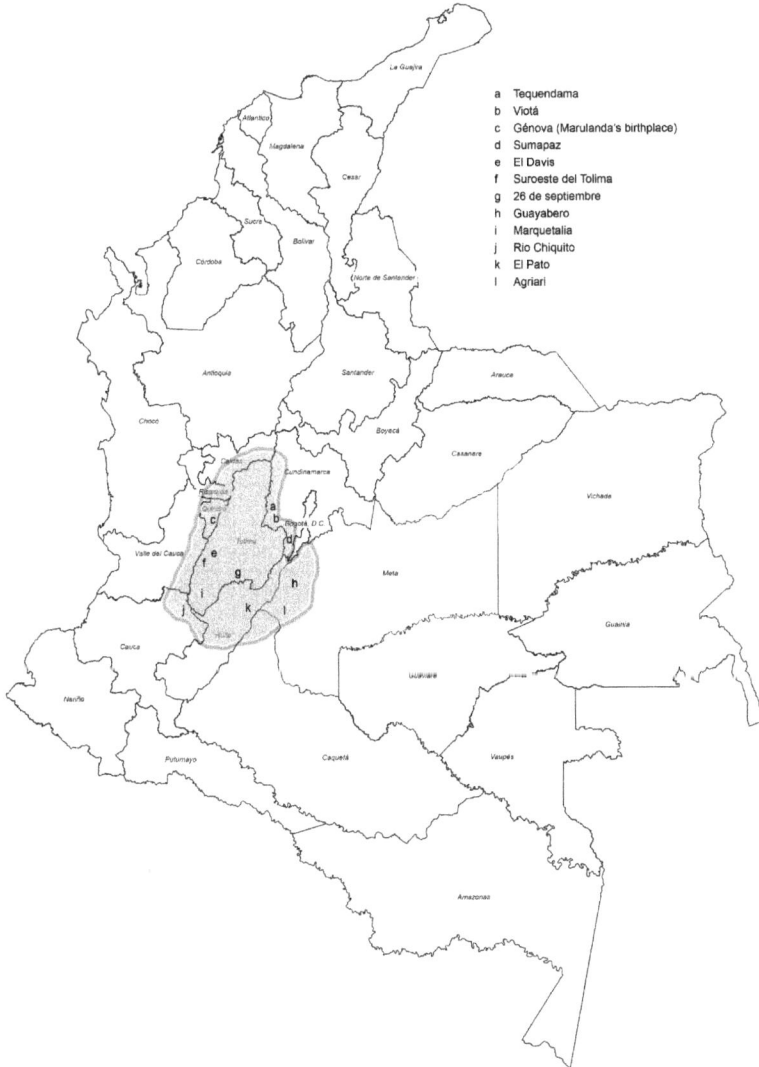

a   Tequendama
b   Viotá
c   Génova (Marulanda's birthplace)
d   Sumapaz
e   El Davis
f   Suroeste del Tolima
g   26 de septiembre
h   Guayabero
i   Marquetalia
j   Rio Chiquito
k   El Pato
l   Agriari

Map 1.1 Area of PCC self-defense communities and early FARC-EP extension, late 1950s to mid-1960s
Sources: Safford and Palacios, 2003: 355; Richani, 2002a: 60; Osterling, 1989: 280; Walton, 1984: 75; Gott, 1973: 282; 1970: 233–36; Huizer, 1970: 404–5.
Note: Most likely because of an error in printing, the map utilized within Huizer (1970) should have been more accurately placed within Gilhodés (1970).

There are differing viewpoints on the development and purpose of the self-defense groups. Some recognized the collectives as autonomous passive alternatives to a repressive state (Walton, 1984: 94, 99). Others saw the communities as strategic centers of grassroots communist-based organizing (Osterling, 1989; Gomez, 1972; Pomeroy, 1968). Arguing the former, Avilés (2006: 36) claimed the communities were "attempting to build sanctuaries independent from the national government." Rural sociologist Ernest Feder (1971: 189) stated that the groups were made up of a "peaceful nuclei of peasants operating land collectively in relatively isolated regions of the country." LeGrand (2003: 175–6) documented how many peasants came to view the state as the people's primary enemy, and to avoid this threat, fled to create regions of safety. After *la Violencia*, vast numbers "withdrew into isolated frontier regions where they put aside their guns and turned to agriculture once again" (LeGrand, 1986: 163).

In essence, much of the writing related to the communities paints a largely pacifist picture of how "these Communist-influenced rural redoubts became refuge zones for peasants fleeing from the partisan violence" (LeGrand, 2003: 175). Some have even depicted the PCC zones as lacking revolutionary vigor. For example, Petras (1968: 355) portrayed the communities as a stagnant sociopolitical and cultural alternative to state repression.[34]

These almost romantic accounts of communist organizing in rural Colombia are accurate in some respects but fall short in their recognition of the militant construction and political goal of the self-defense groups. Describing her recollection of the PCC's involvement with the self-defense groups of the 1950s and 1960s, Maria Ovidia Díaz stated, "the campesino self-defense groups were an organization that sought to address the daily needs of the farmers. In its origins these campesino self-defense groups were organized to protect the well-being of the community" (quoted in Obando and Velásquez, 2004). Far from docile, these sociopolitical collectives sought a peace-filled life through mechanisms that would defend their alternative development projects from reaction. The self-defense groups did not exist as individualized non-violent social organizations, but rather understood that objective security was needed to face dominant class-interests (see Gomez, 1972: 252–3). Therefore:

> with the overall policy of preparing for guerrilla action (a policy subsequently pursued in other zones as well) intensive work was done to build up stocks of supplies for the future detachments. Large stores of provisions were cached in the mountains .... A plan of hostilities was worked out in advance.
>
> (Gomez, 1972: 253)

Simons (2004: 41) remarked that as a result of *la Violencia*, peasants had to become "organized in self-defense units by the Communist Party ... forced to take military initiatives to avoid extermination." In formation the groups illustrated a significant threat for the rural elite and a potential time bomb for the state (Crandall, 2002: 60). The communities – arranged in a localized dual strategy of sociopolitical cultural development and defensive measures to sustain alternative collective societies – did not promote a non-militant autonomous existence. They were rather organized communists, part of a larger network vying for a revolutionary shift in the social relations of production (see Peace and Socialism, 1966).

Several scholars have described the sociological make-up of the regional self-defense groups as communities that formed themselves into administrative social structures independent of centralized state powers (Simons, 2004: 42; Ramírez Tobón, 1981; Gilhodés, 1970; Guzmán Campos, Fals Borda, Umaña Luna, 1964; 1962). At the beginning of the 1950s, increased migrations of peasants and rural wage laborers were occurring in areas where the PCC was organizing. Some of the first were El Davis, Tolima, and El Pato, situated on the borders of Huila and Caquetá, which later became the first regions to house the FARC-EP.[35] These networks showed how men, women, youths, and children could facilitate alternative social development (Gomez, 1972: 249).

A community leader with executive powers, a parcelador (who distributed the land and assumed the role of judge in the event of conflict), and a general secretary (in charge of publicity and information). They formed a kind of council, together with representatives from each of the veredas (rural neighborhoods), in which the representatives of the party and of the youth and women's organization also participated. The women's organization was responsible for promoting certain elements of cooperativism in the home, such as the collectively used sewing machine and for taking care of the schools. Other elements of collective life were in evidence as well in Pato (and, with variations, in other zones) including a collective cane distillery and a library (in general, of a very political nature). Literacy campaigns were waged and classes in politics, to which attendance was compulsory, were given.

(Gilhodés, 1970: 437–8)

This sheds light on the PCC's relation to the self-defense groups; it is manipulative to call them "independent republics." Led by members of the Central Committee, the networks would later be responsible for founding the FARC-EP (Ferro Medina and Uribe Ramón, 2002: 32–4; de la Peña, 1998: 331; 353). Hence, guerrilla warfare was "the intensification" of an already existing class-based struggle (Lenin, 1965f: 216). As noted by Alfredo Molano (2000: 25), "Marulanda ... organized a community based on economic self-management and military self-defense. This was the first of the guerrilla bases that later came to be known as 'Independent Republics.'" Part of a multifaceted plan of class struggle, the communities soon became a potential risk to the existing class structure, and then had to be suppressed (Gomez, 1972: 249, 251–2; see also Crandall, 2002: 60).

The growth and demise of Marquetalia: The US/Colombian state's response to rural (communist) development

The success of the communities led sectors of the political and economic elite to see:

a threat in the existence of the self-defense zones. It realized that they were not a sign of relative equilibrium in the class balance, but a manifestation of class struggle. Consequently, a plan of aggression against these zones began to be elaborated in 1957. It envisaged five stages: civilian action, economic blockade, military action, unification of the zone, and its "return to the orbit of national life". In 1960–63 the government began to carry out this plan. (Gomez, 1972: 251; see also Sánchez and Meertens, 2001: 178–84)

Under the rubric of Plan Lazo,[36] the United States and the Colombian state implemented an extensive tactical campaign entitled "Operation Marquetalia," to disrupt the progress of the self-defense groups (Sánchez and Meertens, 2001: 204n.4; de la Peña, 1989: 354; Gott, 1973: 299). It was in 1964, however, that the most aggressive military campaign in Colombia's modern history occurred, with orders to "retake the municipality of Marquetalia, a communist hamlet in the extreme south of Tolima, on the border of Cauca and Huila" (Hylton, 2006: 56). The mission suboperations "Cabeza" and "Soberanía" added a two-pronged military attack aimed at killing PCC/guerrilla leader Manuel Marulanda Vélez and eliminating the southwestern self-defense groups (Ruiz, 2001: 110; Lartéguy, 1970: 147–8). Accompanied by Colombia's entire fleet of Iroquois helicopters, over 20,000 Colombian forces and US advisors conducted aerial bombardments and ground assaults against the region (Ruiz, 2001: 109). Well before its use in Vietnam, the Colombian Air and Armed Forces also utilized US-supplied napalm during the campaign to desolate the Marquetalia valley (Hylton, 2006: 40; O'Shaughnessy and Branford, 2005: 25; Dudley, 2004: 10; Sánchez and Meertens, 2001: 204n.4; Cala, 2000: 58; Cockcroft, 1972: 117n.1, 134). Some have even said that Marquetalia gave the United States "the opportunity to try out napalm" (Walker III, 2001: 24; see also Grandin, 2006: 98).[37]

To illustrate the importance of the operation, all we need do is underline its monetary and tactical costs. By mid-1964, the Colombian state had devoted over US$17 million alongside one-third of its entire army to defeat Marulanda and the network of self-defense communities (Alejandro and Billon, 1999; de la Peña, 1989: 354; Gott, 1970: 249; Lartéguy, 1970: 148). Using general inflation rates, the operation would today total almost US$3 billion. Marquetalia became a defining moment in Colombian history.

Winning in Marquetalia was essential for US/Colombian forces. Marquetalia had become an objective and symbolic capacity of the people's ability to fend off the state while partially existing outside a capitalist system. The communities had become "virtually autonomous principalities whose borders were not violated by government forces" because of the defensive measures employed by the guerrilla (Walton, 1984: 94). A very real need existed to quell stories circulating of how peasants and guerrillas were able to create and hold power for themselves (see Gilhodés, 1970: 445). The stories held some truth as the state had been unsuccessful at hampering the PCC's growth inside Marquetalia, Rio Chiquito, El Pato, Guayabero, and other regions through southern Colombia throughout the 1950s and early 1960s.[38] Over a span of several years, the state saw thousands of troops defeated by the self-defense forces in the southwest (Osterling, 1989: 294; Gomez, 1972: 251; Gott, 1970: 248; Lartéguy, 1970: 146).[39] While in some areas "troops easily dealt with groups of young patriots who, influenced by romantic idealism, had taken arms, ignoring the actual conditions in which they had to operate," Marquetalia (and Marulanda) proved far more complex.

> In Marquetalia however – and this is an indicative fact – the resistance offered by the self-defence detachments (backed by a nationwide protest movement against the aggression) repulsed an expeditionary corps of seven thousand men in early 1962 and compelled the [class] enemy to give up the operation.
>
> (Gomez, 1972: 251)

With much of the region destroyed, Operation Marquetalia was a success (see Gott, 1973: 301). Yet in the context of Plan Lazo, it is hard to characterize Marquetalia as a victory: Marulanda remained alive and well, the self-defense groups stayed intact, the organizational presence of the PCC continued in southern Colombia (Hylton, 2006: 56; Stokes, 2005: 73). For example, during Operation Cabeza, "the seemingly easily ensured victory proved much more difficult to achieve. While the government's troops prevailed, that they struggled to defeat a few hundred guerrillas was an embarrassment" (Crandall, 2002: 60). Cabeza characterized both the failure of the state to achieve its goals and the surprising ability of the guerrilla forces to function and defend zones when targeted.

A mere 50–200 combatants were stationed throughout Marquetalia at the time of the attack (Simons, 2004: 41; Crandall, 2002: 60; Osterling, 1989: 295). Alongside preparations for the strike, the guerrillas successfully evacuated all families from the area (Livingstone, 2003: 180; Gomez, 1972: 252). The entire community of 4,000[40] was able to flee due to the intelligence gathering and organizational preparation of the guerrillas (Stokes, 2005: 73; Livingstone, 2003: 180; Ruiz, 2001: 110; Pearce, 1990a: 64; Osterling, 1989: 281, 294; Gilhodés, 1970: 444). The rural leaders in the community knew of the state's mission and "anticipating the attack, the peasants evacuated children, elderly people, and women who could not fight" (Richani, 2002a: 62; see also Gomez, 1972: 252).[41] Within months of Operation Marquetalia the guerrillas were also able to retake the zone (Gott, 1970: 254). The legend of Marquetalia is still shared by everyone from the countryside to the café – a legend that details how Marulanda proved incredibly resourceful in taking on US/Colombian forces (Alejandro and Billon, 1999). It symbolically

> marks the start of renewed armed resistance .... The army symbolically took the Marquetalia region, but in spite of its new anti-guerrilla conceptions, it was militarily impossible to wipe out the seed of struggle, which had sprouted from these lands. The seed is the origin of the FARC-EP.
>
> (FARC-EP, 1999: 17–18)

Marquetalia became the turning point in Colombia's revolutionary struggle. Immediately following the campaign a significant segment of the rural population moved to support the guerrillas (Gott, 1970: 251–2; see also Chernick, 2007: 55–6; de la Peña, 1998: 360).[42] After multiple attempts to find a peaceful solution to the internal strife, even offering to surrender himself so as to protect civilians in the communities, Marulanda claimed that no other avenue but armed struggle was available (Braun, 2007: 29; Maullin, 1973: 131n.13). Contrary to claims that the PCC sought "a peaceful road to revolution,"[43] the Party supported Marulanda and acknowledged that many forms of struggle (including "armed action") were needed to achieve change in Colombia (Ratliff, 1976: 70, 73; Vieira, 1970: 22; 1963: 17–19; Pomeroy, 1968: 312–13).[44] In short, Marquetalia produced both the legend of Marulanda and the victorious rise of the FARC-EP (Gomez, 1972: 253–4).

The linkages between Marulanda, the FARC-EP leadership, and the PCC

As might be expected, the FARC-EP's founding commander-in-chief of the Central High Command[45] (sometimes referred to as the commander in chief of the Central General Staff) was Manuel Marulanda Vélez.[46] Known for having "elements of political and military genius," Marulanda's story is one of great complexity and importance (Ruiz, 2001: 8). Even though he has been cited as the greatest revolutionary peasant leader in the history of the Americas, and will forever remain one of the most important figures in Colombian history, very little is known about the political and sociological origins of "Tiro Fijo" outside Colombia.[47] While any text worth its salt contains an account of the once commander-in-chief, most fail to address the origins of his ideology.

Like many of those who make up the FARC-EP Secretariat,[48] Marulanda was the son of a peasant. As a young adult he became a peasant producer, and at times a wage-based agricultural worker (Alejandro and Billon, 1999; Pearce, 1990a: 56). Other accounts have claimed that prior to his involvement with the guerrillas Marulanda was a lower-level employee in public works, and specifically the Ministry of Transportation in Tolima and Caldas, in the area of highway construction (Braun, 2007: 29; Maullin, 1973: 129n.2; Gilhodés, 1970: 444).[49] Whatever his occupational history, it is imperative to outline Marulanda's politics, especially his relation to the PCC.

Any statement describing Marulanda as a Liberal rather than an orthodox communist and member of the PCC is seriously misleading. It is true that Marulanda briefly associated himself with the Liberal party as an adolescent.[50] Yet his ideology and sociopolitical tendencies resonate with the doctrines of a communist program, a political theory he faithfully followed for well over a half-century without deviation (Lozano Guillén, 2001; Marulanda, 2000; Alejandro and Billon, 1999; Alape, 1989). During his early and mid-teens, Marulanda was, as a result of his socio-geography not his politics, historically aligned with the leftist tendencies of the Liberal Party in rural Colombia. This was due, in part, to the fact that he was born into "a peasant family deeply influenced by the violent political struggles between Colombia's Liberals and Conservatives" (Cala, 2000: 57; see also Wickham-Crowley, 1992: 331). By the time he was in his early 20s, however, Marulanda clearly became aligned with Marxism-Leninism and abandoned any social-democratic ideology (Cala, 2000: 57–8; Alejandro and Billon, 1999; Pearce, 1990a: 56; Maullin, 1973:

129n.2). Already politically astute in Marxism, Marulanda's education in Marxism-Leninism can also be traced to Jacobo Arenas[51] (Cala, 2000: 57–8; see also Dudley, 2004; Molano, 2000).

By the end of the 1940s, Marulanda had become strongly involved in the PCC, and in 1952, at age 24, he officially became a member (Pearce, 1990a: 56; Maullin, 1973: 129n.2). In a few short years Marulanda stood out as an outstanding guerrilla fighter and organizer of the PCC in the Central Cordillera. As an important leader he was elected to the Central Committee in 1960 (Wickham-Crowley, 1992: 331; Pearce, 1990a: 56; Hobday, 1986: 363; Maullin, 1973: 129n.2; Gomez, 1972: 249; Pomeroy, 1968: 312). Marulanda became instrumental in the establishment of all the self-defense groups in southern Colombia, most notably Marquetalia (Molano, 2000: 25; Gott, 1970: 26, 235). Following the military aggressions associated with Plan Lazo, Marulanda pursued the formation of the FARC-EP as a revolutionary political-military organization with a coarse but organized hierarchical structure (Gomez, 1972: 254-255; Gott, 1973, 1970). When looking back on this formation, Marulanda retrospectively explained how the FARC-EP organized itself under a broad, flexible, yet complex, revolutionary strategy.

Faced with the aggression against Marquetalia, for example, we created a single leadership. We were building a new type of general staff as the supreme political and military authority, taking care that militarism did not overwhelm everything. We set up the military structure that corresponds to an extraordinarily mobile struggle, and we adjusted the tactics to the necessities of that needed mobility. The guerrilla detachments and groupings are deployed in the field with the same versatility as a very small guerrilla unit. If we need to, we establish fixed commands for whatever time is required. Discipline is not imposed; rather, it springs forth in the conscious combatant as a necessity of the struggle. The barracks method modeled on that of the units of troops in the bourgeois army is now but a memory of the first days of the guerrilla force. However, our military structure is guided by conscious revolutionary military principles, adjusted to our form of guerrilla force. We maintain a critical and self-critical attitude in the face of our political and military errors, while we are guided by a profoundly respectful conduct in our dealings with the masses and in their interests. We raise and support the immediate and fundamental demands of the masses, which by virtue of our activity are in the fields like us. We were never, and we will never be, a bunch of self-important people trying to dictate the line to everyone else, nor defenders of the absurd thesis that 'the guerrilla force creates the party.' We go forward guided by the orientation of the only party that has always been with us: the Communist Party. And we will always continue to be so guided.

(Marulanda, 2003: 120)

This chapter has demonstrated how the FARC-EP's roots are firmly planted in the PCC of the twentieth century alongside those from the countryside, making it the people's army.[52]

2

EJÉRCITO DEL PUEBLO: A SOCIOLOGICAL ANALYSIS OF RADICAL SOCIAL CHANGE

In the aftermath of Marquetalia, the FARC-EP formed and extended itself across four municipalities. Support from the peasantry grew throughout the mid-1960s and late 1970s (de la Peña, 1998: 353, 360). By the 1980s, the insurgency saw significant growth, with roughly a fifth of the country seeing some form of its presence (Richani, 2002a: 68). It was the 1990s, however – with the rise of neoliberal economic policy and increased state repression – that the FARC-EP saw its most dramatic increase to date (Moser and McIlwaine, 2004: 42; LeGrand, 2003: 176). Reviewing this period, James F. Rochlin (2003: 132) noted that the FARC-EP grew more than it had during the preceding three decades combined. The guerrillas had expanded to more than 60 percent of the country (Vanden and Prevost, 2002: 245). One comprehensive study from the mid-1990s revealed that the insurgency had a tangible influence in 622 munici-palities (out of 1,050) (Avila et al, 1997: 133; see also Petras and Veltmeyer, 2003a: 32; Leech, 2002a: 23). By the end of the decade the guerrillas existed within 1,000 municipalities (Livingstone, 2003: 8; see also Ortiz, 2006: 207). In a few short years, over 93 percent of all areas of recent colonization had a guerrilla presence (Sánchez, 2003: 15; Richani, 2002a: 68).

Table 2.1 The growth of the FARC-EP in municipalities throughout Colombia

Year	Number of municipalities	Percentage of national municipalities
1964	4	0.4
1970	54	5
1979	100	9
1985	173	15
1991	437	2
1995	622	59
1996	800	76
1999	1,000	95
2003	1,050	100
2007	1,050	100*

* continuity in extension.

Sources: Chernick, 2007: 67; Avilés, 2006: 85; Brittain, 2005e: 23; Livingstone, 2003: 8; Rochlin, 2003: 137; Petras, 1999: 30; Avila et al, 1997: 133; Wickham-Crowley, 1992: 109–10; Osterling, 1989: 99; and information obtained through observational research.

This advance did not slow. In Cundinamarca, for example, the FARC-EP stretched over 83 of the department's 116 rural and urban-based municipalities (Norwegian Refugee Center, 2003: 1). Upon the rise of the new century the insurgency had "enough support to move throughout the whole country" (Parrar, 2004). Since the 2000s, it has been said that Ecuador sits on no longer territory controlled by the Colombian state, but rather a geography secured by the FARC-EP (Vieira, 2008e; see also Bajak, 2008b; Kraul, 2008). Such findings are similar to my own research, which discovered entire regions completely fortified by the guerrillas. On many occasions I travelled by land and water, sometimes for days, without any sight of state influence, yet squads of guerrillas were seen on a regular basis. As support varies from region to region,[1] some form of solidarity exists in every municipality, giving the insurgency national fluidity (Livingstone, 2003: 8).

The insurgency has a distinct organizational structure. The Secretariat is the highest level of leadership, and finalizes all tactical and political decisions in cooperation, consultation, and influence with the Central High Command. The Secretariat of the Central High Command consists of seven members (at the time of writing, Jorge Briceño, Alfonso Cano, Pablo Catatumbo, Joaquín Gómez, Mauricio Jaramillo, Timoleón Jiménez, and Iván Márquez[2]). The Central High Command (sometimes referred to as the Central General Staff) is made up of 25 members situated in seven blocks (Caribbean, Centre, East, Iván Ríos, Middle Magdalena, South, and West – see Map 2.1) (Richani, 2002a: 77; FARC-EP, 2001a: 29). Each block holds a number of highly organized fronts, historically averaging 300 to 600 combatants per unit (Ahmad, 2006: 63;

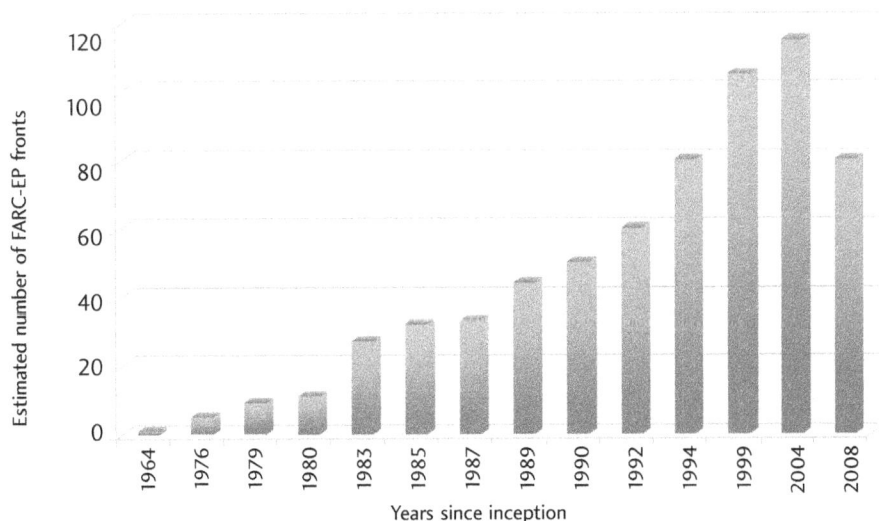

Figure 2.1 Number of FARC-EP fronts in Colombia

Sources: Bristow, 2008; The Current, 2008; Ahmad, 2006: 43; Sánchez, 2003: 15; Murillo and Avirama, 2003: 70; Rochlin, 2003: 99; Scheina, 2003: 271; Richani, 2002a: 76; Crandall, 1999: 226; Petras, 1999: 31; Pearce, 1990a: 167, 173, 281; Osterling, 1989: 266; Ruhl, 1981: 138; and information obtained through observational research.

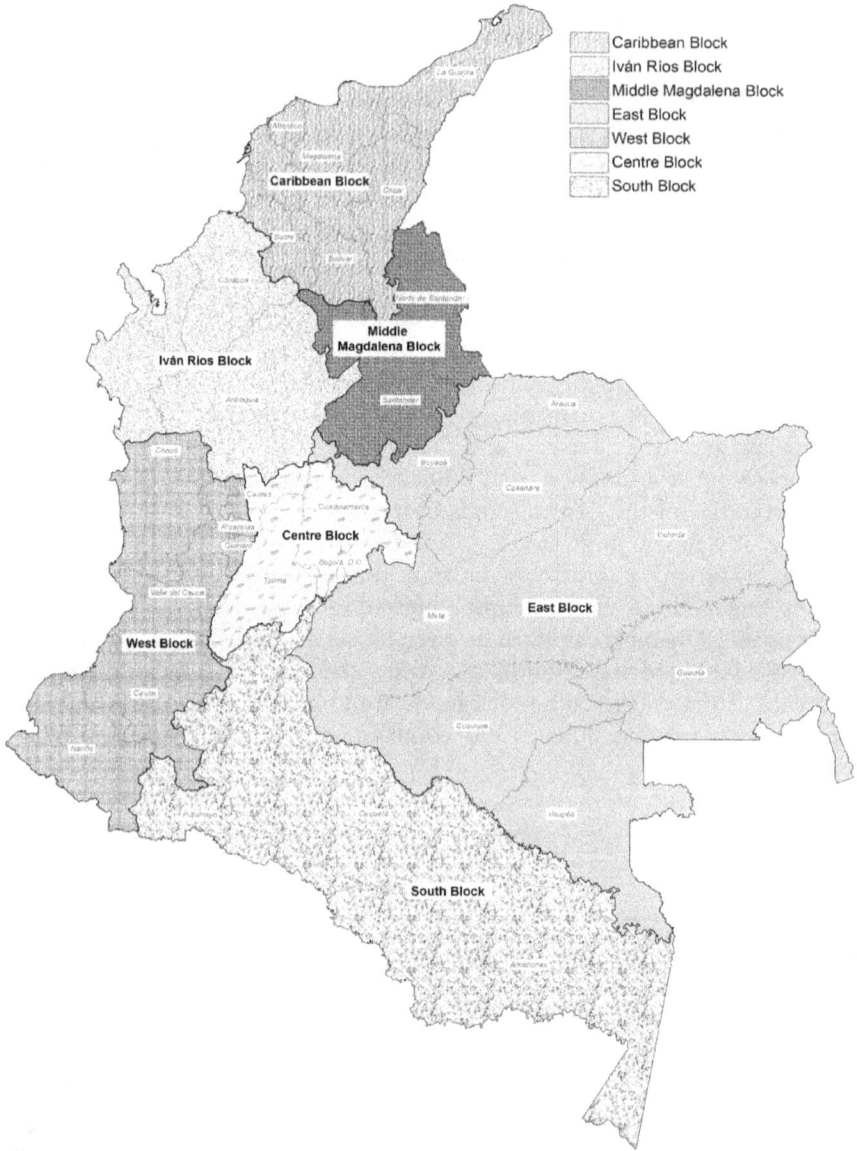

Map 2.1 A visual depiction of the FARC-EP blocks of political geography.
Sources: Adapted from information obtained through observational research alongside documents
provided by the FARC-EP in 2004; see also Ferra Medina and Uribe Ramón, 2002: 53.

Richani, 2002a: 76–7). Each front has a comandante who keeps an updated list
of each member, detailing gender, age, occupation prior to membership, where
they are from, education level, reason for joining, disciplinary record, injuries,
and rank (Gutiérrez Sanín, 2008: 7; see also Colombia Reports, 2008).

By the mid-1990s roughly 105 fronts existed (Hylton, 2006: 89; Petras, 1999: 31). After observing numerous meetings involving the FARC-EP, I collected data that suggested the possibility of at least an additional dozen fronts by the early to mid-2000s. This assessment was shown to be accurate during a heated debate between Roger Noriega, assistant secretary of state for the Western hemisphere affairs under the George W. Bush administration, and Colombian political scientist Daniel García-Peña Jaramillo. Noriega said US intelligence believed an estimated 120 fronts existed throughout the country in 2008 (The Current, 2008). Such a figure seemed high, as the insurgency appeared to have altered its structure around 2008–09 by reducing the quantity of fronts. A more accurate figure of the FARC-EP's front status at this time rested around 80 (see Bristow, 2008).

Collecting information on the number of combatants in the FARC-EP is understandably difficult. Most figures are grossly out of date, yet used repeatedly. This is surprising as numerous assessments found that the FARC-EP exceeded 30,000 in the early 2000s (International Crisis Group, 2009: 7n.57; Chernick, 2007: 67; Petras et al, 2005: 118; Petras and Veltmeyer, 2005b: 378; Vieira, 2004a; Rochlin, 2003: 137, 165n.81). The following information, compiled through first-hand research, highlights far greater numbers than outdated regurgitated records suggest. Collected over several years, my research found the guerrillas had grown substantially over much of the last 15 years. This growth is largely attributed to continued political-economic repression of the rural population and urban working poor. At its peak (from the late 1990s to mid-2000s) the guerrilla organization was estimated to have 40,000–50,000 combatants (Brittain, 2005e). This number may appear high when compared with popular media accounts and state sources, but it must be understood that the FARC-EP remained disproportionately underrepresented for the greater part of the previous two decades, even though a remarkable physical and geographically expansion was realized.

The FARC-EP's membership has grown consistently (see Brittain, 2005g).[3] With over 105 fronts between the late 1990s and early 2000s,[4] at a median of 450 insurgents per front,[5] the number of combatants roughly equated to 45,000. This is quite different from most of Bogotá and Washington's figures, which have argued that more and more guerrillas have been captured, demobilized, deserted, or killed in recent years. In contrast, Colombian mathematicians José Fernando Isaza Delgado and Diógenes Campos Romero noted that recruitment expanded in the mid to late 2000s, a position openly shared by various human rights organizations.[6] Using state-based statistics concerning FARC-EP enlistment and abandonment, Delgado and Romero (2007: 8) noted, "for every 100 subversives who deserted or were killed, the guerrillas were able, in the 2002–2007 period, to recruit 84 new combatants." Utilizing this equation, the number of guerrilla forces exceeds 42,500, with the FARC-EP making up the vast majority (Delgado and Romero, 2007: 9; see also Delgado, 2008). In September 2008 further information was obtained referring to the FARC-EP's size when state forces acquired a database related to one of the guerrilla's seven blocks. The material suggested the Eastern Block alone housed

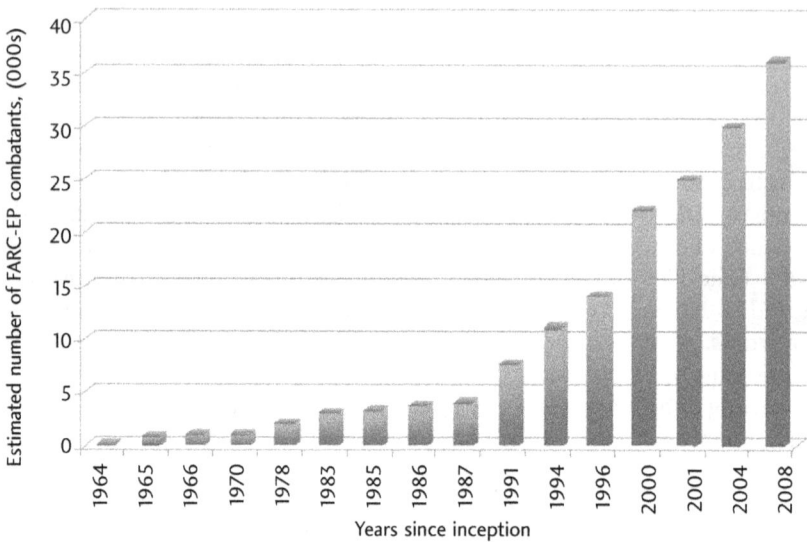

Figure 2.2 Number of FARC-EP combatants in Colombia

Sources: Delgado, 2008; Delgado and Romero, 2007: 9; Wilson and Carroll, 2007: 91; Schulte-Bockholt, 2006: 141n.15; Goff, 2004: 44; Vieira, 2004b; Sánchez, 2003: 15; Kirk, 2003: 218; Rochlin, 2003: 99, 137, 165n.8; Crandall, 2008: 53–4, 74; Richani, 2002a: 76; 2001: 53–4, 74n.33; Alejandro and Billon, 1999; FARC-EP, 1999: 17; Osterling, 1989: 266, 294; Gunther, 1966: 443.

9,387 combatants (Colombia Reports, 2008a). Again, this highlights that the FARC-EP is much larger than popular accounts have suggested.[7]

State sources claimed the number of FARC-EP combatants significantly declined during 2008.[8] While setbacks were said to have occurred in select regions, the actual capacity of the FARC-EP went unhampered. Support remained high in areas with long-established roots (International Crisis Group, 2009; Chernick, 2007). In some locales civil backing was in the 80th percentile (Bajak, 2008b). There were even cases of FARC-EP expansion. Ecuadorian intelligence found insurgent encampments to have doubled by 2008 (Kraul, 2008). In many areas, the guerrillas continued to destabilize state forces, while further concentrating their power over territory (Justice for Colombia, 2008). While some victories over the FARC-EP were realized, such successes occurred largely in blocks where the insurgency's power was significantly less than it was elsewhere. The majority of FARC-EP's blocks have seen little if any destabilization.

> Units that were already weak are being hit hardest. The FARC's regional blocs in northern Colombia have long been smaller than those it maintains in the south and east of the country. Blocs in the central coffee-growing region, the Magdalena Medio region, Antioquia department and the Caribbean have fewer members, operate in more densely populated areas, and have had to contend for more than twenty years with paramilitary groups, which originated in this part of the

country .... It is far from clear, though, whether FARC units elsewhere are in similarly bad shape. The FARC's Eastern and Southern Blocs (and to a lesser extent, its Western Bloc) are far larger and wealthier than those that have suffered the strongest blows. They operate in much more remote and unpopulated areas, including triple-canopy jungles, and they profit enormously from the coca economy and control of drug-trafficking routes. Their region is considered the guerrillas' historical "rearguard" zone. Though key targets of the "Plan Patriota" military offensive, which has somewhat reduced the area in which they can operate freely, these blocs have seen fewer of its leaders killed and captured .... Guerrilla leaders considered more "political" have been hit harder than representatives of the FARC's so-called "military wing" ... many of those killed or captured in the last year are believed to be representatives of the FARC's "political" wing. These include the two Secretariat members (Reyes and Ríos), former peace negotiator Carlos Antonio Losada, and 40-year FARC member "Martín Sombra." There is no way to know why these relatively less hard-line leaders have borne the brunt of the past year's military operations. It is interesting to note that while "military" chiefs like "Mono Jojoy" and "Timoleón Jiménez" remain in the most remote areas, protected by large and powerful blocs, the more "political" leaders have been more exposed – either in less securely held areas like Antioquia, or – in the case of Reyes – in the vulnerable position of meeting with easily tracked foreign delegations. Better intelligence is making these efforts possible – and probably dividing the FARC. For the most part, these successes against the FARC are not the product of massive, costly "Plan Patriota"-style military offensives. These seem to do little more than rack up large "body counts" of dead guerrillas of the lowest rank, many of them easily replaceable teenagers. Instead, the latest successes are the product of far better intelligence-gathering.

(Isacson, 2008)

In light of the above, it is ill-informed to assess that the FARC-EP has seen its end. The number of fronts may have changed, but in no way does this suggest a reduction in the FARC-EP's overall aptitude, support, and measures related to recruitment (Chernick, 2007: 77). For example, in February 2009 Alan Jara, a former governor of Meta retained as a political prisoner by the FARC-EP in 2001, was released from guerrilla custody. During press conferences following the ordeal, Jara spoke of the FARC-EP's current reach and how the insurgency have experienced little if any change in its capacity to obtain clear and imme-diate material solidarity from local populations (see Semana, 2009). Rather than being weakened, research suggests the FARC-EP has reconfigured block formations by creating fewer, yet more concentrated, fronts. Even utilizing interviews, observation, and existing data, we can only offer estimates of the current figure of combatants.

Some might question the numbers given above, as the Colombian state and media claim that the FARC-EP has been considerably weakened. In early 2008 three momentous blows came to the FARC-EP when not one but two of the insurgency's most recognizable leaders were killed, coupled with the natural death of the FARC-EP's commander-in-chief, Manuel Marulanda Vélez. It appeared as though the FARC-EP might have been dealt a mortal blow when Comandante Raúl Reyes *and* Iván Ríos, two Secretariat members, were murdered. It was soon claimed that:

> Colombians are for the first time raising the possibility that a guerrilla group once thought invincible could be forced into peace negotiations or even defeated militarily. Weakened by infiltrators and facing constant combat and aerial bombardment, the insurgency is losing members in record numbers.
>
> (Forero, 2008)

Using state sources, one of Colombia's most popular news magazines wrote how desertion and lack of internal cohesion were leading to the potential internal eradication of the FARC-EP (Cambio, 2008a). While the three deaths were of great significance, reports of the FARC-EP's decline are not new.

The FARC-EP's revolutionary push threatens Colombia's political-economic stability as it erodes the state from below. In recognition of this power, the dominant class periodically portrays the guerrillas as structurally weakened in the hope of discouraging support, both internal and external to the country. Such accounts are repeatedly proven false as time elapses, however. At the beginning of the 1970s, early in the insurgency's formation, the FARC-EP received a devastating blow at the hands of the Colombian state when the Misael Pastrana Borrero administration (1970–74) (and the United States) encouraged a series of counterinsurgency offences against specific guerrilla-extended regions (Premo, 1988: 230; Hobsbawm, 1970: 56). In 1973 the Colombian state launched "Operation Anori," which resulted in the destruction of the FARC-EP's military supplies and sections of its leadership (Avilés, 2006: 154n.25). This was a shift in state-military policy in the fact that "for some years after the attacks on the 'independent republics' ... the armed forces had been content to contain the guerrillas in their isolated rural zones of operation, but in 1973 they decided to enter these areas in force" (Ruhl, 1980: 196). After the campaigns took place it was documented that the FARC-EP had lost 70 percent of its ammunition, with only an estimated 150 armed and trained combatants remaining (FARC-EP, 1999: 24; Premo, 1988: 243n.45; Ruhl, 1980: 196, 205n.63). Remarkably, the FARC-EP quickly bounced back (Petras and Morley, 2003: 101; Castro, 1999: xx–xxi). In fact, the guerrillas were able to "regroup and conduct sporadic actions on an increasing number of fronts" by the mid-1970s (Premo, 1988: 231). Understanding that setbacks are realities of long-term class struggles, true revolutionary movements are able to recognize their errors and use this experience to respond to future attempts to fracture their efforts (see Marx, 1975a: 142; Lenin, 1966a: 220). This is what the FARC-EP was able to do (Hobsbawm, 1970: 56–7).

More recently, several major counterinsurgency campaigns (Plan Colombia, 1998–2006, and Plan Patriota, 2002/03–06) claimed premature victories over the FARC-EP, while in reality the insurgency witnessed combatant growth amidst triumphs over corporate and state interests (Brittain, 2005e). Examples of this were experienced after the 2008 allegations of deterioration, when the guerrillas destabilized Colombia's most important oil infrastructure facility while eliminating an entire military battalion. Between April 29 and May 6 the FARC-EP coordinated a series of attacks which isolated Colombia's largest oil pipeline and subsequently halted production of an estimated 800,000 to 3,000,000 barrels of oil. The guerrillas strategically destroyed important transportation routes needed to control the flow of oil and military supplies throughout various departments in the north of the country. Destroying an essential bridge near Catatumbo, César, the FARC-EP was able to cut off the movement of state and private security forces (Weinberg, 2008c).

At the same time, another front in Norte de Santander pursued an aggressive assault against security forces guarding the 770-kilometer Colombian Ecopetrol and US-based Occidental Petroleum owned Caño-Limón pipeline near Tibu – the true target of the attack. All this occurred only a few short hours after US ambassador to Colombia, William Brownfield, visited the area and applauded the progress made in areas of security and economic prowess as a result of the FARC-EP's decline (Reuters, 2008c). In response to the strike Colombian General Paulino Coronado coordinated a mounted offensive on May 3 to stop the FARC-EP campaign and resume the flow of oil production. The guerrillas quickly eliminated the battalion and continued their assault on the pipeline facilities for an additional 48 hours (Associated Press, 2008b). The coordinated campaign threw off the perceptions of officials from both Colombia and the United States that many sectors of the north were stable.

Showing the operation was not simply a one-time tactical success, the FARC-EP carried out an additional attack on Colombia's largest coal mine – the Cerrejón – on the 44th anniversary of insurgency's inception. On May 27, 2008, roughly one month after the attacks aimed at oil production took place, the guerrillas again attacked multinational corporations (MNCs) and state infrastructure in the region by derailing "around 40 wagons out of the 120-wagon train, carrying 110 tonnes of coal" (Reuters, 2008d). While officials tried to downplay the extensive damage, it was quickly revealed that the FARC-EP had considerably hampered trading by destabilizing export routes (Reuters, 2008e). These are just two actions where the FARC-EP demonstrated a continued capacity to respond to both state and private security forces in relation to corporate interests. As was said by former interior minister Carlos Holguin, Bogotá is far from claiming victory over the FARC-EP (see Otis, 2008b).

Although estimates that there are tens of thousands in the FARC-EP may appear high to some, it has become general knowledge that the Colombian state actively under-represents the numbers of those involved in armed movements throughout Colombia. In 2006 Jorge Daniel Castro, then general director of Colombia's national police, announced that 30,944 paramilitaries had taken amnesty since 2003 under Law 975 (see Badawy, 2006). This was double any published estimate by scholars, military analysts, or government officials of the size of Colombia's largest paramilitary organization, the United Self-Defense Forces of Colombia (*Autodefensas Unidas de Colombia*, AUC) (International Crisis Group, 2004: 2, 2n.7; Murillo and Avirama, 2004: 89, 108; Livingstone, 2003: 269n.15; Crandall, 2002: 88; Ministerio de Defensa Nacional, 2000: 10). The administration of Álvaro Uribe Vélez (2002–) has been widely accused of forcing state officials to alter statistics related to internal security and state policy. Cesar Caballero, former director of Colombia's National Administrative Department of Statistics (*Departamento Administrativo Nacional de Estadística*, DANE), admitted that the state has manipulated and continues to manipulate "statistics to make Colombia appear safer than it is, casting doubt on achievements that have made him popular both at home and with the U.S. government ... the president's policy is ... to maintain the perception that security has improved, no matter what the case" (see Crowe, 2007).

State-enforced misinformation can also be easily recognized through an evaluation of internally displaced persons (IDPs), or what Arturo Escobar (2004: 16) calls "the essence of modernity." Constanza Vieira (2008b) noted that the number of Colombian IDPs jumped 38 percent in 2007. Colombia is second only to the Sudan in its number of IDPs, a growth that began after the rise of paramilitarism in the 1980s. To put this into perspective, Colombia has well over 1 million more IDPs than the entire Middle East combined (including Iraq). The state has stated that there are roughly 1.9 million IDPs (see Internal Displacement Monitoring Centre, 2007). This is half the figure documented by numerous domestic and international human rights organizations and research centers. It is widely agreed that the actual figure of Colombian IDPs fluctuates between 3.9 and 4.3 million (see Consultoría para los Derechos Humanos y el Desplazamiento, 2008, 2007; Internal Displacement Monitoring Centre, 2007; Japan International Cooperation Agency, 2007).[9] This suggests that reports concerning the FARC-EP's numbers are likely to be suspect as well.[10]

While the FARC-EP most certainly experienced unprecedented difficulties in 2008, it must be realized that as long as inequitable sociocultural and political-economic conditions pervade Colombian society, so too will a base of recruitment exist. For decades a major factor that enabled the guerrillas to persist was how the leadership responded to periods of tribulation. Because of his unique, egalitarian, and collegial style it has been argued that Marulanda's passing, while tragic, will have little effect on the insurgency's continuity (Chernick, 2007: 69). The FARC-EP remains the longest-running and most powerful political-military movement in contemporary Latin America, with numbers still in the tens of thousands. To buy into any suggestion that the insurgency has passed into the annals of history is to adopt a false consciousness. As inequality, displacement, and exploitation accelerate further in Colombia, so too will levels of opposition. These are the causes of instability and the true forum through which people become aware of their class position; hence, their subsequent engagement in acts of resistance through more extreme measures (see Grandin, 2006: 218). Put simply, political-economic disparity brings "insurgent movements a ready-made mass of disaffected supporters" (Calvert,

1999: 128). Jennifer Holmes, Sheila Amin Gutiérrez de Piñeres, and Kevin M. Curtin (2006: 178) have clarified how a "lack of economic opportunity contributes to leftist guerrilla violence." The FARC-EP are bound to experience defeats, tactical reformation, and withdrawal, but to think that this implies the movement is over is indicative of a level of ignorance towards both guerrilla warfare and the material conditions that pervade Colombian society and class struggle. The suggestion that the FARC-EP has experienced defeat fails to comprehend the right of self-determination. The struggle in Colombia is far from over. It will continue to be waged through radical and antagonistic forms. As the US and Colombian dominant class continues to engage a war against the poor, so too will they exacerbate "Colombia's internal conflict by robbing families of their livelihoods and leaving them with little option but to join the left-wing guerrillas, particularly the FARC" (O'Shaughnessy and Branford, 2005: 7).

BECOMING THE PEOPLE'S ARMY: THE EVOLUTION OF THE FARC(-EP)

In agreement with the writings of Che Guevara (2006: 13–14), Colombia offers an important example of "revolutionary optimism" and contests the premise that certain countries lack the immediate conditions for radical transformation. The FARC-EP has been applauded for consistently vindicating "the ideological roots of the revolution, with Martí and Bolívar, which moreover undoubtedly found echoes throughout the continent even in countries where conditions were not ripe for insurrection" (Raby, 2006: 105). For decades, the PCC – in accord with the USSR – proclaimed that Colombia was in no position of revolutionary upheaval (Livingstone, 2003: 206; Gott, 1970: 519; Pomeroy, 1968: 308).[11] Yet in the early 1980s, the FARC-EP, independent of the PCC, argued that "for the first time ... a revolutionary situation existed in the country," and therefore, new strategies needed to be developed to take advantage of the sociopolitical situation (Pearce, 1990a: 173; see also Schulte-Bockholt, 2006: 110). After years of cooperation and struggle, at the Seventh Conference of the Guerrilla Movement (May 1982), the guerrillas announced that they had become the "People's Army" (*Ejército del Pueblo*).[12] Doing so meant moving from a solely defensive collective to a revolutionary guerrilla movement taking on "more offensive military tactics" (Simons, 2004: 52).

> This new method meant that the FARC-EP would no longer wait in ambush for the enemy. Rather, it would go in pursuit to locate, besiege, and surround the enemy and if the enemy were to change its method of operation, returning to its old concept, the FARC would attack with an offensive of mobile commandos. For the first time since the revolutionary guerrilla movement arose in Marquetalia, the Seventh Conference gave the movement a clear strategic and operational concept for a revolutionary army.
>
> (FARC-EP, 1999: 26)

Safford and Palacios (2003: 356, 364) described this period as a "metamorphosis," where the guerrilla organization extended its operations while decreasing relations with the PCC. By changing its military structure, the FARC-EP "altered its gradualist strategy and prepared to seize power" (Livingstone, 2003: 207–8). Hylton explained the change by sharing how the guerrilla group:

> abandoned its defensive strategy, in theory (they had already done so in practice), to protect themselves throughout the national territory – a change symbolized by the initials, EP (Army of the People), added to the group's name. The FARC had already expanded from its bases in Caquetá, Meta, and Putumayo, into the Urabá, the Middle Magdalena, and areas of the southeastern plains – Guaviare, Vichada, and Vaupés – which had indigenous majorities. This was the jump-off point from which ... the FARC would become a military enterprise dedicated to territorial expansion and control.
>
> (Hylton, 2006: 65)

Maintaining its Marxist-Leninist roots, the FARC-EP became "an authentically offensive guerrilla movement" (FARC-EP, 1999: 26). By the end of 1982, the guerrillas claimed to be a formidable force for and of the people, "with a centralized hierarchical structure, a general staff, military code, training school and political program" (Molano, 2000: 26–7). This has remained intact as the FARC-EP carry out "political work with its rural and urban popular bases and a hit-and-run war of attrition on the army" (Safford and Palacios, 2003: 364). Through "a readjustment of all its mechanisms of leadership and command" the insurgency changed in name and form (Hylton, 2006: 63; Simons, 2004: 52; Safford and Palacios, 2003: 364; Livingstone, 2003: 207–8).

The FARC-EP has a complex command structure. Although there is a strict and binding hierarchy, the level of constant interaction between the highest sectors of the FARC-EP's leadership and all members is surprising. It was not rare to see those belonging to the FARC-EP's Secretariat involved in dialog, jovial discussion, and seeking general observations and input from the various ranks. On a daily basis, the leadership talked with all members on a variety of issues ranging from camp structure to regional coordination. An example of how combatants are organized and must follow formal levels of authority in the organization was noted during a trip to an educational facility.

When travelling through an immense river system, a small group of guerrillas, who belonged to a different company from those I had been with, quickly surrounded the boat I was on. I was asked a series of questions relating to who I was, what I was doing in that part of the country, and so on. I was then asked to wait. As they walked away, I could overhear three of the squad members who had just interrogated me. They met with what seemed to be a squad commander or deputy. After roughly ten minutes, the commander/deputy proceeded to order one of the squad members to contact the column commander to find out whether my answers were accurate and I truly was who I claimed to be. Within 15 minutes the squad commander, with three squad members,

Commander-in-Chief of the Central High Command
(Superior organism commanding the FARC-EP totality)
Purpose: Organizes, orders, and rules over decisions relating to the entire
movement and all its members

↑↓

The Secretariat of the Central High Command
(High Command of each block of fronts)
Purpose: coordinate the areas of the respective blocks

↑↓

Blocks
(7 [5+ fronts])
Purpose: coordinates and unifies fronts in a specific zone of the country

↑↓

The Central High Command
(Highest command of each front)

↑↓

Front
(1+ column)

↑↓

Column
(2+ companies)

↑↓

Companies
(2+ guerrillas)

↑↓

Guerrilla
(2 squads)

↑↓

Squad
(+/- 12 combatants)

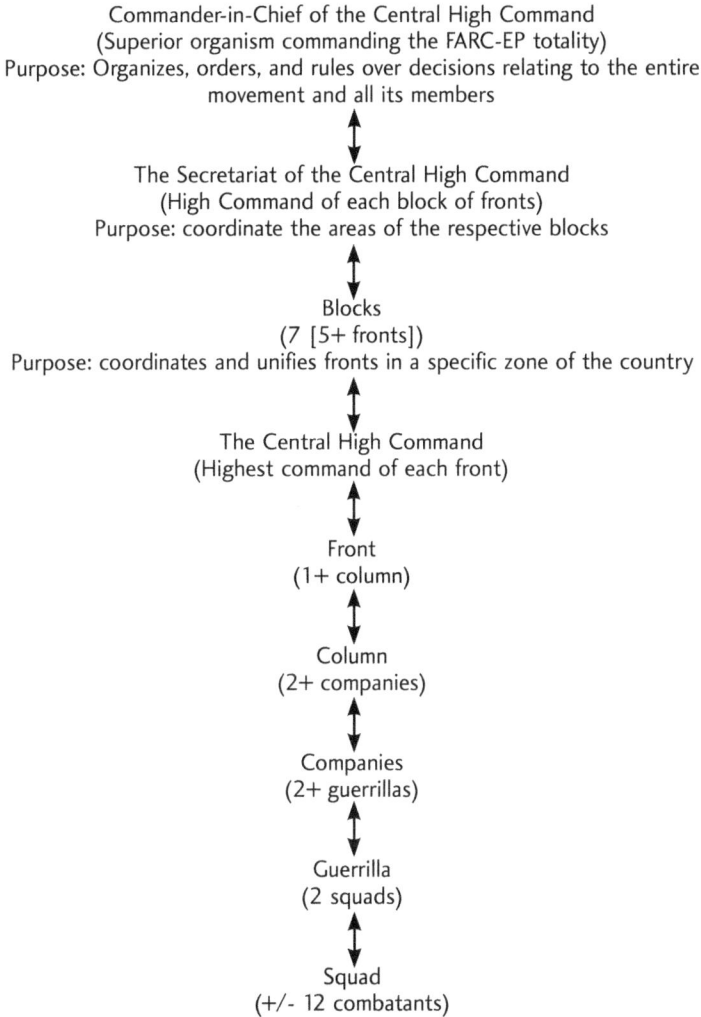

Figure 2.3 Organized formation of the FARC-EP hierarchical command
Source: Adapted from information obtained through observational research alongside documents
provided by the FARC-EP in 2004; see also FARC-EP, 2001 c.

came back and told me to stay safe and proceed further down the river, where I would encounter another checkpoint. I was left amazed at the detailed hierarchy, security measures, and fluid communication that existed throughout a rural-based informal bureaucracy. The experience demonstrated the immense breadth of control held by the insurgency (see Petras, 2003: 100).

In 1964, the FARC-EP was a peasant-based movement, largely consisting of subsistence agriculturists living in relatively underdeveloped regions of the southwest (Leech, 2002a: 13; Osterling, 1989: 294; Feder, 1971: 189). Since its inception, the FARC-EP has developed into a complex force with 65

Table 2.2 Hierarchical leadership structure of the FARC-EP (in comparison with a conventional armed forces structure)

FARC-EP's organic structure	Equivalent in a conventional armed forces structure
Combatant	Soldier
Candidate for commander	Sub-official
Squad deputy	Corporal 2nd class
Squad commander	Corporal 1st class
Guerrilla deputy	Sergeant 2nd class
Guerrilla commander	Sergeant 1st class
Company deputy	Sergeant Major
Company commander	Sub-lieutenant
Column deputy	Lieutenant
Column commander	Captain
Front deputy	Major
Front commander	Lieutenant-colonel
Block deputy	Colonel
Block commander	Brigadier-general
Central High Commander deputy	Major-general
Commander of the Central High Command	Three-star general
Commander-in-chief of Central High Command	No equivalent

Source: Adapted from information obtained through observational research alongside documents provided by the FARC-EP in 2004; see also FARC-EP, 2001c.

percent of its formal members coming from the countryside – 12 to 13 percent derived from various indigenous groups[13] – and the remaining 35 percent from urban sectors. The current membership is dominated by subsistence peasants and small producers, but has grown to incorporate indigenous populations, Afro-Colombians, the displaced, landless rural laborers, intellectuals, unionists, teachers, professionals, doctors, lawyers, priests, and sectors of the urban workforce (Petras et al, 2005: 118; Petras, 2003: 24–5, 99; Petras and Veltmeyer, 2003a: 178–9; Richani, 2002a: 63; Wickham-Crowley, 1992: 214). Attention has also been paid to gender equity with respect to both the rank and file and leadership. Currently, 50 percent of FARC-EP members are female, with 30 to 55 percent of comandantes being women, depending on the region (Gutiérrez Sanín, 2008: 10; O'Shaughnessy and Branford, 2005: 27; Galdos, 2004; Richani, 2002a: 62).[14] Such sociocultural compositions demonstrate how the FARC-EP "became an army of the whole people" (Petras, 2008).

From being heavily centered in the countryside, the expansion of the FARC-EP into the cities is of tremendous importance.[15] For decades it was argued that Colombia's cities remained largely immune from the civil war (see Williamson, 1965: 41).[16] Some analysts even claimed the FARC-EP lacked any formal strength because it had yet to develop urban support (Rochlin, 2003: 143). However there is substantial evidence that over the past two decades the FARC-EP has acquired clandestine allies and constructed counter-hegemonic networks in various cities. The FARC-EP has formed a number of urban militias (Petras, 2003: 161; Petras and Veltmeyer, 2005b: 378). During the 1990s, the FARC-EP mustered support in various cities through "a network of helpers" that provided "logistical support for armed action" (Livingstone, 2003: 208). Prior to the peace talks with the Andrés Pastrana Arango administration (1998–2002), the FARC-EP engaged in combat with state forces and launched major military campaigns just outside Bogotá, while establishing roadblocks along main highways (Simons, 2004: 91; Petras, 2003: 25; 1999: 32). Beginning in 2001, the FARC-EP started to show growth in Cali and Medellín, and increased its technological and organizational capacities in the capital, as was made apparent in its attack on the Casa de Nariño during the first presidential inauguration of Uribe in August 2002 (Crandall, 2005b: 176–7; see also Sweig and McCarthy, 2005: 25; Petras and Brescia, 2000: 134–5). In fact, the insurgency has engaged in, and won, significant confrontations with state forces in various cities since the 1990s (Richani, 2005b: 84; see also Steinberg, 2000: 264). Some suggest that the FARC-EP has acquired an estimated 12,000 members in urban centers over the last ten years alone (Felbab-Brown, 2005: 105; see also Chernick, 2007: 67; Petras and Veltmeyer, 2005b: 378; Petras et al, 2005: 118).[17]

With the urban expansion of the guerrillas, aggression has expanded to areas that had been largely unaffected by the conflict. In the last few years "the escalating dynamics of war in Colombian cities are introducing Colombians to a conflict traditionally restricted to Colombia's rural areas" (Sweig and McCarthy, 2005: 25). While numerically smaller than the countryside, the power of such forces cannot be understated. For example, one urban militia in Medellín required roughly 3,000 state police and military forces to detain 29 combatants (Sweig and McCarthy, 2005: 25; see also Petras and Brescia, 2000: 134–5). The mid-2000s saw the insurgency wage assaults throughout Bogotá by constructing networks that facilitated "attacks on water and electrical infrastructures" and "the country's political elite and middle class, whose political and financial support Uribe depends upon" (Sweig and McCarthy, 2005: 26). Within six weeks of Uribe's re-election (in 2006), the US embassy in Bogotá attested that the FARC-EP had not been weakened since his arrival to office. Intelligence revealed that the guerrillas retained the capacity to launch urban military campaigns, and officials were ordered to stay clear of certain areas of the city (Reuters, 2006b).[18] Two years later, General Oscar Naranjo and Defense Minister Juan Manuel Santos admitted that little had changed and the FARC-EP still held the ability to target the capital (Agence France-Presse, 2008c).

Examples of the insurgency's counter-hegemony in urban locales are also found in community-based health clinics in various *barrios*. In 2006, it was made known the FARC-EP had been providing medical services in some of the most impoverished slums of Colombia (People's Daily, 2006b). The guerrillas had created infirmaries capable of supplying surgical operations, medicine, and healthcare supplies to local civilians. It is for these and other reasons that some have suggested the FARC-EP has taken advantage of "vacuums of legitimate power at local levels" across several cities (Williams, 2005: 161). Hence, what began as a peasant-led rural-based land struggle in the 1960s has since been transformed into a national political-military social movement illustrating a vision of alternative development through a socialist society via armed struggle (Ortiz, 2002: 130–6; Pearce, 1990a: 283). A growing minority of the FARC-EP are outside the country's many small villages and towns (Petras, 2003: 99). By constructing a support base, extensive geographical breadth, and an expanding ideological model of emancipation, the FARC-EP has proven the ability to move its revolutionary ethos beyond the countryside.

AN EVALUATION OF CIVILIAN SUPPORT FOR THE FARC-EP

In her book *My Colombian War*, Silvana Paternostro (2007: 212) wrote that the FARC-EP has "less than 1 percent approval by the population ... perhaps the least-liked revolutionaries in history." These comments were not new, as many have claimed that the guerrillas have very little support from the general public. Such claims are however simplistic, and it could be argued that they are false representations of the realities in parts of the country. Although it is popular to claim there is little support for the FARC-EP, this does not explain why many Colombians choose to keep their political cards close to their chests. There is also evidence of alliances between the insurgents and sectors of the civilian population (Petras, 2003: 24; Petras and Veltmeyer, 2001: 90). We now look at support for the FARC-EP, and how the insurgency can be seen as a people's army.

According to Marx and Engels (1976c: 495), a revolution must be backed by those most exploited under the current political-economic system. In 1966, the FARC-EP (and the PCC) stated that "the guerrilla movement is well aware that it *alone* cannot carry out the revolution" (Pomeroy, 1968: 312). The leadership of the FARC-EP recognized that the insurgency, in its infancy, had yet to form an *Ejército del Pueblo*. They understood that the support of the people was needed in order to create a true emancipatory society. Only through this process could the FARC-EP "play a decisive role in winning power for the people" (Pomeroy, 1968: 313; see also 310).

The simple continuity of the guerrilla movement demonstrates that substantial solidarity has existed at a local level (see Johnson, 1966: 160–3). Contrary to Paternostro's statement, it has been shown that the FARC-EP gained the most support of any guerrilla movement in Latin America during the 1960s (Paige, 1988: 153; see also Vega, 1969: 120). The 1970s then saw peasants (even those of a right-wing political ideology) showing relative, if not extensive, support of the guerrillas based on the revolutionaries' integrity and defense against reactionary forces.

> Communist guerrillas were fairly well received by the peasants in the central part of the country (south of Tolima, northern Huila and Caquetá, southern Meta, northeastern Cauca, the present-day department of Quindío), and avoided useless deaths and pillage, devoting themselves principally to fighting the Army. The Army, in turn, launched further

operations against other Communist strongholds, Pato and Ríochiquito. The total number of families in these areas was not over ten thousand. The guerrillas lost their permanent bases and had to become mobile. They adopted the name of Armed Forces of the Colombian Revolution, FARC, but did not achieve any notable success. Their leaders had great prestige among the peasants, even in Conservative areas, such as the municipality of Colombia (Huila).

(Gilhodés, 1970: 444–5)

Many of those I spoke with echoed similar claims. They had a common theme: that the guerrillas did not represent or fight *for* the masses, but that the insurgency *was* the masses. In no way are the guerrillas separate from the general population (Gibbs, 2008; Kalyvas, 2006; CISLAC, 2001). Areas I visited showed the insurgents living in close proximity to peasants and small producers. Colombian biologist Liliana M. Dávalos (2001: 70) found similar examples of how guerrilla encampments "correspond mainly to frontier and degraded farmland zones of insufficient economic development and near-absence of institutional infrastructure." In short, the FARC-EP is not differentiated from the peasantry, but rather respectfully inhabits the same environment.

Sociogeographical research has shown trends of migration to FARC-EP territories. During the 1998–2002 peace negotiations between the state and the FARC-EP, hundreds of thousands of peasants, small and medium producers, indigenous groups, and Afro-Colombians relocated to FARC-EP-controlled zones, especially San Vicente del Caguán – the center of the negotiations often referred to as *Villa Nueva Colombia* (Felbab-Brown, 2005: 109).[19] Garry Leech (2002a: 78) argued that "many townsfolk enjoyed living in the rebel safe-haven" because it provided a sense of security and the ability to create alternative community-based development projects (see also Villalón, 2004a, 2004b; Clark, 2003: 44).

The next few years saw rural inhabitants enter the FARC-EP-maintained demilitarized zone at a remarkable pace. Prior to the peace negotiations, the "zone" had a population of less than 100,000 (Isacson, 2003: 9; Chernick, 2000: 36; see also Hodgson, 1999: A15). By the time the army invaded the region and ended the peace negotiations in February 2002, roughly 740,000 had migrated to the guerrilla-held territory (Wilson, 2003). A further demonstration of the support amongst the rural populations for the FARC-EP was witnessed after insurgent-held territories were temporarily taken by state and paramilitary forces or abandoned as a result of the devastation of the civil war (fields and farmlands were ruined by bombing, agricultural crops being sprayed by defoliants and so on). Stathis N. Kalyvas (2006: 213n.2) found that in areas where this occurred the peasants regularly emigrated alongside the insurgents. Quite literally, the rural population followed the FARC-EP, and vice versa. A US citizen who documented her experience wrote an excellent comparative depiction of civilian relations in FARC-EP and paramilitary-controlled territory.

During my time in Colombia, I traveled through FARC-controlled territory as well as areas controlled by paramilitaries. As an American, going through government or paramilitary checkpoints involves interrogation, searches, intimidation and harassment. Colombians are frequently disappeared at checkpoints. I heard stories of rape, theft and terrorization by government forces, and consistently saw fear in campesino eyes when they faced military officers. My experience in FARC-controlled area was very different. At FARC checkpoints, I was welcomed and never threatened. In rebel territory, the FARC smile and greet you warmly. In return, average Colombian people openly welcome the FARC fighters. The difference from one area to another is evident beyond roadside checkpoints. Colombians – particularly organizers – assume they are watched and followed by repressive paramilitary forces all the time. They are very cautious about whom they will talk to and what they will say publicly. In a coastal area where paramilitaries have a lot of control, no one would speak above a whisper to me about the paramilitaries or the government because the police openly attended all of their meetings. Police–government–paramilitary collaboration is understood as a fact. By contrast, in FARC territory, people speak freely, without fear of reprisal. Talking politics with campesinos and with FARC soldiers, I experienced freedom of speech at a level I don't even feel in my own country. In addition, the campesinos reported that they felt safer in rebel-held territory. Members of one village told me that the government stopped committing a massacre when a campesino ran up the mountain because they knew that the FARC would be there momentarily to protect the villagers. People in these areas defended themselves with confidence from wealthy landowners who were threatening to push them off their land. They knew the FARC would back them up and defend their right to stay.

(Aby, 2006)

Gauging civilian support for the FARC-EP remains very difficult (see Leech, 2005b; Coghlan, 2004: 19; Livingstone, 2003: 204). It is widely recognized that "in Colombia, US military involvement has intensified the carnage and displaced hundreds of thousands of peasants to deprive the popular insurgents of recruits, food and logistical support" (Petras et al, 2005: 68). As these populations are forcibly displaced, the observable level of support for the FARC-EP becomes fragmented and difficult to calculate. If knowledge of a Colombian individual, community, or municipality, that supported the FARC-EP, were released publicly it would be targeted immediately by national and international counterinsurgency forces. This was made abundantly clear to me when I visited with community organizers and small producers in the department of Meta. Many peasants whom I met characterized themselves as somewhat supportive of the insurgency, yet they wished to remain anonymous for fear of "being found out" by state and "state-connected" forces outside areas of FARC-EP control. One of the reasons they wished to remain secret was not necessarily their own individual protection, but rather because they feared that family members living outside insurgent territory would be in jeopardy if their support became known.

During its initial years of formation, support for the insurgency was extensive, especially in the southwest (Livingstone, 2003: 180; Pearce, 1990a: 60, 167; Gilhodés, 1970: 433, 445; Gott, 1970: 235; Lartéguy, 1970: 143). Throughout the 1970s and 1980s, the guerrillas had support from "a substantial minority" of the rural inhabitants in many departments of the south. However, some have suggested that these sympathies started to decline in the 1990s (Hylton, 2006: 86). Others deny this decrease and suggest social support rose during the period, as a result of the continued deterioration of socioeconomic conditions and state absence (O'Shaughnessy and Branford, 2005: 34; Petras et al, 2005: 105, 113; Moser and McIlwaine, 2004: 42, 138–40). Schulte-Bockholt (2006: 106) claimed that popular support for the FARC-EP grew exponentially for much of the past 20 years as a direct consequence of counterrevolutionary violence and aggression toward the rural population (see also Comisión Andina de Juristas, 1990: 95). He argued that "the strength of the FARC has grown considerably during the 1980s and 1990s, largely due to the polarization of the struggle over land between the local elites in league with criminal groups on one side and the peasants on the other" (2006: 110)

At the beginning of the 1990s it was noted that "several hundred thousand civilian activists, overwhelmingly peasants," were in clear support of the guerrillas, and within a decade roughly 1 million Colombians were in recognizable alliance with the FARC-EP (Petras, 1999: 30; Petras and Veltmeyer, 2001: 90). Over the last decade the FARC-EP expanded support because of "the rural crisis and the government's fumigation campaigns (which led to mass protests in 1995–1996)" (Livingstone, 2003: 208; see also Petras et al, 2005: 105, 113). When asked if the guerrillas helped or hindered the local population one 43-year-old *campesino* from Caquetá gave me an answer that cannot be found in any book, yet spoke volumes of the FARC-EP's role in the countryside.

> The guerrillas are a necessity! ... The insurgency lives with the people and has allowed the community to sustain its way of life. The insurgency is a necessity for if we want to change the state the people of Colombia cannot support or employ one simple form of struggle but many forms of resistance; we must have armed struggle, political education and community organization. It is through the FARC that these methods are constructed. The state does not sustain its power through one form but many; therefore, to alter such inequality and exploitation the people of this country must resist and struggle in all forms that the current exploitation holds ground.

For hours this humble peasant reiterated that entire communities have come to support, interact with and exist through a reciprocal alliance with the FARC-EP. I found this interesting, for how could so many media soundbites and state reports claim that the FARC-EP has minimal or declining support when so much information, both past and present, proved otherwise?

During an interview with a 58-year-old worker from Nariño (now displaced and living in Bogotá), I was told that any "decline" in support during the 1990s was a calculated response from the civilian population. He described how systemic paramilitary violence fell upon anyone who displayed the slightest antagonism toward state policy and/or the economy. It should be borne in mind that state and paramilitary forces murdered 40,000 in this decade alone (Petras, 2003: 25; see also Petras and Morley, 1990: 163). This figure in some ways "suggests the degree to which the guerrillas were and are deeply rooted among the working and peasant population" (Petras, 2003: 25). Even researchers critical of the FARC-EP have noted that the guerrillas have had the support of many living in regions under insurgent control (Rochlin, 2003: 132–3). The reasons for this are many.

After Plan Colombia's multi-year military push (failed) it was clear, once again, that the guerrillas had "solid popular support" in the south (Mondragón, 2007: 43; see also Weinstein, 2007). The more Bogotá and Washington increased efforts to coercively eliminate support for the guerrillas, the greater that support became (Peceny and Durnan, 2006: 109). Rather than destroying the solidarity through counterinsurgency, civil violence, and counter-narcotics programs, the insurgency's social base was solidified.

> Over the past four decades, the FARC has become a formidable guerrilla formation, accumulating a vast store of practical understanding of the psychological and material bases of guerrilla warfare and mass recruitment – not in a linear fashion but through trail and error, setbacks and advances. Throughout its history of championing land reform and peasant rights the FARC has been able to create peasant cadres who link villagers and leaders and communicate in both directions.
>
> (Petras and Morley, 2003: 101)

Accounts have shown that many social movements groups containing significant numbers of civilians have come to assist the guerrillas in urban and rural locales (Bajak, 2008b; Moser and McIlwaine, 2004: 138–40). These have facilitated the mobilization of civilian demonstrations against domestic and foreign state policies (O'Shaughnessy and Branford, 2005: 34; Petras et al, 2005: 92).[20] Such activities further the guerrillas' rapport with rural workers, *campesinos*, landless peoples, and indigenous nations through mutual cooperation. Former US Special Forces trainer Stan Goff (2003: 78) described how civilian assistance has also provided logistical data on state and paramilitary "composition, strength and disposition," enabling the FARC-EP to procure decisive victories over state forces.[21]

Chalmers Johnson (1966: 160–1), a former agent with the US Central Intelligence Agency (CIA) turned influential scholar on issues of unconventional revolutionary conflict, provided a practical account of how a successful guerrilla force must obtain – and retain – grassroots support (see also Wilkinson, 1971: 137–8). Johnson detailed how guerrilla-based struggles evolve over time through alliances with the local population, a progressive change in sociopolitical structures, and a final shift from purely positional warfare to open conflict with the dominant system. Based on Johnson's approach, backing for the FARC-EP is therefore recognizable by its half-century of continuity. Rather than representing a fundamentalist schism, the movement has achieved a "growing ascendancy among the Colombians most affected by the economic, political, and social situation" (Petras and Brescia, 2000: 138).

There exist a number of support networks linked to the FARC-EP:

- The aforementioned combatant forces overseen by the Secretariat, who are life-long members of the insurgency.
- *Militias (milicianos)*, primarily made up of young men and women between 15 and 35 who are directly trained by the FARC-EP but remain in small villages and medium-sized towns. These groups provide technical and communications services to the guerrillas, informing the insurgents of where and when state/paramilitary forces are or have been, and so on.
- *Urban militias (milicianos urbana)*. Somewhat similar to militias, these persons are trained by the FARC-EP and located in the *barrios* of major cities where they provide logistical support. Both urban militias and militias are free to work with the FARC-EP or leave the alliance (see Gutiérrez Sanín, 2008: 32n.41);
- There has also been growth in "Bolivarian cells," where civilians and guerrillas work together through the Bolivarian Movement for a New Colombia (*Movimiento Bolivariano por la Nueva Colombia*, MBNC): a clandestine political organization formed by the FARC-EP (Brittain, 2005c: 36; FARC-EP, 2000c).
- The *Clandestine Colombian Communist Party* (*Partido Comunista Clandestino Colombiano*, PCCC[22]), an independent underground political party located in vast rural locales and certain urban regions (with a significant number of members in various universities throughout the country).[23]
- *Popular militias (milicianos popular)*, numerous men and women, usually of a mature age, in solidarity with the FARC-EP but remaining in their communities to organize support and communication.

Through first-hand experience Johnson (1966: 161–3) asserted that without local support a guerrilla movement would undoubtedly collapse in a short period. Examples of this have been experienced throughout Latin America, most famously in Bolivia with the death of Che Guevara (Ryan, 1998; see also Salmón, 1990; Harris, 1970). If a guerrilla force is able to sustain itself or expand, it could be argued that this is an indication of external solidarity. Some may argue, however, that for a guerrilla movement to persist is not necessarily an indication of voluntary support, but rather it might employ methods of coercion to acquire backing or recruit members (see Lair, 2003: 94). My own experience suggests that this is not the case with the FARC-EP. On numerous occasions I observed civilians being free to support and work with the guerrillas or peacefully refuse assistance.

During a public forum on education, consisting of a few dozen peasants

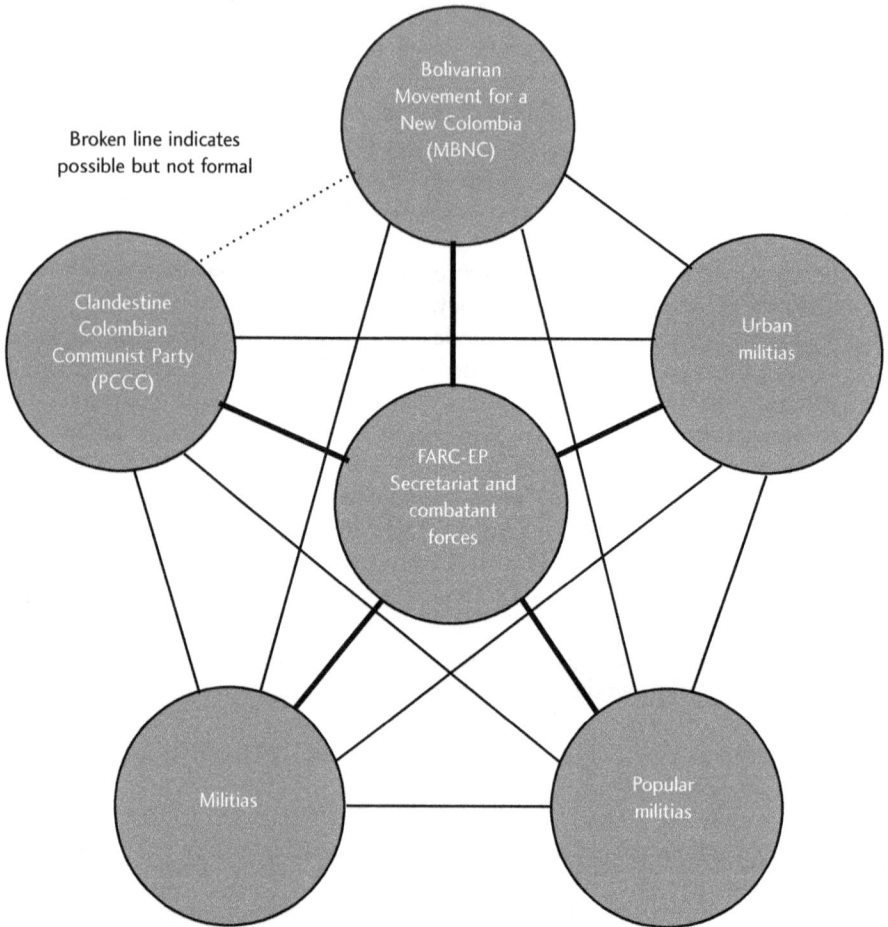

Figure 2.4 The FARC-EP's interlinking support and solidarity structure
Source: information obtained through observational research in 2004.

and seven members of the FARC-EP, it was clear to me that a reciprocal dialog exists between rural civilians and the guerrilla. Certain issues were mutually agreed upon and others aggressively debated. One comandante of the FARC-EP claimed that such differences of opinion were the only way in which the guerrillas and community members could work together to create better community-based policy. While I never experienced a heated argument between any FARC-EP member and local civilians, it was more than evident that differences arose when some locals expressed their desire for the guerrillas to increase the number of educational classes (in literacy, writing, and so on) offered to the public. Roughly six persons in the audience claimed there was a desire and need for classes to be held every morning. In response, the guerrillas tried to explain that they could not hold daily daytime lessons for security reasons. Interested civilians would have to either attend evening classes (held twice a week) or continue to attend the weekly morning class already offered. After the forum ended it was unmistakable that a range of views existed over the availability of and access to education, yet it was clear that there was little fear of reprisal for expressing different opinions. A few years after observing the meeting, I was able to meet with a handful of those in attendance that day. They informed me that while it is difficult, their periodical educational classes continue, as does their support for the guerrillas. As one put it, "We can support the FARC-EP but still debate with them."

A guerrilla force that chooses to hold onto power through terror cannot sustain itself over time.[24] If coercion is the only medium through which a body maintains power, then it will not be long until the base of its power – the local population – withdraws its "solidarity" (see Johnson, 1966: 162–3). The FARC-EP, as the longest-running and most powerful guerrilla movement in Latin American history, illustrates how community support has helped to enabled its continuity (see Brittain, 2005c: 36; Petras and Morley, 2003: 101–2; Petras and Veltmeyer, 2001: 90; Petras and Brescia, 2000: 135, 142). To succeed the FARC-EP must further consolidate the civilian population along revolutionary class lines (see Bottomore, 1973: 31). As alliances continue, interpersonal/community connections between the guerrillas and local society have the potential to create a micro-level testing ground for radical social change (see Johnson, 1966: 162).

I have made a case that support for the FARC-EP exists in Colombia. However, it should also be noted that there is significant protest against it. In February 2008, hundreds of thousands marched throughout Colombia's cities (and around the world) in apparent opposition to the guerrillas and their continued armed struggle. We now need to contextualize this massive event.

Popular protest: February 4 and March 6, 2008

It could never be claimed that the FARC-EP is a universally supported or even universally accepted social movement. February 4, 2008 made this evident, as people flooded Colombia's streets to protest against the guerrillas.[25] While opposition to the insurgency has been present for decades, early 2008 was significant as the protest took on a popular form. It is important to examine the social construction of this parade of disapproval.

The internet has been heralded as an egalitarian medium through which true democratic voices can be expressed and recognized. Facebook is an effective example of this perspective. It could be argued that the social networking outlet is a progressive communication device which provides the public with a centralized digital location through which there can be interaction and organization using non-hierarchical and non-exclusionary methods. Using Facebook a small group of young media-savvy Colombians generated "a website to organize hundreds of thousands for a one-day, worldwide protest against the kidnappings of Colombians and foreigners by that country's leftist rebels. The effect was a public cry against an imposition of fear" (Christian Science Monitor, 2008).[26] If we look closer, however, is it true that this was a spontaneous and egalitarian protest? Did February 4 demonstrate widespread dissent from FARC-EP's aims and methods?

Roughly 96 percent of Colombia's population has no direct access to the internet (Telecom Paper, 2008). With less than 5 percent regularly accessing the Web, notions of democratic expression via the internet are highly exaggerated. Even taking into consideration the country's many internet cafés, only one in four Colombians can gain access, because of issues of cost, time, and surveillance (see Janicke, 2008b). In addition to this, there is no guarantee of reliable electricity supplies on a daily basis in various cities, let alone medium-sized towns (Coghlan, 2004: 205–6). This momentous digital divide should make us question whether the February 4 protest was truly democratically representative. Deconstructing the protest, Kiraz Janicke (2008a) considered the socioeconomic and political realities surrounding it, and how many of the organizers were wealthy young internet users. Much of the event was controlled and promoted by sectors of the Colombian state, with extensive support from the country's primary business owners (see Janicke, 2008a; Vieira, 2008a). As Bill Weinberg put it,

> the campaign clearly had official sanction. Throughout the country, schools cancelled classes for the day or let students out early. In a public square in the northeastern city of Valledupar, President Álvaro Uribe voiced his support for the mobilization. Many marchers openly supported Uribe.
>
> (Weinberg, 2008a)

Most disturbing (and telling of the actual political intentions of the protest) was the fact that some of those leading the anti-FARC-EP parades were "leaders of right-wing paramilitary death squads" (Janicke, 2008b). This made it quite easy for left-of-center politicians to claim that February 4 was nothing more than a "pre-fascist" expression of Colombia's political division (see Archila, 2007).[27] Investigating the dominant classes' role in the event, Deirdre Griswold (2008) saw the demonstration as "widely publicized in advance by all the major pro-government media," while "the Colombian stock exchange closed down for it, bosses pressured their workers to attend, and the government shut down schools and public services for the rally." The protest also went beyond a denunciation of the FARC-EP, as it attacked Latin America's leftward momentum (Janicke, 2008b). Some commentators noted similarities between February 4 and the anti-left protests witnessed in Chile during the administration of Salvador Allende (1970–73), which claimed to be of the people but were in fact structurally orchestrated by reactionaries (Griswold, 2008). It was not long until "the pro-war 'peace' demonstrations dominated by Colombia's wealthy classes revealed deep divisions within Colombian society" (Janicke, 2008b).

After the events of February 4, another domestic and international mass march related to Colombia's civil war took place. In contrast to the well-publicized February protests, the Colombian-based National Movement of

Victims of State-Sponsored Crimes (*Movimiento Nacional de Víctimas de Crímenes de Estado*, MOVICE) and various social justice-based organizations, promoted March 6 as a day of remembrance, homage, and protest against those tortured, murdered, and disappeared by past and present governments, militaries, and paramilitary-linked factions. For months, human rights groups, sectors of organized labor, and politically conscious civilians worked together to create a domestic and international response to state-based atrocities. Luis Alberto Matta (2008) highlighted that 270 cities, towns, and villages across Colombia connected with each other to organize the event. Outside Colombia, an estimated 140 cities in 23 countries across Asia, Australia, Europe, North America, and Latin America coordinated events outside Colombian embassies and consulates in conjunction with the day of protest (see also Martínez, 2008a). After months of preparation and days of travel, Colombian men and women peacefully demonstrated their distaste for the state's activities.[28] Hundreds of thousands from both the countryside and cities came forward to condemn state coercion (Rueda, 2008). Over 40,000 arrived in Bogotá alone to surround the Casa de Nariño and Plaza de Bolívar in protest (BBC, 2008; Weinberg, 2008b).

While the organizers and promoters of February 4 came from a specific social stratum, the urban-based political-economic elite, the March 6, 2008 protest saw Colombians from all socioeconomic brackets, religions, ethnic backgrounds, and racial categories flood the country's dirt roads and paved streets. Although the demonstration proved to be a peace-filled egalitarian success, the state had tried relentlessly to dissuade participation through both direct coercion and psychological intimidation. A few weeks prior to the march, President Uribe's top political adviser, José Obdulio Gaviria, proclaimed that the events scheduled for March 6 were nothing more than a rally coordinated by the FARC-EP (Vieira, 2008a). Coinciding with state threats, Colombia's popular media groups, primarily *El Tiempo*,[29] made a spectacle of FARC-EP comandante Raúl Reyes, who had been killed a few days earlier.[30] News outlets paraded photographs of Reyes' bullet-ridden and mutilated corpse on an hourly basis. This was as a tool to intimidate activists, attack sociopolitical direct action, and deter sympathizers from criticizing the state's political dominance and promotion of far-right economic/military policies. When these tactics proved insufficient, direct methods of intimidation were deployed. In the southwestern department of Nariño, paramilitaries threatened to attack any organization or person associated with March 6 as "military objectives" (Vieira, 2008a).[31]

Days prior to the demonstration, in the face of threats and intimidation, indigenous communities, Afro-Colombians, and rural-based civilians began their procession to the Plaza de Bolívar in the heart of Bogotá. Helda Martínez (2008a) documented how roughly 700 people of various ethnicities and racial backgrounds – all of whom had been displaced by state and paramilitary forces – from Cauca, Chocó, Cundinamarca, Huila, and Tolima joined together at a bridge linking Flandes, Tolima and Girardot, Cundinamarca. The collective then symbolically dropped thousands of "flowers of all colors" into the flowing current of the country's famous Magdalena River, paying homage to those disappeared, tortured, and/or murdered by a select minority that attempts to uphold Colombia's dominant class. While such an organic wide-ranging national and international statement was made by everyday Colombians from every corner of the country, "the peaceful nationwide demonstration ... basically went unreported by the mainstream media, by contrast with the heavy international coverage of the global Feb. 4 march against the Revolutionary Armed Forces of Colombia (FARC) guerrillas" (Martínez, 2008b).

What about the popular polls?

Several times a year Colombians are exposed to national popularity polls that attempt to gauge levels of support for the state. It is assumed that the surveys offer a representation of faith in the government and military, while providing the international community with an apparent picture of stability. The polls are conducted across Colombia, and produce a quantitative measure of endorsement for state policies and programs. During President Uribe's first term (2002–06), they showed approval to be above the 70th percentile, and it was in the mid-80s and low-90s halfway through his second term (2006–10). Some argued that Uribe had the highest level of support of any president in the Americas (Bajak, 2008a). This is unique (and somewhat perplexing), as a variety of factors plagued this administration and would have been regarded as an inhospitable climate for most other Latin American governments.

Aside from the fact that it is one of the most unequal countries in the hemisphere, roughly 10 percent of Colombia's population have been forced to leave their communities as a result of threats from paramilitary and state forces (Consultoría para los Derechos Humanos y el Desplazamiento, 2007). Another factor is Colombia's "*parapolitica* scandal." Since 2006, well over 100 governors, mayors, military officials, and Congressional politicians have been alleged to have, or were found guilty of having, direct connections, meetings, and/or contracts with paramilitary contingents. During these collaborations thousands of political opponents, trade unionists, and community organizers became the targets of threats and assassinations, and/or they "disappeared."[32] Included in this list are Colombia's vice-president, Francisco Santos Calderón, his cousin, former defense minister Juan Manuel Santos, President Uribe's brother Santiago, and their cousin, former senator Mario Uribe, the brother of interior and justice minister Fabio Valencia Cossio, three brothers and the stepson of Colombia's attorney general, Eduardo Maya Villazón, Senator Carlos García Orjuela, the president of Uribe's Social National Unity Party (*Partido Social de Unidad Nacional, Partido de la 'U'*) – the list goes on (Guillen, 2008; Wingerter, 2008; Forero, 2007b; Romero, 2007). It has been alleged that secret paramilitary meetings also took place at the President's personal Guacharacas *finca* (Forero, 2007a; Semana, 2007).[33] According to Salvatore Mancuso, the AUC's principal leader, the actual number of sitting politicians linked to the paramilitary rests around 100 (see Thompson, 2008). When we consider such problematic internal conditions, coupled with an apparent rise in support for the electoral left in the majority of Latin America (including Colombia[34]) during the 2000s, it is surprising that a right-wing government should enjoy such popular support. This paradox calls for a deeper examination of Uribe's popularity.

In March 2008 a Gallup poll found that virtually all Colombians were in support of the Uribe administration (Angus Reid Global Monitor, 2008a). Colombia's most read daily claimed that the president experienced unprecedented support, with record approval ratings (El Tiempo, 2008). The poll was extensive, with 1,000 Colombians in different parts of the country being interviewed (Murphy, 2008). It is seldom understood, however, that the vast majority of these polls are carried out using telephone interviews via landlines (Bajak, 2008a). This is highly problematic for several reasons. First, many Colombians do not use landlines: they are too poor, they do not have access for geographical reasons, or they have personal or political reasons for avoiding them. While mobile phones are widely used throughout much of the country, many areas lack basic infrastructure such as landlines. Some major cities do not yet have the infrastructure to guarantee a stable electricity supply, let alone fixed-line optical networks (see Coghlan, 2004: 205–6). Second, those who are interviewed can easily be traced through their landlines, so the polls are not truly anonymous. This is important to highlight, for it is the state that encourages and partially funds these polls. Third, although polls such as the one quoted claim to be of a representative sample of Colombians, in fact the interviewees are drawn almost entirely from specific zones in the four largest cities.

Alfredo Molano argued that these circumstances create a flagrant example of how the state enables small segments of elite society to express their class-biased political approval (see Feder, 2004). Such polls manipulate information from a handful of dominant urban centers, while the state's most vociferous opponents in the countryside are silenced (Reuters, 2004). As one media outlet brazenly put it, "Colombian pollsters rarely survey the whole country because they consider responses in war-afflicted rural areas unreliable" (Associated Press, 2008c). Fourth, the timing of the March poll was noteworthy. The Gallup interviews took place between March 4 and 6, which directly followed the death of one of the FARC-EP's most prominent leaders a major victory in the eyes of the elite (see Mercopress, 2008). This was also just hours before one of the largest anti-state rallies in Colombia's recent history. When a wider sample were polled over Uribe's popularity weeks later, there was a decline in his approval rating. In May 2008, another 1,000 citizens were polled, but this time in 17 cities. The proportion of respondents in support of Uribe dropped by almost 20 percent (Angus Reid Global Monitor, 2008b). This resembled my own research: I found the further I traveled from the handful of affluent urban centers toward the *barrios*, rural communities, villages, and towns, the more opposition to the state I found. In fact, hostility toward Uribe has been constant, albeit muted (Mondragón, 2007, 2003, 2002).

THE FARC-EP AS A UNIQUE MARXIST SOCIAL MOVEMENT

The FARC-EP has been accused of being "the most dangerous international terrorist organization based in the Western hemisphere."[35] Espousing a Marxist-Leninist ideology, the guerrillas represent a material threat to Colombian administrations, the maximization of profits for foreign-based enterprises operating in the country, and domestic economic beneficiaries.[36] Yet approaches linked to classical Marxism have been characterized as outdated or insufficient under the changing global dynamics of capitalist expansion, leading theorists to call for other forms, avenues, or social constructs to change society (Hardt and Negri, 2004; 2000; Foweraker, 1995; Laclau and Mouffe, 1985). The FARC-EP offers a unique quandary within this scenario, as it has amalgamated characteristics of both Marxism-Leninism and social movement theory (see Petras, 2003, 1997b; Petras and Veltmeyer, 2003a, 2001; Veltmeyer and Petras, 2002). Anything but a dogmatic guerrilla organization trapped in a long-dead ideological framework, the FARC-EP has adapted and adopted an inimitable approach towards Marxism, which could in part be a reason for its longevity.

Understanding the need for multiple forms of struggle, Marulanda acknowledged that the FARC-EP was not the sole route to create a socialist Colombia, and emphasized a need for the Party (Marulanda, 2003: 120). Moving beyond previous exclusionary and inflexible communist regime structures, the FARC-EP promotes a unified democratic collective with various affiliations whose aim is an "equitable redistribution of wealth and resources" on its rise to power (Petras and Brescia, 2000: 135).[37] As the guerrillas distinguish themselves from the "camps" of conventional social movements or Marxist forces, it is important to detail these differences.

The 1990s saw the FARC-EP grow at an immense rate. As numbers of recruits rose, so too did non-combatant support, both materially and ideologically. Aijaz Ahmad (2006) claimed the rise was the result of the exploited responding to their material conditions. Ironically, this was during a period when Latin America, as a whole, experienced a period of revolutionary decline while maneuvering toward a neoliberal political-economic paradigm (Raby, 2006; Castañeda, 1994). With nation-states adopting strategies of increased privatization, decreases in social spending and services, and international tariff reductions placing further strains on domestic workers, it was not difficult to see suffering at the hands of minorities who controlled profits and state policy. Contrary to structural theory, however, declines in states' capacity to govern did not result in radical social change, as revolutions were not on the radar of most countries in Latin America at this time. In what seemed to be a volatile regional situation, revolutionary movements and important struggles appeared to fade as a result of cooptation, coercive force, and/or fatigue (Petras and Morley, 2003: 100; Petras, 2002: 28–9; see also Buscaglia and Ratliff, 2001: vi). Nevertheless, Colombia proved to be an exception where the candle of revolutionary sentiment burned on.

Initially, FARC grew slowly but with the advent of the brutal neoliberal policies of the 1990s it began to expand very rapidly so that, by the end of the decade, its power extended to perhaps as much as half the country. It concentrated on the main productive areas, such as the coffee, banana and petroleum regions, while also penetrating the urban centres and building up forces in rural districts surrounding those centres.

(Ahmad, 2006: 62; see also Petras et al, 2005: 8, 105, 113, 119; Livingstone, 2003: 208)

Throughout the mid to late 1990s, the FARC-EP took center stage as it decimated state forces while expanding control (Hylton, 2006: 90; Marks, 2002; Richani, 2001: 57; Ruiz, 2001: 18–36).[38] It was during this period that Washington and the Colombian state quietly realized that a very real hemispheric threat to capitalist interests was emerging (Bergquist, Peñaranda and Sanchez, 2003: xxi; Rochlin, 2003: 133; Solaún, 2002: 1; Ruiz, 2001: 21; Farah, 1998; NACLA, 1998). While the fashionable postmodernists and reassured conservatives argued that we were seeing the "end of history," Colombia showed that such claims were premature. Questions soon arose: How was any of this possible with the "end" of communism and the cold war? Were not all Marxist-Leninist movements dependent on the USSR, and with its fall did not all remaining communist struggles collapse? Attempts at answering these queries bring into focus the FARC-EP's stability and power from below.

During the cold war Marxist-based insurgency movements around the world could obtain objective and subjective support from the USSR. A number of revolutionary groups (in other words, guerrilla movements) became heavily reliant on "some form of external aid, weapons, personnel and food supplies, and a degree of external ideological and military support" without which they would have been unable to sustain their activity (Wilkinson, 1971: 138; see also Cameron, 1966: 39). The end of the cold war led to a precipitous and immediate decline of revolutionary movements, especially in Latin America, showing that Soviet paternalism had been inefficient. In Colombia, "official *expectations* were that the guerrillas would experience reduced capacity in the years to come," and in time they would become extinct in a growing post-Marxist world (Sánchez, 2003: 31, italics added). Some analysts went so far as to suggest that "after the fall of the Sandinistas and the Berlin Wall, revolution once again disappeared from the left's lexicon" (Castañeda, 1994: 68). Amidst this presumed disappearance the FARC-EP remained, still following a Marxist-Leninist strategy of self-determination.

The collapse of the FARC-EP never occurred. The insurgency not only survived the cold war and the breakdown of Soviet-styled communism, it witnessed a remarkable growth in both numerical size and geographical space controlled. This led to numerous scholars questioning how such a geopolitical occurrence could have taken place. Characterizing this period, Mark Peceny and Michael Durnan (2006: 95–6) described how the FARC-EP's growth during the 1990s was an anomaly caused by "the spread of liberal democracy and withdrawal of international assistance to formerly Cold War-era guerrilla groups," which more or less "shattered the ideological and financial base that has traditionally fuelled revolutionary upheavals." Michael K. Steinberg added to this by stating that:

> the success of the Marxist Fuerzas Armadas Revolucionarias de Colombia (Revolutionary Armed Forces of Colombia, of FARC) is intriguing, given that the Soviet Union, the former sponsor of many Marxist-oriented revolutionary groups in the developing world, officially no longer exists. Initially, one would assume that the power of the FARC would wane without the support of a powerful political sponsor. To the contrary ... the FARC's strength has grown since the end of the cold war, and it now has the Colombian military on the defensive across much of the country.
>
> (Steinberg, 2000: 264)

There are numerous theories about how the FARC-EP was able to sustain its political and ideological organization following the cold war. Many link the FARC-EP's sustainability to the drug economy and other criminal activities (see Peceny and Durnan, 2006: 108–9; Labrousse, 2005: 179; Rochlin, 2003: 100; Steinberg, 2000: 264). The hypothesis behind these popular arguments is that the FARC-EP's power is dependent on the coca industry. This perspective is analyzed later in the book, but it should be stated here that it is historically limited (and politically neglectful) in that it fails to analyze the praxis of the insurgency and its relation to a communist ideal in a post-Cold War geopolitical environment.[39] We can get a better answer to how the insurgency has sustained its ideology and practice through an in-depth investigation of the FARC-EP's Marxism-Leninism. This analysis reveals that the FARC-EP, prior to the collapse of the Soviet Union, took on a non-dogmatic philosophy that was contextually relevant to the writings of Marxism-Leninism, Colombian society, and the realization of radical social change at a national level. To fully understand the FARC-EP's unique Marxism-Leninism coupled with its unparalleled place in the modern world, it is important to further analyze the relations between the FARC-EP, the PCC, and the larger dynamics of the cold war, and also to analyze the FARC-EP's separation from the PCC (and the CPSU/USSR).

The FARC-EP's break from the PCC and the CPSU and its survival

While programmatic debates often arose between the groups, the PCC remained vigilantly aligned with the USSR throughout much of the 1960s and 1970s. The FARC-EP was a different story. As shown by Petras (2003: 99), "while some of the leaders of the FARC, including its legendary leader Manuel Marulanda, are formally members of the Communist Party of Colombia, in fact, the FARC has its own leadership, program, strategy and tactics, with a decidedly distinct social base."

In addition, the guerrilla organization derived only marginal assistance (in the form of arms) from the Soviets during a brief window in the 1960s, and was thus hardly dependent upon any foreign patron for its development (Maullin, 1973: 23–4). Mario A. Murillo and Jesus Rey Avirama (2004: 58) maintained, "the FARC by no means represented a transplanted, externally influenced insurrection, as the U.S. government had at times tried to convey" (see also Ortiz, 2006: 208–9). The insurgency has long gone "without either foreign financial or material contributions ... unlike other guerrilla movements, the FARC did not receive any material support from the outside" (Petras, 2008). Rooted in regional and national class realities, the guerrillas have struggled against immediate problems of domestic exploitation and imperialist encroachments, which predate the Cuban revolution (Premo, 1988: 237; see also Leech, 2002a: 16). Richard Maullin (1973: 24–5) clarified that it was not foreign assistance that constructed or sustained the guerrillas but rather factors from below; hence, "whatever the particulars of foreign contributions to Colombia's revolutionary violence, they seem not to be as important a motive for the existence and scope of insurgent activity as factors inherent in Colombia's internal political life."

As the insurgency did not gain from foreign assistance it was supported almost entirely through PCC members in the cities and countryside (Maullin, 1973: 25; see also de la Peña, 1998: 331). Nevertheless, we must remember that life in working-class Colombia during the 1960s and 1970s was difficult, and many trials and tribulations were experienced by the FARC-EP at this time. "Unlike the other guerrilla groups in Colombia, who received assistance from third parties like the Cuban government, the FARC was dirt poor and got little or no help from its natural ideological ally, the Soviet Union. These were lean years" (Dudley, 2004: 50).

Being self-reliant on local support was partially why the FARC-EP went virtually unscathed by the collapse of the USSR. The guerrillas had "never been dependent upon Soviet-Cuban alliance. Instead the guerrilla ... have been self-sufficient economically, which has permitted them a free and unfettered hand in their political endeavors" (Rochlin, 2003: 4; see also Ortiz, 2006: 210; Schulte-Bockholt, 2006: 137). This organic strategy highlights why the FARC-EP "actually gained military power since the 1980s, while other Latin American leftist groups dependent on Soviet-Cuban support were forced to the bargaining table and subsequently disappeared" (Rochlin, 2003: 100).

The guerrillas recognized that material conditions, not foreign immaterial ideas, lead to social change. As many Colombian intellectuals started to accept radical means of change (see Maullin, 1973: 16), others clarified that revolutionary class conflict must be a verb, not a noun. From this point of view revolution was realized by way of national conditions (Gomez, 1972: 255). Remaining outside material circumstances (both figuratively and literally) can prevent revolutionary goals from becoming necessary (Gomez, 1972: 248).

During the 1960s and 1970s, tensions were realized between varying CPs in relation to the desired programmatic perspectives of the CPSU (and the USSR). Castañeda (1994: 31) wrote how several Latin American communist parties "were split into those which exercised only a marginal, passive role and those that became active players in the political arena." Many continued a dual strategy, as was agreed to be permissible by the Havana Conference (1964) and Tri-Continental Conference (1966).[40]

> The distinguishing feature in the Latin American Left is its emphasis on the *via armada* and rejection of the *via pacífica*, favored by Moscow-line communists. Violence and armed struggle are seen as inevitable; parliamentary democracy has proved a fraud; elections can never truly express the people's will. Armed struggle in the countryside is not simply a tactic; if it were there would be little quarrel with the communists, who are prepared to use violence provided they are in control, and to use guerrilla methods ... as they still are prepared to do in the case of the communist-controlled FARC (Fuerzas Armadas Revolucionarias de Colombia) in Colombia.
>
> (Hennessey, 1972: 15)

By the 1970s, however, all CPs in Latin America abandoned a dual strategy except the PCC (Gott, 1970: 12, 28). Not wanting to lose what successful gains had been made with the peasantry, "the PCC's role differed from that of other Latin American Communist parties, who had distanced themselves from the guerrilla movements in their respective countries following directives from Moscow" (Schulte-Bockholt, 2006: 109).[41] After 1966, the PCC represented:

> the longest and most consistent record of a party combining armed actions with legal and parliamentary activities. Actually, it is the only CP on the continent that did not abandon a dual strategy in response to the 20th Congress of the CPSU.
>
> (Hodges, 1974: 53)

The only country to maintain this position, Colombia saw a balancing of armed class conflict alongside electoral mechanisms well beyond the 1970s and into the 1980s (Miller, 1989: 12; Osterling, 1989: 187; Ratliff, 1976: 190; Alexander, 1973: 47). However, as time went on links between the Party and guerrillas fragmented; hence, the need to clarify how and why the FARC-EP are no longer connected to the official CP.

To claim that at the moment the FARC-EP is associated with the PCC is not only incorrect in its assumption but also ill-informed about the organizational framework and contextual political environment of Colombia's history and present. In the early 1980s, differences between the PCC and FARC-EP started to show, and:

> the FARC evolved from an armed force subject to the Communist Party to an independent guerrilla organization with its own political and military doctrine. At the time the FARC gained more public attention than before, and it underwent a metamorphosis that brought rapid growth, as well as its separation from the Communist Party
>
> (Safford and Palacios, 2003: 356; see also Skidmore and Smith, 2005: 244)[42]

One of the principal reasons for the dissolution was the insurgency's contempt toward "communism's" abandonment of Marxism through the acceptance of capitalist tendencies via the implementation of *perestroika* (FARC-EP, 1999: 47). As a result of its separation from "official" communist relations the FARC-EP went unaffected by the collapse of the Soviet era (Castañeda, 1994: 240–1; Lévy, 2004: 80; FARC-EP, 1999: 47–8).[43] Former Secretariat member Iván Ríos argued that abiding by a Colombian interpretation of Marxist revolution "saved us when the Berlin Wall fell" (as quoted in Lévy, 2004: 80; see also FARC-EP, 1999: 49). Unlike many revolutionary struggles that followed the instruction (and leadership) of the CPSU during much of the twentieth century (see Barlow, 1993: 189), the guerrillas reasoned and responded to national conditions through a contextual knowledge of domestic class relations. With the USSR no longer, the FARC-EP became a leading example of how national struggles can dialectically construct their own strategies, forms, and methods of communist direction (see O'Shaughnessy and Branford, 2005; Ferro Medina and Uribe Ramón, 2002). As a result, "the FARC represented the epitome of the post-Soviet guerrilla threat in the Americas" (Rochlin, 2003: 152; see also Cala, 2000: 56).

The FARC-EP's distinctive Marxism-Leninism

The FARC-EP has shown to be distinct in its approach toward Marxism-Leninism in several ways, in both leadership and strategy. For example, the insurgency was shaped, organized, and remains led by the peasantry.[44] Outside the FARC-EP, there has never been a peasant-founded, structured, directed, or sustained revolutionary organization in modern Central or South American society (Richani, 2002a: 60; Veltmeyer and Petras, 2002: 82; Wickham-Crowley, 1992: 18, 26). Those within the Secretariat have a personal connection to the countryside, as do "most of the commanders of the fronts and columns" (Weinstein, 2007: 289; see also Gibbs, 2008; Richani, 2007: 414-15; 2002a: 63; Wickham-Crowley, 1992: 331). The leadership has been historically made up of people from rural backgrounds rather than doctors, professors, lawyers, priests, or students (Weinstein, 2007: 289; de la Peña, 1989: 353; see also Richani, 2007: 414–15; 2002a: 63).[45] While various guerrilla movements garnished considerable peasant support, their leadership derived from university-trained intellectuals.[46]

The FARC-EP's rank and file also deviate from other Latin American guerrilla movements, including others in Colombia (Wickham-Crowley, 1992). Rather than coming from the middle and upper-economic strata, the membership has had "little or no support from university students or intellectuals" (Petras, 1999: 30). Through an organic response to their immediate socioeconomic and political conditions, not top-down structures, small producers and subsistence peasants have predominantly mobilized the FARC-EP (see FARC-EP, 1999: 9).

Being a peasant-incepted, organized, and maintained revolutionary organization, the FARC-EP represents the only example of such a movement in contemporary Latin America (Veltmeyer and Petras, 2002: 82; Richani, 2002a: 60; Wickham-Crowley, 1992: 18, 26). In regard to its formation and leadership, peasants have been the primary initiators of the FARC-EP's activity and not merely secondary respondents, as has been the case in most insurgencies (Petras and Brescia, 2000; Petras and Harding, 2000). This is not to imply that peasants have been uninvolved in past attempts of self-emancipation, because they have, in Cuba, El Salvador, Guatemala, Nicaragua, Peru, and currently Bolivia, Brazil, Mexico, and Venezuela. Nor does it suggest that Colombia's middle and upper-economic strata, urban-based unionists, or other sectors of society are not in the ranks of, or associated with, the guerrillas – as they most assuredly are. What this does signify is that the FARC-EP offers an alternative example of a Latin American insurgency through leadership and strategy.[47]

Another distinction of the FARC-EP's Marxism-Leninism has been its approach toward nurturing revolution within Latin America. The FARC-EP was one of the only Latin America insurgencies to not adopt a Cuban-applied model of *foco* theory[48] (see Guevara, 2006; Debray, 1967). All too often guerrilla ideology has been over-generalized as lacking ideological premise by simply following the examples of Cuba (see Wilkinson, 1971: 139). Such assumptions could not be further from the truth, as scholars like H. Michael Erisman and John M. Kirk (2006: 162) noted the insurgency was never influenced by Havana (see also Maullin, 1973; Gott, 1970). Contrary to Régis Debray's (1967: 27) claim that the attack on Marquetalia signified the "end of an epoch and attests the death of a certain ideology," the FARC-EP is the clearest example of how a Marxist-Leninist revolutionary social movement, following a platform of emancipation, can exist. Rather than following a *foco* strategy, the FARC-EP maintain a model by which local power is amassed through the establishment of broad support over long periods (Avilés, 2006: 36; Hylton, 2006: 56–7; Petras, 2003: 24; 1999: 30–1; Pizzaro Leongómez, 1992: 181–2; Pearce, 1990a: 168; Gomez, 1972). "The FARC doctrine," according to Schulte-Bockholt (2006: 111), "proclaimed that revolutionary conditions developed over time." Hence, the FARC-EP "has built its power base patiently over time with a precise strategic plan: the accumulation of local power" (Petras, 1999: 30).

The above details how the FARC-EP shaped itself through a unique "form of Marxism-Leninism" (O'Shaughnessy and Branford, 2005: 25; see also Cala, 2000: 59). This was noted by philosopher Bernard-Henri Lévy, who wrote,

> there is something in this Marxism–Leninism that, despite its irreproachable rhetoric, resembles nothing I have ever heard or seen elsewhere ... this is an impeccable Communism; along with Cuba, this is the last Communism in Latin America and, certainly, the most powerful.[49]

> (Lévy, 2004: 82)

Unlike "new" or postmodernist social movements, the FARC-EP has committed itself to a less fashionable, classically oriented Marxism-Leninism (Goff,

2004: 39–41; see also O'Shaughnessy and Sue Branford, 2005: 26).[50] It has been suggested that this has paid off, as the FARC-EP possesses the potential to be victorious and in some ways is succeeding (Goff, 2004: 44, 47; see also Petras et al, 2005: 126; Röhl, 2004: 2). It has even been speculated that the FARC-EP may become "the first leftist guerrilla movement to achieve success in the post-cold war era" (Cala, 2000: 56).

3

THEORIZING REVOLUTION: THE IMPORTANCE OF COLOMBIA

The struggle of the proletariat with the bourgeoisie is at first a national struggle. The proletariat of each country must, of course, first of all settle matters with its own bourgeoisie. In depicting the most general phases of the development of the proletariat, we traced the more or less veiled civil war, raging within existing society, up to a point where the war breaks out into open revolution, and where the violent overthrow of the bourgeoisie lays the foundation for the sway for the proletariat.

Karl Marx and Frederick Engels (see Marx and Engels, 1976c: 495)

In 1872, Marx suggested that there are some countries where the proletariat "may achieve their aims by peaceful means" yet "we must also admit that in most countries" this is not the case and "force ... must be the lever of our revolution" (Marx, 1988a: 255; see also Raby, 2006: 5). Along these lines E. J. Hobsbawm wrote,

the road to socialism cannot be the same in, say, Britain and Brazil, or its perspectives equally bright or gloomy in Switzerland as in Colombia. The tasks of Marxists is to divide the countries of the world into realistic groupings and to analyze properly the very different conditions of progress in each group, without trying to impose any uniformity (such as "peaceful transition" or "insurrection") on all of them.

(Hobsbawm, 1973: 117)

While individual countries share a common denominator of class exploitation, each is affected by capitalism differently. This leads those in each country to create their own revolutionary identity, as "measures will of course be different in different countries" (Marx and Engels, 1976c: 505).[1] According to Marta Harnecker (1986: 128), "the historical transition" from capitalism to socialism "depends upon the concrete form of the class struggle in each country." This begins with the conscious and active deconstruction of the (pre)existing domestic conditions as oppressed movements begin to establish roots for social transformation.

No revolution can be uncompromisingly copied. Radical social change is based upon immediate sociopolitical and economic conditions not a deterministic, and sometimes foreign, rationalism (Marx, 1978: 56; see also Goff, 2004: 180–1).[2] Hence, "instead of creating a new sect alongside the several existing sects, let us develop our program out of a critical analysis of what is going on now, out of the real struggles and the real movement rather than sheer ratiocination" (Draper, 1978a: 107). Such insight emphasizes the potential benefit of guerrilla warfare.[3]

> Marxism differs from all primitive forms of socialism by not binding the movement to any one particular form of struggle .... Under no circumstances does Marxism confine itself to the forms of struggle possible and in existence at the given moment only, recognizing as it does that new forms of struggle, unknown to the participants of the given period, inevitably arise as the given social situation changes. In this respect Marxism learns, if we may so express it, from mass practice, and makes no claim whatever to teach the masses forms of struggle invented by 'systematisers' in the seclusion of their studies .... Marxism demands an absolutely *historical* examination of the question of the forms of struggle. To treat this question apart from the concrete historical situation betrays a failure to understand the rudiments of dialectical materialism. At different stages of economic evolution, depending on differences in political, national-cultural, living and other conditions, different forms of struggle; and in connection with this, the secondary, auxiliary forms of struggle undergo change in their turn. To attempt to answer yes or no to the question whether any particular means of struggle should be used, without making a detailed examination of the concrete situation of the given movement at the given stage of its development, means completely to abandon the Marxist position.
>
>   (Lenin, 1965f: 213, 214; see also 1965e: 176–7)

Various theorists have acknowledged how "different regions of the world experience the impact of capitalism differently; thus, regional and national movements arise that propose specific solutions to these varied strains" (Garner, 1996: 45; see also Hobsbawm, 1989; 1973; Draper, 1978b). Marx discussed this issue in 1877. Although capitalist events are "strikingly analogous" they nonetheless occur "in different historical milieux," leading to "quite disparate results" (Marx, 1989a: 201). As differences exist between regions so too will relations toward development (Marx, 1989b: 362). Based on this position, Marx pleaded that one not manipulate

> my historical sketch of the genesis of capitalism in Western Europe into a historical-philosophical theory of general development, imposed by fate on all peoples, whatever the historical circumstances in which they are placed, in order to eventually attain this economic formation which, with a tremendous leap of productive forces of social labour, assures the integral development of every individual producer.
>
>   (Marx, 1989a: 200)[4]

Certain Marxist sects have argued that the concept of a nation's right to self-determination is an outdated goal for minority-based political positioning

(Teeple, 2005: 68–70). Others reason that change in "backward countries" is not possible without revolutionary shifts first taking place in the most advanced (imperial) countries, as bourgeois–democratic reforms have yet to be realized in those regions. Determinist in structure and dismissive in form, such premises fail to grasp the capacity of revolutionary social movements in the majority world.[5]

In what Lenin called "backward countries" a large proportion of the population was of peasant origin, which already subscribed to bourgeois modes of capitalist relations. Some of these countries were able to obtain independence by centralizing governance firmly "in the hands of workers and peasants" (Lenin, 1966b: 490).[6] Citing these republics, Lenin came to an important conclusion concerning the peasantry. Certain nations, which did not identically replicate advanced capitalist countries, were able to facilitate some form of socialist governance. From this circumstance Lenin (1966b: 490–1) found that "not only in the industrially developed countries" can the shift to socialist dynamics be realized, "but also in those which have the peasantry as their basis." This emphasizes the importance of the majority world within the context of revolution and its linkages to global capitalist expansion.

As bourgeois-democratic reforms took place in France, England, and Germany so too did changes take place in countries like Brazil and Colombia, albeit in different eras and of different types (see, for example, the body of work detailing democratization in Latin America – Isacson, 2005: 21; Crandall, 2005a: 2–3; Munck, 1989; Harding and Petras, 1988: 3–17). The domestic bourgeoisie, far from weak or cowardly, periodically supported electoral politics, populism, social democracy, and so on, as the need for expanding markets increased (Raby, 2006: ch. 2). To not acknowledge that bourgeois-democratic changes have taken place in the majority world would be to negate the fact that internal class structures exist therein, and these structures secure power and class interests in association with imperialist counterparts.[7] Nevertheless, there are some who view the bourgeoisie in these countries as too impaired, limited, small, corrupt, and/or weak to objectively resist imperial power. Such a claim is problematic for several reasons. First, this perception seems to suggest that non-imperial nations fail to have an internal class who assist in controlling the country's economic and political affairs. This mode of thinking is preposterous in the case of Latin America (see Brazil, El Salvador, and Colombia), where an incredibly small domestic population held legal title over the vast majority of the country's resources and capital. Second, this premise fails to understand that capitalists – regardless of national placement – co-align with other members of their class in order to expand surplus profits (see Marx and Engels, 1976c: 481, 508).

A certain kind of brotherhood does of course exist among the bourgeois classes of all nations. It is a brotherhood of the oppressors against the oppressed, of the exploiters against the exploited. Just as, despite the competition and conflicts existing between the members of the bourgeoisie, the bourgeois class of one country is united by brotherly ties against the proletariat of that country, so the bourgeois of all countries, despite their mutual conflicts and competition on the world market, are united by brotherly ties against the proletariat of all countries. For the peoples to be able truly to unite, they must have common interests. And in order that their interests may become common, the existing property relations must be done away with, for these property relations involve the exploitation of some nations by others: the abolition of existing property relations is the concern only of the working class. It alone has also the means for doing this. The victory of the proletariat over the bourgeoisie is, at the same time, victory over the national and industrial conflicts which today range the peoples of the various countries against one another in hostility and enmity. And so the victory of the proletariat over the bourgeoisie is at the same time the signal of liberation for all oppressed nations .... Defeat your own internal enemies and you will then be able to pride yourselves on having defeated the entire old system.

(Marx, 1976b: 388)

Did Marx not write that "whether a tree is large or small it is a tree" (Marx, 1977: 213)? He saw it as naïve to view any bourgeoisie as inferior, subordinate, or different from any other regardless of birth or naturalization. Lenin too addressed how *all* capitalists have the same purpose, power, and unification regardless of the nation in which they reside, as they share

a certain *rapprochement* between the bourgeoisie of the exploiting countries and that of the colonies, so that very often – perhaps even in most cases – the bourgeoisie of the oppressed countries ... is in full accord with the imperialist bourgeoisie, i.e., join forces with it against all revolutionary movements and revolutionary classes.

(Lenin, 1966a: 241–2)

In understanding this we can appreciate that successes can be achieved if national revolutionary struggles are engaged. Such struggles can act as a wedge between capitalist class linkages in majority world countries and imperial nations.[8] Domestic revolutions carry a capacity to increase immediate eman-cipation while potentially destabilizing imperial power. If class-based seizures of state power are achieved through domestic struggles of self-determination, certain material realities soon befall bourgeois alliances. It is argued that the struggle to alter the social relations of production in "one country first" might assist in the deconstruction of an imperial epoch, especially if imperial power is centralized in one country (see Dussel, 2003: 100). Lenin (1964i: 208) supported this strategy, as it generated a global ripple affect via economic, political, and social consequences (see also Raby, 2006: 65–6; Novosti Press Agency, 1969).

Uneven economic and political development is an absolute law of capitalism. Hence, the victory of socialism is possible first in several or even in one capitalist country alone. After expropriating the capitalists and organizing their own socialist production, the victorious proletariat of that country will arise *against* the rest of the world – the capitalist world – attracting to its cause the oppressed classes of other countries, stirring uprisings in those countries against the capitalists, and in case of need using even armed force against the exploiting classes and their states. The political form of a society wherein the proletariat is victorious in overthrowing the bourgeoisie will be a democratic republic, which will more and more concentrate the forces of the proletariat of a given nation or nations, in the struggle against states that have not yet gone over to socialism. The abolition of classes is impossible without a dictatorship of the oppressed class, of the proletariat. A free union of nations in socialism is impossible without more or less prolonged and stubborn struggle of the socialist republics against the backward states.

(Lenin, 1964c: 342)

Timothy Harding (2003: 62) viewed internal struggles of self-determination as having the capacity to weaken imperium both politically and economically.[9] Imperial countries are dependent on "backward countries" for they provide capitalist profits through the transfer of surplus value (see Lenin, 1968; 1964d). If revolutionary social struggle takes place in the majority world, imperial power is restricted from much needed surplus value (Dussel, 2003: 100). Immanuel Wallerstein stated that an internal transfer of state and economic power away from capitalism greatly hampers the once fluid movement of natural resources and total national capital.[10] If a revolution occurs in the majority world, or a strategic segment of a majority-world nation is consumed by anti-systemic conflict, then the flow of capital weakens, as does imperial power (Wallerstein, 1984: 131). Threatened by the potential loss of capital, imperialist countries are forced to respond to class conflicts in nations undergoing socialist transformation. All that is necessary to prove this correct is to graph imperialist transgressions. Conflicts involving dominant geopolitical powers are "frequently responses to initiatives from forces in the exploited countries" (Harding, 2003: 62).

Additional effects may also occur if revolutionary class conflicts are successfully waged in more than one majority world country, leading to an immediate deunification and lessening of imperial political coercive economic power. First, a revised transfer of surplus value occurs if production and services are socialized. Profits once acquired through the extraction of surplus value immediately remain in the majority world. This decrease in the empire's centralization of capital subsequently results in a loss of reinvestment (that is, military and security, economic growth or stabilization, and so on), thus hampering future capital returns. For those newly revolutionized countries this means that a counter-accumulation of once lost capital takes place, resulting in increased stabilization, and thereby enhancing the revolutionized states' ability to respond to the immediate and future needs of the domestic population. Second, imperial power shifts from a hegemonic stage of power, via consent, to one of coercion, leading to a further weakened empire. Reactionism will and must occur to reclaim lost surplus profits and geopolitical power. This inevitably ends in imperial overstretch while placing the newly revolutionized state(s) at a decisive advantage. As a result of the transfer of surplus value, the socialized nations are able to expand militant defensive power, while forcing imperial nations into a two-way political-economic disadvantage. Economically, the empire's already bleeding coffers are further exhausted because of the losses of foreign derived profits. Politically (and militarily), it is forced into unconventional conflicts (that is, guerrilla warfare) on unfamiliar terrain; a field and strategy of battle in which modern imperial powers have proven inefficient.

As the exploited begin to "liberate themselves from the bourgeois yoke" they come to consolidate and unify themselves with other states that have done the same (Lenin, 1964e: 339). Revolutionaries in Colombia, to be victorious, must recognize the country's unique arrangement and relation to capitalism and revolution, and ensure a contextually specific non-dogmatic approach toward social change. This is achieved through a pragmatic response to domestic conditions. Theoretically, this will be dependent on the internal emancipatory dynamics and social organization from below.

EVALUATING REVOLUTION "FROM BELOW": THE IMPORTANCE OF COLOMBIA

A great deal of theory related to the issue of revolution has muted the subject of organic struggles "from below," opting rather for analyses dominated by the question of the centralized state.[11] Take for example Theda Skocpol's (1979) characterization that revolutions are a consequence of competition amongst nation states, or interconflict between those of the dominant class, resulting in the alteration of existing political relations. While some emphasis is placed on those from below, her thesis attests that revolutions occur through and by a dramatic shift at the level of the state, whereby dominant class competition and conflict (through domestic or international political-economic pressure) lead to state deterioration and transformation.[12] Negating agency, Skocpol is chastized for developing a deterministic and dissident elitist political perspective, for only "division among the elites ... increase the probability of the success of a revolutionary movement" (Defronzo, 1996: 12). "No matter what form social revolutions conceivably might take in the future (say in an industrialized, liberal-democratic nation), the fact is that historically no successful social revolution has ever been 'made' by a mass-mobilizing, avowedly revolutionary movement" (Skocpol, 1979: 17).

Skocpol's famous definition of revolution is the "rapid, basic transformations of a society's state and class structures; and they are accompanied and in part carried through by class-based revolts from below" (Skocpol, 1979: 4; see also 163–4). Criticized for marginalizing the latter group, Skocpol attempted to legitimize her approach in a later work by examining the role of peasants in revolutionary situations (1982). Providing a clever overview of multiple theories of revolution (including Marxist), she detailed the revolutionary "contribution" of those in the countryside. Characteristically, Skocpol dismissed this group as unorganized and incapable of responding to state power through class relations or militaristic capabilities.[13] Incapable of revolutionary class-consciousness, peasants are universally argued to have a unified "kinship and community institutions with collective economic functions that may tie richer and poorer relatively closer together than their individual property interests might suggest" (Skocpol, 1979: 116).[14] While this is marginally accurate, numerous examples of peasants organizing around class issues in Colombia prove otherwise (Larios, 2006; Röhl, 2004; Zamosc, 1986).

The significance of Skocpol's work has been its direct challenge to the 150-year canon that revolutions are the product of contradictions related to the social relations of production. She challenged that revolutions "have not conformed to Marx's theoretical expectations" but are a consequence of state crisis (see Skocpol and Trimberger, 1986: 60). Social change is then not a result of historical processes or development, but rather a series of political responses resulting in slight transformations to the social construct. In turn, the state is interpreted as "a potentially autonomous institution" in relation to capitalism (Guggenheim and Weller, 1982: 11; see also Defronzo, 1996: 24; Skocpol, 1992: 42; 1979: 30). Unlike Marxists, such premises approach the state and capitalist class as not intrinsically linked but separate entities with periodically related interests. Viewing the state and the capitalist class as distinct reifies the thesis that "states should be viewed theoretically as conditioned by, but not entirely reducible to, economic and/or class interests" (Skocpol and Trimberger, 1986: 62). This position is of importance to this book, for Skocpol's highly influential structural approach cannot be considered valid in the context of Colombia's revolutionary situation, the FARC-EP's structure, or the Colombian state's relation to political-economic realities in much of the country. Colombia epitomizes how a state is a cemented ally (if not relative) of the dominant class. Suggesting otherwise abstracts economic conditions as secondary participants to the capital system and retards any understanding of the social relations of production (see Gilly, 2003: 108).

Any theory separating capital from politics is misleading in the context of domestic capitalism and imperialism. The conjoined promotion and defense of property and surplus profits via state and class perpetuate capitalist expansion. To look at either as independent of the other is to negate the historic and present conditions of modernity.[15]

Antonio Gramsci noted how two superstructures exist in society: *civil society* (that is, the capitalist class) and *state*. Some have used this to imply that the state and the capitalist class, while mutually dominant, are distinct (see Skocpol, 1979: 6). Gramsci's work, however, clarified that both superstructures combine to produce a mutually beneficial hegemony (Gramsci, 1971: 12). Essentially, class interests are extended through a united force of state and (elite) civil society (Gramsci, 1971: 263). When a (capitalist) state's centralized power is threatened, it is "civil society" that employs reactionary forces, external to the official coercive arm of the allied state, to assist the continuity of the paradigm (Gramsci, 1971: 238).[16] Apart from this, progressive forces have also been known to be co-opted through conventional political mechanisms and/or upon their rise to power, simply continuing this vicious cycle (Petras and Veltmeyer, 2005a; Gramsci, 1973).[17] A "from below" strategy could then be a sound tactic to respond to issues of political and economic class alliances, as it provides those most marginalized by capital to revolutionize society well outside the lines of convention.

State breakdown: a consequence – not cause – of revolution

One of the suggested causes of grassroots involvement in revolution is a "rapid deterioration in material living conditions" and/or "a decline in capabilities of attaining them" (Defronzo, 1996: 11). Another assumption "is the breakdown of a mode of social control which prompts and allows social revolution" (Skocpol, 1976: 181). Yet such accounts fail to encapsulate the reality of social conditions and the state's role in much of Colombia. At virtually every interview I participated in or rally I attended the phrase "*ausencia del estado*" was heard, as in "state authority has only weakly reached the countryside," while negative socioeconomic and political conditions have remained constant for generations (Wickham-Crowley, 1991: 35; see also Saunders et al, 1978: 132–4; Gilbert, 1974: 142–7; Felstenhausen, 1968a, 1968b; Galbraith, 1953: 59–60, 94–5). It has even been suggested that an altogether material absence of the state has existed across the Colombian territory since independence (Sweig, 2002).[18]

Rapid declines in healthcare, education, human rights, and so on, are not the basis on which revolutionary sentiment has pervaded Colombia for decades, nor has social welfare and state confidence suddenly deteriorated, simply because such conditions have never been present. Those in the countryside have yet to experience a degeneration in living conditions, as they have experienced a constancy of squalor and exploitation through capitalist and state forces. In fact, the only measure of state presence in much of rural Colombia has been that of the state forces, which does not constitute state authority (see Kalyvas, 2006: 113n.2; Gutiérrez Sanín, 2004: 275–6). On the contrary, it demonstrates a lack thereof (Henderson, 1985: 109).

While a potential for the state to break down is real, the revolutionary dynamic being experienced in Colombia is not a consequence of fractured centralized power in Bogotá. Dominant class power remains very much intact as noted by Francisco Gutiérrez Sanín (2004: 276): "Colombia has a quite stable democratic institutionality vis-à-vis its level of development, and a state that can't be reasonably described as being in a breakdown process; on the contrary, in several key domains it has visibly modernized and strengthened."[19]

Colombia then breaches structural theories to more accurately reflect a Marxist theory of revolution. Rather than the state, it is the FARC-EP that has undercut class power through a long-term strategy of mobilizing via dual power. Any breakdown of the state is therefore inexplicitly the consequence of those from below.

A seldom-presented argument supporting the radical power of those from below has been the intimate influence of a revolutionary culture within (Latin America and) Colombia. Not only were names like Che and Marulanda brought up regularly during interviews with civilians and the guerrillas, but so too were Bolivar and Martí. Latin America provides an important example of how agency, culture, and history create a trinity promoting the realization of social change. The region has a "legacy of revolutionary activity" which has undoubtedly influenced the sociopolitical ethos for some of those inside its borders. Well versed in the study of Latin American emancipatory struggle, political scientist Eric Selbin (1997: 125) argued that "the cult of the heroic revolutionary has produced in many places a popular political culture of resistance, rebellion, and revolution," which has little to do with structure but rather the hearts and minds of those in struggle throughout the region. Historian D. L. Raby (2006: 11–12) also noted that within Latin America there exists a historical consciousness that not only critiques power but also approaches the issue of social change outside typical Western-political forms (that is, electoral politics, constitutional government, and so on).

> It needs to be pointed out that Latin America has an outstanding tradition of popular armed struggle which long predates the Cuban revolution, having its roots in the Independence Wars of the early nineteenth century. It is based on a concept of popular collective insurgency which has nothing to do with militarism or with the "individual right to bear arms" of the US Constitution. The idea of the people taking up arms to achieve liberation is central to Latin American political culture, and it by no means excludes other forms of struggle and participation. It embodies a distrust of institutionalized politics and a radical rejection of all forms of paternalism: rights are gained by struggle, whether armed or peaceful, and not granted by benevolent authority. It is intimately linked to the concept of popular sovereignty, that sovereignty really does reside in the people as a whole and not in the propertied classes or in any hereditary group or privileged institution. The people, moreover, constitute themselves as political actors by collective mobilization, not merely by passive reception of media messages or individualized voting .... Hence the resonance of the term "revolutionary" tends to be positive, unlike in contemporary Europe or North America where it has come to be associated with irrational violence or dogmatic sectarianism.
>
> (Raby, 2006: 11–12)

Recognizing that human development evolves through revolution enables it to be viewed as an acceptable methodology for social change. Revolution is simply "a particular strategy to which actors resort when conventional constitutional ways for progressive change are closed" (Vilas, 2003: 104; see also Goodwin, 2003: 138–9). In Colombia, traditional attempts to challenge the country's political-economic structure have been met with devastating outcomes for the left. Recognizing the exclusionism of capitalist power, the FARC-EP continues outside convention. In most cases the insurgency does not impose social transformation but rather facilitates change of/by/with segments of the populace (that is, community action groups, public forums, and so on). As centralized state power continues to function in Bogotá, the countryside witnesses the FARC-EP fusing power.

State-centered approaches have also fallen short in their analyses in that they do not theorize revolutionary movements that exist outside the state (see Goodwin, 2001: 55; Wickham-Crowley, 1992). Jorge Gilbert suggested,

> the Cuban revolution, the Nicaraguan revolution, and the revolutionary situation in El Salvador, Guatemala, and the increasing organization of the resistance movements in South America, indicate a change in the correlation of forces and a new era for the social movements and the social forces which compose them.
>
> (Gilbert, 1982: 1)

Social movements in Latin America have, for quite some time, demonstrated an important reconstitution toward radical social change, not always coinciding with conventional models and theories (Isbister, 1998). As revolutionary social movements seek to alter existing socioeconomic and political systems, they do not necessarily reflect nor seek legitimacy within the parameters of formal politics (Defronzo, 1996: 8). Unlike electoral parties they exert power over the state through venues apart from "acceptable" means. Revolutionary movements (including insurgencies) then carry a potential to be system-antagonists through their emphasis on changing society from below (see Johnson, 1966: 164; 1964: 66).

> Unlike political parties social movements are not organized to pursue power as such. Although they are clearly engaged in the struggle over state power this struggle is an inescapable consequence of their quest for social change and anti-systemic politics of mass mobilization ... While the electoral road to political power requires conformity to a game designed and played by members of "the political class," social movements generally take a confrontational approach to change and pursue a strategy of mass mobilization of the forces of resistance against the system and the political regime that supports it.
>
> (Petras and Veltmeyer, 2005a: 220–1)

Social change from below is important for it looks at revolution beyond the confines of politics. The crumbling of a political form does not, in fact, constitute a revolution, but rather a window of opportunity for the next most dominant political faction to usurp power (see Draper, 1978a: 180–1; Tucker, 1969: 11). Understanding this, Marxists are not overly concerned with the "conception of the state, as such, but the relation between this conception and Marx's attitude to the proletariat (or, rather ... 'the poor' ...)" (Löwy, 2005a: 29).

Revolutions, by their very nature, cannot come through those already empowered, but are made real only through the conscious and organized action of the unempowered. Hence, revolutions can best be defined by the extent to which those exploited under the dominant paradigm of capitalism are emancipated (Löwy, 2005b: 24). Marxism-Leninism then emphasizes the potential power of the powerless to respond to the contradictory social relations of productions as *the* important factor when concerning revolution. It is not solely the political in which the majority is exploited; therefore, it is more than the state that must be altered (see Engels, 1990b: 59; Draper, 1978a: 180–1; 1992; Marx, 1975b: 184; 1975c: 205–6; Avineri, 1968: 193–4).

Although it might appear simplistic, it is useful to categorize revolutionary theories into two modes: those that sustain order and those that create change (Naiman, 2004; Sacouman, 1999; Greene, 1990). Instead of accrediting state-based power transfers as the defining act of a revolution, broader analyses consider whether peoples experience societal transformation, which created such conditions, and what, if any, these changes entail for those marginalized.

THE POTENTIAL FOR DUAL POWER IN COLOMBIA

Emphasizing the role of the state in revolution is shared by both "state-centered and Marxists analysts alike, even though the latter are otherwise keen to emphasize how class struggles are supposedly the driving force behind revolutions" (Goodwin, 2001: 42). Some state-centered theories have even utilized the work of Lenin as a vehicle to justify top-down revolution (Goodwin, 1997: 15; Skocpol, 1979: 26). True, Lenin's contribution had a consistent theme, that a revolution must, to be successful and sustained, incorporate and consolidate state power (Paige, 2003: 20). However, what these theorists who employ Lenin as a proponent of top-down approaches tend to leave silent is Lenin's lifelong contribution to how a truly emancipatory revolution comes to fruition.

As clearly noted in *Dual Power*, Lenin argued that a true revolution does not occur from above through the consolidation of power through a pre-existing sociopolitical class system, but rather from below though an alternative class-based construct (both governing and militaristically prepared), which exists beyond the conventional model (Lenin, 1964g: 38–9). Some have tried to define dual power as the existence of "two or more political blocs (including, typically, extant state officials and their allies), both or all of which claim to be the legitimate state, and both or all of which may possess significant means of coercion" (Goodwin, 2001: 12).

According to Charles Tilly (1978: 191–3), the situation of dual power, or what he labels "multiple sovereignty," occurs when contending groups vie for authority over a given population, thereby weakening one "state" power in favor of another.[20] However, this is not what Lenin said. He argued that an alternative state must exist in dismissal of, not competition toward, the existing model. Within such a situation people "set up their own organized power without having achieved political independence" (Lenin, 1969: 401). Dual

Top-down (state-centered) approach

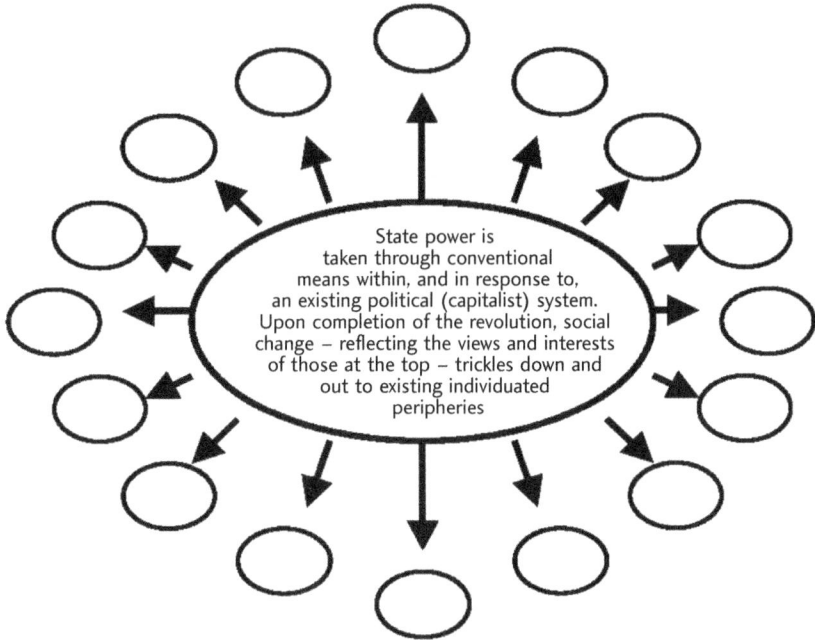

State power is
taken through conventional
means within, and in response to,
an existing political (capitalist) system.
Upon completion of the revolution, social
change – reflecting the views and interests
of those at the top – trickles down and
out to existing individuated
peripheries

From below (dual power) approach

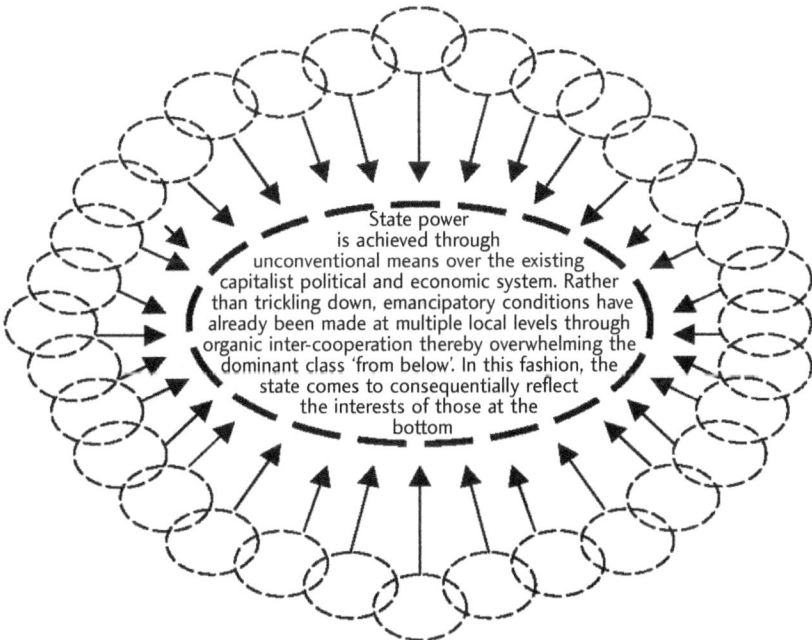

State power
is achieved through
unconventional means over the existing
capitalist political and economic system. Rather
than trickling down, emancipatory conditions have
already been made at multiple local levels through
organic inter-cooperation thereby overwhelming the
dominant class 'from below'. In this fashion, the
state comes to consequentially reflect
the interests of those at the
bottom

Figure 3.1 Varying approaches toward (and outcomes from) the taking of state power and revolutionary social change

power then promotes a provisional state formed from and supported by the most exploited (in arms) through an entirely different form of self-governance whereby the people emancipate themselves and their class apart from the capitalist model (Lenin, 1964g: 38–40).

Ernest Mandel offered a more recent account of dual power as "reflecting a territorial division of the country into liberated zones, in which a new state is *emerging*," while other segments of the country remain entangled in the structure of the old (Mandel, 1994: 194, italics added; see also Bookchin, 1996: 9–10). In time, new states consolidate more of the population as the once exploited establish additional zones apart from the previous system (see Wickham-Crowley, 1992: 155).

For Lenin, dual power does not come from those at the bottom *joining* external political groups that compete against the conventional political–economic order. Those from below construct their own alternative sociopolitical, economic, and culturally distinct state. This dual power does not witness a continuity of competition between those seeking power – as argued in state-centered and structural theory – but an evolutionary progression within distinct regions whereby emancipatory conditions have been *made by those from below* and *outside* the capitalist political-economic model.[21] The provisional state refrains from claiming legitimacy beside the capitalist state, for that which exists from below does not regard, nor does it associate with, the conventions of a capital system. Those from below grasp their newly emancipated provisional state (and actions) as an evolved sociopolitical, economic, and cultural formation existing apart from capitalism, not in competition with it. Created outside pre-existing elite control, the new state alters the class dynamics of sociopolitical and economic relations (Petras and Veltmeyer, 2005a: 224). This form of revolution repudiates the idea of reassigning power through capitalist politics, but substantively takes power from below.

Taking power is not only essential in order to improve inequitable social conditions but is the most realistic method through which social change can remain a consistent reality in a given country. Yet the taking of state power and the creation of a revolution can, and arguably must, take on different forms than those offered in popular approaches. Rather than utilizing imposed models that emphasize the existing state structure as the ideal primary trajectory for change via existing political processes (that is, electoral politics), or more extreme strategies by which power is taken from existing governing bodies (that is, *coups d'état*), dual power facilitates revolution "from below." Instead of creating changes from the top down, it is realized that a change can begin through the creation of a war of position while the struggle to improve localized conditions remain ongoing. This strategy can facilitate a situation of dual power created at levels of local support and territory. Conventional state structures become inundated as more and more municipalities take *power over the state rather than through existing conventional structures*. Such a strategy creates a noose-like effect that strangles the existing capitalist (political-economic) power structure from outside, and as a result takes state power.[22]

4

COLOMBIA'S RURAL POLITICAL ECONOMY IN HISTORICAL AND CONTEMPORARY PERSPECTIVE

Many years ago, Che Guevara drove through the Andes on a small motorcycle and stated that the country of Colombia, recognized on paper as the oldest democracy in Latin America, had "more repression of individual freedom" than any other country in the hemisphere (2004: 157). The famous revolutionary went on to write that "the atmosphere [in Colombia] is tense and it seems a revolution may be brewing. The countryside is in open revolt and the army is powerless to suppress it" (Guevara, 2004: 157; see also Leech, 2002a: 12).[1] This historical proclamation eerily foreshadowed the reality of Colombia's countryside, where civil conflict disproportionately continues a half-century after Guevara wrote these words. How did Colombia come to be a place of such angst, and how have such insecure conditions been sustained? This chapter examines these issues through a detailed account of the country's rural political economy, broken into two main sections. First, it is shown how Colombia's dominant class worked to enact legislated policies that partially destroyed the peasantry. An exploration of how the state and capitalist class cooperated to centralize land and its resources enables us to understand from whom and how the FARC-EP was able to draw support.[2] Second, the chapter provides an analysis of the overall rural political economy of Colombia from both historic and contemporary perspectives. This section details the devastating consequences of land centralization and neoliberal economic policies toward small producers. Highlighting the consequences of these policies (income inequality and fiscal disparity, rising rates of rural poverty, continued land centralization, the formal decline of small-scale agriculture, and so on), the chapter provides an explanation why, out of devastation, some of the rural population responded to negative conditions through the cultivation of coca (and alignment with the narcotic industry) – an issue addressed in Chapter 5.

LAW 135: A MEANS TO (INCREASED) LAND CENTRALIZATION AND SEMI-PROLETARIANIZATION

As capitalists seek to exploit rural methods of production for (class) gain, it is important to note that such conditions can only occur with the united and receptive support of the state. In rural Colombia, the state has hardly filled the role of a representative for the majority. On the contrary, Colombia is an example of how a state, in conjunction with domestic (and foreign) monetary interests, assisted in creating exploitive conditions for the rural population. For over two centuries Colombia's dominant class has coercively encroached upon rural lands for the purpose of expanding economic control over specific resources, which were otherwise rationally underexploited (Simons, 2004; Bergquist, Peñaranda and Sánchez, 1992; Bergquist, 1986; LeGrand, 1986; Lipman and Havens, 1965).

During the last half century, it has been the state that has used coercive techniques to push people off the land. This process of expulsion occurred through a conscious dual approach of direct violence compounded by the inactivity of governing institutions (Stokes, 2005: 78; LeGrand, 2003: 175–8).[3] For decades the state has remained absent, consistently neglecting the rural regions where a substantial majority of the population lived until the 1970s (Weil et al, 1970; Fluharty, 1957; Currie, 1950). Even though most of the country's constituents inhabited these areas, the Colombian government failed to provide even basic health and medical services, agrarian security, and the most limited of social services (Saunders et al, 1978: 132–4; Gilbert, 1974: 142–7; Galbraith, 1953: 59–60, 94–5; see also Bryant, 1969).[4] The next paragraphs detail how a political and economic elite formatted policy to expand class interests at the expense of the rural majority. This enables the reader to look at today's circumstance – a half-century after Che's journey – and discern whether any change has transpired in the realm of class-based apathy and exploitation.

In the development context, Colombia is an interesting topic of analysis. The country experienced several "firsts" in relation to state aid and economic progress within Latin America. Colombia was the first country to be analyzed and receive assistance from the World Bank (then called the International Bank for Reconstruction and Development) (Leech, 2002a: 17; Dix, 1967: 148–9; see Currie, 1950). It was the first Latin American state to receive formal counter-insurgency and military assistance from the United States (Chasteen, 2001: 277; Bushnell, 1993: 231; Randall, 1992: 221–5, 238). Also, Colombia was the first recipient of the most noted regional development program adopted during the mid-twentieth century, devised by W. W. Rostow under the John F. Kennedy administration (1961–63) (Clark, 2003: 42; Latham, 1998; Gott, 1970: 487; see also Keen, 1966: 237–45). In 1961, Colombia became the first state through which the Alliance for Progress claimed to provide the foundation for a decade of economic development. It was soon realized, however, that its ambition "meant more than economic aid" (Rabe, 1999: 10).

The Alliance for Progress provided a development strategy accompanied by a strategic military component known as Plan Lazo – a regional "security" campaign to quell left-wing movements in a post-1959 Cuba setting (Stokes, 2005: 71–4; Latham, 1998; Pearce, 1990a: 65; see also LaFaber, 1972: 220–1).[5] Benjamin Keen and Keith Haynes (2000: 534) referred to the Alliance for Progress as a systemic "program combing reform and repression." In the midst of the cold war the Alliance for Progress/Plan Lazo correlation was in essence a plan "to reduce revolutionary pressures by stimulating economic development and political reform" (Chasteen, 2001: 277). Jacques Lambert (1971: 97), addressing the rural strategy of the model, conservatively added that its reforms were designed to quickly subdue the peasantry's emancipatory "imagination in a pre-revolutionary situation," while Stephen J. Randall (1992: 238) argued that the "alliance was founded on the desire of U.S. capitalists to gain easier access to Latin American markets and resources." While all these statements are correct, none captured the essence of the policy better than Richard Gott. Gott (1973) characterized how the Alliance for Progress was the first formal binational anti-guerrilla strategy coordinated between the United States and Latin America; a plan that became a staple for counterinsurgency/rural oppression throughout Central and South America for decades to follow (see also Stokes, 2005). The United States hoped to "drain the water from the fish" by supplying rural-based reforms together with counterinsurgency activities. The Alliance for Progress became the strategy to do it.

As the Alliance for Progress was a large-scale regional geopolitical strategy, to domestically "drain the water" the Colombia elite needed to address the rise of rural political organizing and direct action in their own backyard. To do this an agrarian reform program was soon established (Livingstone, 2003: 70; Pearce, 1990a: 66). As have many land reform programs, the entire Colombian development paradigm systematically excluded the peasantry from any part of the process (Braun, 2003: 89; Collier and Collier, 2002: 683; Richani, 2002a: 11–35; Handelman, 2000: 104; Sanders, 1981: 84–101; Gilbert, 1974: 142–5). What actually happened through the state-based land reform was that Colombia's rural political economy (d)evolved from peasant-based production to centralized agrarian capitalism. Simply put, the Colombian state – in conjunction with the United States – created top-down strategies to distract peasants from mobilizing with oppositional political movements or communally based peasant groups (Rabe, 1999). By 1961, the Colombian state had implemented Law 135, the Agrarian Social Reform Law (*Ley de Reforma Social Agraria, Ley 135*).

Law 135 was executed through a newly devised state mechanism, the Colombian Institute of Agrarian Reform (*Instituto Colombiano de la Reforma Agraria*, INCORA) (Richani, 2002a: 5; Bushnell, 1993: 232).[6] The stated objective of INCORA and Law 135 was to expropriate unused or fallow lands from the rural elite[7] and present the newly acquired properties to the larger population, thus assisting the development of Colombia's countryside (Livingstone, 2003: 70; Richani, 2002a: 27; Smith, 1967: 241).[8] Many blindly trusted large landholders and the state to effectively carry out Law 135. There were even scholars who believed that INCORA, the state, and the rural elite would altruistically assist the land-starved rural population with a better future of equitable land distribution and subsequent modernization. Such a position was reflected in Michael B. Whiteford's assumption of the dominant classes' capability to accommodate the needs and wishes of the rural poor, as if the impoverished were the social strata that held political and economic power in Bogotá:

Due to a changing social climate and the efforts of the government land reform, Instituto Colombiano de la Reforma Agraria (INCORA), wealthy families will no longer be able to retain their large landholdings; they must take the initiative in the establishment of local industry if they wish to have any voice.

(Whiteford, 1976: 118)

Accounts spoke of INCORA's efficiency and the eventual benefits that were derived by the rural population from the land reform (Shaw, 1976: 126–7; Sumwalt, 1974: 53–5; INCORA, 1972; Adams and Montero, 1965). Critical observers, however, quickly announced that Law 135 was nothing more than "a fraud," which "had done little to expand income or employment opportunities for peasants or to reorder the over-all distribution of land" (Cockcroft, 1972: 134; Dorner and Felstenhausen, 1970: 223). Paul Harrison (1993: 118), for one, viewed INCORA, and other state machinery focussed on land reform at the time, as nothing more than a political tool created to consolidate land interests and objectives in the hands of already large landholders, while defusing rural support for revolutionary movements (see also Feder, 1971: 245). When looking at the process and quantitative results of the law, Harrison was not far off. Law 135 did nothing more than transfer land from the left hand of the dominant class to its right. Many analysts who studied the land reform period support this claim. For example, Jorge P. Osterling (1989: 25–7, 272) noted that the "redistributed" land acquired during the reform period was actually appropriated from either private or public holdings and handed to urban-based large landowners[9] via clientelism.[10]

On paper, the state declared that the "land reform was a great success," with INCORA distributing roughly 4 million hectares to 130,000 people (Lindqvist, 1979: 102; see also INCORA, 1972). Scholars analytically studying Law 135 came to a different conclusion. They discovered that these numbers were not just greatly misleading, they contradicted the real conditions. Tad Szulc (1964: 245) noted that in its first year, the achievements of Law 135 "were barely noticed," an apathy that continued after 1962 when the state had "little stomach for pushing it ahead" (see also Duff, 1968: 61). In fact, only a minority of land was "reformed" in Colombia; "by the end of 1970 – a mere 2.0 per cent of the nation's total agricultural land" had been expropriated, and of the 2 percent annexed, only a slight portion was "given" to those struggling in the countryside (Gilbert, 1974: 161). After further study it was revealed that between 1962 and 1978, "less than 1 per cent of the total surface of land was affected" (Rojas and Molano, 1986: 332). In recent years additional accounts found that the amount of land redistributed was, in fact, even more marginal. Nazih Richani (2002a: 28) highlighted that "less than 1 percent of the lands subject to expropriation were distributed, and most of that was public land" (figures also supported by Hylton, 2006: 60; Palacios, 2006: 183; and Kline, 1983: 105).[11]

The vast majority of land expropriated under Law 135 was public. With little redistribution occurring, the state indirectly transferred land that, politically speaking, already belonged to the people via the Colombian Republic (Richani, 2002a: 28). Some estimates cited that of the 4 million hectares of land utilized in the reform, roughly 94 percent had already been land under

state control, while the lands expropriated – or, more accurately, purchased
– from large landholders accounted for a minuscule 2–4 percent (Lindqvist,
1979: 103; Gilbert, 1974: 161; see also Sanders, 1981). In reality, "no significant expropriation of big estates occurred, and there was no change in the rural
power structures. Rather, the reform ground to a halt when it came up against
them" (MacEoin, 1971: 91). The reason was that the vast majority of those
in the Colombian state "were landholders or sympathetic to" dominant class
interests, so they sustained the existing socioeconomic and political structure
(Sanders, 1981: 89). "Landed and agribusiness interests" were able to co-opt,
manipulate, or beat out any policies implemented through INCORA (Walton,
1984: 99). By 1964, it was claimed that the actual number of peasant families
who had received and settled on the so-called expropriated land was less than
0.4 percent of those involved in agriculture (Havens, Flinn and Cornhill, 1980:
356).

   This can be illustrated with an analysis of lands expropriated and redistributed throughout the southwestern department of Tolima. In one of the
most inequitable regions of land distribution in the country, "only 1,115 out
of 90,000 landless agricultural workers had received titles to land by 1969"
(Keen and Haynes, 2000: 534). After a decade of land reform, roughly "1 to
2 percent of all the agricultural families in Colombia had gained access to land
through INCORA" (Berry, 1980a: 299). According to Jenny Pearce (1990a:
94), "from 1961 and 1985, INCORA bought up 4,009 farms totaling 472,470
hectares and expropriated only 254 farms totaling 66,035 hectares. This land
was distributed to just 30,000 families." Suggesting reasons for land reform
failure, R. Albert Berry (1980a) and Thomas G. Sanders (1981) claimed that
the state and economic elite had no intentions of assisting the rural population, but rather intended to construct a coalition to sustain dominant class
conditions and future interests (see also Berry and Solaún, 1980).

> From the outset, the government agency created to administer the reform
> (INCORA) was submerged in legalistic quicksand that made expropriations
> almost impossible; the Ministry of Agriculture, which largely represented
> the interests of the large landholders, retained great latitude in deciding
> which lands would be off limits for redistribution.
>
>   (Palacios, 2006: 182–3)

In addition to disguising the reform program by expropriating publicly owned
lands, the state largely collected lands "of very low quality" (Gilbert, 1974:
161; see also Palacios, 2006: 183; Beals, 1974: 34, 312).[12] Through engineered
agreements the state "expropriated" the worst lands belonging to the large
landholders. Gonzalo Sánchez (1992: 119) provided a telling account of how
some "hastened to offer for sale unproductive *latifundio*, abandoned over the
previous decade." This process saw the state further enrich the economic elite
through utilizing public coffers to purchase inoperative lands. Roughly 350,000
hectares of "largely unusable land" was purchased by INCORA through this
method (Pearce, 1990a: 94). Hence, the land "expropriated" was "almost

without exception ... worthless" and soon left fallow by peasants because it had little productability, or the state denied new landowning peasants the ability to borrow credit to develop it (Lindqvist, 1979: 102–3; see also Palacios, 2006: 183; Harrison, 1993: 123; Beals, 1974: 34, 312; Feder, 1971: 246).[13]

Contrary to its stated objectives, Law 135 did not see a decrease in rural impoverishment or a growth in small producers with access to land (see Havens, Flinn and Cornhill, 1980: 358). On the contrary, by 1969, "the total number of landless families" had increased to 400,000, with an annual increase of "40,000 each year" (Gott, 1970: 516n.1; MacEoin, 1971: 91; see also Kline, 1983: 105; Havens, Flinn and Cornhill, 1980: 358–60).[14] Between the mid-1960s and the late 1970s the proportion of those in the countryside that were landless or near-landless hovered between 66 and 70 percent (Christodoulou, 1990: 13, 33). Some sectors of the country saw roughly 81 percent of the population being labeled landless or near-landless (Deere and León de Leal, 1982: 41). In light of such skewed expropriation decisions we need to ask, if it was not to give land to peasants, then why was Law 135 introduced?

It has been strongly suggested that the Latin American land reforms of the 1960s were nothing more than measures to dissuade farmers, peasants, rural workers, and indigenous people from joining the revolutionary struggles that had been arising throughout the region.[15] Colombia's Law 135, however, appears to have had an additional purpose: the monopolization of land in the hands of urban-based rural-owning capitalists. As economist Neil Ridler wrote,

> in developing countries agrarian reform frequently refers to the expropriation of large farms and their fragmentation into smaller units. However agrarian reform can also refer to the opposite procedure, that of land consolidation. In Colombia two alternative reforms strategies have been proposed. One strategy would implement agrarian reform directed towards land fragmentation; this strategy would result in small non-mechanized farms (hereafter called family farms). The other strategy proposes a policy of land consolidation; which would result in large-scale mechanized farms.
>
> (Ridler, 1978: 37)

What materialized following the land reform was a legitimate structural recentralization of land in the hands of already large landholders who controlled the means of production (Palacios, 2006: 182–3; Pearce, 1990a: 92, 94).[16] With legislation (such as Law 1 of 1968) allowing and encouraging greater mechanized large-scale agro-production and the elimination of sharecropping, the state had little moral problem with displacing peasants (see Livingstone, 2003: 70; Rochlin, 2003: 98; Richani, 2002a: 29; Pearce, 1990a: 81; Kline, 1983: 107–8; de Janvry, 1981: 134). There was then a further process of land centralization because peasants could not utilize what little plots they had, or those given by INCORA, because of their poor quality or a lack of capital to finance increased production, eventually leading to them sell the "redistributed" properties to the elite, who reconsolidated property relations once more

(Pearce, 1990a: 94; Latorre and César, 1988: 44). According to Pearce (1990a: 92), the implementation of Law 1 resulted in "a massive expulsion of tenant farmers and sharecroppers, and by the end of the decade, farms under ten hectares had diminished substantially in number and size." Alain de Janvry (1981: 133–4) provided an account of this process: "The decline in the number and area of small farms is due in large measure to the liquidation of sharecropping and rental agreements of small parcels traditionally used as a means of tying labor to the land in precapitalist estates."

Official land titles and state-based policies provided the capitalists with a formal method through which they could further exploit (and expel) the peasantry in these regions by turning them into systematic wage laborers or semi-proletarians (de Janvry, 1981: 108, 132).[17] As a result of these conditions, rural Colombia witnessed a unique application of a dual system of subsistence peasants increasingly becoming aligned with, but not eliminated by, capitalism (Walton, 1984: 84; de Janvry, 1981: 98–9).[18] In the case of rural Colombia, a "lack of access to sufficient means of production to produce the household's subsistence is what compels some household members to join the ranks of wage labour" (Deere and León de Leal, 1982: 5).[19]

Prior to Law 135, the rural populace was very much structured around a different mode of production, both socially and economically. Throughout the early to mid-twentieth century, a considerable portion of the rural population consisted of subsistence-based laborers working to support their immediate family and/or community (Kalmanovitz, 1978). Throughout the 1930s and 1940s, this structure stayed relatively consistent, with many producers remaining at least partially at subsistence level. From the 1950s onwards, however, there was a substantive shift, with a growing number of rural producers working their own land and that of another for wages (Kalmanovitz, 1978: 38).[20]

> [T]wo systems of agricultural production existed side by side under antagonistic social relations. Small-holders and tenants struggled for survival under increasingly disadvantageous terms. On one hand, the large-holders wanted to consolidate more land and rid themselves of anachronistic tenant obligations. On the other, they needed their labor .... The Colombian peasant was drawn into the world market.
>
> (Walton, 1984: 84; see also Angell, Lowden, and Thorp, 2001: 47)

For those rural workers that labored outside subsistence production, many did not earn wages as such, but worked exceedingly long hours for "low wages in low-calorie foodstuffs" (Gerassi, 1965: 154; see also Dumont, 1965: 12–18; Rodríguez, 1949: 298). The 1950s and 1960s, however, saw a transfer from labor-based rents to monetary rents (cash trumping sweat). Hence, "the growth of manufacturing, as well as favorable state policies toward agriculture, helped the development of agrarian capitalism in Colombia in the 1950s" (Deere and León de Leal, 1982: 30).[21] As guerrilla and radical peasant mobilizations struggled for real agrarian reform, posing an increasing threat to the elite-based ownership of land and natural resources, both the state and urban-based large landholders began to see the importance of increased production and the elimination of subsistence-based localized rural production. To best engage this process, support went out for the means of production to be monopolized by industry; that is, *increased centralized ownership accompanied by wage labor*.

As it protected the *latifundistas* from peasant encroachments through the construction of rural-based wage labor, Law 135 acted as a buffer from revolution. Taking a risk, the elite hoped that the "water" in which the guerrillas swam would be too overwhelmed to assist in radical anti-systemic endeavors. Hence, as long as peasants were disenfranchised *enough* (no longer able to devote their time fully to family or community subsistence production), they would be overly preoccupied, by means of wage labor, thus incapable of organizing alongside insurgents (Brittain, 2005b). As peasants became excluded from their previous subsistence lifestyle, poverty quickly followed. With this poverty, peasants increasingly competed against each other in order to survive and satisfy their immediate needs. Doing so enabled peasants to stay alive, while ensuring stability for the owner of the means of production because the rural mass were overly consumed with combating their neighbor/competition rather than their employer and state (Harrison, 1993: 121; see also Marx, 1977: 225–6).

As noted by most scholars in the field of development and rural sociology, land is of the utmost importance to any social group (Fals Borda, 1976; Ortiz, 1973; Galeski, 1972). Andrew Pearse (1982: 63) illustrated the need by emphasizing the external competition for land that evolved between Colombians capitalists and peasants. This competition did not subside in the shadow of Law 135, but increased the desire for opposing parties to consolidate their material aspirations. Reminiscent of Rosa Luxemburg's ideas of protest, spontaneous peasant revolts erupted throughout the region based on a need to acquire land as a means of sustenance (2004: 169–99; see Harrison, 1993: 117). The state used such actions to justify coercion and rectify legal property relations. Pearse (1982: 63) argued that state-led coercion (through direct and indirect forms)[22] "contributed to the expansion of large-scale commercial enterprises on to land formerly worked by peasants." These conditions led once subsistent peasants to seek other means of living because of their lack of land and resources.[23] Such a reality saw "the transition" of peasant-based communities and landless laborers "to capitalist agriculture" controlled "by landowners or commercial companies" (Pearse, 1982: 63). During the early 1960s Charles Wagley (1964: 43) found that "the land shortage of the peasant is aggravated by the presence of large commercial holdings" (see also Bushnell, 1993: 241). An interesting image of this polarization was given by Harrison:

> In the Magdalena valley, Colombia you can see four-wheel drive tractors ploughing hundred-hectare fields, combine harvesters trundling through man-high maize, and crop-spraying planes taking off from private landing strips – while ragged sharecroppers and smallholders pause over their hoes or wooden ploughs to watch them fly over.
>
> (Harrison, 1993: 112)

The late 1960s showed that "large landowners had largely expropriated peasants from within their estates and shifted to a semiproletarian labor force of free peasants" (de Janvry, 1981: 108–9). The strategy worked in favor of capital, as the majority of rural-based workers became waged laborers by the 1970s (Sanders, 1981: 85–7). Subsistence-based peasants were no longer the majority.[24] By the late 1970s and early 1980s over two-thirds of the rural Colombian population were close to landless and, faced with no other option, forced to sell their labor power (Christodoulou, 1990: 13).

The noted anthropologist Michael Taussig (1980: 83) found that by the early 1970s, 80 percent of arable land was concentrated in a handful of large farms. Figures showed ownership was "becoming increasingly concentrated," thus ensuring that the dispossessed sold their labor power to the large capitalist landholders (Pearse, 1982: 63–7). Harvey F. Kline (1983: 21) found that "after more than a decade of agrarian reform ... there were more *latifundios* of more than 2,500 hectares."

> Nearly forty years after the enactment of the first agrarian reform law, land in Colombia continues to be among the most concentrated in the world, according to a recent report of the World Bank. In 1988 a million peasant units, 62.4 percent of all agricultural properties, held only 5.2 percent of the area farmed; the mean size of their parcels was 1.2 hectares (not quite acres). These small plots often are on sloping, eroded, and/or not very fertile land that produces little, requiring peasant smallholders to hire themselves out part of the year to try and sustain their families.
>
> (Safford and Palacios, 2003: 309)

Many scholars and institutions have cited similar figures throughout this period. During the 1950s, the majority of land holdings were well below 5 hectares (see Christodoulou, 1990: 136; Kline, 1983: 21; Shaw, 1976: 27; Galbraith, 1953: 87), a position that was also recognized through the 1960s, when 63 percent of rural producers worked on lands less than 5 hectares (Berry, 1991: 83 (revised September 26, 2006); Shaw, 1976: 27; World Bank, 1972: 10).[25] The situation continues today: the majority of rural producers still exist on 2–5 hectares (Díaz Montes, 2005; Obando 2005; Safford and Palacios, 2003: 309; Taussig, 1980: 83).[26]

It can be conservatively estimated that Law 135 helped structurally solidify landownership in the hands of the Colombian economic elite (that is, capitalist class). Within an incredibly short period of time this underscored purpose was obvious. Rural sociologist T. Lynn Smith (1967: 37) provided statistics showing how 7,500 Colombians controlled 60–65 percent of the country's farmland following Law 135's implementation. The Canadian International Development Agency (CIDA), showed that 70 percent of all farmland had become concentrated in the hands of 5.7 percent of the population after Law 135 (large landholders owned 45 percent and medium multi-owners controlled 25 percent) (Feder, 1971: 244). Most telling were the findings of political scientist Harvey F. Kline (1983: 21), who learned that after a decade of land reform there were more large landholdings equaling 2,500 hectares (or more) than in the years preceding Law 135. Ironically, INCORA (1964: 7–22) argued that no monopoly over land existed in Colombia following the land reform (see also Berry, 1991: 94; Adams, 1964: 78).[27]

The country's most fertile land, which could have supported the impoverished peasantry, remained completely unused (see *Tolima* – Table 4.1). Worse still was that the vast majority of these unused plots were located in the southwestern departments of Colombia (Nariño, Tolima, Cauca, and so on). Paradoxically, these regions held the largest region of land available for expropriation yet saw the least percentage of land expropriated (Feder, 1971: 246). Today one can travel for hours in these departments and never leave the same property, for entire regions, equaling tens of thousands of hectares, are regularly owned by one large landowner who lives in Medellín, Bogotá, or another major city (Brittain, 2006c: 7). The data presented supports the claim that the state's agrarian reform was nothing more than "a piece of paper, and Colombians are no better off than before" (Gerassi, 1965: 154; see also Lindqvist, 1979: 102). Ironically, the "subsequent progress" of Colombia's land reform became "disheartening" to those it was stated to benefit (Bonilla, 1964: 203).

Harrison (1993: 118–19) has asserted that Law 135 divided organized struggles while creating a thriving reserve army of labor for domestic and foreign capitalists to easily exploit by way of displacing peasants and privatizing lands.

> Colombia's land reform ... was instituted to defuse guerrilla actions and spontaneous peasant rebellions, which in the 1950s and 1960s succeeded in

Table 4.1 Utilized and stagnant land in selected departments of southern Colombia in 1960

Department	Percentage of minifundios* (under 5 ha.)	Total hectares utilized
Cauca	63	60,120
Cundinamarca	69	113,037
Huila	47	20,359
Nariño	67	77,139
Tolima	52	49,887

Department	Percentage of latifundios (over 500 ha.)	Total hectares not utilized
Cauca	0.3	7,981
Cundinamarca	0.2	11,197
Huila	0.7	5,928
Nariño	0.1	5,472
Tolima	0.6	29,313

* Minifundios are defined as "small subsistence farms that produce barely enough to enable the cultivator to sustain the family"; hence, "most minifundistas (one who farms a minifundium) must augment their earnings elsewhere" even though "their principal occupation is that of a farmer" (Saunders et al., 1978: 16).

Source: Adapted from Shaw, 1976: 115–16.

setting up autonomous zones in the central provinces. It was a purely cosmetic measure; but it raised expectations among the landless, and peasants started invading and occupying the estates they worked on. The state responded with a two-pronged approach. With one hand they threw a few more crumbs before the peasants ... and with a boot, in the shape of the army and police, they stamped down fiercely on occupations wherever they arose.

(Harrison, 1993: 118–19)

The state not only gave protection to the capitalist large landholders but also provided them with the tools to control how the land reform was to be carried out (Christodoulou, 1990: 142; Deere and Leon de Leal, 1982: 30–3; Sanders, 1981: 89). State officials (from both Liberal and Conservative camps) "undermined the redistributive aspects of the reform," thus creating "a tendency toward the reconcentration of landholding" (LeGrand, 1986: 166). Even officials working in INCORA admitted that they had "placed all the cards in the hands of the landowners" (Harrison, 1993: 118; see also Sanders, 1981: 89). If peasants sought land through Law 135 they had to apply formally through INCORA.[28] If they were able to get this far, they then endured the long bureaucratic process by which lands were socially and geologically examined for expropriation by the state, obviously taking a great deal of time, energy, and resources (see Duff, 1968; Smith, 1967). At this stage INCORA would undertake:

a thorough and expensive agronomic, geological and social survey of the area and decides whether it is suitable for a "project." If it decides it wants to buy land, it first has to approach the landlord and *negotiate a price* with him. Usually only those with poor land or especially tiresome labourers are willing to sell voluntarily. If the landlord does not want to sell, the matter goes to law, which is long, laborious, formalistic and nitpicking .... The law is so weighted in favour of landlords that for every ten properties INCORA has *tried* to buy (and these were all estates that, on the face of it, seemed candidates for takeover) it has been in it for landlords to escape through the colander .... The few landlords who cannot squeeze through any of these holes have other tactics at their disposal.

(Harrison, 1993: 118–19, italics added)

The land reform acted as a legitimate method for large landholders, in cooperation with the state,[29] to formally consolidate lands while, first, ensuring a legal mode of ownership that enabled the owners to call on the state to "protect" interests through coercive means of displacement, violence, torture, and intimidation; and second, creating a landless or below-subsistence reserve army of labor forced to sell its labor power for their (family's) continued existence (see Zamosc, 1986: 97).[30] This was arranged by large landholders who sought to "evict the tenants and rehire them as labourers. In five years after 1968 there were twice as many evictions as in the previous 25. The evicted tenants swelled the surplus army of labourers and kept wages down" (Harrison, 1993: 119).

It is known that "capitalist agriculture requires wage workers, and disposed and displaced peasants form a 'reserve' of labour for such employment" (Pearse, 1982: 63–4). Bushnell (1993: 241) suggested that "the displacement of tenant farmers by the advance of large-scale commercial production ... tended to increase the supply of manual labor in relation to demand and thus hold down wages." Demonstrating this process, Carmen Diana Deere and Magdalena León de Leal commented how

> the new conditions of production were no longer to depend on a dependent labour force. Rather, what was required was a free labour force as well as large expanses of land for irrigated and mechanized agricultural development. The peasantry, displaced and dispossessed, was to form the rural labour reserve for the capitalist enterprises.
>
> (Deere and Leal, 1982: 33)

Such a strategy was important, as many peasants creatively settled on lands of fertile or lucrative yields regardless of to whom they formally belonged (LeGrand, 1986: xvi).[31] What partially enabled this encroachment was that the lands were largely controlled and owned by professionals (doctors, lawyers, academics and so on) located mainly in Bogotá.[32] The land reform made allowances for the large landholder to remove, with the coercive backing of state forces, anyone who unlawfully inhabited land, thus enabling them to "reinstate" landless peasants as easily exploitable wage laborers (Harrison, 1993: 119).

There are, however, always exceptions to the rule, and there are still some rural producers who have been able to hold title to, or utilize, some form of land. In such rare cases it is important to note that "landownership is no guarantee to livelihood," for "two thirds of farms were below subsistence level," leaving peasants with little to do but sell their surplus labor power in the hopes of sustaining their small plots (Harrison, 1993: 109; similar comments were made by Pearse, 1982: 63 and Taussig, 1980: 85). As the state consistently failed to provide social services to the countryside, the vast majority of peasants remained educationally and physically deprived. Taussig (1980: 85) illustrated that as land was increasingly centralized peasants had little choice but to sell their labor power for a wage in order to nourish their family's needs, thus leading to less devotion to their own land and more toward another's (that is, the capitalist's).

During the 1960s, large segments of the rural population had "been denied certain sanitary and medical services, educational facilities, occupational mobility, and general socioeconomic advance" (Williamson, 1965: 37). John Bryant, a medical doctor with the Rockefeller Foundation, compiled a significant amount of data related to the deplorable medical conditions of rural Colombia during this period. His findings showed that in certain locales the leading causes of death in children was diarrhea related to malnutrition caused by poor political-economic conditions; "42 percent of children under six years of age were malnourished and 30 percent had diarrhea at any one time" (Bryant,

1969: 103). It was also noted that these appalling conditions could have been easily rectified but remained structurally untreated as the state kept per capita annual health expenditure at US$3.50 per person (Bryant, 1969: 85).[33] Another way to deal with malnutrition was to send trained doctors to affected areas. This was never adopted as half of the bucolic populace failed to receive any formal healthcare service (Bryant, 1969: 88).

Conditions outside the countryside were little better for the poor, as many in major urban centers witnessed unacceptable medical services. In Bogotá, Colombia's largest city, 40 percent of deaths occurred without a doctor present (Bryant, 1969: 320). Throughout the mid to late twentieth century Colombia's largest cities witnessed roughly 36 percent of deaths "occurring without the attention of a physician" (Bryant, 1969: 240). It cannot be said that this absence of physicians was caused by a lack of trained medical practitioners. On the contrary, in Cali the doctor-to-physician ratio was 910:1, and Bogotá had a 1000:1 quotient (Bryant, 1969: 87, 320). What this rather symbolizes is the systemic apathy toward the poor – in both city and countryside – as the state continued its complacency.[34] This left "virtually the entire region" of southern Colombia and its population "in a desperate predicament" (Lindqvist, 1979: 89).

The deplorable malnutrition and health standards throughout rural regions during the 1930s and 1950s did not improve after the 1961 land reform (Henderson, 1985: 233; Galbraith, 1953: 95; Smith, Rodríguez, and García, 1945: 62).[35] Under-nourishment throughout southern Colombia became an inescapable reality of rural life (Dumont, 1965: 9). Evidence showed that "the average weight of men over the age of twenty was 56 kg in the coffee districts and 52 kg in the cattle district; 70 per cent were seriously undernourished; 49 per cent were illiterates; only 10 per cent had shoes" (Lindqvist, 1979: 89).

James D. Henderson documented that in the southwest:

> teams of health workers sent to 'Tolima 1' in 1962 were appalled by the infrahuman conditions they found. Starvation stalked the mountains, and a score of serious diseases were endemic among the people. Adult males averaged but 5' 5" in height and 119 pounds in weight, and women were only 5' tall and weighed 112 pounds. Near-universal malnutrition played a dominant role in the high levels of infant mortality.
>
> (Henderson, 1985: 233)

Colombia was a reported underdeveloped country at the time, and it could be suggested that it simply lacked the adequate resource supply to meet the physical and nutritional needs of the population. However, after several decades conditions continue to be inadequate for the rural populace even though the country is now considered to be an increasingly "developed" country. By the 1980s,

> the population of the rural areas of the country is that which shows the highest levels of these social evils; open malnutrition in children reaches 24.2 per cent; infant mortality is 80 per thousand; 56.6 per cent of homes do not

satisfy normal nutritional needs; 84 per cent lack running water; 60.5 per cent lack treated drinking water; only 21.4 per cent have sewage or a septic pit and to complete the panorama of the rural areas, 31 per cent of women between 15 and 49 have never been to school.

(Pearce, 1990a: 222–3; see also Lang, 1988: 57–60)

Things were not much better in the 1990s, with 80 percent of those living in the countryside having little if any access to a formal healthcare system, while malnutrition remained "widespread" (Clark, 2003: 24; Harding, 1996: 60). During this period, only 10 percent of the populace was covered by social security, yet this tenth consumed "50 percent of all public sector health expenditure" (Doyal and Pennell, 1994: 279). Current accounts do not find standards any better. Today "27 percent of all households in the countryside live without access to water" (Emcke, 2007: 207). In 2006, 73 percent of Colombia's poorest cannot even meet the basic needs of sustenance, according to Christina Rojas (2006: 3).

In relation to gender, there is a disproportionate rural political-economic attack on women, revealed by the fact that "rates of maternity-related mortality deteriorated while child mortality is at a standstill" (Rojas, 2006: 3). Yet, Colombia does not lack the medical facilities or professionals to address such issues. On the contrary, its health system is quite efficient. On September 24, 2008, Colombia's minister of commerce and trade, Luis Guillermo Plata Páez, made a speech praising the industry and presented how the state has supported a shift in the country's health services (Uribe and Plata Páez, 2008).[36] Plata detailed that Colombia's health sector was now the perfect center for business process outsourcing (BPO). Ironically, Colombia's healthcare system is not for domestic use but rather foreign consumption.

The state of education provides no comfort either. For decades young people throughout countless rural regions of Colombia have been routinely disenfranchised from obtaining any form of schooling past mid-primary levels.[37] During the 1960s some researchers argued for higher levels of education and domestic training for those living in the periphery (Adams, 1968: 94–6). However, with the support of the United States, the Colombian government refused to offer any educational facilities or opportunities to people in the countryside past the most basic levels – which were already grossly lacking in structural construction, formal arrangements, and teacher qualification (Jallade, 1974: 33; Adams, 1968: 89, 92–3). Ninety percent of the countryside remained deprived of any formal education (Saunders et al, 1982: 100; Adams and Havens, 1966: 213; Gunther, 1966: 432).[38] By the 1970s, the figures saw slim improvement, with 85 percent being unable to obtain education past primary level (Jallade, 1974: 32). In rural regions of the country, 94 percent of homes had only 33 percent of children enrolled in school (Jallade, 1974: 32). When accessible, the Colombian state only offered primary educational services in rural regions and did not support anything beyond this level (Jallade, 1974: 33). The result, roughly 100 percent of children who remained in the countryside were denied the ability to obtain any model of formal education past the age of nine years (Shultz, 1970: 15).

As with healthcare, education services have not become better with time. Recent findings show the state's lapse in assistance has remained intact. As a result of the countryside's deplorable political economic situation, "many of the [impoverished] children are forced to abandon school in order to help support their struggling families" (Leech, 2002a: 54). However, the primary reason social services have not been realized is the government's systemic attack on the countryside. It has been well documented that contemporary education facilities, if offered at all, are (de)constructed from providing any true benefit to the bucolic population. Coghlan (2004: 103) reported that "in rural communities there might be two teachers for three hundred children," who, in fact, live hours away from the facility. He also found a case where "there were only ten teachers" who knew the local dialect of 40,000 students. It was a systemic practice to have teachers placed in rural areas only to have the state not pay them, resulting in the workers being forced to leave out of necessity for their own subsistence or career aspirations (Coghlan, 2004: 103, 95).

Such realities illustrate how the government appears to have programs in place but has no intention of implementing educational needs (see also Quintanilla, 2005). From this, we can understand how "up to 40% of Colombia's children do not attend school" (Ramírez, 2005: 33). It is hard not to recognize how the state and associated foreign development agencies structurally sustain class relations that result in a continuity of inequitable social relations. Taking note of the situation, Dávalos commented that:

> the national and local government and their resources have been largely absent – even relatively stable settlements, e.g., San Pedro Frío, are removed from the closest health centre by a 12-h journey by mule and jeep, and children must walk for hours to the nearest elementary school, run by a teacher who has not received a high school diploma. Settlements in San Pedro are even further removed from these basic public services.
>
> (Dávalos, 2001: 72)

While the state projects an image of rural support, in reality it negates health and education services and therefore is slowly creating what Samir Amin (2004) has labeled the genocide of the peasantry. Such conditions shed light on the state's consistent structural lack of social support and control throughout the countryside. When asked about such issues and what the state had done for his community, one respondent, demonstrating an incredible intuitive awareness of current sociopolitical conditions, replied:

> What else is there to say, repression is repression; it is the violent reaction of the state, the armed forces, the paramilitaries, and the elite within these groups that does not want to offer support or assist the people they are stated to help but rather our government is constructed to ensure that existing economic conditions is sustained over time .... The problem with the state not only in our department but through much of rural Colombia is not the state per-se but those who are in power at the state level. Our country

needs a true democratic structure that represents the interests and needs of its people, the current problem is not the state itself but the laws that are made and the persons who have made them; laws made to benefit a select few .... The state vocalizes or expresses that it is in the community and that it is actively working for, providing education, health care, development and progress for the people, but in reality, if you look in our and other communities [laughingly scoffs], anyone can see that the government does nothing for our people. Social services [scoffs again], social services have never been offered in our community. The state is non-existent in providing any social services to the vast majority of people in our department. The only service [holds up his fingers to symbolize quotation marks] that the Uribe government provides to our community is repression and violence through the state's battalions and the paramilitary. The only service provided is that which keeps the current rulers in power.

Again, some may come to the defense of the Colombian state and capitalists by arguing that inequality, malnourishment, or poverty are not related to issues of class exploitation and land monopolization, but are rather consequences of Colombia being a developing nation, which has an insufficient volume of accessible domestic or regional natural recourses to sustain the rural population effectively. This has, however, been countered by those who have taken the time to research this issue. It has been shown that the conditions are a direct result of the concentration of landholdings by the dominant class, as peasants are unable to access goods that can materially sustain their existence. There is no lack of resources but rather an increase in centralized ownership (Deere and León de Leal, 1982). At present, Colombia finds itself in an inequitable political economy, the throngs of civil war, and a ruling class that subscribes to a development model of neoliberal economics – as supported by the United States. Within such an environment there remains a small group of very wealthy landowners and capitalists who, as illustrated through Law 135, have the ability to directly influence governmental policy and economic conditions. This chapter therefore moves to an analysis that examines how, in many ways, the past looks very much like the present. The difference, however, is that unlike the poor conditions of earlier decades, today rural populations have responded to inequity through unconventional methods.

AN INTRODUCTION TO THE POLITICAL ECONOMY OF COCA IN RURAL COLOMBIA

For over a century, the country of Colombia has been described as an incredibly wealthy country due to its numerous natural resources and impressive commodity-based export potential (Beals, 1974: 115; Currie, 1950). Recognized as one of the world's few "mega-diverse" countries, Colombia has global ecological relevance due to its significant variety of plants, flora, and fauna. It has even been claimed that the country contains "a high percentage of all species existing on the planet" (Dieppa, 2007: 203–4). Former US attorney-general Ramsey Clark demonstrated the extensive surplus of primary resources available throughout the Andean nation. He illustrated how Colombia has more than enough resources to meet the social needs of the country's constituency.

> The nation's productivity is enormous. Colombia has 26 million head of cattle, 60% more in proportion to its population than the United States, a chicken for every pot and abundant fish. Annually, Colombia grows 180 pounds of plantains for every man, women and child; 130 pounds of potatoes; 110 pounds of bananas and 90 pounds of rice and 50 pounds of corn. Colombia produces 830,000 tons of the best coffee in the world and 32 million tons of sugar cane a year …. It extracts close to 200 million barrels of oil a year with new fields awaiting development and 24 million tons of coal, the largest coal deposits in South America. More than 700,000 troy ounces of gold are mined annually and more than 6 million carats of emeralds are mined, half the world production.
>
> (Clark, 2003: 24)

In the midst of this surplus, consumption levels remain devastatingly skewed and malnourishment is rampant throughout rural Colombia. Murillo and Avirama (2004: 38) acknowledged that "notwithstanding the relative stability and wealth of the country, one cannot erase the fact that the majority of Colombians are poor," with the second "most inequitable distribution of wealth in the Western Hemisphere" (see also Escobar, 2004: 19; Rochlin, 2003: 100). Former political counselor to the Canadian Embassy in Bogotá, Nicholas Coghlan clarified how:

> considerable wealth is concentrated in fewer hands than in most of Latin America. Much is actually centered on just four prominent industrial groups, headed by 'Los cacaos' (the big cheese) …. This inequitable distribution of wealth (translated in rural Colombia into inequitable land distribution) continues to fuel both the guerrilla insurgency and the paramilitary response to it by large landowners.
>
> (Coghlan, 2004: 153–4)

This inequitable income distribution is easily shown in the fact that throughout the 1960s and 1970s, Colombia consistently had a Gini coefficient of 0.57 (Berry and Urrutia, 1976: 40–1; Díaz-Alejandro, 1976: 5). Coghlan (2004: 153; see also Comisión Colombiana de Juristas, 2004; Rochlin, 2003: 100) noted that the country of Colombia "has one of the highest Gini coefficients on the continent." It has been documented that of selected countries throughout Central and South America, Colombia consistently had the highest Gini coefficients during the 1980s and 1990s combined (Korzeniewicz and Smith, 2000: 10–11; see also Ramírez, 2005: 83).

In 1997, Colombia had the second highest rate of economic inequality in all of Latin America – a status that has for the most part remained consistent (Avilés, 2006: 91; see also Coghlan, 2004: 153; Comisión Colombiana de Juristas, 2004; Contraloría General de la República, 2004: 43, 44). During the first few years of the 2000s Gini coefficients averaged 0.570 (World Resources Institute, 2003: 2). The current figure is between 0.591 and 0.576 (Rojas, 2006: 3). Brazil holds the greatest rate of economic disparity in Latin America, but its distribution figures have remained stable (Sachs and Santarius, 2007: 15). Meanwhile Colombia's rates of inequitable income distribution continue to rise, resulting in ever greater disparities between rich and poor.

Aside from monetary divergences, people in rural Colombia have experienced extremely inequitable distribution of land ownership (and of natural resources) for decades. During the 1950s, 0.7 percent of *latifundios* controlled an estimated 41 percent of arable lands, with 0.06 percent consolidating 63 percent a decade later (Shaw, 1976: 27, 112; see also Powelson, 1964: 36). John Gerassi (1965: 154) documented, over four decades ago, that "3.5 percent of landowners control 65 percent of the land" (see also Duff, 1968; Smith, 1967; Fluharty, 1957; Smith, Rodríguez, and García, 1945). In 1966, only 1.1 percent of all agricultural-based families controlled more than 45 percent of the nation's arable lands (Christodoulou, 1990: 27). When looking at land concentration based on plots of land less than 10 hectares, Sanders (1981: 90) discovered that in the 1960s roughly 76.5 percent of the population (small producers and/or peasants) had access to a mere 8.8 percent of available land. This inequitable distribution saw a minimum shift during the 1970s, when 73.1 percent had access to only 7.2 percent of arable land (see also Powelson, 1964: 36). If we exclude farm size from the ratio, 6.9 percent of large landowners had access to roughly 75.8 percent of land during the 1960s, with the 1970s seeing the ratio equal 8.4 percent to 77.7 percent (Sanders, 1981: 90). The 1980s saw a rise in land concentration, with roughly 3 percent of the landed elite owning over 71 percent of arable land, while 57 percent of the poorest farmers subsisted on less than 3 percent (Washington Office on Latin America, 1989: 9; see also Taussig, 2004a: 13; Giraldo, 1996: 14). In 2003, Clark wrote that:

> in the midst of this vast potential for social and economic justice, the human condition in Colombia is desperate. Per capita income is barely over $2,000

Table 4.2 A quarter-century of Colombian Gini coefficients

Time period	Gini coefficient
1980	0.518
1989	0.532
1994	0.505
1999	0.566
2004	0.562
2006	0.584

Source: Rojas, 2006: 3; Ramírez, 2005: 83; Comisión Colombiana de Juristas, 2004; Korzeniewicz and Smith, 2000: 10–11.

with more than half the population living on less than $500. The gap between the rich few and many poor is a human and national tragedy. A very small part of the population holds most of the wealth. The richest 1% control 45% of the wealth. Half of the farmland is held by 37 interests.

(Clark, 2003: 24)

By 2004, 97 percent of people in rural Colombia could access only 25 percent of the country's arable land, while 1.1 percent controlled over 55 percent (see Avilés, 2006: 24; Escobar, 2004: 19).[39] One year later, Francisco Ramírez Cueller (2005: 83) showed that five economic groups[40] controlled the vast majority of the nation's capital, and ten specific companies captured 75 percent of the assets in the domestic financial market. Such disparities were further increased in work done by the Comisión Colombiana de Juristas (2004), which showed that 61.2 percent of all officially registered land was owned by roughly 0.4 percent of the population (see also Ahmad, 2006: 60; Avilés, 2006: 24). With the considerable growth in the concentration of land over the last decade, there has been a significant surge in enormous farms, even when compared with those amassed following Law 135. Between the 1950s and 1970s, *latifundios* grew roughly 40 percent in size; however, by the 1990s these properties increased by another 21 percent, becoming colossal property holdings (Livingstone, 2003: 70; Berry, 1991: 83; Fernández, 1979: 56; Shaw, 1976: 27; World Bank, 1972: 10; Powelson, 1964: 36).

For the past half-century, high rates of concentrated wealth and landownership have occurred throughout rural Colombia at the majority's expense (Harrison, 1993: 109; Feder, 1971: 10–11). Some have suggested "the inequality of Colombia's land structure has changed little despite much legislation and many reports on agrarian reform" (Safford and Palacios, 2003: 309; see also Restrepo, 2003). With such a concentration of property in the hands of a minority, there are obvious economic effects.

According to Safford and Palacios (2003: 309–11), rates of land centralization and rates of poverty are deeply interrelated; therefore, alongside the rise in monopolization, Colombia's rural populace has experienced a systemic increase in impoverishment. Over the past 15 years the growth has become precipitous. Table 4.3 illustrates how presently, more so than any other time in Colombia's recent history, the vast majority of peasants live in poverty.

Disproportionate allocations of resources compounded by an inequitable distribution of wealth have resulted in increased rates of poverty. Figure 4.1 reveals how general rates of rural poverty varied slightly during the 1970s and 1980s, but have since showed steady growth. Interestingly, this period of increased rural poverty was also the period when Colombia formally implemented neoliberal economic policies throughout the countryside. There was a clear and sustained 12 percent jump in poverty when neoliberal economic policies took hold in the mid-1990s, heavily targeting Colombia's agricultural sector (see Avilés, 2006: 90; Stokes, 2005: 130; Green, 2003: 235–7).[41]

The most devastating consequences of poverty have persisted in rural regions. Former Colombian Senator Apolinar Diáz-Callejas (2005) stated that over 69

Table 4.3 Five decades of disproportional land concentration – capitalist percentages

Time period	Percentage of owning population	Percentage of land
1950s	3	50
1960s	4	66
1970s	5.7	70
1980s	2.8	71
1990s	1.8	53
2000s	0.4	61

Sources: Ahmad, 2006: 60; Avilés, 2006: 24; Ramírez, 2005: 83; Berry, 1991: 83; WOLA, 1989: 9; Feder, 1971: 244; Smith, 1967: 37; Gerassi, 1965: 154; Fluharty, 1957: 204.

percent of the Colombian population now lives in poverty; however, it is the countryside where the highest rates of poverty are realized, currently hovering at 87 percent (Rojas, 2005: 210; Contraloría General de la República, 2004: 43, 44; UNDP, 2003: 42). In the rural regions of Putumayo and Caquetá rates are even higher, with averages in the 80 percentile since the 1980s (Palacios, 2006: 225). Holmes, Gutierrez de Piñeres, and Curtin (2006: 178), however, claimed that real levels of poverty in Colombia are likely under-represented and income distribution even more skewed than existing data suggests.

While these figures are staggering, the levels of absolute poverty[42] are diffi-cult to gauge. The rates increased sporadically between the 1960s and 1970s, yet the figures for the 1980s and 1990s seem inconsistent with general rural poverty rates (see Figures 4.1 and 4.2). In 1964, the proportion of urban and rural people living in absolute poverty hovered at 25 percent, while in 1973 it rose to roughly 43 percent in the cities and 68 percent in the countryside (Keen and Haynes, 2000: 534). General rates of rural poverty accelerated with the implementation of neoliberalism, but the 1990s saw the numbers in absolute poverty decrease. In 1986, the percentage of Colombians living in absolute poverty was roughly 18 percent, a figure that then grew to 27 percent in 1991, 31 percent by 1993, and in 1996 a whopping 40 percent (see Avilés, 2006: 90; Chomsky as quoted in Giraldo, 1996: 14). The rises in absolute and general poverty are more in line over the last few years.

Neoliberalism has not only cost the rural populace their land and plunged them further into poverty, it has also created huge differences in socioeconomic status across the country (see Table 4.4). The political and economic policies have disproportionately organized the country into clear divisions based on income levels. Stokes (2005: 130) showed that "in 1990 the ratio of income between the poorest and richest ten per cent was 40:1. After a decade of economic restructuring this reached 80:1 in 2000" (see also Avilés, 2006: 24; Coghlan, 2004: 153; Comisión Colombiana de Juristas, 2004; Contraloría General de la República, 2004: 47).[43] Analysts such as R. Albert Berry and Francisco E. Thoumi (1988: 64) have characterized this inequitable wealth distribution as the principal cause of Colombia's sociopolitical and economic ills (that is, poverty, malnutrition, extensive antagonisms between classes, and

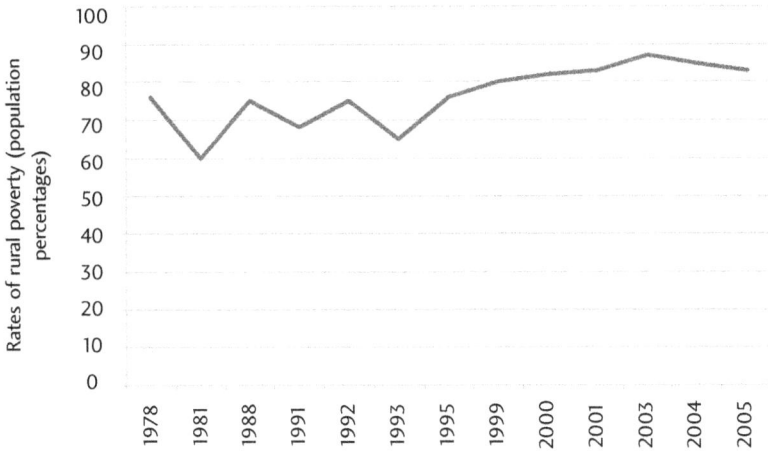

Figure 4.1 Comparative leaps in general rates of rural poverty
Sources: Avilés, 2006: 24; Hylton, 2006: 118; Richani, 2005a: 118; Rojas, 2005: 210; Comisión Colombiana de Juristas, 2004; Murillo and Avirama, 2004: 38, 129; Livingstone, 2003: 100; Safford and Palacios, 2003: 307; UNDP, 2003: 42; Lang, 1988: 99.

so on). Inequality has grown even worse over the past few years (Sachs and Santarius, 2007: 15; Diáz-Callejas, 2005) in both urban and rural regions (see Leech, 2002a: 17; Keen and Haynes, 2000: 534). According to development theorist and sociologist Henry Veltmeyer (2005: 97), this is specifically linked to the implementation of neoliberal economic policies.

One of the clearest reflections of the effect neoliberalism has had on

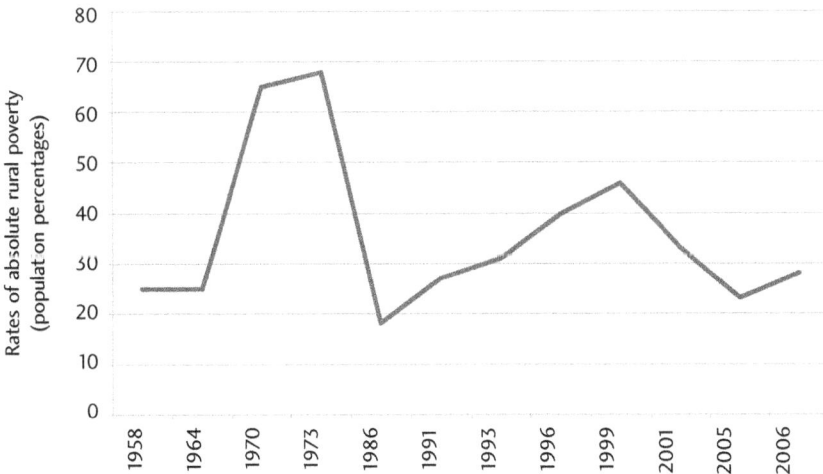

Figure 4.2 Rates of absolute rural poverty in Colombia, selected dates
Sources: Avilés, 2006: 90; Prensa Latina, 2006c; Ramírez, 2005: 80; Murillo and Avirama, 2004: 129; Livingstone, 2003:100; Leech, 2002a: 17; Keen and Haynes, 2000: 534; Berry, 1999: 14n.22; Chomsky as quoted in Giraldo, 1996: 14; Bushnell, 1993: 241; Reinhardt, 1988: 130.

peasants is seen in the coffee industry. Once a thriving coffee-growing region, sectors of southwestern Colombia witnessed a dramatic shift in the return from this once lucrative commodity. At its peak in 1955, coffee accounted for roughly 84 percent of Colombian export income (Kofas, 1986: 17; Arrubla, 1970: 136; Mandel, 1968: 460). The 1970s and 1980s saw roughly 300,000 to 350,000 farmers cultivating coffee and 2 million Colombians benefiting from the industry in some form (O'Shaughnessy and Branford, 2005: 29; Harding, 1996: 40). As neoliberal policies encouraged unfettered international trade, however, tariffs were increasingly removed, and the US withdrawal from the International Coffee Agreement (ICA)[44] in 1989 drastically altered the historic yet modest returns for coffee producers (Harding, 1996: 41).[45]

> For many years, the cultivation of coffee beans had provided farmers in the coffee-growing regions with a measure of security and stability in the midst of Colombia's violence. However, the international market price for coffee – Colombia's leading legal export for most of the 20th century – plummeted in the post Cold War era, forcing many farmers to seek alternative means of survival. Consequently, increasing numbers of farmers began replacing their coffee plants with coca plants ... The dilemma now faced by Colombia's coffee growers began with a World Bank development project in Vietnam that, during the 1990s, encouraged Vietnamese farmers to grow coffee. The program was so 'successful' that in 2001 Vietnam surpassed Colombia to become the number two coffee producing country in the world behind Brazil. However, a resulting global glut in coffee caused the market price to plummet from over $2 a pound at the end of the 1980s to 58 cents by the end of 2001. Consequently, coffee growers around the world, including those in Vietnam, are now desperately struggling to survive by growing a crop that sells for less than it costs to produce.
>
> (Gibbs and Leech, 2009: 51; Leech, 2002a: 51)

William Avilés demonstrated the negative effect of the ICA's marginalization on producers in the highlands of Colombia.

> The liberalization of the international price of coffee in 1989 after the collapse of the International Coffee Agreement, which ended restrictive quotas on supply, brought the price of coffee to a thirty-year low by 2003,

Table 4.4 Incremental leaps in inequitable income distribution

Decade	Distribution of income (richest 10% and poorest 10%)
1950s	11:1
1980s	18:1
1990s	40:1
2000s	80:1

Sources: Stokes, 2005: 130; Pearse, 1990a: 70; Lambert, 1971: 46.

exacerbating already extensive rural poverty. The collapse of coffee prices led thousands of small coffee farmers to switch to growing poppies for heroin production, as coffee input fell by 25 percent.

(Avilés, 2006: 90)

According to Colombian political economist Héctor Mondragón, responsibility for reduced coffee returns is squarely on the shoulders of international financial institutions (IFIs) such as the World Trade Organization and international lending institutions (ILIs) such as the International Monetary Fund and World Bank. These institutions had countries reduce or eliminate national protection arrangements, leaving farmers unable to maintain any level of subsistence and subsequently resorting to unconventional agricultural production.[46]

Thanks to free trade, the Colombian farmer has no other options. The agricultural sector has been ruined. We import 8 times more food than we did ten years ago. Starting last year, we've been importing coffee, to meet our export quotas. The quotas can't even be met because the price is too low. Latin America is destroying the coffee harvest. In the last 2 months, coffee prices dropped 22% for the grower. It was already at a low – 1/3 of the price 10 years ago. Selling coffee is now a losing proposition. Production costs are higher than the sale price .... The US broke the world coffee pact, which provided some stability for growers and consumers alike, in order to make the WTO happen. Before that Colombia had a fund used to stabilize the price of coffee. Now such a fund is illegal.

(Mondragón, 2001; see also Ross, 2006: 62)[47]

Gabriel Silva, an official from the National Federation of Coffee Growers of Colombia (Federación Nacional de Cafeteros de Colombia, FEDECAFE), stated that from a US$4 cup of coffee bought in North America, "around one cent will go back to the farmer" (ABC, 2004). In 1997, Colombian-based coffee farmers were reportedly paid US$3.80 for every pound of coffee they produced, while in 2004, the producers received about 0.70¢ (ABC, 2004). Accounts from popular US and British business reports, however, show that the true returns are lower still. In the fall of 2005, the Associated Press (2005) quoted Silva saying that during the 2003–04 coffee season the price per pound was roughly 0.77¢, but Stephen Farr's (2004) Bloomberg report found that Colombian coffee's highest return in years, in January 2004 (during the 2003–04 season), was "$690 a metric ton." A metric ton equals 2,204.6 lbs, so a little arithmetic shows that this was 0.31¢ per pound. A more efficient example of coffee growth would be to gauge whether or not the localized producers are deriving an increase in direct revenue gains: according to my meetings with small-scale coffee farmers in the coffee zones between 2003 and 2007, they are not.[48]

Losses as a result of neoliberal economic policies were not confined to the coffee sector, but occurred throughout the entire agricultural industry (see Table 4.5). Thus the rural population have had few options to sustain their socioeconomic and cultural situation. Historically, times of negative political-economic circumstances have seen peasants leave for urban centers in hopes of a better life.

> The peasant is not bound to the land to the same extent as his counterparts in certain other Latin American countries. The limitation is almost solely economic; in general, and increasingly during the last twenty years, the farm worker and smallholder readily abandons the land whenever opportunity presents itself of transferring to an urban activity.
>
> (Galbraith, 1953: 88)

There clearly was a significant out-migration of peasants from the countryside throughout the 1950s to 1970s, which continues to this day, but it has been argued that there were also growing numbers of small producers. Mike Davis's important work in *Planet of Slums* (2007) contextualizes the ever-increasing rates of peasant immigration to urban centers, but some sectors of Colombia's countryside have witnessed an increase in their peasant population.

Labor organizers, social movements, and human rights organizations have detailed that *campesinos* have remained and raised families in the countryside even when their situation there was dire (Díaz Montes, 2005). Mondragón (2006) found that alongside a very real exodus from the countryside there has been an influx in the number of rural producers in Colombia. While not a new phenomenon, this marks an important distinction in the context of rural production and socioeconomic identity throughout Latin America.

> The most evident impact of capitalism, both rural and urban, has been the high rate of farm-to-city migration that has taken pace in Colombia since the 1950s. Pushed out by worsening conditions in the rural economy and attracted by the possibility of high-wage industrial jobs in the urban centers, rural migrants contributed to urban growth rates that were on the order of 6 percent per year by the 1960s. Notwithstanding these high rates of

Table 4.5 The declining importance of conventional agriculture in the Colombian economy

A: Drop in agriculture's proportion of in GDP since the implementation of neoliberalism

Industry	1980	1990	1999	Average decade reduction percentage
Agriculture	22%	19%	13%	5

B: Decline in annual growth of the rural economy per decade

Industry	1980–89	1990–99	Decade reduction percentage
Agricultural	2.9%	-2.6%	5.5%

Sources: Adapted from Avilés, 2006: 58, 118; Richani, 2005a: 117-118; 2002a: 141; Decker and Duran, 1982: 29.

migration, the density of the rural population increased from 80 persons per square kilometer in 1960 to 98 persons in 1970. Undoubtedly, this concentration is higher on the farms under 10 hectares.

(de Janvry, 1981: 135)

More recently, there has been comparative population growth in the Colombian countryside, even when weighed against the emigration of rural producers to urban centers.

Although the rural population has dropped in relative terms, it has continued to increase in absolute terms from 6 million people in 1938 to 11.6 million in 1993. A similar dynamic occurred with the economically active population in the farming sector, which went from 1.9 million in 1938 to 2.7 million in 1993. Moreover, "self-employed workers" in the sector (medium scale campesinos) went from 600,000 in 1938 to 700,000 in 1964 and to 800,000 in 1993.

(Mondragón, 2006: 165)

One of the ways rural producers found to remain in the countryside and respond to the land question was, again, by migrating to and colonizing less fertile lands in remote regions. Because of the deep concentration of fertile arable land in the hands of large landholders, many peasant families came to inhabit the mountainside, literally. Even though the practice became illegal in 1951, some "decided" to remain in the countryside by living on and farming incredibly dangerous inclined slopes throughout the three mountain ranges of south-central and southwestern Colombia (Palacios, 2006: 225; Gomez, 1972: 250; Smith, 1970: 165; Rogers, 1969: 384n.3; Thayer, 1963: 143; Galbraith, 1953: 88). Another avenue enabling many *campesinos* to remain in the countryside was to increase activity in the informal sector. Over the last two decades, roughly 500,000 peasants have begun to directly cultivate coca, while an approximate 1 million turned to the coca industry as a marginal source of socioeconomic security (Richani, 2002a: 97, 75).

These figures are significant particularly because of their parallels with the once-strong coffee industry. As noted, prior to neoliberalism coffee provided an estimated 300,000 to 350,000 small producers with a form of livelihood (O'Shaughnessy and Branford, 2005: 29; Harding, 1996: 40). By the 1980s, roughly 300,000 were directly involved in the coca industry as a means of subsistence (Felbab-Brown, 2005: 112; see also Schulte-Bockholt, 2006: 98). As neoliberalism increasingly disenfranchised peasant producers, coca cultivation quickly doubled in Colombia during the mid to late 1990s (Leech, 2002a: 43).[49] It seems evident that former coffee growers have shifted to coca (Peceny and Durnan, 2006: 109; O'Shaughnessy and Branford, 2005: 29).

Peasant producers derive several benefits from growing coca. The crop has partially if not fully eliminated "the high transaction costs otherwise incurred by transporting legal crops to markets in areas with very poor transportation systems," of which there are many in rural Colombia, (Felbab-Brown, 2005:

108–9; see also Richani, 2002a: 71). Coca remained one of the only crops that could be grown in the poor lands inhabited by many peasants, which could keep "the *campesinos*' heads above water" (Goff, 2004: 33; see also Castaño, 2006; Rochlin, 2003: 135–6). For many, the crop enables families to receive a "small portion of the profit from the cocaine market, the illegality of coca means that they reap substantially more than producing this commodity than from any other crop" (Peceny and Durnan, 2006: 99).[50]

> This livelihood [illicit crop cultivation] is not only stable, but also far more comfortable than the alternatives open to poor, minimally-mobile peasants. The price that traffickers can offer for coca leaves surpasses the price peasants can get for cocoa pods by between two and eight times, for rubber by four times, and for maize by more than 40 times.
>
> (Felbab-Brown, 2005: 108)

By 2000, coffee only accounted for 13.4 percent of Colombia's exports because tariff reductions had flooded the global market with cheap and excessive product (Ramirez-Vallejo, 2003). As a result of the fall in coffee returns, "many small farmers were forced off the land through bad debts. Some of the displaced families moved south and began to cultivate coca" (O'Shaughnessy and Branford, 2005: 29). While cultivating coca does not make a small producer wealthy, it does guarantee an income based not on speculation but on material production and delivery (Castaño, 2006; Richani, 2002a: 111).

Much of this chapter has demonstrated how the state and capitalist class monopolized land and capital and how this disenfranchised the peasantry. Nevertheless, it is important to note that the growth and expansion of the coca industry has not been based solely on the increased concentration of land and inequitable distribution of income. Such conditions are simply subcategories of a larger problem within the national economy, which exists amidst a globalized capitalist reality centered on the centralized accumulation of wealth. Many small producers I interviewed believed that as the state increasingly adopts neoliberal economic patterns of perceived development, worse days are sure to be on the horizon. Stemming from this critique, it is now important to see what relation the FARC-EP has had to coca, and how and to what extent the insurgency is connected to the industry today.

5

THE POLITICAL ECONOMY OF COCA IN COLOMBIA, PAST AND PRESENT

Numerous state-based reports, scholastic papers, and popular media accounts have reiterated, to the point of uncritical acceptance, that the FARC-EP is directly involved with the Colombian coca industry. These articles hypothesize that the FARC-EP has intimately connected itself to differing sectors of the coca trade (cultivation, processing, production, and trafficking) to financially sustain its revolutionary efforts against the Colombian state or for mere individual monetary gain. Rather than regurgitating these simplified claims, this chapter chooses to look at the insurgency's relation to this informal economy from another perspective. As the rural population continues to be exploited through a detrimental political economy, the FARC-EP has attempted to create a pre-revolutionary program by manipulating the conventional coca industry in the hopes of strengthening sociopolitical and economic conditions for the marginalized. A detailed account of the insurgency's relation to coca is presented; a much-needed analysis in light of Colombia's contemporary economy and the lack of research relating to the FARC-EP's actual position toward the country's drug trade. This account, moving beyond unfounded descriptions, demonstrates the insurgency's historic and contemporary relation to coca, and how the guerrillas have created a program to respond materially to the socioeconomic and cultural needs of the Colombian peasantry by delinking their dependence on illicit crops through a process of alternative crop substitution.

THE FARC-EP'S HISTORIC RELATION TO COCA

Within sectors of the popular media and in countless US/Colombian state reports, a strategic attempt has been made not only to paint the FARC-EP as an ideologically empty political-military organization but to embellish, without credible evidence, the insurgency's relation to the coca industry. Such claims have been under-evaluated and uncritically accepted by large sectors of the population. It is most unfortunate that such unsubstantiated allegations tend over time to be adopted by "experts" and the academy. Some have concluded from them that the FARC-EP is a degraded post-ideological criminal movement seeking nothing more than to expand the coffers of its members (Sweig and McCarthy, 2005: 18; Collier, 2000; Collier and Hoeffler, 2000). Supporting this acceptance, LeGrand (2003: 179) cited former Colombian attorney-general Alfonso Gómez Méndez: "just as drug money has corrupted society and the establishment, it has also corrupted the anti-establishment." Such "analysts" insisted the FARC-EP has failed to retain "an ideological vision" of political organization or the expansion of class consciousness (LeGrand, 2003: 179). In short, the guerrillas are characterized as devising a strategic coca-alliance/dependence in negation to their historic Marxist-Leninist positioning (LeGrand, 2003: 176-180).

Some scholars, however, have argued against these claims. They have criticized such positions as failing to explain "the character of the Colombian civil war"; "identify the origins of an insurgency that has recently celebrated its 40th year in existence"; or illustrate "the longstanding ideological vision of the FARC or its social base among some sectors of the Colombian rural proletariat" (Peceny and Durnan, 2006: 96). Research has suggested that depicting the FARC-EP to be a purely profit-based collective pursuing greed demonstrates a false and oversimplified understanding of the insurgency's history and contemporary political ideology (Peceny and Durnan, 2006; Gutiérrez Sanín, 2004; Röhl, 2004; Molano, 2000).

Some have argued that the FARC-EP's power (and cancellation of ideology) is based exclusively on the insurgency's sociogeographical location; far from state eyes the guerrillas have been able to exploit the cultivation and production of coca (Ortiz, 2006: 207; LeGrand, 2003: 176). One of Colombia's most renowned critical scholars published a brief history of the FARC-EP. Through this work Alfredo Molano was able to clarify that the insurgency is by no means a narco-guerrilla organization. He explained that the narcotic industry exists outside the insurgency and remains a consequence of the region's political economy (Molano, 2000: 27). In addition, Molano identified that the FARC-EP's longevity is not related to the drug trade or to state breakdown but rather to historic conditions of exploitation and rural organization. Of those who have examined the FARC-EP, all acknowledge that the insurgency was established long before the processing of coca, poppy, or even marijuana.[1] This is evidence that the FARC-EP's expansion and support cannot be loosely attributed to the coca industry (see Schulte-Bockholt, 2006: 135; Petras and Morley, 2003: 100).

> Cultivation of illegal crops was established in the colonization areas not simply because of weak army presence, but because the colonists were on the brink of ruin. And the guerrillas were in the colonization regions long before coca cultivation appeared. Their growth was due mainly to the repression unleashed against popular protest, and by the growing impoverishment of the population – not to participation in the drug trade.
>
> (Molano, 2000: 27)

Alain Labrousse (2005: 179) assessed that "the FARC had developed for many years without resorting to coca trafficking, and in some departments, Cordoba and Urabá for instance, their fronts had multiplied without the support provided by illicit crops" (see also Labrousse, 2005: 171). Francisco Gutiérrez Sanín (2004: 265) commented that "the organizational take off of the FARC *preceded*" coca. Nevertheless, many academics, journalists, and politicians have opted to dismiss this important historical and cultural connection between the FARC-EP and the socio-geography of the countryside (see Johnson, 1972: 289–92). Hence the importance of detailing the FARC-EP's past relation to coca.

The FARC-EP's historic position toward coca

The FARC-EP claims to follow a Marxist-Leninist ideology; however, the coca industry revolves around a social relation of production based upon a capitalist framework. In light of this dichotomy, would it not be theoretically erroneous for a political-military organization steeped in the Marxist tradition to materially support such an industry? Some have argued that its relationship to the coca (capitalist) industry illustrates the FARC-EP's ironic departure from Marxist-Leninist ideology (Labrousse, 2005: 172, 181). Therefore, does the FARC-EP today lack a political foundation? Has the insurgency bastardized its principles by accepting coca cultivation in regions under its control? A review of existing literature on the subject, coupled with a proper review of Marxist-Leninist theory, suggests that the answer is no. On the contrary, it is as a direct result of the FARC-EP's *Marxist–Leninist ideology* that the organization has recognized and responded to not only national realities but also the socio-economic conditions of its supporters.

Lenin (1965a) condemned guerrilla organizations that distort their material objectives by not altering activities to the needs and social environments of the working classes in which they are embedded. On several occasions, Lenin clearly stated that "guerrilla actions must conform to the temper of the broad masses and the conditions of the working-class movements" (Lenin, 1965g: 224; see also 1965f: 213–23). After recognizing the material needs of the peasantry, coupled with the deteriorating rural political economy, the FARC-EP altered its political doctrine from the ground up, allowing, albeit under restriction, a means of subsistence through the cultivation of coca (Molano, 1992: 210–12). It is not well known that the FARC-EP was stringently against drugs from the 1960s to the early 1980s. However, the insurgency directly responded to the contextual conditions and subsistence needs of the peasantry through a distinct Marxist strategy (Hylton, 2006: 154n.196; O'Shaughnessy and Branford, 2005: 26). Based on a Marxist-Leninist positioning, the FARC-EP became "involved with the security of coca growers in their zones of influence for much of the 1980s as the guerrillas found it difficult to oppose an industry that potentially could improve the lives of peasants" (Avilés, 2006: 155n.38).[2]

This suggests that the FARC-EP effectively analyzed the economic condition of the Colombian peasantry and decided to support them from their own class dynamic. This support is not based on a specific crop, but on a class position and goal for revolutionary emancipation. As noted in Chapter 2, the FARC-EP understands that revolution can only be implemented with the popular support of the people. Asserting this idea, the insurgency assisted those peasants who felt they must cultivate coca to survive.[3] In recognition of this, *the FARC-EP does not support coca but it does support the class that must produce it.* This emphasizes two important points. First, the FARC-EP has proven to analyze and grow in revolutionary consciousness by supporting the needs of the marginalized. The second demonstrates how the insurgency continues to seek social change from below.

Based upon its interpretation of Marxism the insurgency has been heavily involved in transgressions aimed at the state and members of the dominant class (Ampuero and Brittain, 2005; Ferro Medina and Uribe Ramón, 2002; Pizarro Leongómez, 1992; 1991; Gilhodés, 1970; Fletcher, 1967).[4] The FARC-EP has long been a threat to the rural political and economic elite as it has "acted as a defensive organization with deep roots among the peasant colonizers, and acted to protect their interests from large cattle ranchers aligned with the Colombia military. They also provided basic social services in the absence of the Colombian state" (Stokes, 2005: 73; see also Wickham-Crowley, 1990: 202).

For decades the dominant class organized with the state in reaction to the insurgency's breadth and support (Lindqvist, 1979: 89; Gilbert, 1974: 116–24; Gilhodés, 1970: 434–51).

> By the end of the 1970s, the state's efforts at repression of the peasant movement and the use of armed militias by large landholders had effectively pushed the settlers into the arms of the guerrillas. For the peasants, the presence of the FARC guaranteed that the cattlemen would not be able to expel them from those lands that they had painstakingly maintained in the preceding years.
>
> (Labrousse, 2005: 172)

In the years to follow, narcotic cultivation rose across Latin America, especially in Colombia. By the 1980s, "the business had grown to the point where the drug trade accounted for 10 to 25 percent of the country's exports" (Holmes, 2003: 88). During this period the FARC-EP maintained a stringent anti-narcotic policy, seeing the industry as a form of domestic and imperial exploitation creeping into the countryside (Weinstein, 2007: 290, 293; Felbab-Brown, 2005: 112; Molano, 2000: 27).

> From the time they were founded ... the FARC did not want to have anything to do with drugs or drug money. When the Medellín Cartel came to the department of Caquetá in 1978 to distribute coca seeds, the FARC forbade farmers from planting the new crop.
>
> (O'Shaughnessy and Branford, 2005: 26)

One of the reasons for the FARC-EP's disdain was the increased centralization of wealth derived from the industry. With the rise of the Colombian cartels many large landowners and cattle ranchers established themselves as a narcobourgeoisie (Richani, 2007; 2005a; 2002a; 2000; Leech, 2003; Scott, 2003). The 1980s saw this group, and their paramilitary allies, consolidate millions of hectares of arable land (Schulte-Bockholt, 2006: 107; Thoumi, 1995: 239–40).

> [I]n the early 1980s, the paramilitaries were strongest in Córdoba and the Magdalena Medio region, where agricultural land was among the most concentrated in the country. By the late 1980s, the distinction between big farmers and ranchers on the one hand, and narcotraffickers on the other, became blurred. In fact, during the mid-1980s narcotraffickers invested their illicit wealth through the purchase of 4 to 6 million hectares of land.
>
> (Rochlin, 2003: 107)

Class-based tensions soon prevailed as narcotraffickers added to the traditional social conflicts between large landowners and the landless by buying up huge tracks of land in the pursuit of cleansing illicit profits and simultaneously becoming members of the domestic elite (Holmes, Amin Gutiérrez de Piñeres and Curtin, 2006: 167). With the insurgency seen as a mouthpiece for the peasantry, it was easily recognized how such conditions "invariably led to tension between the FARC and the traffickers" (Stokes, 2005: 86–7).

> Narcotrafficking kingpins have been renowned for being fiercely capitalistic, and have considered themselves to represent the legitimate bourgeoisie of Colombia. Hence the obvious ideological clash with the socialistic FARC, which, for example, has insisted upon land reform that threatens the huge estates controlled by narcotrafficking executives.
>
> (Rochlin, 2003: 100)

To fight against the FARC-EP's continued protection of the rural population, and consistent spontaneous attacks and harassment of the unused arable lands, "traffickers collaborated with traditional landowners, the military and other elements of the local power structure to combat predatory guerrilla attacks and infrastructure" (Clawson and Lee III, 1998: 52; see also Scott, 2003: 86). For much of the 1970s and 1980s, the FARC-EP remained in constant opposition (and armed conflict) with the primary drug cartels in Colombia (Camacho Guizado and López Restrepo, 2007: 80; Felbab-Brown, 2005: 113; Dudley, 2004: 57, 102; Gutiérrez Sanín, 2004: 282n.40; Rochlin, 2003: 107; Clawson and Lee III, 1998: 52, 58, 180). In contradiction of Labrousse (2005: 177), who stated that relations between the FARC-EP and the cartels "were relatively nonproblematic," numerous accounts showed the ferocity between the two groups.[5]

Rensselaer W. Lee III (1988: 98) pointed out how the cartels combated the FARC-EP through violent aggressions aimed at unionists and civilian supporters (see also Gugliotta, 1992: 113). The Medellín and Cali cartels had a detailed "history of sponsoring violence against the revolutionary left" (Clawson and Lee III, 1998: 180; see also Leech, 2002a). One of the ways in which the narco-bourgeoisie did this was by developing a systemic working relationship with armed forces. Drug lords began operating "hand in hand with the paramilitary death squads to fight the FARC-EP" (International Action Center, 2001: 3; see also Lee III, 1991: 98). Álvaro Camacho Guizado (1988: 144), quoting Pablo Escobar, depicted how the cartels fought against the guerrillas because of their clear ideological differences. Escobar noted, "that they try to present me as an associate of the guerrilla ... hurts my personal dignity .... I am a man of investments and therefore I cannot sympathize with the guerrillas who fight against property" (see also Schulte-Bockholt, 2006: 95).

Some have gone a step further to reveal that not only had paramilitary forces worked with the cartels, so too had the conventional military: "although officially involved in the war against drug lords, sectors of the armed forces ... allied with the lords against the guerrillas and their suspected civilian supporters" (Pearce, 1990b: 19). The FARC-EP's critical stance toward the cartels remained solid until their official demise in the early 1990s. However, based on the changing political economy of rural Colombia the organizational structure of today's narcotics industry is greatly different from what it was during the 1970s and early 1990s.

There is a recognized problem concerning the FARC-EP's relation to the coca industry in contemporary Colombia. While the FARC-EP once denounced drug trafficking, some speculated that the insurgency took up the trade in recent years (Dudley, 2004: 52). Others have argued that the guerrillas never deviated from their ideological opposition to drug trafficking (Richani, 2002a: 99). Evidence of the latter has been noted by numerous academics and multi-national organizations such as the United Nations (see Stokes, 2005). To think of the FARC-EP as drug-traffickers or "narco-guerrillas" is, in short, absurd (Holmes et al, 2006: 167; Peceny and Durnan, 2006: 96; Schulte-Bockholt, 2006: 129; Leech, 2002a: 62; Molano, 2000: 27; Chernick, 1996).[6] Former military advisor to the Uribe administration, Alfredo Rangel Suárez, stated, "it is a mistake to treat the FARC like a drug cartel because it ignores the fact that the principle [sic] goal of the FARC is not to make money from drug-trafficking but to take political power through violence" (Associated Press, 2006a).

Rangel Suárez went on to suggest that "if you reduce the FARC to just a drug cartel, you make the possibility of negotiating a political settlement more difficult" (Kraul, 2006). Depicting the FARC-EP as a drug-linked guerrilla organization has strategically hijacked any negotiated solution to the civil war, while simultaneously delegitimizing the organization's sociopolitical and economic ideological intentions (Schulte-Bockholt, 2006: 104). Others have verified that there is no proof to support the claim that the FARC-EP is directly involved in the coca-industry (Röhl, 2004). Even representatives from the Colombian and US governments have agreed (International Action Center, 2001: 3).

High U.S. officials have challenged the claims of their own government. For instance, Donnie Marshall, the former Administrator of the U.S. Drug Enforcement Administration (DEA), and James Milford, the former Deputy Administrator, have said that there is no evidence that the guerrillas participate in the drug trade by producing it or by selling it to the smuggling syndicates.

(Ahmad, 2006: 63)

For years, DEA documents indicated that the agency "has no evidence that [the insurgents] have been involved in the transportation, distribution, or marketing of illicit drugs in the United States or Europe" and that the FARC-EP "never will be major players in Colombia's drug trade" (Stokes, 2005: 87; see also Gutiérrez Sanín, 2004: 266; Shannon, 1989: 161–6). Donnie Marshall also testified to the US House Committee that no conclusion could be made supporting the claim that the insurgency is involved in the narcotic industry (see Hart, 2000). He testified that there was nothing to substantiate the claim that the FARC-EP is connected to smuggling, trafficking, or laundering narcodollars (Ahmad, 2006: 63; Coghlan, 2004: 207; Shannon, 1989: 161–6).[7] Former US ambassador to Colombia Myles Frechette pointed out that there is no clear evidence that the FARC-EP is directly involved with the drug trade (Goff, 2004: 33). According to Robin Kirk (2003: 246), both Frechette and Colombia's former chief of police, Rosso José Serrano, "routinely iced down these allegations as a ruse that the generals used to wrangle money to fight the FARC." Former US Special Forces (Green Beret) officer Stan Goff (2003: 81) joined the chorus and stated that:

[M]y own personal experience as a military advisor in Colombia in 1992 leads me to conclude that the "war on drugs" is simply a propaganda ploy, a legitimizing story for the American public. We were briefed by the Public Affairs Officers that counter-narcotics was a cover story for curious journalists, friends, and family that our mission, in fact, was to further develop Colombians' capacity for counterinsurgency operations.[8]

(Goff, 2003: 81)

Past Colombian president (1998–2002) and ambassador to the United States (2005–06) Andrés Pastrana Arango also stood by the position that the FARC-EP was in no way linked to drug trafficking (Ruiz, 2001: 151; Hart, 2000). Pastrana revealed that the Colombian state had been unable to find "any evidence that they're involved directly in drugs" (Weymouth, 2000).

Moving beyond the issue of involvement, it has been extensively noted that the FARC-EP have consistently worked to prevent the coca industry from completely taking over rural sectors of the country (Holmes et al, 2006; Glenn, 2003; Stokes, 2002). Following the FARC-EP's open refusal to support coca cultivation during the 1970s and early 1980s, the insurgency shifted its position to some degree in the late 1980s and 1990s. Remaining in opposition to coca, the FARC-EP began to work with the United Nations during the 1980s on numerous projects related to crop substitution in zones under the insurgency's control (Labrousse, 2005: 175). Working outside the Colombian state, the United Nations embraced the FARC-EP as a partner in programs related to social development and crop substitution (see also Ahmad, 2006;

Schulte-Bockholt, 2006; Labrousse, 2005; Glenn, 2003). Several officials stated that the insurgents were anything but narco-guerrillas. One was Klaus Nyholm, former Director of the United Nations International Drug Control Programme (UNDCP) in Colombia, who said, "The guerrillas are something different than the traffickers, the local fronts are quite autonomous. But in some areas, they're not involved at all. And in others, they actively tell the farmers not to grow coca" (quoted in Stokes, 2002).

Throughout his career as the UN special advisor on Colombia (1999–2005), James LeMoyne repeatedly argued that the FARC-EP were not linked to narcotrafficking but rather subscribed to an ideological position that opposed the Colombian state through class struggle and the pursuit of self-emancipation for both workers and peasants (UN News Centre, 2005; LACIC, 2004; Coghlan, 2004: 10; LACYORK, 2003; O'Donoghue, 2003). LeMoyne was anything but quiet in his evaluation of the FARC-EP and the Colombian civil war. Aside from defending the insurgency's application of Marxism, he criticized the Colombian elite for distancing their own children from combat while sending the poor to die for dominant class interests.[9]

The FARC-EP has never promoted the production of coca. The insurgency has long encouraged and assisted crop substitution projects in several municipalities (Richani, 2002a: 99; FARC-EP, 2000d). It has not just resisted the drug economy, it has purposely sought alternative development programs of substitution (see Coghlan, 2004: 207; Livingstone, 2003: 130; Gamboa, 2001: 100 Ruiz (2001: 62). One example found,

> a government official in charge of administering alternative development programs visited villages where the FARC was known to operate. His expectation was that the FARC would oppose the programs since the diminished cultivation of coca would reduce the guerrillas' income. In each village he visited, however, the FARC not only failed to oppose the programs but encouraged them.
>
> (Felbab-Brown, 2005: 122)

During the 1990s and 2000s the FARC-EP successfully supported a shift from coca to legitimate crops in the mayoralty of Micoahumado in the Morales municipality of the Bolivar department (Richani, 2002a: 193n 12; 2001: 59–60). Similar projects were implemented in regions of the Casanare department in the central northeast (Richani, 2001: 60). While the FARC-EP has fronts extended throughout the country, only a minority have a coca industry in their territory (Clawson and Lee III, 1998: 179).[10] Rochlin (2003: 100, 137), too, pointed out that "not all members of fronts of the FARC have been involved in the illicit drug trade." Arguably this is based on the premise that sectors of the FARC-EP fully reject the insurgency's indirect involvement in the industry and/or that the substitution programs have proven successful (Holmes et al, 2006: 167).

In 1999, after several years of trying to establish formal international arrangements related to crop substitution (and attempted consultation with the

United States and the Colombian state), the FARC-EP independently outlined a program entitled *For a Government of Reconstruction and National Reconciliation* and later *Planning Mechanisms for the Substitution of Illegal Crops: Municipality of Cartagena del Chairá (Caquetá)* (Gamboa, 2001: 100; FARC-EP 2001a: 7). One year later, the guerrillas organized a four-month experiment involving crop substitution in the largest narcotic-producing country in the hemisphere (FARC-EP, 2000d). With the full support of the European Union and the United Nations, the FARC-EP's platform was implemented in select regions of Caquetá. After several months, the FARC-EP hosted a conference related to its alternative development and legalization strategies, allowing hundreds of members from the international community, domestic government officials, and peasant groups from the department of Caquetá to review and critique its work.

On June 29–30, 2000, the FARC-EP organized the *International Conference on Illegal Drug Crops and the Environment* in the town of Vereda Los Pozos, in the municipality of San Vicente del Caguán, Caquetá. The purpose of the conference was to discuss and construct an official policy toward altering coca cultivation over a larger Colombian territory. Using the region of Cartagena del Chairá, Caquetá as an example, the insurgency provided evidence of already existing alternative crop-substitution projects, which demonstrated both ecological and socioeconomic methods of successful eradication without bringing excessive cultural, economic, or physical harm to the rural population.

During the two-day conference community leaders, spokeswomen, *colonos*, small producers and representatives from over 50 peasant-based organizations delivered lectures, held seminars, and discussed issues related to their agricultural activities. Over 20 international and government representatives were in attendance to listen to these colloquiums and talk about coca cultivation and the need to alter Colombia's dependency on the drug economy over the next decade (representatives from the Vatican and the United Nations included those in attendance). Presenting the need for rural crop substitution, the FARC-EP emphasized how peasants were forced to shift from traditional agriculture to a neo-dependency on coca as a monoculture crop. The insurgency offered to act as an overseer of manual eradication efforts over a controlled territory – giving credibility to both the local population and insurgency to cooperate in directing infrastructure. The FARC-EP did not seek to be in control of the project, but rather proposed that a grassroots collective should facilitate the venture.

According to Monica Somocurico (2000), "the revolutionaries called for forming a local authority comprised of community, union and environmental representatives that would oversee the implementation of the plan." Supported by the United Nations, numerous members of the European Parliament, different international observers, and foreign governmental agencies and delegates, the project was immediately opposed by the Colombian state (whose representatives were present) and the United States (which refused to send representatives to the conference).[11] On March 8, 2001, the FARC-EP followed up the June conference and Cartagena del Chairá experiment with another symposium, again with numerous international representatives in attendance. The insurgency stressed "that the solution of the problem of illicit crops will be achieved by social investment and not through repression" (FARC-EP, 2001a: 9). With the participation of representatives from 28 countries (including Canada, Cuba, France, Italy, Mexico, Norway, Portugal, Sweden, Switzerland and Venezuela), a program was mapped out in an official document; *Planning Mechanisms for the Substitution of Illicit Crops* (FARC-EP, 2000d; see also 2001a: 8–10).[12]

As mentioned, prior to the FARC-EP's formal international proposal addressing the national drug issue in the period from 1999 to 2001, the insurgency had been working on alternative social development projects with the United Nations as far back as the Belisario Betancur Cuartas administration (1982–86) (Labrousse, 2005: 175). This is an important point for it demonstrates that the FARC-EP was, in fact, the first organization in Colombia to support crop substitution – long before the problem of coca became too much to control. Unfortunately, any chance of implementing the multi-million-dollar UN/FARC-EP projects "to replace coca crops with new forms of legal alternative development" came to an abrupt end in 2002 when the US/Colombian state supported a military invasion on the agreed demilitarized zone of San Vicente del Caguán, destroying the insurgency's ability to devote time, energy, and security to the project (see Stokes, 2002; FARC-EP, 2000a). In spite of all of this, the FARC-EP has remained engaged in autonomous projects that encourage peasants to grow subsistence and traditional crops (Villalón, 2004b; Richani, 2002a: 99, 193.n12).

The FARC-EP's relation to coca

To try to offer a clearer picture of the FARC-EP's present association to coca, the next section examines how the insurgency has *indirectly* involved itself with the industry. Although this might appear to be in contradiction with previous statements concerning the FARC-EP's Marxist-Leninist position on narcotics, it is argued that the insurgency altered its position toward coca after re-examining the peasantry's declining social conditions amidst the rural political economy. The guerrillas recognized that growing numbers of people were financially forced to move away from traditional crop production as a result of low returns and/or the need to abandon subsistence agriculture as a result of increasing land centralization via coercive land acquisitions by large landowners.

Based on these circumstances, it can be argued that the FARC-EP, if truly applying Marxism-Leninism, had to adapt its earlier anti-narcotic principles in order to generate a program that was and is most beneficial for the exploited class. If the FARC-EP is to wage a revolutionary war beside those marginalized (and protect the rural masses), the insurgency is "compelled to accept the peasants' shift to illicit crop plantations as a supplementary income" (Richani, 2002a: 71; see also Molano, 2005: 32).[13] The manner in which the FARC-EP eventually chose to "accept" the peasants' "shift" was through a class-based model of taxation imposed by the insurgency on specific sectors of the coca-industry.[14] We now look at this model, and at the contemporary political economy of the coca-industry at a peasant-based level.

The FARC-EP has established a complex series of taxes for persons and corporations throughout regions where it holds power (Ortiz, 2006: 216; Stokes, 2005: 86; Holmes, 2003: 88; Chernick, 1996).[15] The levies imposed by the insurgency are based on a person's association to the social relations of production; hence the taxation must be examined within a class framework. This class-based model provides for an intricate system of levies and tariffs on sectors of the coca industry, as well as on all corporate or economic activity throughout the rural political economy (including oil production, bananas, and all other commodities and services). This exemplifies how the FARC-EP is interested not in the drug economy *per se* but rather in overseeing (and taxing) all aspects of class-based production (see Kirk, 2003: 227–8). This authority explains why some have wrongly analyzed the FARC-EP as a narco-guerrilla organization.

As noted by Marc Chernick,

> the guerrillas do not constitute another "cartel." Their role in the drug trade is in extorting a percentage of the commercial transaction of coca and coca past, just as they do with many other commercial products in the areas which they operate, be it cattle, petroleum, or coffee.
>
> (Chernick, 1996)

As well as this intricate class-based taxation model, the FARC-EP has been involved in much simpler excise practices in some rural communities. These levy systems saw the guerrillas collect a tax on amenities such as toothpaste, soap, and in some cases beer, which was reciprocally repaid in full to a community-based body. The taxes were collected but not spent by the FARC-EP. They are forwarded to "an elected committee from the locality" called *Juntas Accíon Comunal* (JAC) – a locally elected neighborhood council – which implements social programs and infrastructure with the collected funds (Richani, 2002a: 70, 80).

Through the JACs the FARC-EP-imposed levies are used for schools, health services, and infrastructure in rural locales (Leech, 2005b; Stokes, 2005: 86; Brittain, 2004c; Richani, 2002a: 80). In Remolinos del Caguán, Caquetá, for example, the JAC and an "elected committee of students and teachers" used the money "for the construction of a local school" (Richani, 2002a: 70). When discussing such funds during an interview a *campesino* from the Putumayo revealed how:

> sometimes the guerrillas give it to us directly and sometimes it is given to local community officials. There have also been times when the guerrillas have paid for peasants to visit other towns and coordinate trade with other struggling communities. This allows us to not become reliant on obtaining money but rather accustomed to trading surpluses of one, or a few crops,

with other communities who, too, have a surplus of crops. This helps all of us who cannot always afford to take our goods to markets [several years ago the Uribe administration placed a cap on oil and gas use and availability in rural regions of the southwest, making it very difficult to get goods to market by road or water].

This levy structure seems rather simplistic, but the class-based taxation model is far more complicated (see Table 5.1). In relation to coca, it is formulated around the many differing sectors of the narcotic industry. For convenience I have allocated these to four categories. Labeled *informal*, the first sector includes peasant cultivators (*cocaleros*) and/or pickers (*raspachines*) of coca. Neither sector is taxed in any way by the FARC-EP (Peceny and Durnan, 2006: 107; Felbab-Brown, 2005: 126n.42; Molano, 2005: 186; Goff, 2004: 33; Richani, 2002a: 70). When asked their view on the FARC-EP's relation to the coca industry, the class-based taxation model, and whether the guerrillas tax all people equally, one coca cultivator stated:

> One of the greatest misconceptions people have when concerning the FARC is that many believe the guerrilla are involved in the narcotic industry. This is completely false! .... This is a good question that needs to be answered. The FARC do not tax any of the poor, including those who cannot work or those who can. The guerrillas tax those who have the means and the capacity to pay; therefore, the poorer sectors of the peasantry are exempt. The guerrillas do not want to take away what little we have and therefore they tax those who have the money. In actuality, the FARC, on a regular basis, provides many of us with tools or credit so that we can keep our small plots going. This money comes from the wealthy peoples in our regions and is then given to those of us who most need it.

This contradicts countless reports by scholars, journalists, and state officials, most, if not all, of whom have never examined or interviewed local populations in FARC-EP-extended regions.

The second and third sectors in the taxation model, labeled *semi-informal* and *semi-formal*, target those involved in the production, processing, and internal distribution sectors of the industry. The *semi-informal* segment includes the merchants (*revenededoras* or *traqueteros*) and small-to-medium-scale distributors, while the *semi-formal* group aims more at large-scale distributors (Murillo and Avirama, 2004: 19; Molano, 2000: 27).[16] Persons in these sectors pay an imposed tariff ranging from 7 to 15 percent, usually based on the fluctuating price of coca paste (Labrousse, 2005: 172; O'Shaughnessy and Branford, 2005: 26–7; Richani, 2002a: 75, 193n66). The FARC-EP has also been known to force these groups to pay an additional fee for natural resource exploitation and labor equity (see Taussig, 2004b: 142–3, 304–5; Villalón, 2004a: 49; McNeely, 2003; Satchell, 1999).[17] In return for the taxes, the FARC-EP agrees not to disrupt the processing or redistribution, thereby stabilizing current and future returns for the *informal* sector.[18] The insurgency cannot then be thought

Table 5.1 Class-based taxation model employed by the FARC-EP

Tax implemen-tation	Sector of society taxed	Percentage taxed	Tax distribution	Method of payment
Informal	Landless and subsistence peasant farmers	Not taxed	Directly receive grants and bursaries from tax model	Monetary support and/or goods provided through the FARC-EP and/or JAC
Semi-informal	Merchants	7-15%	JAC and/or Individual peoples	Monetary, goods, or services
Semi-formal	Drug merchants and/or large cattle ranchers	7-15%	JAC and/or Individual peoples	Monetary
Formal	Colombians/ MNCs worth over $1 million (Law 002)	10%	FARC-EP (with some surplus devoted to public infrastructure)	Monetary

Sources: Adapted from Brittain, 2004b, with original data collected from Richani, 2005a: 125–6; 2002a: 70, 75, 80, 142, 193n.66; Stokes, 2005: 86; Murillo and Avirama, 2004: 19; Taussig, 2004a: 52; Leech, 2002a: 17–18; Galvis, 2000: 136; plus observational research of both FARC-EP and rural civilians from Cauca, Cundinamarca, Huila, Meta, Nariño, Putumayo, and Tolima between 2003 and 2007.

of as having direct contact with the industry's activities via the cultivation of leaves, processing paste, or distribution of the product (Schulte-Bockholt, 2006; Goff, 2004; Leech, 2002a; Richani, 2002a; Stokes, 2002).

Probably the most famous tax established by the FARC-EP was formulated under its Law 002, proclaimed in March 2000.[19] Law 002 stated that a "TAX FOR PEACE" is collected "from those persons or corporations whose wealth is greater than $1,000,000 US" within insurgency-extended regions (FARC-EP, 2000a). The justification for this is founded on the claim that "trans-national corporations continue to loot our natural resources and the labor of our majorities" while in return, the people who most suffer from this exploitation (through crop contamination, labor manipulation, displacement, and so on) are given nothing (FARC-EP, 2000a; see also Villamizar, 2003: 29).

Unlike the other three tax models, where the levy is handed over to the JAC, the "peace tax" stays with the FARC-EP and is seldom disseminated directly to the civilian populace. Those well read on this aspect of the class-based taxation model have documented how it is used for the FARC-EP's militaristic purposes in conjunction with development projects in regions under its presence. Garry Leech (2002a: 18) noted how the guerrilla organization acquires the "peace tax" and uses it to "improve its military capabilities by modernizing its weaponry and improving the standard of living of its fighters," with a portion of the levy used for "social and economic services, such as credit, public works, and cultural programs to the local peasantry." Stokes (2005: 86) confirmed that "the taxes raised tend to go towards sustaining the insurgency as well as providing local services such as schools and other social infrastructure." The revenue is regularly invested "in public projects such as vocational schools, road paving, public health, and environmental protection," while assisting in the FARC-EP's capacity to wage revolutionary assault on the dominant class (Richani, 2002a: 80). This policy has distinguished the FARC-EP from a cartel, mafia, paramilitary group, or organization involved in the drug economy, as its guerrillas "use the funds not for personal enrichment but to finance their conflict and to supply a minimum of services in the territory under their control" (Schulte-Bockholt, 2006: 138).

> In regions where the FARC has been present for decades, such as Caquetá, Meta and Putumayo, the rebel group functions as a de facto government that has developed and maintains close relations with local communities. In fact, it is clear in these communities that local residents are at ease with the guerrillas and that their greatest fear is of the Colombian military. The military is often the only branch of the state with which the peasants have had substantial contact, and that contact has usually consisted of aerial bombings .... In these regions, the FARC has implemented its own judicial system and has carried out agrarian reforms. A rare investigative piece that was published by the *Washington Post* in October 2003 reported that during the previous two years the FARC had broken up ten large ranches in southern Meta and redistributed the smaller parcels of land to subsistence farmers. The guerrillas have carried out similar programs in Caquetá, Putumayo and other regions. The FARC has also implemented a national tax system whereby the income from kidnapping, extortion and the taxation of wealthy landowners and businesses is used to fund military operations. The revenue from taxes imposed on local communities in FARC-controlled regions, however, is turned over to municipal leaders ... this revenue is used to fund local social and economic projects.
>
> (Leech, 2005b)

In various regions the FARC-EP has continued to assist the rural populations by providing community-based security and law enforcement, infrastructure projects – like road construction and free electricity, numerous forms of economic and social assistance, free medical supplies and services, and a revolutionary judicial system.[20]

> With the complete failure of the government to even attempt to provide any basic services to the local population, it is the FARC that has filled the void by helping to build roads and provide electricity, law enforcement, judges and other public services traditionally supplied by the state. As one local peasant notes, "When farmers or their families get sick and can't afford

medicine, it is the FARC that gives them money to purchase what they need" .... Until the government offers peasants like Cecilia something more than military repression, the local populations in areas such as the Macarena will continue to see their welfare and survival as inextricably intertwined with that of the FARC. Consequently, violence will continue to wreak havoc on another of the country's national treasures: its people.

(Leech, 2006b)

Such circumstances led some to illustrate that the FARC-EP:

are clearly a "government of the people." Many households in the region have at least one family member in the FARC and the local population interacts with the rebels as naturally and comfortably as rural citizens in the global North do with their local government officials and law enforcement officers. As one peasant explains, "When someone has a problem with another person, perhaps a fight or something, they can take their complaint to the FARC. The FARC then investigates and determines who is at fault and what the sentence will be." He goes on to point out that there are no prisons under the FARC, that the sentences handed down to guilty parties include repairing the roads or working in the fields of communal farms.

(Leech, 2006b)

Significant infrastructure projects have been erected by the FARC-EP. These could not have been created by simple community-based levies on soap and toothpaste but only through larger-scale taxation aimed at the elite. The insurgency has utilized Law 002 to construct social services for the most impoverished sectors of Colombian society, a need the conventional state has never addressed objectively or subjectively.

The FARC rebels have gained support among coca-growing peasants by protecting them against the military, the paramilitaries, the drug police, and the drug traffickers. Moreover, the guerrillas provide a number of services as they take over some of the functions of the state they replace such as policing, as the FARC impose its own brand of law and order in areas often reigned by lawlessness and violence. The Colombian rebel groups supply services, such as giving peasants cheap credit, providing health and education, issuing land registrations, and dispensing justice. Allegedly, the rebels are even involved in protecting culture and the rain forests' ecosystem.

(Schulte-Bockholt, 2006: 135)

In light of such a reality it is no surprise why support towards the insurgency remains.

Within the guerrilla territory, FARC runs schools, medical facilities and popular judicial institutions while providing protection to peasants, trade unions, women's associations, and so on. A remarkable feature of its base among the peasants is that tens of thousands of such peasants are said to have migrated into the FARC-controlled but embattled guerrilla zones, seeking protection against the savagery of the state in the zones that the state controls.

(Ahmad, 2006: 62–3)[21]

Detailing the complex class-based taxation model provides a clearer understanding of pre-revolutionary policies established by the FARC-EP. Through such strategies the insurgency has not only proven its credibility by supporting local rural populations' efforts to benefit themselves and their community, the strategies legitimize the guerrillas' capacity to act in an ethical economic framework. Hugh O'Shaughnessy and Sue Branford (2005: 27–8) acknowledged that "although large sums of money are involved, there is little personal corruption" in the FARC-EP, on any level. "There is no evidence," according to Chernick (2007: 73) "that leaders or fighters in the FARC are accumulating individual wealth." Very much ideologically based in their actions, the insurgency has demonstrated collective rather than individually-led motivations, especially concerning the tremendous amount of monies obtained (Gutiérrez Sanín, 2004: 268–9).

Even though the FARC is flush with cash ... looting for individual benefit is nearly inconceivable .... Leaders of the FARC have so far resisted pressures to distribute resource wealth, instead investing in new assets in the growth of the military movement.

(Weinstein, 2007: 292, 294)

Supporting this claim, Colombian political scientist Francisco Gutiérrez Sanín (2008: 13) has noted that "looting for individual benefit is nearly inconceivable." After reviewing hundreds of cases of guerrillas in several separate databases, Gutiérrez Sanín found that cases of corruption are "relatively rare, especially taking into account the magnitude of the sums handled by the guerrillas," and commented that "indeed, I am not aware of any reports of individualistic looting by the FARC; all the goods coming from military or illegal economic activities go to the organization" (Gutiérrez Sanín, 2008: 14, 13). He added that no evidence suggests comandantes are involved in activities of personal enrichment (Gutiérrez Sanín, 2004: 268–9). This is something I can attest to. I met with one of the FARC-EP's highest ranking Secretariat leaders during a field study, and the "special supper" being eaten by the comandante was stewed *guatin* – a cross between a rat and a guinea pig – captured in the jungle earlier that day. Even Marulanda, the FARC-EP's founder and long-time commander-in-chief, was reported to exist like any other rural peasant, living his entire life without any luxuries and never deriving benefit from the insurgency's activities (see Hudson, 2002: 160). Such untarnished practices have more than "facilitated the accountability of the FARC" (Stokes, 2005: 86).[22]

In addition to the procurement of funds, the FARC-EP class-based taxation model has created offshoots that have enabled the peasantry to secure "a stable economic base for the colonos and small peasants by regulating the market relations and prices and by providing financial and technical assistance to the peasants and protection of the colonos"(Richani, 2002a: 70; see also Kenney, 2007: 230n4). The guerrillas have been able to do this by forcing those involved in the middle and upper echelons of the industry to consistently pay peasants and rural wage laborers the going market price for coca leaves, coupled with an additional payment for the labor power exhausted by the worker (Rochlin, 2003: 136; Richani, 2002a: 70). The FARC-EP determines an equitable and fair return and makes certain that middle persons abide by the set wage (Peceny and Durnan, 2006: 107; Labrousse, 2005: 172). It should be said that it is not the FARC-EP that pays the peasants directly; it acts as an intermediary ensuring local coca cultivators are treated and paid fairly (Weinstein, 2007: 291; Gutiérrez Sanín, 2004: 266).

A more accurate assessment is that "the FARC have ... tended to act as arbitrators between drug traffickers and peasant cultivators through the regulation of local markets through ensuring fair prices for peasant cultivators" (Stokes, 2005: 86). As the insurgency makes certain that the buyers pay the coca growers a fair price, the class-based taxation model has translated into better wages for peasants in FARC-EP-controlled areas (International Action Center, 2001: 3). There is proof of this, as in "areas in which the guerrillas' presence is weak or nonexistent, the price of labor is lower than in areas where it has a strong military presence" (Richani, 2002a: 110; see also Felbab-Brown, 2005: 109). In addition to the guaranteed fiscal return policy, Neil Cooper found that the FARC-EP has:

> developed a sophisticated social safety net which is supported by the profits made from various illicit activities. This includes a minimum wage for coca leaf pickers, a minimum price that must be paid to farmers and a social security system which, amongst other things, provides pensions for retired guerrillas.
>
> (Cooper, 2002: 946)

While this is in no way suggests an economic boom for the peasants, it does provide them with a guaranteed income that is not based on speculation, as traditional crops would be, but on guaranteed returns (Castaño, 2006; Felbab-Brown, 2005: 108; Villalón, 2004a; 2004b; Richani, 2002a: 70).

> The FARC taxes coca (the buyers, not the campesinos), a far cry from trafficking. Coca also is the only crop left that keeps the campesinos' heads above water. The peasant who grows standard crops will have an average annual income of around $250 a year. With coca, they can feed a family on $2,000 year. These are not robber barons. They are not getting rich.
>
> (Goff, 2004: 33)

This claim is important. O'Shaughnessy and Branford (2005: 7) have shown that "out of every $1,000 that a buyer spends on cocaine in a rich country, the Colombian peasant cultivating the coca bushes receives only $6" (see also

Peceny and Durnan, 2006: 99).[23] It needs to be realized that it is not the Colombian peasant who makes the highest return. On the contrary, "the Colombians who profit the most from the drug trade are members of the armed forces, the paramilitaries, and police; government officials; and the 'big businessmen of the urban centers'" (Goff, 2004: 33; see also Castaño, 2006). During the 1980s, "only an estimated 8–10 percent of cocaine profits actually remained in or returned to the producer countries, while a mere 0.4 percent went to the coca-growing peasants" (Schulte-Bockholt, 2006: 134). Molano interviewed several persons connected to the drug trade in his book *Loyal Soldiers in the Cocaine Kingdom: Tales of drugs, mules, and gunmen*. One of the persons interviewed, an upper-level distributor, was very clear about who obtains the greatest proportion of profits from the coca industry, and, according to him, it is not the Colombians at all.

> You have to look closely at who's filling their pockets from this business. For a kilo of crystal we Colombians pocket let's say ten thousand dollars, and the monkeys sell it for twenty five thousand. What happens to the fifteen thousand pieces of green in between?
>
> (Molano, 2004: 31)

Breaking down the mechanics of the industry Goff, too, highlighted that the most lucrative returns exist outside Colombia altogether.

> Once the coca is processed, a kilo fetches about $2,000 in Colombia. Precautions, payoffs, and the first profits bring the price to $5,500 a kilo by the time it reaches the first gringo handler. The gringo sells the kilo, now ready for U.S. retail, for around $20,000. On the streets in the United States, that will break out to $60,000. There are some high rollers at the end of the Colombian chain, but as with cheap manufactured goods from overseas sweatshops, the real makeup winners are the American dealers.
>
> (Goff, 2004: 33)

Not making the peasantry rich, the FARC-EP's measures have nevertheless ensured a level of protection for those in the agricultural sphere.[24] In the past, the cartels financially pitted impoverished peasants against one another, thus driving down the price of coca leaves once Colombia became a processing zone. Such a practice flourished after the Medellín and Cali cartels had been decentralized into micro-cartels (see Coghlan, 2004: 154). Since the FARC-EP's class-based taxation model was implemented, monetary and physical security has been partially afforded to peasants within insurgency-extended zones.[25] Unfortunately, with the paramilitary's increasing involvement in the coca industry there has been a greater need for the FARC-EP to maintain its material protection and support for the peasantry.

As paramilitary threats have increased against peasant cultivators, the FARC-EP has increasingly sought to protect small producers from such intimidation. While my research found no evidence of this, it has been suggested that "citing the danger of the paramilitary infiltration, the FARC gradually took over control of the whole production process, although not the most profitable activities – trafficking, shipping and selling"(O'Shaughnessy and Branford, 2005: 27; see also Labrousse, 2005: 178).[26]

This may help clarify why the FARC-EP has appeared to be "suppressing intermediaries" (Peceny and Durnan, 2006: 107). Here the insurgency acts as another defensive barrier for cultivators and pickers. Some may see this as an admission to the guerrillas' immersion in the industry; however, if the FARC-EP wanted to maximize profits, it would be far more lucrative to enter the most profitable aspect of the Colombian drug trade: production, trafficking and selling. Scholars continue to show that no such correlation exists (Schulte-Bockholt, 2006: 133; Röhl, 2004: 4).

This account has showed how the FARC-EP has enabled peasants to cooperate with each other to reduce production costs, maintain environmental standards, and preserve peasant economic models of cultivation and production (Richani, 2002a: 99). As noted, the insurgency has supported cultivators in a twofold process; insuring that workers are given a fair monetary return for their labor power and through physical protection. One female respondent from Putumayo explained how the insurgency's actions enable her community to enact extensive reforms which otherwise have been impossible because of the likely state reaction.

Well, it is important to say that without the guerrillas we would not have a community at all. Over the past few years the state has increasingly been using paramilitaries to threaten rural people, especially here. Doing this not only allows for foreign MNCs to take our land and oil resources but it enables the paramilitary and large landowners to consolidate further landholdings by claiming they are being unutilized or are being left fallow. It has been the guerrillas that have enabled many of us to stay on our land by keeping the paras away from us, or when they might not be able to, they inform us about where the paras are so that we can prepare to leave for few days or hide …. These are just the defensive measures that the guerrillas have been able to do for us. The guerrillas have also established schools to teach our children and any adults who want to learn about reading, writing, math, history, etc. You would be surprised, but math can come in very handy for many of us because of the rates of illiteracy and the lack of education in the countryside. The state has negated any forms of education in the countryside for decades and it is only through the FARC's schools that someone in the rural areas can have a chance of learning. The guerrillas also take care of our community's health needs by bringing in and giving medical supplies to us while sometimes offering doctors, nurses, and even dentists to look over our children and families and providing free care and services.

However, there are many other ways the guerrilla support the people here. The FARC provide funding for campesinos within our community to work with other compañeros in other parts of the country so as to better enable cooperation in trade, cultivation, organic fertilizers, etc. … To many of us, the FARC are the government, they provide us with protection from violence, they give our communities roads and means of trading our products with other communities. They also ensure that we are paid fairly for our goods and that the merchants and local employers respect us and our family. Uribe and Pastrana gave us nothing but grief. The [department] has had the FARC since before I was born and our towns, communities, and families lived in unity with them. It was only when the government started to threaten and attack our lands and communities that the trouble started. Unlike what the papers and television says, it was not the FARC that caused us problems, but it is certainly the FARC who protects us as best they can from them .... [W]hen you have a state that restricts the amount of gasoline each home is allowed to have [this is in response to the Uribe administration's claim that all persons in rural Putumayo use gasoline to produce coca paste] you quickly understand what their true purpose is. It is the FARC that not only support us to provide a living for our families but they protect us in the process. This is more than a protection of physicality but true representations of how a revolutionary force can socially, politically, and economically assist those in the most need while making those who can afford it pay the costs.

All this sounds noble and addresses the FARC-EP's activities on a localized level, but realistic consideration must be given to how the insurgency plans to deal with the subject of coca once it has achieved state power. The insurgency has proven capable of making significant policies that assist the rural popula-tion – its class-based taxation model, social services, infrastructure, and so on – but how will the FARC-EP address the narcotics industry upon consolidating power in Bogotá? Would the United States and other countries not immediately condemn the newly socialist country as a narco-state? Do the guerrillas have a plan of action to dispel the negative reliance on monocrop coca produc-tion? How does a Marxist-Leninist political-military organization plan to alter regions of Colombia that have increasingly become disassociated from subsistence-based production to a capitalist model, if at all? Has the FARC-EP prepared for a post-revolutionary rural society that has become dependent on the coca industry as a means of subsistence? The subject of the coca industry poses a series of interrelated dilemmas that will undoubtedly face the FARC-EP if it achieves its objective of taking state power. The next subsection considers these issues.

The FARC-EP's pre-revolutionary coca development strategy: An analysis of preparatory post-capitalist crop substitution

The history of Latin America has proven that monoculture (or something close to it) economies do not and cannot sustain national incomes through what appears to be the rational productive approach of comparative advantage. It has also been shown that Colombian peasants are unable to survive under the expansionist system of capital. Even so, many have turned to "illicit" crop production in order to scratch together a modest monetary existence.[27] The problem with this practice is that coca cultivation maintains a capitalist relation of production, which enables the negative structural conditions that cause sociopolitical and economic exploitation to continue. Some development agencies, alongside the Colombian state, have sought crop substitution programs that deter peasants from coca production and processing. This form of development, while highly important, cannot alter and has not altered the industry for one principal reason; the structural political and socioeconomic consequences of a capital system. Until capitalism is structurally altered, sustained micro-level changes will remain unattainable, hence the importance of the FARC-EP's program of crop substitution.

Nations that subscribe to monoculture only hold value for an erratic period. Such a system, while producing some benefits, is incapable of sustaining consistent returns because of the global capitalist concentration and undervaluation of commodities. Monoculture disables a country's capacity to establish productive and economic equilibrium during periods of socioeconomic volatility because of a lack of productive diversity and/or the ability to derive profits from other sectors. Harry E. Vanden and Gary Prevost (2006: 153) noted, "by making the entire economy dependent on one primary product, the nation's economic health becomes heavily tied to the fortunes of that product on the international market. Devastating busts often follows boom periods."

Present throughout the late 1980s and 1990s, the FARC-EP witnessed the consequences of monoculture as it related to the coffee industry, where busts greatly affected Latin America as a result of neoliberal policies of deregulation coupled with neo-mercantilist protectionist measures securing returns for imperial nations. Small and medium-sized producers became devastated not only during "busts" but throughout the entire post-bust period as well. A rural producer unquestionably feels the greatest devastation following the collapse of a boom period. A once-productive crop becomes worthless, resulting in the producer having nothing to sell to get an income until the next harvest. Following this period is the post-bust phase, when rural producers must find a way to procure some means of subsistence for themselves and associated family. This necessity leads to peasants having to obtain loans and/or credit, which will be repaid during the next "boom." When the boom comes, if it does, the little returns realized by the producer are subdivided. First, debts acquired during the bust and post-bust period are repaid, and second, there is an expansion of crop cultivation so returns can be made as rapidly as possible, in the hope of keeping pace with domestic inflation until the next post-boom period. However, it is not merely loans and neoliberal economic policies that can affect the returns from monoculture for Colombia's rural population. Ironically, other peoples and regions in shared opposition to neoliberalism may hinder development.

As noted, numerous peoples in Colombia increasingly took up coca cultivation in response to the devastating results of neoliberal economic policies, which eliminated national tariffs, devalued currencies, increased overproduction, and so on, eventually leading to the complete devaluation of traditional crops. However, Colombia was not alone in this imposed economic predicament. Other Andean countries such as Peru and Bolivia experienced increased coca cultivation during the late 1980s and 1990s, which continues to this day (UNODC, 2008). Hypothetically, if the FARC-EP were to support a coca-based monocrop economy then rural workers would be in direct competition with other coca producers in other (neighboring) countries. This would not only lead to a complete devaluation of the crop, it would additionally place strain on the increasingly center-left movements in this region of (Bolivarian) Latin America (that is, Evo Morales' (2006–10) Movement for Socialism (*Movimiento al Socialismo*, MAS)).

Whatever the economic paradigm, monocrop production is unsustainable (Vanden and Prevost, 2006: 151–2). A socialist system – as was recognized in Cuba with sugar, and the collapse of the USSR – while providing numerous social benefits to the population, can be devastated and prone to crisis after the removal of monoculture-based revenue (Moore, Núñez Sarmiento and Sacouman, 2004). Since the 1980s, Colombia, while not as dependent on one crop as Cuba, has become increasingly reliant on coca as a means of sustaining its national economy (see Schulte-Bockholt, 2006: 97; Sweig and McCarthy, 2005: 28; Thoumi, 1995: 199; Arango-Jaramillo, 1988: 126). To alter this reliance the FARC-EP has promoted alternative crop substitution. Encouraging such reforms, while giving the insurgency credibility, does not necessarily relieve the problematic outcomes of monocrop production. In light of this, the FARC-EP has shown opposition to monoculture, made steps toward crop substitution, and attempted to restore rural cultural traditions via agricultural practices.

For over two decades, the FARC-EP has worked on reducing the rural population's dependence on coca by providing crop substitution programs so the peasantry can adapt and reduce their structural reliance on the industry. Yet, if all sectors in FARC-EP-extended territory supported and maintained a simple systemic formula of crop substitution, moving to the next most lucrative crop, then a cyclical effect would take place because of the nature of capitalist expansionism.

> If the number of campesinos turning to alternative crops continues to increase, production will likely surpass local demand and drive prices down, and impoverished campesinos will once again face the same economic problems that forced them to turn to coca cultivation in the first place.
>
> (Leech, 2002a: 74)

It is important to highlight this, for it exemplifies how mere reformist measures cannot be sustained over extended periods of time in a capitalist environment. Even if peasants successfully replace their illegal product with another that is legal, it is only a matter of time before the restrictions of capital drive the commodity to be devalued domestically and globally. In light of this readily unspoken reality, it is realized that the primary problem facing rural Colombians is the capitalist model itself.

Capitalism forces constant exploitation in the pursuit of economic gain.

In this quest any restrictive barriers to increased surplus profits must be eliminated. As a result, the peasant is materially unable to maintain a positive income from the production of the newly adopted (legitimate) crop, and has little alternative but to return to the coca industry. The FARC-EP seeks to eliminate this top-down economic model while understanding that the progression to socialism takes time. A socialist society does not arise through the simple negation of capitalism or taking state power. It is construed by gradually altering the private relations of production so as to create a socialized economy. Sympathetic to this dialectic process, the insurgency has melded a realistic practice that first encourages a more democratic process of production by allowing members of "communities that have found themselves forced to take up illicit crops as a means of subsistence" to decide on whether crop substitution is possible as well as practical (FARC-EP, 2001a: 6; 2000d).

Its acceptance of the rural population's reliance on coca has had a tremendous effect on the FARC-EP's objective for a socialist revolution in economic form. The FARC-EP, while not being in support of capitalism or of narcotic use, has understood that the rural poor in Colombia need a way to survive, and this has led it "to accept the peasants' shift to illicit crop plantations as a supplementary income" (Richani, 2002a: 71). The insurgency has not only provided physical protection from paramilitary forces and crooked middlemen, but has enabled peasants increasingly to dissociate themselves from the tools used within the capitalist process of production (banks, lending institutions, and so on).

The FARC-EP has implemented a structural opposition to the state/ capitalist alliance by providing a micro-level solution to the immediate problems of Colombia's rural population. In the immediate period, it has been able, at a grassroots level, to lessen the rural workers' attachment to exploitative neoliberal methods of competition or outmigration (urban wage labor), bringing workers more time to spend with their families and/or devote to activities in the community.[28] On a macro level the insurgency is, however, "providing market stability and protecting peasant coca plantations," while making it possible for a peasant-based subsistence economy to be linked to "international markets with minimum 'structural adjustment' and economic dislocations as opposed to the experience of peasants subjected to the market forces of legal economy" (Richani, 2002a: 71; see also Petras and Veltmeyer, 2003b: 60).

The peasant movements within Colombia have resisted neoliberal policies by promoting the growth and cultivation of alternative crops, some being coca. This is very interesting, regardless of your position to cocaine, for the peasants have saw that they do not want to subscribe to this system of economic imperialist activity so they have altered and resisted this by growing and finding their own methods of economic sustenance. This maintains their agricultural activities and culture while at the same time allows the campesinos to provide a small living for themselves.

(Petras and Veltmeyer, 2003a: 176)

While substituting illegal crops for legal ones is important, it does not, however, address the negative consequences specifically resulting from a domestic capitalist framework. For the greater part of the past 20 years, there have been three specific outcomes for those peasants who moved away from coca cultivation. First, as numerous peasants adopted crop substitution there was a glut of some crops in some regions, driving down prices. This subsequently caused a cyclical effect of poverty. Once more rural producers fell back into the coca industry as a means of survival (Leech, 2002a: 72–75). The second dilemma saw peasants, who agreed to state-imposed crop substitution, not receive promised incomes from the state, development agencies, or NGOs. Suffering from a lack of capital, producers were forced to return to coca as no other means of subsistence was available (Gibbs and Leech, 2005: 68, 70–1; O'Shaughnessy and Branford, 2005: 51–2: Murillo and Avirama, 2004: 131; Solaún, 2002: 4). Third, peasants who once refrained from growing coca saw legal crops sprayed with poisonous defoliants during Colombian/US anti-narcotic campaigns. This left many of them with little option but to leave for the city or ironically move to coca to cover their losses (O'Shaughnessy and Branford, 2005: 13–14, 112). [29] These are some of the common realities that have been witnessed throughout Colombia as a result of so-called alternative crop substitution projects amidst the confines of a capitalist paradigm. To relieve such quandaries, the FARC-EP has prepared a more efficient program to slowly transform an individuated capitalist model to a socialized system.

One of the most interesting policies concerning coca in insurgent-held territory is that the FARC-EP "urges peasants to dedicate parts of their parcels for foodstuff production and to retain only a part for coca growing" (Richani, 2002a: 70; see also Schulte-Bockholt, 2006: 133, 134; Pearce, 1990b: 33). It is not well known that a cultivation program has been established whereby peasants who chose to grow coca devote a certain percentage of lands to alternative crop production (Brittain, 2007a; see also Villalón, 2004a, 2004b; Labrousse, 2005: 172).

> We are planning a different solution for the problem of narcotrafficking. It consists of providing a better life for the poor campesino through agrarian reform, by giving them good lands, technical assistance and low-interest loans to change from growing illicit crops to legal crops; such as, coffee, yucca, bananas, sugarcane and ranching. An alternative development that facilitates commercialization for these products. But it's a slow process to change them; it's not just destroying the illicit crops and then telling them to grow different ones. We have to educate the campesinos about how to produce them. Give them tools, credits and time so they can make a living from these crops and become a different kind of campesino.
> (Simón Trinidad, as quoted in Leech, 2000b; see also 2000a)

In consultation with small producers and certain JACs, the FARC-EP's program sees producers who choose to grow coca devote a percentage of their cultivation to another crop, which might be a subsistence crop, a traditional Colombian crop, or a crop for regional bartering. I witnessed this on two different occasions, one with a peasant-based coca-cultivator and another with a FARC-EP member. This model arguably prepares the rural sector for a smoother transition from capitalist forms of production in the aftermath of a political-revolutionary victory. The method and reasoning behind this process has been in the works for over two decades in selected regions of FARC-EP control, and it has increasingly been implemented across most of the insurgency's territory.

Dating back to the 1980s, "the FARC guerrillas ... encouraged the peasants in the coca growing areas they control to grow food crops as well as coca" (Pearce, 1990b: 33). This strategy continued throughout the 1990s where the FARC-EP compelled "farmers to grow foodstuffs in addition to coca" (Schulte-Bockholt, 2006: 133, 134). In 2004, Carlos Villalón made a documentary film entitled *Cocaine Country*, which recognized how the FARC-EP has increasingly instituted this program. In the regions visited by Villalón (2004b), all peasants who chose to grow coca were required to devote a minimum of three acres of land to alternative crop production for every seven acres of coca. In 2005, much higher percentages were realized in Labrousse's work, which documented how the FARC-EP was encouraging a 75 percent devotion to subsistence crops with only a quarter of the land allotted to coca (2005: 172).

During discussion with both FARC-EP members and civilians, I noted that the alternative crop ratio program prepares peasants for crop substitution in the event of the insurgency seizing centralized state power. The political-economic reality of coca cultivation and production is the by-product of necessity. The peasants' sole reason for cultivating coca is that it is the only means by which they can procure some level of stability. In recognition of this, the drug economy is a direct result of the deteriorated rural political economy. If a large-scale socialized economy were provided – with education, healthcare, redistribution of land, and so on – peasants, having their social requirements met, would have little need for individualized wealth. Vast segments of the rural sector could then cease coca cultivation. This could potentially result in a large proportion of the rural population, once dependent on growing coca, working with the FARC-EP to shift production to traditional agriculture, providing growth in caloric intake and nutritional sustenance for the, future, socialized, Colombian population.

Another benefit from the alternative crop ratio model can be recognized through a sociological examination of rural Colombia in the context of neo-liberalism. By the 1970s, subsistence-based agricultural had largely been abandoned in the south. It was at this time that the cartels slowly started to gain momentum. With the "opening" of the Colombian economy in the 1980s, and the thoroughgoing policies of neoliberalism that were implemented during the 1990s, many in the south shifted to coca cultivation as a means of survival. The sociological result is that contemporary southern Colombia has a second and third generation of coca growers. Unlike those who were working the lands from the 1950s to the 1970s, many of the present generation have never known any alternative model of agricultural production. The older generation, once experienced in traditional crop production (coffee, yucca, lemons, maize, and so on), were forced to deviate to coca as a direct result of land central-ization, state-based coercion, and neoliberal economic policies. The current generations do not share this cultural history nor do they relate to any other model of crop production. Many of the rural producers I interviewed under the age of 34 acknowledged that they had little experience in crop diversification. They did, however, have considerable knowledge concerning highly advanced methods of cultivating coca – such as genetically modified strands of coca resistant to aerial fumigation. The ratio program enables these generations to become reacquainted with classical crop cultivation and production, skills that will be much needed upon the FARC-EP's potential victory.

As the FARC-EP supports a nationally applied partial crop substitution model, accompanied by regions under total crop substitution, the insurgency is actively involved in rural Colombia's delinking from a capitalist produc-tion process. If the insurgency is to assist the creation of a socialist society, based on Marxist-Leninist principles, it must dissociate from capitalist models of production and trade. This will not be immediate or sudden, but realisti-cally takes time. Facilitating a crop substitution model begins a structure that acquaints peasants and other Colombians with an alternative non-capitalist method of subsistence, communal models that reinvigorate cultural methods of production, and socialist practices that derive domestic benefits.

This demonstrates how the FARC-EP is not only preparing to act as a legitimate government in a socialist Colombia, but readying the population for a post-capitalist society not monetarily dependent on the coca industry. Such conditions are disconcerting to those at higher levels in the drug trade, which derive extensive profits from the informal economy. It is more troubling to these individuals that this clear pre-revolutionary project implemented from below has already worked in areas of the country. In reaction, the state and rural/urban capitalists have, for some time, worked to prevent such methods from continuing. It is necessary to look at one of the most explicit methods by which sectors of Colombia's dominant class have responded to the FARC-EP's power and support. Such reactionary measures suggest why few options of social change are available other than revolution.

6

DOMINANT CLASS REACTIONISM: FAR-RIGHT POLITICS AND PARAMILITARISM

Paramilitarism was state policy .... I am proof positive of state paramilitarism in Colombia.

Salvatore Mancuso (see Forero, 2007b)

The FARC-EP cannot be seen as a passive political-military movement. The insurgency must be recognized for what it is – an organized body of men and women engaging in revolutionary direct action against Colombia's political and economic elite. A plethora of media accounts, state reports, and certain non-governmental organizations have criticized the FARC-EP for their methods. Commentaries that demonize the insurgency are presented daily and readily accessible. Yet amidst this flurry of widely available critique is the failure to address or analyze one simple question – why revolution? Why is it that sectors of the population feel they must support armed struggle to bring about social change? Here we try to contextualize Colombian reactionism, in an attempt to shed light on why many have consciously chosen a life of resistance via guerrilla warfare.

A CONTEMPORARY HISTORY OF COLOMBIAN PARAMILITARISM

It is essential to understand that paramilitarism[1] does not exist in itself but is rather a sociopolitical and economic by-product of dominant class continuity. There have long been reactionary responses to class struggle throughout Latin America, but Colombia's use of right-wing death squads is in some ways unique. The country not only witnessed the devastation of paramilitarism before and during the tumultuous period of the cold war, it continues to suffer from death squads well into the twenty-first century (Simons, 2004; Green, 2004; Romero, 2003; Sánchez and Meertens, 2001; LeGrand, 1986; Taussig, 1980; Fals Borda, 1969; Urrutia, 1969; Dix, 1967; Fluharty, 1957). Development theorists Dirk Kruijt and Kees Koonings (2004: 28) have argued that the "most comprehensive case of paramilitary forces ... can be observed in the context of the still ongoing Colombian conflict." Without dismissing the horrors committed, some even asserted that "the death squads, paramilitary groups and peasant patrols of El Salvador, Guatemala and Peru pale in comparison" to Colombian paramilitarism (Richani, 2002b: 18; see also Brittain, 2005a).

Much of this is because of the country's unique model of hegemony.[2] Colombia's dominant political and economic structures offer:

> a distinctive example of continuous leadership by an upper-class modernizing elite, based on long dominant families, that has succeeded in retaining power despite periodic electoral changes and precarious challenges to its hegemony. In other Latin American countries, by contrast, the traditional upper class has had to yield at least part of its control and allow the participation of new classes and interest groups. Though Colombia's upper class has experienced many similar threats to its domination – populism, Marxist movements, organized labour, and reformist military interventions – the governing elite has managed to prevent them from seizing control or even sharing significantly in power.
>
> (Sanders, 1981: 82)

Seen as a threat to internal stability, the twentieth century saw an emerging organized urban proletariat amidst a rural-based guerrilla movement. The state responded by passing class-based legislation to strengthen prevailing political and economic allies. While similar methods were utilized in the 1920s, 1965 saw the implementation of Decree 3398, which permitted the formation of security forces to protect large landowners, cattle ranches, and officials. By 1968, the decree was succeeded by Law 48.[3] According to Richani (2002a: 104–5), the legislation "opened the door for the emergence of private armies and consequently became an inherent part of the security of the social order.' Over the coming decades, additional edicts would be passed legitimizing the construction and continuance of paramilitary forces (Murillo and Avirama, 2004: 101; Leech, 2002a: 20; Giraldo, 1996).

After various massacres and human rights abuses, President Virgilio Barco Vargas (1986–90) rendered these private security forces temporarily illegal in 1989 through Decrees 815 and 1194. However, segments of the Colombian state (with pressure from the United States) successfully reformulated the legislation. By 1991, through Order 200-05/91, not only were private forces reinstated, they were granted the ability to specifically confront the FARC-EP (Avilés, 2006: 47, 89–122; Simons 2004: 58; Leech, 2002a: 22, 25; Ruiz, 2001: 28, 181; Giraldo, 1996: 94). Two years later, Decrees 2535 and 356 (1993) further empowered these groups to protect interests related to large landowners and MNCs (Livingstone, 2003: 232; Richani, 2002a: 50, 52, 104–5). Broadening policies associated with the cold war, the new edicts did not only permit forces to secure state faculties and defence property, they opened the door for paramilitaries to act as offensive supplementary mechanisms in areas of dominant political-economic importance.

Throughout this period, Álvaro Uribe Vélez was a senator for the department of Antioquia (1986–94) and instrumental in supporting these statutes (Livingstone, 2003: 26; Scott, 2003: 71–2; Leech, 2002a: 88; Defense Intelligence Agency, 1991). Once he became governor (1995–97), Uribe broadened his promotion of security forces to include the creation of a nationalized "civilian-military force" known as CONVIVIR,[4] sanctioned under the presidencies of César Augusto Gaviria Trujillo (1990–94) and Ernesto Samper Pizano (1994–98) (Avilés, 2006: 135; Murillo and Avirama, 2004: 103; Simons, 2004: 310–11; Livingstone, 2003: 26). Warned of the potential for the CONVIVIRs to develop into paramilitary groups, the state went on to facilitate and fund the formation of armed networks (García-Peña Jaramillo, 2007: 107; Avilés, 2006: 119; Hylton, 2006: 94; Rochlin, 2003: 150; Leech, 2002a: 26; Giraldo, 1996: 115).[5] By the mid to late 1990s, over 500 existed throughout the country, with an estimated membership of 10,000 (Avilés, 2006: 119; Richani, 2002: 52). Known to be "a strong supporter of CONVIVIR, promoting their development through the department," Uribe saw Antioquia become the epicenter of these units with roughly 67 – the capital city of Medellín housed 45 (Avilés, 2006: 135; see also Simons, 2004: 310–11; Riaño-Alcalá, 2006: 4; Scott, 2003: 71–2).[6] Based on his endorsement of the civilian military networks, Uribe was later heralded by some as a "paramilitary president" (Murillo and Avirama, 2004: 103; see also Livingstone, 2003: 26).[7]

The stated reasoning for the CONVIVIR was to "allow armed civilians to establish rural security cooperatives for the purpose of providing the Colombian military with intelligence information" (Leech, 2002a: 26; see also Richani, 2002a: 52). It became clear that this was not their true intention. According to Luis Alberto Restrepo M. (2003: 118), "they in fact served as armed protection for different personages and for different regions of the country and, in many cases, they exercised their own brand of justice." An equation soon arose: the more the elite supported supplementary forces, the more human rights were ravaged (see García-Peña Jaramillo, 2007: 109). In violation of international humanitarian law, the CONVIVIR "made civilians both potential victims and victimizers in the military conflict" (Murillo and Avirama, 2004: 103; see also 204n.4). The armed civilian networks, heavily involved in displacing rural populations throughout Urabá, Córdoba, and Antioquia, "became a network of murderous vigilantes" (Simons, 2004: 310–11; see also Hylton, 2006: 93). "What emerged," says Geoff Simons (2004: 316), "were private armies, funded and armed by the state, and associated with a dramatic increase in the number of massacres, assassinations, forced disappearance, forced displacements and 'social cleansing' operations."

Resembling methods used by other Latin American governments, the CONVIVIR became an explicit example of the state supporting a civilian-based counterinsurgency force to combat the growing support and power of the guerrillas (Sánchez, 2003: 22; see also Hylton, 2006: 93).[8] Uribe especially supported changing the CONVIVIR from localized civilian–military units to strategic counter-insurgency forces that would react to FARC-EP counter-hegemony (Livingstone, 2003: 57; see also Murillo and Avirama, 2004: 103). According to Crandall (2002: 84–5), the state purposely sanctioned the militarization of the CONVIVIRs with the goal of combating the guerrillas (Murillo and Avirama, 200: 103; Livingstone, 2003: 57).[9] Uribe's strategy of having the CONVIVIR expand throughout Antioquia was a means by which the state could further legalize and regulate "anti-guerrilla militias," a strategy he sustained into his first term as president (Hylton, 2006: 93; Murillo and Avirama, 2004: 103; see also 113, 204n.4; Scott, 2003: 71–2).

The CONVIVIRs were finally "outlawed in 1999 after many of them were implicated in human rights abuses, including massacres of civilians" (Leech, 2002a: 26; see also Murillo and Avirama, 2004: 103, 204n.4). However, what eventually arose from the ashes of the CONVIVIRs was what had been predicted by its original opponents; the inclusion of the civilian forces into paramilitary organizations (Sánchez, 2003: 22; Crandall, 2002: 97n.78). While some saw the elimination of the CONVIVIR as a progressive move to restrict paramilitarism, in reality the "cooperatives" inflated the existing paramilitary networks throughout the country (see Simons, 2004: 316; Restrepo M., 2003: 103). The networks did not evaporate but were "instrumental in the accelerated growth" of the country's largest paramilitary organization during the 1990s – the AUC (Murillo and Avirama, 2004: 103–4; see also Sweig and McCarthy, 2005: 19).

Colombian sociologist Fernando Cubides (2003: 131) revealed how the CONVIVIR "became semi clandestine, and, according to various sources and the declarations of some of their leaders, put themselves at the disposition of the paramilitaries." While the AUC witnessed growth outside the formation of the CONVIVIRs, once it was outlawed paramilitary membership saw a significant influx (Hylton, 2006: 93). In short, "when the Constitutional Court banned the Convivirs for numerous massacres of unarmed civilians, their foot soldiers simply passed into the ranks of the AUC" (Hylton, 2006: 95; see also Holmes, 2003: 90; Leech, 2002a: 26). By relinquishing its "formal" involvement with the CONVIVIR and not ensuring its disintegration, the state facilitated aggressions against suspected guerrilla supporters via civil society (Brittain, 2006d).[10]

The justification behind institutionally validating paramilitarism was to defend the conventional economic and political stability of a select minority. The result, however, has been an offensive mechanism that propagates far-right conservatism. Rather than rectifying the reasons for antagonism to the dominant class, the state – assisted by Washington – put its energy into counterinsurgency in an attempt to decimate resistance (Ampuero and Brittain, 2005). As this account emphasizes the state's link to "regulating" paramilitarism, it is important to detail where the ideology and persona of contemporary Colombian paramilitarism came from.

THE CASTAÑO CONNECTION

As the FARC-EP increased its presence in the country by the mid-1970s, so too did it adopt the practice of "retention." This is regularly referred to as kidnapping, but in fact the practice of retention is quite complex, with a clear class target and political motive. First the guerrillas collect intelligence on persons whom they view as representing the interests of the dominant class.[11] This usually includes right-wing ideologues, members of the political elite, those with relative wealth, military personnel, and so on.[12] The insurgency then conducts a "study" of the individual's political-economic status, and decides whether to "retain" the person against their will. In most cases, the individual remains in custody as a prisoner of war until a monetary fee has been acquired *or* a humanitarian prisoner exchange has taken place.

In the late 1970s, the insurgency carried out such intelligence gathering on one *Don* Jesús Castaño. A staunch far-right Conservative, *Don* Jesús was a dominant capitalist in Segovia, Antioquia. In addition to his class position and political ideology he was a director of community affairs, making him a textbook case for "retention." By 1981, the FARC-EP made the decision to retain the right-wing cattle rancher and landowner.[13]

Don Jesús fathered twelve children, eight of whom were boys, the eldest named Fidel. Leaving home at 16, Fidel became involved in the lucrative emerald industry, though illicitly, as a smuggler (Livingstone, 2003: 133; Ruiz, 2001: 172). Always keeping his foot in the waters of the infamous Colombian emerald trade, Fidel stretched out into the profitable and growing economy of narcotics by using his contacts and experience. A competent smuggler, he soon tried his hand at trafficking marijuana and cocaine. In a relatively short period of time the one-time thug established himself as a principal figure in the Colombian drug trade. Fidel quickly became excessively wealthy, enabling him to acquire extensive tracts of land in the north (Livingstone, 2003: 221). He and his younger brother Carlos purchased over 1.2 million hectares of land throughout Antioquia, Córdoba, and Chocó (Mercedes Pereira, 2001: 19–20). By the 1980s, Fidel had become one of "the most powerful capos in Colombia and the world" (Dudley, 2004: 98).[14] Aside from being first and foremost an illicit entrepreneur, Fidel was brought up a staunch Conservative in socio-economic opposition to egalitarian forms of production. The experience of their father's retention and death changed the Castaño brothers' ideology from mere economic protectionism to reactionary aggression aimed at the FARC-EP.

The two wealthiest sons of *Don* Jesús organized a private military to both protect their property and business interests in northern Colombia and avenge their father's passing. The Peasant Self-Defense Units of Córdoba and Urabá (*Autodefensas Campesinas de Córdoba y Urabá*, ACCU) became one of the most powerful and well-funded paramilitary forces up to that point in Colombian history.[15] The brothers, through the ACCU, began to work with sectors of the military to combat the guerrillas.[16] By utilizing their wealth, they began "an explicit anti-guerrilla agenda – and offered its services, particularly in the area of intelligence, to the army's Bomboná battalion, which was operating in the areas where the brothers owned land" (Richani, 2000: 38–9). Southeast of the Castaño brothers, another paramilitary organization was beginning to form as well. Unlike the ACCU this anti-guerrilla collective was not formulated around an individual family or regional context, but through a much wider coordinated effort of mercenaries, drug cartels, large landowners, cattle ranchers, foreign MNCs, state officials, and high-ranking members of the Colombian army.

THE REACTIONARY FORMATION OF THE MAS AND ACDEGAM

The early 1980s saw an immense interwoven web of support for another paramilitary force that emerged in Colombia. At the end of 1981 and through the early months of 1982, members of Medellín's thriving drug cartel, the military, Texas Petroleum, numerous political representatives, and several cattle ranchers from the Puerto Boyacá region came together and "created an armed organization to defend their interests and deter guerrilla attacks and extortions" (Richani, 2002a: 38). Labor researcher and unionist Francisco Cellular Ramírez (2005: 68) cited paramilitary chief Black Vladimir's account of the historic meetings in the department of Boyacá, where "representatives of the Texas Petroleum Company in addition to ranchers, mafiosos and small industrialists" collaborated to cover expenses needed to train paramilitary forces using "U.S., Israeli and English mercenaries." The Medellín cartel helped fund the paramilitary's formation, alongside army officers, large cattle ranchers, and numerous landowners from the Magdalena Medio region, which included Pablo Escobar, Jorge Luis Ochoa, and González Rodríguez Gacha (Livingstone, 2003: 133; see also Caballero, 2006; Kline, 1999: 68). Strategically, military personnel worked to convince dominant class sectors (and US-based MNCs) to create this "independent" paramilitary organization in regions of interest so as to target the sociopolitical networks of the guerrillas (Dudley, 2004: 42). By 1982 the force was coordinated, and aptly named Death to Kidnappers (*Muerte de Sequestradores*, MAS).

After the MAS's inception, the same partners created an organization to exist alongside yet appear separate from the paramilitaries. This association would facilitate the collection of funds and subsequently forward capital to the newly constructed death squads, while using far-right populism to bait peasants to support their endeavours.[17] Shortly after the formation of the MAS, the Association of Peasants and Ranchers of the Middle Magdalena (*Asociación Campesina de Agricultores y Ganaderos del Magdalena Medio*, ACDEGAM) was constructed (Kline, 1999: 68).

> In 1984 a new organization, the Association of Peasants and Ranchers of the Magdalena Medio (ACDEGAM), was created to give the paramilitary and self-defense groups legal cover .... It took responsibility for the political and military defense of the region and gave socioeconomic assistance to the peasants who supported it. The campaign against "subversion" reached new heights when ACDEGAM started to eliminate trade unionists (from, for example, the Nare cement works), peasant organizers and even dissidents from the Liberal Party. [President] Belisario Betancur himself visited the region in 1985 (at the invitation of Luis Alfredo Rubio Rojas, Pablo Guarín and the president of ACDEGAM) and highly praised the people of the Magdalena Medio, particularly General Yanine Díez, for restoring peace.
> (Pearce, 1990a: 247)

In the early and mid-1980s, the ACDEGAM worked hard to legitimize reaction to the threat of communism via insurgents. With its far-right rhetoric compounded by nominal acts of charity, the association gave unspoken and spoken legitimacy to the newly armed paramilitary groups. "Puerto Boyacá had become a kind of independent paramilitary republic," with the ACDE-GAM organizing schools and health clinics, providing light road building and repair, and even constructing a communication center (Pearce, 1990a: 247). But this infrastructure was not set up for altruistic reasons: it was a paramilitary project to facilitate the narcotics industry, create training centers for new MAS recruits, build hospitals to tend to wounded mercenaries, and construct schools to disseminate anti-communist propaganda to the young and old alike.

The illusion of populism was revealed as the paramilitary began to target anyone who opposed the centralized landholders of the area (that is, narcotraf-fickers) or the MAS's counter-insurgency objectives, while simultaneously rewarding those aligned with what increasingly resembled a fascist movement. Simons (2004: 56) noted that the MAS and the ACDEGAM were more than willing to reward or offer assistance to peasants who were accommodating or sympathetic to their activities.

Within this context, a growing sentiment of anti-communism pervaded areas of the Magdalena Medio alongside anti-worker policies and opposition to orga-nized labor. The ACDEGAM openly threatened "any attempt to protect worker and peasant rights," while the MAS followed up the rear with death threats, covert attacks, and assassination of suspected insurgent supporters (Simons, 2004: 56). Apparent benefits once given to peasants were largely cancelled as the MAS and the ACDEGAM consolidated activities in the pursuit of benefit for the rural elite and narcobourgeoisie. It was soon realized that the facilities and infrastructure paid for by the ACDEGAM(/MAS) were, in actuality, mediums to expand dominant class wealth and power.

> The association set up more than thirty schools in different parts of the Middle Magdalena Valley. These schools created what ACDEGAM called a "patriotic and anti-Communist" educational environment. The association also established health clinics and cooperatives where local farmers could get technical and financial assistance. ACDEGAM built roads and bridges. Financing for these projects came from all types of businesses, including Texas Petroleum Company, a Texaco subsidiary. Yet behind the non-profit façade, ACDEGAM was the *autodefensas'* center of operations. Recruiting, weapons storage, communications, propaganda, and medical services were all run from ACDEGAM headquarters. The association had a printing press that put out anti-guerrilla pamphlets, and it had a clothing store that furnished uniforms for paramilitary soldiers. It had "Medical Brigades," who spent most of their time curing injured paramilitary soldiers.
>
> (Dudley, 2004: 68)

Within this context the ACDEGAM was able to present an image of, first, providing security to large landowners and cattle ranchers in the face of the growing FARC-EP threat; and second, delivering benefits to peasants if they supported the association's expansion. The ACDEGAM's dual stratagem of supporting elites (protection) alongside peasants (services) was possible only through the association's centralized control of information over the Magdalena Medio. As propaganda was created and disseminated faster than reports of death threats and disappearances, the MAS, and its supportive partners, could extend their domain of resource concentration and influence.

THE MAS/ACDEGAM'S FORMATION OF MORENA

By the mid-1980s, the ACDEGAM, alongside the MAS, had grown considerably, and with it the need grew for financial resources.[18] After 1985 this need was mostly taken up by Colombia's prominent drug traffickers: "Pablo Escobar, Jorge Luis Ochoa and Gonzalo Rodríguez Gacha," who had also become exceedingly large rural landowners (Pearce, 1990a: 247). However, funding is never free and certain strings were attached. Patrons demanded that any funding previously promised for social projects was to be abandoned and all surplus capital was to be specifically directed towards strengthening the MAS. The cartels then constructed "a school for training assassins," which saw the paramilitary become an organized army rather than a band of mercenaries (Pearce, 1990a: 247; see also Kline, 1999: 73–4; Livingstone, 2003: 133). Assistance was specifically targeted "to increase the supply of weapons to the MAS paramilitaries and to improve the group's intelligence gathering and other activities" (Simons, 2004: 57).

> There was no doubt that Puerto Boyacá, cradle of these groups and what one functionary called "a kind of paramilitary independent republic," continued to be the epicenter from which the principal bases and schools were controlled and from which policies and objectives were designed. In the municipality, the paramilitary organization had a clinic, printer, a drug store, an armory, a computer and (a datum that most concerned the government officials) a center of communication that worked in coordination with the state-run telecommunications office. A second satellite center was located in Pacho, Cundinamarca. Rodríguez Gacha also had a farm in that small town. The organization had thirty pilots and a flotilla of airplanes and helicopters. It had 120 vehicles, principally jeeps, but also bulldozers and levelers, without counting the boats. It collected a monthly fee from ranchers. The one paid by narcotraffickers was much higher, and, according to some sources, the paramilitary organizations were financed almost completely by them. One high functionary said, "In addition one can think that these men [narcotrafficking leaders] have stopped bring mere common delinquents, as they were when they dedicated their activities to narcotrafficking only, and have begun to get a certain political status since they have changed themselves to the sponsors of the subversion of the right."
>
> (Kline, 1999: 73–4)

Before the 1980s would end, the MAS had become:

active in eight of the 32 regions of Colombia, enjoying the support of local political and military leaders. The weapons rifles used by the MAS paramilitaries included R-15, AKMs, Galils, FALs and G-3 rifles, all nominally prohibited for civilian use, but supplied through drug-funded private sales, by the military, and by Military Industry (Industria Militar, INDUNIL).

(Simons, 2004: 57)

Yet, with the groups becoming a more formally organized force subscribing to a specific ideology, a growing fascist tendency started to pervade both the MAS and ACDEGAM.[19]

Now in partial control over blocks of territory in the country's central-north, there was one area in which this network of elites had to solidify their legitimacy; politics. It was believed that an official far-right political organization would not only open the door to the legal conventional realms of Colombia's municipal, regional, and national politics, but that a political party would enable the paramilitary to achieve complete authenticity as an army. Hence, in August 1989, the Movement of National Restoration (*Movimiento de Restauración Nacional*, MORENA) was formed – in the dogma of anti-communism, as it promoted policies of capitalist expansion and economic centralization at any cost (see Pearce, 1990a: 250).[20] The fascist foreshadowing of the mid-1980s was now a reality.

One of the first shadows cast by MORENA was the "assassination of the father of Martha Lucia González, judge of public order, who had indicted the leaders of ACDEGAM – Pablo Escobar, Gonzalo Rodríguez Gacha, and various officials of military intelligence – for massacres in Urabá" (Kline, 1999: 77). Amidst a growing environment susceptible to fascism, such actions did not see significant condemnation, revealing that MORENA (and its ACDEGAM and MAS counterparts) could conduct their activities with little state opposition. This is not to imply that the majority of Colombia's traditional rural elite supported the praxis of the far right, but rather that the apathy of the dominant class demonstrated where it leaned (Pearce, 1990a: 8). It even began to look as though "the radical right in Colombia" could emerge as a participatory actor in the country's political reality (Rochlin, 2003: 106). Colombian journalist Jorge Child went on to view sectors of the elite as a sanctioning a national fascist paradigm.[21]

It has been proven that the "narco-fascists" do have connections with traditional capitalists and with government, administrative, military and police personnel. This makes one think that Colombian capitalism which has been pumped full of drug money for the last twenty years is now becoming a fascist-capitalist project. A project which enthusiastically embraces the appearance of its legal, political arm: MORENA.

(quoted in Pearce, 1990a: 266)

More telling were comments made by those in MORENA itself. In no way did party members hide their far-right tendencies; they rather defended them. Shortly following its official proclamation as a party, Ivan Roberto Duque

García, general secretary of the ACDEGAM, openly declared, "if fascism implies defending private property and the family with vigor and energy, defending the state, defending democracy and shaking off the dangerous specter of communist totalitarianism, then let them call us fascist" (quoted in Pearce, 1990a: 250).

Certain members of the Colombian state had begun to fear a loss of electoral seats to the new party, and that international trade might erode as support grew for ACDEGAM/MORENA (and quietly, the MAS). It was well known that the ACDEGAM had already created a pseudo-state in Puerto Boyacá.[22] As Colombian General Miguel Maza Márquez put it,

> the drug traffickers no longer operated like ordinary criminals, like the mafia. They were becoming a small state within the Colombian state .... This small state has a very organized military infrastructure and a political arm in formation in the MORENA party in the Magdalena Medio region.
> (quoted in Pearce, 1990a: 3)

Alongside the organization having "links with all the region's political representatives, including Congress," it was recognized that "the paramilitary groups had become as important as the guerrilla with regard to their affect on Colombian society" (Pearce, 1990a: 247; Kline, 1999: 75). As members of the ACDEGAM, such as Luis Alfredo Rubio Rojas who won a mayoral election in March 1988, were becoming politically successful prior to the formation of MORENA, it was assumed they could do so again, albeit as representatives of a fascist party.[23] Soon after its formation, Rubio announced his membership and potential candidacy via MORENA. Resistance quickly poured out against Rubio from the rural poor, echoed by some in government (Pearce, 1990a: 248; Kline, 1999: 77–8).[24] Wishing to diffuse the potential power of MORENA, sectors of the state capitalized on the grassroots protests.

The sitting Barco administration realized there were few ways of restraining MORENA from legally conducting its "political" activities in preparation for the elections (Kline, 1999: 77–8). Therefore, knowing MORENA would not agree to such conditions, Barco ordered prospective parties to severe all ties to unsanctioned paramilitaries, agree to endorse all national laws, and follow the rules of the Colombian constitution (Simons, 2004: 58). In response and protest, "MORENA leaders replied that if it were not approved as a political party, it would be a clandestine group" (Kline, 1999: 77–8). While the legislation did facilitate the demise of MORENA's legitimacy, it could not ensure the end of the fascistic ideologies from some members of the elite. These people simply shifted their far-right sympathies toward expanding the breadth of paramilitarism across the country.

THE MAS/ACCU PARTNERSHIP AND THE MANIFESTATION OF FASCISM VIA THE AUC

During the MAS's formation a working relationship had formed with the Castaño brothers (and the ACCU).[25] The Castaño brothers increasingly supported the MAS by way of force or profits derived from transactions connected to the narcotic industry and protection rents (Livingstone, 2003: 221). By the 1990s, the MAS and the ACCU were individually providing intelligence information to state forces while conducting operations against suspected guerrilla supporters. Through their mutual relations with the Colombian military, the ACCU and MAS forces soon began coordinating "major counterinsurgency against the guerrillas" (Richani, 2000: 38–9). This relationship continued into the mid-1990s until the principal architect of the ACCU, Fidel Castaño, was murdered in 1994 and his younger brother assumed leadership of the paramilitary organization. This caused things to change concerning the two paramilitary forces.

Unlike his brother Fidel, noted for relishing the spoils of power, Carlos moved away from a pure desire to establish himself as a wealthy capitalist or right-wing populist and specifically concentrated his activities toward eliminating the FARC-EP (Rojas, 2005: 227; Dudley, 2004: 144–51). For the next few years, he worked tirelessly to unify the two regionally based paramilitary forces into one distinct national organization (Livingstone, 2003: 220; see also Leech, 2002a: 23; Richani, 2000: 39). With the ACCU and MAS already having a working history, coupled with their co-aligned ideology and economic interests, a successful consolidation of the two took place in the late 1990s. In April 1997, Carlos Castaño succeeded in expanding operations from a regionalized level to a national scale, and announced the AUC to be a national paramilitary association (Pearce, 2007: 263n.11; Leech, 2002a: 23).[26]

THE AUC: AN APPENDAGE OF COLOMBIAN FASCISM

The AUC is the most recognized paramilitary organization in Colombian history.[27] Known for its ruthlessness, the organization initiated itself by carrying out the greatest array of violent massacres in Colombia's recent memory (Richani, 2002a: 93–132). Between 1997 and 2000, it allegedly conducted over 1,145 massacres (International Crisis Group, 2003a: 33). As if making a concession, Carlos Castaño agreed that after 1999, the AUC would only involve itself in massacres of no more than three persons at any one time (Holmes, 2003: 91). Yet the AUC cannot be thought of as an independent reactionary armed force simply supporting Colombia's far right. Rather, the AUC is a segment of a complicated and important history, a past which holds relevance in the context of today's civil war throughout the countryside and, in many respects, explains why the violence continues to rage.

Organizationally, the AUC can be thought of as an umbrella organization linking tens of thousands of armed combatants from various paramilitary groups under one principal leadership comprised of "a joint operational staff, and regional and local field units" (Kruijt and Koonings, 2004: 29; see also Livingstone, 2003: 219–20). The founding Carlos Castaño acted as leader of the AUC from 1997 to 2001/02, at which time his second in command and militant hardliner Salvatore Mancuso became the paramilitary's commander

(Simons, 2004: 178; Crandall, 2005b: 178; Livingstone, 2003: 219).[28] Frictions have long existed within the AUC. The paramilitary organization cannot be seen as a consolidated army, similar to a conventional nation state; rather it is an amalgam of autonomous groups with a shared anti-guerrilla pro-capitalist ideological mission. In comparison with the insurgency, the AUC "are far more loosely organized and much less disciplined than the FARC. Unlike the guerrillas, they have their own turf wars, often fighting between themselves for control of drug networks" (O'Shaughnessy and Branford, 2005: 41).

Some have considered the AUC to be the "largest and most notorious force in the history of Latin American paramilitaries" (Kruijt and Koonings, 2004: 27). It is, however, important to not simplify the AUC as a simple pseudo-mercenary force. Such a characterization fails to display the reality of why and how this paramilitary organization became the most perverse fascistic presence to sweep across the continent of contemporary South America. While the AUC did "espouse a conservative ideology," a closer examination of its coercive methodologies reveals far more than mere support for the continuity of the existing order (Kruijt and Koonings, 2004: 29). Researcher Robin Kirk (2003: 144) and anthropologist Michael Taussig (2004a: 11) have both compared Castaño's ideology and the AUC's practices with the Third Reich. "With the MAS, things rarely went further than a bullet in the head and the utilitarian slit in the belly, to ensure that the body sinks in water," yet such actions are conservative in relation to the AUC (Kirk, 2003: 144). Castaño's paramilitary:

> mutilated bodies with chain saws. They chained people to burning vehicles. They decapitated and rolled heads like soccer balls. They killed dozens at one time, including women and children. They buried people alive or hung them on meat hooks, carving them. They threw their dozens of victims like damp and flyblown trash to the side of the road. Rarely were their victims uniformed guerrillas .... Castaño's victims were civilians accused of supporting the guerrillas by supplying them with food, medical supplies, and transportation. The Germans have a word for what Castaño did – *Schreck-lichkeit*, meaning frightfulness. It was applied in their invasion of Belgium and France, to circumvent the civilian resistance that did not threaten but could delay troops. German soldiers burned homes, shot whole families, and pillaged and raped. It was not homicidal mania, but deliberate, part of the plan.
>
> (Kirk, 2003: 144)

The disturbing depictions of such offenses shed a light on how the AUC is in ideology and practice an organization with fascist intentions far beyond conservatism. Under the pretence that fascism is a system through which political and economic interests become fully unhindered, it is recognized that the AUC are an acute representation in present-day Latin America. Colombia's dominant class have long utilized "social fascism and political fascism (networks of paid informants, suppression of rights) ... to maintain a pattern of capital accumulation that benefits an increasingly narrow segment of the world population" (Escobar, 2004: 20).[29]

THE HISTORIC INTERCONNECTIONS BETWEEN LAND, THE NARCOBOURGEOISIE, AND THE AUC

One of the most important resources in Colombia, as with most regions of the world, is land. Land has long been concentrated in the hands of a relative few in Colombia. Unlike past decades, however, this concentration has now surpassed the mere desire for capital accumulation. In years past, urban-based rural landholders utilized land for acquisitions, agricultural production, cattle ranching, or profits through speculation on future returns. While such activities continue, other sociocultural and political-economic benefits are derived for those holding legal title.

Owning land has provided capitalists with the ability to derive profits without having to engage their own labor power. Holding title to land has enabled the owner to retain an income from peons and later peasants who would work the land and subsequently hand over goods or rents based on semi-proletarian conditions. Nevertheless, apart from its purely productive merit through surplus profits and use value, land has ironically carried worth in the absence of its usage. The Colombian state has routinely voiced that "significant property holdings, such as rural land" are to "remain immune to taxation" (Sweig and McCarthy, 2005: 22). Resulting from this, land, apart from being a marker of one's socioeconomic and political stature, can be utilized by the wealthiest sectors of the country to reduce or eliminate personal taxation. It is not, however, formal tax exemptions alone that can secure capital for an owner but rather the state's approach toward stagnant land.

In 2001, the Colombian state enacted directives that not only exempted the urban-based rural landowners from formal property levies but enabled these elites paradoxically to make money from "fallow" lands. Through Law 685 Chapter XXIII, Article 256, large landowners have been afforded the ability to borrow from the state's public coffers on the basis of proposed projects and/or projected earnings. In turn, the large landowners purposely declare a loss on the expected profits, return to the state lender, affirm the shortcoming, and subsequently obtain a repayment of the loss from the Colombian government's loan guarantee fund. Some have even used the repayments by the large landholders to cover costs related to AUC services (Ramírez, 2005: 60, 101n.37). This analysis helps to explain why large land areas remain underutilized and why the Uribe administration, while paying lip service to its prospects, objectively sustained a hostile position toward a real land reform strategy (see Sweig and McCarthy, 2005: 32–3).

Apart from monetary wealth, non-utilized land also provides sociocultural prestige, as centralized ownership over extensive tracts of land brings status (Dudley, 2004: 147; Richani, 2000: 41). Land is a symbolic representation of political-economic superiority. The Colombian bourgeoisie have an obsession about land titles that is almost a fetish. A great deal of power is attributed to those who have excessive amounts of land and leave it to stagnate. This is not because the land is unusable – Colombia has some of the most fertile soil in the world – but because keeping land underutilized is a sign of wealth. The owner does not use the land because he does not need to. A small producer from Cauca shared his thoughts on what this means to the impoverished rural poor.

> Those who own land around here do not even use it! They use the unused land as a sign of their wealth and power. As we starve trying to eke out an existence on what little poor land we have, for those of us who have some, they drink wine and laugh about their excess riches. This is the irony of the countryside. The rich are so rich they do not have to use their land.

Pragmatically, this practice had a particular appeal for the growing narcobourgeoisie, as it facilitated "respect" while enabling them to launder large sums of money. In an effort to legitimize themselves as productive members of society, they set up a system to "cleanse" their income from the drug trade (Holmes, Amin Gutiérrez de Piñeres and Curtin, 2006: 167; Decker and Duran, 1982: 46–7). With profits extending into the billions, the cartels had to find outlets for their earnings (Bowden, 2001).[30] From as far back as the mid to late 1970s, they purchased and/or funded "legal" investments in service and commercial sectors, and used offshore sales, overbilling, and international trade to launder capital (Decker and Duran, 1982: 46–7).

Schulte-Bockholt (2006: 97) argued that such practices enabled Colombia to adopt a model of socioeconomic progress through what he calls "narco-development." Industrialists provided a venue for economic stability during the rise of neoliberal economic policies while recirculating overwhelming flows of surplus capital into legitimate domestic enterprise (Thoumi, 1995: 199; Arango-Jaramillo, 1988: 126; see Table 6.1). This enabled those who were once criminals to associate with Colombia's traditional ruling class. In Schulte-Bockholt's words, "it seems clear that this wealth provides trafficking groups with the resources to infiltrate the nation's power structure" (2006: 97; see also Bagley, 1988: 85). Some have gone so far as to suggest the traffickers, specifically the AUC, were an economic partner assisting the Colombian economy to maintain structural macroeconomic constancy and growth through their input of narcodollars.

> Although economists disagree on the drug economy's impact on Colombia's macroeconomic stability, there is little disagreement that drug money provided a boon to the Colombian economy, helped establish fiscal stability in the 1990s, and continues to buttress the nation's balance of accounts.
> (Sweig and McCarthy, 2005: 28)[31]

The drug economy temporarily circumvented some of the economic trials that many Latin American nations experienced during the "lost decade" (the 1980s) and early 1990s by stimulating other sectors of the Colombian economy through capital reinvestment (Schulte-Bockholt, 2006: 97, 99, 100). Table 6.1 illustrates some of the areas in which the narcobourgeoisie laundered surplus profits during this period.

When asked about the AUC's more recent investments and money-laundering practices, one respondent from Cundinamarca told me the:

> paras control an intricate gambling program in the city [Bogotá] and have invested in the highest sectors of Colombian business and the financial industry; however, there are many other service investments that the para-military have involved themselves in over the past several years. Probably the most upsetting is the paras' control over child prostitution through-out central and Northern Bogotá [Northern Bogotá is the wealthiest part of the capital, populated by the middle-upper and upper strata of Colombia's dominant class]. You can go anywhere at any time of day and see the rise of child prostitution, especially young boys, throughout the capital; all of which is controlled or indirectly related to the paras.

Although this refers to the AUC's involvement in the contemporary urban sphere, the paramilitary has not forgotten how the countryside is one of the most important mediums of political-economic and cultural power.

By the early 1980s, the narcobourgeoisie "found in land the perfect way to deposit their cash into something of value, and, at the same time, achieve the social status that had eluded most of them" (Dudley, 2004: 147; see also Richani, 2000: 41). It a short time they managed to acquire millions of hectares of the most fertile lands (Rochlin, 2003: 107; Richani, 2002a: 34).

> By the mid-1980s, the Middle Magdalena Valley had become a drug traffickers' haven. All over the region, drug traffickers were buying up land in startling quantities. To the south of Puerto Boyacá, Pablo Escobar's strongmen and business partner in the Medellín cartel, José Gonzalo "El Mejicano" Rodríguez Gacha, owned large swaths of property .... A smattering of smaller traffickers were picking up other plots with or without

Table 6.1 Narcobourgeoisie/paramilitary leadership investment portfolio, 1980s

Area of "legitimate" investment	Percentage of narco-profits allocated
Land consolidation (urban and eural)	45
Cattle ranching and production	20
Financial commerce and investment	15
Private and commercial construction	10
Service industry	10

Sources: Adapted from Richani (2000: 41); Arango-Jaramillo (1988: 126) Lee III (1988: 92). This covers "legitimate" investments and not ventures in narcotics, gambling, and child prostitution.

the permission of locals. Just north of Puerto Boyacá, in a dusty cattle village called Puerto Triunfo, Escobar himself established a fifteen-thousand-acre ranchhouse, the Hacienda Napoles .... The narco-landgrab in the Middle Magdalena Valley was originally a way to launder money and gain the social status that had eluded many of the ones who, like Escobar, came from poor families. Drug traffickers bought cattle and carved out huge spaces for their opulent mansions. It was a trend that would continue throughout the 1980s and eventually change the face of the Colombian conflict forever. The drug traffickers were purchasing their way into the landed gentry.

(Dudley, 2004: 72–3)

The narcobourgeoisie's primary activities of land acquisition and concentration were a means to cleanse surplus narcodollars, while bringing the traffickers and elite ever closer through direct contact (see Schulte-Bockholt, 2006: 107; Richani, 2005b: 91; Lee III, 1988: 92). During the mid-1980s "narcotraffickers invested their illicit wealth through the purchase of 4 to 6 million hectares of land" (Rochlin, 2003: 107; see also Richani, 2002a: 34). In a decade, the traffickers came to own over 21 percent of all arable land in Colombia (Schulte-Bockholt, 2006: 107; Carrigan, 1995: 9). By 2000, it was said that "the total amount of land acquired by the drug traffickers is difficult to assess ... estimates range from 7.5 to 11 million acres – some 10% of Colombia's most fertile lands" (Richani, 2000: 41).[32] Some estimates related to earlier periods showed that lands had been violently usurped from roughly 3 million rural-based Colombians (see Bond, 2006: 1), equaling upwards of 7 million hectares (Haugaard, 2006: 2). By the turn of the century, "about 48 percent of the country's most fertile lands" had been concentrated in the hands of the new narcobourgeoisie (Richani, 2007: 411; see also 2005b: 91).[33] Recent figures have supported these findings, suggesting that the narcobourgeoisie and the AUC held title to well over half of all the country's arable land (Neira, 2006: 15n.15).[34] However, as the traffickers became the new rural elite, the FARC-EP ideologically saw them as the enemy.

As Escobar and his allies amassed billions of dollars during the 1980s, they invested in millions of acres of prime cattle-grazing lands, becoming a major part of Colombia's agrarian elite in a short time. The FARC attempted to extract taxes from the new landlords using techniques it had successfully used with the existing landed elite; threatening retribution if those elites refused to pay, or kidnapping for ransom. Instead of paying the FARC, however, the new landlords, led by Rodríguez Gacha, created powerful paramilitary forces that attacked the FARC and its civilian allies.

(Peceny and Durnan, 2006: 103)

The narcobourgeoisie were no longer mere merchants and unlawful traffickers of emeralds, marijuana, and cocaine, but were now directly disenfranchising the peasantry and therefore became a target of the guerrillas. As a result of the FARC-EP's threat of attack, retention, and/or class-based taxation, the cartels backed paramilitarism to respond to the hostilities and sustain revenues. In response the AUC targeted the insurgency's support base, increased private property holdings, and prevented equitable land reforms (Richani, 2005b: 91; 2000: 41). A cyclical relation began where coercive displacement was followed by a legitimate land acquisition. First, the AUC strategically deployed violence in FARC-EP territory. This was to intimidate sympathizers in the hopes of decentralizing resistance. Second, Colombian law at the time made allowances for particular lands – abandoned, failing to be used productively, or without legal title – to be acquired by interested parties. If peasants were physically removed – via massacre, displacement, or flight – then capitalists could gain ownership.

> Since land titles are disputed in the areas where the conflict is concentrated, the expulsion of poor peasants and the colonos meant a transfer of the claim over the land. The expelled peasants had no legal right to return to the land before the introduction of the Law 387 in 1997. In this manner, property could change hands, and violence became a profitable vehicle as a means to this end. Against the institutional loopholes regarding property rights, massacres became an effective tool in the process of concentration of land.
> (Richani, 2002a: 119–20)

In short, "the right-wing offensive began to look like good business, the exodus of peasants enabled others to appropriate their lands" (Pearce, 1990a: 247–8). However, how did the narcobourgeoisie materially consolidate political-economic power and by what means was this achieved? The next section looks in detail at the AUC's actual transgressions, illustrating how fascist practice has ensured the stability of the existing sociopolitical construct.

COLOMBIAN FASCISM IN ACTION

After interviewing Carlos Castaño, the French philosopher Bernard-Henri Lévy concluded that the leader of the AUC was an unquestionable fascist and "a psychopath confronting mafiosi" (Lévy, 2004: 71, 89). Although Lévy accurately depicted Castaño as the AUC's sadistic mastermind, attributing fascism to one charismatic authority fails to explain the larger context of the far right in Colombia. Attempting to remove any restrictions to political and economic growth, fascism has long needed the ability to facilitate violations against those that pose a potential deterrent to such interests. The AUC has done this not by targeting the FARC-EP specifically but brutalizing non-combatants. It would be impossible to outline all that it has done, but here are some samples to illustrate the objective realities of contemporary Colombian fascism.

A recognized tactic of the far right has been to impose a model of morality through the practice of "cleansing" society. Taussig (2004a) devoted an entire text to this subject by documenting the paramilitary's activities over a two-week period in May 2001. Within Taussig's work the AUC was repeatedly involved in eliminating those deemed detrimental to Colombia's social fabric. These ranged from persons who displayed an incorrect understanding and practice of a perceived conservative morality to people who did not support economic growth (Lévy, 2004: 74; Livingstone, 2003: 107; Shah, 2002).[35] Suspected guerrilla sympathizers, unionists, community organizers, street-kids, homosexuals, independent prostitutes, drug addicts, beggars, small-scale street merchants, and the homeless are regularly besieged. Even:

> Catholic Church workers and human rights activists, who used to be seen as unbiased mediators between the military and guerrillas, have become targets for the paramilitaries, who view them as apologists for the guerrillas. In February 1998, for example, in the southern state of Putumayo, paramilitary groups entered into a town and listed the names of priests and other activists to signal that they had been marked for death.
>
> (Crandall, 1999: 229)

Unlike US forces that claim "collateral damage" as a consequence of war, the AUC has repeatedly violated international law and Geneva conventions by specifically coordinating attacks against civilians and the public infrastructure. Healthcare facilities and workers in predominantly FARC-EP influenced regions are embattled under the pretence of disabling social services for their community and/or the guerrillas (Brittain, 2006c; Isacson, 2006a; Coghlan, 2004: 31). Such military actions are quite different from those employed by the FARC-EP. While not always successful, the guerrillas tactically target state and corporate infrastructure, trying to keep civilian casualties to a minimum (Holmes and Amin Gutiérrez de Piñeres, 2006: 112–13; Molano, 2005: 191, 195; Coghlan, 2004: 107).[36]

A surprising issue concerning the AUC has been the lack of open denunciation of the organization's involvement in human rights abuses against non-combatants. It seems that little quantitative analysis has been conducted in relation to the paramilitary's extensive actions against unarmed civilians during the civil war. For example, much of the AUC's leadership was extradited to the United States in May 2008 not on charges of assassination, disappearances, or genocide – even though they have admitted as much – but rather on the grounds of drug trafficking. While numerous groups condemn their activities, the vast majority of human rights-based organizations and NGOs seem to criticize the FARC-EP. Such enthusiasm is ironic given the fact that the insurgency commits a much lower proportion of abuses against non-combatants. Furthermore, it could be argued that when looking at this issue through a lens of class warfare that the people targeted by the FARC-EP predominantly belong to, or are associated with, Colombia's dominant class.[37] In the context of class struggle, the guerrillas perceive this section of society as legitimate targets as they are members of the elite, class enemies. In contrast, the AUC (and state forces) have done the direct opposite in targeting poor unarmed civilians.

Figure 6.1 shows two specific outcomes. First, the AUC, alongside its state allies, is responsible for most human rights violations. Over 140,000 victims

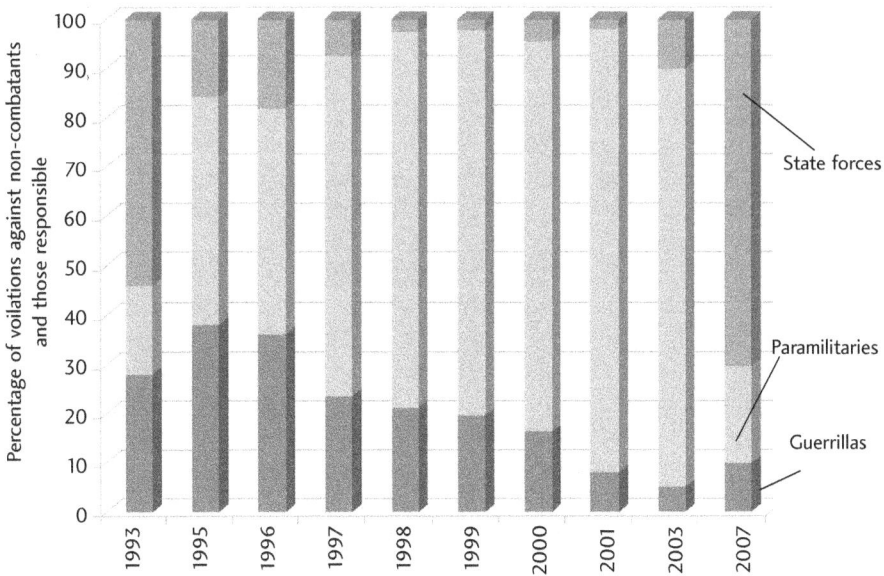

Figure 6.1 A re-examination of groups responsible for human rights violations against non-combatants in Colombia
Sources: Coalición Colombiana Contra la Tortura, 2008: 8; Gareau, 2004: 214; Murillo and Avirama, 2004: 89, 185–6; NUPGE, 2004: 2; HURIDOCS, 2003; Stokes, 2003a: 11; 2003b; Valenzuela, 2002: 10; Comisión Colombiana de Juristas, 2001. Data for between 2003 and 2006 has been very difficult to obtain, possibly because of the attempt to make the AUC/state negotiations (2003–06) appear effective.

of the paramilitary have been identified in the past few years alone (Haugaard et al, 2008: 11). The "guerrillas" were responsible for only 5–10 percent of all violations, while the combined state/paramilitary forces were responsible for approximately 90–95 percent.[38] From these figures the insurgents' human rights record has actually improved over the past decade. This is not to argue that the insurgents have not committed human rights abuses: they have, but the trend has generally improved since 1995. Second, the level of abuse at the hands of the state is directly related to the legitimate installation of the paramilitary via Decrees 2535 and 356 (1993), especially since the formal creation of the AUC (in 1997). As the figure demonstrates, there was an immediate and precipitous decrease in violations by state security forces, which correlates with the paramilitary's maturity. Pearce has supported this assessment and the "miraculous" shift in the state's proportion of responsibility of violations toward non-combatants.

The Colombian army has a long history of human rights abuse. It was deemed responsible in 1993 for 54 per cent of political killings in Colombia according to the US State Department annual report on human rights in Colombia. Over the next few years its record apparently improved and by the mid-1990s only 4 per cent of killings were attributed to it and 60 per cent to paramilitary groups.

(Pearce, 2007: 263n.12)

Not surprisingly, upon the AUC's so-called demobilization (in 2006) non-combatant abuses quickly reverted back to state forces (see and compare years 1993 and 2007 in Figure 6.1), who were subsequently responsible for over 71 percent of violations.

Failing to examine the larger domestic issue of human rights abuses, or examining them through a class perspective, has resulted in minimal information being released about who commits the majority of atrocities in Colombia. Much of the popular media has generalized that such violations are the result of Colombia's civil war and its "actors." When abuse data is quantitatively analyzed, however, it is apparent that this claim is a misrepresentation. In reality, the state/paramilitary forces are the leading architects of violence, torture, rape, and murder throughout the country. This is not difficult to deduce from the simple fact that those assaulted – unionists, left-of-center political elements, community organizers, and large portions of a critical civil society – maintain a sociopolitical ideology in promotion of social welfare.[39] Obviously, this does not align with the far-right conservatism of the paramilitary and the Álvaro Uribe Vélez administration. Under the paramilitary pretence, the state has co-perpetuated violence, intimidation, and acts of murder to prolong political stability and economic influence. The Colombian state and military, in collaboration with the AUC, are as a result responsible for perpetuating the preponderance of human rights violations against the civilian population. In spite of this, popular domestic and international media outlets have made conscious decisions to under-examine or more blatantly silence analyses that present the state's role in public violence.

Although it is an incredibly well-armed organization, the AUC also uses ad-hoc assault techniques. It regularly uses sharpened machetes, gas-propelled chainsaws, hammers, and even rocks as tools of war (Webb, 2004; Leech, 2002a: 23). Using such weaponry, the AUC slit throats, committed decapitations, and threw acid in the faces of suspected subversives (Coghlan, 2004; 12, 77; Taussig, 2004b: 18; Livingstone, 2003: 34). With the support of the military, its operatives have been known to travel from village to village with prepared lists of persons connected to the FARC-EP or other organizations that it has been declared need to be "cleansed" (Taussig, 2004b: 18; Shah, 2002). During one massacre Carlos Castaño and Colombian military Colonel Lino Sánchez organized an attack on Mapiripán, Meta. Here the AUC seized the listed individuals from their homes or places of work and "according to eyewitness accounts, hacked them to death with machetes or decapitated them with chainsaws" (O'Shaughnessy and Branford, 2005: 49). Another account noted how members the AUC cut off the head of 17-year-old Marino López after hacking off his legs and testicles (Pérez, 2003; see also Ramírez, 2005: 50). After the decapitation, the paramilitary, alongside members of the army, proceeded to use López's head as a ball during a soccer game in front of the village of Bijao del Cacarica in the Ríosucio municipality of the Chocó department (Pérez, 2003). At the end of the match, the forces took the lifeless, severed, and now fractured skull, and spitted it on a post as a threatening reminder to the remaining residents (Ramírez, 2005: 50).

> Once the teams were on the field, the referee sounded his whistle. Each team took up positions on the field. Then a helper brought a large bag to the center of the field, emptying its contents at a point equidistant from the two forwards who would start the game with the initial kickoff. The audience cried out in horror. The soccer ball was the head of Marino Lopez .... For long minutes the only sound heard by the inhabitants was the cracking of the players' feet on the man's destroyed skull. In the oppressive sun of that unending morning, the paramilitary team passed the defense of its opponent and scored twice. After the second goal the captain announced that the soccer ball would no longer serve, and so the game would have to end. The members of the Army team had to follow. They didn't like to lose, but the game had been clean. The forward, who had come close to scoring twice, apologized to his companions. "The ball was terrible", he said. "Hopefully next time they will inflate it properly before the game."
>
> (Garavito, 2004)

Taussig (2004b: 18) has written about paramilitaries hanging subversives "on meat hooks" in slaughterhouses for extended periods of time, sometimes days, before their execution. Multiple observers witnessed this during a massacre of roughly 100 peasants living on the San Miguel River, Putumayo.

> Survivors who fled the massacres say the paramilitaries forced residents of the villages to stand in columns, then tied them up, interrogated them and tortured them physically and psychologically before hanging them from beams and cutting them to pieces with machetes and chainsaws. Some of those killed were Ecuadorans who were working as day laborers on coca plantations. Witnesses say the bodies remain in the villages, since no one dares to retrieve them and bury them.
>
> (Weekly News Update on the Americas, 2004c)

Transgressions against youths have also risen. Assaults range from the suffocation of a six-year-old girl by placing a plastic bag over her face (Leech, 2002a: 53); amputating a teenage girl' s hands before cutting her abdomen open (Livingstone, 2003: 35); the enigmatic murder of a mentally challenged, deaf mute child (Coghlan, 2004; 12); decapitating infants or children having their hearts, while alive, ripped out of their bodies (Herman and Conde, 2005; Galvis, 2000: 28). It is also widely known that the AUC, supported by local merchants, "cleanse" orphaned children who have had to turn to the streets to survive (Molano, 2005: 113; Taussig, 2004a: 15).[40]

Over the last several years, the AUC increased practices of decapitation and the sexual mutilation of suspects while conscious. While such counterinsurgency practices are not new in Colombia,[41] they are acknowledged as being more prevalent today than during *la Violencia*. In one interview, Castaño actually chuckled during a discussion of how the AUC utilizes castration (Lévy, 2004: 87; see also Coghlan, 2004: 77; Pérez, 2003). The paramilitary has "raped both women and men and then dismembered them in front of the townspeople" (Ramírez, 2005: 51).[42]

On May 5, 2003, planes flew over the department of Arauca and approached an indigenous community in the Betoyes region, Tame. Parachutes began to open as armed combatants began to leap from the visible military aircraft (Donahue, 2003). Upon landing,

> armed individuals – identified by survivors from the indigenous Guahibo reservation as National Army troops wearing armbands of the paramilitary United Self-Defense Forces of Colombia (AUC) –raped four adolescent girls and massacred four people, including a pregnant teenager who was one of the rape victims.
>
> (Engqvist, 2003: 7)

The Guahibo girls assaulted were aged 11, 12, 15, and the pregnant 16-year-old, Omaira Fernández. Following the raping of Fernández, "the attackers reportedly cut her womb open to pull out the fetus, which they hacked apart with machetes," then "according to the Regional Indigenous Council of Arauca, witnesses from the reservation" saw the state/paramilitary forces throw "both mutilated corpses into the river" (Fitchl, 2003; Engqvist, 2003: 7; see also Obando, 2004). Reports soon appeared claiming that the US-trained 18th Brigade of the Colombian army was responsible for the atrocity (Leech, 2006d: 155; Donahue, 2003; Fitchl, 2003).[43] On the heels of the attack Castaño was cited saying,

> if any man, or any woman, has even the vaguest link with the guerrilla movement, then they stop being civilians and become guerrilla fighters dressed in civilian clothes, and as such deserve to be tortured, have their throats cut, to have a living hen sewed in their wombs in place of a foetus.
>
> (Lévy, 2004: 88)[44]

In 2003, the UN Commission on Human Rights (UNCHR), under the direction of Rodolfo Stavenhagen, began an examination into atrocities carried out by the AUC. Aside from finding the AUC responsible for the execution of indigenous peoples belonging to the Kogui tribe from the Sierra Nevada de Santa Maria in Arauca, the paramilitary were thought to engage in acts of cannibalism with the lifeless bodies. Upon the revelation of the massacre and the findings of the remains, "the fleshy parts of their legs and buttocks were missing" because "their captors had apparently fried and eaten them" (O'Shaughnessy and Branford, 2005: 109). It is in light of these horrors that Jorge Child stated, "the fundamental cause of Colombia's political violence" is the "narco-fascist paramilitary groups."

Unless we are clear about the nature of the real enemy in this historical moment in Colombia's democratic development – the narco-fascist paramilitary project ... An increasing number of political crimes will continue with impunity until home-grown fascism strikes its final blow.

(Child as quoted in Pearce, 1990a: 266–7)

THE ROLE AND RELATION OF THE COCA INDUSTRY TO THE PARAMILITARY (AND GUERRILLAS)

The appellation of "narco-fascist paramilitary" is significant; therefore, it is important to address how and to what extent the AUC aligned itself with the drug trade, particularly to coca. During the 1970s the Castaño brothers became deeply involved in narcotics, and later in assisting other localized narcobourgeoisie and large landowners to expand their wealth through increased land acquisitions by displacing peasants and securing increased shipping/smuggling routes. However, by the early 1990s, pressure from the United States and the Colombian state toward narcotrafficking hit new heights.

For more than a decade a central goal of the international war on drugs waged by the United States was to reduce the supply of illicit drugs being cultivated and exported from the Andean region of South America. In the case of Colombia in particular, for most of the 1990s this strategy involved pressuring the government to go after the leaders of the cocaine cartels based in the provincial cities of Medellín and Cali. Washington thought that this "kingpin strategy," if successful, would deal a mortal blow to the cartels' ability to ship drugs to the United States. In many ways the strategy worked. By 1995, all of the Cali and Medellín cartel leaders were either dead or in prison in Colombia or the United States.

(Crandall, 2005b: 179)

Working together, Washington and Bogotá deconstructed the two infamous cartels by aligning with those who had once worked closely with them (Dudley, 2004; see also Scott, 2003: 89; Taussig, 2004b: 18; NACLA, 2003: 2). The Castaños were quick to support this top-down approach both ideologically and materially, as both brothers had reasons for cutting ties with the cartels, particularly with Escobar. Fidel felt Escobar had watered-down his stringent anti-communist ideology, while Carlos saw the drug lord withdraw his once extensive support for the MAS (Kirk, 2003: 156). The brothers then re-routed their approach to the industry by working with "the police, the Cali Cartel and dissidents from the Medellín Cartel (Henao brothers) to defeat Pablo Escobar" (Livingstone, 2003: 133; see also Avilés, 2006: 71–87; Peceny and Durnan, 2006: 102; Bowden, 2001).

Upon the demise of the cartels a looming void was left vacant for the drug trade to redevelop itself in the pursuit of supplying the global demand for cocaine.[45] With Fidel dead (in 1994), and the paramilitary needing an additional outlet to fund its actions, the AUC filled this void and became one of the primary organizations involved in the Colombian narcotic industry.[46]

> The demise of the Medellín and Cali cartels in the 1990s allowed the paramilitaries to diversify their operations into other aspects of drug production and trade .... Due in part to its control of Urabá and other areas close to the border of Panama, a main contraband route, the AUC was able to inherit the narcotrafficking network and contracts in the interior of the country and international markets. In addition to taxing the coca farmers, the paramilitaries provide protection for processing labs, and at least some of the paramilitary groups appear to be directly involved in cocaine production and actual trafficking.
>
> (Felbab-Brown, 2005: 113)

The paramilitary were soon involved in the direct production of coca, and became financed primarily through trafficking, as was admitted by Carlos Castaño himself (Molina, 2001: 205; see also Murillo and Avirama, 2004: 100–1; Crandall, 2002: 88). Throughout the 2000s, the AUC conservatively attributed 80 percent of its income directly to trafficking, involving itself in roughly 40 percent of all narcotic activity in Colombia (see Richani, 2007: 409; 2005b: 102n.77; 2002a: 108–9; Scott, 2003: 39). What is interesting about these figures in relation to the FARC-EP is that the guerrillas derive only a minority of their income from taxing drug merchants and have no direct involvement in trafficking (Holmes et al, 2006: 163; Schulte-Bockholt, 2006: 130; El Tiempo, 2005; Miami Herald, 2005; Semana, 2005; Röhl, 2004: 4; Cooper, 2002: 951; Richani, 2002a: 64; Rangel Suárez, 2000: 585; Halliday, 1989: 88; Shannon, 1989: 161–6). Furthermore, the FARC-EP's indirect involvement with the industry only equates to roughly 2.5 percent of all drug activity in the country (Scott, 2003: 39, 52n.1, 71, 72, 74–5).

In recent years, contrary to claims that the FARC-EP is involved in processing and trafficking, findings have demonstrated that the insurgency actually decreased export rates of coca from regions under its control while sustaining (and increasing) levels of gross domestic product and employment (Holmes and Amin Gutiérrez de Piñeres, 2006: 111–13). Hence, the FARC-EP has stabilized domestic production and economic activity while limiting coca (see Munck, 2008: 191). Such an analysis supports my research related to the FARC-EP's class-based taxation model and its pre-revolutionary strategy of alternative development via crop substitution. As export levels do not increase and domestic products grow, an argument could be made that the insurgency's program of commodity sharing via JACs has worked. There is no decline in gross domestic product but there is one in rates of export; therefore, in certain locales the insurgency has enabled small producers to fairly trade surplus goods with other rural-based producers rather than competing against each other in a formal capitalist market. If, in fact, the FARC-EP were heavily involved in trafficking, levels of illicit export would be high in areas under its control, for it would be the medium through which commodities are transported – as is the case in areas controlled by the paramilitary (Holmes and Amin Gutiérrez de Piñeres, 2006: 112–13).

What has been found in areas of FARC-EP territory is simply an involved relation between the guerrillas and the rural population in making sure peasants remain protected from external threat so as to enable them to produce what they need to subsist. One reason for this FARC-EP success may be its distinct approach toward coca growers when compared with the AUC. The FARC-EP protects peasants who choose to cultivate coca (on incredibly small plots of land) whereas the AUC violently forces peasants to harvest coca on immense land tracts or coca plantations (Stokes, 2001: 65–7; see also Schulte-Bockholt, 2006: ch. 5; Cassidy, 2005).[47]

Explanations for the AUC's structural involvement in the drug trade have been the removal of the Cali and Medellín cartels coupled with the systemic over-attention given to fumigating coca in regions predominantly controlled by the FARC-EP (O'Shaughnessy and Branford, 2005: 5, 35, 62; Sweig and McCarthy, 2005: 15; Kruijt and Koonings, 2004: 75).

> [F]or all the success in apprehending narco-traffickers, the kingpin strategy did little to reduce the overall drug trade. Instead, a drug production atomized from the large, visible Medellín and Cali cartels to a much greater number of small drug producers. These "boutique" drug traffickers became harder to track and apprehend, making subsequent operations much more difficult.
>
> (Crandall, 2005b: 179)

As the large cartels of the 1980s and 1990s decentralized, the AUC – that is, their former employees and security – established micro-level drug processing labs (Kenney, 2007: 90; Brittain, 2006d; Padgett and Morris, 2004; Selsky, 2004; Livingstone, 2003: 84–5; Richani, 2000: 40). This was facilitated by Washington and Bogotá's support for the AUC's counterinsurgency efforts (Peceny and Durnan, 2006: 111–13). As argued by Mark Peceny and Michael Durnan:

> the coercive military and police activities of the United States and its allies often determine which set of private actors in which countries benefit the most from the drug trade. As the United States focuses its prohibition efforts on one set of actors or countries, the profits of the drug trade shift to other actors.
>
> (Peceny and Durnan, 2006: 96)

It has been suggested that this strategy was systemically orchestrated to enable the United States and the Colombian state to keep a close tab on the narcotics industry and/or take up the "slack" following the demise of the cartels (Taussig, 2004b: 18; NACLA, 2003: 2; Scott, 2003: 89).

In 2003, the Uribe administration's policies "coincided with the 'strong expansion' of paramilitary groups" enabling the "ultra-right groups" to increase "their presence in various regions of the country" (NACLA, 2003: 2). This is no mere coincidence according to former Canadian diplomat Peter Dale Scott, who suggested this inter-connection is the true purpose of the US narco-methodology, which has no means or desire to eliminate the narcotic industry. On the contrary, Scott (2003: 89) has argued that Washington and Bogotá seek to "alter market share: to target specific enemies and thus ensure that the drug traffic remains under the control of those traffickers who are allies of the Colombian state security apparatus and/or the CIA" (see also Taussig, 2004b: 18). Putting this into perspective from an economic standpoint, Carlos Oliva Campos demonstrated the tremendous amount of (prohibited) capital that the narcotic industry provides US-based banks. Washington has no systemic interests of curbing the dynamics of the global drug trade because of its economic spin-offs. Campos (2007: 38) noted that "there are many unclear questions on the real interest of the United States to put an end to drug trafficking due to the economic benefits received by the big American transnationals, especially the main banks of the nation" (see also Petras, 2001b; Petras and Morley, 1995: 86). As one commercial bank executive astonishingly revealed, considerable fiscal benefits are derived from illicit transfers:

The 500 billion dollars from the illegal origin coming into the main American banks and circulating among them exceed the net income of all computer companies in the United States and, of course, their benefits. This annual income exceeds all net transfers made by the main oil and military companies and aircraft manufacturers. The largest banks in the United States – the Bank of America, J.P. Morgan, Chase Manhattan and, above all, the Citibank – receive a high percentage of their banking benefits from services provided to the accounts of criminal dirty money. The larger banks and financial institutions in the United States support the global power of the United States through their laundering operations and management of illegal funds. The Citibank, the first money laundering bank, is the largest bank in the United States, with 180,000 employees across the world distributed throughout 100 countries, 700,000 well-known deposits and over 1 billion deposits of private individuals in secret accounts and carries out private bank operations (investment portfolio management) in more than 30 countries thus turning it into the bank with the largest global presence compared with all financial institutions in the United States.

(quoted in Campos, 2007: 38–9)

Regardless of whether or not this hypothesis is true, scholars have clearly demonstrated that US involvement in counterinsurgency tactics has allowed criminal bodies to increase their political, monetary, and militaristic foothold (Peceny and Durnan, 2006).

US LINKS TO COLOMBIA'S NARCOTIC POLITICAL ECONOMY
AND PARAMILITARISM

US foreign policy has purportedly targeted the narcotic industry for well over a century; however, its punitive opposition to drugs became most significant during the latter decades of the twentieth century. Under the Republican guidance of Richard Nixon (president 1969–74), Washington formally announced its "war on drugs" in the late 1960s. This was the catalyst for a conjoined foreign and domestic policy that sought to combat the usage of narcotics in sectors of United States, which paved the way for future anti-drugs policies under the Reagan, (both) Bush, Clinton, and Obama administrations.[48] Interestingly, such a policy has not aimed at combating usage via treatment, understanding why sectors of society consume mind/mood-altering substances, or improvement of socioeconomic conditions, but rather at targeting producer nations (Isacson, 2005: 19; Neild, 2005: 68; O'Shaughnessy and Branford, 2005: 21–2; Livingstone, 2003: 173; Leech, 2002a: 41).

In the mid-1980s, the time of important revolutionary struggles throughout Central America, the United States stated that the FARC-EP was heavily involved in Colombia's internal and external drug trade (Scott and Marshall, 1998: 96–103). Following these allegations, proven false years later,[49] Washington claimed that "the narcotics trade threatens the integrity" and "national security of the United States," and established the National Security Decision Directive Number 221: Narcotics and National Security (NSDD 221) on April 8, 1986[50] (White House, 1986: 2; see also Avilés, 2006: 48; Williams, 2005: 168; Scott, 2003: 39, 71, 87–8; Solaún, 2002: 5). Formalizing the NSDD 221 as a national security policy enabled Washington to aid and construct "foreign assistance planning efforts" allowing state forces to legally carry out direct actions, militaristic or otherwise, in regions other than their national jurisdiction (Avilés, 2006: 48; Crandall, 2005b: 168; Parenti, 2002: 79, 82; Jackson, 1994: 170; White House, 1986: 3). The legislation strategically defined the coca industry "as a national security matter, allowing for the use of U.S. troops in Colombia in alliance with the CIA" (Scott, 2003: 87).[51]

On the heels of the NSDD 221, the Ronald Reagan (1981–89) and George H.W. Bush (1989–93) administrations encouraged the Andean region to adopt economic reforms under the argument that they would stimulate agricultural producers to move away from the drugs trade. Each country in the region was encouraged to open (*apertura*) their economies to greater trade, which in turn would lead to development. For Colombia the argument was that a liberalized economy would deflate the coca industry, as increased trade – compounded by a reduction in tariffs – would translate into the primary sector, assisting the expansion of both secondary and tertiary production. Enter in the Andean Trade Promotion and Drug Eradication Act (ATPDEA).[52]

Neoliberal trade pacts did not lead to a reduction in coca. The production of coca is a consequence of social and economic conditions (factors of exclusion, poverty, systemic absence of social services, and so on). The lowering of trade barriers, while addressing macroeconomic restrictions to domestic and international corporations, does not guarantee a decrease of socio-economic problems at a grassroots level. In actuality, preferred market access for agricultural commodities did little more than benefit a select minority of owners through increased profits. Some have, however, argued that benefits from the ATPDEA were witnessed in Colombia's flower industry, which was transformed "into a $600 million national business that now accounts for 14 percent of the world export market" (Sweig and McCarthy, 2005: 32). While it was suggested that the ATPDEA "helped" the flower industry, it is important to note that flower workers remained mostly teenage women who received less than US$0.60¢ an hour, and were denied the ability to receive formal education (Friedemann-Sánchez, 2006).[53] As rates of poverty escalated in both urban and rural sectors over the last two decades, it is clear whom the Drug Eradication Act helped – certainly not the many young women in the flower industry trying to survive.

A consequence of the ATPDEA has been an attack on workers. While some aspects of the economy, such as the flower industry, were applauded, less attention was placed on the devastating societal effects of such neoliberal policies. There was an inequitable increase of imports in sectors of the rural economy, leaving a deficit the economy was unable to respond to. Producers in the countryside either continued or went back to coca as a means of subsistence. In short, the ATPDEA witnessed an increase in US economic power at the expense of Colombia's overall economy (see Williams, 2005: 164).

> World Bank statistics show that between 1989 and 1993, Colombia's average tariff decreased from 44 percent to less than 12 percent, resulting in lower prices for imported goods. Consequently, the country's trade surplus soon became a trade deficit. In 1989, Colombian exports totaled $7.3 billion and imports $6.4 billion – a surplus of almost one billion dollars. But only nine years later, exports of $13.6 billion were surpassed by imports totaling $17.5 billion, resulting in a deficit of close to $4 billion. It soon became apparent that the government's policies were negatively impacting domestic producers who were unable to compete with the high-tech industries of scale in developed countries.
>
> (Leech, 2002a: 45)

As coca activity increased, commercial investment deflected attention from the growing rates of impoverishment in the countryside. Over the last decade, Colombia has witnessed a two-way exploitation of the dual economy, a great deal of which is tied to narcodollars. First, problems in the rural political economy led peasants to increasingly colonize new lands to grow coca out of necessity. Second, urban-based textile and commodity export factories saw capitalists drive down wages to maximize surplus profits (Richani, 2005a; 2005b). On paper, Colombia soon "saw its legal and illegal exports to the United States jump dramatically" as the ATPDEA assisted in cleansing monies generated through the coca industry (Williams, 2005: 164; see also Richani, 2005a). All this helped further justify Washington's foreign policy via NSDD

221 and the future deployment of the largest counterinsurgency operation in the hemisphere, given the façade of a war on drugs.[54] Paradoxically, the US and the Colombian state's policy towards coca resulted in the expansion of the narcotic industry with unhindered ease. However, if measures were established to institute "a comprehensive attack on the trade – from eliminating production at the source," then why did coca cultivation levels increase (see Bureau of Western Hemisphere Affairs, 2001)? The answer lies in the fact that as Washington and Bogotá specifically targeted peasants in areas of FARC-EP control, the AUC implemented devastating aggressions against the rural populace while expanding its power over the narcotics industry, with serious consequences.

First, US-sponsored fumigation practices have had an indisputable affect on the rural population and environment of Colombia. The destruction of peasant crops has hampered the capacity for communities to sustain themselves – let alone develop – subsequently leading people to colonize forested regions (Leech, 2006b; Petras and Veltmeyer, 2003a: 179; Ungerman and Brohy, 2003; CISLAC, 2001; KAIROS, 2001). Aerial spraying of defoliants has forced many to leave their homes, villages, and regions, only to further spread coca cultivation over greater territories. This has greatly eroded the environment as peasants have little choice but to cut down trees and inhabit previously unpopulated territories. As fumigation soon follows, so are more soils and water supplies contaminated, thus affecting present and future food production, economic stability, and health conditions (Ungerman and Brohy, 2003; Leech, 2002a: 71). It could be argued that the US and Colombian states are carrying out an attack against the poor through the use of such methods.

Second, the rural population has been horrified by (internationally backed) domestic reactionism. Through a "drain the water" mentality the state has utilized financial assistance from the United States to destroy "peasant links to the FARC" by driving "the peasantry out of the countryside and isolating the guerrillas" (Petras and Veltmeyer, 2001: 143; see also Petras, 2002: 17). Since they seldom initiate confrontations with the FARC-EP, state and paramilitary forces have targeted peasants, small landowners, and rural workers who are presumed supporters of the guerrillas. In order for this to be legitimated on a national or global scale, a justification must be and has been presented.

> Although presented as fighting the war against narcotics, the Plan is actually directed against suspected peasant sympathizers and peasant guerrillas linked to the left. The use of paramilitary forces to repress civilians allows Washington and its military clients "plausible denial" (in fact, Washington even criticizes the "paras") while channelling arms, funds and protection via the Colombian military command.
>
> (Petras and Veltmeyer, 2003a: 178)

Such a policy has seen the causalities of the civil war reach unprecedented heights. In service of foreign political and economic interests, the Colombian state has greatly feared any escalation in support for the FARC-EP (see Petras, 2002: 17; see also Petras and Veltmeyer, 2003a: 40). As a result a massive "polarization of civil war proportions between the oligarchy and military, on one side, and the guerrilla and the peasantry, on the other" has been established (Petras and Veltmeyer, 2003a: 122). Such tactics are explicitly designed to combat revolutionary objectives. As expressed in Chapter 2, it can only be with the people that the FARC-EP can generate emancipatory and transformative action, hence the real war that is taking place in Colombia is not against drugs, but against the consequential threat of the people implementing a socialist revolution from below.

Contrary to popular reports, the result of class reactionism has been an increase in the FARC-EP's numbers and support base in many locales. Without protection peasants have understood all too well the realities of extermination, thus the guerrillas have proven to be "the only ones left who can protect the *campesinos*" (Braun, 2003: 68; see also FARC-EP, 2002b: 28–9; 2001–02: 5, 14). This being the case populations periodically flock to, or remain in, FARC-EP-held territory. Inadvertently, broad numbers of people become involved in reflecting/conversing about social conditions, political circumstance, the history of US interference in Latin America, and the overall situation of their country. Such conditions arguably foster an environment of "heightened anti-imperialist consciousness," leading segments to unify with the FARC-EP (Petras and Veltmeyer, 2003a: 179). This goes to the heart of class analysis and the contemporary geopolitical relevance of Marxism. Because of Washington's fear of a Marxist insurgency actually taking power[55] – coupled with the possibility of it happening – the very structure of imperialism may be threatened.

A third consequence has been the rapid increase in coca growing. Several years after NSDD 221, Washington alleged coca levels had decreased as a result of their involvement. To their embarrassment and discredit, external findings revealed that cocaine productivity was 2.5 times higher than previously speculated (Scott, 2003: 83n.35). None of this is surprising in light of the fact that the AUC was now deriving four-fifths of its income from trafficking, and had control of just under half of all narcotics activity in the country (Richani, 2007: 409; 2005b: 102n.77; 2002a: 108–9; Scott, 2003: 39).

THE AUC'S STRUCTURAL CONNECTION TO COCA

Since the implementation of NSDD 221, a considerable rise in coca cultivation has shadowed the comparative growth of paramilitarism (Avila et al, 1997). The most significant jumps took place during US/Colombian counternarcotic and counterinsurgency campaigns alongside the formal inception of the AUC, around 1997 (see Figure 6.2). As Washington and Bogotá increasingly focused on defeating the FARC-EP, they simultaneously provided leeway for the AUC to expand its economic and militaristic activities. This cost–benefit approach has been regularly shown in US foreign policy, whereby one set of actors are targeted while others enrich themselves provided their activities benefit the United States in some form, political or otherwise (Peceny and Durnan, 2006: 96, 112).[56]

A more telling sign of the AUC's involvement in the drugs trade was the considerable freeze in coca cultivation coupled by the increase of proclaimed AUC members at the beginning of the formal demobilization negotiations with the Uribe administration in 2003. The state agreed to negotiate with the AUC in July 2003, and stated that an amnesty for AUC combatants would be considered, coupled with protection of all property and assets members had acquired over the past decade (FENSUAGRO, 2005; Ramírez Lemus, Stanton and Walsh, 2005: 134; Simons, 2004: 331; Dudley, 2004: 206–7). By 2005, this was passed into law via Law 975 (Goffman, 2005; NACLA, 2003). The so-called "Peace and Justice Law" sought

> the demobilization of up to 20,000 members of the rightwing paramilitary group the United Self-Defense Forces of Colombia (AUC), while granting its leaders broad concessions. Under the legislation, AUC commanders will receive sentences as short as 22 months and at most eight years, with the possibility of serving the time on private farms instead of in state-run prisons. A "double jeopardy" provision also makes extradition to the United States unlikely. In addition, the legislation does not require AUC commanders to dismantle the group's organizational infrastructure, nor to give up any profits they have made from drug trafficking, kidnappings or other criminal activities.
>
> (Goffman, 2005: 50)

At the passing of Law 975, Colombian congresswoman Gina María Parody d'Echeona criticized the legislation as it paradoxically gave "benefits to people who have committed the worst crimes" (Goffman, 2005: 50–1). Furthermore, traffickers, once connected with the paramilitaries, were able to manipulate the legislation by "acquiring" official AUC member status, thus enabling them to cleanse all assets obtained during their years in the narcotics industry (that is, production, smuggling, trafficking, and so on) while going virtually unpunished for any crimes committed (Goffman, 2005: 50–1; Forero, 2004). By the summer of 2006, Jorge Daniel Castro, then general director of Colombia's national police, announced that about 31,000 paramilitaries had claimed amnesty via Law 975 (see Badawy, 2006). This skyrocketing figure was almost double any estimate by scholars, military analysts, or governments officials of the size of the AUC (International Crisis Group, 2004: 2, 2n.7; Murillo and Avirama, 2004: 89, 108; Livingstone, 2003: 269n.15; Crandall, 2002: 88; Ministerio de Defensa Nacional, 2000: 10). Political and security analyst Vanda Felbab-Brown (2005: 113) suggested that numerous drug traffickers "bought themselves leadership positions in the AUC to take advantage of AUC peace negotiations with the Colombian government and avoid extradition under the resulting lenient treatment of the paramilitaries."

Trying to add legitimacy to the negotiations with Uribe, the AUC and narcobourgeoisie quashed coca cultivation, processing, and distribution during the early stages of the demobilization process, making it appear as though the organization was sincere in disbanding. According to Holmes and colleagues

(2006: 168), "with the goal of making itself more acceptable to participate in government peace talks ... the AUC needed to appear less implicated in drug trafficking." This explained the pronounced reduction in coca cultivation in 2003 and 2004. When negotiations started to go awry in 2005 and 2006, there was a parallel rise in coca cultivation, again highlighting that the AUC had not demobilized. After an initial decrease in coca production in Colombia during 2003, record-high aerial spraying in 2004 not only failed to achieve any decrease in the acreage of cultivated coca, but failed to prevent a renewed increase in acreage despite proclamations from US officials that by the end of 2004 there would be no significant plantations of mature coca left in Colombia (Felbab-Brown, 2005: 116).

COMPARING COCA CULTIVATION IN AUC AND FARC-EP TERRITORY

A significant correlation between the AUC's combatant forces and the systemic ascent in coca cultivation is clearly apparent. However, could this relation not also apply to the FARC-EP? Examining this question may provide some reflection on which armed groups are dependent on the illicit drug trade to effectively maintain their actions. Economically speaking, for the coca industry to increasingly and proficiently thrive a proportionate number of facilitators are

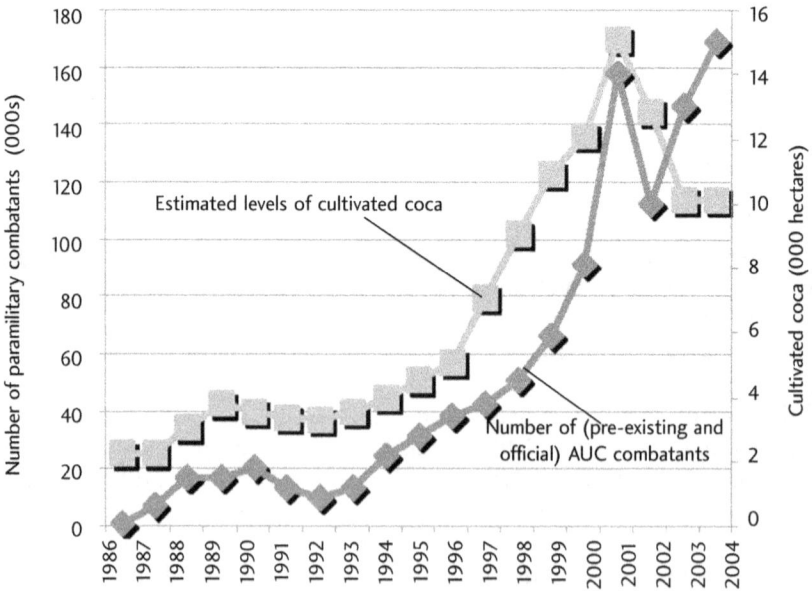

Figure 6.2 The links between coca growth and AUC paramilitarism
Sources: *AUC Data* – International Crisis Group, 2004: 2, 2n7; Murillo and Avirama, 2004: 89, 108; Livingstone, 2003: 269n15; Crandall, 2002: 88; Ministerio de Defensa Nacional, 2000: 10; *Coca Data* – ONDCP, 2005; Latin American Working Group, 2003; US Department of State, 2003; Abruzzese, 1989.

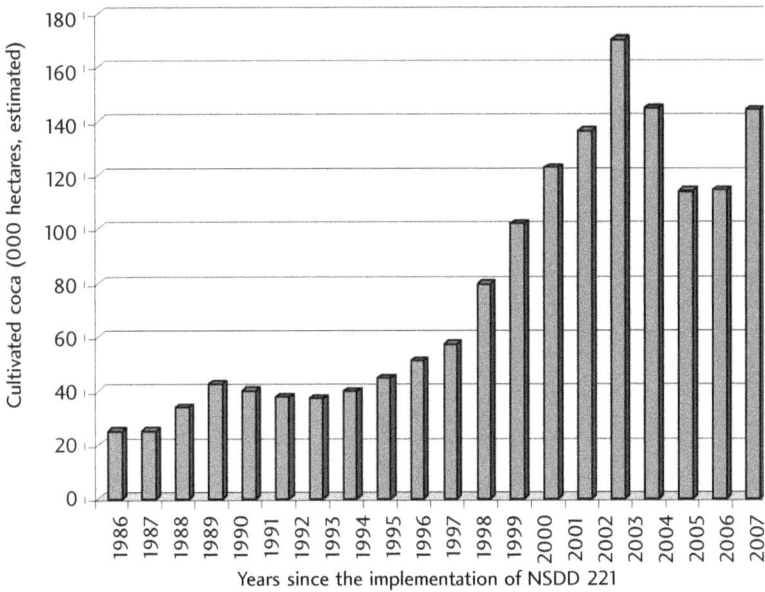

Figure 6.3 Growth in national coca cultivation
Sources: ONDCP, 2008; 2007; 2006; 2005; Latin American Working Group, 2003; US Department of State, 2003; Abruzzese, 1989.

needed. If the AUC and/or the FARC-EP are heavily involved in processing and trafficking, a parallel growth in numbers (combatants) will shadow cultivation. If ambiguities, bloating, or dissimilar levels are identified, then an argument could be made that the group is less influential and/or less tied to the structural activities of the coca industry.

Figure 6.4 compares coca growth and the number of AUC and FARC-EP combatants for a selection of dates following the implementation of NSDD 211. It is apparent that FARC-EP combatant growth rates are not closely or consistently aligned with levels of coca cultivation. For the most part, the number of FARC-EP combatants has grown consistently since 1964, a date which long precedes the coca industry. The AUC/coca cultivation figures, however, show a much closer correlation.

Figure 6.5 examines levels of coca cultivation in FARC-EP and AUC-controlled regions between 2003 and 2004. Did US/Colombian counternarcotic programs, which disproportionately targeted regions under FARC-EP control, ignoring areas under AUC control, result in an increase in coca processing in zones where the paramilitary were active? This would be the case if the AUC were heavily involved in the coca industry.

Antioquia, a region where the AUC has long-entrenched roots, saw coca cultivation increase by 71 percent in a mere two-year period (UNODC, 2005: 15). The region of Putumayo, long associated with the FARC-EP, saw a remarkable 68 percent drop in coca production between 2002 and 2004.

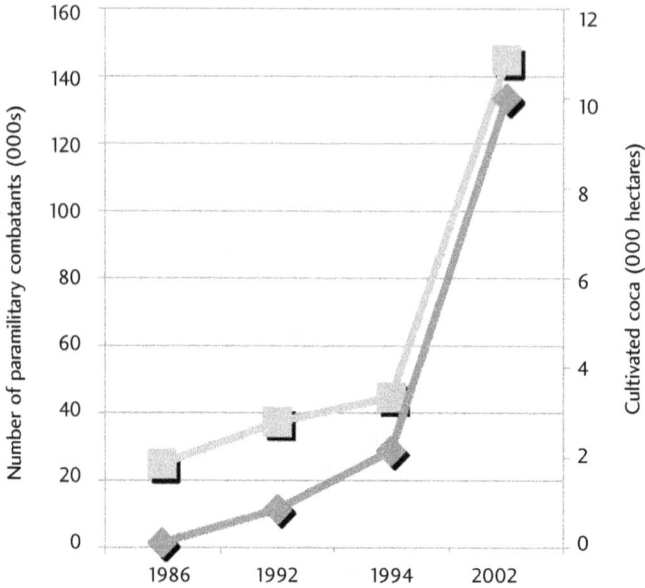

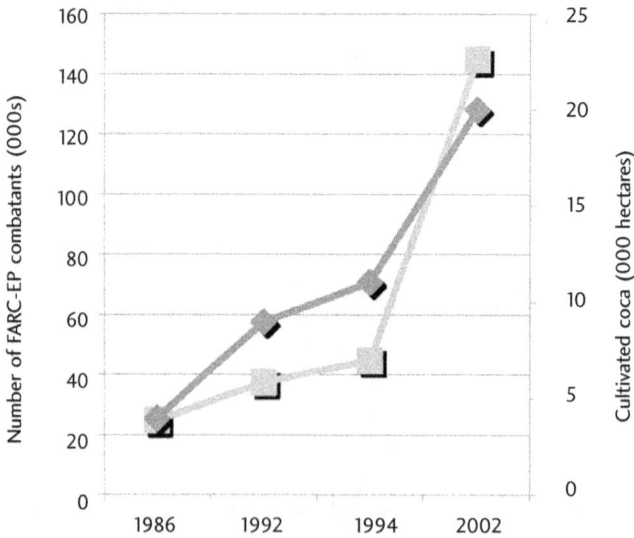

Figure 6.4 A comparative examination of the insurgency/paramilitary relationship to coca cultivation

Sources: *AUC Data* – International Crisis Group, 2004: 2, 2n.7; Murillo and Avirama, 2004: 89, 108; Livingstone, 2003: 269n.15; Crandall, 2002: 88; Ministerio de Defensa Nacional, 2000: 10; *FARC-EP Data* – Schulte-Bockholt, 2006: 141n.15; Goff, 2004: 44; Sánchez, 2003: 15; Kirk, 2003: 218; Rochlin, 2003: 62, 74–9, 137, 165n.81; Crandall, 2002: 61, 68; Richani, 2002a: 76; 2001: 53–4, 74n.33; FARC-EP, 1999: 17; Osterling, 1989: 266, 285, 294–5; Gunther, 1966: 443; *Coca Data* – ONDCP, 2005; Latin American Working Group, 2003; US Department of State, 2003; Abruzzese, 1989.

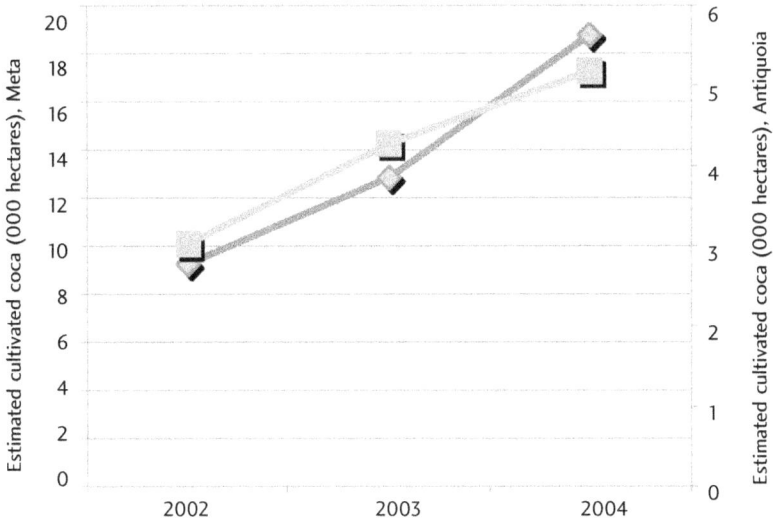

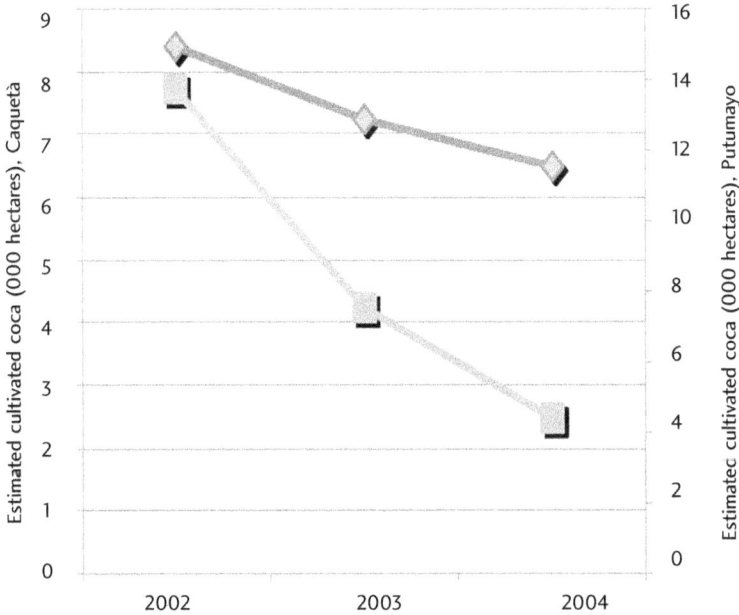

Figure 6.5 Rates of coca cultivation in departments associated with the AUC (Meta, Antioquia) and FARC-EP (Caquetá, Putumayo)
Sources: Adapted from UNODC (2005). Since the AUC's inception and supposed demobilization there was no aerial fumigation or manual eradication of poppy cultivation in either Meta or Antioquia (UNODC, 2005: 66).

Adam Isacson highlighted that areas controlled by the FARC-EP showed explicit signs of coca reduction, while areas under the AUC showed sustained, if not increased, levels of cultivation and related industry activity. Isacson (2006b) noted that narcotic cultivation intelligence data explicitly illustrates that in "FARC ... and AUC zones of action, one immediately notices that coca has stayed stable or increased in regions controlled by paramilitary groups." AUC-controlled territories witnessed a significant rise in coca cultivation while FARC-EP regions saw a prominent decline in relation to the rest of the country (Brittain, 2006b; Brittain and Sacouman, 2006a; 2006b). To further test these findings additional departments associated with the FARC-EP and AUC are considered.

Numerous peasants and rural organizations, organized labor groups, indigenous peoples, afro-Colombians, human rights institutions, and representatives from women's organizations have acknowledged that "paramilitary elements have increased their presence" in central Meta (Isacson, 2006a). During field studies in Meta, local residents told me the AUC had significantly increased its presence in the department, making it an important area for examining cultivation levels.[57] Caquetá was another important department to investigate not simply because it is a major center for coca cultivation but for its historic connection to the FARC-EP (Hylton, 2006: 88; Labrousse, 2005: 179; Richani, 2005a: 139n.10; Pearce, 1990a: 167; Marsh, 1983: 123–4). These departments too showed that coca cultivation increased in areas under recent paramilitary control, and declined in FARC-EP-associated regions, suggesting a structural relationship.

This is evidence against the frequent claims that the FARC-EP is dependent on coca as a means to fund its armed actions against the state and capitalist infrastructure. Contrary to popular rhetoric, reductions in coca cultivation do not materially affect the FARC-EP's capacity to wage military campaigns. However, since reductions in coca cultivation translate into less income for the population, one of two outcomes is often seen. First, small producers become increasingly uninterested in supporting the FARC-EP, because of the insurgency's inability to sustain dual power. Second, resentment increases against those who have encouraged anti-coca programs in guerrilla territory.

Although the first response is possible, it goes against the long history of peasants who have, time and time again, even during periods of difficulty, supported the FARC-EP as a result of their ideological and practical attempt to systemically challenge the inequitable conditions in the countryside. As one respondent stated:

The insurgency lives with the people and has allowed the community to sustain its way of life. The insurgency is a necessity for if we want to change the state, the people of Colombia cannot support or employ one simple form of struggle but many forms of resistance; we must have armed struggle, political education, and community organization. It is through the FARC that these methods are constructed. The state does not sustain its power through one form but many; therefore, to alter such inequality and exploitation the people of this country must resist and struggle in all forms that the current exploitation holds ground ... There are many forms of struggle and all peoples must understand that they [FARC-EP] are the wives, sisters, brothers, fathers, sons, and daughters of the people who live throughout the countryside of this country. Our country is their country.

There is a perception however told to those within the cities, many of which, I might add, have never traveled throughout this country, that the guerrilla are not revolutionaries but that they are violent war mongers, kidnappers, narcos, and bandits. This is important for it then makes people dissociate the guerrilla as an inhuman group, a collective that is not made up of Colombians, and therefore presents an image that the FARC are not of the people but rather another "armed actor" [holds up his hands and makes quotation gestures] struggling for individual wealth and power. This is quite interesting for many of us in the countryside who see, live, and interact with the guerrillas on a weekly or monthly basis, who receive information about where the military is, or who are invited to attend a reading and writing class put on by the guerrillas, or are offered free medical information and care through the FARC. All communities, be they in the city or the country, must understand that the insurgency is not an independent organization or rogue group that is separate from the people and the conditions of this countryside but a much needed revolutionary movement with the closest ties to the people who have a right to struggle. It is not necessarily important that we know the truth of what the guerrillas are doing, because we live it, but that you inform the people in the cities that the guerrillas are our brothers and sisters, sons and daughters, and that they are intimately connected to those of us who live in the countryside because ... they are us. This is a truth and reality that has to be accepted by all Colombians and all foreign nations.

As rural antagonism toward the dominant class becomes increasingly acute during declines in coca cultivation, so too does the FARC-EP's ability to maintain revolutionary efforts against the state. This was seen from 2002 to 2004, when the insurgency launched devastating offenses against both US and Colombian forces (Brittain and Sacouman, 2006a; 2006b; Brittain, 2005e). However, after 2004, growths in cultivation were realized (Selsky, 2005). After repeated efforts to withhold annual reports on levels of coca cultivation, both the United Nations and Washington revealed that it had increased significantly. A 20 percent growth was recorded in 2005, 19 percent in 2006, and by 2007 levels reached one of their highest points in history. Interestingly, the highest levels of total coca cultivation (including coca fumigated by aerial spraying and manual eradication) in Colombia's history occurred under the Uribe administration.

With such significant growth it is hard to think that the FARC-EP will be unable to continue its dual power. If anything, declines in coca rates from 2002 to 2004 demonstrated the resilience and aptitude of the guerrillas to withstand efforts from Washington and Bogotá to combat the rural population and their political economy.

SHIFTS IN THE AUC'S FOCUS

A growing move away from the AUC's historic formation and ideology was experienced by the early 2000s. During this period the paramilitary organization increasingly moved away from its original goal of conducting operations against the FARC-EP, and toward more lucrative control over the drug trade (Isacson, 2006a; Felbab-Brown, 2005: 112–13; Sweig and McCarthy, 2005: 28). According to Taussig (2004b: 117), many AUC actions changed from direct counter-insurgency to a practice of taking over coca fields harvested by peasants in guerrilla territory. Sectors of the leadership began relieving themselves from counter-insurgency altogether in order to solely devote their activities to the coca industry (Forero, 2004).[58] In time Carlos Castaño would condemn the ideological disjuncture of certain leaders, and resigned, "saying he could no longer control the death-squad extremists" (Simons, 2004: 290). After Castaño's resignation, the AUC's leadership was increasingly based on who could facilitate greater economic returns for the organization, as the rank and file became ever more attracted to economic incentives, rather than defeating the guerrillas.[59]

> The paramilitary federation disintegrated in 2002 (as an organization, not as a Mafia-type phenomenon), and was survived by the FARC ... it was an organizational no-go, as it failed to establish a minimal internal cohesion to maintain stable regional structures, let alone build a national anti-subversive project ... due to the fact that the paramilitaries are a "cadre army," led by members of the legal or illegal economic elites, which offers economic

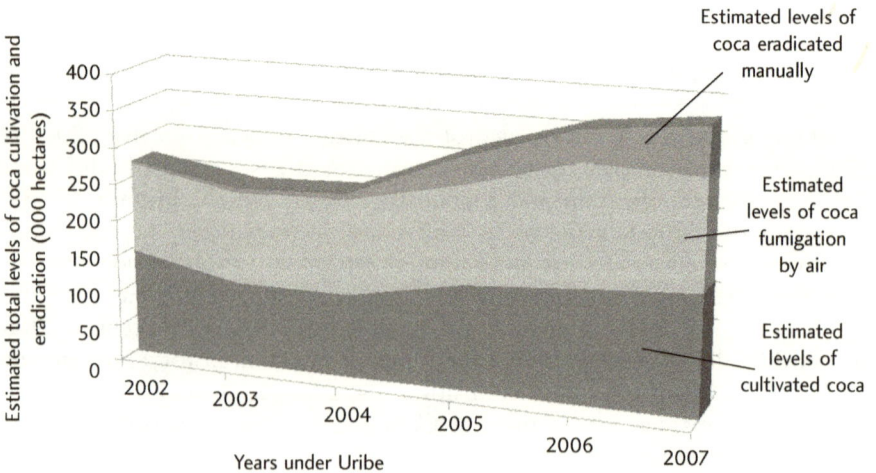

Figure 6.6 Growth of total coca cultivation in Columbia under the Uribe administration, 2002–07
Source: ONDCP, 2008. Ironically, as these statistics come from the ONDCP, other US intelligence suggests even higher figures (see Bureau of International Narcotics and Law Enforcement Affairs, 2008).

incentives to its members, and works like a loose network of security providers, they have evolved towards a Mafia-type scheme ... the idea, so common in the political economy of conflict, that the provision of selective economic incentives to fight is translated into military and organizational strength in some "natural" way is both wrong and naïve.

(Gutiérrez Sanín, 2008: 16–17, 28)

It would not be long until Castaño himself "disappeared." Many believed Castaño's death was directed by "rival paramilitary leaders who were unhappy with his repeated criticisms of the AUC's ever deeper involvement in drug trafficking" (O'Shaughnessy and Branford, 2005: 50; see also Crandall, 2005b: 178). Accounts suggested he was executed under the direction of Salvatore Mancuso, who wished to silence Castaño's opposition to the paramilitary's escalation in the coca industry (see Crandall, 2005b: 178; O'Shaughnessy and Branford, 2005: 50).[60] However, on August 25, 2006, Jesús Ignacio Roldán, a one-time member of the AUC, confessed to killing Castaño on April 15, 2004, under the order's of Jose Vicente Castaño (an older brother of Carlos) and five other paramilitary leaders (Deutsche Presse Agentur, 2006).[61] Fearing he would reveal information to the international community of the AUC's links with the state, involvement in narcotics, and counterinsurgency techniques, Castaño was executed. Ironically in similar fashion to what he himself did to many civilians, Castaño was brutally murdered in a barrage of bullets by Roldán and 20 AUC members (Deutsche Presse Agentur, 2006; Dudley, 2006b; Muse, 2006b).

Under Castaño the AUC was founded on a strategy of targeting suspected FARC-EP supporters. Based on this foremost ideological position, Castaño justified the AUC's activities in narcotics as a means to fund its anti-communist counter-revolution. After 2001, Castaño began to take a more vocal line about the need to distance the AUC from narcotics in order for it to become a credible political medium (Felbab-Brown, 2005: 114; Dudley, 2004: ch. 15; Livingstone, 2003: 222). While at one time the AUC saw the drug trade as a means (to acquire funds) to an end (to combat FARC-EP's social base), its fascist inclinations moved to armed action as a means of ensuring complete unfettered individualized economic growth – the means becoming an end in itself. Murdering non-combatants increasingly involved killing those who disrupted profit maximization, not simply insurgent supporters. Aggressions against the FARC-EP declined (although the guerrillas did not lessen their attacks on paramilitaries) (Restrepo and Spagat, 2004: 12–13).

This chapter paints a disturbing picture of why some have felt revolution may be the only means to bring about social change in Colombia. State-sanctioned paramilitarism, created and carried out to deter people from taking part in any form of conventional social transformation, has conversely led many of those seeking change to move to radical means. The next chapter details what this unconventional revolutionary and pre-revolutionary situation looks like, and what the FARC-EP is doing to facilitate such conditions.

7

THE FARC-EP'S RELATION TO (PRE)REVOLUTIONARY SOCIAL CHANGE

A need has long existed for the FARC-EP's unique approach toward revolutionary social change to be analyzed. This chapter does this through a threefold process. First, the chapter theorizes the insurgency's activities. An argument could be made that the FARC-EP has displayed characteristics of Gramsci's war of position/war of maneuver[1] to create emancipatory conditions at a localized level.[2] Second, an analysis contextualizes how the insurgency has revolutionized one-time mechanisms of dominant class hegemony. This section demonstrates how certain *Juntas Acción Comunal* (JACs), created to pacify bucolic populations, have come to work alongside the FARC-EP, exemplifying how the guerrillas are not autonomous but tied to the disenfranchised via pre-revolutionary frameworks. Finally, the chapter provides a thorough examination of initiatives and methods promoted by the FARC-EP within frameworks of society, culture, and politics.

THE FARC-EP'S CONTEXTUAL APPLICATION OF GRAMSCI'S WAR OF POSITION

Gramsci viewed modern capitalist societies as having two separate superstructures: civil society (private) and the state (political society), which combine to produce a hegemonic system of dominant class rule (Gramsci, 1971: 12). This hegemony maintains "the supremacy of a social group" and manifests its power "in two ways: as 'domination' and 'intellectual and moral leadership'" (Gramsci, 1971: 57). This exercise witnesses "the combination of force and consent variously balancing one another, without force exceeding consent too much" (Gramsci, 1971: 80n.49; see also 263).[3]

If dominant class interests are extended solely through the use of force, then hegemony is susceptible to weakness in both objective and subjective terms. Objectively, the fragility of an elite dependent on oppression is quickly realized if its coercive mechanisms are deconstructed. Subjectively, an over-reliance on coercion rather than consent empowers those exploited to increasingly recognize the dominance of the economic and political minority (Gramsci, 1971: 275–6). Therefore, tampering with the delicate balance of coercion/consent assists in the creation of counter-hegemony (Gramsci, 1985: 104–5).

At various times throughout Latin America ruling classes have deviated from equilibrium in the hopes of sustaining power (Shnookal, 2003; Blum, 1998;

Chomsky, 1987). In Colombia, however, little emphasis has ever been placed on consent to facilitate stability (Giraldo, 1996; Beals, 1974: 229).[4] Such an environment, according to Gramsci (1971: 275–6), nurtures the development of a revolutionary counter-hegemony. It is in this theoretical circumstance that the FARC-EP has constructed pre-revolutionary measures that respond to repressive class relations. We now examine how this counter-hegemonic shift has been constructed in localized zones through a Gramscian "war of position."

Throughout his prison writings, Gramsci developed a specific two-pronged approach toward revolutionary tactics depending on a country's distinctive, yet related, superstructures. Some countries have a unified political and civil society, where little differentiation is realized between the two (Gramsci, 1971: 234). Under these conditions, a direct frontal assault, or war of maneuver, can demobilize conjoined class structures because of their strongly concentrated character via the state (Gramsci, 1971: 237–8). Other countries, adopting an over-developed capitalistic political economy, have a more defined civil society external, but nevertheless related, to political society. Here a focused war of position is necessary, where social, cultural, and political shifts occur, creating the initial conditions for counter-hegemony, which are followed by a frontal assault over the conventional system ("war of maneuver") leading to a successful taking of power (Gramsci, 1971: 236–8).

While some have suggested Colombia could still see change through a war of maneuver (see Dashti, 2003: 170), a war of position is the most realistic avenue for revolutionary success because of the country's distinctive decentralized political-economic structure (Escobar-Lemmon, 2006; 2003; Angell, Lowden and Thorp, 2001; Fiszbein, 1997; Montoya, 1991). The stated goal of decentralization was to strengthen democracy through the separation of superstructures and centralized state power (LeGrand, 2003: 179). However, in practice, "the process of administrative decentralization had advanced to the point of seriously undermining and weakening the working of local municipal governments, which had more or less been displaced by the decentralized agencies of the central government" (Veltmeyer, 1999: 77–8; see also Pearce, 2007: 242; Bell Lemus, 1988). As Bogotá (once again) demonstrated its incapacity to centralize authority, the FARC-EP furthered its war of position – and arguably war of maneuver – across sectors of the countryside.[5]

On the ropes during the late 1980s and 1990s, the state, unable to respond to the FARC-EP's increasing military aptitude in the countryside or prop up class interests via private security forces,[6] focussed on securing specific urban centers of the country, namely the capital (Richani, 2002a; 2001; 1997). Doing so only increased the insurgency's ability to sustain offences against the state's weak coercive apparatus, construct a localized war of position, and partially erect a regionally focussed war of maneuver in several areas of rural Colombia.

> The guerrillas shifted their strategy .... Rather than seize political power by assuming the state central apparatus and institutions, they deconstructed state power at the village and municipal levels and moved upward. The

guerrillas are responding to the state's failures in mitigating rural conflicts and are filling a hegemonic void left by the state.

(Richani, 2002a: 89)

In light of all this, Gramsci's theory can be adapted to fit the Colombian dynamic as the FARC-EP creates pre-revolutionary rural-based centers of dual power at a grassroots level.

Several years after the 1982 shift in strategy, the FARC-EP demonstrated a tangible change in political-military positioning (FARC-EP, 1999: 26; Pizarro Leongómez, 1996). The guerrillas "began to move away from the rigid top-down bureaucracy to one more dependent on a system of regional blocs and fronts operating throughout the country" (Murillo and Avirama, 2004: 75). Emphasizing a "local power" strategy, regional linkages and increased acceptance and support were obtained in predominantly rural areas (Avilés, 2006: 36; Hylton, 2006: 56–7; Schulte-Bockholt, 2006: 111; Williams, 2005: 161; Murillo and Avirama, 2004: 75; LeGrand, 2003: 178, 181; Petras, 2003: 24; 1999: 30–1; Rochlin, 2003: 132–3; Pizzaro Leongómez, 1992: 181–2; Pearce, 1990a: 168; Gomez, 1972). In these regions, many of which are impoverished, various socio-political, economic, and cultural alternatives were grounded (Botero, 2006).

> In regions where the FARC has long maintained control, and where the national government has never had a presence, the rebels function as a de-facto government and have implemented redistributive projects. In recent years, for example, the FARC has broken up almost a dozen large ranches in southern Meta department and redistributed the smaller parcels of land to subsistence farmers. The guerrillas have carried out similar agrarian reform programs in Caquetá, Putumayo and other regions .... The FARC has also implemented a national tax system whereby the income from kidnapping, extortion and the taxation of wealthy landowners and businesses is used to fund military operations. The revenue from taxes imposed on local communities in FARC-controlled regions, however, is turned over to municipal leaders and used to fund local social and economic projects.
>
> (Leech, 2005d; see also 2006d: 124; 2004b: 16; Wilson, 2003)

A more specific example of a transfer from positional warfare to the consolidation of power over distinct territory is Miraflores, Guaviare: an area with a considerable population (over 5,000) where for a decade the guerrillas had a wide social base, expanded recruits, formulated an alterative economic system, and defended civilians (Richani, 2005b: 79, 99n.35).

The last 15 years have, for the most part, seen the guerrillas expand social and cultural programs while escalating security measures over state and paramilitary reactionism (Avilés, 2006: 36). The FARC-EP has been able to do this because it has become "more sophisticated, shifting from small guerrilla units using hit and run tactics to 'mobile warfare,' employing a large number of combatants (battalion-strength) and targeting well-armed garrisons in peripheral cities" (Richani, 2005b: 84; see also 95). In these areas, the

FARC-EP has moved beyond mere guerrilla combat and matured to a place of political-militaristic control (González, Bolivar, and Vázquez, 2002: 54). This, however, does not suggest that the insurgency refrains from moving in and out of guerrilla tactics (FARC-EP, 1999: 26). Rather it has periodically "adapted its military to offset the government's air power advantage by re-employing guerrilla warfare tactics, moving in small units, and dispersing its forces into larger areas" (Richani, 2005b: 89).

The FARC-EP has opted against taking centralized state power through an immediate win over the governing apparatus or a series of revolutionary pushes aimed at the capital (Petras, 1999: 30; see also Granada and Rojas, 1995). Adopting a war of position has facilitated a "system of dual power in several regions of the country," offering an alternative to conventional state power (Petras, 2003: 25; see also Schulte-Bockholt, 2006: 201–2; Williams, 2005: 161; Petras, 1999: 31).[7] By extending influence through a slow, realistic, ideologically motivated program, the FARC-EP has created a distinct counter-hegemony via "the accumulation of local power" (Petras, 1999: 30). Although the situation is fluid, specific rural territories are under guerrilla control and experience the fulfillment of needs left unmet by the state's absence (Rochlin, 2003: 132–3; Petras, 1999: 31; see also LeGrand, 2003: 178, 181).

The insurgency has tried to sustain regionalized social-based welfare programs that provide individual and communal benefit to the immediate populations (Pizzaro Leongómez, 1992: 181–2; see also Avilés, 2006: 36; Hylton, 2006: 56–7; Petras, 2003: 24; 1999: 30–1; Pearce, 1990a: 168; Gomez, 1972). This reflects Gramsci's argument that socialism is a process, an intermediary evolving series of developments for the betterment of a given society (Gramsci, 1977: 55). A socialist revolution must be a "continuous and systematic revolution of a people," not merely the taking of state power: "a continuous process of formation and superseding of unstable equilibria," always in process and response to the societal conditions of a revolutionary epoch (Gramsci, 1977: 55; 1971: 182).[8] Over the past several years, the FARC-EP has tried to achieve this using dual power. Nevertheless, an explanation is needed of how this is being realized within contemporary Colombia.

THE FARC-EP'S CONTESTATION OF URBAN-CENTRIC POWER THEORIES

James F. Rochlin (2007; 2003) has characterized the FARC-EP as a revolutionary movement trapped in the framework of pre-modernity, modernity, and postmodernism. By pursuing a political-military model in the countryside, and not taking steps to first procure centralized state power by taking control of Bogotá, the FARC-EP is said to be engaged in a "premodern disposition toward space and politics" (Rochlin, 2003: 144; see also 2007: 48). This is quite ill-informed as it lacks any theoretical understanding of what the FARC-EP is doing within modernity itself (see also Hardt and Negri, 2004: 83). Much of the FARC-EP's capacity to create substantive change is ignored under the assumption of limited power in metropolitan centers. As the insurgency

is perceived to lack urban strength it is believed to be restricted from implementing revolutionary shifts. Essentially, the position equates counter-hegemony to the ability to consolidate urban power (Rochlin, 2003: 139). "[T]he
most profound debility of the FARC has been the group's failure to cultivate
meaningful popular support outside its enclaves in the countryside. The rebels
have not attracted a measurable following in cities, where the vast majority of
Colombians reside" (Rochlin, 2003: 143).

Urban-centric ideologies have long suggested that true change can only
prevail as revolutionary movements take power over those regions where the
vast majority resides. Arguments depicting "the city" as key socio-geographical
mediums of power pragmatically lack understanding of the agency of those in
the rural setting.

Neo-liberal structuralists tend to assume a one-way flow of influence and
pressure: from the cities to the countryside – from the globalized economy
inward. Their concept of power is based exclusively on an institutional or
market conception of power in which the top institutional position and the
flows of capital are the only source of power. *Although institutions and
markets are important modules of power, they are not the only source of
power. Organized masses of people are also sources of power. Power is a class
relation in which the dominant class has resources like money and what it can
buy and state instruments of armed forces while the peasants/rural workers
have large numbers, a new form of (potential) organization and grass-roots
support ....* Implicit in most neo-liberal structuralist arguments is a virtuous
view of the city. Urban economies are seen as dynamic, creative and the wave
of the future. A corollary to the dynamic city is the image of a static, stagnant
countryside .... In their negative view neo-liberal structuralists fail to examine
the class context of agricultural activity. Where rural movements have been
successful in expropriating productive lands and securing credit and technical
assistance they have produced virtuous outcomes, demonstrating that there
are many roads to agrarian modernization. By examining the class context
of modernization we can understand the facile incorporation of elite classes
and the difficult and insurmountable obstacles to popular incorporation and
hence their resistance, not to modernization per se, but to a particular form
of it. The issue of realizing modernization goals is less a problem of "peasant
embrace of traditional values" or resistance to "structural adjustments" and
"short-term pain", but the lack of access to available alternative employment,
housing and security in the urban setting. *Staying in the countryside and
attempting to improve rural livelihoods is a modern, rational decision based
on cost–benefit analysis*: the real possibility of change based on perceptions
or information of other successful activity in other regions or adjoining
territories. The diffusion factor is also operative: positive activities in one
region have a multiplier effect; successful occupations have a demonstration
effect. The demonstration effect is only successful if peasants or landless
laborers already have a predisposition to want to remain in the countryside
and farm if the opportunity presented itself. Illustrating what we could call

'modernization from below' is evidenced by peasant/rural worker demands for technical assistance, credit, infrastructure and marketing. These demands are associated with raising production and acquiring market shares, obviously associated with modernization, albeit in capitalist form. *Today the issue of agrarian reform is not a simple replay of traditional demands of 'land for the tiller,' counter posed to capitalist modernization associated with large-scale corporate export farming. It is an alternative modernization strategy built around modern social classes. Peasants/rural workers or at least their cadres/ leaders view land distribution as only the first step in an agrarian reform. Thus the conception of "the peasant" or "landless workers" today is vastly different from past images of atomized subsistence farmers, relying solely on traditional farming know-how and barely aware of markets, alternative cropping, non-traditional marketable crops and resistance to technological innovation. It is precisely the emergence of a different peasantry and rural workers, with modern attitudes and with positive attitudes toward the possibility of significant, even transformative, change, that accounts for the resistance to being displaced or 'proletarianized' (more likely joining the urban reserve army of unemployed).*

(Petras, 2003: 92–4, italics added)

Numerous historic and contemporary examples are available to demonstrate how an "urban-centric conception of power" is a fallacy. The FARC-EP exemplifies how "rural movements can reverse urban and external flows of influence and exercise hegemony on a national basis" (Petras, 2003: 93). In regions of FARC-EP control a pre-revolutionary dynamism has introduced new forms of development outside metropolitan capital systems (see Richani, 2002a: 66, 71). Through this process, the insurgency's political and military capacity, has, on multiple occasions and at specific times, demonstrated a domestic and international threat to national capitalist hegemony. From this it can be understood that the FARC-EP's support and sustained position in the countryside is not a demonstration of pre-modern conditions but rather a clear presentation of the insurgency's unique political and ideological framework within modernity itself. Again, the FARC-EP attempts to create a "war of position" not by taking centralized power but through an organized ongoing consolidation of newly revolutionized socio-geographical environments across rural Colombia. It is important to demonstrate how this has occurred, so I offer an analysis of one counter-hegemonic strategy where a once state-based mechanism, shaped to co-opt the peasantry and rural populations, was transformed into a pre-revolutionary medium of grassroots power.

THE TRANSFORMATION OF JAC: FROM PACIFYING STATE MECHANISM TO REVOLUTIONARY COMMUNITY-BASED INSTITUTION

The 1950s and 1960s saw a class structure in rural Colombia ripe for political organizing because of the disparities in ownership of capital and land.

Sociologist T. Lynn Smith noted that community-based development projects were:

> badly needed in rural society, such as that in Colombia, in which the two-class system of social stratification has prevailed for centuries, in which the mass of the rural people are either agricultural laborers or at most the owners or renters of very small plots of relatively poor land, in which hoe culture and the still more primitive system of felling and burning are the principal ways of getting products from the soil, and in which the smallest subdivision of government is really an administrative division of the national government and not a unit that by any stretch of the imagination is entitled to be called an entity for local self-government.
>
> (Smith, 1967: 315)

Recognizing the historic and volatile situation of this turbulent period (after *la Violencia*, the National Front's political exclusion, the PCC's involvement in the countryside, and so on), the state attempted to mitigate tensions through a localized development strategy. *Juntas Acción de Comunal* (JAC) offered pseudo-self-government across the countryside while distracting attention from leftist politics. Historian Marco Palacios presented a formal description of the JACs' creation.

> The most durable state-directed mobilization initiative of the FN [Frente Nacional] era, the Juntas de Acción Comunal (Community Action Boards, or JACs), created in 1958, were a Liberal initiative. JACs were organized by rural subdivision or urban neighborhood and were assigned funds by the state for specific development goals such as the construction of schools, clinics, and roads, or the extension of water and sewer lines. In return the communities provided volunteer labor and some funding, although the latter often came from aid organizations.
>
> (Palacios, 2006: 185)

Colombia's governing structure has long been arranged through a hierarchical lineation. Conversely, Law 14 (1958) appeared to decentralize power through the creation of community action boards that shaped development projects via state funds, private institutions, NGOs, and the rural communities themselves.[9] Law 14 required that the JACs:

> be made up of local residents of rural and urban neighborhoods, and could be delegated "functions of control and vigilance and a certain intervention" in the management of various public services. Through the boards the government was to permit popular participation in a number of activities, including school construction and repair; health programs and construction of health centers and public restaurants; construction and administration of irrigation and drainage systems; low-cost housing, roads, and bridges; improvement of agriculture; encouragement of sports as well as recreational

and cultural activities; and the organization of cooperatives and labor exchanges.

(Bagley and Edel, 1980: 260)

A year later, Decree 1791 saw further services bestowed upon JACs, such as "adult education, reforestation, preparation of residents of overpopulated areas for migration, and the development of animal husbandry for dietary improvement" (Bagley and Edel, 1980: 260). Nevertheless, the state did not permit JACs to participate in politics or local decision making, which mattered little as authority appeared to be held at the level of the community. As time lapsed JACs became a façade of "power," as they provided an image of local control while the political remained restricted.

JACS AND POLITICAL PACIFICATION

The official state line was that JACs were constructed under the premise of supporting rural "development, through community self-help" and to "alter the passivity of the Colombian campesino" (Dix, 1967: 151–2). The goal, however, was to sociopolitically pacify the rural population during the rise of agrarian capitalism (Zamosc, 1986: 38; Bagley and Edel, 1980: 258–60). Resembling the National Front in the cities, the state needed to appear sympathetic to the peasantry but restrict political control. The reasoning was threefold, to:

- pacify active state-antagonists in the countryside
- decrease PCC political work and alliances throughout the rural sector
- sever ties between peasants, the landless, indigenous groups, small producers, workers, and the militant revolutionary goals of the guerrillas.

In pursuit of these objectives, Colombia's dominant class supported the implementation of JACs as a means to "make communities less receptive to anti-elite sentiments and movements" (Richardson, 1970: 44).

As the local action boards spread, so too did "the presence of the state in the countryside" (Henderson, 2001: 400). Although they appeared to be rural-based peasant organizations, JACs were in fact strategic state-induced mechanisms created to pacify class-conscious peasants. Far from organic, they were "created by government officials" and used by the local elite to procure increased political clout and/or garnish centralized state funds (Pearce, 1990a: 149).[10] In most cases JACs, completely guided by state-based development officials and the dominant class, rejected local input (Henderson, 1985: 231; Richardson, 1970: 44; Dix, 1967: 151–3). Robert H. Dix (1967: 153) suggested the action boards manufactured an image of social change; a "motivation to improve rural conditions without altering the real balance of social power in the countryside." It is not difficult to see why the state greatly expanded JACs in the hopes of gaining a political foothold over the countryside.

JACs were systematically directed towards areas of organized left-wing political action (Pearce, 1990a: 127; Zamosc, 1986: 195; Bagley and Edel, 1980: 260–2). Working with the action boards, the state tried to limit (or eliminate) "rural enclaves of Communist Party strength" (Collier and Collier, 2002: 466; see also Bagley and Edel, 1988: 262; Solaún, Flinn and Kronus, 1974: 152–3). The intention was to not only persuade people to relinquish peasant political activity, alliances with radical groups, and introspection as a class, but to emphasize the importance of localized apolitical community-based development, thereby stabilizing the centralized state (Zamosc, 1986: 38, 51–2, 195; Bagley and Edel, 1980: 258).

Others noted that the JACs were formed to discourage alliances between the rural populace and "rural left-wing guerrilla movements" (Collier and Collier, 2002: 683, 686). The state's hope was that JACs would undermine "the degree of loyalty which the campesinos of some regions continued to hold toward certain former guerrilla leaders" (Dix, 1967: 378). Bruce M. Bagley and Matthew Edel (1980: 261–2) revealed that where "ideological revolutionary groups had some roots among the peasantry" JACs, the state, NGOs, and private corporate interests quickly arrived to gain "central control by bringing peasants groups into closer contact with national agencies. This tactic, accompanied by military and police action in most cases, succeeded in gradually reducing the organizational and ideological coherence of the radical peasant groups."

JACs and capitalist economic development

Action boards took on an "important role in government plans to stimulate economic development" (Collier and Collier, 2002: 686). If revolutionary movements could be weakened, the state was free to broaden rural-based projects for capital expansion. One of the most readily implemented activities was the building of schools. JACs became an active partner in infrastructure related to the construction of rural schools. The end of the 1960s saw roughly 1,000 built through their assistance (Bagley and Edel, 1980: 264). Ironically, this was not done with the intention of escalating rural education, but to stimulate monetary growth outside the urban-industrial sector.[11] In reality, rural education was discouraged as the state refused to establish services past the primary level, a practice that remains largely present to this day (Marsh, 1983: 63–4; Jallade, 1974: 33; see also Gutiérrez Sanín, 2008: 6, 12; Dávalos, 2001: 72). The rural school system was grossly deficient in its formal structure and teacher qualifications (Adams, 1968: 89, 92–3). As years passed, it became clear the state had little aspiration of reforming the rural education system or the insufficient services therein (Williamson, 1965: 37). Throughout the 1960s and 1970s "only 10.8 percent of the [rural] population had had five or more years of schooling" (Saunders et al, 1978: 100; Adams and Havens, 1966: 213). During the 1960s, literacy rates exceeding a grade five level were 10 percent while 37 percent of all people above 15 years of age were unable to read at all (Gunther, 1966: 432). By the 1970s, the numbers had barely improved, with 85 percent of rural-based children being unable to obtain any formal education at even the primary level, while 94 percent of homes had only one-third of their children enrolled (Jallade, 1974: 32).

> Over three-quarters of the rural schools offer only two years of education, and only 15 percent of those enrolling in the rural first grades can expect to enter the third grade in a rural area .... Only three percent of those entering rural primary education later register in the fifth and final grade of primary school in rural areas.
>
> (Adams, 1968: 89)

The state cared little for rural education but rather sought to stimulate economic expansion (while making Bogotá appear to be an active supporter of the peasantry). Failing to offer education at secondary or post-secondary levels, the young migrated from the countryside en masse (Jallade, 1974: 33). Of those who remained, almost 100 percent were denied the ability to obtain any formal education past the age of nine (Shultz, 1970: 15). Ironically, at a time of proposed rural prosperity and development – specifically through the construction of schools – young people wanting to obtain an education were forced to leave the very areas the JAC "helped" (see Shultz, 1970: 14-18, Jallade, 1974: 32n.1).

Not necessarily intentionally, certain non-government organizations (NGOs) that worked with action boards patronized what little education was given to the rural population. For example, accounts showed how indigenous peoples, who have cultivated agro-based crops for millennia, were seen as rationally unable to comprehend how to "grow vegetables" (see Sumwalt, 1974: 34; Reichel-Dolmatoff, 1965: 52). Demonstrating their supposed lack of cultural understanding, these US-based NGOs "taught" them how to properly nurture crops in the Colombian countryside. We can recognize the state's intentions concerning rural education through such practices. The "students" did not receive any applicable education, nor was it within a formal education facility. Certain documents suggest that rural infrastructure was unavailable or non-existent amidst the "development" construction boom (Sumwalt, 1974: 36). Rather, the state-supported foreign NGOs pushed rural producers to better conduct manual labor, an already all-too-familiar activity. Dale W. Adams (1968: 94–6) argued that what was truly needed was a developmental program that encouraged a model of higher education and domestic training of localized production. Adams (1968: 91) opposed Colombia's development programs as a platform organized and carried out by persons completely disassociated from the realities of rural life and the social relations of production there. One of the reasons was that the Colombian state, with the support of Washington, did not offer any educational facilities or opportunities to people in the countryside (Marsh, 1983: 193; Jallade, 1974: 33; Adams, 1968: 89, 92–3). In short, JACs (alongside the state, associated foreign development agencies, and/or NGOs) assisted capital development and not a change in inequitable rural-based social relations.[12]

The politicization of JACs

While excluded from formal politics, JACs did enable large numbers of small producers, landless peasants, and rural workers to increase their understanding of functions related to local governance.[13] In pursuit of financial support from Bogotá, those from the countryside became acquainted with managing finances and lobbying. Apart from the state, JACs also developed relations with industry. In Arauca, for instance, action boards:

> became one of the main mechanisms for BP's [British Petroleum's] relationship with the communities. In addition, the idea that oil would bring new developments to communities and that BP was willing to help with social projects led a number of communities to organise their own community development associations. These associations also became involved in protests about the impact of oil on their environment.
>
> (Pearce, 2007: 239–40)

Such conditions "led the community boards to see themselves as local semi-governments able to represent their communities in matters outside the search for project grants" (Bagley and Edel, 1980: 265). This empowered the once-pacified JACs to become pseudo-autonomous political organizations. "Though in many ways effective, these organizations ... began to escape from central government control and various local JACs began to form regional organizations to increase their ability to pressure the government" (Collier and Collier, 2002: 696–7). In turn, some JACs sought reformist measures to better satisfy the wants and needs of their community, while distancing themselves from centralized state control and the promotion of capitalist expansion via development agencies.

Nearing the end of the 1960s and early 1970s certain JACs began to work alongside rural federations and unions at municipal and regional levels. This unification of interests antagonized the state and increased the influential power of the community action boards (Bagley and Edel, 1980: 265). Southern-based JACs particularly rallied around issues of land and were becoming radicalized (Pearce, 1990a: 149). Several carried out actions against local state representatives who had supported elite interests over the peasantry, small producers, and the landless. Throughout Caquetá, Cundinamarca, Nariño, and Putumayo, JACs were demanding land, credit, irrigation, and various social services (Zamosc, 1986: 45–6).

> A large number of community action boards had presented government agencies with petitions for land redistribution, complaints about government services, demands for transportation services, and had made other grievances known. In 1966, three-quarters of the juntas had experience with petitioning for matching funds, and slightly over one-third had presented petitions or demands on other matters.
>
> (Bagley and Edel, 1980: 265)

While some reforms were carried out as early as 1962 due to such demands, radicalized JACs began to obstruct the state in their communities (Bagley and Edel, 1980: 266). JACs in Tolima attacked "public officials who favored large landowners over small farmers in the distribution of services," while letter and telegram campaigns concerning land reform flooded Cauca (Bagley and Edel, 1980: 265). As the National Front restricted oppositional party viewpoints from entering the conventional governing sphere, the more radicalized JACs formed their own local governments, imitating what had been done during the 1920s and early 1960s through the PCC (Osterling, 1989: 296; Henderson, 1985: 318n.38; Gott, 1970: 231–2; Alexander, 1973: 46; 1957: 252; Hobsbawm, 1963: 17).

After witnessing the politicization of these JACs, the state grew concerned about destabilizing scenarios in various sectors of the country (Berry and Solaún, 1980: 448). Those in Bogotá feared the action boards "were in danger of escaping from central influence," and therefore "had to be brought back under control" (Bagley and Edel, 1980: 266). To rein them in, the state implemented clientelist policies, which saw JACs that supported official state policies being pleasantly rewarded with financial assistance, and those that wavered experiencing a withdrawal of monetary support (Bagley and Edel, 1980: 266, 269; see also Collier and Collier, 2002: 687). Additional restrictions were implemented through Decree 2263 (1966). This permitted the state to appoint representatives directly to JACs as a means to divide "the community action movement by creating new organizations to compete with or replace" the growing unity within (Bagley and Edel, 1980: 267).[14] The administration of Misael Pastrana Borrero (1970–74) even tried blackmail to depoliticize the JACs (Bagley and Edel, 1980: 269). Those seen as too political (that is, radical) were charged with violating government policy and denied state support.

While some JACs became radical, many wished to remain neutral. As time went on, however, the realities of state apathy led to more moving outside Liberal and Conservative party structures (Berry and Solaún, 1980: 439; Richardson, 1970: 44–5). In one study, 52 percent of those surveyed felt that state-based JACs "benefited few or none" of the rural populace (Henderson, 1985: 232).[15] As government financial support wavered, action boards were forced to find funding within their impoverished communities (through for example horse races, fiestas, or dances) (Richardson, 1970: 44–5). Though noble, such efforts proved unsustainable because of the local socioeconomic conditions. Exploiting this problem, rural elites offered to fulfill this need for capital, thereby establishing themselves as the primary financers of local projects. By the 1970s, non-politicized JACs were associated less with small and landless peasants and more with the propertied class (Bagley and Edel, 1980: 262; Richardson, 1970: 44). These JACs saw "substantial participation by politicians, who used their special legislative allocations ('parliamentary assistance') to assist projects" (Palacios, 2006: 185). Once again the elite became the decision makers.

For centuries, state absence, repression and fiscal insecurity led to rural disarray and political unrest. After decades of clientelist politics, and after

Law 14 (1958) had failed to change the rural political economy for the better, it became customary for JACs to become even more radical. "As time passed, *campesinos* became skeptical that much would come of Accíon Comunal programs, and a majority came to view them cynically as proof that the government wanted to save money at their expense" (Henderson, 1985: 232). From below, JACs engaged civic protests and rejected political convention by the mid-1980s (Pearce, 1990a: 161). On the one hand, "under the impact of rapid urbanization, regional inequalities, and lack of state provision, the Juntas began to lose their legitimacy, along with the traditional parties" (Pearce, 1990a: 149). On the other, certain JACs radically reformatted their structure to one of revolutionary alliances with the FARC-EP.

The shift to revolutionary alliances

On the surface, state-induced community action boards "intended to encourage community participation and self-help projects to improve local services, uniting communities across class lines" (see Pearce, 1990a: 149). Structurally, they were mechanisms to *renounce* the peasantry as a class (Zamosc, 1986: 38, 52). Leon Zamosc (1986: 195) claimed JACs had two principal functions: "they provided a channel for the expression of the peasants' needs and they created vertical lines of submission that ... subordinated the peasantry to the executive agencies of the state." To achieve these methods peasants had to be disengaged from material class relations, "by vertically integrating all sectors of the population around 'shared community concerns,' Accíon Comunal was opposed in principal to horizontal class associations" (Zamosc, 1986: 38).

> The committees of Accíon Comunal were based upon the principle of vertical integration of the different rural sectors, and since they reproduced local patterns of clientelist domination, they could not be used to promote the demands of the peasantry as a class .... The committees of Accíon Comunal were able to obtain tangible improvements for the peasants, at the price of reinforcing vertical "communitarian" channels that abolished the horizontal bases of class association and strengthened the power of the *gamonales* and local political clientelism.
>
> (Zamosc, 1986: 51–2, 195)

Colombian history has shown that rural populations are susceptible to organizing around political and socioeconomic class interests (LeGrand, 1986; Gilhodés, 1970). The countryside houses a unique mix of ingenuity, motivation, and solidarity toward community-based development (Payne, 1968: 308). That the state recognized this aptitude for progressive peasant mobilization arguably explains why it established so many JACs over the past half-century. One explanation for why action boards grew so exorbitantly was that they met the state's need to quell rural protest. By the 1970s and 1980s, JACs were strategically placed in areas where peasant activism was most concerted, moving beyond grievance to radicalism (Pearce, 1990a: 127). "The state gave priority to the promotion of Acción Comunal in those regions in which the peasant movement had been stronger and more radical: The number of Acción Comunal committees doubled between 1966 and 1979 throughout the country" (Zamosc, 1986: 195).

For decades the state sought to restrict the FARC-EP by periodically offering charity (Gomez, 1972: 251). When peaceful methods proved unsuccessful in procuring hegemony, the state "turned to threats and repression. The consequence was the continued failure of rural opposition movements and a growing perception, especially among the landless peasants, that the only alternative was to join the guerrilla" (Collier and Collier, 2002: 685; see also Lemus, Stanton and Walsh, 2005: 102; Marsh, 1983; 204–5).

> Despite the efforts made by the government to win over the people in these peripheral zones, the latter are continuing to give strong support to their fellow peasants in the guerrilla units. The correct policy pursued [by] the revolutionary movement has borne fruit.
>
> (Gomez, 1972: 253)

Rather than abandoning the gains achieved through JACs many ideologically joined the FARC-EP and sustained the very structures once created to pacify them (see Richani, 2002a: 80). As clientelism and repression increased, the state and JACs collided over issues of rural politics and development. The 1980s and 1990s saw altercations become common as select JACs allied with the guerrillas in class struggle against the state (Collier and Collier, 2002: 687; Marsh, 1983: 205).

> When the government's and peasants' interests diverged, the government tended to rein in the newly created groups. However, by constraining these organizations, the government created new groups of angry, cynical peasants who were, as a consequence, more likely to support the very guerrilla groups that these organizations were originally intended to combat.
>
> (Collier and Collier, 2002: 687)

Historically, JACs were "successful in limiting the impact of the left insurgent movements, even though they could not end the conditions that gave rise to

Table 7.1 Growth of state-supported Juntas Acción de Comunal (JACs) since 1958

Time period	Number of JACs
1960s	9,000
1970s	8,000
1980s	32,000
1990s	45,600

Sources: Palacios, 2006: 185; Safford and Palacios, 2003: 327; Pearce, 1990a: 149; Bagley and Edel,1980: 263; INCORA, 1971. In 1966 roughly 4,500 JACs were functional (Bagley and Edel, 1980: 263). By 1974 allegiances between many JACs and the elite declined (see Henderson, 1985: 232).

the guerrillas in the first place" (Collier and Collier, 2002: 687). Yet in time alliances would be formed with the guerrillas as a means of responding to socioeconomic and political conditions. Having few alternatives, these JACs adopted a position of revolutionary struggle alongside the FARC-EP (Molano, 2005: 186–7).

> The objective, once again, would be to force government authorities and private individuals to recognize the political power of the rural sector, and to elicit from them a reaction that will bring concrete benefits – better services, more credit, higher wages, more input in development planning, etc. – to Caquetá's poor, rural population. In the case that such peaceful pressures do not lead to positive change or, in fact, provoke more repression and neglect, it would be folly, in light of Caquetá's current political instability, to deny the inevitability of increased political participation, possibly leading to wider local support for the guerrilla campaigns.
>
> (Marsh, 1983: 204–5)

By the late 1970s and early 1980s, JACs were far from docile or apolitical. Coalitions formed between the insurgency and many JACs as the state lacked the capacity to influence change (see Röhl, 2004: 3; Marsh, 1983). During an interview with one JAC representative from Valle del Cauca, the importance of this partnership became clear. The community leader provided an account of how the FARC-EP and the JACs work together to create emancipatory conditions, not through neo-clientelist relations but by way of class consciousness.

> While my view may not be what you want to hear it is my personal belief that the FARC should not provide social services at this stage in the struggle. It is not their responsibility to offer, provide, or distribute social services for they are not the state. If some fronts decide or choose to provide such services this may cause some peoples within certain communities to become apolitically reliant on the guerrillas to provide social services. It may also restrict people in some communities from coming to a political place of understanding or supporting the struggle and the need for revolution in this country because some are receiving services without comprehending that the state [in Bogotá] has failed to support them. The most important service that the FARC provides is their support for the struggle of the people through the defense of our rights and needs for change. It is through our Accíon Comunal that the services are to be provided and through the FARC-EP that our communities can exist to do so.

While it cannot be thought that all JACs are revolutionary, it is demonstrated that some are working hand-in-hand with the FARC-EP, establishing localized rules of conduct and security while engaging in class-based taxation models where capital is handed over to revolutionized action boards for organic infrastructure projects such as the construction of healthcare facilities, schools, and education centers (Leech, 2006b; Ampuero and Brittain, 2005: 370; Richani,

2002a: 70–1). Contrary to arguments that the FARC-EP retains collected monies, the guerrilla organization has:

> crafted its state-making project by helping in channeling funds to public works. The guerrillas have two main sources of funds: private companies such as multinational corporations, national companies, and public enterprises; and state resources devoted to municipalities. Most of these moneys end up in investments in public projects such as vocational schools, road paving, public health, and environmental protection. The taxation mechanisms of FARC, developed and enhanced in the 1990s, are complex because they involve intermediaries such as neighborhood councils (Juntas Accíon Communal, JAC).
>
> (Richani, 2002a: 80)

As previously noted, the FARC-EP acquires levies which are given to JACs for needed localized development and cultural advancement, not top-down programs as incepted and carried out through NGOs or development agencies. It cannot be said that the insurgency hoards collected revenues, nor does it decide how the funds are to be disbursed to the community. Rather, taxes are gathered by the FARC-EP and passed on to the JAC, where "an elected committee from the locality decides on disbursement and allocation of the taxes collected" (Richani, 2002a: 70). In many cases it is not even the guerrillas who negotiate the tax system, as JACs have taken on a greater role in negotiating agreements with local companies or MNCs (Richani, 2002a: 80–1).

This highlights the revolutionary evolution of JACs from mediums of centralized state manipulation to revolutionary organizations aligned with the FARC-EP. Members of the insurgency have even been invited to run for certain positions in community action boards: some have won, some lost (Richani, 2002a: 89). Again, this demonstrates the interrelation that has been formed between the FARC-EP and some JACs, a relationship where the guerrillas are not using their power as a tool to coerce a counter-hegemony, but trying to legitimize power from below. JACs have demonstrated, how, when linked with the guerrillas, rural class consciousness has the potential to transform a society. In short, this provides yet another example of how the FARC-EP is organizing pre-revolutionary models to potentially construct a socialist Colombia. However, why is such information largely hidden from the public? We now address this question by considering the role of censorship through the popular media.

THE MEDIA'S STRUCTURAL SILENCING OF COLOMBIA'S REVOLUTION

Although it is labeled "the most dangerous international terrorist group based in this hemisphere" and a threat to US national security, there is ironically little known about the FARC-EP's operations, activities, or ideology (see Ashcroft, 2002; Randall, 2001; Taylor, 2001; US Department of State, 2001; White

House, 1986). Outside claims of being involved in state-targeted violence and pseudo-relations with the drug economy, minimal understanding exists of what the insurgency is doing in the jungles and mountains of Colombia. Much of what is related is suspect because of the centralized ownership of Colombia's media and its reliance on state-based sources (Murillo and Avirama, 2004: 160–9; see also Emersberger, 2008; Haste, 2007). The state and monopolized media outlets have over-reported certain aspects of the FARC-EP revolutionary project and greatly under-reported others, if they are addressed at all. This is not to say that some mediums neglect important information: rather, most reports are structurally skewed, inaccurate, or manufactured.[16]

Structural state-supported media censorship in Colombia dates back to the 1950s through Decree 3000 (1954), which legalized control over critical media operators (Estep, 1969: 62; Martz, 1962: 198). The past decade, however, witnessed a more specific filtering of what is released to the public, factual or otherwise. In the mid-1990s, social justice advocate Father Javier Giraldo (1996: 22–3) argued that Colombia's media owners had come to rely exclusively on the government or armed forces for information related to sociopolitical issues, especially surrounding the civil war. As time went on it was argued that journalists increasingly became "hyper dependent on official [state] sources, which ... resulted in an increasingly distorted coverage of the conflict" (Leech, 2005b). Alfredo Molano noted this centralization of information by describing how the military refuses to:

> allow journalists to enter the combat zones. This kind of control leaves the public essentially blind, and no one knows what happens in these areas. There is a very tight control over information in Colombia, and it gets tighter every day. Ninety, maybe one hundred percent of the news about the conflict or about public order in general are literally produced by the army. So one never completely knows what is going on.
>
> (quoted in Feder, 2004)

Such practices not only censor the reality within but they subsequently misinform peripheral media outlets which unknowingly reproduce the "findings" (Giraldo, 1996: 23).

Repression of public thought and critical media commentaries continued in Colombia, but experienced a significant rise under the Uribe administration (Brittain, 2006e; 2006f; Feder, 2006; 2004; Coghlan, 2004: 13).

> That the reality of the country's conflict is rarely reflected in the mainstream media is largely due to the way journalists operate in Colombia. Foreign reporters mostly cover the country's civil conflict from the safety of the capital Bogotá, rarely venturing into dangerous rural zones except on press junkets organized by the Colombian military or the US embassy .... The mainstream media often echoes official claims that the FARC has lost its ideological motivation and are simply terrorists – a convenient label that has been added since 9/11 to the equally useful

moniker narco-guerrillas. While it is true that the FARC has utilized strategies such as kidnapping and reckless bombings that have alienated sectors of Colombian society, the rebels still retain widespread support in rural areas that have long been under their control. Most media reports and government statements claim that Uribe's high approval ratings are evidence that he has widespread public support and that the FARC's low ratings illustrate the rebel group's marginalization. But these reports often fail to point out the flawed methodology used in the polls. Virtually every opinion poll taken in Colombia is conducted by telephone with some 500 people in the country's four largest cities: Bogotá, Medellín, Cali and Barranquilla. Logically, the likely respondents are members of Colombia's middle and upper classes who support Uribe, despise the guerrillas and constitute about 30 per cent of the population. The results are thus clearly not derived from a random sampling of the Colombian population: most urban shantytown dwellers do not have phones. Indeed, the methodology used tellingly illustrates that the opinions of the rural poor still don't count for much ... the rebels do possess significantly more backing than that acknowledged by the opinion polls, government officials and the mainstream media.

(Leech, 2005b)

In short, the state restricted disparaging reports from being released to the domestic and international public by threat of coercion. More than a simple opponent of a free press, Uribe's administration openly suppressed any who criticized its power.

Uribe is also pushing for tighter control of the Colombian media by seeking to pass laws which censor reporting on Colombian "counter terrorism measures" and Colombian military activity. One of the "anti-terrorism" bills seeks to hand down sentences of eight to twelve years in prison for anyone who publishes statistics considered "counterproductive to the fight against terrorism", as well as the possible "suspension" of the media outlet in question. These sanctions will apply to anybody who divulges "reports that could hamper the effective implementation of military and police operations, endanger the lives of public forces personnel or private individuals", or commits other acts that undermine public order, "while boosting the position or image of the enemy" .... The media censorship laws also mean that the reporting of human rights abuses will be harder.

(Stokes, 2005: 108–9)

When referring to the Uribe government, Eberto Díaz Montes and Juan Efrain Mendiza[17] (2006) claimed that "the prevailing regime in Colombia violates all the fundamental rights of the citizens, especially when they are left-of-centre." They argued that the voices of those inside the media (and society) are increasingly allowed to only transmit ideas parallel to those of the elite. If they publish another perception they are immediately exposed to persecution. Within this context, Garry Leech (2005b) suggested the dominant classes' hegemonic presence has forced journalists to self-censor findings because of fear of political reaction or occupational reprimand.

Broadening the scope to include Washington, it becomes clear that there exists a campaign to filter information related to the civil war and especially the FARC-EP.

> An intense disinformation campaign organized by the U.S. government is being propagated by all the corporate media .... The media distort the situation [in] Colombia .... Whenever there is an incident, they immediately blame the rebels. They become the judge and jury with a single mouse click, long before any evidence has been gathered.
>
> (Gutierrez, 2003: 50)

Adding to this scenario, Stan Goff (2003: 81) asserted that the guerrillas are demonized through:

> an active, energetic, and highly sophisticated collaboration of the corporate media. Through innuendo, lie, and repetition, they can create an overwhelming impression about the reasons for various U.S. foreign policies. As a result, grotesque distortions like 'narco-guerrillas' ... are taken by most people in the United States almost as articles of religious faith.
>
> (Goff, 2003: 81)

In September 2005, Maria Anastasia O'Grady, from the *Wall Street Journal*, recounted a story of a FARC-EP attack on the small hamlet of Santo Domingo, Arauca in 1998. O'Grady (2005: 17) wrote how the FARC-EP booby-trapped a truck, meant for state forces, but the bomb went off prematurely, resulting in the death of 17 local civilians. In the ironically titled article ("Seeking the truth about a massacre in a Colombian hamlet"), O'Grady published how the FARC-EP forced community members to testify the killings were the result of an air force bombardment. Two weeks after O'Grady's article was released, Luis Alberto Galvis Mujica, a survivor from Santo Domingo, forwarded a letter condemning O'Grady's falsified account of what happened on December 13, 1998 and the *Wall Street Journal* for publishing such disinformation. Galvis Mujica clarified how the attack on his community was undoubtedly (in the fact that he saw it carried out) conducted by state and paramilitary forces, not the FARC-EP (Galvis Mujica and Kovalik, 2005). The article exposed the propaganda disseminated by the centralized media in Colombia and the United States.

Some journalists, however, fearlessly continue to work. Their diligence has found various examples of "FARC-EP attacks" that never occurred. To the contrary, they exposed paramilitaries and state forces conducting bombings and blaming them on the FARC-EP (Leech, 2008a; Al-Jazeera, 2006; International Herald Tribune, 2006; Prensa Latina, 2006b; Vieira, 2006c; Pravda, 2005).

An investigation by journalists revealed that the Colombian Army had planted car bombs to accuse FARC of a terror campaign in Bogotá to scare people, build support for the Army and against FARC. It turned out these bombs were not planted by FARC, it was all a frame-up by the Army. One of the bombs actually exploded and killed one civilian and wounded 26 soldiers. The commander of the army went out and said that the bombs had been planted by the Army. The details appeared in the print media, and they involved the purchase of false witnesses and false confessions. The use of money to get witnesses and confessions is part of the perverse politics of rewards for information .... Part of 'Democratic Security' is paying people for information and it has led directly to arbitrary detention and false accusation. And inside the army it's created a career for finding "positives" – "positive" evidence of guerrilla activity that, in many cases, turn out to be "montajes" [to frame]. This craziness for finding "positives" is a product of the president's own pressure on the armed forces .... So "Montajes" starts with the information from the investigation of the Bogotá bomb plot. But then we showed other montajes in recent history, like the case of Cajamarca. There, a family was killed and the president called it an "accident" of the army. The president effectively made himself the judge to absolve the army. He went on television immediately after the massacre, during prime time, and spoke for half an hour, to explain how it was a mistake made by the army. The truth is that those soldiers had never made a mistake – they planned the killings in detail, including who was going to kill who. It was a young campesino family, including a baby and parents in their twenties. It was a murder, a homicide, an assassination. And when the truth came out, a year later, this news weren't worth 3 minutes of commercial television on the air. After a year of profusion of lies, we were treated to a fragmented 3 minutes of truth. This is how the media prevents memory. So we showed the elements of the truth of the case of Cajamarca, the case of the recent "montajes", and we showed how the President justified both.

(Morris, 2006)

Rifle de cuadre was another tactic found regularly used. Here state and paramilitary forces would murder civilians and subsequently dress them in guerrilla fatigues, making it appear as though they were defeated in battle (Isacson, 2006a; Vivanco and Sánchez-Moreno, 2006; Aceveda, 2005; BBC, 2005; United Nations, 2005; Glenn, 2003: 71; Holmes, 2003: 91; Scott, 2003: 78; NACLA, 2000: 42). A two-way strategy, it presented an image of state efficiency in fighting the FARC-EP and intimidated insurgent supporters, as they wondered who would be targeted next. Other accounts documented the planting of evidence to make the FARC-EP appear to be involved in illicit activity (Hardy, 2004; Scott, 2003: 92n.19). It has also emerged that paramilitaries and petty criminals have pretended to be guerrillas to gain intelligence on, or loot, rural communities, thus blame is placed on the FARC-EP (Molano, 2005: 134; Taussig, 2004b: 140–1).

This offers a seldom-presented critique of how the FARC-EP has been deemed to be terrorists rather than revolutionaries. Now let us counter this manufactured image by highlighting the guerrillas' project of radical social change.

THE FARC-EP'S RELATION TO REVOLUTION

A revolution cannot simply entail political change, as this would leave inequitable social relations of continued exploitation. Nor can a revolution be purely social, for it might allow the political construct that made allowances for elite interests to persist (see Draper, 1978a: 180–1). Contrary to reformist measures, that have long suggested social change can occur without deconstructing the capital system, it has been shown that the only way to emancipate a society is through a "radical reconstruction" (Engels, 1990b: 59). As political revolutions have time and again proven insufficient, it must be understood that to take state power alone "leaves the pillars of the house standing" (Marx, 1975b: 184; see also Avineri, 1968: 193–4). In this reasoning a full and sustained revolution has to encompass various facets (Marx, 1975b: 184; 1975c: 205–6). The social, cultural, and political are not autonomously affected by capital but are systematically manipulated through its interrelated process. Liberation from one, without addressing those remaining, negates full emancipation. Hence, any momentary relief from a single sphere of exploitation translates into increased repression in those areas left untouched. For this reason, we now examine the FARC-EP's interconnected approach toward revolution and its effects.

HOW THE FARC-EP HAS AFFECTED SOCIAL CONDITIONS

One of the aims of the FARC-EP's revolution has been to distort capitalist relations through the betterment of social conditions. One area where this can be seen is education. As Colombia's dominant class excludes the poor from a formal education, the FARC-EP attempts to create a platform from which those marginalized can learn, critically think, and broaden their social positioning through rational endeavors. Marx and Engels (1976c: 502, 505) argued that education must be not only provided to all, but rescued from the ruling class through revolutionary action (see also Marx, 1996b: 367–8). Therefore, as the state disenfranchises logic, the insurgency must instill it. True societal transformation, however, cannot exist by feeding the mind while the body remains malnourished. Health and the environment are then other areas of focus for the insurgency.

Education

According to Tom Bottomore, "a high level of general education is a *precondition* for the social transformation which will create a socialist society" (1973: 31, italics added). Hence, a revolutionary movement may choose to amend immediate objective conditions of exploitation and construct a pre-revolutionary subjective platform onto which a new mode of thinking can be constructed (see Marx, 1976a: 5; Marx and Engels, 1976a: 8). Change therefore arises not from material shifts alone but from immaterial ones as well (Marx, 1987c: 263–4; Marx and Engels, 1976b: 23, 59–61; 1976c: 503). Marx (1987a: 91) demonstrated that such conditions could occur amidst the realties of capitalism (see also McLellan, 1971: 141–3). In times of socioeconomic and/or political turbulence the bourgeoisie "supplies the proletariat with its own elements of political and general education, in other words, it furnishes the proletariat with weapons for fighting the bourgeoisie" (Marx and Engels, 1976c: 493).

As noted in the discussion on Colombia's media, the dominant class controls the means of information for the purpose of maintaining socioeconomic and political conditions. However, if a revolutionary body was able to "alter the character of that intervention, and ... rescue education from the influence of the ruling class" then such mediums could release an emancipatory message (see Marx and Engels, 1976b: 23; 1976c: 502). Hence, movements like the FARC-EP can become "engaged in the construction of" a "new revolutionary subjectivity" (Petras and Veltmeyer, 2001: 91).

Upon visiting areas controlled by the FARC-EP I observed educational facilities in both public spaces and guerrilla camps that loosely resembled small makeshift schoolhouses. The encampment schools were plastered with pictures of Che Guevara and past comandantes of the FARC-EP, and were referred to as "cultural centers." They were heavily used and resembled a jungle-like revolutionary museum; filled with pamphlets, books, music, and information related to Marxism, Colombia's political economy, and Latin American society. The centers were also outfitted with a public television and a stereo/radio. Apart from these existed public civilian education centers, which were in many ways similar to the "cultural centers" in their simple construction. They remained civilian-based and all teaching materials were removed after each lesson. These centers were built in semi-open areas where a small portion of land had been cleared and an oversized-camouflage tarp/brush acted as a roof (they were essentially small huts or shacks that housed no more than 50 people). While the overall structure of the building matched that of the "cultural centers" (benches, a blackboard, some FARC-EP publications, and so on), electronic goods were seldom provided as electricity is often unavailable.[18] Males and females, of various ethnicities and ages, attended classes. Depending on the time, classes differed in ratio of gender and age. Afternoons saw more women and youths whereas early evenings witnessed teenagers, equal proportions of men and women, and adults ranging from their 20s to 50s.

The civilian educational facilities could be best described as "community guerrilla centers." Within these public spaces, courses were offered in a wide variety of subjects, and varied in level of difficulty. While the buildings were primitive in structure, the educational material provided was not, ranging from basic math skills to complex social and political debates. During the sessions, students were occasionally subdivided into groups based on their education levels. Some groups worked on the alphabet and letter recognition, number identification, and elementary writing skills. More developed groups had classes in advanced politics, economics, and history. Though concepts and names such as Marx and Lenin did arise at both levels, they were far more prevalent during these upper-level lessons. Such findings support those of Colombian journalist Jorge Enrique Botero (2006), who noted that the FARC-EP not only teaches people to read, it has done so by utilizing the works of Marx (see also Vieira, 2006b). It could be argued that this style of education is selective in that the material has an obvious political slant. It may even be seen as Stalinist in its subtle indoctrinating educational bias. Acknowledging the potential for such criticisms, the centers demonstrated a shared cooperation between the community and the FARC-EP. Rather than rigid programming, they are more empirically (and theoretically) faithful to a Gramscian model of counter-hegemony through their unified approach toward revolutionary upheaval. With the FARC-EP creating conditions for people to read and write, an opening is nevertheless provided to the localized populace to expand their own individual and collective intellectual endeavors, subsequently enabling people to make their own informed decisions. In light of this, topics such as imperialism, agrarian reform, political economy, wages, class structure, and hegemony were regularly used during upper-level sessions.

In each rural area visited there was, at a minimum, one "community guerrilla center" providing some form of educational service. The instructors were both FARC-EP members and civilians from surrounding villages. At two different centers civilian instructors discussed how they had traveled to various areas to discuss crop substitution and how to decrease weeds through organic cultivation practices, reducing economic and environmental costs related to pesticides. This was highly important for it showed the guerrillas were not dominating the educational format, and that civilians, who may not have been politically active in the past, had come to work alongside the insurgency. Nevertheless, the funds to facilitate these educational networks are collected through the FARC-EP's class-based taxation model.[19] This enables the insurgency to "provide social services that would otherwise be lacking in the regions they command" (Felbab-Brown, 2005: 110; see also Molano, 2005: 32). Underling all this is the fact that the "community guerrilla centers" have created grassroots cross-regional alliances for educational advancement.

In much of the countryside, however, peasants live alongside waterways or in remote regions. As a result, services like "community guerrilla centers" are relatively worthless because people cannot access them. The FARC-EP, recognizing this, constructed small campaign groups of 10 to 12 guerrillas who are sent out to try to assist these far-off families, who otherwise have minimal access to education, knowledge of what is happening throughout the country, or of the guerrillas' intentions (Millar, 2003; Pothecary, 2001). This enables those living in secluded peripheries to also benefit from programs offered by the guerrillas. One young woman from such a location noted that the FARC-EP was her only link to an education when she was growing up.

The guerrillas were good people, not rude or bad-mannered. Sometimes they'd stop by the house and chat or teach the kids songs: 'Long live Viotá the Red, long live the Revolution ...' was one we all knew without having any idea where Viotá was or what a revolution was. The guerrillas taught me how to read and write.

(quoted in Molano, 2005: 179)

The reality of such work is far from safe; state and paramilitary forces have destroyed numerous community guerrilla centers, causing temporary loss of access to education. I saw one center that had been bombed and subsequently torched by members of the AUC, who left graffiti threatening all those who participate in activities with the FARC-EP. Such conditions have led the guerrillas to include armed defensive cadres to accommodate those who volunteer to educate the rural populace. Such groups do not sit in on the classes but rather clandestinely surround the exterior of the center, acting as a security force during the lessons (see FARC-EP, 2001b: 14).

As noted, the FARC-EP also provides educational services to its members. Combatants, many of whom received little if any (formal) education prior to membership, are provided with the opportunity to develop mentally (Gutiér-rez Sanín, 2008). Apart from courses on subjects relating to history, math, science, and political economy, coupled with full access to library facilities and classroom lectures, the guerrillas continue to experience schooling outside the camps. During treks through the countryside, members may utilize a small chalkboard and begin to give "mini-lessons in math, science, English ... perform plays and write poetry ... geometry by playing billiards with them and explained physics by kicking around a soccer ball" (Dudley, 2004: 62; see also Wickham-Crowley, 1992: 139). In some cases, the guerrillas have even begun to support combatants to attend universities throughout Colombia (Van Dongen, 2004). This is paid for by the insurgency, and enables those with academic promise to leave the mountains and theoretically develop their ideas in the country's most prestigious institutions (Ortiz, 2006; Easterbrook, 2003). Support and recruitment has also risen from students already attending post-secondary education institutions (Fuerza Aérea Colombiana, 2006). These conditions offer a reply to those that suggest the FARC-EP employs a Stalinist method of manipulating intellectual endeavors. The university system has no direct relation to the insurgency. Post-secondary institutions create their own course curriculum; hence a clandestine guerrilla attending a university has the capacity to retain and adopt any form of thinking. If it were Stalinist, the FARC-EP would never allow this, as it would potentially facilitate modes of thought other than the revolutionary.

The FARC-EP's presence in universities has become so significant that the state has established a specific wing of the Department of Administrative Security (*Departamento Administrativo de Seguridad*, DAS) whose exclusive purpose is to gain intelligence on campuses. In 2007, Cecilia María Vélez White, Colombia's then minister of education, stated that the state must "watch those students who might be recruited by rebels after the army reported that fighters are infiltrating the country's higher education centers." She then suggested that universities and the state must start working together "to follow up on students and their professional futures to prevent them joining guerrilla groups ... This is why we will insist on a campaign that strengthens young people's social values" (as quoted in Xinhua, 2007). By the mid-2000s, it was estimated that the FARC-EP had members at about ten universities, 30 percent of whom were in the capital (Easterbrook, 2003). Román D. Ortiz (2006: 212) argued that this expansion has been related to the insurgency's emphasis "on improving the education and training of its militants."

> In fact, the substantial investments made by the guerrilla organization for the training of its members enabled innovative activities in two ways. On one hand, it expanded the base of technicians available to the group as it increased the number of militants with the education necessary to work on the development of different innovations. On the other hand, this allowed the dissemination of new techniques throughout the structure of the organization ... the organization has invested a substantial amount of resources toward sending some of its members to universities throughout the country, so that the organization may benefit from their knowledge after they complete their studies. For this purpose, training centers have been established to provide lengthy training programs in which FARC has invested substantial human and material resources. In fact, it is not unusual to see the development of three-month courses, attended by dozens of guerrillas removed from their usual duties in order to receive training.
>
> (Ortiz, 2006: 212)

It has been suggested that after their schooling, insurgents return to the countryside and teach at both the cultural centers and the community guerrilla centers.[20]

Apart from these endeavors the FARC-EP has been open to sponsoring dozens of forums with academics, scientists, and civilians to discuss crop substitution, peace, agrarian rights, and international humanitarian law (FARC-EP, 2000d; 2000a: 5–6). Supporting academic autonomy, it has allowed international and domestic scholars, journalists, and researchers to evaluate its activities and – unlike the state – express perceptions, either critical or promotional, of the insurgency's outcomes, positions, and beliefs (Dudley, 2004: 173, 179–80; Bergquist, Peñaranda and Sánchez, 2003: 214–23; Kirk, 2003: 215; FARC-EP, 2001–02: 17).

Health

Alongside the creation of education centers, the guerrillas have shaped grassroots medical facilities (Ahmad, 2006: 62–4; see also Botero, 2006; Felbab-Brown, 2005: 110; Molano, 1992: 214). While ideology is important in helping progress a political goal, a revolution in thought cannot cure the physical ills of a population. In distinct locations, the FARC-EP has, directly and indirectly, provided modest medical provisions to those in the countryside and urban *barrios*.

Anyone traveling throughout Colombia's countryside has witnessed the state's coercive presence. Manual spot-checks have become a common occurrence, as have the confiscation of medical material from civilians and the prevention of such supplies from getting to the rural populace. As state and paramilitary forces increasingly block roadways to the countryside, the availability of provisions greatly decreases (Brittain, 2006c; Weekly News Update on the Americas, 2005a; 2004a; 2004b). In other cases, once community guerrilla micro-medical centers are created they are quickly destroyed by reactionary elements connected to the state. Even so, the FARC-EP has had a credible record of facilitating treatment to tens of thousands of destitute Colombians. In one survey alone, 68 percent of those interviewed stated they had been the recipients of "health services offered" by the FARC-EP (Buscaglia and Ratliff, 2001: 9). Using its own resources the FARC-EP has acquired supplies and promoted preventive measures of health care in regions under its control (Leech, 2002d; 2000a; 2000b). In the stability of the demilitarized zone of San Vicente del Caguán, Caquetá, the guerrillas instituted a vaccination campaign where over 20,000 children and adults received free medical attention (FARC-EP, 2001a: 12). The rationale was that precautionary treatment is more efficient than responsive care, which is expensive and difficult to implement.

Medical and dental services have been provided by the FARC-EP directly or through allies. This has been possible due to an increased number of trained professionals (that is, doctors, dentists, nurses, and so on) working in solidarity with the FARC-EP (see also Taussig, 2004b: 140; Villalón, 2004a: 53; Galvis, 2000: 120–2). I witnessed both services being offered to local civilians in certain zones. While dental care was less common, many residents said they had received some form of medical assistance in the past six to twelve months. In exceptional cases, some had obtained visits on a weekly basis. It was said that those providing services were certified doctors and nurses; however, it was hard to be sure whether they were in fact professionals who had become FARC-EP members, or were civilians supporting the guerrillas through their labor power.

When someone is ill, remedial treatment is offered at no cost. I experienced this at first hand when I became severely ill in the jungle. Bedridden for the better part of two days, I was visited and diagnosed to have a virus by one of the FARC-EP doctors. Within a half hour, a traditional treatment of warm liquids, melted sugars, and diluted teas was prescribed. When the violent vomiting and diarrhea failed to subside after two hours, a FARC-EP nurse came to me and candidly asked me to turn around and drop my pants. She then proceeded to give me a small injection. Within 15 minutes, to my utter amazement, the violent outbreak was under control.

Prostitution has become a vivid reality in rural Colombia. The guerrillas have established agreements with doctors to conduct free weekly physical checks for those involved in the sex trade. After each examination, physicians provide healthy sex workers with "formal passes" to continue their occupation for another seven days (Villalón, 2004a: 46). Those who have contracted a virus or transmittable disease are provided with treatment, when available, at no expense. This practice stems from a campaign implemented by the FARC-EP between 1998 and 2002, where HIV-testing facilities were set up in several municipalities across the southwest. The centers offered free examinations to all community members, so the guerrillas and community could create open lines of communication for the betterment of the overall population, and control the spread of the illness. Surprisingly, some deemed this a negative step.

While not outlawing prostitution, the FARC-EP prohibits pimps. With a devastated rural political economy, the insurgency understands that some women may believe that few options are available to them to make a living. In recognition of this, they argue that if a woman must sell her body as a commodity in order to support herself and/or her family, it is the woman herself who is entitled to all monies paid for her services. A pimp is seen as a pseudo-capitalist merchant who profits from the efforts of another without employing their own labor power in the process. However, this, and the medical checkups for the prostitutes, were seen by Amnesty International (2004) as a violation of human rights in the assumption that the guerrillas were acting as "the guardians of a traditional form of sexual morality associated with the idea of order." Such claims are interesting for they illustrate the individualized bias of certain NGOs and human rights groups who fail to understand the reality of Colombia's political economy or even try to comprehend collective benefit and social justice through revolutionary means. Garry Teeple argued that:

> organizations, such as Human Rights Watch and Amnesty International, assume an apparently unassailable moral high ground as critics of injustice ... however much they may draw attention to some violations. They remain supporters of the prevailing property relations of a particular social formation; their self-defined mandates obscure the meaning and significance of social rights, not to mention the rights of women, children, Aboriginal, and marginal peoples, and the rights necessary to protect the environment. Similarly, they cloud the reasons as to why, in certain instances, subordinated classes and peoples are forced to take up arms to defend themselves against corporate or state repression.
>
> (Teeple, 2005: 6–7)

In areas where such measures were taken, local residents stated to me that disallowing pimps and having the health centers available allowed the FARC-EP and community to coordinate democratic structures for the betterment of the community as a whole.

Through the support of domestic and international medical technicians and organizations, the FARC-EP has brought healthcare services to other parts of the country (Galvis, 2000: 120–2). For example, it has increased medical aid in some of the most impoverished *barrios* of Colombia's largest cities (People's Daily, 2006b). This was revealed when the DAS invaded a FARC-EP Bogotá-based health clinic equipped with various medicines, remedies, and supplies, located in a laboratory filled with surgery equipment. At the time of the incursion, over 22 people were being treated in the clinic (14 bedded patients and eight persons being treated for various illnesses). Only six of the 22 were members of the FARC-EP, while the others were civilians needing assistance (People's Daily, 2006b).

Infrastructure

With a landmass equaling that of France, Portugal, and Spain combined, compounded by the enormity of the Andes, Colombia's geography is very inhospitable to travel.[21] Against such huge odds, the FARC-EP has inventively established infrastructure in some of the country's most remote regions (Buscaglia and Ratliff, 2001: 22). Here the guerrillas have worked alongside local populations to generate projects to benefit the countryside. In Meta,

> over the past 50 years, with no support from the national government, the local peasant population has carved a network of primitive dirt roads throughout the rainforest that are only traversable in four-wheel-drive vehicles. They have constructed electrical grids powered by gasoline generators for their villages and small towns. And it is the FARC that has become their government, providing such public services as security, social aid and a justice system among other things.
>
> (Leech, 2006b)

For decades, the FARC-EP has provided modest installations of electricity, plumbing, and water treatment facilities at local levels (FARC-EP, 2001b: 14; Galvis, 2000: 165; Molano, 1992: 214). During the 1990s and early 2000s, however, infrastructure projects were established on a regional scale. Roadways were constructed and ensured civilians had some access to imports while enabling small and medium-sized producers to export surplus goods with greater ease. Creating a passage for rural-based trade also created avenues for municipalities to communicate. These cross-linkages empowered communities to carry out more efficient ways of expanding and sustaining mutual goals. Apart from roadways there were projects to revitalize rural airspaces throughout controlled territory (see FARC-EP, 2001a: 12). At first, the FARC-EP used the landing strips to better supply the insurgency's material and military needs. In time, however, the guerrillas, in consultation with local civilians, allowed transportation pathways to be used by peasants in order to export and receive goods (at the expense of the insurgency). The FARC-EP even began arranging international trade between small producers and buyers in Canada, Norway, Sweden, and Iran for agricultural products and cattle (see Dudley, 2004: 173).[22]

Transportation-based infrastructure is of significant importance in the countryside. Because of the country's dilapidated secondary and tertiary roadways, the average ratio of distance to time related to rural travel is roughly ten kilometers per hour.[23] Considering this lack of infrastructure, the FARC-EP has cut roads across treacherous terrain while going so far as to pave certain territories (Petras and Veltmeyer, 2001: 142; FARC-EP, 2000–01: 19). For example, the guerrillas coordinated and built over 250 kilometers of new road/highway and repaired another 250 kilometers during the first two years of the demilitarized zone.[24] During this time, San Vicente del Caguán alone saw 64 streets built by the FARC-EP. While some characterized them as poor quality (Young Pelton, 2002), it should be recognized that before 1998, there were fewer than five paved streets throughout the entire municipality (FARC-EP, 2001a: 12). The insurgency also constructed 20 local bridges over rushing waterways for agricultural producers, connecting several communities, villages, and towns (see Molano, 2005: 186; Buscaglia and Ratliff, 2001: 8; Cienfuegos and Cienfuegos, 1999: 21). The past five years have seen gravel roads intersecting major roadways as a measure of support for local needs and preparation for aggressions centered at Bogotá (Webb-Vidal, 2005).

The finances used to build this infrastructure go beyond monies acquired from the class-based taxation model. As a part of its environmental agenda, the insurgency has been involved in studying and carrying out the promotion of local resources. As with any development project, more than mere capital is needed for a venture to come to fruition; therefore, natural resources such as tar, oil, and labor power are necessary. The FARC-EP is then faced with a major problem: how is a clandestine revolutionary movement to procure the investment and resources needed for the construction of rural-based causeways? To respond to this dilemma the insurgency has moved to a socialist model that does not rely on capitalist development via borrowing from international lending institutions (ILIs) or banks.

Under areas of FARC-EP control the insurgency collects information on available natural resources. Communities and insurgents then utilize internal assets instead of going to institutions outside the region for fiscal or social capital. In the case of San Vicente del Caguán all the streets built or repaired were done so using local asphalt, rock, stone, and so on, which eliminated the need for monetary loans or external engineers and construction companies.[25] This also prevented "foreigners" from entering the region and placing the community at risk by revealing civilian alliances with the guerrillas. Through the establishment of these work brigades community members and guerrillas worked together to construct useful infrastructure. In an interview with Alfredo Molano one woman stated how "the guerrillas organized everything" for the people in her town;

> [A] bazaar to raise money for a road, a beauty pageant for a bridge, or a *tejo* tournament to clear a road. When the town's water tank was swept away by the river, it was the community junta that organized people to build another one. There were festivals, and everybody helped out by donating money, a pig to roast, some chickens to eat, or helped making the *sancocho*. Some did more than others, but everybody did something. That was how the town got its water supply back.
>
> (quoted in Molano, 2005: 186)

Such task forces enable both civilians and insurgents to work side by side in the fulfillment of social needs (FARC-EP, 2001a: 12). This is done through the cooperation of local tradespeople, the unemployed, general workers, and skilled guerrillas. Some cooked, several volunteered a truck and driving skills (anyone who has driven in Colombia will know there is a true skill to navigating rural roadways), others shoveled and smoothed out asphalt, children brought firewood or passed out water. Studies outside my own research found that over one-third of all households in areas of guerrilla control participated in these "communal public works coordinated by the FARC" (Buscaglia and Ratliff, 2001: 9). Working with the community, the FARC-EP put in place "work days dedicated to public sanitation," in order to prevent infections and illness through contaminated waterways in rural territories (FARC-EP, 2001a: 12). I observed several latrine projects being implemented in areas where there were none, coupled with an infirmary in case of illness (see also FARC-EP, 2001b: 14; Galvis, 2000: 165). Other infrastructure projects have been proposed, such as an expanded electricity supply, improved schools and medical centers, and a public-initiated campaign to "build a water main since not all houses have running water" (see also Rochlin, 2003: FARC-EP, 2001a: 12; Molano, 1992: 214).[26]

Realizing the degradation of land and water facilities in the countryside, the FARC-EP has given much attention to ecological protection when using local resources. Observing this focus on local labor power and sustainable resources, villages were able to expand cooperation and bypass the need for capital across entire territories (see Cienfuegos and Cienfuegos, 1999: 21). In short, the FARC-EP devised a way to use materials sustainably while satisfying regional needs.

> The FARC-EP has set up a civilian police force and has held many democratic, public forums to discuss and solve the problems of each municipality. In one of these municipalities lies the town of San Vicente, a large and important agricultural centre. Because it was not in the government's interests to look after the farm workers or townsfolk of this area, San Vicente was left to run down. Roads were impassable, the water pumps broke down regularly, the electricity station was extremely unreliable, and there was a horrendous crime rate, homicide being the number one cause of death. Since the FARC-EP took over this municipality, there has not been one homicide, nearly all the roads have been paved, and the electricity and water supplies have been improved. The FARC is also planning a literacy campaign in the area and is demanding that the government build more hospitals and schools in poor country areas .... The townsfolk told us that now the FARC-EP has taken over, the people sleep with their doors open and can go out at any time during the night without any problems. The landowners say the tax they pay to the FARC-EP is fair since the FARC-EP respects them and protects them from the state-controlled paramilitaries. As well, the landowners' work is made easier by the new roads. The farm workers say that no one in FARC-EP controlled areas starves – the FARC-EP always finds ways to ensure that the hungry get food.
> (Cienfuegos and Cienfuegos, 1999: 21)

Rather than looking at infrastructure from an economic perspective, the FARC-EP has given its attention to first bettering impoverished areas, with the private sector being the last to receive services (FARC-EP, 2001a: 12). In most regions of Colombia business has always been given priority at the expense of the majority. Creating a model of infrastructure from below enables the poor to gain access and associations outside their immediate space, potentially creating more egalitarian social dynamics where emphasis is placed on social need before economic want.

Environment

One of the civil war's dichotomies has been the structural attack on the environment. Counter-narcotic aerial and manual fumigation of peasant and indigenous crops has devastated the country's natural flora and fauna while poisoning animal populations and water systems, only to further drive producers to the drug industry.[27] In 2003, after these programs proved to cause health and agricultural defects, local officials, with the support of the Supreme Court, "ordered the spraying of chemicals to be halted" in Cundinamarca (O'Shaughnessy and Branford, 2005: 85). In reaction, the Uribe administration argued that the region's ecology had not been negatively affected by fumigation, but rather from chemicals used by peasants in coca production. This was a weak argument in that the "chemicals" used to harvest coca are sun, water, and soil. In addition, the processing of coca poses no major threat to public health as the elements used to produce coca paste (lime, cement, and unleaded gasoline) are regularly utilized in every town, village, or city. Nevertheless, Bogotá argued that "a suspension of spraying will benefit armed outlawed groups, as the drug business provides them with their resources" and "the Uribe government appealed to the Council of State, a federal court with greater powers than the local Cundinamarca court, and won the right to ignore the ruling" (O'Shaughnessy and Branford, 2005: 85).

It has been shown that fumigation programs have little effect on the FARC-EP (Brittain and Sacouman, 2006a; Brittain, 2005e). Hence, the true purpose of fumigation is to further destabilize the poor and prevent them from mobilizing. For example, Cundinamarca has less that 0.01 percent of the total coca cultivated in Colombia, hence spraying this department has virtually no effect on the drug trade (UNODC, 2005: 15). Why then is this department targeted? The answer lies in the fact that Cundinamarca has become an important department for alternative educational and farming centers that assist displaced peasant, indigenous, and Afro-Colombian families, coordinated by rural-based labor organizations (Brittain and Sacouman, 2008c; Brittain, 2006c). The state's attack on the environment, and those trying to eke out a living, is in the hopes of deconstructing alternatives to dominant class interests.

In Putumayo a state-led development initiative was established in the 1990s. The plan was created to evaluate the problems of this largely rural department, which is home to the Amazon rainforest and, for four decades, the FARC-EP (Taussig, 2004b: 132; see also OAS, Government of Colombia, and

Government of Ecuador, 1995: 2). Mirroring the Cundinamarca case, the stated "strategies, components, goals, and objectives" did not, however, seek betterment for Putumayo's population, but laid the blame for the region's problems on them (OAS, Government of Colombia, and Government of Ecuador, 1995: 4–8). According to state officials the region's ecological ruin was not the result of exploitation or over-use in the pursuit of profits, but rather caused by the poor: landless farmers, small producers, displaced populations, and suffering indigenous communities. Environmental breakdown was the result of poorly developed farming methods and a failure to properly rationalize the consequences of deforestation through increased rural colonization (see Villalón, 2004a; 2004b).

> Studies show that the region is facing serious problems caused by rapid rates of growth and settlement. This, coupled with the fragile ecosystems and the inappropriate use of resources, is seriously altering the natural environment. Resource degradation combined with inefficient production techniques is having a major impact on the functioning of natural systems.
> (OAS, Government of Colombia, and Government of Ecuador, 1995: 1)

These examples demonstrate the state's dismissal of the conditions faced by those in the countryside. They also ignore the fact that most environmental problems are connected to corporate natural resource extraction (Leech, 2005a). In turn, thousands have been forced to flee the regions suffering political economy and state-supported coercion, and in turn the struggle for social change (Bajak, 2007; Brittain, 2006d; Lyderson, 2005; Villalón, 2004a; Richani, 2002a).

Critiquing the state's so-called ecological regulations, one biologist detailed how "in San Lucas [Bolívar] there are no offices, checkpoints, or delegates from the usual host of governmental environment agencies, e.g., the Ministry of Environment and CorpoSur (local government institution for environmental issues)" (Dávalos, 2001: 73). She went on to add that the state has actually withdrawn development and environmental organizations from various rural territories even though repeated sectors of civil society have documented and presented their concerns about natural resources being mismanaged.[28] Responding to such apathy the FARC-EP has constructed projects to slow the degradation of Colombia's social and natural resources (Leech, 2006b; Felbab-Brown, 2005: 105; O'Shaughnessy and Branford, 2005: 87; Taussig, 2004a: 142–3, 304–5; Villalón, 2004: 49; McNeely, 2003: 142, 148; Satchell, 1999: 41).

The guerrillas have an intimate connection with the Amazon that dates back to the 1970s. Over this time the insurgency has witnessed environmental degradation as a result of corporate exploitation in the quest for profit maximization (see Cassidy, 2005; Leech, 2004a; 2004c). Chief scientist at the World Conservation Union (IUCN), Jeffrey A. McNeely (2003: 148), has written about the FARC-EP's militant conservation practices targeting imperial and domestic capitalist interests. This "gunpoint conservation" has ensured "forest conservation *from* drug cultivation and cattle ranching in areas beyond the rule of law and/or contested by armed groups" (McNeely, 2003: 148, italics added; see also Richani, 2002a; Villalón, 2004a). Under the claim of sustainability the guerrillas have promoted a "discourse of sovereignty over biodiversity" where resources belong to the local populace, not foreign or national elites (McNeely, 2003: 148; see also FARC-EP, 2000a). For example, JACs and the guerrillas have created agreements disallowing the large-scale monetary trade of lumber in the Amazon. While members of the local population (residents, artisans, and so on) are free to use "fell trees to build a home and furniture," anyone found violating such rules are "heavily fined and the money turned over to the community" (Taussig, 2004b: 142).

Outside the Amazon the FARC-EP has taken measures to ensure ecological protection. In these regions Michael Satchell (1999: 41) noted the FARC-EP "has long struggled against illegal fishing, unsustainable hunting and logging, and destruction of endangered species. The rebels have closed some of the national parks they control, but they have allowed park rangers and researchers to go about their business unmolested." In Meta the insurgency excluded "almost all agriculture from the southern half of the Macarena region, ostensibly to preserve the wealth and beauty of the forest for future generations" (McNeely, 2003: 148). As one peasant farmer said, "if you simply start cutting down trees to plant more crops, the FARC will fine you. We must obtain permission from the guerrillas before we can cut down the rainforest" (Leech, 2006b). These extreme methods have supported the rejuvenation of regions once under extensive corporate and elite control. "Their protection can be very effective. During the 1997 El Niño droughts, [large landholding] farmers seeking to expand their landholdings burned the lowlands of the Munchique National Park [Cauca], until the FARC threatened to kill the arsonists; the fires quickly stopped" (McNeely, 2003: 148).[29]

Apart from securing reforestation projects, the guerrillas have restricted overfishing on depleted stocks in certain areas; "as a conservation measure, the guerrilla have enforced a moratorium on all shrimp fishing in the estuary of the Timbiquí [Cauca] during February and March," with severe consequences for violators (Taussig, 2004b: 142–3). Not limited to Cauca, the insurgency has established similar policies on various forms of aqua-flora and fauna, fish and water reserves, as well as reforestation projects in regions adversely affected by MNCs and domestic lumber-based capitalists (FARC-EP, 2001a: 12; Satchell, 1999: 41). In 2006, a Colombian biologist told me that this has allowed resources and animals to re-enter and/or rejuvenate in certain regions as they are protected. The only way that this can occur is through established and sustained working relationships with the FARC-EP, environmentalists, researchers, scientists and local residents familiar with local ecology.

In the absence of governmental environmental programs, the guerrillas have bridged this administrative gap with their own set of environmental policies instated in the last decade, as San Lucas attracted larger numbers of colonizers and miners. An environmental group – Groupo Ecológico – operates in Monterrey under the auspices of FARC guerrilla authorities.

They have successfully forbidden hunting and logging in the immediate surroundings of the Eastern lowland villages of Santo Domingo, San Luis and Pozo Azul, compiled information about captive animals in the vicinity (such as the above mentioned Tremarctos ornatus), and plan on setting up a zoo for the local community. The FARC also kept a close watch on the access routes throughout the lowlands and collect taxes in the processed cocaine passing through the roads.

(Dávalos, 2001: 74)

Some environmentalists have suggested that the FARC-EP, while radical, is not a primary threat to the environment or local populace. On the contrary, by cooperating with peasants the FARC-EP has erected policies to reduce production costs while maintaining environmental standards (Richani, 2002a: 99). "Far more damaging are the paramilitaries, essentially mercenaries for cattle ranching and narcotics trafficking interests; once they have cleared regions of guerrillas, they consolidate the landholdings and clear forests for cattle ranching or coca cultivation" (McNeely, 2003: 148; see also Crowe, 2006). Paramilitaries and large landholders have been heavily involved in deforestation and displacement (Díaz Montes, 2005; Lydersen, 2005; McNeely, 2003: 148). On paper:

twenty-three Afro-Colombian communities in the northwestern Chocó region had a total of 123,000 hectares of land (about 393,940 acres) seized by the government in 1997, displacing 7,800 people, to make room for the planting of African palm, the source of highly exported palm oil.

(Cassidy, 2005)[30]

This "displacement has been caused in large part by paramilitaries paid by rich African oil palm growers, intent on expanding their holdings and increasing their production for world markets" (Escobar, 2004: 19). During the 1990s, the paramilitaries acquired lands through threat of force. A great deal of these lands were "turned into an African palm plantation run by the company Urapalma and its subsidiaries," the subsidiaries being the AUC (Lyderson, 2005).[31] Responsible for 95 percent of the Afro-Colombian producers murdered, state and paramilitary forces coercively forced the former owners to:

sell their land at below-market prices under threats from paramilitary members. Then ... Urapalma declared title to 30,000 hectares and planted 8,000 hectares with African palms. To facilitate the palm plantation, they deforested much of the land and drained its rivers and wetlands with a system of canals .... The palm farms are a major way for paramilitaries to launder money from narco-trafficking ... four million hectares of land have been acquired in this way and used for mono-industries like cacao and palm that are ecologically destructive and used for narco money laundering.

(Lydersen, 2005)[32]

The FARC-EP is arguably the only mechanism that can and has the capacity to conserve rural wildlife and biodiversity (McNeely, 2003: 148). It has proven its ability to keep "timber mafias from destroying forests and colonists from settling in fragile regions" (see Satchell, 1999: 41). Therefore, small producers and peasants have expressed hope that the guerrillas can do the same in relation to the palm industry. Both civilians and the guerrillas, however, informed me the only realistic way to continue this process and prevent environmental destruction is through defensive measures.

The FARC-EP program of conservation, to help sustain the environment amidst the confines of civil war and extreme natural resource extraction, is intensely militant (Coghlan, 2004: 207–8). As one environmentalist noted while working with the guerrillas, "villagers or colonists who get caught fishing, hunting, or logging illegally usually get a warning ... second time, they get fined and a really stern warning. Third time, they get shot" (Satchell, 1999: 41; see also Molano, 2005: 90; Coughlin, 2004: 207; Taussig, 2004a: 142–3; Villalón, 2004a: 49; Pearce, 1990a: 173). This is not to suggest that the guerrillas target civilians. On the contrary, locals are insulated from the very real dangers of the FARC-EP's stringent environmental policies (see McNeely, 2003: 148). Rather, violators are dealt with harshly. Placing this in the perspective of war, McNeely (2003: 142) argued that in order to sustain and protect the "biodiversity-rich tropical forests ... peace can be even worse, as it enables forest exploitation to operate with impunity." While not pleasing to some, reality demonstrates that if the FARC-EP refused to maintain strong-arm tactics then capitalist expansion would most assuredly further degrade the regional environment. Although it is extreme, without the FARC-EP's conservational praxis Colombia's biodiversity would be open to "full-blown, large-scale unplanned exploitation in areas that are now off-limits" (McNeely, 2003: 148).

HOW THE FARC-EP HAS AFFECTED CULTURE

Spending time amongst the FARC-EP I noted that the average day for insurgents begins around 4:00 am. Everyone awakes at this time and starts the day by eliminating any trace of their existence from the previous evening. This is followed by a communal breakfast at 6:00 am proceeded by the first educational class of the day, commencing at 8:00 am (see also FARC-EP, 2001b: 14). Depending on the front, after morning tasks have been completed a division of labor is established and daily assignments are given out: patrolling (and possible combat), community outreach, additional classes in literacy training, reading skills, and for more academically mature members readings in Marxism-Leninism, economics, and history (see also FARC-EP, 2001b: 14-15; Wickham-Crowley, 1992: 139). After routine or appointed activities are completed all return to their encampment for an evening meal, followed by additional classes where one or a few members prepare further educational lectures for their comrades (see also Braun, 2003: 56). Every day begins within a collective context and ends in the same way.

I outline this to show that the FARC-EP is more than an armed force tramping through the jungle; rather it is a movement acting beyond purely militarist functions. It also has some egalitarian features: the organization is trying to establish an active equity based on shared experience, not gender pre-speculation, exclusion, or bias. To paraphrase one *guerrillera*, "since the dynamics of poverty, social exclusion, and violence affect all rural Colombians equally as a class, women and men join the FARC-EP to combat this exploitation through a spirit of collective action."

While little is known about the FARC-EP, substantially less is known about the lifestyle and culture of those in the guerrilla organization. Marulanda once stated:

> it's been many years now that we've been in this struggle. We've had, I think, one enemy, the worst of all enemies. You know what it is? I'm talking about the isolation of this struggle, which is worse than going hungry for a whole week. Between you, you of the city and us, we who've been out here, there is a huge mountain. It's not a distance of lands and rivers, of natural obstacles. Your voices and ours don't speak to each other. There is little about us that is known among you.
>
> (quoted in Alape, 1989: 19)

The guerrilla culture must be analyzed, or we would ignore one of the most important aspects of the revolutionary struggle; the immaterial and material context of those involved.

Capitalism's reach moves well beyond politics and economics to include the sphere of culture (Sacouman, 1999: 125). In response, a "dual position" must develop where an alternative culture creatively develops alongside existing class structures (see Jay, 1984: 165; Gramsci, 1971: 169–70). Enter the FARC-EP, which, "in the face of the globalization of capitalism," has assisted in the creation of a new "citizenry that creates its own culture and aspires to its own hegemony" (FARC-EP, 2002a: 24). During gatherings I attended, many guerrillas commented on the need for a new ethos in Colombia that does not resurrect an imagined past but moves beyond the manipulated and increasingly marginalized conditions of the present. With an emphasis on art, music, and theatre, they demonstrated how a socialist culture could provide progressive shifts in gender equality, indigenous rights, and the defense of existing domestic and regional cultural forms from imperial degeneration. There follow some examples.

Guerrilla culture

The FARC-EP is an entrenched feature of Colombia's identity (Ortiz, 2002: 130-136, FARC-EP, 2000b: 14–15; Pearce, 1990a: 283). More than an enigma, the guerrillas have become a part of the national narrative (Petras, 1968: 334). As they cohabit with, work with, and come from the marginalized populations, so too does a newfound human and social connection arise between guerrillas and non-guerrillas.[33]

> "National" revolutionary movements have a strong cultural basis. The culture of the colonized has a quality lacking in underclass class culture: a sense of community and individual identity that can, under certain circumstances, give rise to radical class consciousness and pride, the formulation of assertive ideologies, and action for change.
>
> (Johnson, 1972: 289)

The FARC-EP has asserted that the country's problems must be dealt with and resolved by the Colombian people themselves (FARC-EP, 2000b: 2). External actors have repeatedly inhibited peaceful resolutions to the civil war or alternative development (Avilés, 2006; Felbab-Brown, 2005; Murillo and Avirama, 2004; Leech, 2002a). Therefore, a positive outcome for Colombia is seen as possible only through domestic shifts in objective and subjective conditions. With the FARC-EP's goal being to consolidate state power, the insurgency's immediate intention is to organize and consolidate dual power – local, regional, and national (Röhl, 2004: 3–4). This will only be possible if it has a membership from varying backgrounds and geographies (see Petras et al, 2005: 118; Petras, 2003: 24–5, 99; Petras and Veltmeyer, 2003a: 178–9; Richani, 2002a: 63; Wickham-Crowley, 1992: 214). Once a member, the life of a guerrilla is ultimately a life of sacrifice for the cause of revolution.

Gender

While changes in the sociopolitical sphere may arise during revolutionary periods, the residue of inequality can remain. Implicit cultural disparities experienced during previous hegemonic structures do not immediately evaporate once state power is achieved or the relations of production become socialized. Though substantive social change may occur at a distal level and radical improvements be experienced at proximal levels, no revolution can be claimed until discrepancies of gender or ethnic inequality are undone. Just as class conditions must be replaced, so too must the subjective chains that restrict full emancipation. According to Gramsci, a person's:

> theoretical consciousness can indeed be historically in opposition to his activity. One might almost say that he has two theoretical consciousnesses (or one contradictory consciousness): one which is implicit in his activity and which in reality unites him with all his fellow-workers in the practical transformation of the real world; and one, superficially explicit or verbal, which he has inherited from the past and uncritically absorbed .... Thus the unity of theory and practice is not just a matter of mechanical fact, but a part of the historical process.
>
> (Gramsci, 1971: 333)

A true revolution will not merely assume political power but will produce a new culture prevented under the capital system. Hence, the liberation of women must co-evolve alongside sociopolitical shifts (Marin, 2004). If women are not a significant part of the revolutionary effort than how can one call the changing face of society a revolution?

> If women are not drawn into public service, into the militia, into political life, if women are not torn out of their stupefying house and kitchen environment, it will be impossible to guarantee real freedom, it will be impossible to build even democracy let alone socialism.
>
> (Lenin, 1964f: 329)

One of the most important areas of analysis concerning the culture of the guerrillas is how the FARC-EP has dealt with *machismo* and gender equity. Approaching the issue from a Marxist perspective, the insurgency contests that gender-based inequality is based on primitive theories of natural insufficiencies or inadequacy (see Engels, 1990a: 129–276; Reed, 1969). It is rather a "sociocultural construction" to maintain the subjugation of women within the "private realm" of economic conditions (FARC-EP, 2000–01: 29). At the level of the community the FARC-EP has long voiced its opposition to the inequitable treatment of women by constructing workshops related to wage equity, informal "second-shift" labor, lack of social benefits, and so on (see FARC-EP, 2001b: 19–20). This is perhaps partly because women have been a significant part of the movement since its inception (Richani, 2002a: 62).[34] Women like Miryam Narváez and Judith Grisales, who fought alongside Marulanda in 1964 and came to form the FARC-EP, have been a cornerstone of the guerrillas (Arenas, 1985: 35; FARC-EP, 2001-2002: 23).[35] According to Olga Lucia Marin (2004), the women in the guerrilla movement were some of the first in Colombia to experience fundamental rights.

As leaders at various levels in the organization, women established guerrilla–civilian hearings on gender issues (Millar, 2003; Alape, 2000: 2–3; Braun, 2003: 277; Leech, 2000b). For example, in the face of extreme threats from reactionary forces, over 800 women from every class, ethnic background, and region of Colombia attended the Public Hearings for Women held in June 2000 (FARC-EP, 2001–02: 22–3). Coordinated by FARC-EP Comandante Maiana Páez in cooperation with Ana Teresa Bernal of the Citizens Initiative for Peace Work, the hearings proved to be a significant breakthrough in two different areas: first, a demonstration of the FARC-EP, once again, working alongside civil society for shared goals of social justice; and second, a demonstration of a Marxist-Leninist organization placing an emphasis on gender egalitarianism (see Sargent, 1981). Other mechanisms used to promote gender issues both within and outside Colombia are local events, conferences, and publications (FARC-EP, 2004b; 2002a: 21–2; 2001a: 11–12; see also Roman, 2000: 12; Leech, 2000b). In addition, the FARC-EP has supported feminist researchers to critique conditions of their encampments, female members, and compare its programs with other Latin American social movements (Gibbs, forthcoming).

Within the insurgency women are treated no differently from their male counterparts. If policy is violated significant penalties are dealt out to offenders (FARC-EP, 2004b). "Equal treatment of men and women with respect to rights and duties is a strictly observed policy within our organization. Anyone who discriminates against women, no matter what the person's rank, is punished according to the Disciplinary Code" (FARC-EP, 2000–01: 29). The FARC-EP has been particularly harsh toward sexual assaults of female civilians. In certain areas, those found guilty of rape are liable to the death penalty (Botero, 2006; Vieira, 2006b). Members from one women's collective told me that their communities, trying to respond to sex-based assaults largely carried out by state and paramilitary forces, support such harsh penalties. They noted how concerned members approached (local Fronts of) the FARC-EP and asked the guerrillas to help them respond to these assaults "with extreme prejudice." While this may appear excessive to some, it is again an example of how the guerrillas are responding to requests from below.

It has been said that "there are a lot of women on the side of the FARC" (Howe, 2004; see also Molano, 2005; Alape, 2000). One woman I interviewed talked of how she regularly interacts with the guerrillas, especially female members, as they share a true interest in her daily needs and activities:

I talk with them all the time. Many of them are friends of mine who I grew up with. They come around quite often to see how I am doing or to ask how my mother and father are or how my children are doing. It is not really that I see them as FARC but rather that they are old friends, or friends of friends, seeing how we are coping .... These are real mothers, they are real daughters, they are real women who have learnt that they can be more than child bearers or sex machines, that they can be more than slaves who clean homes or work in the fields. One woman in the FARC told me that when she joined she learnt how to read and write and now she teaches other men and women in and out of the guerrillas to read and write. This woman, who could not even read, is now a revolutionary who is teaching others who would never have had the opportunity to read or write. The women also seem to have a sense of confidence unlike many women in our and other communities. There are many who are Comandantes ... how many women do you think are leaders of squads in the [Colombian] armed forces? I really believe what friends of mine have told me, that the women in the FARC are not looked upon as women but as comrades, people involved in struggle. If they were looked upon as women, or as many Colombians see women, they would be cooks, camp cleaners, or private comforts [likely referring to a sex-worker]. This is not the case. When you see them in town, the men in the guerrillas treat these women with the most respect. You can also tell when this is not sincere. They are all comrades, they are all friends, and they are all in the struggle together. This cannot be said for many men and women in many parts of the countryside.

Others interviewees revealed how gender equity is greater among the guerrillas than in civil society. A respondent in her 30s explained that she regularly wonders if her plight would be better as a member of the FARC-EP rather than remaining "just a women" in her town.

> I have actually asked myself many times what it would be like to be in the guerrillas, to be treated as a equal and to have a real say in what happens, in not only my life but to have a say in helping the lives of others. The problem though is that I start to think of my children and I do not have the strength to leave them. You do know that many of the men and women in the FARC have had to leave their children with family or friends to do what they are doing. Can you imagine having that type of love for your country that you decide to leave your children so that all children will have a better future than we did? When I think of that love I start to weep. That is the sign of not only a truly loving parent but also the type of people that we need in power [she slowly starts to cry]. These people, who live in jungles, eating whatever they can find, not receiving any salary, do this all in the purpose of creating a better Colombia. They give up everything ... everything for nothing. This is why none of us believe they are terrorists [earlier in the conversation we had talked about the United States and the Colombian state's constant referral to the FARC-EP as terrorists], we know these people, we know what they have given up for us and for those Colombians who have yet to be born.

As moving as the above statement is, it hints that more could be done to alter the discrimination of women who are not members of the guerrillas. One comandante assured me that the insurgency has been trying to address this, especially in remote rural locales. Interviewing one elderly woman showed me how such measures might be working. She recounted how, by empowering women in the insurgency, the FARC-EP indirectly empowered women in her community. Both men and women, through their interactions with women in the FARC-EP, were faced with their own prejudices (and abusive relationships) at home.

> While growing up, I do not really remember hearing much about the 'guerrillas' [uses quotations with her hands]. It was very seldom that one heard any reference to what is now the FARC, but rather we were told that they were bandits that would rape us and take our food, or that they were Communists trying to organize our communities against the government. It was not really until the 1980s that I really remember them being referred to as guerrillas, or maybe it was the 1970s .... Well, I must say that I am always amazed whenever they come to my home or into town at how many women there are. When he was alive, my husband used to talk about them as well. He used to question why so many women were involved in the FARC. You see, the women are very powerful .... I am not saying they are mean but that they are as strong as the men. Like the men, they come and talk to us and have a glass of lemonade and you see that the women seem to be the same as the men. The women in the guerrilla are treated by the

men in the FARC and men from the local towns as equals ... and, actually [begins to chuckle], in some cases the women are the men's superiors. This was always quite unusual for my husband who never saw women as equals. It is not that my husband was a cruel man but he grew up thinking, and being taught, that women could not be equal to a man so when the FARC started coming around regularly, seeing how we were doing, my husband began to see things through a different window. By seeing how women in the guerrillas were equal to the men my husband increasingly came to see me as his equal. Forgive me, but I sometimes talk about my husband more than I should.

Since its inception, the number of women in the FARC-EP has grown consistently. Part of the attraction might be that women wish to leave patriarchal conditions for a revolutionary movement where both genders have equal right to membership and the ability to develop through their own volition (Alape, 2000: 2; see also Wickham-Crowley, 1992: 216; Hodgson, 2000). In the 1960s, the FARC-EP maintained a continual flow of support from women (Marin, 2004). This continued into the 1970s where the number of women involved grew to represent over 20 percent of the total organization (Richani, 2002a: 62). Numbers remained constant throughout the latter part of the decade and into the 1980s. Then, in the 1990s, a dramatic increase in the insurgency brought the proportion of women up to 30 percent (Richani, 2002a: 62). From the beginning of the twenty-first century to the mid-2000s, the number increased from 40 to 45 percent (Galdos, 2004; Marin, 2004; FARC-EP, 2001b: 25). Present figures show women now account for half of all FARC-EP members (Lewis, 2007: A6). According to O'Shaughnessy and Branford (2005: 27), women in the insurgency are explicitly equal to their male counterparts. For example, there are hundreds of female members under the command of female comandantes (Marin, 2004). Francisco Gutiérrez Sanín (2008: 10) found that 30 percent of the Central High Command is comprised of women. The female leaders have had an effect on civilian gender relations, as one woman explained to me:

I cannot remember the first time I saw a female in the guerrilla because I always remember women being in the FARC; however, what surprises me is the number of women. There must be one woman to every man in the group now .... They seem to be equal in every way. They can all read and write, they do not do any more chores than the men do and most important, the men, all men [emphasized], treat them as equals. You see, they are around us a lot; some are the sons and daughters of friends of ours. We watched them grow up and we can see who treats who like what, and I must say they seem to treat each other with respect. Not like a brother and sister but more like a person you work with that is also your friend.

To further illustrate the FARC-EP's attitude to gender equity we can compare the gender dynamics of conventional political and military forms.

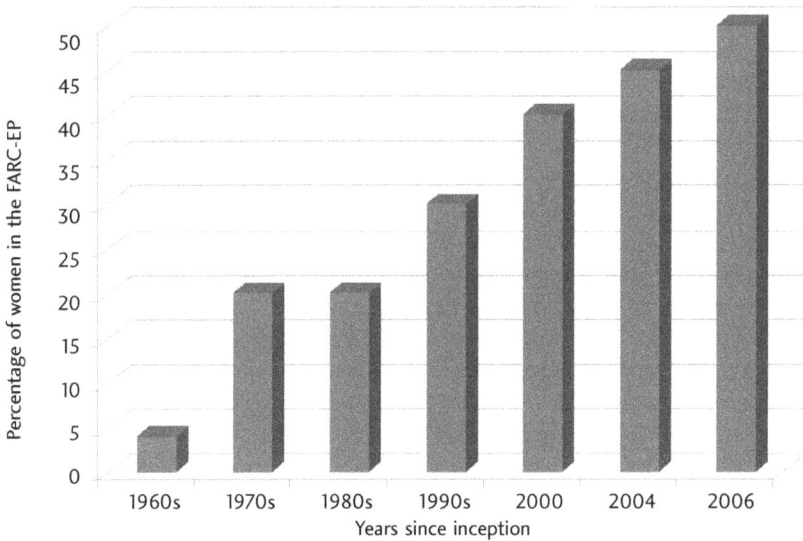

Figure 7.1 The percentage of women in the FARC-EP since 1964
Sources: O'Shaughnessy and Branford, 2005: 27; Marin, 2004; Richani, 2002a: 62; Galdos, 2004; FARC-EP, 2001b: 25.

The percentage of women in the central Colombian government is on average 10 percent, while municipal levels average 5 percent (Cordoba Ruiz, 2002: 3). Looking at the military, only 2 percent of soldiers on average are female while the FARC-EP has a 1:1 sex ratio (Penhaul, 2001: 6).[36] It is equally important that not all members trained in combat hold rifles. Both men and women in the movement share roles as "accountants, cooks, fundraisers, logistics specialists, medical doctors, or recruiters" (Hudson, 2002: 18–19). All this is significant, as some "revolutionary" movements have boasted of their female representation but the women's place in the organization simply reflected conventional roles. They were seen as second-class members, and confined to food production, cooking, cleaning, and other patriarchal duties (see Mies, 1986; Sargent, 1981). This is not the case in the FARC-EP. All members, regardless of gender, share duties – from combat to cleaning. Even civilian women appeared to be well represented in FARC-EP territory. On a number of occasions I found women equaling males at community meetings, guerrilla–civilian open forums, collectives and JACs, and in some cases outnumbering them.

Indigenous relations

A discussion concerning indigenous relations with the FARC-EP is greatly needed. As noted, the guerrillas have incorporated people from all regions of the country into their ranks, including members of Colombia's 84 indigenous groups, to the extent that they make up 12–13 percent of members.[37] Historically, the PCC was in close contact with many indigenous communities. According to Paul Oquist (1980: 92), the groups worked closely together dating as far back as the 1920s and 1930s (see LeGrand, 2003: 175; Osterling, 1989: 185). It was this interrelation that facilitated the foundation of the FARC-EP, and later alliances between the guerrillas and indigenous population. For example, take Charro Negro, alias Jacobo Prías Alape, whose civil name was Charry Rincón (see Hyams, 1974: 168n.2). Not only a member of the Central Committee, Charro Negro was an original founder of Marquetalia and one of the first leaders in the FARC-EP (Gott, 1970: 235–6).

During the 1960s, the guerrillas obtained large-scale support from various indigenous groups in the southwest, specifically Chaparral, Ortega, Natagaima, and Marquetalia (Gilhodés, 1970: 430). Much of this was due to the organizing efforts of Charro Negro. However, in contrast to this historic relationship, coupled with the fact that indigenous people were some of the insurgency's first members, the FARC-EP did not always have good relations with all indigenous groups. In fact, in some areas, the FARC-EP was not welcomed by sectors of the population, leading to periods of turbulence between the FARC-EP and a handful of indigenous peoples.

During the establishment of the self-defense communities, certain tensions arose between some rural communists (and their peasant supporters) and certain members of the Páez tribe.[38] Capitalizing on this, the army strategized a campaign to enhance the frictions by enticing the Páez with economic incentives. It informally enlisted indigenous informers living in or near the self-defense communities who would forward intelligence to the military. In time, this information assisted the historic attack on Marquetalia. Following the offensive on the self-defense communities, the FARC-EP posed several questions. How were these attacks able to take place? From whom was the (poorly[39]) collected intelligence derived? How did it get to the Colombian military? The answers pointed at members of the Páez.

> The army actually recruited informers from FARC regions who had "personal contradictions" with the peasant guerrilla leadership ... the army recruited Páez Indians – who had had conflicts with the "peasant republic's" leaders – to scout and guide for the military in its campaign against Marquetalia. Their role was crucial in the army's taking of the region.
>
> (Wickham-Crowley, 1992: 146)

Both Russell Crandall (2002: 60) and Dennis Rempe (1995: 321) commented how the state used numerous Páez to help flush out the FARC-EP during the 1964 aggressions. Wickham-Crowley (1992: 56) referred to "the cooperation of the Páez Indians" as helping "the government to subdue the peasant republic of Marquetalia." Years after the attack, Jacobo Arenas (1972: 107–8) proclaimed that without this sector of the Páez turning on the guerrillas (and the local peasantry), the state would not only have had extreme difficulty finding Marquetalia, they would have experienced significant causalities as the guerrillas would have been more prepared (see also Kirk, 2003: 54). Yet, while some of the Páez jeopardized the security of those living in the self-defense communities, other indigenous peoples came to the aid of the rebels. Numerous indigenous groups have long supported the PCC, and constructed escape routes in the event of an evacuation of the region. As a result of the cooperative networks that developed between the communists and indigenous people, those within Marquetalia had a venue to flee the bombings (Ruiz, 2001: 110).

Although it is seldom documented, the FARC-EP has long promoted the rights of "native minorities" (Bernard et al, 1973: 316). For the most part, the guerrillas, like the PCC, have coexisted alongside many indigenous communities throughout much of the south, especially Caquetá and Cauca (Findji, 1992: 128). This is likely to be because the guerrillas have supported indigenous self-representation and in no way express an anti-indigenous position (Warren and Jackson, 2002: 82; FARC-EP, 1999: 118–19). It is important to note that issues between the FARC-EP and the Páez[40] were not related to the Páez as a people, but rather derive from political ill will as a result of the lives lost at the hands of the state. Tensions then cannot be seen as ethnic-based but rather class-based.

During the mid-twentieth century the Páez sought to increase their consolidation of land. Some believed eliminating the guerrillas would facilitate this. The Páez have long populated areas of the southwest (Ortiz, 1971: 324–5). However, during the 1930s, the region saw an influx of poor farmers, small producers, and their families, people who would later form the FARC-EP (Sanchez and Meertens, 2001). While there was some good will and trading between the existing and new residents, a proportion of the Páez felt "foreigners" had intruded on their territory. Cooperating with the military, they hoped to expel these *campesinos*, which would make it easier for them to increase their landholdings. As a result of this collaboration, historic tensions – even leading to armed confrontations – between the guerrillas and the Páez took root. However, in 1997, the FARC-EP acknowledged that to facilitate change from below they had to improve their relations with the Páez. The FARC-EP established a series of bipartisan meetings with the Páez, and established a commitment to peace with the indigenous group (Richani, 2002a: 188n.15).[41] Negotiations commenced and an agreement was signed, ending decades of disagreement.

The reality of periodical tensions between the FARC-EP and indigenous groups should not be dismissed; sometimes these have even resulted in deaths, as witnessed in February 2009 when the guerrillas – responding to a request from the indigenous community itself – executed eight Awá members who had been working with the army and established a vigilante group (Vieira, 2009b). In fact, the FARC-EP are responsible for perpetrating a very small percentage of abuse of indigenous groups, yet they appear to be primary culprits because there is such an overemphasis on guerrilla/indigenous confrontations in state and media sources (Leech, 2005a).[42] "According to several displaced Awá," Leech (2006c) said, "it is the army, not the guerrillas, that has threatened them in the past and is primarily responsible for their displacement." It has been shown that the guerrillas have had a lower rate of aggression toward indigenous peoples than state forces, paramilitaries, or criminal gangs (see

Weekly News Update on the Americas, 2005b). Testimonies I collected also contradicted claims that the FARC-EP threaten indigenous communities. When asked about his community's position toward the FARC-EP, one indigenous respondent said:

> the guerrillas have allowed us to continue our way of life so that we, our children, our families, and our village can exist with less fear; however, things were not always like this. Some indigenous communities have had a difficult past with the guerrillas. For many years some persons in certain communities did not want the FARC anywhere near their towns in fear of being caught in the middle of the war. If the government forces, including the paramilitaries, found out guerrillas were near indigenous communities then they would either be found or assumed to be working with or support-ing the guerrillas, making the community a target. Because of this, many communities wanted all its members to separate or not interact with the guerrillas at all.

When asked whether the guerrilla have supported indigenous peoples and whether their community supports the FARC-EP, the same respondent described how the insurgency, over time, adapted its revolutionary strategy to recognize different groups.

> I do not think it is necessarily one or the other but a combination of the two. As you know, some indigenous peoples did not get along with the guerrillas during the middle of the twentieth century for many felt that the guerrillas were too violent or were encroaching upon their traditional lands. However, as the repression of the state became too much to bear, many, especially the young, have come to increasingly align themselves, or join, the FARC as a means of fighting against this violence .... Creating a broad revolutionary force against that which commonly and equally represses all peoples in Colombia; not merely blacks, peasants, or members of indigenous tribes. I am not saying I support all their methods but it is time that we as a people [pointing to me and him] resist repression. We are all affected by this injus-tice; therefore, all must resist in order to build, as they [the guerrilla] say, a new Colombia. This position has taken a long time and some still resist this position but many feel that it is the only answer because the repression is far more violent and ongoing than it was in the past; a violence not only against our people but all those who are not members of the rich.

Rather than taking sides with the guerrillas solely for protection, I have found that a deeper political consciousness has emerged, leading indigenous communities to align with the ideology of the FARC-EP (see also Rizvi, 2006). Researchers have documented how some, seeing no other option but to directly combat state-based reactionism and class repression, are moving away from purely identity/autonomous-based politics to more distal revolutionary movements (Valetta, 2004). The events described by one father from a Wayuu community in La Guajira help to show why this mode of reasoning has come to fruition.

> You can not imagine how it is to have to escape on the run so that they [state and paramilitary forces] won't kill you, and then hear the cries of the kids, of my two little sons who they burned alive without me being able to do anything .... They burned them alive inside my pick-up. Also, they beheaded my mother and cut my nephews to pieces. They didn't shoot them, they tortured them so we would hear their screams, and they cut them up alive with a chainsaw.
>
> (quoted in Valetta, 2004)

Others have documented how some groups have not only aimed their sights against the state but have opted to support the FARC-EP as a consequence of the insurgency's promotion of indigenous rights (coupled by their military capacity to respond to state and paramilitary threats) (Brittain, 2005d; Lobe, 2004). During an interview, a member from one indigenous community acknowledged how people cannot expect change to take place if reformist or non-structural ideas are at the fore.

> Many indigenous communities want to remain or struggle for autonomy but many do not know what this word really means. Many want to be left alone by the state, by the paras, by the guerrilla, etc. but the reality is that once the large landowners or the paras want more land they come into our communities. Mind you, this is not a new phenomenon but one which all indigenous peoples have experienced for centuries. In Colombia, many indigenous communities hoped for the day when their individual clans would be left alone and allowed to exist in and of themselves. The last 20 years have shown us that this is not and will never be the case. While the state may not have bothered us in the past, as long as we do not politically organize, our people are witnessing growing violence against our communities for no reason other than to consolidate more land and resources for the rich in this and other countries. This truth has led to many of the young to support, and even join, the guerrillas to stop this from continuing. This is a good thing ... it has brought an increased understanding of indigenous cultures to the guerrillas. With more and more indigenous peoples joining groups like the FARC, the leadership in these organizations has become more familiar with our history, our culture, and our desire for a new Colombia that respects differing peoples and their ways of life.

When asked, "Do you think this has helped relations between the FARC-EP and differing indigenous groups throughout the country?" he immediately responded; "Undoubtedly! With more indigenous peoples joining the guerrillas a broader sense of Colombia's reality had to come about. There are even elders who now sit and eat with the guerrillas where at one time they would have fled."

Fine arts

The FARC-EP has viewed imperialism as "an overdeveloped and highly effective machine for manipulating the thinking of large sections of the population" (FARC-EP, 2002a: 13). Capitalism has influenced a culture that has, in many ways, facilitated an "apolitical and apathetic" society "submerged in the notions of individualism and consumerism," which fractures unified progressive solutions to inhospitable conditions (FARC-EP, 2002a: 14). To offset this manipulation the FARC-EP have tried to nurture an alternative culture outside foreign and domestic class control. Establishing a cultural alternative to imperialism creates the potential for a more collectively conscious opposition to arise. This section examines said alternatives via art, music, and theater.

Jacobo Arenas promoted culture as being the common bond that will continue to unite the Colombian people after the guns of revolution fall silent (FARC-EP, 2001–02: 30). Amidst a country in conflict the "cultural hour" acts as a mechanism of expression and enjoyment for and of the guerrillas.

> The FARC-EP guerrilleros play, sing, write poetry and books, tell stories, put on plays and paint, etc. The most sensitive men and women, reflecting the reality around us, transform our culture into an orally and visually attractive form, nourishing the patriotic and revolutionary sentiment of thousands of fighters, their friends and thousands of people who today listen to the songs, read books, recite poetry and watch films made by the guerrilleros ... Culture occupies a very large space and plays an important role in the life of each guerrillero in the FARC-EP .... There is a cultural hour from 7 to 8 p.m. in all guerrilla camps, when the public order situation permits. In this hour there may be a book reading, a lecture, the reading of a poem, singing, or a *fiesta* to dance the current rhythms and compositions of the guerrilleros. This is a space created so that culture is present in the struggles of our people.
>
> (FARC-EP, 2000–01: 30–1)

The "hour" however is not exclusive to the insurgency but has expanded to involve civilians in sharing their own revolutionary ideas and creativity (see FARC-EP, 2001b: 14). Organizing community plays, dances, concerts, and art exhibits has created a medium through which the imaginations of the guerrillas and civilian populace can be expressed (FARC-EP, 2001a: 12). Artists, musicians, playwrights, poets, and writers are frequently asked to voice their feelings and share their gifts with others (see Angel, 2002). In the area of music various composers have emerged from the guerrillas who might otherwise never have had the chance to develop their talent: Luke Iguarán, German Martinez, Cristian Perez, Juan Polo, Camilo Germán Vargas, and Los Compañeros: Jaime Bernardo, Jairo Padilla, and Prudencia Arijuna have recorded dozens of albums in traditional musical styles like Vallenato, Porro and Llanera (see Buch Larsen, 2008; FARC-EP, 2001b: 30). The most famous representative of the FARC-EP's promotion of culture through music has been

Julián Conrado, a member of the Central High Command who has written and recorded hundreds of songs related to Colombia's revolutionary struggle.[43] A member of the FARC-EP for almost three decades, Conrado was born in 1954 in the town of Turbaco, Bolivar, and established himself as an influential representative of the guerrillas during the 1998–2002 peace negotiations through his activism and community concerts (Semana, 2008a). Conrado's passionate kind demeanor has promoted this positive alternative culture, leading some to suggest that "the popular and quick-to-smile 'rebel' seemed out of place in Latin America's most brutal civil conflict" (Buch Larsen, 2008).

The FARC-EP has also delved into (multi)media as a tool to disseminate its propaganda. For several years informational films have been produced that depict guerrilla campaigns and victories, to respond to false reports of state-based successes propagated by corporate outlets. Beginning in 2006 a news program entitled *Revista Resistencia* was created and distributed throughout urban areas and rural enclaves via the Bolivarian Movement for a New Colombia (MBNC) and various fronts. It is shown in settings from community halls to individual laptops. A full-length soap opera, *El Mito del Hombre Zorro* (The Myth of the Fox Man), was released in 2007. The film touches on two issues: first, encouraging peace negotiations alongside a prisoner exchange, and second, demonstrating camaraderie and solidarity between combatants. The FARC-EP has also broadened its long-time use of radio. It changed its old format, *Radio Resistencia*, transmitted to and easily obtainable in rural locales in Caquetá and Putumayo on 95.9 fm (see Penhaul, 2000), to a more extensive Bolivarian Chain Radio (*Cadena Radio Bolivariana*, CRB). The CRB or Voice of the Resistance (*Voz de la Resistencia*), can be heard throughout Valle del Cauca, Cauca, Nariño, and some parts of Caquetá and Putumayo by tuning to 106.8 fm.

As preliminary alternative cultural measures are established, a basis for expression is made possible in a country where it is greatly suppressed. The FARC-EP has stated that:

> revolutionary culture is present and is nurtured by the people. It is the expression of rebellion charged with social content that has flourished in spite of everything throughout our history – in spite of the massacres, the bullets and the negation with which they think they can silence the voice of the people.
>
> (FARC-EP, 2002a: 31)

As one member of the Secretariat told me, "to have peace a people must also have an environment to express the joys of peace."

The church

It may seem irrelevant to some to include any discussion of religion when examining a Marxist–Leninist revolutionary movement. The topic did however come up several times when I was interviewing people both within and outside the guerrilla movement. Obtaining information related to the FARC-EP and the (Roman Catholic) church proved to be informative, if nothing else. My research contradicted claims that the guerrillas are anti-religious or violently opposed to the church, and provided an interesting view of those still practicing their faith amidst the civil war.

A few years ago, corporate and state media reported news of a tape on which Mono Jojoy (Jorge Briceño), a member of the FARC-EP's Secretariat, discussed the need for the FARC-EP to target and execute priests throughout the countryside (United Press International, 2005). This claim alarmed many in a country where 90 percent of the population is Roman Catholic. Doubts about the tape's credibility soon arose, for several reasons. The guerrillas have long encouraged their members to support all "priests sensitive to the cruel arrogance of the powerful" (FARC-EP, 2000b: 14–15). The FARC-EP has also partnered with congregations to construct churches in the countryside, especially during the 1998–2002 peace negotiations (see Otis, 2004).[44] Since 2002, sectors of the church have fought for peace talks between the FARC-EP and state. My own research found several cases of FARC-EP members who were once priests but left the institution to struggle alongside the people in a more direct manner, or remained priests keeping their alliances with the insurgency quiet (see Wickham-Crowley, 1992: 214). Former secretary-general of Colombia's Catholic Bishops Conference, Monsignor Fabian Marulanda Lopez, even questioned the authenticity of the reports demonizing Mono Jojoy. He argued that the tape "should be analyzed because it's not understood why that group would go after those who are trying to reach them to discuss peace."[45]

One person I interviewed was a young man who had recently stopped studying to become a priest. Once stationed in a rural part of one southern department, he vehemently contested all notions that the FARC-EP target members of the church in the countryside. On the contrary, he noted that many guerrillas are quite religious, and some continue to practice their faith even though they are Marxist-Leninists. When asked if he could "talk about the relationship between the guerrillas and the Church in the rural regions" and clarify his position on whether "the FARC-EP are quite repressive toward the religiosity," he said,

> I am always interested in claims of how the guerrillas are in opposition to the church because it demonstrates one of two things: one, how much control there is over information, and two, how little people understand about the guerrillas. I do not really want to talk about the media and how it is controlled by a small few in this country; however, I would like to answer your question concerning this important relationship. As you know, many people in Colombia have a deep devotion to their faith. One can travel throughout the country and see people that are steeped in their affection toward the church, which is practiced by the majority of people in the cities and in the countryside. In understanding this one has to then ask where do the guerrillas come from? Who are the people who have formed the FARC? In answering this question one must then follow with another question, "If the guerrillas come from our towns, villages, cities, which are steeped in the

teachings of Christ, then why would the guerrillas not be made up of many Catholics?" What I mean is, just because one joins the FARC or that those involved are communists does not mean that they abandon their faith. On the contrary, some are members as a result of their faith .... I remember one instance when we were asked to baptize children and new-born babies in one town, which included FARC members located throughout the region. I had met, or more accurately crossed paths, with members of the guerrillas many times, but this was my first time seeing how large and faith-filled many who belonged to the guerrillas were. While I know some no longer follow the church in their beliefs, it was astounding to see the loyalty, solidarity, and love that they all bestowed for their fellow comrades in attending the holy sacrament. The church where we held the baptisms was bursting at the seams with literally hundreds of townspeoples and guerrillas, side by side, having their children brought into the church. That day will always remain with me as a true statement of the unity that exists between many civilians and the insurgency, and the hope that the FARC are doing what they are doing for the right reasons.

When asked to expand on the above, the former would-be priest quietly looked out into the countryside and peacefully said,

The teachings of Christ and the Apostles are interpreted in various ways, which greatly depend on what part of the world one comes from. In the North, many see the Church as teaching tolerance, acceptance, and to carry the burdens of life in the image of Christ so as to benefit in the life thereafter. This was an important way of teaching Christ, especially considering the development of capitalism in that part of the world, the trade of African slaves, and the treatment of blacks during the nineteenth and twentieth centuries in the United States. This interpretation creates a relationship that is individualistic. In the South, especially in Central and South America, many people have internalized the Church not as an institution but as a relationship with others. The Church is not a building per se but our brothers and sisters, our neighbors and friends, the people that surround our lives. If we are to live like Christ, if we are to be true Christians, than it is our community that must come first, it is the person who has the least amongst us that is important, and as long as they suffer, so do we all. When we look at Christ, he was constantly battling the authorities and was always with the most impoverished. I am not saying that I condone all their actions, but this is important to understand. Some revolutionaries see this as being their struggle, a struggle to work with and fight for the most repressed peoples as Father Camilo[46] did.

HOW THE FARC-EP HAS AFFECTED POLITICS

We cannot think of the revolutionary struggle in Colombia as existing inside a political system that abides by conventional democratic forms (Goodwin, 2003:

139). "While officially a democracy, the Colombian state is part of a protection racket that employs violence against the excluded to maintain supremacy
of the oligarchic structures" (Schulte-Bockholt, 2006: 105). Some have even
classified the country as a "bureaucratic authoritarian state" (Munck, 1984a:
358).[47] Colombian political scientist Jaime Zuluaga Nieto (2007: 117) argued
that, at best, Colombia is nothing more than a "precarious democracy", "one
with permanent recourse to a state of siege, suspension of fundamental free-
doms, criminalization of social protest and political opposition, militarization
of the official response to social conflicts, and the overall authority of military
officers rather than civilians over 'public order'."[48]

For such reasons, Colombia "should not be regarded as a democracy,
but rather as a civilian dictatorship because of the rampant violence
wrought by army-backed paramilitary groups" (Lilia Solano Ramírez as
quoted in Bond, 2006: 1). Looking upon this reality Arturo Escobar (2004:
16) concluded that Colombia suffers from "selective inclusion and hyper-
exclusion – of heightened poverty for the many and skyrocketing wealth for
the few – operating through spatial-military logics" which creates "a situation of widespread social fascism." Those who would promote Colombia's
political system as functional or legitimate refuse to acknowledge that it
structurally negates the vast majority of the population (see also Mészáros,
2006: 41; Goodwin, 2003: 138). It should then come as no surprise when
people move to a position of support for, or even formal membership of,
the FARC-EP. Even the president of Venezuela, Hugo Chávez (1998–), has
weighed in on this controversial issue by asserting that Colombia's politick
is not a democratic arrangement but rather a pact, which purposely strait-
jackets any transformation of the country's socioeconomic and governing
system (see Harnecker, 2005: 32, 42).

Such a system of elite control is not new or the fault of one specific
administration, but rather the by-product of entrenched class relations
(Cherry, 2002: 55; see also Alejandro and Billon, 1999; Kline, 1988a).
While numerous attempts have been made to alter these conditions, here
is some evidence of how those showing even the most non-threatening
forms of political will have been prevented from participating in Colombia's
"democracy." Efforts, including those of the FARC-EP, to work within the
conservative system have only witnessed violent reaction. In response a revolutionary series of laws, policies, and justice has been created from below.
Before we look at the current situation, there follows a historic overview of
Colombia's exclusionary political structure.

The fallacy of Colombian democracy

In early 1964 Tad Szulc (1964: 297–8) warned that excluding Colombia's
electoral left, together with the growing influence of guerrilla movements in
the countryside, could ignite "long-range revolutionary potential" (see also
Mészáros, 2006; Guevara, 2004: 157). Far from heeding Szulc's warning, the
state spent the next two decades further segregating the left via attacks on

peasant-based self-defense communities and the National Front agreement (1958–74). The 1980s and 1990s were no different, with the onslaught of paramilitarism and its targeting of critical political opponents. Others have shown that more human rights violations were committed per year during the Uribe administration than during the entire Chilean dictatorship of Augusto Pinochet (1974–90) (Colombia Reports, 2008b). With a shocking rate of political casualties, Colombia has been put in the same company as Latin American countries that once experienced authoritarian rule. Cynthia McClintock (1998: 6) even cited Colombia as being substantially less democratic than the highly publicized Argentinean state during the "dirty war." Other see Colombia as a "death-squad democracy," where "rightist paramilitary forces and death squads acting with the tacit approval, if not active participation, of armed forces" murdered any opposition, especially those on the left (Petras and Morley, 1992: 20, 21). It is for this and other reasons that Ronaldo Munck (2008: 40) has continued to categorize Colombia's regime as hardly democratic.

Evaluating these deplorable political conditions, István Mészáros (2006: 41) criticized Bogotá and Washington for blocking processes that could lead to the betterment of the country.

> For forty years the forces of oppression – internal and external, U.S. dominated – tried to suffocate the struggle of the Colombian people, without success. Attempts to reach a negotiated settlement – "with the participation of all social groups, without exception, in order to reconcile the Colombian family," in the words of Manuel Marulanda Vélez, the leader of FARC-EP – have been systematically frustrated. As Vélez wrote in an open letter addressed recently to a presidential candidate: "No government, liberal or conservative, produced an effective political solution to the social and armed conflict. The negotiations were used for the purpose of changing nothing, so that everything should remain the same. All of the political schemes of the governments were using the Constitution and the laws as a barrier, to make sure that everything continues the way as we had it before."
>
> (Mészáros, 2006: 41)

Here Mészáros provides an important commentary on how the Colombia's internal conflict is a consequence of class-based reaction to the explicit will and agency of those from below. State-centered theorists may depict Colombia's conflict as a derivative of "the historic and contemporary institutional failure of the state" (Richani, 2007: 405). On the surface, this may seem accurate; however, a proper evaluation of the state shows that it never held authority over the entire country – especially the countryside. This makes it impossible to argue the state has fallen into a period of decline, loss of power, or failure, as it never had control. The revolutionary situation developing in Colombia is not the cause of the state, but rather the result of class consciousness in action.[49] Hence, it was not the left's promotion of change (and peace) that brought violence to the countryside, but rather the response to these alternatives.

Table 7.2 A comparative review of politically motivated assassinations in selected Latin American countries

Country	Period of analysis	Estimated number of political assassinations
Argentina	1976–1983	9,000
Brazil	1964–1979	125
Chile	1973–1990	2,666
Colombia	1986–2006	62,833*

* This figure is actually below that of other scholars and human rights groups that suggest the number of politically motivated assassinations over the past two decades hovers around 70,000 (Torres and Torres, 2005).
Sources: Adapted from Dudley, 2004, front flap; Livingstone, 2003: 30; Stokes, 2003b; Giraldo, 1996: 18; with additional data from Chernick, 2007: 54; Petras, 2003: 25; Leech, 2002a: 53.

Revisiting the slaughter of the Unión Patriótica (UP)

On paper, Colombia is proclaimed to be one of the longest-running democracies in the Western hemisphere. Since independence, it has held presidential and congressional elections through an electoral college system, coupled with a constitution to ensure ethical, political, and civil matters (Bushnell, 1993; Randall, 1992). However, it should be questioned whether this makes the country a democracy, as a minority has historically placed restrictions on those eligible to engage in politics through requirements of property ownership (the Congress of Cúcuta, 1821), bipartisan alliances as "codified in the restrictive Constitution of 1886" (see Bergquist, 2007: 671), and the direct implementation of political genocide against leftists, as recognized in the case of the Unión Patriótica (UP).[50]

With a firm place in the hearts of many, the UP has a significant role in Colombian political culture as one of the most important examples of civil society coming together for change through non-violent means (Aldana, 2002). It is argued that the unique ideology, support, and broad spectrum of those who came to form the UP were, in part, the reasons it was subjected to violence, repression, and extermination. Numerous statements, comments, and quotes from renowned scholars of Colombian social and political history provide the basis for the analysis that follows. Those cited do not share a homogeneous perspective on the Colombian civil war, or support a single political philosophy or faction. Nevertheless, there is one common denominator: they all take the informed position that the UP was a legitimate political party in Colombia, which sought, through peaceful means, an end to the civil war and an opening to democratic representation.

Historically speaking, the UP, much like the PCC, had indirect associations with the FARC-EP, as did many political institutions and organizations. Following peace negotiations with the Conservative government of Belisario Betancur (1982–86), "many guerrillas laid down their arms and integrated themselves into the orthodox political system, with a good number of them forming a new political party Unión Patriótica" (Crandall, 2002: 33). Hence, in some ways the party was constructed of "former guerrilla members, who in good faith put down their weapons and who, through the UP, participated in the so-called legitimate political arena" (Rochlin, 2003: 102). The UP, however, was a distinct organization with a dramatically different political project from the insurgency, a program that sought a peaceful path to political change.[51] Pearce (1990a: 180) clarified how the FARC-EP was an altogether separate entity at the time, which had organizationally disassociated itself from the UP in ideology and practice. The UP never based itself on a militant doctrine but was "established as a left political party in response to government promises of 1984 at La Uribe that aimed to bring the revolutionary left into peaceful political activity" (Safford and Palacios, 2003: 356). Many believed "the UP was made up of some of the most articulate voices and brilliant political minds of the Colombian left" (Murillo and Avirama, 2004: 63).

On May 28, 1985 the UP became an official state-sanctioned political party. As noted, "the foundation and consolidation of the Patriotic Union political party" resulted from governmental agreements where "amnestied members of the FARC-EP were provided legal and constitutional guarantees to organize politically" (Osterling, 1989: 163). The constituency, however, consisted of far more than former insurgents who had left the war behind, and included members of the PCC, trade unionists, and other sectors of the Colombian population who cooperatively worked to establish the UP "as the country's third political force and main opposition party" (Pearce, 1990a: 175–6, 279; see also Sánchez, 2003: 6; Urrego, 2003: 171; Osterling, 1989: 299).[52] While some, such as historian David Bushnell (1993: 258), stated that the UP was partially constructed of ex-guerrillas who had turned their back on violence, researcher Grace Livingstone (2003: 208) suggested the vast majority of the UP rank and file were civilians who had had no direct association with the guerrillas. Only "two FARC comandantes left the mountains, won election, and took up seats as members of congress," because "most of the UP's other candidates were not recruited from the FARC, but from other sectors of the left or the Communist Party" (Chernick, 2007: 62; see also Wilson and Carroll, 2007: 85; NACLA, 1990). The most important point to understand is that the UP was never a political arm of the FARC-EP, and to think otherwise is to negate the lateral support and unification of various elements of Colombian civil society.

Programmatically, the UP formed itself around the goal of opening a democratic system in Colombia for the purpose of expanding social welfare. The UP sought "political reforms to end the Conservative and Liberal domination of Colombian politics, the popular election of local mayors, rural land reforms and the nationalization of foreign business, Colombian banks and transportation" (Stokes, 2005: 75). Far from armed revolution, or even direct action politics, the UP "advocated constitutional reform, decentralization, grants of land to peasants, increased health and education spending" and "a civilian defense minister" (Livingstone, 2003: 228–9).

The UP stresses that Colombia needs major social, economical, and political structural changes which should be achieved through peaceful means. Among these is the struggle to achieve more political space – the Apertura

Democratica – which would imply the most urgent political opening, such as more access to national institutions and to the mass media, an authentic agrarian reform, various economic reforms which would provide the poor with better educational and health facilities.

(Osterling, 1989: 195)

From an electoral standpoint, the UP was a valid institution which worked in unison with the state. For example, members actively participated with other political parties, government officials, clergy, and former Liberal President Julio Cesar Turbay (1978–82), when drafting a response and review of governmental positions toward the notorious narco-trafficker Pablo Escobar (Kline, 1999: 54). In the field of popular support, the UP showed "significant electoral performance," which "temporarily demonstrated a plural support base for the emerging 'legitimate' left" (Rochlin, 2003: 113). "This support ranged from traditional members such as peasants who endured the brunt of the nation's poverty, to newcomers in the form of urban and middle-class residents who felt excluded from the elite politics of the Liberals and Conservatives" (Rochlin, 2003: 113).

Contrary to conventional political structures of centralized power, the UP proved most prominent at the local level. It was here where "the UP's gains were more significant," as "entire areas of the sparsely populated regions east of the Andes comprising almost half of the national territory came under its electoral influence" (Chernick, 2007: 62). By March 1986, less than a year after it had become official, the party had:

succeeded in electing two Senators and three Representatives from its rank, and four more Senators and five Representatives in alliance with members of various liberal or leftist political movements .... The UP won both a Senate and Chamber seat alone both in the department of Antioquia and in Cundinamarca; and alone it won a third Chamber seat in the department of Santander.

(Osterling, 1989: 196; see also Livingstone, 2003: 229)[53]

In all, the UP gained 12 elected congressional members, 21 representatives to departmental assemblies, 170 members of city councils and 335 municipal councillors (Osterling, 1989: 196–7; Livingstone, 2003: 229). While it has been noted that the 1970s saw a growth in left-of-centre parties, the 1986 presidential elections proved to be the highest vote for the Colombian left up to that point in history (Pearce, 1990a: 198; Cusicanqui, 1987: 129; Maullin, 1973: 16). In a very limited time the UP acquired a significant base throughout the country. Politically speaking, if there was to be electoral continuity the "left" had the potential to become a formidable player in the duopoly of Colombian political culture. Perceiving a threat to traditional political stability, reactionary responses took aim.

Doug Stokes reported that the UP was conceived of "as a broad political movement to represent the left in Colombian politics and to articulate peasant and working-class interests within a democratic framework" (Stokes, 2005: 75). Yet, during the rise of the party, policies of economic liberalization were being introduced to Colombia that targeted organized labor and social-based public spending. This translated into the far right perceiving the UP to be a "liability." Members became "indiscriminately linked with the armed movements to justify repression" (Pearce, 1990a: 157). Many "hard-line antileftists" felt that:

> UP members were still committed to the violent overthrow of the existing system and had formed the party to undermine that system from within – a strategy whereby UP elected officials would be defending the interests of those still under arms in the back country.
>
> (Bushnell, 1993: 266)

After its inception:

> more than one thousand UP militants were assassinated, including Jaime Pardo, its presidential candidate in 1986, and Bernardo Jaramillo, its nominee for the election of 1990 (slain before the election took place). Even more UP candidates for mayoral and city council posts were killed.
>
> (Bushnell, 1993: 266)

Over 70 percent of all presidential candidates in 1990 – and 100 percent from left-of-centre parties – were murdered (Braun, 2003: 232). From an ideological and strategic position it became beneficial for some to associate political

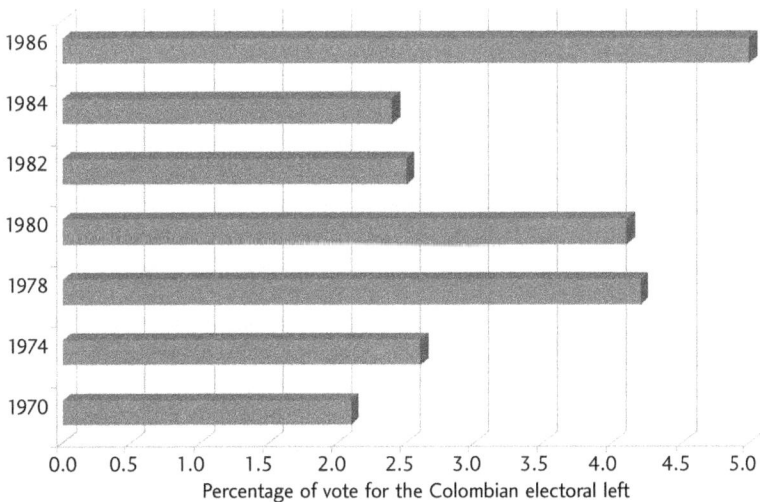

Figure 7.2 National percentage showings of left candidates in congressional elections, 1970–86 (UP –1986)
Sources: Stokes, 2005: 76; Osterling, 1989: 197; Ratliff, 1976: 69.

activism with armed struggle, as it meant that a large number of individuals, and the organizations with which they were associated, could not be considered legitimate democratic participants. Since 1986, it is estimated that 6,000 members of the UP have been assassinated (Holmes, 2003: 93; see also Aldana, 2002). As a result of these staggering figures various organizations have tried to work with the Inter-American Commission of Human Rights and the Organization of American States (OAS) to propose that the targeting of the UP be classified as (political) genocide (Murillo and Avirama, 2004: 63; see also Dudley, 2004: 188; Restrepo, 2003: 99; Giraldo, 1996: 101).

The massacre of the UP is "evidence of the Colombian elite's intolerance and the impossibility of achieving change through parliament" (Livingstone, 2003: 208). The Commission for the Study of Violence (1992: 269) declared that the UP was structurally prevented "from expanding and from launching new political activities outside the two-party system." From this standpoint we can see why the FARC-EP is justifiably "reluctant to give up their arms because the UP experience proved disastrous. After guerrillas reinserted themselves into society, they were systematically decimated by right-wing groups" (Thoumi, 2005: 154–5).

Attempts to demonize the UP under false pretences of FARC-EP associations only led to conditions of political instability.[54] In many ways, domestic and international accusations, followed by violent reaction, motivated certain politicos on "the left to work outside Colombia's official political system" (Rochlin, 2003: 149). Rather than eliminating the UP from Colombia's political spectrum, the opposite took place, as many came to recognize that support had to now be given to the FARC-EP's program (Eckstein, 2001: 399). In short, "repression, particularly against the UP, has served to perpetuate the violence in Colombia and insulate Colombia's political system from reformist pressures" (Stokes, 2005: 77).

This overview offers an important insight into the UP. The party continues to be an integral actor in Colombia's political culture because of its broad support from various sectors of the rural and urban population, its methodology of trying to alter Colombian politics through conventional means, and its violent demise. It was following the history of the UP that the FARC-EP saw the need to re-emphasize how centralized politics are an impractical venue for change.

Methods of localized governance via organic politics

Colombia has had a turbulent past in the realm of state politics. For much of the twentieth century elite rule was secured in Bogotá while the military flexed its muscle across the countryside. Ironically, in Latin America's "oldest democracy," a significant minority experienced displacement, exploitation, or were simply left out of the political process. With the FARC-EP establishing itself as a pseudo-state mechanism in certain regions, such apathy only further germinated a climate for radical politics (Richani, 2002a: 60–91; FARC-EP, 2000b: 23; Arnson, 1999: 197; Clawson and Lee III, 1998: 180; Boudon, 1996: 289–90). On a local scale the FARC-EP:

struggles on behalf of basic peasant interests (land, credit, roads, etc.), the social services and law and order they provide, and their political education and ideological appeals. In most of their dealings with the rural population, the FARC represents order, rectitude, and social justice .... The strength of the FARC is based on the interplay of ideological appeals and the resonance of its analysis and socio-political practices with the everyday reality of peasant life.

(Petras and Morley, 2003: 102)[55]

Apart from establishing localized sociocultural alternatives, the FARC-EP have also addressed the political alternatives, leading some to take note of its "state-making capabilities complementing its military and economic power" (Richani, 2002a: 90). Beyond supporting schools, medical centers, and infrastructure, the guerrillas have attempted to establish a political model counter to the conventional state, suggesting the "ideal-rational state should represent the people's interest as a communal collectivity, rather than the narrow selfish interests of parts of society" (FARC-EP, 2000–01: 29).

Laws and municipal governance

Marx (1992b: 83) once wrote that "shouting and doing are irreconcilable opposites." It can be easy to criticize those in power, yet difficult to know how and with what the existing model should be replaced. To reconfigure policy is an arduous task, yet this is exactly what has been attempted by the FARC-EP. In certain areas under its control, codes of conduct or Rules of Coexistence (*Reglas de Convivencia*) have been established, which "stipulate laws and sanctions regarding issues such as carrying arms, fishing, hunting, working hours, liquor consumption, prostitution, interfamily violence, drug abuse, and cutting trees" (Richani, 2002a: 89). These laws have been viewed as effective and to an extent applauded by local residents. One of the most noted benefits has been a consistent reduction in crime (Kalyvas, 2006: 70n.15; Molano, 2005: 90; Coghlan, 2004: 188, 207; Dudley, 2004: 52; Taussig, 2004a: 142; Petras and Morley, 2003: 102; Rubio, 1999: 129; Pearce, 1990a: 173). Even those critical of the guerrillas acknowledged how these methods saw the insurgency decrease if not eliminate "thievery, drunkenness, and prostitution; [they have] repaired roads and infrastructure; and been good stewards of their jungle environment" (Satchell, 1999: 41).

There are some, however, who argue that this policy is potentially harmful if not repressive. LeGrand (2003: 178), for one, labeled such activities as negative, as the FARC-EP seem to have taken "on the role of local government," enabling the insurgency to "have [a] major say in who is elected and how municipal funds are spent. In such zones, the guerrillas are de facto the law, adjudicating disputes and punishing thieves, while taxing most productive activities, including the highly profitable coca crop." People living in these areas, however, told me the regulations are highly community-based and have proved useful in protecting sectors of the environment and population. Schulte-Bockholt (2006: 201) agreed the insurgency does "indeed police the territory they control," yet "those living under guerrilla law do not necessarily consider themselves unfortunate about the imposition of 'revolutionary justice.'"[56] Susceptible populations have on many occasions requested the FARC-EP to protect their communities (see Weinstein, 2007: 293–4; Molano, 2005).

> Prior to the arrival of the FARC in 1999, it inhabitants regarded San Vicente as a "lawless frontier town." The killings which the community suffered on a daily basis while the Colombian military was present stopped almost completely once the heavily armed rebels began patrolling the streets. The FARC also drove out the official local judges, replacing the country's judicial system with their own. As long as the rebels were in control of the territory, most criminal cases involved domestic disputes, 90 percent of which were resolved by the rebel courts. In cases of domestic violence and wife abuse, the perpetrator would be "locked in the town jail for a few days or set to work sweeping streets or building roads."
>
> (Schulte-Bockholt, 2006: 202)

Some have put these measures in historical context and understand that many in the countryside cannot regard the state as upholding security, as the state – including paramilitaries and large landholding allies – has been the greatest threat to the peasantry. Years ago,

> the FARC was authoritarian and harsh in punishing wrongdoers, but it established rules in a situation where the law of the jungle would otherwise reign. Its law of the mountain, as it was called, gradually won legitimacy and support. Corruption ran high within the army and police, further reducing their authority among the peasantry already deeply hostile after years of abuses at their hands ... . This is how the FARC's influence spread between 1965 and 1976 from Caquetá, the Meta and Guaviare to the middle Magdalena valley, Bajo Cauca and Alto Sinu. In a number of areas the FARC took over the role of the negligent or absent state to become a governing authority for large numbers of peasants. Zones of self-defense became guerrilla fronts. In the Magdalena Medio, the FARC became a virtual rural civil guard, supported for a period by landowners as well as peasants as the only force to provide law and order. These roots enabled the FARC to survive the 1970s.
>
> (Pearce, 1990a: 173, 168)

Dismissing the FARC-EP's Rules of Coexistence as undemocratic or repressive fails to recognize that such rules were and continue to be supported by sectors of the populace to which they apply. While facilitated by the guerrillas, they are regularly agreed, discussed, and debated by and through the community. Here is an excellent before-and-after account of the system from one community.

Before the FARC laid down the law, this region was like the Wild West, where going into town meant risking your life. Much of the trouble came from migrant workers who'd poured in to pick and process the coca harvest. Working long hours and making pretty good money, they roamed the streets at night and spent recklessly. Parties rocked bars, which today bear the name Saigón and Tronco Mocho, or Tree Stump. Alcohol flowed, gamblers crowded the cockfights, and customers kept the brothels busy around the clock. Saturdays were in a class by themselves: Full of beer and *aguardiente*, the local liquor, the men would pick a fight over anything – a woman, a wager, a perceived insult. With most of the population carrying a machete or a gun (customary gear in the countryside), several drunks and passers-by would turn up dead on Sunday morning. By the time I arrived for the first time in December 2000, the FARC had long since taken control, and the crazy days were over. In fact, in all the weeks I spent here, I came across just one murder – a mysterious case of a cattle rancher shot dead from a passing boat, which stunned everyone. The FARC had produced a strictly enforced code of conduct: No drinking from Monday to Friday. No brawling. And, ironically, no drug use. These days, anyone caught breaking a rule is sentenced by the FARC to work on a development project in the trackless interior of the forest – building a bridge, for instance, or opening a road – things that a government would usually take care of. Drinking on a weekday or a first-time offense may get the culprit a couple of months. Murder brings a year-long penalty, at the very least. After investigating the infraction, the town's FARC commander sends word for the guilty party to show up at the FARC office with his bags packed and his affairs in order for the time he'll be away from home. Few dare to ignore the summons.

(Villalón, 2004a: 42–3)

One account expressed how "the guerrilla bring justice, big time," and in regions prone to decades of violence, "nothing could be more important to the people than stopping theft and violation, and the guerrilla are right on the money in having seen and acted on this" (Taussig, 2004b: 142). Stathis N. Kalyvas (2006: 70n.15) went so far as to claim that in regions under FARC-EP control, "crime all but vanished" (see also Taussig, 2004b: 142). Beyond monitoring criminal activity, the FARC-EP has also responded to those who would disrupt the individual and collective needs of the social fabric (see Richani, 2002a: 70). The insurgency has been known to punish "drunks, adulterers, and murders. They also protected villagers from aggressive drug traffickers and forbade the use of dangerously addictive coca derivatives" (Dudley, 2004: 53; see also Schulte-Bockholt, 2006: 133–4).[57] The overall effectiveness of these measures has been clear. In San Vicente del Caguán, "when the Cazadores Battalion and the official police station were there, there were 366 violent deaths" in the year prior to the town being officially handed over to the guerrillas as the DMZ (FARC-EP, 2001a: 12). Once consolidated under FARC-EP control, there were eight deaths over a three-year period, while "muggings and robberies diminished to almost nothing and women no longer live in terror, threatened by imminent rape."[58]

The manner through which the FARC-EP partially sustains order may be through warnings or levies. Those who violate community-based rules are cautioned by a stringent "three-strike" policy (Coghlan, 2004: 207). The model is far from lenient; "anyone who breaks our law will get two chances before we kill him or her. The first, to correct their mistake. The second, to go. The third is the end" (Molano, 2005: 90; see also Taussig, 2004b: 142–3; Satchell, 1999: 41; Pearce, 1990a: 173). The FARC-EP also utilizes aspects of its class-based taxation model and fines those committing misdemeanors. Monies obtained are then passed onto the community, usually through a JAC. There have been extraordinary accounts of the FARC-EP forcing thieves to return the goods they pillaged. This is a delicate process when people are desperately poor, and the socioeconomic conditions caused them to commit crimes against the community. Where it is not realistic to ask for monetary recompense, the insurgency – alongside JACs – has criminals repay the community through laboring on communal projects and social-based infrastructure. It has even been said that some have been made "to build trails through the forest so as to enhance the mobility of the guerrilla" (Taussig, 2004b: 143). When talking with a member of the Secretariat about such penalties I was told that crime:

> is quite often an expression of individualism. Therefore, those who have violated the community must be shown that the community is a part of them. Applying their labor power for the betterment of all it is hoped that one will lose their need for self-promotion for the betterment of the many.

Measures have even been applied to state and paramilitary forces that have stolen from communities. As noted by Goff (2003: 77), "money, goods, and livestock that the unit [AUC and members of the Colombian Army's 11th Brigade] was suspected of having stolen from peasants in Peque and Ituango were recovered and returned to those who said they were robbed."

As the "rules" reduce violence, crime, public drunkenness, and prostitution,[59] the laws could be considered to be authoritarian directives given the insurgency is not brought to power through electoral processes. To some of those I spoke with this meant very little, as the local populations stated they were choosing to adopt a different form of representation that is directly local and outside existing political forms. Support for the FARC-EP has been gained through proximal action not distal politics. Learning from the atrocities against the UP, the FARC-EP has taken a different approach in how it organizes politically. This strategy sees sociopolitical coalitions from the bottom up; a revolution from below that directly coincides with a Marxist-Leninist position of emancipatory action (Lenin, 1964g: 38; see also Petras and Veltmeyer, 2003a: 222). The FARC-EP does not disagree that the state needs to be drastically altered,[60] but believes it must be done through an ongoing mobilized process (Röhl, 2004: 3-4; CISLAC, 2001).

It could, however, be said that establishing "rules" is far from revolutionary.

In fact, it may even be oppressive if no forum for justice is set up. We need to further analyze the FARC-EP's activities to address the issue of community-based judicial reform.

Judicial transformation: restorative (with punitive)

In areas of control the FARC-EP has moved to abolish "traditional" judicial institutions, if ever they existed. In 2000, Simón Trinidad (as quoted in Leech, 2000b), a former negotiator during the peace negotiations in San Vicente del Caguán, expressed how:

> for many years the state hasn't been present in many regions. There have been no state judges, no justice system and no public administration in many regions of the country. The society has had to resolve their own problems because they don't believe in the ministry of work, they don't believe in Colombian justice, they don't believe in the Colombian army and police. They came to us and we were there for them in the country.

In place of an absent state, the guerrillas have worked to establish communal judicial bodies alongside localized municipal-based unarmed police forces instituted by, and of, the townspeople. In conjunction with communities and/or JACs they helped establish counter-hegemonic methods of dispersing justice (Ahmad, 2006: 62, 64; Leech, 2006b; Murillo and Avirama, 2004: 68; Richani, 2002a: 89; Buscaglia and Ratliff, 2001: 9; Murch, 2000).[61] These formations have not replicated capitalist (or Stalinist) models, where the judiciary is simply an extension of those in power.[62] Their logic is based on the guerrillas calling for:

> a radical transformation of crime policy and the whole legal apparatus; in line with the political, economic and social changes Colombia requires, and the overcoming of the inequalities between humans, while destroying the retrograde Colombian penal and penitentiary legislation that alone favors the petty interests of the dominant class; this is the proposal of the FARC – People's Army.
>
> (FARC-EP, 2001b: 17)

Consolidating cooperative links with given communities creates a socio-political environment capable of addressing offences within a localized context while negating existing judiciary forms seen as objects of dominant class perpetuation. Such structures:

> contribute to the pursuit of solutions for the most varied conflicts in the communities, be they large or small. In every case, decisions to determine responsibility and achieve justice for those affected are made considering the authorized opinion of the neighbors and those who know the issues.
>
> (FARC-EP, 2000–01: 29)

The function of the revolutionary judiciaries is to respond to criminal activity, violations, or disputes related to the Rules of Coexistence. Claims of a community or personal offence are first presented to the Office of Claims and Complaints (*Oficina de Quejas y Reclamos*), which is made up of community members and occasionally one representative from the guerrillas. Upon recognition that a violation has occurred a gathering of community members takes place. The process does not have a judge as such, but rather involves those most affected by the alleged crime. The FARC-EP has a representative (or sometimes more than one, but not many) accompany those involved, and these individuals participate in a collective hearing, making sure civility is maintained (Murillo and Avirama, 2004: 68; Buscaglia and Ratliff, 2001: 9; Murch, 2000). The affected parties are brought together and encouraged to come to a mutual agreement about how any grievances can be rectified. If an immediate solution is not found, the FARC-EP representative may act as a further mediator and speak with the person(s) most affected by the alleged act. The representative then recommends the parties to privately work together to reach an equitable solution to the grievance. If a mutual agreement is reached the hearing is dissolved until a follow-up consultation takes place to check that the matter has been rectified. Such community-based judiciaries are widely used throughout FARC-EP-controlled regions to oversee issues of marriage and divorce, personal disputes, theft, and so on (Botero, 2006; Vieira, 2006b). One study found that over "57 percent of the heads of households" had been involved or "knew someone who had used the informal dispute resolution mechanisms provided by neighborhood councils or directly from the FARC" (Buscaglia and Ratliff, 2001: 9).

An extreme example of this process occurred when a homicide took place in Caquetá. The person accused admitted to killing a young man while intoxicated. Because of the severity of the crime, the FARC-EP decided to organize a conference between the dead man's parents and the killer's parents, which the entire community was invited to attend. A guerrilla representative asked the mothers to talk privately about the situation of their families and the plight of both those involved in the crime. After deliberating for several hours they agreed that the man who had committed the crime was an alcoholic who had never intended to kill. The mothers mutually agreed that for the safety of the community the perpetrator should be ejected for a minimum of one year and could only return if a fine of 25 million pesos (US$10,000) was paid to the victim's family. This was based on the reasoning that a young person provides a great deal both financially and physically, not only to the community but also to their family. The dead man's family (and largely his mother) would suffer financially as well as emotionally, so the fine was meant to act as a form of compensation (Murch, 2000).

In addition to radical judicial shifts in parts of the countryside, the FARC-EP has also tried to support the establishment of non-insurgent law enforcement through a prototype group called the civic (*el cívico*). The civic enables a community to regulate itself. While the FARC-EP maintains the larger responsibility of securing a given region, the civic has people from each village act as a support group. They make sure civil peace is maintained and are even allowed to use small amounts of force to detain or apprehend criminals (FARC-EP, 2001a: 12). The guerrillas assist by "checking criminal and delinquent activity and the possession of weapons and adjudicating social conflicts and disputes between individuals, such as marital problems and domestic violence," and larger-scale situations where the civic would have very little positive effect or ability to control the situation (Richani, 2002a: 70).

Peace through political representation

The enormous power and magnitude of the FARC-EP's military strategy of armed struggle has been, and continues to be, well documented by researchers, journalists, scholars and statespeople. Although they are important, such analyses can detract from the guerrillas' constant position toward peace and repeated attempts to implement non-violent change in Colombia. After three national peace negotiations, several ceasefire agreements, and numerous humanitarian accords, the Colombian state has refused to halt dominant class reactionism from both internal and foreign factors.[63] While countless people are eager to shed light on the guerrillas' militancy, few have discussed the insurgency's 25-year promotion of a negotiated settlement to the civil war. Let me buck this trend and offer a brief synopsis of the insurgency's past and present policies for resolving the conflict through non-violence.

One of the most important points that must be addressed in relation to the FARC-EP is that the movement arose not from conflict but out of a peaceful philosophy. It has been well argued that the roots of the guerrillas lie in the peaceable creation of self-defense communities. After many years of trying to maintain a passive subsistent social economy, the collectives experienced a frontal attack at the hands of the state (with the financial and political-military support of Washington), as the state recognized how efficient the self-defense communities were (see Obando and Velásqeuz, 2004). This was achieved by strategically labeling the peasant-held territories as "independent republics," promoting an image of a larger domestic and international communist threat in order to obtain the external support and extra-national acceptance needed to attack the rural enclaves (Murillo and Avirama, 2004: 49–53, 58). During the 1950s and 1960s, the communities expanded and other pseudo-socialist rural collectives started to flourish as a result of the successes in the southwest (Hylton, 2006: 54; Schulte-Bockholt, 2006: 109; Safford and Palacios, 2003: 356; Petras and Morley, 1990: 176; Osterling, 1989: 294). After the 1964 events at Marquetalia, armed assaults were carried out against various rural collectives over the next several years. It is important to reevaluate this history in order to situate an analysis of how the insurgency has for close to three decades tried to negotiate a process towards peace.

Limited success towards achieving peace was realized with every administration the guerrillas have dealt with. Each series of negotiations has fallen as a result of paramilitary forces targeting civilian populations or the state's refusal to address socioeconomic policy (Murillo and Avirama, 2004: 64; see also

Lozano Guillén, 2001; 2000; Shifter, 1999: 19). If the FARC-EP is to protect the rural population, it has little choice under such conditions but to resort to defensive measures, and this gives the state justification to end negotiations (Restrepo M., 2003: 99; Hylton, 2003: 81; Scott, 2003: 98; Molano, 2000: 25–7; Hobday, 1986: 364). Historian Herbert Braun (2003: 65), recognizing the negotiations as a fraud, argued that "one of the main purposes of the various amnesties over the years has been to get the guerrillas out of the mountain and into the city, where they are easy prey."

During the first peace negotiations (January 1983 and October 1987), which were initially between the FARC-EP and the Conservative Belisario Betancur Cuartas administration (1982–86), a new government came to power, headed by the Liberal Virgilio Barco Vargas (1986–90). This Barco administration not only silenced the discussion for peace but also began numerous military campaigns targeting the FARC-EP, dismissing ceasefire agreements. Very little was accomplished during the second peace talks (June 1991 and March 1992) with the Liberal César Augusto Gaviria Trujillo administration (1990–94), which stalled after only ten months (García-Peña Jaramillo, 2007: 92–9, 109–15; correspondence with James Petras, February 17, 2007). The most notorious peace negotiations (July 1998 and February 2002) were those during the Conservative Andrés Pastrana Arango administration (1998–2002). Within the first 48 hours of these talks, over 200 civilians were slaughtered at the hands of AUC as a sign of protest (FARC-EP, 2002a: 6).

Pastrana understood the FARC-EP was not involved in narcotics trafficking, and felt the two parties could come to an agreement for peace (see Ruiz, 2001: 151; Galvis, 2000: 11). After consolidating a demilitarized zone to ensure peace, the FARC-EP and state began negotiations that resulted in a series of concessions in the government's favor. After sporadic, but nevertheless successful talks, a "humanitarian accord" was established on February 9, 2001. The *Los Pozos Accord* stated that both sides would release retained combatants. On June 2, 2001, the FARC-EP released 55 soldiers and police, while the state released 15 guerrillas (FARC-EP, 2001b: 1). As a sign of good faith, the FARC-EP proceeded to release an additional 300 prisoners in the "interests of peace and social justice" (FARC-EP, 2001b: 7, 1). In total, the FARC-EP released over 400 militia troops, officers, military and political detainees. Despite the demilitarized zone being "a large peaceful island in the turmoil of Colombia," negotiations came to an end in 2002 (Clark, 2003: 44). Similar to the unfortunate circumstances seen during the negotiations of the mid-1980s, the talks broke down on February 20, 2002, immediately preceding the election of Álvaro Uribe Vélez. In similar fashion to the 1980s peace talks the arrival of a new administration saw negotiations cease as the state invaded guerrilla-inhabited zones.[64] During Uribe's time in office, the FARC-EP continually tried to establish new rounds of negotiations.[65] Invitations fell on the deaf ears, or once successfully established were ended on the claim that the state refuses to negotiate with "terrorists."[66]

The FARC-EP has long agreed that political awareness is needed to establish peace. Therefore, the guerrillas knew that outside the Party (that is, PCCC) there is a need for political organization, albeit clandestine, so as to ensure the safety of those involved. In light of this reasoning the MBNC became a new political venue for education and collective action. Since 2000, it has remained an underground organization "because no other way is possible at the present time" (FARC-EP, 2000b: 16; see also Murillo and Avirama, 2004: 54).

As noted, the 1980s peace process enabled some once related to the insurgency to become involved in politics through the creation of the UP, whose goal was to lead Colombia – without arms – to a peaceful democratic situation where all could be represented. Dominant political-economic interests, however, took precedence over the popular needs of representation. The guerrilla movement then concluded that there was no solution other than armed conflict. The state demonstrated it would not allow conventional peaceful methods of change. Even today, 4,000 Colombians are killed annually for their political beliefs (Chernick, 2007: 54). Given these circumstances, the FARC-EP, rightly or wrongly, decided the most pragmatic method for organizing political activity was through a clandestine broad-based movement.

The FARC-EP established the MBNC with the aim of providing the political groundwork needed to contend with the bourgeois political system that has dominated Colombia since independence. While there has been much attention paid to "independent" candidates in Colombian elections over the past several years, those "independents" are typically rooted in the Liberal and Conservative camps (Stokes, 2005).[67] They are entrenched in ruling-class ideology: supporting counter-insurgency and the fulfillment of domestic and imperialist economic interests. A systemic lack of public support has been recognized through the decreasing turnout rates at both presidential and municipal elections (Williams, 2005: 154). Trying to strike back, the FARC-EP has tried to devise a unified and safe approach to counter dominant political forms (see Petras and Veltmeyer, 2003a: 130).

Alfonso Cano (now commander-in-chief) and Iván Ríos (deceased), two members of the Secretariat, oversaw the creation of the organization. In addition to providing a political space for popular participation, the MBNC acts as a mechanism through which concerns are brought to the FARC-EP, reconstructing the conventional top-down political mechanisms. This has enabled a broad range of supporters of all professions, educational backgrounds, and ethnicities to become actively involved with the guerrillas (FARC-EP, 2000c). The MBNC can be thought of as a cyclical model through which the most exploited work within their own communities while at the same time informing the FARC-EP of their needs, wants, and politics (see Figure 7.3). This program is designed to ensure the FARC-EP responds to the people, and not vice versa. Thousands of these small "Bolivarian cells" have been established throughout rural and urban Colombia, allowing members to secretly "hold political positions" and "voice the movement's position" to communities without being recognized (Dudley, 2004: 175).

Throughout the 2000s, every major city in the country saw an increase in cell formation. It has even been estimated that millions may belong to such groups, as the secretive design has provided protection from the kind of violence experienced during the 1980s and 1990s. At the induction of the MBNC, Manuel

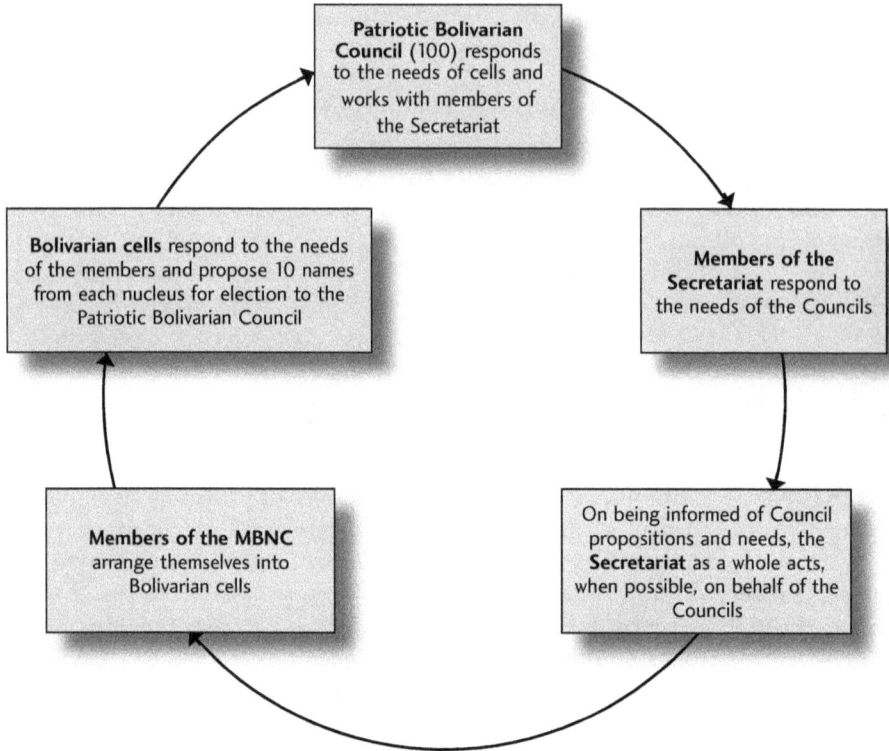

Figure 7.3 MBNC (PCCC) model of political organization
Source: observational research between 2004 and 2006.

Marulanda Vélez stated, "we must make changes to the government through the Bolivarian Movement in cities and the countryside with the help of the FARC to avoid what happened to the UP" (quoted in Dudley, 2004: 178). The FARC-EP is therefore directly related to and supports the MBNC.

This chapter has detailed extensively how the FARC-EP has and continues to create conditions of social change through, of, and with those from below. Offering numerous examples of how the FARC-EP has created a platform on which radical measures are being created alongside revolutionary projects throughout parts of the countryside, it highlights the insurgency's war of position and unique Marxist-Leninist approach towards substantive change. It has demonstrated how the FARC-EP has worked closely with local communities to create a dual power which repudiates top-down revolutionary perspectives. The insurgency has employed a model of social change that has facilitated pre-revolutionary mechanisms throughout various social, cultural, and political spheres of Colombia's rural and urban regions. This approach from below not only obstructs the conventional state without taking centralized power, but also continues to hamper existing pillars of capitalist political-economics that seek further opportunities for exploitation.

8

PROSPECTS FOR THE FUTURE: FROM "DUAL POWER" TO TAKING POWER

This chapter reflects upon why the FARC-EP has remained at the margins of centralized power even though it had the military capacity to take power. On several occasions the guerrillas held the capacity to carry out a *coup d'état* and simply usurp power through the military efficiency of a small collective, as numerous anti-systemic movements, militaries, and state antagonists in Latin America have done in the past. For example, from 1999 to 2003, the guerrillas maintained an average distance of 16 to 50 miles from Bogotá's downtown (correspondence with Petras, November 26, 2004; see also Simons, 2004: 203–5; Housego, 2003; Petras, 2003: 25; 1999: 32). It would have been more than plausible for them to seize power through one or several major offensives targeting the capital. When asked why this line of attack was not deployed, a comandante told me, "to do so would have gone against the (Marxist-Leninist) ideology of the insurgency."

A *coup d'état* enables a select group to consolidate centralized state power. Potentially effective, as it enables those without power to obtain it, a *coup* generally negates any broad alignment between the political-military movement of power takers and the exploited. While a new consolidation of power transpires, a transformation of the capitalist paradigm does not, because of a lack of mass class-conscious direct action.[1] The FARC-EP has opted to consolidate "political power at the local municipal levels instead of seeking outright military victory," whereby "political consciousness" rises from the periphery of the city and countryside (Richani, 2002a: 153; Bernard et al, 1973: 326). This then begs the question; can the FARC-EP establish radical transformation on a national scale? The preceding chapters highlighted how social change has occurred at a local level; however, can similar conditions extend across the whole of Colombia? Is such a feat even possible under current geopolitical conditions? This final chapter therefore weighs the FARC-EP's potential to move from a place of dual power to state power, and assesses its ability to further challenge the political stability of the Colombian state and the capitalist system itself.

THE FARC-EP'S APTITUDE TO TAKE STATE POWER: THE DIA BOMBSHELL

Under the auspices of the Democratic administration of John F. Kennedy (1961–63), the US Defense Intelligence Agency (DIA) was established. The DIA's objective is to "provide timely, objective, and cogent military intelligence" through the "integration of highly skilled intelligence professionals with leading edge technology to discover information and create knowledge that provides warning, identifies opportunities, and delivers overwhelming advantage to our war fighters, defense planners, and defense and national security policymakers" (DIA, 2007). Since 1961, the DIA has become the United States' "principal military intelligence service" (Ruiz, 2001: 21).[2]

In November 1997, a top-secret report prepared by the agency criticized the Colombian state as being too militarily inefficient to withstand the expansion of the FARC-EP. In April 1998, a summary report of the November study was obtained by (in other words, leaked to) the *Washington Post*. The newspaper proceeded to examine the document, interviewed "sources with direct knowledge of the full text" and published an article of the findings (Farah, 1998). Journalist Douglas Farah (1998) exposed how "the guerrillas have been fighting the government for the past three decades but have never before evinced the strength now attributed to them." Alongside his presentation of the FARC-EP's growing power from below, Farah went on to warn that "the Colombian military has proved to be inept, ill-trained and poorly equipped," causing General Charles Wilhelm (former chief of US Southern Command, SouthCom) and General Manuel José Bonnet (then commander of the Colombian military) to admit that the Colombian army was unable to defeat the guerrillas (Farah, 1998; see also Ruiz, 2001: 21–3; Crandall, 1999: 223–4). The report asserted that increased direct foreign intervention was needed, as did the DIA when it forewarned that without heightened counter-insurgency through the guidelines, leadership, and military of the United States, the FARC-EP could realistically be the first post-cold war Marxist insurgency to take state power by 2002 or 2003 (Simons, 2004: 181; Bergquist, Peñaranda, and Sánchez, 2003: xxi; Ruiz, 2001: 21).

A barrage of support for foreign intervention soon came from sectors of Colombia's elite. Former US ambassador Mauricio Solaún applauded the notion of Washington becoming militarily involved in the civil war, as he himself had published that "63 percent of the respondents" from a 1998 national survey "opined that the guerrillas were capable of seizing power by force" (Solaún, 2002: 1). In fact, "by 1998, there was wide agreement within Colombia's ruling circles that the Colombian military could not defeat the insurgency" (McInerney, 2003: 62). The dominant class was however not alone in fearing the FARC-EP's promotion of a socialized economy, as various US-based political-economic interests showed signs of distress (Ross, 2006: 63; McInerney, 2003: 60). Immediately following the 1998 DIA summary, the Democratic administration of Bill Clinton (1993–2001) drastically adjusted its foreign policy and significantly increased its counter-insurgency assistance and military funding to Colombia (NACLA, 1998: 46).[3]

During the mid to late 1990s, the FARC-EP had demonstrated its growing political-military prowess, placing the military on the defensive (Ruiz, 2001). In light of this, Washington sought to increase Colombia's anti-guerrilla leverage with the hope of decreasing the FARC-EP's authority.

The impact of the United States' involvement was to strengthen the bargaining position of the government's armed forces, the agribusiness elite and their right-wing paramilitary allies, thereby reducing any incentive for them to negotiate under the 1996–98 balance of forces, which they perceived to be more favorable to the FARC.

(Richani, 2005b: 84)

The United States could not afford, politically or economically, to have a Marxist-Leninist insurgency movement come to power on a hemispheric or geopolitical level.

Washington sees the Colombian guerrilla ... as the major threat to its empire in Latin America. A victory of the popular forces in Colombia would establish an alternative socio-economic system to U.S. directed neo-liberal model. In addition it would encourage neighboring countries to break with U.S. tutelage by demonstrating that mass struggle can win against the empire. Furthermore, Colombia has oil, gas, agriculture and industry in a country for 40 million – a capacity to resist U.S. economic pressures. Finally, a Colombian–Venezuelan–Cuban alliance would be a formidable economic-political-military force capable of resisting imperial aggression and aiding other countries in the region seeking to move in the direction of social transformation.

(Petras, 2001a)

The United States had been well aware of the FARC-EP's growth and increasing threat to domestic and international political-economic interests long before 1997–98. Evidence has shown Washington was involved in training Colombian forces in counter-insurgency techniques and deploying US troops in specific regions of the country since the early 1990s (Hinojosa, 2007; Gill, 2004; Goff, 2004: 31–2). In 1990, for example, the Central Intelligence Agency's (CIA) Colombia post was the largest of its kind in the world (Scott, 2003: 88; see also Bowden, 2001: 159). Anthropologist Winifred Tate (2000: 19) characterized the deployment of US officers from "the Defense Department, the Defense Intelligence Agency, the CIA and the Drug Enforcement Agency (DEA)" during this period as resembling tactics employed in Central America when US/Contra preparations began against the FMLN and the FSLN. Apart from the above, the end of the 1990s witnessed the US and Colombian states establishing the largest counter-insurgency campaign in Latin American history, Plan Colombia (1998–2006)[4] (Chavez, 2007: 95). Washington and Bogotá perceived that an increased counter-insurgency assault, through an influx of US-backed military aid, would decrease the insurgency's revolutionary potential and offset its ability to procure state power. Ironically, this never occurred.

As mentioned above, 1998 saw the DIA report that the Colombian state could fall to the FARC-EP in about five years unless a significant binational counter-insurgency campaign was deployed. Interestingly, after this pronouncement, and military spending periodically averaging US$9 million per day, the same plea was made six years later. In 2004, yet another administration appealed for the United States to increase its military presence. On April 1, President Uribe declared that "without an extension of U.S. aid under the multibillion dollar 'Plan Colombia'" Colombia would be defeated by the FARC-EP (Stewart, 2004). As repeated counter-insurgency campaigns failed, further calls for increased US assistance were expressed in 2005: "barring unforeseen U.S. congressional action to re-evaluate the war on drugs in Colombia, what little is left of the South American country's democratic institutions could die prematurely despite U.S. efforts" (Morales, 2005). The following year Colombia's vice-president, Francisco Santos Calderón, confessed, "if we don't make decisions quickly, if we do not strengthen our intelligence capacity and our legal system to fight them, criminals [FARC-EP] will destroy the state" (as quoted in Xinhua, 2006). Trained military specialists suggested that "without air support from the U.S. and its surrogates there, the Colombian armed forces could not match the FARC's military prowess, nor do they have a popular base outside the urban petit-bourgeoisie and ruling classes" (Goff, 2004: 45).

Numerous analysts have affirmed the FARC-EP will not and cannot be defeated. In fact, some have noted that:

> despite the steady increase of the state's military capacity, the state is still not capable of defeating the guerrillas today or in the foreseeable future ... its organizational structure, recruitment base, and ability to wage guerrilla warfare in all areas of the national territory remain undiminished.
>
> (Chernick, 2007: 76–7)

Experts, from former US ambassador to El Salvador Robert White to Colombian historian Herbert Braun, have claimed that in no way can Bogotá or Washington militarily defeat the FARC-EP (Braun, 2003: 66; Ungerman and Brohy, 2003; Murch, 2000; KAIROS, 2001). By the close of Plan Colombia over US$7.7 billion had been poured into a counter-insurgency strategy that had not only failed to see the FARC-EP collapse but saw some of the most ferocious guerrilla campaigns launched in a decade (Mondragón, 2007: 42; Brittain, 2005e). Ecuador's President Rafael Correa's (2007–) assessment of Plan Colombia was direct: "it's a complete failure ... The coca crops are still there and there are still vast areas that are not controlled by the Colombian State" (see Colombia Reports, 2008c). Correa has even referred to Ecuador as not bordering on Colombia but rather on the FARC-EP (see Vieira, 2008e). Nevertheless, 2009 saw yet another Colombian state official (President Uribe) pronounce the familiar refrain that "we can only defeat these criminals completely with the help of the United States and the international community" (Colombia Reports, 2009a).

Alongside the FARC-EP's expansion, the social and psychological repercussions of counter-insurgency have begun to show. Segments of Colombia's military fully believe the FARC-EP has the political and material potential to topple regional centers, while the state lacks the ability to respond to revolutionary surges from below. Sectors of the rank and file have even said that it is only a matter of time until the insurgency achieves its objective of state power (see Coghlan, 2004: 68). Demoralized, growing numbers of infantry are suffering from post-traumatic stress disorder (see Engqvist, 2005; Coghlan, 2004: 105). Many cases exist of troops suffering emotional problems, bouts of insanity, and delusion. In 2005, it was said that "the fighting spirit and morale of Bogotá's soldiers seem at an all-time low after a series of defeats against the guerrillas" (Engqvist, 2005). Lacking the facilities to respond to rising rates of psychological fatigue, some troops and commanding officers have lashed out: throwing acid in the faces of battalion members while asleep; gunning down groups of fellow soldiers during patrols; multiple attempts of suicide or homicide, and so on. The murder of civilians has also gravely affected soldiers psychologically. "I can't sleep. I'm awake all night, tossing and turning in bed .... I have this psychosis that at any moment someone could come, something could happen to me, that they are going to kill me" (Bajak, 2008c). From this scenario we can recognize that the military, while considerably larger, are no more emotionally advanced, efficient, or prepared to handle counter-insurgency warfare than they were in 1997.

Katharina Röhl (2004: 2) suggested that "there is no sign of the FARC losing its momentum. On the contrary, despite extensive counterinsurgency, persisting paramilitary presence, and massive US military and financial aid all contributing to stop and destroy it," the guerrillas have established dual power in many locales. Over time the guerrillas have advanced their tactical competence over domestic and imperial counter-insurgent forces. Not only is the FARC-EP triumphant in that they are structurally able to withstand tremendous military aggression, its capacity to respond to the same reactionary forces time and time again demonstrates its fortitude.[5]

Goff commented, "I have been questioned as to whether I really believe the FARC is winning, I do .... They have survived and counterattacked one of the most well-financed military offensives in this hemisphere" (2004: 44; see also 47).

Apart from sustaining its movement, the FARC-EP has arguably contained the expansion of US imperialism in Colombia, blocking the spread of foreign multinationals, and exposing "the vulnerability of imperialism" (Petras et al, 2005: 126; see also 94, 102).[6] As a result of the FARC-EP's aptitude as a revolutionary force, additional factors have arisen leading to a potential collapse of conventional power. If such conditions prevail, a significant threat to the interests of the dominant class, within and outside the Andean country, is sure to be realized – centralizing power in favor of the FARC-EP.

A POTENTIAL FOR COLLAPSE

Prior to his first presidential term, Álvaro Uribe Vélez promised he would defeat the FARC-EP during his political tenure. Such pronouncements were disproved as 2002 through 2006 saw the most sustained and powerful escalation of FARC-EP aggression toward state and paramilitary forces in years

(Fundación Seguridad & Democracia, 2006; 2004; Brittain, 2005e).[7] As some successes were, however, realized during his second term (2006–), the fact remains that very little scholarship has been devoted to Uribe's militaristic inability to eliminate the FARC-EP or Colombia's ongoing political-economic restructuring under his administration. Here we shed some light on these issues, and consider potential challenges facing the state as a consequence of the revolution from below (see González, Bolivar and Vázquez, 2002).

Contextualizing Uribe's failure to respond militarily to the FARC-EP

Prior to his coming to power in 1998, former president Andrés Pastrana, while not fully supportive of the idea, based much of his electoral campaign on negotiating a peace with the guerrillas (O'Shaughnessy and Branford, 2005: 43; Ramírez, Stanton and Walsh, 2005: 106; Leech, 2002a: 4). While many saw this strategy as problematic, as the state spoke of peace while it prepared for war (see Richani, 2005b: 95; CISLAC, 2001), it was based on this program that Pastrana found a home in the Casa de Nariño. On the heels of Pastrana's failed attempt to find a resolution to the war, Uribe started his run for the presidency from a completely different perspective (see Santiso, 2006: 216). He too promoted peace, but not through negotiation; rather, he called for the violent annihilation of the FARC-EP (O'Shaughnessy and Branford, 2005: 54; Ramírez et al, 2005: 111; Leech, 2002a: 74; Randall, 2002). If elected, Uribe declared he would rid the nation of the guerrillas in four years, a promise which gave him resounding support from the dominant urban class and elites throughout the periphery (Avilés, 2006: 123; Richani, 2005b: 93).

Within days of coming to office, Uribe augmented the counter-insurgency directives of Plan Colombia adopted under Pastrana by introducing draconian rule in areas thought to support the FARC-EP. Policies implemented saw massive numbers of peasants become rural soldiers for the state, the creation of a clandestine civilian information network, and the placement of entire regions of the country under military control via controversial zones of "rehabilitation and consolidation" (Crandall, 2005b: 177; Ramírez et al, 2005: 111–12; Sweig and McCarthy, 2005: 23–4; Bland, 2004: 5–6; Helweg-Larson, 2003; Leech, 2002c; 2002e). These methods were familiar to Uribe, as similar measures had been applied on a regional scale when he governed Antioquia. As noted in Chapter 6, Uribe promoted the legal creation of the CONVIVIR to combat the guerrillas. Before it became illegal many suggested the CONVIVIR model worked well at decreasing the FARC-EP's power in sectors of the northeast (Sweig and McCarthy, 2005: 19; Livingstone, 2003: 26; Scott, 2003: 71-72; Leech, 2002a: 88; Richani, 2002a: 52, 144). The reasoning was that if reactionary approaches proved effective regionally, similar successes could be achieved nationally. The FARC-EP, however, proved to be far more powerful than previously anticipated.

Near the middle of Plan Colombia it had become clear the mission was not working. In response, a more emphatic military campaign was devised to deal with the insurgency (Mondragón, 2007). Officially beginning in 2003, a new subcategorical counter-insurgency strategy was implemented concentrating on the Putumayo, Caquetá, Meta, and Nariño, and entitled Plan Patriota.[8] There was unprecedented growth in state aggression toward the FARC-EP, as military-initiated attacks against the guerrillas increased by 73 percent (Richani, 2005b: 89, 95). Immediately, reports surfaced claiming Plan Patriota had started to "wear down" the guerrillas (Acosta, 2004). There were assertions that Colombian and US forces were winning in their offensive against the FARC-EP alongside decline in support, a lowering of recruitment numbers, and a significant withdrawal from one-time socio-geographical strongholds (Crawley, 2005; Garamore, 2005; Pablo Toro, 2004). US officials announced that the FARC-EP had "been significantly degraded," and now "there is no portion of the country where Colombian forces cannot go" (as quoted in Garamore, 2005). By 2005, Uribe looked as though he would not go back on his electoral promise, especially when US Air Force General Richard B. Myers praised Plan Patriota for unequivocally defeating the FARC-EP (see Garamore, 2005).

As state reports affirmed the effectiveness of Plan Patriota and Uribe guaranteed the defeat of the FARC-EP, numbers on the ground proved quite different. In fact during Uribe's first two years as president the FARC-EP had conducted the same number of attacks against state forces as it had during the entire four-year term of Andrés Pastrana (Fundación Seguridad & Democracia, 2004).

Russell Crandall (2005b: 177) noted that 2003 saw FARC-EP attacks increase by a remarkable 23 percent. The next year proved even worse for the state, as assaults on state infrastructure increased by 100 percent and oil pipeline attacks grew by 21 percent, especially in the south (Brittain and Sacouman, 2006a; Fundación Seguridad y Democracia, 2006; Vieira, 2006a). Throughout Uribe's first term FARC-EP-initiated campaigns swelled, "from 227 percent between 1998 and 2002 to 450 percent per year in the 2002–04 period," while state-initiated attacks decreased 22 percent between 2003 and 2004 (Richani, 2005b: 95). Contrary to state and media accounts, the FARC-EP had put the state on the defensive, especially in the areas where Plan Patriota was deployed (see Chernick, 2007; Brittain, 2005e; Restrepo and Spagat, 2004). During an interview with a member of the Secretariat I was told, "Look around, here we are. Do you see any troops? Plan Patriota has not destroyed the FARC-EP. We move freely throughout the region as we have for the past several years." The fact remains that apart from the verbal rhetoric of the state and corporate media, the Uribe administration has failed to establish legitimate authority across vast areas of the country (see Williams, 2005: 160–1).

The blowback of neoliberal economic policy

Issues quite apart from the state's militaristic inability might have contributed to the weakness of the government. One such problem has been a lack of capital to combat the FARC-EP. Attempts have been made to try and rectify this problem, yet within the context of neoliberal economics the spending has proven unsustainable and could, in fact, increase instability. Traced back to the Betancur administration (1982–86), neoliberalism has become entrenched policy (Avilés, 2006). Deregulation and the privatization of domestic resources, especially energy-based primary industries, has significantly limited the availability of accessible state revenue, and this in turn has affected funding for the war (Leech, 2005a; Richani, 2005a: 115; 2005b: 89–90, 101n.69). One example of this was the once-lucrative "war tax" implemented to assist the state in its fight against the guerrillas.

Established on February 11, 1991, Decree 416 empowered the state to apply a "war tax" on "oil, gas, coal and nickel exports and on international telephone calls," and a 5 percent tax on those who earned more than 1 million pesos annually (Avilés, 2006: 157n.15). The most important aspect of the levy was its attachment to the natural resource industry, specifically oil. It was designed to enhance the state's capacity to confront the growing power of the FARC-EP, as the state acquired US$1–1.50 from every barrel of oil sold (Renner, 2002: 38). However, in 2001 several energy-based MNCs voiced their opposition to the tax, arguing it was a deterrent to trade, investment, and profit maximization (Richani, 2005a: 116). Ironically, as a direct result of increased neoliberal economic policy, and an internal decrease of state controls over multinational activity, the "war tax" on oil was removed (Richani, 2005a: 128; se also Leech 2006d: 147–51; 2005a).

With the threat of the FARC-EP not subsiding, the state had to find other sources of revenue to sustain military operations. One option chosen by the Uribe administration was to increase reliance on the Colombian elite through taxation. During Uribe's first year in office, a 20 percent hike in income taxes was applied (Muse, 2004: 22–3).[9] This was followed by an additional one-time 1.2 percent excise on liquid assets (Daily Journal, 2006b). At the time, these measures were supported under the belief that financially backing increased militarization would keep the guerrillas out of the country's cities.[10] However, when the pressure from below did not subside, elite-based tax structures continued. In 2006, an additional proposal was implemented for another "one-time" elite-based tax to expand military spending (Reuters, 2006a). This tax reform sought to increase the military's coffers by $1.2 billion through imposing a tax structure which placed a low percentage levy on financial holdings in excess of US$1 million (People's Daily, 2006a).

Some have suggested that these taxes upset the dominant class and their support for Uribe (Bronstein, 2006b; Stratfor, 2006; Sweig and McCarthy, 2005: 26). However, it should be borne in mind that any increased taxation directly applied to the wealthy will be indirectly transferred onto the backs of the urban and rural working class (Leech, 2006a; Martínez, 2006; LACY-ORK, 2003). Emphasizing elite-based taxation fails to address the fundamental question why a small minority pays such a disproportionate percentage of the overall tax bill.

There are several reasons why the majority do not pay a formal income tax. One is that Colombia has one of the most inequitable income distributions in Latin America (Holmes, 2003: 87–8; Green, 2003: 157; Röhl, 2004: 6n.29). As the majority of the population live in poverty, legitimate sustainable employment – the basis from which income tax is realized – is far from attainable.[11]

Beyond woeful overall employment levels, rural land has also remained central-ized in the hands of a limited few. These conditions, in the context of a national economy in decline (see DANE, 2008), prevent the majority from becoming constructive contributors to the domestic economy via a consistent taxable income.[12]

Dismissing such realities the Uribe administration nevertheless expanded an existing national value-added tax (VAT) system in 2007, which dispropor-tionately affected those with low incomes (see Lines, 2008: 57).[13] Economic development analysts and foreign financial advisors applauded such changes under the belief that "if more Colombians start paying taxes, they will be able to lower overall tax rates, which would have a positive impact on the overall competitiveness of the economy" (Bronstein, 2006a). The VAT expan-sion included a 1.6 percent tax on private cleaning and security services, a 10 percent levy on basic food supplies, a 16 percent excise tax on a vast array of consumer products, and finally a 23–35 percent tariff on items such as vehicles and boats. With increasing rates of both urban and rural poverty, the VAT expansion fiscally devastated the vast majority of the population, and badly affected small domestic-based business and agricultural producers (Bernardi, Fumagalli and Fumagalli, 2007; Bronstein, 2006b). In short, the VAT put mini-mal strain on the elite yet placed a heavy burden on the underemployed or unemployed. In fact, after passing the VAT expansion, the Uribe administra-tion reduced formal income tax levels for the dominant class (see Bronstein, 2006a).

In many ways VAT and the overall neoliberal approach broadened the state's fiscal dilemma. Not only have domestic industries experienced a reduction of capital, as people in the middle and lower-income brackets have reduced their spending as a result of the increased taxation, continued tariff reductions have decreased the returns from foreign direct investment.[14] Such activities affect all Colombians, as existing or potential domestic entrepreneurs, industry, and regional business groups are marginalized while largely foreign investors are supported. In contrast to numerous Latin American countries that are "moving away from neoliberalism by reclaiming sovereign control over their economies and natural resources," the Colombian president "has once again made evident his commitment to serving the interests of global capital at the expense of the welfare of Colombia's poor majority" (Leech, 2006a). Ricardo Duran, chief analyst with the Bogotá-based brokerage firm Corredores Asociados, added that the real goal of such policies is to benefit not those in Colombia but a minority beyond its border (see Muse, 2004).

"Free trade": assisting the revolt from below

There have been objections throughout Colombia to the continued promotion and adoption of free-trade agreements (FTA):

> Colombia's 28,000 rice growers – as well as corn, cereal and poultry farmers – say the trade pact threatens to put them out of business for good. That's

because, like farmers everywhere, many struggle to eke out an existence while their U.S. counterparts receive generous government subsidies. To lessen the impact, trade barriers for sensitive agricultural goods will be removed gradually over a period of 12–19 years. Nevertheless, in the first year Colombians must import a 87,000-ton quota of U.S. white rice – representing nearly 6 percent of Colombia's annual production – and the quota increases by 4.5 percent every year thereafter. In the short term, a feared flood of cheap imports could depress the price Colombian farmers get for their rice by as much as 30 percent, says Rafael Hernandez, general manager of Fedearroz, the country's rice growers association. But a bigger concern is what happens if farmers, unable to compete, turn to illegal crops like coca or poppy, the base ingredient of heroin. Especially in the central, rice-growing province of Meta, where coca and rice grow almost side by side, "if the government doesn't help farmers, the drug traffickers will," said Hernandez.

(Goodman, 2006a)

Those in the countryside have long complained how bilateral trade agreements between minority world countries and Colombia marginalize small and medium-sized producers that harvest traditional crops for local consumption.[15] However, in April 2006, Hernando José Gómez, Colombia's chief FTA negotiator, guaranteed that in the event of poor returns the state would assist those most affected with fiscal security measures and/or programs (Goodman, 2006a). President Uribe then promised "lower prices for foodstuffs, machinery that increases crop yields as well as the opportunity to export high-margin crops like mangos and other exotic fruits" (Goodman, 2006a). There was also a commitment that $220 million would be provided to local producers through subsidized loans to offset any FTA-related strains or losses.[16]

In mid-2006, however, Bogotá (and Washington) shifted to a policy that would only escalate anti-systemic sentiment throughout rural regions and guarantee the continuity of coca cultivation. Soon after the state's "commitment" to the rural producers was announced, it was leaked that the Uribe administration had quietly cut the proposed monetary support by 41 percent, and suggested it might be reduced further (Prensa Latina, 2006a).[17] Furthermore, on the heels of a US Embassy warning that the FARC-EP had the capacity to carry out assaults on Bogotá,[18] the US Agency for International Development (USAID) decided to cut its largest mission in the Western hemisphere and suspend all economic aid to the south of the country – the region most socioeconomically dependent on the coca industry (Reuters, 2006b; O'Shaughnessy and Branford, 2005: 32).[19] USAID indirectly stated that the political-military power of the FARC-EP had far exceeded the acceptable limits for the agency to work effectively. Another way of looking at this scenario is that USAID has failed to offer any lasting alternative development programs (Goodman, 2006b; Gibbs and Leech, 2005).[20] Hence, after roughly $8 billion in funding, the deployment of 20,000 US-trained forces, and immense weapons supplies, Washington and Bogotá have once again proven to be unable to assist those most exploited or debilitate the insurgency.

Needless to say, a wary populace, already distrustful of a government that has repeatedly abandoned it, is now more skeptical than ever about the rhetoric emanating from Bogotá and Washington. As Mario Cabal of PLANTE succinctly stated, "We have money for helicopters and arms for war, but we don't have money for social programs."

(Gibbs and Leech, 2005: 70–1; see also Bloomberg, 2006)

A STICK WITH NO CARROT: SUPPORTING REVOLUTIONARY ALLIANCES

It has been well referenced that Colombia's negative socioeconomic conditions, with limited prospects of structural change, have led to an increased ideological, political, and social growth in radical political activity (Brittain, 2007b; Holmes, Amin Gutiérrez de Piñeres, and Curtin, 2006: 178; Peceny and Durnan, 2006: 98; Felbab-Brown, 2005: 14, 107; O'Shaughnessy and Branford, 2005: 7; Klare, 2001). Rather than reducing social discontent, the realities of neoliberalism and conventional models of development have continued the marginalization of the poor in rural and urban Colombia, facilitating a sociopolitical equation that potentially increases alliances with, or reliance on, the FARC-EP (Leech, 2006b). For example, the methods employed by Washington and Bogotá to eliminate coca applied military strategies to what is clearly a socioeconomic and political problem (Peceny and Durnan, 2006: 109).

As was noted in preceding chapters, many cases of increased support toward the FARC-EP have been the result of state violence or its sociopolitical and economic absence (Grandin, 2006: 218; Holmes et al, 2006: 178; Peceny and Durnan, 2006: 98; O'Shaughnessy and Branford, 2005: 7, 34; Calvert, 1999: 128). Disproving assumptions that the insurgency's support and power are linked primarily to the coca industry, coca eradication programs have repeatedly failed to decrease its political-military capacity or hamper localized support for the guerrillas' objectives. In August 2006, a FARC-EP comandante said, "the fumigations hurt the peasants more than the guerrillas. They are the ones who are most dependent on coca for their survival" (Leech, 2006b). He went on to state that such "tactics are only further entrenching popular support for the guerrillas in remote regions of the country."

Reactionary policies have, in actuality, allowed the FARC-EP to remain "organically linked to the local peasant population – a fact that the same governments choose to ignore" out of either ideological and political support or socioeconomic sustainability (Leech, 2006b).[21] In turn, the guerrilla organization is seen as a proto-government and the army "of the people" (see Petras, 2008; Leech, 2006b).[22] Felbab-Brown (2005: 107) claimed that pursuing a system of eradication without the defeat of the FARC-EP or the implementation of sustainable alternative development projects "does the opposite of winning the hearts and minds of the people." Restrictions in social aid and an expansion of FTAs simply escalate the social base, recruitment numbers, and counter-hegemonic legitimacy of the movement (Brittain and Sacouman, 2006b; Leech, 2006b). Such a vacuum only solidifies the FARC-EP pre-revolutionary programs, enabling the guerrillas to be the ones who win the hearts and minds of the local rural populations (Felbab-Brown, 2005: 104).

What has resulted from these socially supportive activities is a sense of communal alliances between the rural populace and the FARC-EP. Such conditions have led people to view their relationship with the guerrillas as a socio-political, economic, and cultural link to their community's survival, which is sustained by the FARC-EP's continuity (Ross, 2006: 64).

> With the complete failure of the government to even attempt to provide any basic services to the local population, it is the FARC that has filled the void by helping to build roads and provide electricity, law enforcement, judges and other public services traditionally supplied by the state. As one local peasant notes, 'When farmers or their families get sick and can't afford medicine, it is the FARC that gives them money to purchase what they need' .... Until the government offers peasants ... something more than military repression, the local populations ... will continue to see their welfare and survival as inextricably intertwined with that of the FARC.
>
> (Leech, 2006b)

As reactionary economic and militaristic state policies take shape, shifts in FARC-EP support and consolidation may take hold. These shifts have the ability to further the revolutionary capacity of the guerrillas in the country-side, leading to an ever-increasing inability of domestic and foreign elites to withstand radical social changes there. This increase in class opposition reveals the frailty of the Colombian state. There are, however, external factors not yet mentioned that have a great effect on the availability of the resources that the state relies on to sustain its stability.

BETWEEN A ROCK AND A HARD PLACE: THE REALITIES OF CONTEMPORARY GLOBAL CAPITALISM

At a time where there has been considerable resurgence in Colombia's electoral left, alongside muted internal political support from one-time allies, the Colombian state has needed to procure ever more financial resources to keep revolutionary sentiment out of the Plaza de Bolívar. This saw the Uribe administration look to foreign institutions to help it retain or expand its revenue as a means of combating the FARC-EP. Here we look at two examples of this process, and suggest that such external dependencies are unsustainable and only increase the government's political-economic decline.

The FARC-EP's political-military capacity, coupled with the country's economy, has placed the state in a very difficult position. Colombia's civil war, which Uribe said he would end by 2006, is very much alive. In light of this reality, the government cannot increase its already over-reliance on the pocketbooks of the country's elite or the backs of the working class to help it retain power. As a result, "to finance the war, the Uribe government is running a budget deficit of 6 percent of the country's GDP, which is well above the 2.5 percent limit set by the IMF" (Richani, 2005b: 89). The rationale behind increasing Colombia's long-term debt was to offset political-economic instability, as many Latin American countries have done before. Such a position, however, cannot be prolonged. With the hindsight of the last 30 years, some in the IMF called for a decrease of support for Colombia in order to prevent a problematic debt ratio in the future (Muse, 2004: 22–3). Uribe himself acknowledged that difficulties in acquiring loans, financing, and monetary credit are to appear in the coming years as a result of his military-based security spending (Sáenz V., 2008). The Colombian state is therefore caught between a rock (IMF) and a hard place (a growing opposition to expanded taxation and FTA exploitation). Some have even argued that a potential backlash may arise from Colombia's elite and leading economic groups[23] "against paying any more taxes, thereby increasing the pressure on Uribe to draw foreign reserves to finance his war" (Richani, 2005b: 89–90, 101n.69; see also 2005a: 115).

Much of Colombia's elite has supported an expansion of the country's debt. It is believed that increased foreign aid and intervention will, first, assist state capacity to combat the FARC-EP, a considerable threat to dominant class interests; and second, decrease the elite's immediate taxable income by placing partial expenses on the backs of foreign taxpayers (Richani, 2005b: 93). The problem with this line of thinking is that Washington, Colombia's primary donor, has become economically crippled by its own problematic military campaigns (Iraq and Afghanistan) and domestic economic strife (debt crisis and the $1.5 trillion banking bail-out). As a result of this imperial overstretch, increased military support from the United States is no longer as likely as it once was (Markey, 2008b; Semana, 2008b, 2008c). This gives the Colombian state fewer options, as it continues to exhaust its borrowing opportunities as a result of deficit percentages unacceptable to the IMF (Richani, 2005b: 89–90).[24] Reviewing this scenario, Richani wrote:

> in light of the current structure of the military and the limited fiscal capacity of the Colombian state, a military build-up needed to match the insurgency's challenge will not be possible. Preoccupied with its own domestic deficit and the spiraling costs of its Iraq adventure, as well as its commitments to rebuilding Afghanistan, the US is clearly in no position to shoulder more of the burden .... US intervention has not been decisive enough to enable the Colombian military to defeat the guerrillas. Five years after the introduction of Plan Colombia there is no victor in sight, nor have the guerrilla forces shown signs of serious weakening.
>
> (Richani, 2005b: 90)

While neoliberalism has constrained the state's capacity to confront the FARC-EP, an argument could be made that a reduced state may be just what is needed, as MNCs can provide "extra income to sustain its war against a growing armed insurgency" (Richani, 2005a: 115).[25] The use of these private security forces, acting as a mechanism of stability for economic and political

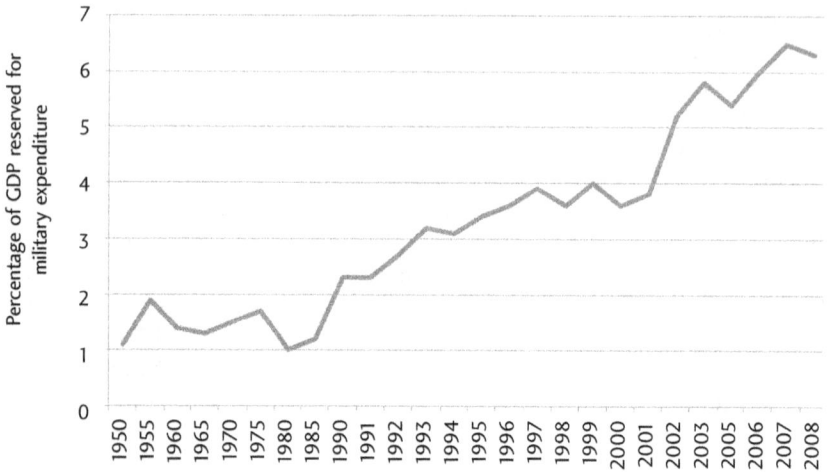

Figure 8.1 Colombia's military expenditure as a percentage of GDP, 1950–2008
Sources: Adapted from Brockner, 2008; Vieira, 2008b; Avilés, 2006: 84; Bloomberg, 2005; Bureau of Western Hemisphere Affairs, 2005; Richani, 2005b: 94; SIPRI Military Expenditure Database, 2005; Brittain, 2004a; Committee of Government Reform, 2004; UNDP, 2004; US Embassy of Colombia, 2003; World Bank, 2002; Federal Research Division Library of Congress, 1988; Ruhl, 1980: 187.

interests, has risen in recent years (Richani, 2005b: 48; O'Shaughnessy and Branford, 2005: 115, 128–30). However, such mercenaries are not without problems. Private forces will only maintain counter-insurgency activities as long as they remain profitable. The more the Colombian state reduces its economic surplus, through the selling-off of public industries and services alongside greater reductions in foreign-based corporate taxes, the greater the monetary pull on maintaining these private forces. The state, needing to sustain these forces, is therefore forced to increase exploitation over the social relations of production, resulting in greater human and natural resource degradation. This only furthers discontent, which increases state antagonism and can generate even more extreme reactions (such as expanded support for the FARC-EP). With there being a limit to the sustainability of using for-profit private security forces, and the finite realities of human and environmental resources, the state's withered internal forces will again be faced with little option but to confront the counter-hegemony of a superior armed movement.[26]

This book demonstrates that a struggle from below is being made real through a united force of the FARC-EP and sectors of the most exploited. This dual power has contributed to a partial breakdown of Colombia's centralized political-economic paradigm. As the civil war rages on, along with neoliberal economic policies, monetary-driven development, increased deficit spending, and the potential for the United States to draw back its support, a crisis exists that could see Colombia's conventional politics collapse. The complexity of these conditions may assist the FARC-EP to expand its sociopolitical footing and eventually succeed in bringing about the first Marxist-Leninist revolution of the twenty-first century. As one *campesino* succinctly stated when asked if he believes the FARC-EP will succeed in its revolutionary endeavors:

> Your question makes it sound as though they are not already [winning] or that their victory is something that will come in the future. The FARC are and have been winning for a long time. Look around ... the paracos are here because the FARC are winning. If the guerrillas and the people who support them were losing the state would not send the paracos to repress us. So many think that if the guerrilla do not take Bogotá they are not winning but they control vast territory throughout the countryside. This is no easy feat, the FARC are winning .... When you look around the southern parts of this country it becomes apparent that the state only exists as an instrument to continue elite rule. Therefore, I think it is very realistic that the guerrillas can preserve control and gain further power over much of the countryside, especially when the United States is so preoccupied with its other wars in the Middle East. Bogotá is a totally different beast .... A few years ago the FARC had the ability to invade Bogotá. They had surrounded it and had people in the barrios ready to fight. For whatever reason, they chose not to do this. Rather the guerrillas have sought to consolidate power in the countryside, where they have the greatest and most open support. Once the guerrillas have consolidated power in the outskirts it will be easier to increase their numbers and march to the Plaza [Plaza de Bolívar]. Bogotá will not be easy but I think they can do it. Support is there, you know. There have been dips here and there, but for the most part, especially here in the south, the FARC cannot be beaten, and the more they try, the stronger the guerrillas will become. The more the paracos come in, the more this forces people into a political and moral corner, leaving them to question, "What else can we do but rebel for a better Colombia?" I do not know if this answers your question. I would never say that the FARC will lose but I will certainly tell you that the state and elite that repress the people of this country will never win.

NOTES

PREFACE

1   Some disregard Marxism-Leninism as a sufficient theory to facilitate radical social change; "The Leninist model has been so thoroughly discredited that it is difficult to see how anyone could revive it now or ever .... The collapse of the Soviet Union also marked the end of Marxist-Leninist revolution as a historical form" (Paige, 2003: 27).

2   Forrest Hylton (2006: 6) referred to Colombia as Latin America's "least understood and least studied" country, and emphasized the need to counter this unsettling "silence in English-language scholarship and public debate."

3   The term "ethnic groups" is employed to uphold anonymity. To name specific groups would partially divulge the socio-geographical locations visited.

CHAPTER 1

1   Works on the Latin American left have paid little attention to the contribution of the PCC (and less still to the FARC-EP), whose roots predate the Cuban revolution (see Hansen, 1972).

2   Marx never promoted a "pure" urban industrial proletariat as the sole force of emancipatory struggle (Avineri, 1973: 112; see also Löwy, 1992; Burke III, 1988; Baranski and Short, 1985; Melloti, 1977; Bottomore, 1973).

3   The term "dual economy" refers to a socioeconomic model where industrial commodity-based workers exist alongside agricultural subsistence/wage-laborers (see Vanden and Prevost, 2006: 158).

4   Vast numbers were organized across urban and rural sectors during this period. By 1938, 83,000 unionists existed, with the agricultural sector almost entirely mobilized by the PCC (Weil et al, 1970: 425; see also Ross, 2006: 60).

5   The Party supported a view that (urban and rural) members learn from each other and their differing socio-environmental conditions, which would be essential upon a revolutionary seizure of power (see Rochester, 1942).

6   Eric B. Ross (2006: 60) noted that "by 1939, more than 150 peasant leagues had been formed; many affiliated with the Communist party, and many that persisted as guerrilla groups in the early 1960s and beyond."

7   During the 1950s, alliances between city and countryside were assisted by the falling price of coffee, which paralyzed the national economy and affected both localities (Chavez, 2007: 94).

8   None of this belittles the PCC's accomplishments in the cities:

> the Communists had gained considerable ground, particularly in the labor movement. In 1958, they recaptured control of the majority of the unions petroleum industry. They also made considerable gains among the workers in the industrial city of Cali and in other important centers. For the first time in a decade the Communists were "an element of importance in the Colombian labor movement, particularly in the ranks of the Confederación de Trabajadores de Colombia (C.T.C.)." (Alexander, 1963: xiv; see also Safford and Palacios, 2003: 293–6, 326; Decker and Duran, 1982)

Disproving claims that the PCC and radical sectors were unable to organize workers (see Bergquist, 2007; Posada Corbá, 2006), Jorge Castañeda (1994: 222–3) noted that the Colombian labor movement "has often been considered the most powerful in Latin America." Munck knew that:

> in Colombia the communist-influenced trade unions pioneered a new form of social mobilization in the 1970s known as the *paros cívicos* (civilian stoppages). These centered less around traditional trade union issues (like wages and conditions) but also on the provision of public services such as water, electricity and waste disposal. A very wide range of social sectors were usually involved including professional associations, in completely paralyzing the major cities. (Munck, 2008: 141)

He added that the Party's importance in relation to social movements has been marginalized due to "the intense repression ... unleashed by the state."

9   Accounts of Colombians utilizing the works of Marx to organize date back to 1849 (Liss, 1984: 149).

10   It was *after* Colombian Marxists had already organized the Party's foundation that Savisky assisted a formal Marxist collective (see Sharpless, 1978: 195n.46; Urrutia, 1969: 82-83; Poppino, 1964: 57, 83).

11   Raúl Eduardo Mahecha, José Mar, Diego Mejía, Roberto García Peña, Moisés Prieto, Armando Solano, Luis Tejada, Gabriel Turbay, and Alejandro Vallejo Dionisio Arrango Vélez were but a few of the original organizers (Sharpless, 1978: 24, 44; Urrutia, 1969: 82; Cuéllar, 1963: 131; Comisión del Comité Central, 1960: 12).

12   Some identify the FARC-EP's inception as during the 1950s–1960s through "agrarian reform experiments of the radical liberal Juan de la Cruz Varela and the organizational and military experiences of the Communist Party" (Richani, 2002a: 62). Any discussion of Cruz Varela as a Liberal during this period is misleading, as he became a member of the PCC in 1950 and "organized the Communist defence of the Sumapaz region" (LeGrand, 1986: 259n.42).

13   One important characteristic that has distinguished the communist guerrillas from Liberals was that during times of strife, violence, and/or political opportunism, the latter repeatedly opted to abandon armed struggle for the chance to involve themselves in the very conventional political arena they once contested (see Buscaglia and Ratliff, 2001: 14; Kline, 1999; Carrigan, 1993; Pearce, 1990a; Gomez, 1972: 250). In some cases, Liberal-based guerrillas were, in practice, nothing more than glorified gangs "formed by the victims of government violence," which "dedicated themselves to steal and plunder" or employ acts of vengeance (Chavez, 2007: 93).

14   Far too many scholars have overweighed or loosely united the actions of the PCC and the Liberal Party. Few have properly explained the PCC–Liberal partnership for what it was, a structured internationalist strategy in sync with the dictates of the USSR during the 1930s. The Comintern expressed grave concern about the growth of fascism, and promoted national (communist) parties to align with domestic anti-fascist groups to help prevent the far right from amassing power (Osterling, 1989: 228; see also Grandin, 2006: 40–1; 2004: 5–6; Crandall, 2002: 22; Beals, 1974: 236, 241). Manipulating the "partnership period" the PCC actually used sectors of the Liberal Party to procure logistical support and intelligence for its self-defense communities (Sánchez and Meertens, 2001: 18).

15   In many ways the Liberal Party worked extensively to destabilize the potential for social change. Charles W. Bergquist (2007: 671) found that influential Liberals feared "the radical potential of their popular allies, leading them eventually into an alliance with the Conservatives to limit popular power." For example, when a leading left-of-center Liberal candidate had a clear lead over a Conservative, the Liberal-right would support the implementation of a second candidate (Chavez, 2007: 93). This electorally assisted the Conservative Party as the Liberal vote would be divided, enabling the ruling class – regardless of party affiliation – to

stay in power. (Similar practices were also seen in the 1980s, see Calvert, 1999: 117.) Liberals also periodically employed social-democratic policy to "divide and conquer the workers movement" and deconstruct the PCC's influence over the CTC (Chavez, 2007: 92).

16 *La Violencia* has been cited as "the largest civil conflict in Latin America since the Mexican Revolution" (Bergquist, 2007: 671). The general review of this period depicts extreme partisan violence between leftist sectors of the Liberal Party and right-wing elements of the Conservative Party. Many claim *la Violencia* was divided between these factions, yet effective researchers have shown that rural peoples, and specifically PCC supporters, were those most targeted. Harvey F. Kline (1999: 18) stipulated that from the 1940s onwards, the Conservative Party directed armed offences against those on the left, and in areas where communists were most powerful and growing. During the 1950s the state declared illegal "any regions thought to harbour Communists," and "indiscriminately" attacked them using ground forces and aerial bombardment (Simons, 2004: 42). For a well-mapped account of the progression from a Conservative–Liberal conflict to a structural targeting of communist influence, refer to Gonzalo Sánchez and Donny Meertens' "phases" (2001: 36, 40).

With the PCC's rise in rural support, it is no surprise why the vast majority of the 300,000 killed during *la Violencia* were those living and working in the country-side: peasants, rural-based wage-laborers, sharecroppers, the landless, subsistence producers, and so on (Richani, 2002a: 23–28; Zamosc, 1986: 15; Lindqvist, 1979: 89; Kalmanovitz, 1978: 302–4; Gilhodés, 1970: 421–51). "While order returned in Bogotá and other cities" after *la Violencia*, "political violence became the pattern for much of rural Colombia" (Williamson, 1965: 36). Recognizing this, Richard Gott (1970: 10–11) described *la Violencia* as nothing short of a civil war, not a dominant political partisan conflict (see also Williamson, 1965: 43). At the same time severe political–economic conditions began to affect the capital, only adding to the country's sociopolitical and economic combustibility (Raby, 2006: 246; Gurr, 1970: 115; Fluharty, 1957: 84–99). Nevertheless, it should be noted that Colombia's current situation is viewed as more severe than *la Violencia* (see Munck, 2008: 145).

17 Prior to the agreement, the PCC had 50,000 open members and significant union influence (Beals, 1974: 240).

18 Not seeing this system as structurally unrepresentative or unequal, some have suggested Colombia never suffered "prolonged periods of counterinsurgent dicta-torship aimed to crush an increasingly radicalized mass movement" (Grandin, 2004: 177; see also Skidmore and Smith, 2005: 243). It is also said the country was insulated from the "wave of brutal military dictatorships that swept the rest of the continent" (Grandin, 2004: 272n.28). Such pronouncements are question-able and fail to comment on, or even regard, the regime of General Gustavo Rojas Pinilla (1953–57), which preceded the National Front (see Henderson, 2001; 1985; Pearce, 1990a: 60–1; Graciarena and Franco, 1978: 37; Beals, 1974: 254; Dix, 1967; Szulc, 1959; Fluharty, 1957). Hylton's work properly clarified such inac-curacies: "if Colombia was spared the experience of the military dictatorships that decimated middle-class, labor, and peasant radicalism elsewhere in Latin America during the 1960s and 1970s, it is because the National Front was a semi-authori-tarian parliamentary dictatorship" (Hylton, 2006: 54; see also Munck, 1984a; Collier, 1979; Williamson, 1965: 37).

19 Stokes offered an important geopolitical insight into the "agreement" and its deep ties to US counterinsurgency during the Cold War:

> under the National Front arrangement ... the USA stepped up its commitments to Colombia as part of its new Cold War crusade of anti-communism. This

period of US intervention marked a watershed in Colombian and US relations, with the Colombian military consistently remaining one of the largest recipients of US military aid and training throughout the Cold War. It was also the first country in Latin America to adopt US CI measures in relation to its perceived problems of insurgency and civil unrest and also hosted the first Latin America counter-insurgency training school. (Stokes, 2005: 5)

20 Some, however, claimed the left's marginality to be a self-induced predicament. Bergquist (2007: 672) suggested that the lack of progressive social change in Colombia is not the fault of the elite systematically excluding alternative political bodies from gaining ground, but rather caused by the failure of the left to act as a vanguard.

21 Albeit limited, the PCC was seen as a viable alternative to Colombia's historic two-party system (Osterling, 1989: 187; Dix, 1980: 131, 138; Weil et al, 1970: 267; Martz, 1962: 13). Much of Colombia has been divided into sociopolitical geographies of Liberal and Conservative support, as has the PCC: "In Colombia, it is often said, one is born either a Liberal or Conservative. What is less often recognized is that the same sort of regional and familial base of partisanship applies to the Communists as well" (Shugart, 1992: 134n.13; see also Alexander, 1957). Such political geography is recognized as certain areas vote for parties that express ideologies similar to the guerrillas (Shugart, 1992: 134). Hence, people have been killed by state and paramilitary forces simply "because of the place of origin shown on their identity card" (Pearce, 2007: 232).

22 Formally ended in 1974, the National Front has effectively persisted since "Colombia's political and economic elite have continued to govern in a manner inconsistent with the interests of a majority of Colombians, despite democratic reform" (Avilés, 2006: 4; see also Gibbs and Leech, 2009: 50; Schulte-Bockholt, 2006: 102; Stokes, 2005: 4; Lieuwen, 1961: 87, 89).

23 Colombian political economist Héctor Mondragón (2003; 2001) has argued that this process was partially legitimized through Currie's capitalist developmental policy (see also Ross, 2006; Brittain, 2005b).

24 Since the 1930s and 1940s, increasingly rural-based large landholders moved to the cities and became absentee owners (that is, urban-based rural landowners) or "capitalist entrepreneurs" while aligning with industrialists, thereby changing the rural dynamic of the social relations of production (Sánchez and Meertens, 2001: 11).

25 In the 1950s, Currie was the largest cattle owner in the country (see Currie, 1966: ix).

26 Dating back to the 1920s and 1930s, the PCC "orientated their efforts toward disrupting the operations of North American companies in Colombia," especially in the areas of agriculture and oil (Decker and Duran, 1982: 81). This is interesting in comparison with Marx's discussion of the Irish Fenians and England (see Marx, 1988b: 449).

27 Two officials, Liberal Victor Mosquera Chaux and Conservative Alvaro Gómez Hurtado, coined the term "independent republics" (see Dudley, 2004: 156; Lozano Guillén, 2001: 19; FARC-EP, 2000b: 22; Pearce, 1990a: 64; Osterling, 1989: 294; Gomez, 1972: 251–2; Gilhodés, 1970: 437). The "opposing" politicos manufactured an expansionary communist threat to procure capital for counterinsurgency/anti-communist measures.

28 Some have even labeled this as the "evolutionary path" of the peasant struggle (Sánchez, 2000: 35).

29 The military assault was made possible through extensive economic, armaments, and guidance from the United States through the Latin American Security Operation (Plan Lazo) (Safford and Palacios, 2003: 355–6; Pearce, 1990a: 64; US Department of State, 1964).

30 The guerrillas had been active prior to this period. Preceding the First (September 1964) and Second (April 1966) Conferences of the Guerrillas, the FARC-EP produced formal statements concerning issues of agrarian reform and imperialist interference. Released July 20, 1964, the *Agrarian Programme of the Guerrillas* detailed revolutionary strategies towards agricultural, land reform, worker-peasant alliances and so on (Peace and Socialism, 1966: 12–18).

31 While the military was directly involved in coercive activity against the rural population, the government was sociopolitically inactive in providing health and medical services, agrarian security, and a lengthy series of social services such as education, for 70 percent of the populace (Saunders et al, 1978: 132–4; Gilbert, 1974: 142–7; Felstenhausen, 1968a, 1968b; Bernstein, 1964: 74–5; Galbraith, 1953: 59–60, 94–5).

32 The progression and expansion of the networks was working well throughout the late 1950s and early 1960s (Petras and Morley, 1990: 176). Prior to 1964, over 16 self-defense communities had been established (Hylton, 2006: 54; Schulte-Bockholt, 2006: 109; Safford and Palacios, 2003: 356; Osterling, 1989: 294).

33 It has been said the "FARC is the heir of a long and endogenous process of accumulation of peasant armed resistance" (Gutiérrez Sanín, 2004: 263).

34 Garry Leech demonstrated how the peasant-based self-defense groups:

> did not find the autonomy they sought, as large landowners intent on increasing their own holdings began laying claim to newly cleared areas. The national government, meanwhile, condemned the peasants and communist bandits and subjected them to an economic blockade. The Colombian military launched massive offensives against the independent republics, which included using U.S.-supplied B-26 bombers against peasant communities. The republics fell one by one, and once under government control, the land was usurped from the peasants and became concentrated in the hands of large landowners. (Leech, 2002a: 13)

> With respect to theories of anti-power or no-power (see Holloway, 2002a, 2002b, 2002c; Hardt and Negri, 2004, 2000) the United States and the Colombian state could not and would not allow autonomous movements to exist, as they presented a real or imagined deterrent to capitalist expansion. For the duration of the 1960s and 1970s, Washington and Bogotá formulated a conjoined economic and militaristic plan to target the peasant-based enclaves (Ampuero and Brittain, 2005). Movements (and theorists) can learn from this: that selective autonomous non-transformative movements cannot create a sustainable response to the capital system, but rather block sustainable pathways to social change (see Brittain, 2006a; Draper, 1978a: 101).

35 El Davis was "the first major center of guerrilla struggle in Latin America led by the party of the proletariat" (Gomez, 1972: 249; see also Gott, 1970: 234n.7).

36 Tad Szulc (1964: 20–1) asserted that "United States antiguerrilla advisers" had placed "a special emphasis on Colombia where the fourteen-year-old backlands bandit wars could well turn into political revolutionary movements" (see also Grandin, 2006: 96; Stokes, 2005: 71–4, 108–9; Rabe, 1999: 140; Barnet, 1972: 73, 74n.12). Demonstrating the geopolitical significance of what the PCC and peasant communities were achieving in Marquetalia, Grandin (2006: 97) illustrated how, "for a time in the early 1960s, the budding civil war in Colombia between the state and breakaway Communist-organized peasant republics was seen as a potentially greater crisis than the one in Vietnam." Commencing July 1, 1962, Plan Lazo became the prominent strategy to eliminate guerrilla movements and re-establish state control over areas of communist presence, influence, and colonization.

37 Disturbingly, it was noted that:

not only were Green Berets working with the Colombian military, the country, according to investigative reporter Gerard Colby, served as a "pre-Vietnam experiment in [Robert] McNamara's 'systems' approach to integrating communications (command and control), rapid air mobility, concentrated firepower, and computer-assisted intelligence for finding and tracking an enemy." (Grandin, 2006: 97–8)

38 It was in these locales that:

hundreds of peasant families and former guerrillas [Liberals who had given up arms or left the struggle] fleeing from government reprisals had taken refuge. The new settlers, without any aid from the state, cleared the mountain slopes and jungles, planted crops and set to raising livestock. In time these zones became major suppliers of produce to nearby markets. (Gomez, 1972: 250)

39 During one attack on Marquetalia in 1962, the peasantry not only defeated the army but inflicted significant losses while procuring arms and heavy military equipment from the overwhelmed state forces (Lartéguy, 1970: 146).

40 The size of Marquetalia tripled from 2,000 square miles in the late 1950s to 5,000 by 1964, with a conservative estimate of 4,000 peasants living in the area, while some claim the number was in the tens of thousands (Schulte-Bockholt, 2006: 109; Livingstone, 2003: 180; Gilhodés, 1970: 433; Gott, 1970: 235; Lartéguy, 1970: 147). This is not outlandish, as an estimated 60,000 assisted in the development of the guerrilla-controlled zones (Lartéguy, 1970: 143). Drawing "on the support of relatively large numbers of mobilized, anti-Conservative peasants," 10,000 peasant families migrated and lived within the self-defense communities, with Marquetalia having 4,000, according to Guillermo de la Peña (1998: 353; see also Pearce, 1990a: 60; Gilhodés, 1970: 445). Most interesting was that these communities and the guerrillas there, specifically Marulanda, were supported by lower-level sectors of the official Colombian military (Sánchez and Meertens, 2001: 148–9).

41 Some peasants knew a major state-based aggression was coming in response to the army's failed attempts to displace the communities (Sánchez and Meertens, 2001: 178–9).

42 Shortly after one mission had taken place, then minister of war, Major-General Alberto Ruíz Novoa, demonstrated the precariousness of the conflict and the class-rooted intentions therein:

[I]t seems that this battle is not of the people of the Cauca, but of some land-owners of this department who want to take over rich lands the peasants of Ríochiquito now farm, for which they do not hesitate to enjoin the army to enter the region with "blood and fire" (quoted from FARC-EP, 2000b: 22–3; see also Maullin, 1973: 28; Gilhodés, 1970: 444)

43 See Leech, 2002a: 14.

44 This is not to imply that the PCC did not support armed struggle prior to 1966. The Party had been involved in establishing guerrilla fronts from the 1930s onwards (Simons, 2004: 51; Safford and Palacios, 2003: 355; Sánchez and Meertens, 2001: 18; Kline, 1999: 18; Gomez, 1972: 249–50; Petras, 1968: 335). During *la Violencia*, for example, the PCC urged proletarians, especially in the countryside, to defend themselves (Kline, 1999: 18). As stated by Alberto Gomez (1972: 248): "in 1949 the Communist Party issued a call to the masses to reply with their own organized violence to the violence unleashed by the reactionaries. The slogan found a response among the peasant masses." If the PCC was to truly represent the interests of the domestic working class, it had to support the right of the people to defend themselves and their communities from class-based repression. In 1961, at the Ninth Congress of the PCC, the Party officially adopted the call

for various forms of struggle, including armed struggle, to be supported (Safford and Palacios, 2003: 356). All this is interesting, for it was during this period that the USSR discouraged armed struggle as a means of revolutionary social change in Latin America. Therefore, the PCC's actions were, to put it mildly, a balancing act. During the 1950s, under the "request" of the USSR, numerous CPs distanced themselves from armed struggle (Poppino, 1964: 147). Hence, in 1959, at its Seventh Congress, the PCC chose to "protest" guerrilla activities in its borders (Aguilar, 1968: 43–4n.2).

The real basis for this shift in policy, especially when concerning support for the guerrillas, was in fact a mechanism to keep relations between the Party and the USSR cordial. One example of the PCC trying to appease the Soviets was during the Liberal administration of Carlos Lleras Restrepo (1966–70]). The Colombian state had sought to boost trade with the USSR (and vice versa); therefore, Lleras requested the Soviets to place pressure on the Party to reduce its support for the guerrillas, and in return Colombia would increase bilateral trade with the communist superpower (Maullin, 1973: 33–4; see also Angell, 1998: 112). Hence, during certain periods, the PCC appeared to oppose the guerrillas, while clandestinely supporting their activities, so as to appease Soviet power. This is how some, such as Gerard Chaliand (1977: 61), may have come to the conclusion that in 1967 (only a few months after the PCC at the Tenth Congress proclaimed further promotion of armed struggle) the Party moved toward a social democratic position of political change and away from armed methods of struggle.

45 This is the highest-ranking position in FARC-EP's hierarchal structure.

46 Marulanda's civic name was Pedro Antonio Marín; he was born on May 12, 1928, in Génova, Quindío (Safford and Palacios, 2003: 354; Osterling, 1989: 295; see Map 1.1).

47 This does not dismiss the valued work of Eduardo Pizarro Leongómez (1996; 1992; 1991) or Arturo Alape (1989), but rather highlights that outside their work little is understood of Marulanda's sociopolitical history.

48 The FARC-EP Secretariat of the Central High Command is made up of Jorge Briceño, Alfonso Cano, Pablo Catatumbo, Joaquín Gómez, Mauricio Jaramillo, Timoleón Jiménez, and Iván Márquez, all of whom, excluding Cano and Jaramillo, come from rural backgrounds (Richani, 2007: 414–15; 2002a: 63; see also Chernick, 2007: 56). While all offer a significant ideological component to the insurgency, Cano, who replaced Marulanda as commander-in-chief (and joined the struggle in 1968), has an academic background and therefore has been said to be more ideological than tactical (Otis, 2008b). Most importantly, the entire leadership's political tendencies are entrenched in communist policy (see Lozano Guillén, 2001).

49 Such reports are nonetheless suspect, because of many discussions and observations that I carried out with the guerrillas and/or the peasantry concerning Marulanda. Research has suggested Marulanda's occupations did not extend outside the countryside, as his only formal education, apart from four years of primary school, was during his time in the army (see Richani, 2002a: 63; Wickham-Crowley, 1992: 331). Some, however, have reported Marulanda was "a woodcutter, butcher, baker, and candy salesman" (Hudson, 2002: 159).

50 It must be clarified that Marulanda's involvement with the Liberal party – during his teens – was due to his family's affiliation, compounded by his father's murder at the hands of the Conservative Party (Hylton, 2006: 58; Alejandro and Billon, 1999; Osterling, 1989: 295). During *la Violencia*, Marulanda would have found immediate solace and support in the Liberal cadres. For a sociological account of the historiography of these family-based links in rural Colombia during the mid-twentieth century, refer to Williamson (1965: 42).

51 Arenas' civic name was Luis Alberto Morantes Jaime. He was born on January
    23, 1924, in Bucaramanga, Santander. First a blue-collar worker in Bucaramanga,
    Arenas became a member of the PCC in the mid-1940s. A militant oil worker in
    Barrancabermeja, he later became a labor organizer/union leader before leaving
    for the countryside to assist the communist-based peasantry as an equal and essen-
    tial ally in revolutionary struggle (Dudley, 2004: 47–8; Osterling, 1989: 295–6;
    Gilhodés, 1970: 445).
52 While some have refused to see the FARC-EP as the "people's army" (LeGrand,
    2003: 180), the guerrillas have nevertheless demonstrated themselves to be such
    (Petras, 2008; Leech, 2006b; Gomez, 1972: 255–6; Pomeroy, 1968: 314).

CHAPTER 2

1   Some areas are completely controlled by the FARC-EP, with schools, medical facili-
    ties, and grassroots judicial structures, while others have a more muted presence
    via small enclaves of simplistic community networks.
2   Other essential figures involved in the leadership of the Secretariat over the past
    quarter-century have been Jacobo Arenas, Efraín Guzmán, Raúl Reyes, Iván Ríos,
    and the long-time commander-in-chief Manual Marulanda Vélez. After decades of
    service to the PCC and later the FARC-EP, Arenas died of heart failure on August
    10, 1990. Guzmán passed away on September 7, 2003 of a heart attack and was
    replaced by Ríos the following November (FARC-EP, 2004a; 2003j). Both Reyes
    and Ríos were violently murdered in two separate incidents in March 2008 (Brit-
    tain and Sacouman, 2008a, 2008b; Brittain, 2008). A member of the FARC-EP's
    Central High Command and comandante of the Southern Block, Joaquín Gómez
    replaced Reyes on March 2, 2008 (Agencia Bolivariana Prensa, 2008; Associated
    Press, 2008a; FARC-EP, 2008a). On March 8, 2008, Mauricio Jaramillo, a trained
    physician, replaced Ríos (FARC-EP, 2008b). Marulanda, the longest-surviving
    Latin American guerrilla and the primary leader of the FARC-EP since its incep-
    tion, passed away on March 26, 2008 as a result of cardiac arrest. Long-time
    member of the FARC-EP's Secretariat, Alfonzo Cano was appointed Marulanda's
    successor, and Pablo Cataumbo became the most recent Secretariat member
    (FARC-EP, 2008c).
3   The last decade saw combatants increase in all blocks. In December 2004, I ascer-
    tained that the guerrillas expanded their forces by 100 newly trained combatants
    in one southwestern municipality alone.
4   See Hylton, 2006: 89; Murillo and Avirama, 2004: 70; Sánchez, 2003: 15;
    Crandall, 2002: 62; Petras, 1999: 31.
5   See Ahmad, 2006: 43; Richani, 2002a: 76-77; 2001: 57. Avilés (2001: 50n.13)
    estimated that an average FARC-EP front at the end of the 1990s consisted
    of 100–200 combatants. This estimate is likely a low one as many insurgent
    campaigns utilize from 300 to 1,500 combatants from a specific front (see Richani,
    2005b: 84; 2001: 57; Stokes, 2005: 91; Ruiz, 2001: 23). Doing so removes the
    potential for information to be misconstrued by another front which might have studied
    different tactical strategies. By 2008, however, the number of fronts decreased.
6   CODHES director Jorge Rojas noted that recruitment escalated dramatically in
    recent years (see Vieira, 2008b).
7   One explanation for the 1986–89 incline was the FARC-EP's relation with the left-
    of-center Unión Patriótica (UP) political party during peace negotiations with the
    Conservative Belisario Betancur Cuartas administration (1982–86), enabling open
    regional support.
8   Such accounts are questionable as Colombia became engulfed in a "false positives"
    scandal in 2008. Officials encouraged the army to slaughter civilians and dress

them in FARC-EP fatigues to create military victories (Semana, 2008e). During Uribe's administration:

> they increased from 246 in 2004, to 458 in 2005, to 795 in 2006 and to 911 in 2007. It is a chilling tale: young men of scant resources, drug addicts, homeless people and other vulnerable citizens without strong family ties were assassinated and presented as combat deaths to high military officials. (Semana, 2008d)

In conjunction Uribe:

> started a vigorous program to promote guerrilla desertion, that includes economic incentives, judicial exoneration, and psychological support, and has scored some successes ... the government has invested enormous resources, both in program and in propaganda, to promote desertion. Given this factor, the desertion rate seems surprisingly small. (Gutiérrez Sanín, 2004: 270)

In fact, FARC-EP desertions have remained consistently below 7 percent, as they have for decades, causing some researchers to suggest that "the government's program promoting desertion is clearly losing momentum" (Gutiérrez Sanín, 2004: 283n.60).

9   Ulrich Oslender (2008: 91) asserted how "reliable data on displacement simply does not exist in Colombia."

10   A famed example of statistical manipulation was witnessed when national police chief General Oscar Naranjo claimed Colombia had reduced its share in the global drug-trade by half between 2002 and 2006, a period that saw coca cultivation reach its highest level in history (Agence France-Presse, 2008b; Leech, 2008c; O'Shaughnessy, 2008).

11   The PCC assessed that the country was not yet at a place to successfully create a revolutionary upheaval of capitalist society (see Schulte-Bockholt, 2006: 109, 110; Livingstone, 2003: 206). Ideologically, however,

> a Party of the Leninist type will never stand idly, holding aloof and waiting for the "great hour," the situation which will itself evoke the revolutionary enthusiasm of the working people and weaken the resistance of their enemies. It seeks and finds possibilities for active work among the masses, for an active political struggle, even under the most unfavorable conditions ... bring very much closer the hour of the decisive battle, and prepares for this battle not only itself, but also the broadest possible sections of the working people. (Dutt, 1963: 168–9, 349)

Lenin (1965d: 154) argued that "the paramount immediate object of these [guerrilla] operations is to destroy the government, police and military machinery and to wage a relentless struggle against the active Black-Handed organizations which are using violence against the population and intimidating it." In areas where the proletariat is incapable of responding materially to reactionism, a guerrilla movement must be wholeheartedly promoted to destabilize dominant class forces (Lenin, 1965b: 118; 1965d: 153). From this stance, the PCC noted at its Tenth Congress that "it would be negative and fatal for the Colombian revolutionary movement to stand by and watch the destruction of this force while waiting for a revolutionary situation to mature before beginning the armed struggle" (as quoted in Gott, 1970: 519). From the same event, Pomeroy quoted:

> armed struggle in Colombia began and is developing as guerrilla warfare at a time when a revolutionary situation does not yet exist throughout the country. It would be disastrous for the Colombian revolutionary movement passively to allow the peasant organizations to be destroyed on the plea that it is necessary to wait until the revolutionary situation has fully matured before taking armed action. To the armed aggression of the enemy it is necessary to counterpose in

the villages guerrilla resistance and armed struggle and, when the conditions are ripe for it, the question of armed struggle must be posed also in the towns and working-class centers. (Pomeroy, 1968: 308)

As Lenin (1965h: 347) famously noted, "passivity is the quality of the petty-bourgeois intelligentsia, not of the revolution."

12 For two decades the FARC-EP was actually referred to as the FARC (minus the EP – acronym for *Ejército del Pueblo* or in English, People's Army) (see Gomez, 1972: 255–6; Pomeroy, 1968: 314). The post-1982 period signified a defining shift in structure and tactics.

13 This is a substantial number when Colombia's indigenous population accounts for 1–5 percent of the populace (Palacios, 2006: 251; Lakshmanan, 2004; Murillo and Avirama, 2004: 41; Livingstone, 2003: 124). I was repeatedly told by both aboriginal members of the FARC-EP and civilians that indigenous membership has been based on two primary factors: first, increased assaults waged against native populations and their lands, and second, shifts in consciousness toward class struggle moving beyond segregated identity politics. As 69 percent of the country's 84 indigenous groups live in the department of Putumayo (see Flounders, 2003: 84), I was told that a great deal of indigenous support for the FARC-EP exists in the south – although it is clandestine.

14 Hylton (2006: 89) suggested that females make up 30–40 percent of middle-level comandantes and deputies. My research found significantly higher numbers during counts conducted between 2004 and 2007, where it was not uncommon for women to outnumber men in areas of membership and leadership in certain areas (see also O'Shaughnessy and Branford, 2005, 27). Also important was how leaders and rank and file in various fronts and columns shared similar class backgrounds (see Gutiérrez Sanín, 2008: 10, 12, 24; Weinstein, 2007: 289).

15 This is not necessarily a strong point in the eyes of some theorists. One of the problems of urban-based guerrilla activity is the lack of environmental (social and physical) cover available to combatants (see Gurr, 1970: 262–3). As noted by Paul Wilkinson (1971: 138), "urban guerrillas ... lack the vital security of isolated rural retreats and fastnesses: they have nowhere safe to lick their wounds, to train new recruits or to make contact with external allies." Nevertheless, Wilkinson has claimed that there are some advantages to urban guerrilla activity, such as the ability to "achieve considerable long-term harassment of security forces by terrorization, armed attacks, sabotage and by tricking and evading police and the military deployed by the regime."

16 While state forces are seen in the downtown core and northern sections of Bogotá, the capital resembles any major metropolis (*barrios* excluded). It can be difficult to assess that extreme conflict lies just outside city lines.

17 Though growth in the cities may appear to be a new phenomenon or tactical strategy, the insurgency has, in fact, had urban networks dating back three decades (Ruhl, 1981: 138; Premo, 1988: 230). Throughout the 1970s and 1980s, the state detained thousands of urban-based guerrillas, suggesting the FARC-EP had far more influence in the cities than previously reported (Ruhl, 1981: 139).

18 Such open recognition of the FARC-EP's urban power had not been recognized since the late 1990s when the guerrillas were stationed within a few miles of the capital (correspondence with Petras, November 26, 2004; see also Simons, 2004: 203–5; Housego, 2003; Petras, 2003: 25; 1999: 32).

19 In the first year of negotiations 20,000 had migrated to *Villa Nueva Colombia* alone (Brittain, 2005e: 23-24).

20 During a 2007 visit, President George W. Bush fled Colombia hours after arriving because of security concerns, as universities closed and 20,000

protested in Bogotá (Weekly Update on the Americas, 2007; Prensa Latina, 2007).

21 It has even been suggested that certain peace communities may provide clandestine support for the FARC-EP (Coghlan, 2004: 26–9, 70).

22 The PCCC mirrors the tactics of *dual communism* witnessed during the cold war in several Latin American countries. "Dual communism" saw "more than one communist party in a country. The legally recognized 'official' party usually gave 'critical support' to the government. The 'unofficial' party usually worked underground in opposition to the government" (Herman, 1973: 21; see also Osterling, 1989: 187). In the contemporary framework of Colombian politics the PCCC exists as a clandestine party with no direct relation to the PCC.

23 Not to be confused with a political party, the MBNC is a political organization which promotes dialog, meetings, and reading groups. The PCCC, however, is a clandestine political party. While both are affiliated with the FARC-EP, the two are distinct even though some interrelation between members may exist.

24 Lenin made a strong case against the classification of guerrilla tactics as being similar to acts of terrorism. Resembling Marx (1987d: 501; 1988b: 449), Lenin (1965b: 117–18) approached the subject of terrorism as acts of aggressions targeting individuals, while guerrilla warfare resembled structured class-based insurrection. In many ways this is what other Latin American governments have assessed, leading them to protest about the labeling of the FARC-EP as a terrorist organization (see Brittain and Sacouman, 2008b).

25 During an interview with a female labor leader in 2008, I was told that the February protest had been misrepresented by the international media as "tens of thousands of people in attendance; workers, students, unionists, women, men, children, were protesting against the state. Uribe and the media misrepresented our voices. Saying that February 4th was against the FARC is not true."

26 The article also applauded Facebook as a medium to mobilize against Venezuelan President Hugo Chávez.

27 The Alternative Democratic Pole (*POLO Democrático Alternativo*) released statements disputing February 4, 2008 as nothing more than a reactionary political-economic tactic to further divide the country along fundamentalist terms while destroying the chances for a negotiated peace in Colombia (2008a, 2008b; see also Archila, 2007).

28 Attending the protest was former Colombian senator Luis Eladio Pérez, one of four retained political prisoners released by the FARC-EP on February 27, 2008.

29 *El Tiempo* is Colombia's most circulated newspaper, and is partially owned by the vice-president and former defense minister's family. Vice-president Francisco Santos Calderón was at one time one of the paper's editors (Haste, 2007).

30 Shortly after midnight on March 1, 2008, President Uribe, vice-president Santos Calderón and his cousin, former defense minister Juan Manuel Santos, sanctioned an illegal air strike and ground assault resulting in the death of Comandante Raúl Reyes, two dozen members of the FARC-EP, four Mexican academic observers conducting research (of whom one – Lucía Andrea Morett Alvarez – survived), and one Ecuadorian citizen. Santos explained how intelligence related to a satellite phone used by Comandante Reyes enabled the military to pinpoint the location of the encampment in Ecuadorian territory (Markey, 2008a; Otis, 2008a; Times of India, 2008). During meetings of the OAS, representatives from Argentina, Bolivia, Brazil, Chile, Cuba, Mexico, Nicaragua, Paraguay, and Peru condemned the assault as a violation of international law and sovereignty (Kraul and McDonnell, 2008; Prensa Latina, 2008; Reuters, 2008a, 2008b; Xinhua, 2008b, 2008c). The only backers of the illegal incursion were officials from the United States (Kraul and

McDonnell, 2008). When asked if the Uribe administration had informed Washington preceding the transgression on Ecuadorian territory, Tom Casey, a spokesman for the US State Department, hesitantly stated, "No, I'm not aware that we found out about this other than after the fact" (Agence France-Presse, 2008a).

Less than assuring complete impartiality, Colombia's chief of police, General Oscar Naranjo, declared, "I can say for sure that the operation was autonomous" (Xinhua, 2008a). Shortly following Naranjo's statement, a high-ranking official in Colombia's Defense Ministry leaked that the United States had been involved in the March 1, 2008 operation (Agence France-Presse, 2008a; Times of India, 2008). In actuality, the United States, through satellite intelligence gathering over southern Colombia and northern Ecuador, had retrieved signals from the FARC-EP's 48th Front and handed over the identification of the satellite telephone being used by the insurgency to intelligence sectors of the Colombian police. The informant's account of the satellite phone effectively mirrors that made during defense minister Santos's press conference. At this time it was suggested that the United States was, at the very least, indirectly involved in the attack. That was until March 7, 2008 when Ecuador's defense minister Wellington Sandoval announced that further investigation of the area targeted revealed that the site had been hit by at least five bombs fired with incredible precision (Xinhua, 2008d). Sandoval explained that such an incursion could only be deployed through the use of aircraft with the capacity to fly at a considerable height and velocity – technology and weaponry not found in any Latin American military. In October 2008 it was revealed that the United States was not only involved in the intelligence gathering but most likely provided the bombers (Agence France-Presse, 2008d; see also Williamson, 2008). One of the most unsettling circumstances related to the attack was that Comandante Reyes was scheduled to meet with French officials on the morning of March 1 to arrange the release of numerous political prisoners, including Ingrid Betancourt – leading some to claim that the attack was planned to prevent any FARC-EP-negotiated humanitarian prisoner exchange (Lucas, 2008).

31 In the days to follow numerous civilians involved in the march were murdered.
32 Over 3,700 mass graves remain throughout Colombia (see Bustamante and Chaskel, 2008: 82).
33 As links between the AUC and Uribe became ever clearer in 2008, the president had leader Salvatore Mancuso and other primary commanders extradited to the United States, where interviews (and confessions) would be difficult (Leech, 2008b; Vieira, 2008d). Matthew Thompson (2008) wrote that "such testimony and Mancuso's explosive political revelations were aborted near midnight on May 12, when, without warning, Mr Uribe had the AUC commander and 13 high-level colleagues plucked from detention on the outskirts of Medellin and extradited to the US."
34 Colombia has had the third highest abstention ratings on the continent (Coghlan, 2004: 131–2; see also Avilés, 2006: 157n.12). For decades the FARC-EP supported the contestation of conventional elections (Decker and Duran, 1982: 113; Ratliff, 1976: 68). In 1997, the insurgency institutionally "protested elections and called on Colombians to refrain from voting" – more than 50 percent abstained (Petras and Brescia, 2000: 139; see also Eckstein, 2001: 399). Electoral apathy resumed with the 2002 elections, which had the highest abstention ratings up to that point in Colombian history (Murillo and Avirama, 2004: 174). Voter apathy has always been high in FARC-EP territory, averaging 80 percent (Dudley, 2004: 220). Some areas under guerrilla influence have even witnessed abstention ratings of 95–100 percent (Coghlan, 2004: 24, 212; Petras and Brescia, 2000: 139; see also Brittain, 2005c: 36). In one of Putumayo's largest cities only "177 of the city's twenty thousand registered voters turned out" (Coghlan, 2004: 211).

Some have suggested such abstentions are the result of fear (Coghlan, 2004). Others contextualized the long historical support of the rural population for the guerrillas, and hint that there is a culture of abstention (Murillo and Avirama, 2004: 174). Several months prior to the 2006 elections, the FARC-EP shifted from its 1997 opposition to voting, and encouraged people to participate in elections. The results were magnetic. The left's Carlos Gaviria Díaz, from the Alternative Democratic Pole (*POLO Democrático Alternativo*), received over 22 percent of the national vote, which was 16 percent higher than the center-left's (*Polo Democrático Independiente*, Independent Democratic Pole) run in 2002 (Registraduría Nacional del Estado Civil, 2006; 2002). When the official polls closed, the POLO had more than doubled the votes of the once influential Liberal Party, thus becoming the official opposition. All this also occurred during far-right campaigning by the paramilitary to intimidate potential POLO and PCC voters and those in opposition to the state's right-of-center coalition (Abad, 2006; Wynter and McIlroy, 2006; see also Vieira, 2008c; Ali, 2006: 34n.2; Brodzonsky, 2006; Dudley, 2006a; Garcia, 2006; Logan and García, 2006; Muse, 2006a; Wood, 2005). According to Mark Eric Williams (2005: 154), "since 1996, popular support for democracy has grown increasingly volatile, and the protection of civil liberties – hardly robust to begin with."

35 See Ashcroft, 2002; Taylor, 2001.
36 Over the past decade, accounts emerge every year citing the FARC-EP's capacity to take state power (see Brittain, 2007b; Ross, 2006: 63; Xinhua, 2006; Morales, 2005; Röhl, 2004: 2; Simons, 2004: 181; Stewart, 2004; Bergquist, Peñaranda and Sanchez, 2003: xxi; Solaún, 2002: 1; Ruiz, 2001: 21–3; Crandall, 1999: 223–4; Farah, 1998).
37 If this scenario comes to fruition such a transfer will be telling. Lenin (1965i: 448) argued that guerrilla forces, which give root to the new socialist state, are to decentralize and assimilate into the army.
38 Richani contextualized how:

> between 1996 and 1998, the FARC scored several important military victories (Las Delicias and Purerres, 1996, San Juanito and Patascoy, 1997, Miraflores, El Billar, and Mutata, 1998), suggesting that the FARC had acquired the military initiative and tactical advantage against government forces. These battles continued throughout 1999, increasing the level of insecurity among the military and the right-wing elements in the political establishment and also worrying US decision-makers. (Richani, 2005b: 84)

39 Working from an ideological position, the FARC-EP is "economically self-sustaining" yet is "not flourishing criminal business empires as suggested by some" (Schulte-Bockholt, 2006: 137).
40 Numerous CPs throughout Latin America opposed the USSR's passive stance toward armed rebellion and guerrilla warfare, especially after the 1959 Cuban revolution. In response, the mid-1960s saw a series of conferences between the USSR (CPSU) and these CPs, the two most significant being the Havana Conference in November 1964 and the Tri-Continental Conference in January 1966. During this period the USSR increasingly accepted tactics of guerrilla warfare and took the stance that nations must follow the most appropriate path to socialism in response to their contextual class conditions (Maullin, 1973: 30–1, 132n.17; Fortuny, Delgado, and Salibi, 1966; Pomeroy, 1964: 90). National dual strategies sanctioned both armed (that is, guerrilla) and non-armed (that is, Party) forms of struggle, whether they were legitimate or not in the eyes of the conventional state (Dudley, 2004: 8–10).
41 Schulte-Bockholt (2006: 109–10) provided an excellent account of why the Soviets

restricted guerrilla struggle (and revolutionary victories) in Latin America, as they feared the adoption of Maoist interpretations of Marxism.

42 The FARC-EP was never a simple tool used by the PCC. While some viewed the guerrillas as a subservient coercive appendage of the Party (Safford and Palacios, 2003: 356; Richani, 2002a: 64), others asserted that "the ties between the two groups were never as intimate as some in Colombia and the United States have suggested" (Crandall, 2002: 61). David Bushnell claimed that "the FARC, with its own highly experienced leadership, was no mere military wing of the Communist Party" (1993: 244). In many ways, the FARC-EP and the PCC were distinct organizations with similar political objectives, which strategically cooperated during periods of mutual benefit. For example, the two effectively worked alongside and supported each other in their opposition toward the state and US imperialism (see Murillo and Avirama, 2004: 58; Maullin, 1973: 22; Gilhodés, 1970: 445). Whatever the relation, without question the PCC and the FARC-EP were "clearly allied in the *early years*" (Wickham-Crowley, 1991: 136, italics added; see also Petras and LaPorte, 1971: 353–4; Gott, 1970: 27, 266).

43 Some argued the post-USSR period afforded Colombia the ability to create its own model toward social change rather than a dogmatic subscription (Martello and Lozano Guillén, 2004: 27–41). Referring to the work of Carlos Lozano Guillén, Petras (2004: 8–9) noted a structural and cultural difference "between the ex-USSR's version of communism – rife with bureaucratic and corrupt practices – and the theory and practice of communism in Colombia." Beyond historic subservience to the dictates of the USSR, there now exists a "new road of an autonomous, reflective, *critical Colombian road to socialism, which is embedded in the history, culture and structural specificities of Colombia's class, race and regional structure*" (Petras, 2004: 9, italics added).

44 The FARC-EP proves to be an exception to (accurate) assessments that many Latin American guerrilla leaders have come from a middle economic stratum (Castañeda, 1994: 78).

45 Compare with National Liberation Army (*Ejército de Liberación Nacional*, ELN, Colombia); Farabundo Martí National Liberation Front (*Farabundo Martí para la Liberación Nacional*, FMLN, El Salvador); Sandinista National Liberation Front (*Frente Sandinista de Liberación Nacional*, FSLN, Nicaragua); 19th of April Movement (*Movimiento 19 de Abril*, M-19, Colombia); 26th of July Movement (*Movimiento 26 de Julio*, M-26-7, Cuba); Guatemalan National Revolutionary Unity (*Unidad Revolucionaria Nacional Guatemalteca*, URNG), and so on. The FARC-EP demonstrates a unique dynamic unlike many guerrilla organizations which are paradoxically led from "the same political class as the government they were trying to overthrow rather than that of their followers" (Calvert, 1999: 112).

46 The Shining Path's (*Sendero Luminoso*, Peru) leader was Manuel Rubén Abimael Guzmán Reynoso: once a professor of philosophy at San Cristóbal of Huamanga National University (*Universidad Nacional de San Cristóbal de Huamanga*) in Ayacucho, Peru. The leader of the Zapatista Army of National Liberation (*Ejército Zapatista de Liberación Nacional*, EZLN, Mexico) is a balaclava-wearing pipe-smoking Althusserian named Subcomandante Insurgente Marcos (Rafael Sebastián Guillén Vicente), also a former philosopher from the Metropolitan Autonomous University (*Universidad Autónoma Metropolitana*) in Mexico City. The Shining Path all but disappeared upon the capture of Guzmán, while the EZLN has fared no better, losing considerable power and influence over the past decade. There are some who question whether intellectuals can even be revolutionaries (Walzer, 2002: 7–8).

47 The FARC-EP "cannot be compared to the Central American guerrilla struggles of the 1980s."

Firstly, it ignores the time factor; the Colombian movements have a longer trajectory, allowing them to accumulate an infinitely greater storehouse of practical experiences and making them far more sensitive to the pitfalls of peace accords that fail to transform the state and place structural change at the center of a settlement. The 1980s formal cease-fire between the FARC and the government, in particular, was a salutary learning experience: over 3,000 guerrilla supporters and sympathizers of the newly formed Patriotic Union political party were assassinated by paramilitary death squads and no progress was made in reforming the socio-economic system. *Secondly*, the FARC guerrilla leadership is made up largely of peasants or individuals with deep ties to the countryside, whereas their counterparts in El Salvador and Nicaragua were primarily middle class professionals eager to return to city life and careers in electoral politics. *Third*, the geography of the Colombian conflict could not be more different: it encompasses a far larger territory and a topography much more favorable to guerrilla warfare. The FARC guerrillas' social origins and experiences have made them more familiar with this terrain than was the case with the Central Americans movements. *Fourth*, the FARC leadership has put socio-economic reforms at the center of their political negotiations, unlike the Central Americans who prioritized the reinsertion of ex-commanders into the electoral process. *Fifth*, the Colombian guerrillas are totally self-sufficient and are not subject to the pressures and deals of outside supporters-as was the case in Central America. *Sixth*, and finally, the guerrillas were not impressed by the results of the Central American accords: the ascendancy of neoliberalism; the immunity from prosecution of armed forces' leaders for major human rights abuses; and the enrichment of many of the ex-guerrilla commanders, some of whom have joined the chorus supporting U.S. intervention in Colombia. (Petras and Morley, 2003: 100)

48 Greatly associated with Che Guevara, *foco* theory is largely a strategy shaped by Régis Debray's belief that small groups could themselves induce revolutionary conditions (Debray, 1967).

49 In recognition of the above, some have demonstrated their clear lack of knowledge about Colombia by stating that the FARC-EP "espouse a dogmatic Marxist ideology" (Sweig and McCarthy, 2005: 18).

50 Variations on conventional social movement theory and classical Marxism have emerged. For example, to facilitate true revolutionary change social movements must reinsert the state as a necessary trajectory while incorporating traditional forms of class struggle (Petras and Veltmeyer, 2005a, 2003a: 161; 2001; Barlow 1993: 206–7). While the FARC-EP upholds progressive issues related to women, indigenous peoples, and supports identity-based groups, it unquestionably promotes the thesis that the exploited must create a push for state power. This illustrates a cross-linkage of contemporary social movement strategies (that is, grassroots collectives) with classical Marxist intentions (that is, class-based state power). As one leading theorist of revolution rightly argued, "rebels are not revolutionaries ... unless they seriously contend for state power" (Goodwin, 1997: 17; see also Locher, 2002: 238; Nash, 2000: 132). Non-revolutionary social movements that neglect to target the state fail to create substantive social change, while classical approaches of Marxism, such as the industrial proletariat, may be incapable of solely responding to the concrete class construct of a given nation. This is yet another example of the FARC-EP's unique difference from other guerrilla movements in contemporary Latin America. It seeks to take state power – not establish autonomous networks, exercise simple banditry and anarchical microcosms, or create power without taking power (see Brittain, 2006a; Goff, 2004: 41, 47; Petras and Morley, 2003: 100; Premo, 1988: 230).

CHAPTER 3

1 Many movements utilize theories such as Marxism but adapt them to localized conditions (Isbister, 1998: 89).

2 While Marx found the most developed countries illustrated the future for the less developed, he clarified that this did not mean all would follow suit (Marx, 1996a: 9; 1989b: 352). Marx did not believe that "because primitive communal societies had been obliterated in the Western capitalist countries, all remaining forms of communal society in the world are doomed to extinction" (Le Blanc, 1996: 30). Lenin too suggested peasant-based collectives could act as a benefit for capital in some regions of the world (Lenin, 1964b: 129). While some "pre-capitalist" forms may be altered (that is, peasants are separated from what little means of production they have, becoming wage laborers), capitalists will seek to maintain characteristics of these forms in pursuit of profit. Permit me to explain. A key to capitalist modes of production is to separate land from producers, thereby alienating the socio-productive process (Lenin, 1964b: 116). While Marx, Engels, and Lenin took note of the benefits from "rational agriculture" and collective large-scale production as an undeniably better form than capitalist production, they understood that pursuing communal-based processes may prove difficult because of the individuated reality of peasants (Marx and Engels, 1998: 123, 608–9, 884; Lenin, 1964b: 120–3). Hence, "large-scale production in agriculture is superior to small production only up to a certain limit," as benefits can be derived from the production of specific crops, which gain more from small-scale farming than large-scale production (cocoa, strawberries, and so on) (Lenin, 1964b: 129).

Small production also holds far superior qualitative benefit in the level to which it is possible to exploit peasants (and their families). The peasant conducts far more work than a waged laborer. The small producer does not employ periodic labor power in the fields but rather continues to work even after the fields have been cared for. Lenin understood that the:

> peasant also works in the household, works on building and repairing his hut, his cowshed, his implements, etc., "not counting" all his additional work, for which a wage-labourer on a big-farm would demand payment at the usual rate. It is not clear to every unprejudiced person that overwork has incomparably wider limits for the peasants – for the small farmer – than for the small industrial producer. (Lenin, 1964b: 129)

This illustrates how adapted capitalist relations can be created, and achieved, within the context of pre-capitalist forms; hence, maintaining small-scale production, in controlled regional contexts, can actually result in capitalist gains. Lenin (1964b: 131–7) illustrated that large-scale agriculture begins to rise in the event of land centralization and monopolization, where large estates are purchased and held by one specific owning body, which is the material case in much of Colombia. Large landowners, many of whom are linked to the narcotics industry, encourage newly landless peasants and rural laborers to remain in the area to cultivate coca (Molano, 2005: 117–36). This provides the capitalist with cheap labor alongside a venue to cleanse narcodollars (see Richani, 2002a: 117–19). Hegemonic benefits are also derived as a perception remains of land being in the hands of the peasantry, potentially pacifying those who, in the event of large-scale production, may organize antagonistically.

3 Lenin attacked bourgeois liberals who did not support such methods:

> a Marxist cannot regard civil war, or guerrilla warfare, which is one of its forms, as abnormal and demoralizing *in general*. A Marxist bases himself on class struggle, and not social peace. In certain periods of acute economic and political

crises the class struggle ripens into a direct civil war, i.e., into an armed struggle between two sections of the people. In such periods a Marxist is obliged to take a stand of civil war. Any moral condemnation of civil war would be absolutely impermissible from the standpoint of Marxism. (Lenin, 1965f: 219–20; see also 1965c: 144; Engels, 1977: 171)

4   More bluntly, Hobsbawm (1964: 49) claimed that "no misinterpretation of Marx is more grotesque than the one which suggests that he expected a revolution exclusively from the advanced industrial countries of the West."

5   Much like Ronaldo Munck's (1984a: 1) position toward geopolitical economic structures, the term "majority world" is used to describe the many countries that exist as capitalist nations yet are excluded from imperial power (that is, the minority world).

6   Sociologist Jim Sacouman (1999: 41) argued, "Marx continually tested and revised his developing historical materialist political economy, or social science, in the light of contemporary class struggles and social revolutions." In the last five years of his life, Marx began what can only be described as an intense re-examination of his theoretical perspectives. Specifically, Marx examined whether rural-based communal societies held the capacity to transform their conditions without realizing the confines of private property relations, essentially leaping a transitory stage of capitalist development (Shanin, 1983). In 1881, Marx wrote a letter to Vera Zasulich that explained how, in Western Europe, a transition of primitive accumulation took place where private property, through one's own labor, was violently altered to a system of capitalist private property (1992a: 71–2; see Marx, 1996b: 704–7). Marx suggested that a process by which communal property could be transformed into private property may be plausible (Marx, 1989c: 370–1; 1992a: 71). Prior to this formal proclamation, Marx wrote three separate drafts of the letter.

His purpose for such activities was to examine how Russia, unlike the West, might bypass formal private ownership over rural lands (1989b: 360). In one draft Marx stated:

in Russia, thanks to a unique combination of circumstances, the rural commune, still established on a nationwide scale, may gradually detach itself from its primitive features and develop directly as an element of collective production on a nationwide scale. It is precisely thanks to its contemporaneity with capitalist production that it may appropriate the latter's positive acquisitions without experiencing all its frightful misfortunes. (Marx, 1989b: 349)

In the same document, Marx became more direct in his assertion by announcing that the transition in Russia was not "forced to pass through a long incubation period in the engineering industry, as was the West, in order to arrive at the machines, the steam engines, the railways etc." On the contrary, Russia "managed to introduce to their own country in the twinkling of an eye the entire mechanism of exchange (banks, joint-stock companies, etc.), which it took the West centuries to devise" (1989b: 353). A year after Marx had sent Zasulich the official letter, he and Engels went so far as to contemplate whether "a form of primeval common ownership of land, even if greatly undermined" could "pass directly to the higher form of communist common ownership?" Stemming from this question, posed in the famous "Preface to the second Russian edition of the *Manifesto of the Communist Party*," Marx and Engels went so far as to question "if the Russian Revolution becomes the signal for a proletarian revolution in the West, so that the two compliment each other, the present Russian common ownership of land may serve as the starting point for communist development" (Marx and Engels, 1989: 426). Albeit late, Marx and Engels' accepted that (under certain historical-material conditions) societies could rise out of communal ownership to socialized property relations.

7   Regarding Colombia specifically, class linkages have generated mutual benefits for both the United States and the Andean country. It was not through foreign imperial pressure or lack of national-bourgeois power that the capitalist class in Colombia implemented neoliberalism, counterinsurgency, and so on, but rather for bilateral class gains. Thomas G. Sanders (1981: 100) argued, "Colombia's close linkage to international lending agencies in the past 20 years has not been an expression of conformism, but rather a form of self-interest."

8   Raúl A. Fernández and José F. Ocampo cautioned against seeing imperialism as "an enemy that cannot be confronted in the immediate battle" and repudiated:

> the role the democratic struggle plays in the revolutionary process, the negation of national independence and of the right of self-determination, and the negation of the right of nations to secede …. This is a way to deny in practice the anti-imperialist struggle. (Fernández and Ocampo, 1974: 33)

9   From another perspective, Agustín Cueva philosophically concluded how "the social" allows capitalism to exist. Cueva (1976: 16) ascertained how theories, such as dependency or structural, show that "the nature of our social formation is dependent on how they are integrated with the world capitalist system." Cueva chose to reverse this position, as it is "the nature of our societies that determines their links with the capitalist world" (Cueva, 1976: 16). Proletarians therefore have the agency, locally/regionally/nationally, to reinterpret a socialist paradigm.

10 For additional examinations of the importance of total national capital in global economics, see Buzuev and Gorodnov (1987: 305) and Marx (1987b: 227), while critical arguments can been recognized in Teeple (2005: 68).

11 Whether it is the principal architect of social change (Goodwin, 2001, 1998; Goldstone, 1991; Trimberger, 1978) or abandoned as a target for power (Hardt and Negri, 2004; Holloway, 2002a, 2002b).

12 Several theorists suggested Skocpol *did* acknowledge revolutions as being assisted by mass action from below (Goodwin, 1997: 15; Wickham-Crowley, 1997: 46–7). While partially correct, Skocpol's argument held that they lacked an ideological understanding of the greater revolutionary context and were of marginal influence (Skocpol, 1979: 17; see also Sanderson, 2005: 102–3). In time, even Skocpol's defenders acknowledged her thesis argued, above all, "that the political crises that made revolutions possible … were *not* brought about by revolutionaries; rather, conflicts between dominant classes and autonomous state officials" (Goodwin, 2001: 43). Regardless of her theoretical nod to those from below, Skocpol made a career on the assessment that revolutions are not a consequence of the most exploited emancipating their conditions but determinist outcomes of elite state-centered dynamics.

13 Peasants are viewed as subservient to factors outside the countryside (Skocpol, 1982: 169). Some on the left see peasants requiring "organizational strength from outside the peasant community" as a result of a perceived individualized fragmentation and need for direction (Paige, 1975: 42; see also Scott, 1977: 294; Migdal, 1974: 232).

14 Skocpol (1982: 163) suggested peasants do not engage in revolutionary struggle for a new social relation of production, political paradigm, or economic structure, but rather strive for instant benefit and self-interest.

15 Simply see the state's relation to the World Bank, International Monetary Fund, or World Trade Organization.

16 Dominant class structures, while united in ideological promotion of capitalist development, promote a material separation of private capitalists and the state, thus manufacturing an image of increased democratization alongside capitalist expansion. In part, these measures increase the capacity for capital to be secured

apart from mere state-coercion through an additional unified strength of private security forces. In theory, this model allows for private economic interests to utilize "stabilizing forces" during times of political assault and instability (Gramsci, 1971: 238). If the state is threatened by revolutionary forces then segments of civil society have the capacity to deploy reactionary forces external to the coercive arm of the state (Gramsci, 1971: 232; 1978: 408–9).

17 An organic revolutionary social movement like the FARC-EP can be valuable in such a context, as its power is not based on an immediate attack of the centralized state but rather a war of position facilitating dual power.

18 The CIA also noted this position in 1958 (see Sweig, 2002: 122).

19 Nor can it be said that Colombia suffers from any threat of competition or stability in relation to other nation states. The Colombian state is widely regarded as the United States' strongest ally in Latin America.

20 For Tilly, those from below do not directly construct authority but come to be a part of it through their external support. In reference to the Colombian situation see Wickham-Crowley (1991: 39).

21 Examples closer to this account of dual power can be recognized historically in Bookchin (1998: 114–15, 217).

22 A "from below" strategy also works when explaining revolutionary social change in an imperial context. The center ring is the imperial state and the outer inter-connected rings are unified revolutionized states.

CHAPTER 4

1 After researching Colombia's political dynamics during the 1950s and early 1960s, Carleton Beals (1974: 258) declared, "Colombia is a land on the brink."

2 In 1967, several years after Colombia's most famous land reform was implemented, sociologist T. Lynn Smith warned that:

> if, however, substantial reforms are not forthcoming, a huge and violent erup-tion of the lower social classes is almost sure to ensue; and if this comes about the fact that many of the elite may have deserved no better will be slight solace for the rivers of blood that will flow and the vast destruction of property that will take place. (Smith, 1967: 133)

According to Schulte-Bockholt (2006: 96), the rise of the guerrillas "is largely because Colombia has experienced very few lands reforms." A similar account was presented by economists Albert R. Berry and Francisco Thoumi, who are convinced today's civil war might have been avoided had the elite enacted real land reform in the early twentieth century (Berry, 1999: 3, 7; Berry and Thoumi, 1988: 66–7). Richani (2007: 405) has also highlighted that Colombia's civil war can only be understood as a by-product of land concentration. It is within the structure of land monopoly that the continuity of conflict has been fueled.

3 Powers in Bogotá *chose* to be absent as the regions were deemed politically deficient (Richani, 2002a: 12–35).

4 The state's apathy toward credit, social services, and educational assistance greatly hindered the socioeconomic potential of rural Colombia (Felstenhausen, 1968a, 1968b). While the state received foreign loans intended for development, a significant emphasis was placed on militarization. During the 1960s, national spending on education rose to 14 percent of Colombia's GDP yet the allotment for the army was above 16 percent (see Bushnell, 1993: 238; Burnett and Johnson, 1968: 254). As a whole the military took up 40 percent of the national budget (Lartéguy, 1970: 143). This foreshadowed how external development "aid" for Colombia would be correlated to "security" for decades to come. For years the

state has structurally reduced spending on health, education, housing, and social security (Holmes, 1990: 204–5). Today, the same percentage of GDP as is devoted to military security is dedicated to health, education, and other social services combined (Delgado and Romero, 2007; UN Development Programme, 2004; see also Vieira, 2008b). Currently, the Colombian state utilizes just below 7 percent of its GDP to respond to the FARC-EP. Putting this into perspective, the United States (while at war in Iraq and Afghanistan) averaged 4 percent of its GDP, and European countries (in NATO) averaged 2 percent (Delgado, 2008).

5   Arguably, the Alliance for Progress was a tool to discourage popular support for communism. With Cuba being so close, the Colombian elite and US-based MNCs attacked the 1959 revolution by erecting religious signs that read, "Colombia is a Catholic country. Break relations with Godless Cuba" (Beals, 1974: 295; see also 289, 296).

6   INCORA systematically targeted regions known to have a history of rural mobilizations in opposition to the state, specifically southwestern Colombia (Richani, 2002a: 28; LeGrand, 1986: 172).

7   A definition of the rural elite is "a constellation of social groups that include cattle ranchers, large landowners, and owners of enterprises investing in export orientated cash-crops, such as coffee, flowers, African palm, bananas, rice, and sugar" (Richani, 2005b: 91). This has come to include the narcobourgeoisie, a term referring to cartel directors and/or traffickers who became "a newly emergent social group" in Colombia's upper socioeconomic ranks (see Schulte-Bockholt, 2006: 129, 132).

8   Such statements are somewhat ironic in light of the fact that INCORA (1964: 17) agreed that micro-level rural landholdings underutilized their full productive potential. State-induced development projects that monopolized land for large-scale agricultural industry were soon supported (Brittain, 2005b). Such assumptions have been discredited as small-scale or parceled production has proven to yield higher outputs (Berry, 1999: 4; 1991: 94; Shafer, 1994: 192; Ridler, 1983: 597; Dorner and Felstenhausen, 1970; Grunig, 1969; Adams and Montero, 1965).

9   A small group of Colombians control much of the lands, but they do not reside on their rural properties but rather in major cities; hence the term urban-based large landowner (sometimes loosely referred to as *latifundistas*: see Sánchez and Meertens, 2001: 206) (Ramírez, 2005: 83; Coghlan, 2004: 153–4; Taussig, 2004a: 13; Leech, 2002a: 9; Giraldo, 1996: 14; Harrison, 1993: 122, 154; Roseberry, 1993: 353; Berry, 1980b: 110; Thayer, 1963: 143). Such a practice has amounted to urban control over rural areas (de Janvry, 1981: 109).

10 This illustrates an important distinction when concerning other rural national conditions and reformist measures amidst revolutionary epochs, which capitalized on peasant stratification so as to fracture alliances (as in Russia and Nicaragua). Colombia's peasant population has been reasonably self-sufficient, with more common factors than differences (see Wood, 2003: 76–7). This, however, does not suggest peasants are exempt from differentiations, as "primitive communities are not all cast from the same die" (Marx, 1996b: 686–7).

11 Richani noted:

> the total number of peasants who benefited from the 40 years existence of ... land distribution policy did not exceed 103,084. In contrast, the new landed oligarchy (narcobourgeoisie) in the 1980s and 1990s acquired more than 10 percent of the country's most fertile lands with an estimated market value of $2 billion. (Richani, 2001: 52)

For two excellent timelines of the state's failure to respond to the land needs of the rural population, see Lindqvist (1979: 88–94) and Vertinsky, Geffner and Fox (1972).

12   Sam Summerlin noted:

> another problem is that land reform legislation adopted by many countries involves resettlement of the peasantry on abandoned or state-owned property. Large landholders often have been unaffected by reform legislation, and thus there has been very little transfer of control of the region's most productive lands into the hands of the peasantry. (Summerlin, 972: 269)

13   Adding insult to injury, the state passed Law 1 (1968), which "granted potential rights to tenants and sharecroppers but provoked landowners to expel them on a massive scale," forcing the newly dispossessed to full or semi-proletarianization (Pearce, 1990a: 81; see also Havens, Flinn and Cornhill, 1980).

14   This is a conservative figure, as some estimated the number of landless at 740,000 (Gunther, 1966: 461).

15   As a result of Law 135, and the involvement of international financial institutions (IFIs), class polarization culminated in support for left-wing modes of change and FARC-EP recruitment during the mid-late 1960s (Findji, 1992: 114–15; Beals, 1974: 230).

16   This was quite similar to Laws 100 (1944) and 200 (1936), which saw a land reform provide concessions empowering the elite to increase land centralization and semi-proletarianization (Hylton, 2006: 34; Richani, 2002a: 22–3; Vertinsky, Geffner and Fox, 1972: 369–71). Beals argued that Law 135 was in actuality:

> a costly type of land resettlement, not the break up of large estates or their conversion into cooperatives of the peasants. This resettlement puts peasants, supposedly benefited, on sub marginal lands or undeveloped lands, a process costly for the government, for the peasants, and often benefiting the large holders. (Beals, 1974: 312)

17   No land reform was as efficient in marginalizing workers as Law 135 (Deere and León de Leal, 1982: 46n.20; Motta de Correa, 1980: 133–4; Weaver, 1980: 186; Duff, 1968: 15). After 1961, rural workers received a daily wage of roughly US$0.15¢ (Beals, 1974: 229). In today's currency this is slightly above US$1 per day.

18   Isbister superbly characterized how maintaining peasant production alongside capitalist wage labor was a consequence of empire:

> before the arrival of the imperialists, the majority of the people of the third world were involved in producing food for their own use – as hunters and gatherers in some regions, but for the most part as cultivators of the soil. They typically produced only what they needed to survive. Any surplus food was used to support a ruling group, but this was usually a small portion of production. Imperialism changed this picture. It did not totally displace subsistence production, of course, because people still needed to eat. On top of subsistence production, however, the imperialists imposed the production of primary export commodities. (Isbister, 1998: 89–90)

19   Lenin described such a condition in relation to sectors of the peasantry who increasingly came to sell their labor power for a wage. He never saw the peasantry as a deterrent to the development of capitalism, but rather as one of the most important aspects of it (Lenin, 1964a: 173). It is through this process that the peasantry becomes exploited in the same form as urban workers, and subsequently equal in class consciousness and class position (Saul, 2006: 48–9; Brittain, 2004b: 24–6; Marx and Engels, 1998: 608; Marx, 1989b: 518; Post and Wright, 1989: 151–2).

20   There were, however, areas in southern Colombia that were subsistence-based (Adams and Havens, 1966: 211).

21   "The definitive transition to agrarian capitalism, characterized by highly capitalized enterprises employing a wage labor force, was a phenomenon of the 1950s" (Deere and León de Leal, 1982: 32).

22 Pearse (1982: 63) noted that "the hold of many peasants over land was weakened" by imposed rent systems resulting in peasants having to sell off lands to pay debts, increased litigation over land titles because of generations of inheritance, the implementation of defoliate aerial spraying on peasants yields, and so on (see Leech, 2002a: 13–14; Pearse, 1982: 63–4; Taussig, 1980: 81). The state then usurped the lands and empowered large landowners by handing over the properties, exemplifying the co-relation of class interests (Leech, 2002a: 14). These activities require significant surplus finance and the governing power to pass and enforce laws, hire solicitors who can properly handle land titles, and commission armed forces to displace small producers. Some have referred to such practices as nothing short of the systematic implementation of "class war" against people in the countryside (Lindqvist, 1979: 89; see also Chernick, 2007). For excellent examples of such legal quarrels see Harrison (1993: 303–4).

23 Large landholders limited the self-sufficiency of rural populations – making them easily exploitable – by monopolizing common natural resources such as land, water and timber (see Dumont, 1965: 12).

24 Subsistence producers accounted for 48 percent of the populace at this time; disenfranchising this hefty group translated into significant political and economic gains (Kolmanovitz, 1978: 38; see also Berry, 1980b: 112).

25 Between 1950 and 1965, roughly 63 percent of producers labored on plots of 1.6 hectares (Shaw, 1976: 101). From 1933 to 1967, southern holdings actually decreased from "4.8 hectares ... to 0.32" (Taussig, 1980: 83).

26 Extending the size to 10 hectares saw the proportion rise to 94 percent (Saunders et al, 1978: 17, 133).

27 Land monopolies, in fact, date back to the nineteenth century (Bergquist, 1986: 137; Adams, 1966: 45–6).

28 An important point to address is that the vast majority of peasants were illiterate and unable to assess the documentation needed (see Currie, 1966: 197). During this period, illiteracy rates in rural Colombia were double those in the cities, at 60–88 percent (Weil et al, 1970: 200).

29 For material examples of state and capitalist linkages see Harrison (1993: 121), Christodoulou (1990: 142), Deere and León de Leal (1982: 30–3), Sanders (1981: 89) and interestingly Currie (1966: ix).

30 Leon Zamosc (1986: 97) claimed that after Law 135 the state paradoxically created a counter-reform policy that "would eradicate all traces of reform in state policy, transforming it into an instrument of defense of the landowners' interests, support for capitalist agriculture, and curbing of peasant aspirations."

31 Such practices still exist. I was told of many cases where landless or displaced peasants colonize lands on unused *fincas*, most prevalent in areas of Putumayo, Caquetá, Meta, Huila, and sectors of Tolima and Nariño.

32 Harrison (1993: 121–2, 154) described how many larger landholders are in fact urban-based. Demetrios Christodoulou (1990: 137) noted that one of Colombia's principal land problems is the acute "concentration of the good agricultural land in the hands of relatively few people ... mostly absentee landowners, usually professional and politicians." For example, rural-based cattle farming is greatly owned by those "who are fully or partially absentee" in the actual activities associated with livestock (Berry, 1980b: 110). Again, many of those who control the means of production in rural Colombia are not rural inhabitants. Various peasants told me the largest *fincas* are monopolized by those that have little contact with the land apart from profits, status attainment, and managerial relations.

33 During the late 1960s and early 1970s the cost to construct and maintain modern water purification systems in highly populated regions close to the countryside would

have been "about $20 for the plant and $50 for the distribution system. Allowing forty years for depreciation, the annual per capita cost is $1.75" (Bryant, 1969: 122).

34   Colombia has long been accused of price transferral (see Sklair, 1973: 261). Commodities like medicine have been systemically overpriced so parent companies derive greater profits (Doyal and Pennell, 1994: 267). Treatments like "tetracy-cline, a modern antibiotic increasingly replacing penicillin, was overpriced by 948 to 987 percent" (Müller, 1979: 170). Today, "Colombia has the highest HIV drug prices in Latin America" (Ballvé, 2008: 34). In short, access to drugs is next to impossible for the rural and urban working poor.

35   During the mid-1960s, average life expectancy was 44 years (Gunther, 1966: 432).

36   An alarming statement made during Plata's speech was that Colombia has socially benefited from civil war: "as a result of decades of violence we developed a tremen-dously good and strong health sector" (Uribe and Plata, 2008).

37   This was confirmed by my own interviews with civilians and the FARC-EP. After reviewing databases of thousands of former insurgents, Francisco Gutiérrez Sanín (2008: 6, 12) also found many had less than 4.5 years of schooling.

38   Throughout the 1960s and 1970s rural migration was greatly dependent upon two factors: violence and economic inequality (Schultz, 1970: 7, 10, 19-20). Some, however, suggested outmigration had less to do with violence than with issues of economic security and education (Whiteford, 1976: 17, 14–16). For example, young people left because of a lack of formal services and their hope for a functional education (Shultz, 1970: 14–18, Jallade, 1974: 32n.1).

39   Seventy-five percent of usable land is set aside for cattle grazing while only a fifth of arable land is actually utilized (Sweig and McCarthy, 2005: 32; Restrepo 2003; Deininger, 2001: 319n.12).

40   "Economic groups" are "conglomerates linked together through interlocking directorates, holding companies, cross-financing, and family ownership" (Avilés, 2006: 151n.15). Consolidating monopolies expanded economic power and re-engaged elite political influence. The most noted are "the Santodomingo group, the Sarmiento group, the Ardilla Lulle group, and the Antiqueño Syndicate" (Avilés, 2006: 78; see also Harding, 1996: 46–7).

41   Colombia was an exception to the usual neoliberal effects until the mid-1990s when it experienced the "worst economic recession" of the last half-century (Green, 2003: 235; see also Holmes, 2003: 87–8; Leech, 2002a: 3).

42   Differentiated from general poverty, in which people have difficulty meeting basic needs, absolute poverty refers to those whose income levels fall below US$1.25 per day (see Ravallion, Chen and Sangraula, 2008).

43   Depending on the region, the income difference between a large landowner and laborer can be 80, 200, or as much as 480 times (Harrison, 1993: 109; Feder, 1971: 10–11).

44   The ICA placed limitations on coffee export and ensured all growers received a minimum of US$1.20 per pound (Gibbs and Leech, 2009: 51; Vanden and Prevost, 2006: 153; Nelson, Shultz, and Slighton, 1971: 249).

45   "Because the United States was by far the world's largest consumer of coffee, its with-drawal from the ICA rendered the pact null and void" (Gibbs and Leech, 2009: 51).

46   If Colombia's third largest legal export (coffee) cannot derive a positive return for small producers, than what chance do maize, bananas or other legal crops have (see Kirk, 2003: 264)? A 50 lb sack of lemons may cost 3,000 to 5,000 pesos (about US$2.00) to produce. It is taken to market and sold solely on speculation of beneficial returns and demand. It is necessary to take into account the time and labor power involved in the actual production of fruit, the cost of the land that was used to grow it, the transportation costs to get the product to market, and

other hidden expenses associated with its production and sale. In many cases the peasant experiences a loss in continuing this mode of production (see also Richani, 2002a: 71; Castaño, 2006). In addition, the Uribe administration restricted access to gasoline in several rural regions during the 2000s, making the transport and sale of goods still more difficult. Dozens of small producers in Putumayo told me the state justifies such measures by arguing they use petrol for coca processing. Even when goods can be dispatched, state forces have been known to restrict "shipments of food and medicine" from these regions (Zuluaga Nieto, 2007: 118).

47 Teresa Gutierrez (2003: 52) shared how "opening the nation's economy to so-called world competition meant that Colombia would now import more than it exported. The once-healthy agricultural sector was devastated."

48 The "rise" in Colombian income during 2004 was based on unsustainable economic conditions. A "6.7 magnitude quake struck the west coast of Colombia," and devastated coffee-growing regions, producers, and their families, which reduced production for the interim and increased demand. Interestingly, the last jump in coffee returns before 2004 was realized in 1999 when yet another 6.2-magnitude earthquake hit the coffee-growing zones, taking the lives of over 1,000 coffee harvesters (Farr, 2004).

49 Schulte-Bockholt (2006: 96) claimed the peasantry only became involved in the coca industry as a consequence of the state's social absence – not to mention a monopolized (neoliberal) political economy (see also Berry, 1999).

50 Little is derived, as "the product is worth far less at this stage of its production and distribution cycle" (Schulte-Bockholt, 2006: 146n.43).

CHAPTER 5

1 See Holmes, Amin Gutiérrez de Piñeres and Curtin (2006: 162); Peceny and Durnan (2006: 100); Labrousse (2005: 171); Richani (2005a: 139n.10); Gutiérrez Sanín (2004: 265); Röhl (2004: 9–10); Ferro Medina and Uribe Ramón (2002); Pizarro Leongómez (1991); Wickham-Crowley (1990: 202); Marsh (1983: 12–4); Fletcher (1967: 3).

2 During this shift, Marulanda detailed how coca was a means of survival in a neoliberal context (Cala, 2000: 58; see also CISLAC, 2001).

3 This is significantly different from trafficking. The FARC-EP has never been directly involved in the drug trade, unlike Colombian (and US) state/paramilitary forces (Daily Journal, 2005).

4 Some researchers have claimed the FARC-EP only became interested in certain regions, like Arauca, when resources such as oil or coca were found (Sweig and McCarthy, 2005: 12). Such "experts" obviously do not know that oil and coca were discovered in Arauca in the 1980s (Pearce, 2007: 227, Tamminen, 2006: 98; Scott, 2003: 72). The FARC-EP, however, have been politically-militaristically present there since the 1960s (Richani, 2005a: 122).

5 Ironically, Labrousse (2005: 177) detailed how the FARC-EP frequently attacked the cartel infrastructure in Meta.

6 Credited with coining the term narco-guerrilla – meant for a branch of the Medellín cartel – Lewis Tambs, former US ambassador to Colombia, applied it to the FARC-EP during Ronald Reagan's administration (1980–88):

> In 1972 Richard Nixon was the first president to use the phrase "war on drugs." A decade later, Ambassador Louis [sic] Tambs went a step further when he coined the word "narco-guerrilla" to refer to the FARC, since the group levied taxes on cocaine. There was both manipulation and truth to the description. When Tambs used it, the relationship between the FARC and drug trafficking existed, but it was no more pronounced than the FARC's relationship with

other business. He could have called them "cattle-guerrillas" or "oil-guerrillas." Guerrillas "taxed" *coca* and charged fees but did not themselves make or sell cocaine. Nevertheless, the choice of term served a political purpose. It worked as a hinge to connect what had been a war in communism to a new campaign, waged with the same tools and against similar targets. (Kirk, 2003: 227–8)

Ironically, Tambs was later "accused of involvement in cocaine trafficking" via the Contras in Central America (Schulte-Bockholt, 2006: 129, 144–5n.38).

7   After September 11, 2001, however, the DEA immediately produced reports contradicting this decade of evidence. For an excellent overview of the DEA's "shift" refer to Schulte-Bockholt (2006: 136, 146n.44).

8   To relieve opposition toward increased counter-insurgency funding and actions in Colombia, the Clinton administration (1993–2001) shrouded the topic of direct US military intervention in the rhetoric of counter-narcotics. To pacify sectors of Congress, Clinton's appointed drug czar Barry McCaffrey presented that "as a matter of administration policy, the United States *will not* support Colombian counterinsurgency efforts" (US Department of State, 2000, italics added). Believing this statement and reassured that the United States would not intervene in Colombia's civil war, Congress voted to allow US troops and private contracted forces to engage in Colombian missions. Once the vote was passed McCaffrey acknowledged the war on drugs was, in reality, a strategy to combat the growth of the FARC-EP rather than a pure attack on coca production (Goff, 2004: 32). This was soon clear as US troops worked alongside Colombian counter-insurgent forces in the sphere of intelligence and combat (Gentile, 2007; Grandin, 2006: 219). Apart from Ambassador Frechette taking note that "there was no clear evidence to support McCaffrey's claims," the promise to not intervene in Colombian's civil war has since been "forgotten" (Goff, 2004: 33).

9   The basis behind such reasoning is that the dominant class has the ability to bypass military service by attending university (O'Shaughnessy and Branford, 2005: 54; Crandall, 2005b: 185). Hence, in many respects, "Colombia's military is a drafted lower-class army fighting for elite interests" (Schulte-Bockholt, 2006: 146n.45),

10   The guerrillas employ a class-based taxation model linked to the coca industry, and, according to the above authors, it was implemented in roughly 37 fronts in the late 1990s. At this time of publication, the FARC-EP had over 60 fronts, hence only a proportion of fronts had indirect involvement in the industry (see Rochlin, 2003: 100, 137; Craig, 1987: 29). Rangel (1998) argued that a clear number of the FARC-EP's comandantes ideologically and tangibly reject the coca industry and refuse to have anything to do with its activities.

11   Throughout 1998 and 2000, the FARC-EP repeatedly invited the United States to discuss issues related to crop substitution. The United States responded by militarizing the region (Gamboa, 2001: 100; Cala, 2000: 59; Somocurico, 2000).

12   In the 1990s and early 2000s, sustainable alternative development programs were established for small producers in insurgent-held regions. One ambitious example was *Unidad Agricola Familiar*, which prompted the rural population to "build a new city, the capital of the Caguán, with every advancement possible and every scientific provision to guarantee its success, and the standard of living of its inhabitants" through establishing "different model farms," which would be a "productive exploitation of natural resources; the development of alternative systems of for construction using banana, plantain and sugar cane; using goods confiscated from illegal accumulation of wealth; encouraging cooperatives; an indigenous agro-industrial park." (FARC-EP, 2000b: 6)

13   My research places the formal shift in the early to mid-1990s. Realizing that their anti-coca position could be interpreted as anti-peasant – thereby eroding support

amongst *campesinos* – the FARC-EP implemented the class-based taxation model (O'Shaughnessy and Branford, 2005: 26; see also Labrousse, 2005: 172 Molano, 2000: 27).

14 The model implemented a tax targeting middle and upper-level purchasers and distributors (Molano, 2000: 27). Doing so actually supported lower-level workers and growers, as merchants regularly threatened and/or swindled illiterate peasant cultivators. The class-based taxation model protected the latter while forcing the former to hand over a percentage of their profit to the peasantry through a localized collective tax structure.

15 The model has been very effective and able to withstand state attempts to disrupt it. Even in areas where the FARC-EP was temporarily expelled by state or paramilitary forces, the tax system stayed intact because of the insurgency's counter-hegemony. MNCs and individuals knew the insurgency would in time retake the territory and re-implement the tax and/or respond to those who periodically stopped payment (see Ortiz, 2006: 216–17).

16 This area of the taxation model is regularly misunderstood and has been the recipient of repeated misanalysis. Simply put, the FARC-EP places a levy on those who obtain the greater portion of the profits – the middle and large processors, merchants, and traffickers. The guerrillas do not tax peasant cultivators but rather those formally involved in the drug industry and its related trafficking activities. If some people are periodically unable to pay the tax in money, the FARC-EP introduced a program where they can provide animals, food, grain, materials and so on (see Galvis, 2000: 136). Resembling a Leninist agricultural strategy (Trapeznikov, 1981a; 1981b; Rochester, 1942), these goods are distributed to marginalized sectors of the immediate or outside communities. I personally witnessed the FARC-EP providing free grants to peasants in need (see also Sánchez, 2003: 6–7; Leech 2006b; Molano, 1992: 214).

17 Instead of a monthly levy the FARC-EP may impose a one-time annual payment on cattle ranchers and medium or large landowners (see Richani, 2002a: 142).

18 The US State Department claimed the FARC-EP provides "advance warning of government raids" for those involved in the coca industry (Lee III, 1985: 155). During interviews, peasants clarified how the FARC-EP periodically notifies segments of the populace about upcoming attacks from state and paramilitary forces or anti-state campaigns carried out by the guerrillas (see also Molano, 2005: 191, 195; Roldán, 2003: xvi).

19 It should be known that "the FARC have long taxed numerous businesses within their areas of control" (Stokes, 2005: 86; see also Holmes, Amin Gutiérrez de Piñeres and Curtin, 2006: 164; Peceny and Durnan, 2006: 107; Felbab-Brown, 2005: 107, 126n.33; Leech, 2002a: 46–7; Alejandro and Billon, 1999). For instance, they force MNCs to fiscally support public projects, employment, and small producers. In 1997 the guerrillas established contact with several foreign-based MNCs which were planning on building an electrical plant in Barrancabermeja. The guerrillas' argument was that the land, resources, and labor to be used for the project were Colombian, thus the territory and those within it must receive benefit from their use. With the help of a local JAC, the guerrillas stipulated that before work was to begin the MNCs were to provide US$2 million for the construction of a vocational school, and ensure steady employment for 200 locally trained residents during the construction of the plant. In return, the FARC-EP would not impose Law 002 against the plant in the future. The event demonstrated the FARC-EP's political negotiating skills, its socially motivated positioning, and ability to devise equitable agreements with oppositional figures (Richani, 2002a: 80).

20 As described by Schulte-Bockholt (2006: 133), "the FARC relies on income from

the drug economy and protects the coca farmers against abuses from government security forces and traffickers."

21 An argument can be made that the only reason the FARC-EP has civilian support is the insurgency's tolerance toward those linked to the coca industry:

> The FARC's most loyal followers since the 1980s have been peasants who cultivate coca in the south of the country. It is a relationship that has been based largely on the immediate economic interests of poverty-stricken peasants, rather than any ideological devotion. (Rochlin, 2003: 99–100)

Petras and Morley (see also Molano (2005; 2000) have shown that such assumptions fail to recognize the reality that the FARC-EP:

> struggles on behalf of basic peasant interests (land, credit, roads, and so on), the social services and law and order they provide, and their political education and ideological appeals. In most of their dealings with the rural population, the FARC represents order, rectitude, and social justice ... *this cannot buy class loyalties or village allegiances*. The strength of the FARC is based on the interplay of ideological appeals and the resonance of its analysis and socio-political practices with the everyday reality of peasant life. (Petras and Morley, 2003: 102, italics added)

Rural support for the FARC-EP is far more complex than merely allowing a few peasants to grow coca but rather an intricate model of pre-revolutionary efforts alongside historic sociocultural alliances.

22 To make sure funds are used for their intended social purpose, local officials are contacted by the FARC-EP via secret meetings and "are lectured and threatened for stealing community funds and for other forms of corruption" as part of Law 003, which prohibits fiscal corruption (Taussig, 2004b: 143; see also FARC-EP, 2000f).

23 The "peasant farmers get a larger income from coca than from any of the other crops they cultivate" (O'Shaughnessy and Branford, 2005: 7; see also Felbab-Brown, 2005: 108; Richani, 2002a; 2001).

24 No registered human rights violations were reported in FARC-EP-held regions where peasants grew coca until the arrival of the paramilitary (Kirk, 2003: 247; see also Coghlan, 2004: 81).

25 Both peasants and insurgents benefit through this model: "the FARC relies on income from the drug economy and protects the coca farmers against abuses from government security forces and traffickers" (Schulte-Bockholt, 2006: 133). Eric B. Ross (2006: 64), discussing the growing levels of coercion deployed against the peasantry (economic and physical), went so far as to suggest the FARC-EP enable the peasantry to sustain its cultural socioeconomic existence: "There may be nothing but the FARC ... standing between them and oblivion."

26 More accurately, the insurgency has for years acted as a go-between making sure peasants receive equitable returns (Stokes, 2005: 86). Nevertheless, some, without evidence, are convinced the FARC-EP "independently produce its own narcotics and develop its own networks to market them" (Ortiz, 2006: 211). These statements have not only been shown false but are not supported by any serious scholarship.

27 The word "illicit" is placed in inverted commas because many coca cultivators are in no way connected to the drug economy. One female community leader I interviewed from Cauca adamantly explained this point:

> First of all there is something that all of you in the North need to understand. Our crops are not illicit, I repeat, not illicit. There is nothing inherently illegal or wrong about some of the crops that some people choose to produce. Look at coca for example. Coca is not illicit, on the contrary, people throughout Latin

America, and specifically the Andes, have been producing coca for thousands of years and commercially for hundreds. This plant is not illicit in our communities! It is not us [the local rural producer] who makes this crop illicit and it is not the plant that is the problem, it is those that produce the final product [cocaine]. The coca plant has been and continues to be made for many things that are not illicit: tea, cookies, wine, soap, etc. We and all peoples have a right to grow and produce this crop for commercial purposes; however, it is you in the North that fail to understand that we use this crop for many other things other than drugs used by people in your countries. We have a right to make an income off of tea made from coca, we have a right to make coca wine, we have a right to make a living .... Everyone who lives in out region grows crops but only a small number of people in our community grow coca alongside many other crops. Our community conducted a study and found that 70 percent of all the coca grown in our region is used for commercial crops and only a small portion is sold for other reasons [the drug economy]. You must tell people that all those who grow coca do not do so for drugs but for domestic consumption through legitimate commercial products. When countries like the United States spray our communities they kill and destroy not only the small number of coca plants used for cocaine but they destroy our entire commercial industry; plantain, yucca, lemons, etc., which also affects our livestock and children whose immune systems are not as strong or developed as the adults.

Fumigation chemicals such as glyphosphate bleach into the soil and contaminate various aspects of the communities water supply.

28 Similarities to this mode of thinking and social interconnections can be recognized in Marx (1975d: 294–306).

29 One US official admitted the goal of fumigation was to structurally displace peasants in order to increase cheap labor in the cities while privately centralizing rural resources (Barstow and Driver, 2003).

CHAPTER 6

1 Paramilitaries have commonly been "backed by economic elites for whom armed groups served to defend property, to repress social protests or to carve out space in (local) political arenas" (Kruijt and Koonings, 2004: 27).

2 Colombia offers one of the strongest examples of class rule in Latin America. The political and economic elite therein "demonstrated that elected governments in Latin America were creatures of the ruling classes just as much as the open dictatorships which have heavily punctuated their existence" (MacEoin, 1971: 137). Furthermore Colombia's middle economic stratum has been far from leading or organizing movements in structural opposition to the state, but has rather sought to imitate the elite in hopes of becoming part of it (Sanders, 1981: 83).

3 Such legislation:

allowed the formation of paramilitaries as an explicit part of the state's strategy to combat the insurgency. This law was promulgated in the context of the Cold War, and consequently marked by the US counterinsurgency doctrine which Colombia's military had incorporated at least in part as a result of training programs at the School of the Americas, then based in Panama. This law laid the legal foundation for the paramilitaries and opened a new phase in the Colombian conflict, with far reaching effects. (Richani, 2007: 406).

4 Referred to as *Asociaciones Comunitarias de Vigilancia Rural, Asociaciones Comunitarias de Seguridad, Cooperativas para la Vigilancia y Seguridad Privada*. This work will address the collectives by acronym only.

5   Officially, CONVIVIRs were authorized by Rafael Pardo Rueda, the defense minis-
     ter under the Gaviria administration (Avilés, 2006: 118; Hylton, 2006: 93; Murillo
     and Avirama, 2004: 103; Cubides, 2003: 131; Richani, 2002a: 52). However, their
     formal inception came under the legalization of paramilitarism during the Liberal
     administration of Ernesto Samper (1994–98) (Avilés, 2006: 118; Hylton, 2006: 93–
     4; Livingstone, 2003: 223; Leech, 2002a: 26; Richani, 2002a: 51; Giraldo, 1996:
     115). Technically, the CONVIVIR were "put under the supervision and control of
     an agency of the Ministry of National Defense"; however, it was soon clear that
     the Ministry was "unable to manage" the armed civilian networks (Gallón, 2007a:
     377; 2007b: 419).
6   Salvatore Mancuso, who became informal leading commander of the AUC in 2001
     and formal leader after Carlos Castaño's murder in 2004, was a commanding offi-
     cer of a Córdoba-based CONVIVIR in the mid-1990s (Hylton, 2006: 94). He was
     also Uribe's neighbor during his time as governor (Avilés, 2006: 136).
7   Members of the AUC openly supported Uribe ideologically and financially (see
     Vieira, 2009a; FENSUSGRO, 2008). His campaign posters, for instance, were
     plastered throughout their compounds in Urabá (Lazzaretti, 2003).
8   The FARC-EP continued to gain support at this time. For example, the late 1980s
     saw the insurgency establish itself throughout Antioquia while founding "the first
     labour unions of banana workers" (Chernick, 2003: 196).
9   Large landholders used them "for economic ends, expelling communities from
     areas where landowners would like to graze cattle or expand crop plantation, often
     disrupting threatened rural communities" (Crandall, 1999: 228).
10   The state is responsible for both the creation of the CONVIVIR and its continu-
     ation once "outlawed." When formed, the Samper administration "devoted few
     resources to the supervision of this new counterinsurgency force" (Avilés, 2006:
     119). When demobilized, the state failed to put forth any program to guarantee
     the collection of the weapons/ammunitions distributed (Richani, 2002a: 52). Not
     only did the networks "still function in rural areas controlled by large landowners
     and narcotraffickers, their two staunchest supporters," they enabled a "legal cover
     for their paramilitary groups," ensuring their growth and increased organizational
     expansion (Richani, 2002a: 52).
11   Retentions are aimed at politicians, MNCs, and large landholders (Avilés, 2001:
     50n.16). This is, in part, because some local merchants support the guerrillas
     while MNCs employ paramilitaries to eliminate small-scale enterprise in order to
     create monopolies over certain local industries (see Coghlan, 2004: 34). The use of
     retention often makes headlines yet the FARC-EP's voluntary shift away from this
     practice has been given little press.
12   The most widely publicized figure of FARC-EP retention was Franco-Colombian
     Ingrid Betancourt. A politician herself, Betancourt's mother, Yolando Pulecio, was
     a congressional representative and assistant to President Barco (1986–90). Her
     father, Gabriel Betancourt, was a minister under the Gustavo Rojas Pinilla dictator-
     ship (1953–57) and became head of the education commission during the Alliance
     for Progress.
13   It is difficult to know how *Don* Jesús perished, as differing accounts have appeared.
     Members of the AUC argued he was murdered by the FARC-EP, while other
     reports cited the cause of death as repeated blows to the head as a result of *Don*
     Jesús banging his head against the tree he was tied to while in custody (Kirk, 2003:
     149).
14   Fidel experienced virtual impunity in northwestern Colombia, regardless of the ille-
     galities associated with his actions. On January 14, 1990, under his order, 43 men
     were violently abducted from the small village of Pueblo Bello in the municipality

of Turbo, Urabá in Antioquia. The reasoning for their capture was that guerrillas were claimed to have taken 43 head of cattle from Castaño's land. In reaction, Fidel demonstrated not only how the paramilitary equate human lives to those of animals, but that such forces do not target insurgents but rather the social base that supports the guerrillas. Shortly after the detentions, 23 bodies were found mutilated on Castaño's land, all believed to be among the 43 abducted earlier in the year. State officials, at all levels of government, declared their inability to prosecute Castaño on a lack of evidence, witnesses, or knowledge of the event – even though eyewitness accounts existed and reports had been filed (Browne, 1994).

15 The Castaño brothers, like all AUC leaders, came from privileged class backgrounds (Richani, 2007: 410, 414). Richani (2007: 415) noted, "the main social base from which AUC members are drawn is the petty bourgeoisie and it is this social class that has effectively formed the backbone of the right-wing militias."

16 Such devotion illustrates the irony of patriarchal constructs. Fidel, alongside his siblings, was violently abused by his alcoholic father, leading him to loathe Don Jesús (Dudley, 2004: 144–5; Kirk, 2003: 148). Fidel's hatred was so deep that he, a multimillionaire during the 1980s, refused to offer one peso for his father's release but rather mortgaged Don Jesús' property holdings to finance the ransom (Kirk, 2003: 148; Ruiz, 2001: 172).

17 Liberal president Alberto Lleras Camargo used a similar tactic entitled "rehabilitation" during his second term in office (1958–62) to detract support from the PCC (Gomez, 1972: 251).

18 During this period the MAS had control throughout much of the Magdalena Medio (Puerto Berrío, San Juan Bosco de Laverde, San Rafael de Chucurí, and so on) (Pearce, 1990a: 248).

19 Escobar, for example, notoriously worked with German-Colombian Carlos Lehder Rivas and was enamored of other Colombian politicos known for their neo-fascist ideas (Harding, 1996: 29; see also Bowden, 2001).

20 During the late 1980s and early 1990s, Colombia increasingly reflected the El Salvador of the late 1970s and 1980s. This "Central Americanization" of Colombia was based on the far-right activities of elite political control and the silencing of subversives. Hence MORENA came to resemble the Salvadorean National Republican Alliance (Alianza Republicana Nacional, ARENA). For Kline (1999: 77), "MORENA would be for the paramilitary groups what … ARENA (Alianza Republicana Nacional, Nationalist Republican Alliance) was for the death squads in El Salvador."

21 This is an imperative point to understand in the context of class conflict from a Colombian perspective. As noted by Pearce (1990a: 8), numerous sectors of Colombia's dominant class financially supported the formation and continuity of this openly fascist organization and paramilitary elements. Acknowledging such information enables us to better understand the FARC-EP's broad opposition to the Colombian elite as supporters of reactionism.

22 At the entrance to Puerto Boyacá a billboard once read "anti-subversive capital of Colombia" (Pearce, 1990a: 248).

23 Dudley (2004: 121) claimed MORENA had won an election in 1988. This is not correct, as Rubio's election preceded the establishment of MORENA (Kline, 1999: 77; Pearce, 1990a: 250).

24 Immediately after his election "many peasants began to flee altogether," while "the problem of internal refugees became increasingly serious," as ACDEGAM encouraged paramilitaries to displace peasants (Pearce, 1990a: 248).

25 State forces facilitated much of this inter-cooperation. The military and internal high-ranking officials acted as a glue linking both paramilitary organizations throughout the 1980s and 1990s (Richani, 2002a: 103).

26 Salvatore Mancuso was also instrumental in the AUC's organizational model at this time (Richani, 2005b: 91).

27 In 2008, José Obdulio Gaviria, one of Uribe's primary advisors, confidently claimed that "there is no paramilitarism," "no armed conflict," or "displacement" in Colombia (see Bustamante and Chaskel, 2008: 77; Cambio, 2008b). On paper, the AUC had demobilized yet in reality it simply experienced a new stage of development. No longer able to dismiss its relevance, embarrassingly the president had to acknowledge the continued power of the AUC in 2009 (Colombia Reports, 2009b). In short, "the AUC is not pulling out of the war system, but rather is simply modifying its role" (Richani 2007: 415).

> At the municipal level there is no evidence that the influence of the AUC has diminished after the demobilisation of some of its armed structures. Informants in the Middle Magdalena reiterated that the AUC command and control structure and its coercive capacities are still imposing their political will on the citizens of these areas. These findings are consistent with the new political strategy articulated by Mancuso. This strategy consists of three basic elements, two of which are relevant here: "one that the AUC functions will not cease to exist with the demobilization. Secondly, the AUC will not cede the territories under their control to the insurgency, but rather will continue protecting these regions within an integrated defense strategy, that will safeguard the established socio economic order which includes the new political and economic power acquired by members of the AUC." This political strategy could explain why little has changed on the ground in the wake of the ostensible demobilisation of 31,000 AUC fighters or members of logistical support units …. Furthermore, the local structures of the AUC will be able to continue co-ordinating with the state in their common fight against the insurgency, without causing national or international uproar, as was the case in the past. (Richani, 2007: 412)

Chernick (2007: 59, 76) provided an excellent discussion of how the state cannot "afford" to have the AUC entirely demobilize in the fact that it would leave a vacuum open for the FARC-EP to fill.

28 Some accounts reported:

> Carlos Castaño gave up his position as military commander in 2001 and as political leader in 2002. With the installation of the Uribe government in that same year, Castaño briefly returned as paramount leader of the AUC, but this time in order to "participate in a peace process" while publicly rejecting practices such as drug trafficking and terrorism. (Kruijt and Koonings, 2004: 30).

29 The state and paramilitary have both utilized paid secret civilian informants (Pearce, 2007: 265–6n 31; Bland, 2004: 5). Within 48 hours of becoming president (in 2002), Uribe inaugurated an organized network of 1 million civilian informants paid to divulge information on the FARC-EP and state antagonists (International Crisis Group, 2003b). However, the Red de Cooperantes "are not only paid a small amount for helping with intelligence, but they could also receive large payoffs ($190 to $770) for particularly important tips that lead to arrests or the prevention of an attack" (Washington Office on Latin America, 2002). In one year, over $40,000 was paid out via "Reward Mondays," where live televised broadcasts would "feature informants in ski masks receiving thick wads of bills from military commander." How credible such information was, however, is another story, as roughly three-quarters of the country experiences substandard economic conditions. This makes information obtained highly suspect, as political-economic need trumps patriotic duty. While the use of informants is a sign of political fascism (Escobar, 2004: 20), the state doubled the number of those involved in 2004, and

by 2006 it reached 4.6 million (Ejército Nacional República de Colombia, 2006; Isacson and Vaicius, 2004).

One displaced civilian from Meta, now living in Bogotá, told me how many informants are used in the city:

Not well known outside Colombia, it is well known here that the paras took control over the downtown districts of the capital [Bogotá]. As you can see, there are thousands involved in the formal and informal economy [*formal* – small-merchants, bakeries, corner-stores, etc. *informal* – street-merchants selling CDs and DVDs, books, clothes, etc.]. These people do not earn much and a few years ago Uribe put in place a secret informant network paid to give information about neighbors, teachers, family members, etc. who may be involved in revolutionary activity. The paramilitary capitalized upon this strategy by targeting sectors of the formal and informal economy in the cities .... As in any revolutionary situation, the cities are important. The paras established extortion links, either by threat or financial incentive. On a weekly or even daily basis they patrol the streets asking merchants if anything suspicious has been going on and they either provide reward or retribution depending on the information given.

When asked '"What might the paras see or interpret as suspicious activity?" the respondent replied:

First, I would like to say that if you are a merchant, struggling to get by, you are going to tell the paras whatever they want to hear. This is why this strategy fails to bring any results. What ends up happening is a flood of false information being given to the paras, or Uribe, due to fear of repression, a need for money, or pettiness – to create hostile reactions against competitors [other merchants] or persons not liked. To answer your question, suspicious activity can be anything from groups of teenagers hanging out putting up posters, people wearing t-shirts with a picture of Che, the distribution of *Voz* [PCC's weekly newspaper], or talk of organizing protests.

I too experienced this during meetings with one labor organization in Bogotá's downtown circa 2006, when civilians and police took photos of those going in and out of the union's office.

30 Salmon Kolmanovitz, an economist and member of Central Bank's board of directors, estimated narcobourgeoisie earnings during this period at US$76 billion (see Richani, 2002a: 181n.54).

31 The paramilitary acts like an economic partner for sectors of the elite. For example:

the AUC collects "rent" from wealthy landowners and narcotraffickers. In part of Colombia's "counter land reform" in the 1980s and 1990s, drug traffickers purchased about 10 percent of Colombia's most productive agricultural land. The AUC has continued this practice by selling land to traffickers who pay the group for security and split the profits from trafficking. (Sweig and McCarthy, 2005: 28)

Going even further, Diana Duque Gómez (1991) argued that paramilitaries/traffickers have benefited Colombia's economy and should be applauded for defending it from Marxism. Similarly, Uribe claimed that the Colombian people are "defended by paramilitaries" (BBC, 2004).

32 Estimates of the amount of land acquired by the narcobourgeoisie by the end of the 1990s ranged from a low of 8 million acres to a high of 33 million (Richani, 2000: 48n.12).

33 The Castaño brothers acquired almost a quarter of all the land obtained (as adapted from Rochlin, 2003: 107; Mercedes Pereira, 2001: 19–20; Richani, 2000: 38).

34 In economic terms, if the narcobourgeoisie held even a portion of this, say 2.5 million hectares, they would have an annual income of roughly US$3.5 billion, 4 percent of Colombia's GDP (see Richani, 2007: 408).

35 Rochlin (2003: 107) described how the AUC possesses a "neofascist agenda" and promotes "ultra-right-wing social policies against the backdrop of a society beset with a shifting moral code."

36 State and paramilitary forces have been known to take over civilian dwellings knowing the FARC-EP will not deliberately attack non-combatants (Shah, 2002).

37 There are clear ideological and political differences between FARC-EP-based "human rights violations" and those carried out by paramilitary forces (see Holmes and Amin Gutiérrez de Piñeres, 2006: 112).

38 Although it is the largest by far, the FARC-EP is only one of several guerrilla organizations in the grouping "guerrillas."

39 Richani (2007: 411) noted that "the mode of development presided over by the narcobourgeoisie is in line with the neoliberal economic paradigm and various free trade agreements." Hence, the AUC aligns with the politics and ideals of the right and not towards social justice, marginalized workers, or collective rights (Richani, 2007: 413).

40 Youths and young adults are not unaffected by the war but are increasingly counter-insurgent targets (Bond, 2006: 1).

> Not even girls and boys were excluded from "vigilante citizen" initiatives. In some cases children were asked to police and report on their own parents. Furthermore, as described by the Comisión Colombiana de Juristas, military personnel were involved in health brigades and advertisements in schools, even implementing a "soldier for a day" program in the conflict-ridden region of Arauca. (Rojas, 2006: 2)

Penny Lernoux (1982: 9–10) provided a chilling account of how the targeting of youth is not new to Latin America but was introduced by the United States during the cold war via counter-insurgency institutions, which methodologically trained Central and South American soldiers to look at youths as targets indoctrinated by communistic ideologies. Course materials used by the School of the Americas (SOA), now the Western Hemisphere Institute for Security Cooperation (WHINSEC), taught that "the disappearance or movement of youths" in a community indicates there is "recruitment to form guerrilla bands in the area" (Lernoux, 1982: 180). Counter-insurgents were trained to be critical of the families of such young people, and that soldiers "should report the reluctance of families of said missing youths to speak about them" (Lernoux, 1982: 180–1). This historical reflection is important for it illustrates that young people have become the principal targets of counterinsurgency forces because of the financial, ideological, and political backing of the United States (see Leech, 2006d: 155–7). Ironically, authors such as Sanjay Suri (2004) have argued that "influential groups such as the G8 (the leading industrialized nations comprising the Untied States, Canada, Britain, France, Germany, Italy, Japan and Russia), the United Nations and the European Union (EU) have all adopted positions against use of child soldiers," yet it is these nations who were once, or remain, the primary financers and military backers of the organizations that continue to recruit them.

41 Structural acceptance of torture toward the left has been prevalent in Colombia for decades (Cleary, 2007: 13). In 1962, US forces became intimately involved in training Colombian soldiers in counter-insurgency techniques (Dix, 1967: 378; see also Colby and Dennett, 1995: 391–5). A leading US general, William Yarborough, met with members of the Colombian state (and military), advising them that a:

> concerted country team effort should be made now to select civilian and military personnel for clandestine training in resistance operations in case they are

needed later .... This structure should be used to pressure toward reforms known to be needed, perform counter-agent and counter-propaganda functions and as necessary execute paramilitary, sabotage and/or terrorist activities against known communist proponents. It should be backed by the United States. (McClintock, 1992: 222)

Yarborough's activities in 1962 compelled Colombia to adopt extreme tactics in an attempt to discourage communist sympathies in the countryside (Stokes, 2005: 70–1). At the time, the United States advocated "physical and mental coercion" against civilians as a means to combat insurgents (Stokes, 2005: 60–1). After their training the Colombian army immediately targeted non-combatants throughout suspected rebel-extended regions. Wickham-Crowley noted how:

> personal testimony providing particular examples of government torture, beatings, and killings was given before the Colombian Congress in November 1964 (that is, at the beginning of the guerrilla movements proper). Among the techniques reported were the placement of a grenade in a prisoner's mouth and threatening to pull the pin; faked firing squads; punching, kicking, and walking on prisoners; electric current applied to the genitals, hands, and ears; burning with cigarettes; and outright execution. (Wickham-Crowley, 1990: 212)

42 As abuses are carried out against the individual the purpose is a psychological method of warfare aimed at the collective. The principal goal is not to engage individual human rights abuses but create an environment of fear. While the sexual molestation of any human being is an atrocity, the AUC used male rape as a systemic tool to engulf fear in patriarchal communities. In rural Colombia, *machismo* is prevalent. When a dominant male figure is violated in such a societal context, sociocultural notions of power, trust, and security are destroyed, with significant ripple effects. Axel Honneth (2001: 40–1) argued that "the suffering or torture of rape, is always accompanied by a dramatic breakdown in one's trust in the reliability of the social world and hence by a collapse in one's own basic self-confidence." If a society believes in the construct of man as defender, the humiliation and structure on which it is partially built is subsequently shattered as the idea of security is eroded. A community may then fear that no recourse to state/ paramilitary aggression is possible and stop organizing in opposition to economic and political exploitation – the true purpose of human rights abuse in Colombia.

43 There are numerous accounts of US links with Colombian paramilitarism (Stokes, 2005; see also Ramírez, Stanton and Walsh, 2005: 102–3, 124; Ramírez, 2005: 68–71; Goff, 2004: 34). Since the mid-twentieth century, Green Berets (US Special Forces) have been used "in combat in Colombia ... as "advisors"" (Barnet, 1972: 73, 74n.12; see also Stokes, 2005: 60–1, 70–1; Wickham-Crowley, 1990: 212; Dix, 1967: 378; Szulc, 1964: 20–1).

44 Kruijt and Koonings (2004: 82) argued the AUC is as vicious as any group was during *la Violencia*. When these atrocities are evaluated, parallels can be seen with those implemented from the 1940s to the 1970s by early Conservative death squads: 1) "ripping the foetus out of a pregnant woman and substituting a cock" (Hobsbawm, 2000: 69); 2) Slitting the throat and pulling the victim's tongue through the neck, called a *Corbata* (tie); 3) Cutting off limbs and head, called a *Franela* (sleeveless shirt) (Hylton, 2006: 44; Galvis, 2000: 28); 4) the murder not only of peasants but the violent molestation and rape of their female offspring and family members; 5) the immolation of babies (Gilhodés, 1970: 446); 6) the spitting of children on pitchforks; 7) unarmed civilians having their "lips, noses, or ears cut off" (Gunther, 1966: 439); 8) the "mutilation of ears, fingers, penises, and breasts"; 8) disemboweling civilians and throwing their bodies into rivers (Hylton, 2006: 45). Not only do these continue, they are far more widespread then during *la Violencia*.

45 As the Cali and Medellín cartels declined in the 1990s much of their power transferred to the paramilitary leadership. Capitalizing on the death or imprisonment of their former employers, the AUC consolidated property holdings and activities associated with the industry.

46 Such conditions linger, as the AUC and its allies remain involved in all facets of the industry (Richani, 2007: 409).

47 Unlike the AUC, the FARC-EP "use the funds not for personal enrichment but to finance their conflict and to supply a minimum of services in the territory under their control" (Schulte-Bockholt, 2006: 138).

48 The four-decade "war on drugs" has shown bias in relation to class and race (Gibbs and Leech, 2005; O'Shaughnessy and Branford, 2005: 20–2).

49 Scott (2003: 86–7) discovered that in 1984 US authorities falsified evidence to make the FARC-EP appear to be involved in narcotics production, processing, and trafficking. It has also been said officials planted evidence trying to link the FARC-EP to the drugs trade (Scott, 2003: 92n.19).

50 This same period saw US-based Occidental locate one of the continent's largest untapped oil reserves in the northeast, and Colombia became a net oil exporter (Pearce, 2007: 277; Tamminen, 2006: 98; Scott, 2003: 39, 72; Renner, 2002: 36). By 1989, oil production at Caño-Limón had increased by 80 percent (Scott, 2003: 100).

51 Former SouthCom commander, General James Hill, provided a more contemporary phrase, calling coca "a weapon of mass destruction" (Hill, 2003: 8; see also O'Shaughnessy and Branford, 2005: 61).

52 The ATPDEA had a timeline of completion (December 31, 2006). By 2007, a new bilateral US/Colombia free trade agreement, FTA (or *Tratado de Libre Comercio*, TLC) was being arranged. It was claimed to transcend the original (Goodman, 2006a; Noticias Aliadas, 2006). On February 27, 2006, the Bush and Uribe administrations signed a promotion agreement accepting this new FTA, which resulted in both states taking it to Congress for approval. At the time of this writing the administration of Barack Obama (2009–) was pushing for its acceptance.

53 Sarah Cox (2002) found that:

> about 70 percent, are women who earn just (US) 58 cents an hour and work up to 60 hours a week, often without full overtime pay, before special occasions like Mother's Day and Valentine's Day. The workers, by many accounts, suffer from a myriad of health problems linked to exposure to pesticide cocktails that are applied up to several times a week to guarantee elegant, pest-free blossoms.

54 The counter-insurgency funding implemented by Bogotá and Washington far exceeds the amount devoted to Central America during the 1970s and 1980s. "Washington spent roughly ten billion dollars in Nicaragua and El Salvador throughout the wars of the 1980s" (Grandin, 2006: 204). Within six years almost $8 billion was spent in Colombia (Campos, 2007: 38; Chavez, 2007: 96; Mondragón, 2007: 42). At times, the Colombian state was spending $7.3 million a day, while the United States provided $1.65 million, equaling almost US$9 million per day to fight the FARC-EP (Murillo, 2005; Latin American Press, 2004).

55 The United States has tried to restrict this evidence, as Marxism is "dead." Not a Soviet holdout, the FARC-EP demonstrates a distinct contemporary relevance of revolutionary Marxism-Leninism (Murillo and Avirama, 2004: 58; Löwy, 1992: 12; Aguilar, 1968: 227–9; Pomeroy, 1968: 308–14).

56 Similar accounts were seen in Afghanistan throughout the cold war; Iraq and the Middle East during the 1980s; the Contras during the important struggles in Central America; and again in Afghanistan with the Northern Alliance.

57 This is a new phenomenon. Meta was once recognized as FARC-EP territory (Leech, 2004b; Wilson, 2003).

58 Such information is interesting, for this is what happened to sectors of the Colombian army during the 1980s. Numerous factions of the national forces became considerably corrupt by the spoils and indirect offshoots of the domestic and international drug trade, which resulted in more concern for the drug trade than any moral, political, or military goal of sustaining counter-insurgency (Decker and Duran, 1982: 11).

59 While the FARC-EP targets the state and capitalist class to advance political objectives, the AUC increasingly seek personal gain (Gutiérrez Sanín, 2008, 2004; Peceny and Durnan, 2006: 111). An example of this can be shown by assessing claims that the guerrillas attract combatants by offering money (Hudson, 2002: 155). Some have stated "the FARC and the paramilitary groups are the two most stable employers of the region, guaranteeing them a salary, a uniform, regular meals, and, most tragically, a weapon" (Murillo and Avirama, 2004: 70; see also Koonings and Kruijt, 2004: 14). To depict the FARC-EP and the AUC as similar "employers" reveals a deep rejection of the "job qualifications." To state that both organizations offer a salary is to fail to examine the ideological distinction and empirical methodologies of how each group organizes its members (Gutiérrez Sanín, 2008; Richani, 2002a: 148).

It is very much true that the AUC provides a formal monthly income for members (Gutiérrez Sanín, 2008: 14; 2004; Howe, 2004; Taussig, 2004b: 153; Livingstone, 2003: 219; Richani, 2002a: 148; NACLA, 2000: 42). The FARC-EP, however, does not pay its members or provide a formal income, but rather supplies necessities to meet daily requirements (Weinstein, 2007: 289, 292; Peceny and Durnan, 2006: 100; Allende La Paz, 2004; Gutiérrez Sanín, 2004: 268; Ferro Medina and Uribe Ramón, 2002: 90). As clearly noted by Gutiérrez Sanín (2008; 14, see also 17, 19), "the FARC does not pay its members. FARC deserters, government and NGO reports, the data gathered in JUDICIAL, FARC leaders, paramilitary leaders, and the population in the areas of influence of the organization, all concur on this point." A member of the FARC-EP Secretariat told me that the insurgency does not directly pay any of its combatants, for to do so would detract from the Marxist-Leninist position of class consciousness and the ability for a person, of their own volition, to emancipate themselves and their class from its "chains." The guerrillas have, however, been known to provide a modest monthly stipend for a family who have lost a member (FARC-EP combatant) as a result of conflict or capture (Chernick, 2007: 74; Richani, 2002a: 148).

Historically, the paramilitary were paid a proportion of the amount that large landowners, drug cartels, and businesspeople in specific regions paid to have them act as "security forces." In recent years the AUC has come to offer a formal monthly salary, because of its increasingly bureaucratic form as a result of its involvement in the narcotics industry. Gutiérrez Sanín, who has done extensive research on this subject, noted:

> the rank and file are normally paid a salary of about $200–250 a month, though there is regional and longitudinal variance. Sometimes they also have access to rents coming from trafficking, extortion, and kidnapping, though this is a privilege mainly awarded to the middle and high leadership. (Gutiérrez Sanín, 2008: 14–15).

Overall, members of the AUC make between US$190 and $1,000 per month, which averages out to be roughly 70–900 percent more than the state-regulated minimum wage.

60 After Castaño "disappeared" on April 16, 2004, Mancuso was formally declared the official leader of the AUC.

61 Vicente was himself brutally murdered by former paramilitary allies on March 11, 2007: he was hacked into pieces which were placed inside tires and set ablaze.

CHAPTER 7

1   Similar to Lenin's *dual power* in many ways, Gramsci's theory can be argued as an empirical account of what the FARC-EP is materially doing in preparation of a provisional state.

2   Unlike classical definitions of positional warfare the FARC-EP has a distinct approach. As stated by Rodrigo Granda, member of the FARC-EP's International Commission:

> we are not waging a war of positions in Colombia. We are a nomadic guerrilla force. When we are in certain areas for a time, we develop direct democracy as it has never been seen in any other type of organization promoted by the state or the oligarchic parties .... This is open, participative democracy and true mass democracy such as Colombia has never seen before. (see Batou, 2008: 28)

3   This is very much a Leninist standpoint – "we have always known and repeatedly pointed out that the bourgeoisie maintains itself in power *not* only by force but also by virtue of the lack of class-consciousness and organization, the routinism and downtrodden state of the masses" (Lenin, 1964h: 46–7).

4   Interestingly, former Liberal president Eduardo Santos Montejo (1938–42) claimed that revolution only comes as a consequence of people's needs; therefore, "what we would defend against communism would be our own freedom but if we have already been stripped of them, we have nothing left to defend. It is thus that the gateway to communism is thrown open by the anti-Communists" (quoted in Beals, 1974: 48–9). According to Richani (2001: 66), Colombia suffers from a "chronic crisis of hegemony," caused "by the state's failure to project its authority either by democratic means or by coercion. Such chronic crisis was partially due to the failures of any sector of the dominant class to lead with the support of a consenting critical mass."

5   While there is a correlation between the rise of civil warfare and political decentralization, the latter also enabled the expansion of the paramilitary (Richani, 2007: 407, 416n.12).

6   Throughout the twentieth century state-hegemonic structures were absent in various regions, resulting in a lack of security for civil (private) society (Richani, 2002a). This resulted in a disproportionate stress on private security forces, but these alone could not respond to the insurgency. According to Richani (2005a), the state questionably furthered its reliance on private forces rather than the army in the hopes of rectifying this dilemma.

7   Ernest Mandel (1994: 195) claimed that this strategy is practical in majority-world countries. According to Robert H. Chilcote (1990: 6), the essence of a Marxist-Leninist strategy is to emphasize a "dual power" through which both workers and popular forces construct "their revolutionary base outside the state apparatuses" and create conditions to confront class rule. The FARC-EP has done this by creating "a much more efficient and formidable strategic-military rival for the government" (Murillo and Avirama, 2004: 75).

8   Gramsci approached revolutionary change as a constant evolution and progression, not a simple reality upon the proletariat's seizure of power. Hegemony "is a process, not a thing ... a daily bid to achieve support for a political and social project, not a once-and-for-all achievement of total domination" (McKay, 2005: 61).

9   Initially, JACs were supported by and worked alongside the military, Peace Corps, the church, and the state (Dix, 1967: 354). However, many JACs functioned only as long as foreign NGOs stayed round (Kline, 1988b: 90).

10 A strong argument could be made that JACs flourished throughout the country as a means for public and private funds to be raised for small sectors of the rural elite (see Barkin, 2001: 194; Veltmeyer, 2001: 54).

11 Throughout this period, Lauchlin Currie, prominent economic advisor to several Colombian administrations, promoted construction as a means to ensure economic growth (see Brittain, 2005b; Currie, 1966, 1971, 1976, 1981).

12 For an excellent account of such activities see Petras (1997a).

13 Since the 1970s, millions have been associated with JACs (Safford and Palacios, 2003: 327).

14 While some saw JACs as a means to defuse radical mobilization in the south, the region actually saw many become quite militant (see Zamosc, 1986: 253n.57; Richardson, 1970: 44).

15 In contrast, JACs that witnessed state absence saw increases in grassroots community involvement (Marsh, 1983: 143). Far from docile, rural populations worked in solidarity during such periods (see Payne, 1968: 308).

16 The FARC-EP make an important distinction between the media executives and journalists:

> Many media have become press chiefs, publicity and propaganda of the owners of power, of the system, of the military and their paramilitaries and they fulfill a military-strategic role .... we must say that the media is not the same as the reporter, and that on our path toward peace we have found many of them who are aware of the national situation, who firmly believe in the need for peace, who fight every day to do their job well and to say the truth, in spite of the pressures, as a contribution to the country's way out of the serious crisis. The majority of the reporters are good and dedicated people who have different ideals from those that pay their salaries. (FARC-EP, 2000–01: 20)

17 Díaz Montes is president and Mendiza general secretary of the National Federation of United Agricultural Farming Unions (*La Federación Nacional Sindical Unitaria Agropecuaria*, FENSUAGRO).

18 This contradicts claims that the state, IFIs, and ILIs successfully administered such services during the 1980s (Lang, 1988: 47). Twenty years later, many cities, let alone rural regions, have yet to obtain reliable electricity. While it is available to MNCs, many individuals, even in Puerto Asís, Putumayo (with a population of roughly 40,000), still lack access to consistent electricity (Coghlan, 2004: 205–6).

19 MNCs are targeted more than small businesses (Moser and McIlwaine, 2004: 86). Some MNCs even adopted a strategy of:

> accommodation and coexistence with the guerrillas by satisfying their demands for social investments in the areas where these companies operated. The guerrillas' demands included building vocational schools, paving roads, supporting clinics, and subcontracting projects to guerrilla-owned enterprises, or taxing 5 percent of subcontracts' value offered to other companies. (Richani, 2005a: 125; see also Felbab-Brown, 2005: 110)

There are a few cases, however, where the FARC-EP refused such agreements to prevent corporate influence (correspondence with Leech, December 10, 2005; see also Moser and McIlwaine, 2004: 43, 86–8; Leech, 2002a: 46–7).

20 It is dangerous to flatly link post-secondary education with the FARC-EP. Some have even suggested leftist academics are the reason liberal democracy has yet to exist in Colombia (see Posada Carbó, 2006).

21 "Until the end of the 19th century it took less time to travel from the Caribbean port city of Cartagena across the Atlantic Ocean to Paris than to the nation's capital" (Leech, 2002a: 7).

22 Bartering networks were scheduled between the FARC-EP and purchasers in North America and Europe. Projects discussed included sanitation and indoor water facilities, electrical hook-ups, and the creation of schools and medical centers. These plans were annexed when the DMZ was attacked after the state recognized the progressive achievements the guerrillas were able to accomplish alongside "mere peasants" in San Vicente del Caguán.

23 This ratio was not of remote rural communities alone but of towns and cities with populations exceeding 35,000.

24 The infrastructure may have begun to develop before 1998, however, as the five municipalities in Meta and Caquetá that made up the "zone ... [were] already under the FARC-EP's control" before the DMZ (Gutierrez, 2003: 53).

25 San Vicente del Caguán has two asphalt mines, which were unutilized by government officials. The FARC-EP put in place measures that guaranteed employment while utilizing community-based human and natural resources by pushing for all roads and the construction of schools to be built from these resources (FARC-EP, 2001a: 12).

26 One plan was to generate power through crafting a micro-tidal generator (FARC-EP 2000b: 6).

27 The Uribe administration in particular – with Washington's aid – expanded this ecological assault by spraying (chemicals illegal in the United States) over national parks (Leech, 2006b; O'Shaughnessy and Branford, 2005: 87–9).

28 Numerous requests made to local and national officials concerning environmental issues and development projects were repeatedly dismissed: Bogotá (May 1998), Cartagena Cathedral (November 1997), San Pablo (October 1997), Santa Rosa (March 1997), San Pablo (1996), and Santa Rosa (October 1996) (Dávalos, 2001: 73–4).

29 Colombia's parks offer 10 million hectares of biodiversity, the largest number of different species of birds on the planet, the second largest "stock of plants and amphibians," and the "third largest stock of reptiles" (O'Shaughnessy and Branford, 2005: 87; see also Dieppa, 2007: 203–4). The FARC-EP has made attempts to protect these resources while the state "weakened environmental protection" over them (O'Shaughnessy and Branford, 2005: 87).

30 In contrast, the FARC-EP has coexisted with Afro-Colombians for decades (Coghlan, 2004: 77; Richani, 2002a: 188:15).

31 AUC "members are official or de facto employees of Urapalma, a major Colombian company, and the other outfits planting African palm for palm oil export on the campesinos' land" (Lydersen, 2005). "A good number of African palm plantations and processing plants are owned by paramilitary leaders in various regions of the country, including Chocó, Córdoba, North Santander and Middle Magdalena" (Richani, 2007: 413).

32 It has been noted that "military guards also control entrance to the palm plantation, and don't allow campesinos in even though they have been awarded title to the land by the government," exemplifying "the tight ties between companies like Urapalma, paramilitary groups and the military" (Lydersen, 2005). For example, the AUC subcontracted small producers and/or employees of paramilitary supporters to cut down existing trees and crops from once fruitful lands to create more room for palm and the processing of palm oil. In one region, the AUC sold local workers 87 chainsaws on installment plans. The workers were then told to deforest peasant and indigenous land to procure mahogany for a local company, which sold each tree for roughly $600 to foreign consumers (the workers were paid $40 a day) (Crowe, 2006). The guerrillas charged the wood outfits roughly 12.5 percent on each shipment of a half-dozen trees and regulated how much could be forested,

something the paramilitaries do not practice. Hence, the local wood company denounced the FARC-EP and worked with the AUC, stating that the guerrillas' environmental policies were a deterrent to profit (Crowe, 2006).

33 The arena of sports has been an interesting meeting ground for guerrillas and communities. Soccer, for example, has provided a psychological and physical release for the FARC-EP and civilians, while enabling non-combatants to become engaged with the guerrillas as a people's army rather than faceless insurgents with guns.

34 Georgina Ortiz was one of the FARC-EP's original members and the first *guerrillera* causality of the civil war.

35 Narváez and Grisales were instrumental in designing the Agrarian Programme of the Guerrillas (Marin, 2004).

36 The number of women in the military mirrors those associated with the AUC (Gutiérrez Sanín, 2008: 10).

37 Figures obtained through observational research between 2004 and 2006.

38 The Páez have long been located in the department of Cauca (see Ortiz, 1973; 1971).

39 The US Joint Chiefs of Staff (1964), for one, argued that the FARC-EP was "oriented toward Cuba whence they receive direction and financing." Countless scholars have shown the FARC-EP was never associated with Cuba, but rather with communists in Colombia wanting to establish a movement apart from other groups (Wickham-Crowley, 1991: 135–6; Pomeroy, 1968: 308–14; Gott, 1970; Murillo and Avirama, 2004: 58; Aguilar, 1968: 228). In fact, it was never strongly influenced by Havana (Erisman and Kirk, 2006: 162).

40 The Páez cannot be generalized, as it was only a segment that betrayed those in Marquetalia (Kirk, 2003: 54).

41 Similar reconciliations were also witnessed with the U'wa (Richani, 2002a: 188n.15).

42 An example of this arose after the FARC-EP was responsible for the murder of three US U'wa supporters. On receiving news of the incident an outraged Secretariat reprimanded the perpetrator, suggesting the incident was isolated, and made an international apology to the indigenous community. While a great deal of attention was given to this incident, minimal consideration was given to the 300 indigenous people killed by the AUC in 2001 alone (Leech, 2002a: 58; see also Murillo and Avirama, 2004: 67).

43 It has been said Conrado was killed alongside Raúl Reyes but others suggest he is still alive (Williamson, 2008).

44 For years, the Vatican, priests, laypeople, and bishops (who are partly persecuted by paramilitaries) supported the FARC-EP's promotion of peace (Washington Post, 2004; FARC-EP, 2001–2002: 6–7).

45 Guerrillas have been seen as complementing the church's struggle for social justice (Molano, 2005: 24, 95–6).

46 Camilo Torres was a well-known Colombian sociologist and Roman Catholic priest who came to join the ELN in the 1960s and died in combat in 1966. Torres was famous for his quote that "the duty of every Catholic is to be a revolutionary ... the Catholic who is not a revolutionary is living in mortal sin" (as quoted in Gerassi, 1971: xiii).

47 Paradoxically, others said that "Colombia never had to endure a 'bureaucratic-authoritarian' regime or a state-sponsored 'dirty-war' against subversives" (Skidmore and Smith, 2005: 243; see also Grandin, 2004: 177; 272n.28).

48 Zuluago Nieto (2007: 114, 117) described how the US "national security doctrine emphasized the security of the state rather than of the citizen," while "Uribe's policy, like Washington's, is focused more on the defence of the state than on the

defence of the individual, and it fails to recognize that Colombian democracy is also under siege from poverty, inequality, and social exclusion."

49 Revolutionary situations have repeatedly arisen in Colombia without the state ever being in or near collapse (Richani, 2002a; see also Röhl, 2004: 11).

50 Some even simplify and equate democracy with capitalism (Lee, 2003: 7). My favorite quote is "although Colombia is the oldest democracy in South America, a privileged class rules the country" (Cherry, 2002: 55).

51 The UP was a political organization while the FARC-EP promoted armed struggle (Crandall, 2002: 69). Nevertheless, after several years of separation, the UP declared itself to be an "autonomous political organization separate from the FARC-EP" in February 1987 (Osterling, 1989: 300; see also 197; Kline, 1999: 35–6). In fact, the first UP presidential candidate, Jaime Pardo Leal, was never a member of the FARC-EP, which demonstrated how guerrilla connections to the party were based on immaterial grounds (Osterling, 1989: 196). Leal clarified that the UP was not the FARC-EP's political mouthpiece and it would continue (self-governing) political activities whether the insurgency supported peace negotiations with the state or not (Kline, 1999: 35–6). Wickham-Crowley (1992: xx, 212) has claimed that if any connections did ever exist between the UP and the FARC-EP, it was solely based on the presumption that some members had left the conflict to pursue lawful political solutions.

52 The coalition included former guerrillas, unionists, social justice advocates, some PCC, and the Fourth Internationalist Workers Socialist Party (*el Partido Socialista de los Trabajadores*, PST-CITO) (Premo, 1988: 235).

53 The UP actively worked with Liberals through political alliances/coalitions (Osterling, 1989: 196).

54 As with its break with the PCC, no political unification remained between the UP and FARC-EP. I have found no connection between these groups, especially since the FARC-EP created the MBNC and is affiliated with the PCCC.

55 The FARC-EP has enabled those who need to survive through the cultivation of coca to do so. Hence, where "the state brings no justice, prohibits cocaine, and is as utterly corrupt," the FARC-EP is seen as supportive (Taussig, 2004b: 142; see also Villalón, 2004a; 2004b).

56 Some accounts have documented civilians fondly describing the FARC-EP as those who have brought security to their community in the absence of the state (see Molano, 2005: 179).

57 The FARC-EP openly discourages substance abuse (Molano, 2005: 90; Coghlan, 2004: 188).

58 Violent attacks against women have been known to carry the death penalty (Botero, 2006; Vieira, 2006b).

59 Once state forces were removed, San Vicente del Caguán saw death rates drop by 98 percent and prostitution became virtually nonexistent (Brittain, 2004c; Murch, 2000).

60 "What must really change are the Regime and the State, which are deeply rooted in the corrupt and anti-democratic customs that have submerged Colombia in the present" (FARC-EP, 2000b: 8).

61 Traces of these policies date back to the 1970s (Simons, 2004: 44).

62 The FARC-EP does not politically dominate regions nor does it monopolize policing. On the contrary, many communities organize their own law enforcement patrols. This counters statements that the guerrillas have centralized the use of force in each given community (Sánchez, 2003: 30). The FARC-EP has not maintained a dogmatic form of Marxism but has rather attempted to facilitate the development of civilian–guerrilla projects (see Murillo and Avirama, 2004: 58; Harnecker, 1986: 128; Hobsbawm, 1973: 117; Draper, 1978a: 101, 155).

63 Chernick (2007: 61) highlighted the predominant issues that resonated across three decades of talks: "(1) land reform and state investment in rural development, and (2) political reforms leading to greater political participation, particularly at the local level." Not radical, the "demands were modest and within the realm of democratic political reforms." The peace negotiations were repeatedly stunted by state and paramilitary aggression and the state's lack of response to the social grievances of the rural populace (Chernick, 2007: 62–3).

64 Post-September 11, 2001 pressure was placed on Pastrana to end negotiations (Murillo and Avirama, 2004: 20).

65 The guerrillas remained open to new humanitarian accords (FARC-EP, 2003a; 2003b; 2003c; 2003d; 2003i; 2003k; 2003l; 2002b: 7–8; 2002c; Dayani, 2001), public forums for dialogue (Washington Post, 2004; FARC-EP, 2003f; 2003g; 2003h; 2002c; NACLA, 1999), support for certain NGOs (FARC-EP, 2003b; 2003g), and negotiations held in the international sphere (FARC-EP, 2003e; 2000e; Reuters, 2003; Castro, 2003).

66 Such a claim is highly suspect because talks and funding were provided to the AUC through the Uribe administration and the United States (Crandall, 2008: 155; Chen, 2006; Daily Journal, 2006a; Harper, 2005; Hutchinson, 2002; NACLA, 2003: 1). Despite proof of AUC involvement in drug trafficking, human rights abuses, and the systemic slaughter of unionists, political opponents, social movement activists, and journalists, Washington provided millions to the AUC (even though it is listed as a foreign terrorist organization (FTO) in the United States). At a US Embassy press conference in Bogotá on March 23, 2006, Harry A. Crumpton (2006), then US Department of State coordinator for counterterrorism, argued that "Colombia has made excellent progress" when concerning "the demobilization of the AUC," and went on to add that:

> Colombia provides many important lessons for nations and governments that are combating the menaces of drugs, terrorism, and transnational crime. Thus, I would like to recognize the Colombian people, for their stamina, determination, and courage; and to thank the government of Colombia, under the leadership of President Alvaro Uribe, for its steadfast commitment to overcome these challenges. We stand with you. Moreover, as President Uribe stressed yesterday, counterterrorism and counternarcotics policy must focus on the long-term social, economic, and political goals, to address the needs of all of our people.

Based on Uribe's "excellent progress," Crumpton stated that the United States would commit another $2.25 million to Colombia, part of which went to the AUC for demobilization. During this same period some claimed that the United States had made a mistake placing the AUC on its list of FTOs and that the Bush administration should have supported the paramilitary more (Hutchison, 2004).

67 As stated by Röhl:

> it could be argued that recent developments of independents rather than liberal or conservative candidates being elected into some of Colombia's highest political offices (such as the President and the Mayor of Bogotá) heralds a decline of Colombia's elitist *bipartidismo*. It remains doubtful though whether this trend will contribute to a more representative democracy. (Röhl, 2004: 12n.61)

CHAPTER 8

1 For discussion related to this topic see Marx (1989d), Tucker (1978: 543–4) and Pomeroy (1964: 89).

2 In 1991, the DIA published a report entitled *Narcotics – Colombian Narco-Trafficker Profiles*. The document listed the Andean country's leading traffickers

and internal collaborators. Not surprisingly, internationally renowned drug lord Pablo Escobar was a principal figure throughout the expose; however, listed just below the famed director of the infamous Medellín cartel was a rising Colombian politician, Álvaro Uribe Vélez (DIA, 1991: 10–11; see also Contreras, 2002). An excerpt from the report read:

> Álvaro Uribe Vélez – A Colombian politician and senator dedicated to collaboration with the Medellín cartel at high government levels. Uribe was linked to a business involved in narcotics activities in the US. His father was murdered in Colombia for his connection with the narcotic traffickers. Uribe has worked for the Medellín cartel and is a close personal friend of Pablo Escobar Gaviria. He has participated in Escobar's political campaign to win the position of Assistant Parliamentarian. (DIA, 1991: 10–11)

3   "Funding tripled from $89 million in 1997 to $289 million in 1998" (International Action Center, 2001: 2).
4   Said to have begun in 2000, Plan Colombia actually started in 1998 following the DIA reports (see McInerney, 2003: 63).
5   Since 2002, the FARC-EP "have decimated the paramilitaries, destroying at least ten percent of their forces (probably substantially more) ... The paramilitaries are neither the FARC-EP's equal on the battlefield nor do they command any loyalty from the rural population" (Goff, 2004: 44).
6   It is not difficult to obtain information related to the social reforms taking place throughout contemporary Latin America, including Bolivia, Ecuador, and Venezuela. Alongside these shifts remains the FARC-EP, a consistent threat to dominant class interests in both Colombia and the United States. Hence, Washington and Bogotá coordinated Plan Colombia to create a militarized environment through which the United States could politically and economically stabilize at least a portion of Latin America's territory for their interests (Campos, 2007: 31; Chavez, 2007: 97). John Perkins described Colombia as the last bastion of US imperial power in Latin America. Washington has attempted to sustain the basis of conventional power in Colombia financially and militarily, to ensure some geopolitical opening remains in the grasp of the United States (Perkins, 2008: 149). If the Colombian government can hold onto power, the United States has hope of regaining regional political-economic authority. Losing Colombia would likely decrease the capacity to gain financially from regional natural resources, cheap labor, and exportable commodities, as it would further signal the ability of those "from below" to continue building collective power through a united (Bolivarian) Latin America that can withstand dominant monetary, political, and militaristic imperial pressures.
7   This is not to imply that the previous years were unfavorable to the guerrillas. Throughout 2002–04, a significant increase in FARC-EP aggression towards the state was witnessed (Rangel Suárez, 2004).
8   Following September 11, 2001, Bogotá and Washington escalated the "war on terror" to include the FARC-EP (Leech, 2004b). In October 2002, US Marines were ordered to increase counter-insurgency activities in Colombia's countryside (Gorman, 2002). It was during this dynamic period that Plan Patriota was concocted.
9   Elite-based taxes did not begin with Uribe, as the Samper administration compelled the wealthy "to buy war bonds to obtain $421 million specifically for police and military operations" (Avilés, 2006: 83).
10 Some have even argued that Colombia's upper economic strata have been disproportionately burdened with costs associated with the civil war, as 1.7 percent of the population cover the costs for the majority to experience national security (Crandall, 2005b: 177; Sweig and McCarthy, 2005: 22; Richani, 2005b: 90).

11 For much of the decade, Colombia has had one of the highest rates of under and unemployment in Latin America (see Rochlin, 2007: 58; Holmes, 2003: 87–8; Green, 2003: 157; see also Röhl, 2004: 6n.29). In 1992, temporary employment was 18 percent. By 2000, the figure was 27, while half of permanent jobs paid below minimum wage (Röhl, 2004: 6n29). In 2003, the number of unemployed in Colombia's 13 major cities was over 33 percent (Röhl, 2004: 6n.29). By 2006, under-employment averaged 36 percent (Rochlin, 2007: 58).

12 Ironically, the largest urban-based rural landholders' lands are tax-exempt (see Sweig and McCarthy, 2005: 22).

13 All sectors of the population have paid a series of monetary levies on most general items through VATs. The VAT expansion came into effect on January 1, 2007 (Congreso de Colombia, 2006).

14 Under Uribe, significant cuts were made in corporate taxation (Leech, 2006d: 147–51).

15 With one of the highest consumption rates of domestically produced agriculture goods in the hemisphere, small producers provide 42 percent of Colombia's total consumed food (Díaz Montes, 2005). Expanding neoliberal policies, which work against localized production, jeopardizes food security (see Richani, 2007: 411).

16 Some have argued that this "subsidized loan model" is "a pittance compared to the $17 billion that U.S. producers receive annually in government subsidies," resulting in Colombian producers, especially small farmers, being further disenfranchised as a result of foreign protectionism (Goodman, 2006a).

17 Salting the wound, Uribe then pushed to reduce departmental decentralization payments (Bronstein, 2006b).

18 On October 19, 2006, a major attack was carried out against a military post-secondary institution in the capital, resulting in the injury of 23 military personal and the destruction of roughly six vehicles (Associated Press, 2006b; CNN International, 2006). While not offering any sustainable proof, vice-president Calderón and defense minister Santos suggested those responsible for the bombing were the FARC-EP (Associated Press, 2006b). Calderón stated that the attack displayed a clear "security lapse" in the state's forces (CNN International, 2006). Many believe that the blast was targeting not so much the military institution as Colombia's then supreme general, Mario Montoya (Associated Press, 2006b).

19 A half-century ago Robert J. Alexander (1957: 22–3) noted the most efficient way for the United States to discourage revolutionary sympathies in Latin America was to implement socioeconomic culturally specific political measures to ideological disrupt opposition toward capitalism. Apparently US administrations have missed this.

20 Some have argued that capital investment may fall, as numerous private ventures will refuse to invest in FARC-EP territory (Goodman, 2006b; Leech, 2004a, 2004c). Nevertheless, some investment has continued, as Nestlé South America (via the United Nations) has facilitated a Caquetá-based dairy facility (Goodman, 2006b).

21 In parts of central and southern Colombia, for example, the FARC-EP was instrumental in creating alternative development strategies with the local population (Leech, 2006b; 2006d: 124; 2004b).

22 As previously shown, the FARC-EP has provided services otherwise lacking in areas where they hold power (see Felbab-Brown, 2005: 110). Services provided include public clinics with free medical supplies and educational services, infrastructure (roads, public transportation services, irrigation, the offering of free electricity to local residents, and so on), alternative community-based judiciaries, protection for the environment (hunting, fishing, forestry and so on), designated fair labor hours,

regulation of prostitution (medical check-ups and the prohibition of pimps), and offering economic aid related to inter-community information sharing (such as agro-production and surplus trade programs) (Felbab-Brown, 2005: 104; Molano, 2005: 32: Taussig, 2004b: 142; Villalón, 2004a).

23 A definition of a Colombian economic group is "conglomerates linked together through interlocking directorates, holding companies, cross-financing, and family ownership" (Avilés, 2006: 151n.15). Most prominent are the Antiqueño Syndicate, the Ardilla Lulle group, the Santodomingo group, and the Sarmiento group (Avilés, 2006: 77–8).

24 Demonstrating this point, 2009 witnessed the state requesting a one-year US$10.4 billion loan from the IMF (Mercopress, 2009).

25 An argument exists that increased margins of foreign direct investment (FDI) occurred during the 1990s as a result of MNCs seeking "potential favorable concessions" as a result of the civil war (Richani, 2005a: 115). This, however, gives little credence to higher FDI due to the rise of neoliberalism in Colombia during this period, which ended the protectionist policies of the previous decade, which had restricted foreign extraction and tariffs. As Leech put it:

> Colombia's high levels of FDI in the 1990s resulted from the opening of the economy in 1990 more than specific conditions related to the conflict. FDI was much higher than in the 1980s because Colombia maintained a protectionist economy during that decade compared to most Latin American nations, which were already implementing extensive neoliberal policies. I would argue that Colombia did not open its economy to increase its war budget, but opened it as a consequence of the global economic climate and corresponding international pressures, particularly from the United States, which was also forcing other countries that were not at war to open their economies. (correspondence with Leech, December 10, 2005)

While Richani (2005a: 117–18) alluded to this premise, excessive credit was given to MNCs for their role in the civil war, with not enough attention being given to the Washington Consensus and the neoliberal policies that have been adopted by Bogotá over the past 15 years.

26 For a conventional army to effectively battle guerrilla forces it is conservatively recognized that they require well-trained forces that outnumber the opponents 10 to 1 – costing tremendous sums (Williams, 2005: 167; see also Sweig and McCarthy, 2005: 21). The Colombian civil war demonstrates a more complex scenario. Crandall (2005b: 185) argued that the FARC-EP are a much more impressive political-military organization, and, as a result, US/Colombian forces will need "at least 15 or 20 to 1" to pose any real threat. Others presented that *to even begin* to respond to the FARC-EP the state would need a ratio of 20:1 (Richani, 2005b: 90, italics added).

BIBLIOGRAPHY

Abad, Susan (2006) "The left's loss is a win," July 13 [online] http://www.lapress.org/article.asp?IssCode=&lanCode=1&artCode=4756 (accessed August 3, 2006).

ABC News (2004) "In designer coffee age growers go hungry," December 19 [online] http://abcnews.go.com/WNT/story?id=287548&page=1 (accessed December 19, 2004).

Abruzzese, Renzo (1989) *Coca-leaf Production in the Countries of the Andean Subregion.* New York: UN Office on Drugs and Crime (UNODC).

Aby, Meredith (2006) "Rebels with a cause: The FARC-EP in Colombia," October 27 [online] http://www.pulsetc.com/article.php?sid=2784 (accessed October 29, 2006).

Aceveda, Ramón (2005) "Colombian military attacks campesinos: paramilitaries continue to be a key arm of the Colombian government," November 14 [online] http://www.narconews.com/Issue39/article1488.html (accessed November 15, 2005).

Acosta, Luis Jaime (2004) "Victory years away in Colombia jungle offensive," September 7 [online] http://www.alertnet.org/printable.htm?URL=/thenews/newsdesk/N07583583.htm (accessed September 17, 2004).

Adams, Dale W. (1964) *Landownership Patterns in Colombia.* Madison, Wis.: University of Wisconsin-Madison.

Adams, Dale W. (1966) *Colombia's Land Tenure System: Antecedents and problems.* Madison, Wis.: University of Wisconsin-Madison.

Adams, Dale W. (1968) *Leadership, Education and Agricultural Development Programs in Colombia.* Madison, Wis.: University of Wisconsin-Madison.

Adams, Dale W. and A. Eugene Havens (1966) *The Use of Socio-Economic Research in Developing a Strategy of Change for Rural Communities: A Colombian example.* Madison, Wis.: University of Wisconsin-Madison.

Adams, Dale W. and L. Eduardo Montero (1965) *Land Parcelization in Agrarian Reform: A Colombian example.* Madison, Wis.: University of Wisconsin-Madison.

Agence France-Presse (2008a) "US played role in rebel strike," March 4 [online] http://www.news.com.au/heraldsun/story/0,21985,23316749-5012753,00.html (accessed March 4, 2008).

Agence France-Presse (2008b) "Colombia's share of world cocaine plummets: general," July 31 [online] http://afp.google.com/article/ALeqM5hqHRJV15SJjs7GvWvr-eRWitHHxgg (accessed August 1, 2008).

Agence France-Presse (2008c) "Colombian police thwart car bombings by FARC rebels," August 6 [online] http://afp.google.com/article/ALeqM5jE6PBTLQXv4-i3oovjidshMGyVLpg (accessed August 7, 2008).

Agence France-Presse (2008d) "CIA knew of Colombian attack on FARC in Ecuador: Quito" October 30 [online] http://afp.google.com/article/ALeqM5hjZqDpKtcwKA-vsrf2NOP7Rm8ZnZw (accessed October 31, 2008).

Agencia Bolivariana Prensa (2008) "Joaquín Gómez sucederá a Raúl Reyes en el secretariado de las FARC-EP," March 4 [online] http://www.abpnoticias.com/boletin_temporal/contenido/articulos/colombia_asesinato_r eyes23.html (accessed March 5, 2008).

Aguilar, Luis E. (1968) *Marxism and Latin America.* New York: Alfred A. Knopf.

Ahmad, Aijaz (2006) "Colombia's lethal concoction," *Frontline,* 23(6): 59–65.

Alape, Arturo (1989) *Las Vidas de Pedro Antonio Marín Manuel Maruland Vélez: Tirofilo.* Bogotá: Editorial Planeta.

Alape, Arturo (2000) *Women in the FARC Guerrilla*. Mexico City: International Commission.

Aldana, Luis Alberto Matta (2002) *Poder Capitalista y Violencia Política en Colombia: Terrorismo de estado y genocidio contra la Unión Patriótica*. Bogotá: Ideas y Soluciones Graficas.

Alejandro, Pablo and Yves Billon (1999) *50 Years of Guerrilla Warfare*. Documentary film (Les Films de Village, Odyssee, Cityzen TV).

Alexander, Robert J. (1957) *Communism in Latin America*. New Brunswick, N.J.: Rutgers University Press.

Alexander, Robert J. (1963) *Communism in Latin America*, 3rd edn. New Brunswick, N.J.: Rutgers University Press.

Alexander, Robert J. (1973) "Impact of the Sino-Soviet split on Latin-American communism," pp. 35–74 in *The Communist Tide in Latin America: A selected treatment*, ed. Donald L. Herman. Austin, Tex.: University of Texas.

Ali, Tariq (2006) *Pirates of the Caribbean: Axis of hope*. New York: Verso.

Al-Jazeera (2006) "Colombia soldiers in 'fake attack,'" September 8 [online] http://english.aljazeera.net/NR/exeres/D84E3EC7-846D-46BD-AA1B- B93C923D6C31. htm (accessed September 8, 2006).

Allende La Paz (2004) "¿Por qué se meten a la guerrilla?" October 4 [online] http://www.anncol.org/side/421 (accessed October 4, 2004).

Amin, Samir (2004) *The Liberal Virus: Permanent war and the Americanization of the world*. New York: Monthly Review Press.

Amnesty International (2004) "AI Index: AMR 23/040/2004," October 13 [online] http://web.amnesty.org/library/index/ENGAMR230402004 (accessed June 14, 2006).

Ampuero, Igor and James J. Brittain (2005) "Land, insurgency, and state apathy: The agrarian question and armed struggle in Colombia," pp. 359–82 in *Reclaiming the Land: The resurgence of rural movements in Africa, Asia, and Latin America*, ed. Sam Mayo and Paris Yeros. London: Zed Books.

Angel, Gabriel (2002) *La Luna del Forense*. Bogotá: Ediciones Magdalena Medio.

Angell, Alan (1998) "The left in Latin America since *c*. 1920," pp. 75–144 in *Latin America: Politics and society since 1930*, ed. Leslie Bethell. Cambridge, UK: Cambridge University Press.

Angell, Alan, Pamela Lowden, and Rosemary Thorp (2001) *Decentralizing Development: The political economy of institutional change in Colombia and Chile*. Oxford, UK: Oxford University Press.

Angus Reid Global Monitor (2008a) "Colombia's Uribe more popular than ever," March 19 [online] http://www.angus- reid.com/polls/view/30184/colombias_uribe_more_popular_than_ever (accessed March 19, 2008).

Angus Reid Global Monitor (2008b) "Two-thirds in Colombia back new term for Uribe," May 5 [online] http://www.angus- reid.com/polls/view/30618/two_thirds_in_colombia_back_new_term_for_uribe (accessed May 5, 2008).

Arango-Jaramillo, Mario (1988) *Impacto del Narcotráfico en Antioquia*. Medellín: Poligráficas.

Archila, Mauricio (2007) "Democratizing 'democracy' in Colombia," pp.60–3 in *The State of Resistance: Popular struggles in the global south*, ed. François Polet. London: Zed.

Arenas, Jacobo (1972) *Diario de la resistencia de Marquetalia*. Bogotá: Abejon Mono.

Arenas, Jacobo (1985) *Cese El Fuego: Una historia politica de Las FARC*. Bogotá: La Oveja Negra.

Arnson, Cynthia J. (1999) *Comparative Peace Process in Latin America*. Stanford, Calif.: Stanford University Press.

Arrubla, Mario (1970) *Estudios Sobre el Subdesarrollo Colombiano*. Medellín: Editorial la Oveja Negra.

Ashcroft, Jon (2002) *Prepared Remarks of Attorney General Jon Ashcroft: News conference, November 13*. Washington: United States Department of State.

Associated Press (2005) "Colombia coffee export revenue up 58 pct.," November 30 [online] http://biz.yahoo.com/ap/051130/colombia_coffee.html?.v=1 (accessed December 1, 2005).

Associated Press (2006a) "Indictments won't faze FARC," March 23 [online] http://www.thedailyjournalonline.com/article.asp?CategoryId=12393&ArticleId=232155 (accessed April 12, 2006).

Associated Press (2006b) "Bomb at university in Colombia wounds 23," October 19 [online] http://www.chron.com/disp/story.mpl/world/4274471.html (accessed October 20, 2006).

Associated Press (2008a) "Colombian rebels replace felled leader," March 4 [online] http://www.foxnews.com/wires/2008Mar04/0,4670,ColombiaRebelCommander,00.html (accessed March 5, 2008).

Associated Press (2008b) "Five Colombian soldiers killed in clash with leftist rebels," May 4 [online] http://www.jpost.com/servlet/Satellite?cid=1209627000639&pagename=JPost%2FJPArticl e%2FShowFull (accessed May 5, 2008).

Associated Press (2008c) "Poll: Colombian president's popularity soars after hostage rescue," July 7 [online] http://www.iht.com/articles/ap/2008/07/07/america/LA-Colombia-Presidential- Poll.php (accessed July 8, 2008).

Avila, Jesus Bejarano, Camilo Enchandia, Roldolfo Escobedo, and Enrique Querez (1997) *Colombia: Inserguridad, Violencia y Desempeno Economico en las Areas Rurales*. Bogotá: Universidad Externado de Colombia.

Avilés, William (2001) "Institutions, military policy, and human rights in Colombia," *Latin American Perspectives*, 28(1): 31–55.

Avilés, William (2006) *Global Capitalism, Democracy, and Civil–Military Relations in Colombia*. New York: SUNY.

Avineri, Shlomo (1968) *The Social and Political Thought of Karl Marx*. London: Cambridge University Press.

Avineri, Shlomo (1973) "The proletariat," pp. 102–12 in *Karl Marx: Makers of modern social science*, ed. Tom Bottomore. Englewood Cliffs, N.J.: Prentice-Hall.

Badawy, Manuela (2006) "Colombia monitors ex-rebels, measures success," July 7 [online] http://today.reuters.com/news/newsArticle.aspx?type=worldNews&storyID=2006-07- 08T004240Z_01_N07392270_RTRUKOC_0_US-COLOMBIA- REBELS.xml&archived=False (accessed July 8, 2006).

Bagley, Bruce M. (1988) "Colombia and the war on drugs," *Foreign Affairs*, 67(1): 70–92.

Bagley, Bruce M. and Matthew Edel (1980) "Popular mobilization programs of the National Front: Cooptation and radicalization," pp. 257–84 in *Politics of Compromise: Coalition government in Colombia*, ed. R. Albert Berry, Ronald G. Hellman, and Mauricio Solaún. New Brunswick, N.J.: Transaction Books.

Ballvé, Teo (2008) "Colombia: AIDS in the time of war," *NACLA Report on the Americas* 41(4): 30–4.

Bajak, Frank (2007) "The real battle in Colombia is for land. Paramilitaries took farms; poor are losers again," January 28 [online] http://www.americas.org/item_30684 (accessed February 3, 2007).

Bajak, Frank (2008a) "Colombia's popular president hovers above scandal," May 4 [online] http://ap.google.com/article/ALeqM5hlOFs7LbJ6rTaFCHXDEyFwN5-o3AD90EVU381 (accessed May 5, 2008).

Bajak, Frank (2008b) "Ecuador's challenge: dislodging Colombian rebels," August 30 [online] http://ap.google.com/article/ALeqM5isFf4FDh7j8SLAU_dG5H8WsNAry-AD92SOB8O0 (accessed September 2, 2008).

Bajak, Frank (2008c) "Who to kill? Colombia army picks soldier's brother,"

November 13 [online] http://ap.google.com/article/ALeqM5hx7D8zSRQDgU1FRi-OXpH0NhR3dGwD94DTV6 O1 (accessed November 13, 2008).

Bara ski, Zygmunt G. and John R. Short (1985) *Developing Contemporary Marxism.* New York: St. Martin's Press.

Barkin, David (2001) "Neoliberalism and sustainable popular development," pp. 184–204 in *Transcending Neoliberalism: Community-based development in Latin America,* ed. Henry Veltmeyer and Anthony O'Malley. Bloomfield, Conn.: Kumarian.

Barlow, Barry H. (1993) *Revolution in the Americas.* Halifax, N.S.: Fernwood.

Barnet, Richard J. (1972) *Intervention and Revolution: The United States and the Third World.* Scarborough, ON: New American Library.

Barstow, Anne and Tom Driver (2003) *Colombians Speak Out about Violence and U.S. Policy.* Documentary film (independent),

Batou, Jean (2008) "The guerrilla in Colombia: An interview with Rodrigo Granda, member of the FARC-EP International Commission," *Monthly Review,* 59(10): 14–32.

BBC (2004) "Uribe defends security policies," November 18 [online] http://news.bbc.co.uk/2/hi/americas/4021213.stm (accessed November 21, 2004).

BBC (2005) "Colombian Army accused of cover up," October 14 [online] http://news.bbc.co.uk/2/hi/americas/4340496.stm (accessed October 14, 2005).

BBC (2008) "Colombians march against violence," March 7 [online] http://news.bbc.co.uk/2/hi/americas/7282872.stm (accessed March 7, 2008).

Beals, Carleton (1974) *Latin America: World in revolution.* Westport, Conn.: Greenwood.

Bell Lemus, Gustavo (1988) "The decentralized state: An administrative or political challenge?" pp. 97–107 in *Colombia: Politics of reforming the state,* ed. Eduardo Posada-Carbó. London: Macmillan.

Bergquist, Charles W. (1986) *Coffee and Conflict in Colombia, 1886–1910.* Durham, N.C.: Duke University Press.

Bergquist, Charles W. (2007) "Book review – Eduardo Posada Carbó, *La nación soñada: Violencia, liberalismo y democracia en Colombia* (Bogotá: Editorial Norma; Virtal; Fundación Ideas para La Paz, 2006)," *Journal of Latin American Studies,* 39(3): 670–2.

Bergquist, Charles W., Ricardo Peñaranda and Gonzalo Sánchez G. (1992) *Violence in Colombia: The contemporary crisis in historical perspective.* Wilmington, Del.: Scholarly Resources.

Bergquist, Charles W., Ricardo Peñaranda, and Gonzalo Sánchez G. (2003) *Violence in Colombia 1990–2000: Waging war and negotiating peace.* Wilmington, Del.: Scholarly Resources.

Bernard, Jean-Pierre, Silas Cerqueria, Hugo Neira, Helene Graillot, Leslie F. Maniget, and Pierr Gilhodés (1973) *Guide to the Political Parties of South America.* Middlesex, UK: Penguin Books.

Bernardi, Luigi, Laura Fumagalli, and Elena Fumagalli (2007) "Colombia updated," in *Tax Systems and Tax Reforms in Latin America: Country studies,* ed. Luigi Bernardi, Alberto Barreix, Anna Marenzi, and Paola Profeta. Unpublished paper. University Library of Munich, Germany.

Bernstein, Harry (1964) *Venezuela and Colombia.* Englewood Cliffs, N.J.: Prentice-Hall.

Berry, R. Albert (1980a) "The National Front and Colombia's economic development," pp. 287–325 in *Politics of Compromise: Coalition government in Colombia,* ed. R. Albert Berry, Ronald G. Hellman, and Mauricio Solaún.New Brunswick, N.J.: Transaction.

Berry, R. Albert (1980b) "Technology choice and technological change in agriculture: The case of Colombia," pp. 105–23 in *Democracy and Development in Latin*

America, ed. Louis Lefeber and Liisa L. North. Toronto, ON: Centre for Research on Latin America and the Caribbean (CERLAC)-LARU.

Berry, R. Albert (1991) "Colombian agriculture in the 1980s," pp. 77–100 in *Modernization and Stagnation: Latin American agriculture into the 1990s*, ed. Michael J. Twimey and Ann Itelwege. New York: Greenwood.

Berry, R. Albert (1999) *Could Agrarian Reform Have Averted Colombia's Crisis?* Draft paper, Department of Economics, University of Toronto (December).

Berry, R. Albert, Ronald G. Hellman, and Mauricio Solaún (1980) *Politics of Compromise: Coalition government in Colombia*. New Brunswick, N.J.: Transaction.

Berry, R. Albert and Mauricio Solaún (1980) "Notes toward the interpretation of the National Front," pp. 435–60 in *Politics of Compromise: Coalition government in Colombia*, ed. R. Albert Berry, Ronald G. Hellman, and Mauricio Solaún. New Brunswick, N.J.: Transaction.

Berry, R. Albert and Francisco E. Thoumi (1988) "Post-war and post-national front economic development of Colombia," pp. 63–85 in *Democracy in Latin America: Colombia and Venezuela*, ed. Donald L. Herman. Westport, Conn.: Praeger.

Berry R. Albert and Miguel Urrutia (1976) *Income Distribution in Colombia*. London: Yale University Press.

Bland, Daniel (2004) "Democratic security in Colombia: At what cost?" *Focal Point: Spotlight on the Americas*, 3(8): 4–6.

Bloomberg (2005) "Colombia seeks to reduce dependence on U.S. Aid within 2 years," February 23 [online] http://www.bloomberg.com/apps/news?pid=10000086&sid=a Of0r7CCbXQg&refer=latin _america (accessed February 23, 2005).

Bloomberg (2006) "Colombia coca growers find quitting hard amid anti-drug assault," February 3 [online] http://quote.bloomberg.com/apps/news?pid=10000086&sid=aN K5nuwu0Mxg&re fer=news_index (accessed February 3, 2006).

Blum, William (1998) *Killing Hope: U.S. military and CIA interventions since World War II*. New York: Black Rose.

Bond, Alison P. (2006) *Voices of the Victims: Their proposals for peace and justice in Colombia*. Toronto, Ont.: CERLAC Bulletin, Vol. 5, No. 4.

Bonilla, Frank (1964) "The urban worker," pp. 186–205 in *Continuity and Change in Latin America*, ed. John J. Johnson. Stanford, Calif.: Stanford University Press.

Bookchin, Murray (1996) *The Third Revolution: Popular movements in the revolutionary era, Vol. 1*. London: Cassell.

Bookchin, Murray (1998) *The Third Revolution: Popular movements in the revolutionary era, Vol. 2*. London: Cassell.

Botero, Jorge Enrique (2006) *Últimas Noticias de la Guerra*. Bogotá: Testimonio.

Bottomore, Tom (1970) *Classes in Modern Society*. London: George Allen & Unwin.

Bottomore, Tom (ed.) (1973) *Karl Marx: Makers of Modern Social Science*. Englewood Cliffs, N.J.: Prentice-Hall.

Boudon, Lawrence (1996) "Guerrillas and the state: The role of the state in the Colombian peace process," *Journal of Latin American Studies*, 28(2): 279–97.

Bowden, Mark (2001) *Killing Pablo: The hunt for the world's greatest outlaw*. New York: Atlantic Monthly Press.

Braun, Herbert T. (1986) *The Assassination of Gaitán: Public life and urban violence in Colombia*. Madison, Wis.: University of Wisconsin Press.

Braun, Herbert T. (2003) *Our Guerrillas, Our Sidewalks: A journey into the violence of Colombia*, 2nd edn. New York: Rowman & Littlefield.

Braun, Herbert T. (2007) "¡Que haiga paz!" The cultural contexts of conflict in Colombia," pp. 23–59 in *Peace, Democracy, and Human Rights in Colombia*, ed. Christopher Welna and Gustavo Gallón. Notre Dame, Ind.: University of Notre Dame Press.

Bristow, Matthew (2008) "Among the FARC's true believers," July 3 [online] http://www.time.com/time/world/article/0,8599,1820099,00.html (accessed July 3, 2008).

Brittain, James J. (2004a) "The economics of violence: Uribe's plan to increase military spending," *People's Voice*, 12(16): 5.

Brittain, James J. (2004b) *The Revolutionary Armed Forces of Colombia—People's Army: A Marxist analysis of a revolutionary social movement*. MA thesis. Wolfville, N.S.: Acadia University.

Brittain, James J. (2004c) *Revolution in Colombia: Organized in the heart and breath of the people*. Paper delivered in Winnipeg, Manitoba for the Society for Socialist Studies (SSS) at the Congress for the Social Sciences and Humanities, University of Manitoba, June 4.

Brittain, James J. (2005a) *International Solidarity and Organized Labour: The need for hemispheric unification*. Paper delivered in St John, New Brunswick for the 2005 National Convention of the Union of Taxation Employees (UTE-PSAC), July 14.

Brittain, James J. (2005b) "A theory of accelerating rural violence: Lauchlin Currie's role in underdeveloping Colombia," *Journal for Peasant Studies*, 32(2): 335–60.

Brittain, James J. (2005c) "Clandestine politics within Colombia: The Bolivarian movement for a new Colombia," *Socialism and Liberation*, 2(5): 34–6.

Brittain, James J. (2005d) "Run, fight or die in Colombia," March 12/13 [online] http://www.counterpunch.org/brittain03122005.html (accessed March 12, 2005).

Brittain, James J. (2005e) "The FARC-EP in Colombia: A revolutionary exception in an age of imperialist expansion," *Monthly Review*, 57(4): 20–33.

Brittain, James J. (2005f) *Systemic Silencing of Political Voice: The relevance of the National Front Agreement (1958–1974) within Colombian society*. Paper delivered in Fredericton, New Brunswick for the 7th Annual International Graduate Student Conference at the University of New Brunswick, October 21.

Brittain, James J. (2005g) "The objective reality of Plan Patriota: A response to subjective propaganda," January 24 [online] http://colombiajournal.org/colombia201.htm (accessed January 25, 2005).

Brittain, James J. (2006a) "The necessity of revisiting social change theory: Negri, Hardt, and Holloway's absence of objective reality within a Latin American context," paper delivered in Fredericton, New Brunswick for the 14th Annual Graduate Student Association Conference on Student Research at the University of New Brunswick, February 23.

Brittain, James J. (2006b) "Forms of unconventional and illicit development: Rural Colombia's complex narcotic industry," paper delivered in Bogotá, Colombia for the 9th Congreso Nacional de Sociología through the Universidad Nacional de Colombia and presented at the Universidad Santo Tomás, December 7.

Brittain, James J. (2006c) "Organizing rural labor in rural Colombia: A federation of unions struggles to exist in the face of state reaction," *Dollars & Sense*, 268: 7–9.

Brittain, James J. (2006d) "Human rights and the Colombian government: An analysis of state-based atrocities toward non-combatants," *New Politics*, 10(4): 124–9.

Brittain, James J. (2006e) "Censorship and hegemony in Colombia: The arrest of journalist Freddy Muñoz," November 25 [online] http://counterpunch.com/brittain11252006.html (accessed November 26, 2006).

Brittain, James J. (2006f) "Censorship, hegemony, and the media in Colombia," November 27 [online] http://colombiajournal.org/colombia248.htm (accessed November 28, 2006).

Brittain, James J. (2007a) "Formas de desarrollo poco convencionales e ilícitas: La compleja industria del narcotráfico en Colombia," *Cuadernos de Sociología*, 41: 13–68.

Brittain, James J. (2007b) "La vacilante economía política de Uribe: Aumento de la tributación dual de clases, acuerdos bilaterales comerciales dilatados o prolongados, y la creciente inestabilidad rural," *Controversia*, 188: 247–89.

Brittain, James J. (2008) "Colombia: Was the US involved in the murder of FARC-

EP leaders?" March 13 [online] http://links.org.au/node/306 (accessed March 14, 2008).

Brittain, James J. and R. James Sacouman (2006a) "Is the FARC-EP dependent on coca?" March 24 [online] http://anncol.org/uk/site/doc.php?id=240 (accessed March 25, 2006).

Brittain, James J. and R. James Sacouman (2006b) "Colombia's internal conflict: A period of discontinuity or prolonged revolution?" paper delivered in Calgary, Alberta for the Canadian Association of Latin American and Caribbean Studies Conference at the University of Calgary, September 30.

Brittain, James J. and R. James Sacouman (2008a) "Uribe's Colombia is destabilizing a new Latin America: A response to the murder of FARC Commander Raúl Reyes in Ecuador," March 3 [online] http://www.colombiajournal.org/colombia273.htm (accessed March 4, 2008).

Brittain, James J. and R. James Sacouman (2008b) "A response to the murder of FARC Commander Raúl Reyes in Ecuador: Uribe's Colombia is destabilizing a new Latin America," March 4 [online] http://www.counterpunch.org/brittain03042008.html (accessed March 5, 2008).

Brittain, James J. and R. James Sacouman (2008c) "Agrarian transformation and resistance in the Colombian countryside," *Labour, Capital and Society* 41(1): 57–83.

Brockner, Eliot (2008) "The future of the Colombian military," September 9 [online] http://www.isn.ethz.ch/isn/Current-Affairs/Security-Watch/Detail?lng=en%26id=91145 (accessed September 9, 2008).

Brodzonsky, Sibylla (2006) "Paramilitary still sway Colombian votes," March 10 [online] http://www.csmonitor.com/2006/0310/p07s02-woam.html (accessed March 10, 2006).

Bronstein, Hugh (2006a) "Colombia proposes lower income tax, wider VAT," July 28 [online] http://today.reuters.com/news/articleinvesting.aspx?type=bondsNews&storyID=2006-07- 28T180018Z_01_N28351504_RTRIDST_0_ECONOMY-COLOMBIA-REFORMS- UPDATE-1.XML (accessed July 31, 2006).

Bronstein, Hugh (2006b) "Colombia's tax reform bill bogged down in politics," September 26 [online] http://today.reuters.com/news/articleinvesting.aspx?type=bondsNews&storyID=2006-09- 26T154702Z_01_N26218419_RTRIDST_0_ECONOMY-COLOMBIA-REFORMS.XML (accessed September 26, 2006).

Browne, David (1994) *Getting Away with Murder*. Documentary film (independent).

Bryant, John (1969) *Health and the Developing World*. Ithaca, N.Y.: Cornell University Press.

Buch Larsen, Martin (2008) "Colombia: FARC ideologue and musician killed," March 13 [online] http://www.freemuse.org/sw25939.asp (accessed March 18, 2008).

Bureau of International Narcotics and Law Enforcement Affairs (2008) *International Narcotics Control Stretgy Report*. Washington, DC: US Department of State.

Bureau of Western Hemisphere Affairs (2001) "Why Americans should care about Plan Colombia," February 21 [online] http://www.state.gov/p/wha/rls/fs/2001/1040.htm (accessed September 23, 2003).

Bureau of Western Hemisphere Affairs (2005) "Background note: Colombia," February [online] http://www.state.gov/r/pa/ei/bgn/35754.htm (accessed February 11, 2005).

Burke III, Edmund (ed.) (1988) *Global Crises and Social Movements: Artisans, peasants, populists, and the world economy*. London: Westview.

Burnett, Ben G. and Kenneth F. Johnson (1968) *Political Forces in Latin America: Dimensions of the quest for stability*. Belmont, Calif.: Wadsworth.

Buscaglia, Edgardo and William Ratliff (2001) *War and Lack of Governance in Colombia: Narcos, guerrillas, and U.S. policy*. Stanford, Calif.: Hoover Institution on War, Revolution and Peace.

Bushnell, David (1993) *The Making of Modern Colombia: A nation in spite of itself.* Berkeley, Calif.: University of California Press.

Bustamante, Michael and Sebastian Chaskel (2008) "Colombia's precarious progress," *Current History*, 107(111): 77–83.

Buzuev, Vladimir and Vladimir Gorodnov (1987) *What is Marxism-Leninism?* Moscow: Progress.

Caballero, Antonio (2006) "Nuestros amigos los paras" [online] http://www.semana.com/wf_InfoArticuloNormal.aspx?IdArt=96777 (accessed September 6, 2006).

Cala, Andrés (2000) "The enigmatic guerrilla: FARC's Manuel Marulanda," *Current History*, 99(634): 56–9.

Calvert, Peter (1999) "Guerrilla movements," pp. 112–30 in *Developments in Latin American Political Economy: Status, markets and actors*, ed. Julia Buxton and Nicola Phillips. Manchester, UK: Manchester University Press..

Camacho Guizado, Álvaro (1988) *Droga y Sociedad en Colombia: El poder y el estogmas.* Calif: Universidad de Valle.

Camacho Guizado, Álvaro and Andrés López Restrepo (2007) "From smugglers to drug lords to *traquetos*," pp. 60–89 in *Peace, Democracy, and Human Rights in Colombia*, ed. Christopher Welna and Gustavo Gallón, Notre Dame, Ind.: University of Notre Dame Press.

Cambio (2008a) "El computador de 'Iván Ríos'," March 12 [online] http://www.cambio.com.co/paiscambio/767/ARTICULO-WEB- NOTA_INTERIOR_CAMBIO-4006789.html (accessed May 12, 2008).

Cambio (2008b) "El país según José Obdulio," August 13 [online] http://www.cambio.com.co/portadacambio/789/ARTICULO-WEB- NOTA_INTERIOR_CAMBIO-4445405.html (accessed August 23, 2008).

Cameron, William Bruce (1966) *Modern Social Movements: A sociological outline.* New York: Random House.

Campos, Carlos Oliva (2007) "The United States – Latin America and the Caribbean: From neopan-Americanism to the American system for the twenty-first century," pp. 11–47 in *The Bush Doctrine and Latin America*, ed. Gary Prevost and Carlos Oliva Campos. New York: Palgrave Macmillan.

Carrigan, Ana (1993) *The Palace of Justice: A Colombian tragedy.* New York: Four Wall Eight Windows.

Carrigan, Ana (1995) "A chronicle of death foretold: State-sponsored violence in Colombia," *NACLA Report on the Americas*, 28(5): 6-10.

Cassidy, Veronica (2005) "U.S. Funds Indigenous Persecution in Colombia," December 1 [online] http://www.americas.org/item_23357 (accessed December 1, 2005).

Castañeda, Jorge G. (1994) *Utopia Unarmed: The Latin American left after the cold war.* New York: Vintage.

Castaño, Julian Gutierrez (2006) "Colombia: Why do small farmers cultivate coca?" December 30 [online] http://www.cpt.org/archives/2006/dec06/0031.html (accessed May 12, 2007).

Castro, Alfredo (2003) "Meeting between FARC and UN to be held in Brazil," September 17 [online] http://www.anncol.org/side/123 (accessed September 20, 2003).

Castro, Daniel (ed.) (1999) *Revolution and Revolutionaries: Guerrilla movements in Latin America.* Wilmington, Del.: Scholarly Resources.

Chaliand, Gerard (1977) *Revolution in the Third World: Myths and prospects.* New York: Viking.

Chasteen, John Charles (2001) *Born in Blood and Fire: A concise history of Latin America.* New York: W.W. Norton.

Chavez, German Rodas (2007) "Plan Colombia – A key ingredient in the Bush doctrine," pp. 91–104 in *The Bush Doctrine and Latin America*, ed. Gary Prevost and Carlos Oliva Campos. New York: Palgrave Macmillan.

Chen, Tai (2006) *Washington's Faltering Anti-Drug Strategy in Colombia, and Bogotá's Evaporating Extradition Policy*. Washington, DC: Council on Hemispheric Affairs.

Chernick, Marc W. (1996) *Testimony to the U.S. Congress House Committee on International Relations. Overall U.S. counternarcotics policy toward Colombia: Hearing before the Committee on International Relations, House of Representatives, September 11.* 114th Congress, 2nd session. Washington, DC: US GPO.

Chernick, Marc W. (2000) "Elusive peace: Struggling against the logic of violence," *NACLA Report of the Americas*, 34(2): 32–7.

Chernick, Marc W. (2003) "Colombia: Does injustice cause violence?" pp. 185–214 in *What Justice Whose Justice? Fighting for fairness in Latin America*, ed. Susan Eva Eckstein and Timothy P. Wickham-Crowley. Berkeley, Calif.: University of California Press.

Chernick, Marc W. (2007) "FARC-EP: From Liberal guerrillas to Marxist rebels to post-cold war insurgents," pp. 50–81 in *Terror, Insurgency, and the State: Ending protracted conflicts*, ed. Marianne Heiberg, Brendan O'Leary, and John Tirman. Philadelphia, Penn.: University of Pennsylvania Press.

Cherry, Andrew (2002) "Colombia," pp. 51–74 in *Substance Abuse: A global view*, ed. Andrew Cherry, Mary E. Dillon, and Douglas Rugh. Westport, Conn.: Greenwood.

Chilcote, Ronald H. (1990) "Post-Marxism: The retreat from class in Latin America," *Latin American Perspectives*, 17(2): 3–24.

Chomsky, Noam (1987) *Turning the Tide: The U.S. and Latin America*. New York: Black Rose.

Christian Science Monitor (2008) "Face-off by Facebook," February 15 [online] http://www.csmonitor.com/2008/0215/p08s01-comv.html (accessed March 6, 2008).

Christodoulou, Demetrios (1990) *The Unpromised Land: Agrarian reform and conflict worldwide*. London: Zed.

Cienfuegos, Raul and Sulema Cienfuegos (1999) "Colombian revolutionaries protect the people," *Green Left Weekly*, 362: 21.

Clark, Ramsey (2003) "The future of Latin America," pp. 23–47 in *War in Colombia: Made in the U.S.A.*, ed. Rebecca Toledo, Teresa Gutierrez, Sara Flounders, and Andy McInerney. New York: International Action Centre.

Clawson, Patrick L. and Rensselaer W. Lee III (1998) *The Andean Cocaine Industry*. New York: St. Martin's Griffin.

Cleary, Edward (2007) *Mobilizing for Human Rights in Latin America*. Bloomfield, Conn.: Kumarian.

CNN International (2006) "General may have been target of Colombian blast," October 19 [online] http://edition.cnn.com/2006/WORLD/americas/10/19/colombia.bomb.ap/ (accessed October 20, 2006).

Coalición Colombiana Contra la Tortura (2008) *Informe Sobre Tortura, Tratos Crueles Inhumanos y Degradantes en Colombia*. Bogotá: Coalición Colombiana Contra la Tortura.

Cockcroft, James D. (1972) "Last rites for the reformist model in Latin America," pp. 115–49 in *Dependence and Underdevelopment: Latin America's political economy*, ed. James D. Cockcroft, André Gunder Frank, and Dale L. Johnson. Garden City, N.Y.: Anchor.

Coghlan, Nicholas (2004) *The Saddest Country: On assignment in Colombia*. Montreal, QC: McGill- Queen's University Press.

Colby, Gerald and Charlotte Dennett (1995) *Thy Will Be Done – The conquest of the Amazon: Nelson Rockefeller and evangelism in the age of oil*. New York: Harper-Collins.

Collier, David (1979) "Overview of the bureaucratic authoritarian model," pp. 19–32 in *The New Authoritarianism in Latin America*, ed. David Collier. Princeton, N.J.: Princeton University Press.

Collier, Paul (2000) "Rebellion as a quasi-criminal activity," *Journal of Conflict Resolution*, 44(6): 839–53.

Collier, Paul and Anke Hoeffler (2000) *Greed and Grievance in Civil War*. Washington, DC: World Bank.

Collier, Ruth Berins and David Collier (2002) *Shaping the Political Arena: Critical junctures, the labor movement, and regime dynamics in Latin America*. Notre Dame, Ind.: University of Notre Dame Press.

Colombia Reports (2009a) "The war can only be won with help of the US: Uribe," March 16 [online] http://colombiareports.com/colombian-news/news/3251-the-war-can-only-be-won-with-help-of-the-us-uribe.html (accessed March 17, 2009).

Colombia Reports (2009b) "Uribe warns demobilized paramilitaries," February 14 [online] http://colombiareports.com/colombian-news/news/2891-uribe-warns-demo-bilized- paramilitaries.html (accessed February 15, 2009).

Colombia Reports (2008a) "'Key FARC data' seized after raid," September 22 [online] http://colombiareports.com/colombian-news/news/1342-qkey-farc-dataq-seized-after- raid.html (accessed September 22, 2008).

Colombia Reports (2008b) "HRW director strikes back at Uribe," November 4 [online] http://colombiareports.com/colombian-news/news/1918-hrw-director-strikes-back-at- uribe.html (accessed November 4, 2008).

Colombia Reports (2008c) "Plan Colombia is 'complete failure', says Ecuador," November 15 [online] http://colombiareports.com/colombian-news/news/2042-plan-colombia-is- qcomplete-failureq-says-ecuador.html (accessed November 17, 2008).

Comisión Andina de Juristas (1990) *Violencia en Colombia*. Lima: Comisión Andina de Juristas.

Comisión Colombiana de Juristas (2001) *Share of Responsibility for Non-Combatant death and forced disappearances*. Washington, DC: Center for International Policy.

Comisión Colombiana de Juristas (2004) *En contravía de las recomendaciones internacionales. ¿Seguridad Democrática?, derechos humanos y derecho humanitario en Colombia: Agosto de 2002 a Agosto de 2004*. Bogotá: Comisión Colombiana de Juristas.

Comisión del Comité Central (1960) *Triento Años de Lucha del Partido Comunista de Colombia*. Bogotá: Ediciones Paz y Socialismo.

Commission for the Study of Violence (1992) "Organized violence," pp. 261–72 in *Violence in Colombia: The contemporary crisis in historical perspective*, ed. Charles Bergquist, Ricardo Peñaranda, and Gonzalo Sánchez. Wilmington, Del.: Scholarly Resources.

Committee of Government Reform (2004) "Andean counterdrug initiative backgrounder," October 13 [online] http://reform.house.gov/CJDPHR/News/DocumentSingle.aspx?DocumentID=604 0 (accessed February 11, 2005).

Committees in Solidarity with Latin America and the Caribbean (CISLAC) (2001) *Colombia: Peace at What Price?* Documentary film (director Anne O'Casey).

Congreso de Colombia (2006) *Ley Numero 1111 de 2006 por la cual se modifica el estatuto tributario de los impuestos administrados*. Bogotá, DC: Congreso de Colombia.

Consultoría para los Derechos Humanos y el Desplazamiento (CODHES) (2007) *2007 Año de los Derechos de las Personas Desplazados*. Bogotá: CODHES.

CODHES (2008) *Tapando el Sol con las Manos*. Bogotá: CODHES.

Contraloría General de la República (2004) *Evaluación de la Poiítica Social 2003*. Bogotá: Contraloría General de la República.

Contreras, Joseph y Fernando Garavito (2002) *Biografía no autorizada de Álvaro Uribe Vélez: El Señor de las sombras*. Bogotá: Oveja Negra.

Cooper, Neil (2002) "State collapse as business: The role of conflict trade and the emerging control agenda," *Development and Change*, 33(5): 935–55.

Cordoba Ruiz, Piedad (2002) *Women in the Colombian Congress*. Stockholm: International Idea.

Cox, Sarah (2002) "The dark side of flowers," June 7 [online] http://www.zmag.org/content/Colombia/cox_flowers.cfm (accessed January 14, 2003).

Craig, Richard B. (1987) "Illicit drug traffic: Implications for South American source countries," *Journal of Interamerican Studies and World Affairs*, 29(2): 1–34.

Crandall, Russell (1999) "The end of civil conflict in Colombia: Military, paramilitaries, and a new role for the United States," *SAIS Review*, 19(1): 223–37.

Crandall, Russell (2002) *Driven by Drugs: U.S. policy toward Colombia*. London: Lynne Rienner.

Crandall, Russell (2005a) "Introduction: The pursuit of stability in the Andes," pp. 1–10 in *The Andes in Focus: Security, democracy and economic reform*, ed. Russell Crandall, Guadalupe Paz, and Riordan Roett. Boulder, Colo.: Lynne Rienner..

Crandall, Russell (2005b) "From drugs to security: A new U.S. policy toward Colombia," pp. 173–89 in *The Andes in Focus: Security, democracy & economic reform*, ed. Russell Crandall, Guadalupe Paz and Riordan Roett. Boulder, Colo.: Lynne Rienner.

Crandall, Russell (2008) *Driven by Drugs: U.S. policy toward Colombia,* 2nd edn. Boulder, Colo.: Lynne Rienner.

Crawley, Vince (2005) "SouthCom chief claims progress in Colombia," March 22 [online] http://www.airforcetimes.com/story.php?f=0-AIRPAPER-728235.php (accessed March 23, 2005).

Crowe, Darcy (2006) "Wood a deadly business in Colombia," August 20 [online] http://www.chron.com/disp/story.mpl/ap/fn/4129170.html (accessed August 20, 2006).

Crowe, Darcy (2007) "Critics: Colombia manipulates crime data," February 17 [online] http://www.mercurynews.com/mld/mercurynews/news/breaking_news/16724427.htm (accessed February 18, 2007).

Crumpton, Harry A. (2006) *Transcript of Crumpton's Remarks – U. S. Embassy Press Conference Bogotá, Colombia March 23, 2006*. Washington, DC: Bureau of International Information Programs, US Department of State.

Cruz, Adolfo Lean Atehortua and Humberto Vélez Ramírez (1994) *Estado y Fuerzas Armadas en Colombia*. Bogotá: TM Editores.

Cubides C., Fernando (2003) "From the private to public violence: The paramilitaries," pp. 127–49 in *Violence in Colombia 1990–2000: Waging war and negotiating peace*, ed. Charles W. Bergquist, Ricardo Peñaranda, and Gonzalo Sánchez G. Wilmington, Del.: Scholarly Resources.

Cuéllar, Diego Montaña (1963) *Colombia: País formal y país real*. Buenos Aires: Editorial Platina.

Cueva, Agustín (1976) "A summary of 'problems of dependency theory'," *Latin American Perspectives*, 3(4): 12–16.

Current, The (2008) "Colombia–Ecuador–Venezuela tensions, March 6, 2008," Toronto, ON: CBC.

Currie, Lauchlin (1950) *The Basis of Development Program for Colombia: Report of a mission*. Baltimore, Md.: John Hopkins Press.

Currie, Lauchlin (1966) *Accelerating Development: The necessity and the means*. New York: McGraw-Hill.

Currie, Lauchlin (1967) *Obstacles to Development*. East Lansing, Mich.: Michigan State University Press.

Currie, Lauchlin (1971) "The exchange constraint on development – a partial solution to the problem," *Economic Journal*, 81(324): 886–903.

Currie, Lauchlin (1981) *The Role of Economic Advisers in Developing Countries*. London: Greenwood.

Cusicanqui, Silvia Rivera (1987) *The Politics and Ideology of the Colombian Peasant Movement: The case of the ANUC (National Association of Peasant Smallholders)*.

Geneva: UN Research Institute for Social Development/Bogotá: Centro de Investigación y Educación Popular.

Daily Journal (2005) "Soldier sentenced to eight years in cocaine smuggling," November 9 [online] http://www.thedailyjournalonline.com/article.asp?ArticleId=203759& CategoryId =12393 (accessed November 15, 2005).

Daily Journal (2006a) "Colombian ex-militia chief: Fighters rearming for lack of work," [online] March 26 http://www.thedailyjournalonline.com/article.asp?Catego ryId=12393&ArticleId= 232396 (accessed March 30, 2006).

Daily Journal (2006b) "Uribe proposes tax to finance army," March 29 [online] http:// www.thedailyjournalonline.com/article.asp?ArticleId=233303&CategoryId =12393 (accessed March 30, 2006).

Dashti, Abdollah (2003) "At the crossroads of globalization: Participatory democracy as a medium of future revolutionary struggle," pp. 169–79 in *The Future of Revolutions: Rethinking radical change in the age of globalization*, ed. John Foran. London: Zed.

Dávalos, Liliana M. (2001) "The San Lucas mountain range in Colombia: How much conservation is owed to violence?" *Biodiversity and Conservation*, 10(1): 69–78.

Davis, Mike (2007) *Plant of Slums*. London: Verso.

Dayani, Martin (2001) "Prisoner release represents FARC's first political concession," July 2 [online] http://www.colombiajournal.org/colombia70.htm (accessed September 16, 2003).

de Janvry, Alain (1981) *The Agrarian Question and Reformism in Latin America*. London: Johns Hopkins University Press.

De la Peña, Guillermo (1998) "Rural mobilizations in Latin America since *c.* 1920," pp. 291–394 in *Latin America: Politics and society since 1930*, ed. Leslie Bethell. Cambridge, UK: Cambridge University Press.

Debray, Régis (1967) *Revolution in the Revolution? Armed struggle and political struggle in Latin America*. London: Penguin.

Debray, Régis (1969) "Latin America: Some problems of revolutionary strategy," pp. 499–531 in *Latin American Radicalism: A documentary report on left and nationalist movements*, ed. Irving Louis Horowitz, Josué de Castro, and John Gerassi. New York: Random House.

Decker, David R. and Ignacio Duran (1982) *The Political, Economic, and Labor Climate in Colombia*. Philadelphia, Penn.: University of Pennsylvania.

Deere, Carmen Diana and Magdalena León de Leal (1982) *Women in Andean Agriculture: Peasant production and rural wage employment in Colombia and Peru*. Geneva: International Labour Office.

Defense Intelligence Agency (DIA) (1991) *Narcotics-Colombian Narco-Trafficker Profiles*. Washington, DC: Department of Defense.

DIA (2007) "Employment" [online] http://www.diajobs.us/ (accessed March 13, 2007).

Defronzo, James (1996) *Revolutions and Revolutionary Movements*, 2nd edn. Boulder, Colo.: Westview.

Deininger, Klaus (2001) "Negotiated land reform as one way of land access: Experience from Colombia, Brazil, and South Africa," pp. 315–48 in *Access to Land, Rural Poverty, and Public Action*, ed. Alain de Janvry, Gustavo Gordillo, Jean-Phillippe Platteau, and Elisabeth Sadoulet. Oxford, UK: Oxford University Press.

Delgado, José Fernando Isaza (2008) "Colombia: War by numbers," January 31 [online] http://www.zcommunications.org/znet/viewArticle/16370 (accessed March 9, 2008).

Delgado, José Fernando Isaza and Diógenes Campos Romero (2007) *Algunas Consideraciones Cuantitativas as Sobre La Evolución Reciente del Conflicto en Colombia*. Bogotá: Working paper.

Departamento Administrativo Nacional de Estadística (DANE) (2008) *Segundo Trimestre de 2008*. Bogotá: Oficina de Prensa, DANE.

Desmarais, Annette Aurélie (2007) *La Vía Campesina: Globalization and the power of peasants*. London: Pluto.

Deutsche Presse Agentur (2006) "Killer of Colombian right-wing paramilitary chief confesses on TV," August 26 [online] http://rawstory.com/news/2006/Killer_of_Colombian_right_wing_para_08262006.html (accessed August 27, 2006).

Díaz-Alejandro, Carlos F. (1976) *Foreign Trade Regimes and Economic Development: Colombia*. New York: Columbia University Press.

Diáz-Callejas, Apolinar (2005) "La "seguridad democrática" se hunde," April 27 [online] http://www.anncol.org/side/1315 (accessed April 29, 2005).

Díaz Montes, Eberto (2005) "Organic class-consciousness in rural Colombia," International Development Studies Special Lecture Series for the Department of Political Science at University of New Brunswick, November 21.

Díaz Montes, Eberto and Juan Efrain Mendiza (2006) *¡Pronta Libertad Para Freddy Muñoz! (21 de Noviembre de 2006)* Bogotá, DC: Comunicado Público.

Dieppa, David Alejandro Alvarez (2007) "Geostrategic resources in Latin America and U.S. control mechanisms," pp. 203–13 in *The Bush Doctrine and Latin America*, ed. Gary Prevost and Carlos Oliva Campos. New York: Palgrave Macmillan.

Dix, Robert H. (1967) *Colombia: The political dimensions of change*. London: Yale University Press.

Dix, Robert H. (1980) "Political oppositions under the National Front," pp. 131–79 in *Politics of Compromise: Coalition government in Colombia*, ed. R. Albert Berry, Ronald G. Hellman, and Mauricio Solaún. New Brunswick, N.J.: Transaction.

Donahue, Sean (2003) "Uribe's cruel model: Colombia moves toward totalitarianism," August 19 [online] http://counterpunch.org/donahue08192003.html (accessed October 20, 2004).

Dorner, Peter and Herman Felstenhausen (1970) *Agrarian Reform and Employment: The Colombian case*. Madison, Wis.: University of Wisconsin.

Doyal, Leslie and Imogen Pennell (1994) *The Political Economy of Health*. London: Pluto Press.

Draper, Hal (1978a) *Karl Marx's Theory of Revolution: Vol. I – The state and bureaucracy*. New York: Monthly Review Press.

Draper, Hal (1978b) *Karl Marx's Theory of Revolution: Vol. II – The politics of social classes*. New York: Monthly Review Press.

Draper, Hal (1992) *Socialism from Below*. London: Humanities Press.

Dudley, Steven (2004) *Walking Ghosts: Murder and guerrilla politics in Colombia*. New York: Routledge.

Dudley, Steven (2006a) "Paramilitaries' control of candidates is feared," March 9 [online] http://www.miami.com/mld/miamiherald/news/14052943.htm (accessed March 10, 2006).

Dudley, Steven (2006b) "Paramilitary leader suspected of killing brother," August 25 [online] http://www.miami.com/mld/miamiherald/15355908.htm (accessed August 27, 2006).

Duff, Ernest A. (1968) *Agrarian Reform in Colombia*. New York: Praeger.

Dumont, René (1965) *Lands Alive*. New York: Monthly Review Press.

Duque Gómez, Diana (1991) *Una Guerra Irregular Entre Dos Ideologías*. Bogotá: Intermedio Editores.

Dussel, Enrique (2003) "Marx and the concept of dependency," pp. 93–101 in *Development in Theory and Practice: Latin American perspectives*, ed. Ronald H. Chilcote. Boulder, Colo.: Rowman & Littlefield.

Dutt, Clemens (1963) *Fundamentals of Marxism-Leninism: A manual*. Moscow: Foreign Languages Publishing House.

Easterbrook, Michael (2003) "Colombian guerrillas seek to recruit on campuses," *Chronicle of Higher Education*, 50(2): 52–4.

Eckstein, Susan Eva (2001) "Epilogue – where have all the movements gone? Latin American social movements at the new millennium," pp. 351–406 in *Power and Popular Protest: Latin American social movements*, ed. Susan Eva Eckstein. Berkeley, Calif.: University of California Press. Ejército Nacional República de Colombia (2006) "4 millones 600 mil colombianos cooperan con la Fuerza Pública," June 2 [online] http://www.ejercito.mil.co/index.php?idcategoria=102580 (accessed March 25, 2008).

El Tiempo (2005) "Las cuentas de las FARC," January 31 [online] http://eltiempo.terra. com.co/coar/NARCOTRAFICO/narcotrafico/ARTICULO- WEB- _NOTA_INTERIOR-1957382.html (accessed February 18, 2005).

El Tiempo (2008) "Popularidad del presidente Álvaro Uribe alcanzó nuevo récord durante crisis diplomática," March 13 [online] http://www.eltiempo.com/politica/2008-03- 13/ARTICULO-WEB-NOTA_INTERIOR-4007494.html (accessed March 14, 2008).

Emersberger, Joe (2008) "The *Guardian* covers (up) Colombia's reality: London's 'left leaning' newspaper props up Latin America's most authoritarian government," May 5 [online] http://www.narconews.com/Issue52/article3084.html (accessed May 6, 2008).

Emcke, Carolin (2007) *Echoes of Violence: Letters from a war reporter*. Princeton, N.J.: Princeton University Press.

Engels, Frederick (1977) "The defeat of the Piedmontese," pp. 169–77 in *Collected Works Vol. 9: 1849*. New York: International Publishers.

Engels, Frederick (1990a) "The origin of the family, private property and the state: In the light of the researches by Lewis H. Morgan," pp. 129–276 in *Collected Works Vol. 26: 1882–89*. New York: International Publishers.

Engels, Frederick (1990b) "Preface to the Fourth German Edition (1890) of the *Manifesto of the Communist Party*," pp. 53–60 in *Collected Works Vol. 27: 1890–95*. New York: International Publishers.

Engqvist, Maria (2003) "The slaughter continues," *Justice for Colombia* (Summer): 7.

Engqvist, Maria (2005) "Colombian soldiers go crazy," January 26 [online] http://www. anncol.org/uk/site/doc.php?id=207 (accessed January 29, 2005).

Erisman, H. Michael and John M. Kirk (2006) *Redefining Cuban Foreign Policy: The impact of the "Special Period"*. Gainesville, Fla.: University of Florida.

Escobar, Arturo (2004) "Development, violence and the new imperial order," *Development*, 47(1): 15–21.

Escobar-Lemmon, Maria (2003) "Political support for decentralization: An analysis of the Colombian and Venezuelan legislatures," *American Journal of Political Science*, 47(4): 683–97.

Escobar-Lemmon, Maria (2006) "Executives, legislatures, and decentralization," *Policy Studies Journal*, 34(2): 245–63.

Escribano, Marcela (2003) "Militarism and globalization: Conference synopsis," pp. 296–308 in *Another World in Possible: Popular alternatives to globalization at the World Social Forum*, ed. William F. Fisher and Thomas Ponniah. London: Zed.

Estep Jr, William R. (1968) *Colombia: Land of conflict and promise*. Nashville, Tenn.: Convention Press.

Fairbairn, Geoffrey (1974) *Revolutionary Guerrilla Warfare: The countryside version*. London: Penguin.

Fals Borda, Orlando (1969) *Subversion and Social Change in Colombia*. London: Columbia University Press.

Fals Borda, Orlando (1976) *Peasant Society in the Colombian Andes: A sociological study of Saucio*. Westport, Conn.: Greenwood.

Farah, Douglas (1998) "Colombian rebels seen winning war: U.S. study finds army inept, ill- equipped," April 10 [online] http://www.colombiasupport.net/199804/wp41098.html (accessed March 30, 2003).

FARC-EP (1999) *FARC-EP Historical Outline*. Toronto, ON: International Commission.

FARC-EP (2000a) *Bill 002 Concerning Taxation*. Mountains of Colombia: Central General Staff of the FARC-EP.

FARC-EP (2000b) *Resistencia*, Issue 24 (July-October).

FARC-EP (2000c) *The People Cannot Remain Separated*. Mountains of Colombia: Central Command.

FARC-EP (2000d) *Planning Mechanisms for the Substitution of Illicit Crops Mountains of Colombia*: Mountains of Colombia: Secretariat of the General Central Staff of the FARC-EP.

FARC-EP (2000e) *To the International Community*. Leadership Command of International Commission.

FARC-EP (2000f) *Law 003, About Administrative Corruption*. Mountains of Colombia: Central General Staff of the FARC-EP.

FARC-EP (2000–01) *Resistencia*, Issue 25 (November–February).

FARC-EP (2001a) *Resistencia*, Issue 26 (March–June).

FARC-EP (2001b) *Resistencia*, Issue 27 (July–October).

FARC-EP (2001c) *Belligerence*, Mexico City: International Commission.

FARC–EP (2001–02) *Resistencia*, Issue 28 (November–February).

FARC-EP (2002a) *Resistencia*, Issue 29 (March–June).

FARC-EP (2002b) *Resistencia*, Issue 30 (July–October).

FARC-EP (2002c) *November 30 Communiqué*. Secretariat of the General Central Staff of the FARC-EP.

FARC-EP (2003a) *February 8 Communiqué*. Secretariat of the General Central Staff of the FARC-EP.

FARC-EP (2003b) *February 21 Communiqué*. Secretariat of the General Central Staff of the FARC-EP.

FARC-EP (2003c) *February 24 Communiqué*. Secretariat of the General Central Staff of the FARC-EP.

FARC-EP (2003d) *March 2 Communiqué*. Secretariat of the General Central Staff of the FARC-EP.

FARC-EP (2003e) *March 20 Communiqué*. Secretariat of the General Central Staff of the FARC- EP.

FARC-EP (2003f) *April 9 Communiqué*. Commander-in-Chief Manuel Marulanda Vélez.

FARC-EP (2003g) *April 13 Communiqué*. Commander-in-Chief Manuel Marulanda Vélez.

FARC-EP (2003h) *April 20 Communiqué*. Commander-in-Chief Manuel Marulanda Vélez.

FARC-EP (2003i) *April 27 Communiqué*. Secretariat of the General Central Staff of the FARC-EP.

FARC-EP (2003j) *Falleció el Comandante Nariño*. Mountains of Colombia: Secretariat of the Central General Staff.

FARC-EP (2003k) *September 10 Communiqué*. For the Secretariat of the General Central Staff of the FARC-EP, Manuel Marulanda Vélez.

FARC-EP (2003l) *September 16 Communiqué*. Secretariat of the General Central Staff of the FARC-EP.

FARC-EP (2004a) *Iván Ríos miembro del Secretariad*. Mountains of Colombia: Secretariat of the Central General Staff.

FARC-EP (2004b) *March 8 Communiqué*. International Commission.

FARC-EP (2008a) *Comunicado Marzo 4 de 2008 (Marzo 2 del 2008)* Montañas de Colombia: Secretariado del Estado Mayor Central de las FARC-EP.

FARC-EP (2008b) *Comunicado Marzo 8 de 2008*. Montañas de Colombia: Secretariado del Estado Mayor Central de las FARC-EP.

FARC-EP (2008c) *Comandante Manuel Marulanda Vélez: ¡Juaramos Vencer!* Montañas de Colombia: Secretariado del Estado Mayor Central de las FARC-EP.

Farr, Stephen (2004) "Coffee rises to 3-month high after inventories drop (correct)," November 16 [online] http://www.bloomberg.com/apps/news?pid=10000086&sid=aA4kfyLFu7JM&ref er=latin_america (accessed November 16, 2004).

Feder, Dan (2004) "Increasing repression, U.S. intervention, and popular opposition in Colombia: A conversation with Colombian authentic journalist Alfredo Molano," June 28 [online] http://www.narconews.com/Issue33/article1003.html (accessed June 29, 2004).

Feder, Dan (2006) "Telesur journalist arrested and accused of 'terrorism' in Colombia," November 20 [online] http://narcosphere.narconews.com/story/2006/11/20/211346/16 (accessed November 21, 2006).

Feder, Ernest (1971) *The Rape of the Peasantry: Latin America's landholding system.* New York: Anchor.

Federal Research Division Library of Congress (1988) "Colombia: Military expenditure" [online] http://lcweb2.loc.gov/cgi-bin/query/r?frd/cstdy:@field(DOCID+co0150) (accessed November 2, 2006).

Felbab-Brown, Vanda (2005) "The coca connection: Conflict and drugs in Colombia and Peru," *Journal of Conflict Studies*, 25(2): 104–28.

Felstenhausen, Herman (1968a) *Improving Access to Latin American Agricultural Information through Modern Documentation Centers.* Madison, Wis.: University of Wisconsin-Madison.

Felstenhausen, Herman (1968b) *Economic Knowledge, Participation and Farmer Decision Making in a Developed and an Under-developed Country.* Madison, Wis.: University of Wisconsin-Madison.

Federación Nacional Sindical Unitaria Agropecuaria (FENSUAGRO) (2005) *Comunicado a la Opinion Publica Nacional e Internacional.* Bogotá: FENSUAGRO.

FENSUAGRO (2008) *Denuncia Pública se Sigue Sembrando el Terror a los Miembros de FENSUAGRO- CUT.* Bogotá: FENSUAGRO.

Fernández, Raúl A. (1979) "Imperialist capitalism in the Third World: Theory and evidence from Colombia," *Latin American Perspectives*, 6(1): 38–64.

Fernández, Raúl A. and José F. Ocampo (1974) "The Latin American revolution: A theory of imperialism, not dependence," *Latin American Perspectives*, 1(1): 30–61.

Ferro Medina, Juan Guillermo, and Graciela Uribe Ramón (2002) *El Orden de la Guerra: Las FARC- EP entre la organización y la política.* Bogotá: CEJA.

Ferreyra, Aleida and Renata Segura (2000) "Examining the military in the local sphere: Colombia and Mexico," *Latin American Perspectives*, 27(2): 18–35.

Fitchl, Eric (2003) "The massacre at Betoyes," August 4 [online] http://colombiajour nal.org/colombia164.htm (accessed August 5, 2003).

Findji, Mario Teresa (1992) "From resistance to social movement: The indigenous authorities movement in Colombia," pp. 112–33 in *The Making of Social Movements in Latin America: Identity, strategy, and democracy,* ed. Arturo Escobar and Sonia E. Alvarez. Boulder, Colo.: Westview.

Fiszbein, Ariel (1997) "The emergence of local capacity: Lessons from Colombia," *World Development*, 25(7): 1029–44.

Fletcher, Laraine (1967) "Guerrilla activity in Colombia," *NALCA Report on the Americas*, 1(4): 3.

Flounders, Sara (2003) "Defoliation is Depopulation," pp. 83–89 in *War in Colombia: Made in the U.S.A.,* ed. Rebecca Toledo, Teresa Gutierrez, Sara Flounders, and Andy McInerney. New York: International Action Centre.

Fluharty, Veron Lee (1957) *Dance of the Millions: Military rule and social revolution in Colombia 1930–1956.* Pittsburgh, Penn.: University of Pittsburgh Press.

Forero, Juan (2004) "Colombia drug lords join paramilitaries to seek leniency," November 27 [online] http://www.nytimes.com.2004/11/27/international/americas/27colombia.html (accessed November 27, 2004).

Forero, Juan (2007a) "Colombian senator: death squads met at Uribe's ranch," April 17 [online] http://www.washingtonpost.com/wp-dyn/content/article/2007/04/17/AR2007041702007.html (accessed February 29, 2008).

Forero, Juan (2007b) "Paramilitary ties to elite in Colombia are detailed: Commanders cite state complicity in violent movement," May 22 [online] http://www.washingtonpost.com/wp- dyn/content/article/2007/05/21/AR2007052101672_pf.html (accessed August 6, 2008).

Forero, Juan (2008) "Colombia's rebels face possibility of implosion: Chief threat not deaths, but desertion," March 22 [online] http://www.washingtonpost.com/wp- dyn/content/article/2008/03/21/AR2008032103536_pf.html (accessed March 23, 2008).

Fortuny, Jose Manuel, A. Delgado, and M. Salibi (1966) "The Tri-Continental Conference," *World Marxist Review*, 9(3): 24–6.

Foweraker, Joe (1995) *Theorizing Social Movements*. London: Pluto.

Friedemann-Sánchez, Greta (2006) *Assembling Flowers and Cultivating Homes: Labor and gender in Colombia*. Lanham, Md.: Lexington.

Fuerza Aérea Colombiana (2006) "Appear Farc graffiti in the Caldas University," May 12 [online] http://www.fac.mil.co/index.php?idcategoria=11192&facmil_2007=227406b312943870629 7958888cbb0c6 August 15, 2008).

Fundación Seguridad y Democracia (2004) *Coyuntura de Seguridad: El repliegue de las FARC: ¿Derrota o Estrategia? (Julio–Septiembre)* Bogotá: Fundación Seguridad y Democracia.

Fundación Seguridad y Democracia (2006) *Balance de Seguridad 2005*. Bogotá: Fundación Seguridad y Democracia.

Fukuyama, Francis (1992) *The End of History and the Last Man*. Toronto, ON: HarperCollins.

Galbraith, W. O. (1953) *Colombia: A general survey*. London: Royal Institute of International Affairs.

Galdos, Guillermo (2004) "Eliana Gonzales," May 27 [online] http://news.bbc.co.uk/1/shared/spl/hi/programmes/this_world/one_day_of_war/ht ml/12.stm (accessed May 28, 2004).

Galeski, Boguslaw (1972) *Basic Concepts in Rural Sociology*. Manchester, UK: Manchester University Press.

Gallón, Gustavo (2007a) "Human rights: A path to democracy and peace in Colombia," pp. 353–411 in *Peace, Democracy, and Human Rights in Colombia*, ed. Christopher Welna and Gustavo Gallón. Notre Dame, Ind.: University of Notre Dame Press.

Gallón, Gustavo (2007b) "This war cannot be won with bullets," . pp. 415–32 in *Peace, Democracy, and Human Rights in Colombia*, ed. Christopher Welna and Gustavo Gallón. Notre Dame, Ind.: University of Notre Dame Press.

Galvis, Constanza Ardila (2000) *The Heart of the War in Colombia*. London: Latin American Bureau.

Galvis Mujica, Luis Alberto, and Dan Kovalik (2005) "Santo Domingo massacre in Colombia: A testimony," October 10 [online] http://www.zmag.org/content/showarticle.cfm?SectionID=9&ItemID=8907 (accessed October 14, 2005).

Gamboa, Miguel (2001) "Democratic discourse and the conflict in Colombia," *Latin American Perspectives*, 28(1): 93–109.

Garamore, Jim (2005) "U.S., Colombia will continue pressure on narcoterrorists," April 12 [online] http://www.defenselink.mil/news/Apr2005/20050412_563.html (accessed April 13, 2005).

Garavito, Fernando (2004) "Colombia's (para)military," May 3 [online] http://www.zmag.org/content/showarticle.cfm?ItemID=5455 (accessed May 4, 2004).

Garcia, Cesar (2006) "Entire Colombian city council resigns," May 3 [online] http://seattlepi.nwsource.com/national/1102AP_Colombia_Council_Resigns.html (accessed May 4, 2006).

García-Peña Jaramillo, Daniel (2007) "Colombia: In search of a new model for conflict resolution," pp. 90–131 in *Peace, Democracy, and Human Rights in Colombia*, ed. Christopher Welna and Gustavo Gallón. Notre Dame, Ind.: University of Notre Dame Press.

Gareau, Frederick H. (2004) *State Terrorism and the United States: From counter-insurgency to the war on terrorism*. Atlanta: Clarity Press.

Garner, Roberta (1996) *Contemporary Movements and Ideologies*. New York: McGraw-Hill.

Gentile, Carmen (2007) "Raid on FARC camp highlights limits on U.S. forces in Colombia," March 16 [online] http://worldpoliticswatch.com/article.aspx?id=633# (accessed March 23, 2007).

Gerassi, John (1965) *The Great Fear in Latin America*. London: Collier-Macmillan.

Gerassi, John (1971) *Revolutionary Priest: The complete writings and messages of Camilo Torres*. New York: Random House.

Gibbs, Terry (2008) "Rainforest rendezvous – Interview with Terry Gibbs, Information Morning Cape Breton – March 27, 2008," Cape Breton, NS: Canadian Broadcasting Corporation.

Gibbs, Terry (forthcoming) *Revolutionary Women and Social Transformation in Colombia*, Working paper. Cape Breton, NS: International Development Studies, Cape Breton University.

Gibbs, Terry and Garry Leech (2005) "Race and class dimensions of the war on drugs: A humanitarian crisis," *Rutgers University Journal of Law and Urban Policy*, 3(1): 62–74.

Gibbs, Terry and Garry Leech (2009) *The Failure of Global Capitalism: From Cape Breton to Colombia and beyond*. Cape Breton, NS: Cape Breton University Press.

Gilbert, Alan (1974) *Latin American Development: A geographical perspective*. London: Penguin.

Gilbert, Jorge (1982) "Introduction," pp. 1–5 in *Social Movements, Social Change: The re-making of Latin America*, ed. Jorge Gilbert. Toronto, ON: OISE.

Gilhodés, Pierre (1970) "Agrarian struggles in Colombia," pp. 407–51 in *Agrarian Problems an Peasant Movements in Latin America*, ed. Rodolfo Stavenhagen. Garden City, N.Y.: Anchor.

Gill, Lesley (2004) *The School of the Americas: Military training and political violence in the Americas*. Durham, N.C.: Duke University Press.

Gilly, Adolfo (2003) "Globalization, violence and revolutions: Nine theses," pp. 107–24 in *The Future of Revolutions: Rethinking radical change in the age of globalization*, ed. John Foran. London: Zed.

Giraldo, Javier (1996) *Colombia: the genocidal democracy*. Monroe, ME: Common Courage Press.

Glenn, Carl (2003) "Soldiers for the banks: Paramilitaries in Colombia," pp. 71–6 in *War in Colombia: Made in the U.S.A.*, ed. Rebecca Toledo, Teresa Gutierrez, Sara Flounders, and Andy McInerney. New York: International Action Centre.

Goff, Stan (2003) "The blurring of the lines: U.S. overt and covert assistance in Colombia," pp. 77–82 in *War in Colombia: Made in the U.S.A.*, ed. Rebecca Toledo, Teresa Gutierrez, Sara Flounders, and Andy McInerney. New York: International Action Centre.

Goff, Stan (2004) *Full Spectrum Disorder: The military in the new American century*. New York: Soft Skull Press.

Goffman, Sam (2005) "Colombia: Paramilitaries get sweetheart deal," *NACLA Report on the America*, 39(2): 50–1.

Goldstone, Jack A. (1991) *Revolution and Rebellion in the Early Modern World*. Berkeley, Calif.: University of California Press.

Gomez, Alberto (1972) "Perspectives of the revolutionary armed forces of Colombia

(FARC)," pp. 248–56 in *National Liberation Fronts 1960/1970: Essays, documents, interviews*, ed. Donald H. Hodges and Robert Elias Abu Shanab. New York: William Morrow.

González, Fernán E., Ingrid J. Bolivar, and Teófilo Vázquez (2002) *Violencia Politica en Colombia: De la nación fragmentada a la construcción del Estado*. Bogotá: Centro de Insetagción y Educación Popular.

Goodman, Joshua (2006a) "Trade deal threatens the war on drugs," April 26 [online] http://www.chron.com/disp/story.mpl/ap/fn/3820387.html (accessed April 26, 2006).

Goodman, Joshua (2006b) "U.S. cuts aid for Colombia area," October 11 [online] http://news.yahoo.com/s/ap/20061011/ap_on_re_la_am_ca/colombia_us_aid_cuts _2;_ylt=AjS8YTAxz3.7XWKfI2l5IeSwv7kA;_ylu=X3oDMTBiMW04NW9mBH NlYwMlJVRPUCUl (accessed October 13, 2006).

Goodwin, Jeff (1997) "State-centered approaches to social revolutions: Strengths and limitations of a theoretical tradition," pp. 11–37 in *Theorizing Revolutions*, ed. John Foran. New York: Routledge.

Goodwin, Jeff (1998) *State and Revolution, 1945–1991*. Cambridge, UK: Cambridge University Press.

Goodwin, Jeff (2001) *No Other Way Out: States and revolutionary movements, 1945–1991*. Cambridge, UK: Cambridge University Press.

Goodwin, Jeff (2003) "First thematic discussion – the political economy and geopolitics of globalization: What has changed? What does it mean for the future of revolutions?" pp. 138–9 in *The Future of Revolutions: Rethinking radical change in the age of globalization*, ed. John Foran. London: Zed.

Gorman, Peter (2002) "Marines ordered into Colombia: February 2003 is target date," October 25 [online] http://www.narconews.com/article.php3?ArticleID=19 (accessed November 22, 2004).

Gott, Richard (1970) *Guerrilla Movements in Latin American*. New York: Nelson.

Gott, Richard (1973) *Rural Guerrillas in Latin America*. London: Penguin.

Graciarena, Jorge and Rolando Franco (1978) "Part One: Power transformations and the contradictions of Latin American development," *Current Sociology*, 26(5): 5–83.

Gramsci, Antonio (1971) *Selections from the Prison Notebooks of Antonio Gramsci* (ed. and trans. Quintin Hoare and Geoffrey Nowell-Smith). New York: International Publishers.

Gramsci, Antonio (1973) *Letters from Prison* (selected, trans. from the Italian, and Introduction by Lynne Lawner). New York: Harper & Row.

Gramsci, Antonio (1977) *Selections from Political Writings, 1910–1920* (ed. Quintin Hoare, trans. John Mathews). New York: International Publishers.

Gramsci, Antonio (1978) *Selections from Political Writings, 1921–1926* (ed. and trans. Quintin Hoare). New York: International Publishers.

Gramsci, Antonio (1985) *Selections from Cultural Writings* (ed. David Forgacs and Geoffrey Nowell-Smith, trans. William Boelhower). Cambridge, Mass.: Harvard University Press.

Granada, Camilo and Leonardo Rojas (1995) "Los costos del conflicto armado, 1990–1994," *Planeacion y Desarrollo*, 26(4): 119–51.

Grandin, Greg (2004) *The Last Colonial Massacre: Latin America in the cold war*. Chicago, Ill.: University of Chicago Press.

Grandin, Greg (2006) *Empire's Workshop: Latin America, the United States, and the rise of the new imperialism*. New York: Metropolitan Books.

Green, Duncan (2003) *Silent Revolution: The rise and crisis of market economics in Latin America*. New York: Monthly Review Press.

Green, W. John (2004) *Gaitanismo, Left Liberalism, and Popular Mobilization in Colombia*. Gainesville, Fla.: University Press of Florida.

Greene, Thomas H. (1990) *Contemporary Revolutionary Movements: Search for theory and justice*. Englewood Cliffs, N.J.: Prentice-Hall.

Griswold, Deirdre (2008) "Colombia and Venezuela: Who's behind the rising tensions," February 18 [online] http://www.workers.org/2008/world/colombia_and_venezuela_0221/ (accessed March 6, 2008).

Grunig, James E. (1969) *The Minifundio Problem in Colombia: Development alternatives*. Madison, Wis.: University of Wisconsin.

Guevara, Ernesto "Che" (2004) *The Motorcycle Diaries: Notes on a Latin American journey*. Melbourne: Ocean Press.

Guevara, Ernesto "Che" (2006) *Guerrilla Warfare*. Melbourne: Ocean Books.

Guggenheim, Scott Evan and Robert P. Weller (1982) "Introduction: Moral economy, capitalism, and state power in rural protest," pp. 3–12 in *Power and Protest in the Countryside: Studies of rural unrest in Asia, Europe, and Latin America*, ed. Robert P. Weller and Scott E. Guggenheim. Durham, N.C.: Duke Press Policy Studies.

Gugliotta, Guy (1992) "The Colombian cartels and how to stop them," pp. 111–28 in *Drug Policy in the Americas*, ed. Peter Smith. Boulder, Colo.: Westview Press.

Guillen, Gonzalo (2008) "4 investigated for paramilitary ties," April 16 [online] http://www.miamiherald.com/news/americas/story/497359.html (accessed April 16, 2008).

Gunther, John (1966) *Inside South America*. New York: Harper & Row.

Gurr, Ted Robert (1970) *Why Men Rebel*. Princeton, N.J.: Princeton University Press.

Gutierrez, Teresa (2003) "Demonizing resistance," pp. 48–57 in *War in Colombia: Made in the U.S.A.*, ed. Rebecca Toledo, Teresa Gutierrez, Sara Flounders, and Andy McInerney. New York: International Action Centre.

Gutiérrez Sanín, Francisco (2004) "Criminal rebels? A discussion of civil war and criminality from the Colombian experience," *Politics & Society*, 32(2): 257–85.

Gutiérrez Sanín, Francisco (2008) "Telling the difference: Guerrillas and paramilitaries in the Colombia war," *Politics & Society*, 36(1): 3–34.

Guzmán Campos, German, Orlando Fals Borda, and Eduardo Umaña Luna (1962) *La Violencia en Colombia: Estudio de un proceso social. Tomo I*. Bogotá: Ediciones Tercer Mundo.

Guzmán Campos, German, Orlando Fals Borda, and Eduardo Umaña Luna (1964) *La Violencia en Colombia: Estudio de un proceso social. Tomo II*. Bogotá: Ediciones Tercer Mundo.

Hagen, Everett E. (1971) "The transition in Colombia," pp. 191–224 in *Entrepreneurship and Economic Development*, ed. Peter Kilby. New York: Free Press.

Halliday, Fred (1989) *From Kabul to Managua: Soviet-American relations in the 1980s*. New York: Pantheon.

Handelman, Howard (2000) *The Challenge of Third World Development*. Englewood Cliffs, N.J.: Prentice Hall.

Hansen, Joseph (1972) *The Leninist Strategy of Party Building: The debate of guerrilla warfare in Latin America*. New York: Pathfinder.

Harding, Colin (1996) *Colombia: A guide to the people, politics and culture*. London: Latin American Bureau.

Harding, Timothy F. (2003) "Dependency: Nationalism and the state in Latin America," pp. 61–5 in *Development in Theory and Practice: Latin American perspectives*, ed. Ronald H. Chilcote. Boulder, Colo.: Rowman & Littlefield.

Harding, Timothy and James Petras (1988) "Democratization and class struggle," *Latin American Perspectives*, 15(3): 3–17.

Hardt, Michael and Antonio Negri (2000) *Empire*. Cambridge, Mass.: Harvard University Press.

Hardt, Michael and Antonio Negri (2004) *Multitudes: War and democracy in the age of empire*. New York: Penguin.

Hardy, Charles (2004) "Who dunnit? The FARC? The AUC? The Etc?" October 15 [online] http://www.vheadline.com/printer_news.asp?id=23116 (accessed November 3, 2005).

Harnecker, Marta (1986) *Reflexiónes acerca del problema de la transición al socialismo.* Managua: Nueva Nicaragua.

Harnecker, Marta (2005) *Understanding the Venezuelan Revolution: Hugo Chávez talks to Marta Harnecker.* New York: Monthly Review Press.

Harper, Liz (2005) "Colombian Congress approves controversial bill to revive peace talks," June 24 [online] http://www.pbs.org/newshour/updates/colombia_06-24-05.html (accessed April 16, 2006).

Harris, Richard L. (1970) *Death of a Revolutionary: Che Guevara's last mission.* New York: W.W. Norton.

Harris, Richard L. (1992) *Marxism, Socialism, and Democracy in Latin America.* Boulder, Colo.: Westview Press.

Harrison, Paul (1980) *The Third World Tomorrow: A report from the battlefront in the war against poverty.* London: Penguin.

Harrison, Paul (1993) *Inside the Third World: The anatomy of poverty,* 2nd edn. London: Penguin.

Hart, Peter (2000) "Colombia's cocaine shell game," May/June [online] http://www.fair.org/extra/0005/colombia.html (accessed December 4, 2002).

Haste, Paul (2007) "Colombia's magical realism: Mágico realismo," May 31 [online] http://www.dissentvoice.org/2007/05/colombia%E2%80%99s-magical-realism/ (accessed June 1, 2007).

Haugaard, Lisa (2006) *Longing for Home: Return of land to Colombia's internally displaced population.* Washington, DC: Latin America Working Group.

Haugaard, Lisa, Gimena Sánchez-Garzoli, Adam Isacson, John Walsh, and Robert Guitteau (2008) *A Compass for Colombia Policy.* Washington, DC: Latin American Working Group.

Havens, A. Eugene, William L. Flinn, and Susana Lastarría Cornhill (1980) "Agrarian reform and the National Front: A class analysis," pp. 341–79 in *Politics of Compromise: Coalition government in Colombia,* ed. R. Albert Berry, Ronald G. Hellman, and Mauricio Solaún. New Brunswick, N.J.: Transaction.

Helweg-Larson, Simon (2003) "Bush responds to guerrilla attack," March 5 [online] http://noticiasaliadas.org/article.asp?lanCode=1&artCode=3259 (accessed August 3, 2003).

Henderson, James D. (1985) *When Colombia Bled: A history of the Violencia in Tolima.* Tuscaloosa, Ala.: University of Alabama Press.

Henderson, James D. (2001) *Modernization in Colombia: The Laureano Gómez years, 1889–1965.* Gainesville, Fla.: University Press of Florida.

Hennessey, Alistair (1972) "The new radicalism in Latin America," *Journal of Contemporary History,* 7(1/2): 1–26.

Herman, Donald L. (1973) "Introduction," pp. 9–34 in *The Communist Tide in Latin America: A selected treatment.* Austin, Tex.: University of Texas.

Herman, Melissa and Pablo Conde (2005) *Empire in the Andes: The war against the poor.* Documentary film (Barricade Films).

Hill, James T. (2003) *Posture Statement of General James T. Hill, United States Army Commander, United States Southern Command, before the 108th Congress House Armed Services Committee, March 13.* Washington, DC: Senate Armed Services Committee.

Hinojosa, Victor J. (2007) *Domestic Politics and International Narcotics Control: U.S. relations with Mexico and Colombia, 1989–2000.* New York: Routledge.

Hobday, Charles (1986) *Communist and Marxist Parties of the World: A Keesing's reference publication.* Santa Barbara, Calif.: ABC-CLIO.

Hobsbawm, E. J. (1963) "The Anatomy of Violence," *New Society,* 28: 16–18.

Hobsbawm, E. J. (1964) *Karl Marx – Pre-Capitalist Economic Formations*. New York: International Publishers.

Hobsbawm, E. J. (1970) "Guerrillas in Latin America," pp. 51–61 in *The Socialist Register*, ed. Ralph Miliband and John Saville. London,: Merlin Press.

Hobsbawm, E. J. (1973) *Revolutionaries: Contemporary essays*. New York: Pantheon.

Hobsbawm, E. J. (1989) *The Age of Empire*. New York: Random House.

Hobsbawm, E. J. (2000) *Bandits*. New York: New Press.

Hodges, Donald C. (1974) *The Latin American Revolution: Politics and strategy from apro-Marxism to Guevarism*. New York: William Morrow.

Hodgson, Martin (2000) "Colombian rebels impose law of the gun: Some villagers support actions in demilitarized zone, but officials say they are illegal and may elicit revenge when armys return," *Globe and Mail*, July 19. p. A15.

Holloway, John (2002a) *Change The World Without Taking Power: The meaning of revolution today*. London: Pluto.

Holloway, John (2002b) "¡Que se vayan todos!," *Studies in Political Economy*, 69: 157–66.

Holloway, John (2002c) "Zapatismo and the Social Sciences," *Capital and Class*, 78: 153–60.

Holmes, Jennifer S. (2003) *New Approaches to Comparative Politics: Insights from political theory*. Lanham, Md.: Lexington.

Holmes, Jennifer S. and Sheila Amin Gutiérrez de Piñeres (2006) "The illegal drug industry, violence and the Colombian economy: A department level analysis," *Bulletin of Latin American Research*, 25(1): 104–18.

Holmes, Jennifer S., Sheila Amin Gutiérrez de Piñeres, and Kevin M. Curtin (2006) "Drugs, violence, and development in Colombia: A departmental-level analysis," *Latin American Politics and Society*, 48(3): 157–84.

Holmes, Ralph (1990) "Colombia," pp. 199–223 in *Latin American Adjustment: How much has happened?* ed. John Williamson. Washington, DC: Institute for International Economics.

Honneth, Axel (2001) "Personal identity and disrespect," pp. 39–45 in *The New Social Theory Reader*, ed. Steven Seidman and Jeffrey C. Alexander. London: Routledge.

Housego, Kim (2003) "General: Colombian troops ward off rebels," November 7 [online] http://www.miami.com/mld/miamiherald/7206457.htm (accessed November 11, 2003).

Howe, Jason P. (2004) "Interview with an assassin," February 9 [online] http://www.colombiajournal.org/colombia177.htm (accessed February 9, 2004).

Hudson, Rex A. (2002) *Who Becomes a Terrorist and Why: The 1999 government report on profiling terrorists*. Guilford, Conn.: Lyons Press.

Huizer, Gerrit (1970) "Emiliano Zapata and the peasant guerrilla in the Mexican revolution," pp. 375–406 in *Agrarian Problems and Peasant Movements in Latin America*, ed. Rodolfo Stavenhagen. Garden City, N.Y.: Anchor.

HURIDOCS (2003) "Colombian activist bags Martin Ennals Award," June 26 [online] http://huridocs.org/nl26emea.htm (accessed June 26, 2004).

Hutchinson, Asa (2002) "Press conference at the CNP Headquarters: Question-and-answer session with reporters, March 26," March 26 [online]. http://www.state.gov/g/inl/rls/rm/2002/9234.htm (accessed March 11, 2007).

Hutchison, Harold C. (2004) "Powell and Rumsfeld," September 25 [online] http://www.strategypage.com/the_estimate/articles/2004925.asp (accessed September 27, 2004).

Hyams, Edward (1974) *Terrorists and Terrorism*. New York: St. Martin's Press.

Hylton, Forrest (2003) "An Evil Hour: Uribe's Colombia in historical perspective," *New Left Review*, 23: 50–93.

Hylton, Forrest (2006) *Evil Hour in Colombia*. New York: Verso.

Instituto Colombiano se La Reforma Agraria (INCORA) (1963) *Segundo Ano de Reforma Agraria*. Bogotá: INCORA.

INCORA (1964) *Informe de Actividades de 1963: Segundo Ano de Reforma Agraria, 1963.* Bogotá: Imprenta Nacional.

INCORA (1972) *Reforma Agraria Augusto 1970–Augusto 1972.* Bogotá: INCORA.

Internal Displacement Monitoring Centre (IDMC) (2007) "Almost 4 million Colombians displaced by violence between 1985 and 2007" [online] http://www.internal- displacement.org/idmc/website/countries.nsf/(httpEnvelopes)/CC05B30C4C94EC968025 70B8005A7090?OpenDocument (accessed March 7, 2008).

International Action Center (IAC) (2001) *Fact Sheet – Colombia: The pentagon's new target in Latin America.* New York,: IAC.

International Crisis Group (ICG) (2003a) *Colombia: Negotiating with the paramilitaries.* Latin America Report No. 5. Bogotá/Brussels: ICG.

International Crisis Group (2003b) *Colombia: President Uribe's Democratic Security Policy.* Latin America Report No. 6. Bogotá/Brussels: ICG.

International Crisis Group (2004) *Demobilizing the Paramilitaries in Colombia: An achievable goal?* Latin American Report No. 8. Bogotá/Brussels: ICG.

International Crisis Group (2009) *Ending Colombia's FARC Conflict: Dealing the right card.* Latin American Report No. 30. Bogotá/Brussels: ICG.

International Herald Tribune (2006) "Colombia investigates army officers for deadly attack on eve of presidential inauguration," September 7 [online] http://www.iht.com/articles/ap/2006/09/08/america/LA_GEN_Colombia_Army_I nvestigated.php (accessed September 8, 2006).

Isacson, Adam (2003) *Was Failure Avoidable? Learning from Colombia's 1998–2002 peace process.* Working Paper No. 14. Coral Gables, Fla.: Dante B. Fascell North-South Centre, University of Miami.

Isacson, Adam (2005) "The U.S. military in the war in drugs," pp. 15–60 in *Drugs and Democracy in Latin America: The impact of U.S. policy,* ed. Coletta A. Youngers and Eileen Rosin. Boulder, Colo.: Lynne Rienner.

Isacson, Adam (2006a) "Notes from last week in Colombia," April 5 [online] http://www.ciponline.org/colombia/blog/archives/000239.htm (accessed April 6, 2006).

Isacson, Adam (2006b) "Love those Semana columnists," September 4 [online] http://www.ciponline.org/colombia/blog/archives/000308.htm (accessed September 6, 2006).

Isacson, Adam (2008) "Where the FARC are being beaten – and where they aren't," May 21 [online] http://www.cipcol.org/?p=601 (accessed May 23, 2008).

Isacson, Adam and Ingrid Vaicius (2004) "Plan Colombia 2?" March 22 [online] http://www.ciponline.org/colombia/040322memo.htm (accessed March 25, 2008).

Isbister, John (1998) *Promises Not Kept: The betrayal of social change in the Third World.* West Hartford, Conn.: Kumarian.

Jackson, Ben (1994) *Poverty and the Planet: A question of survival.* London: Penguin.

Jallade, Jean-Pierre (1974) *Public Expenditures on Education and Income Distribution in Colombia.* Washington, DC: International Bank for Reconciliation and Development.

Janicke, Kiraz (2008a) "Venezuela to receive three more hostages held by Colombian rebels," February 6 [online] http://www.venezuelanalysis.com/news/3125 (accessed March 6, 2008).

Janicke, Kiraz (2008b) "War vs peace: Colombia, Venezuela and the FARC hostage saga," February 8 [online] http://www.venezuelanalysis.com/analysis/3134 (accessed March 6, 2008).

Japan International Cooperation Agency (JICA) (2007) "The crisis in Colombia," June 20 [online] http://www.jica.go.jp/english/resources/field/2007/june20.html (accessed March 7, 2008).

Jay, Martin (1984) *Marxism and Totality: The adventures of a concept from Lukács to Habermas.* Berkeley, Calif.: University of California Press.

Johnson, Chalmers (1964) *Revolution and the Social System*. Stanford, Calif.: Hoover Institution on War, Revolution and Peace.

Johnson, Chalmers (1966) *Revolutionary Change*. Boston, Mass.: Little, Brown.

Johnson, Dale J. (1972) "On oppressed classes," pp. 269–301 in *Dependence and Underdevelopment: Latin America's political economy*, ed. James D. Cockcroft, André Gunder Frank, and Dale L. Johnson. Garden City, N.Y.: Anchor.

Justice for Colombia (2008) "More soldiers killed in further guerrilla attacks," September 19 [online] http://www.justiceforcolombia.org/?link=newsPage&story=4 19 (accessed October 5, 2008).

KAIROS (2001) *The Hidden Story: Confronting Colombia's dirty war*. Documentary film (KAIROS).

Kalmanovitz, Salomon (1978) *Desarrollo de la Agricultura en Colombia*. Bogotá: Carretas.

Kalyvas, Stathis N. (2006) *The Logic of Violence in Civil War*. New York: Cambridge University Press.

Keen, Benjamin (1966) *Americans All: The story of our Latin American neighbors*. New York: Dell.

Keen, Benjamin and Keith Haynes (2000) *A History of Latin America Volume II: Independence to the present*. New York: Houghton Mifflin.

Kenney, Michael (2007) *From Pablo to Osama: Trafficking and terrorist networks, government bureaucracies, and competitive adaptation*. University Park, Penn.: Pennsylvania State University Press.

Kirk, Robin (2003) *More Terrible Than Death: Massacres, drugs, and America's war in Colombia*. New York: Public Affairs.

Klare, Michael (2001) *Resource Wars: The new landscape of global conflict*. New York: Metropolitan Books.

Kline, Harvey F. (1983) *Colombia: Portrait of unity and diversity*. Boulder, Colo.: Westview.

Kline, Harvey F. (1988a) "From rural to urban society: The transformation of Colombian democracy," pp. 17–45 in *Democracy in Latin America: Colombia and Venezuela*, ed. Donald L. Herman. Westport, Conn.: Praeger.

Kline, Harvey F. (1988b) "The Colombian state in crisis: Continuity and change," pp. 87–107 in *Democracy in Latin America: Colombia and Venezuela*. ed. Donald L. Herman. Westport, Conn.: Praeger.

Kline, Harvey F. (1999) *State Building and Conflict Resolution in Colombia, 1986–1994*. Tuscaloosa, Ala.: University of Alabama Press.

Kofas, Jon V. (1986) *Dependence and Underdevelopment in Colombia*. Tempe, Ariz.: Center for Latin American Studies, Arizona State University.

Koonings, Kees and Dirk Kruijt (2004) *Armed Actors: Organized violence and state failure in Latin America*. London: Zed.

Korzeniewicz, Roberto Patricio and William C. Smith (2000) "Poverty, inequality, and growth in Latin America: Searching for the high road to globalization," *Latin American Research Review*, 35(3): 7–54.

Kraul, Chris (2006) "U.S. indicts Colombian guerrillas," March 23 [online] http://www.latimes.com/news/nationworld/world/la-fg-farc23mar23,1,6872382.story?coll=la-headlines-world&ctrack=1&cset=true (accessed April 12, 2006).

Kraul, Chris (2008) "Ecuador asks Colombia to send troops to border to contain rebels: The nation says its neighbor must do more to prevent its civil conflict from spilling over," August 29 [online] http://www.latimes.com/news/nationworld/world/la-fg-ecuador29- 2008aug29,0,2760707.story (accessed August 29, 2008).

Kraul, Chris and Patrick J. McDonnell (2008) "Neighbors take aim at Colombia over incursion," March 5 [online] http://www.latimes.com/news/nationworld/world/la-fg-oas5mar05,1,5513384.story?ctrack=5&cset=true (accessed March 5, 2008).

Koonings, Kees and Dirk Kruijt (2004) "Armed actors, organized violence and state failure in Latin America: A survey of issues and arguments," pp. 5–15 in *Armed Actors: Organized violence and state failure in Latin America*, ed. Kees Koonings and Dirk Kruijt. London: Zed.

Kruijt, Dirk and Kees Koonings (2004) "The military and their shadowy brothers-in-arms," pp. 16–32 in *Armed Actors: Organized violence and state failure in Latin America*, ed. Kees Koonings and Dirk Kruijt. London: Zed.

Labrousse, Alain (2005) "The FARC and the Taliban's connection to drugs," *Journal of Drug Issues*, 35(1): 169–84.

Laclau, Ernesto and Chantal Mouffe (1985) *Hegemony and Socialist Strategy: Towards a radical democratic politics*. New York: Verso.

LACYORK Informational listserv on Latin America and the Caribbean (2003) "U.N. envoy sparks debate on guerrilla motives," May 30 [online] http://sundial.ccs.yorku.ca/cgi-bin/wa?A2=ind0305&L=lacyork&F=&S=&P=1134 (accessed May 30, 2003).

LaFaber, Walter (1972) *America, Russia, and The Cold War, 1945–1971*, 2nd edn. New York: Wiley.

Lair, Eric (2003) "Colombia's internal conflict since the 1970s: A strategic approach," pp. 84–101 in *Colombia: Civil conflict, state weakness and (in)security*, ed. David Myhre. PLAS Cuadernos: Latin American Studies Program, Princeton University.

Lakshmanan, Indira A. R. (2004) "Battling for survival: Indigenous Colombians caught between factions," November 16 [online] (accessed http://www.boston.com/news/world/articles/2004/11/16/still_battling_for_survival_indigenous/ (accessed November 16, 2004).

Lambert, Jacques (1971) *Latin America: Social structure and political institutions*. Berkeley, Calif.: University of California Press.

Lang, James (1988) *Inside Development in Latin America: A report from the Dominican Republic, Colombia, and Brazil*. Chapel Hill, N.C.: University of North Carolina Press.

Larios, Nelson Viloria (2006) *30 Años, 1976–2006 – Organización Lucha y Resistencia: Por una reforma agraria democrática e integral*. Bogotá: Primera Edición FENSUAGRO.

Lartéguy, Jean (1970) *The Guerrillas: New patterns in revolution in Latin America – A provocative analysis of post-Castro guerrilla warfare*. New York: New American Librarian.

Latham, Michael E. (1998) "Ideology, social sciences, and destiny: Modernization and the Kennedy-era Alliance for Progress," *Diplomatic History*, 22(2): 199–230.

Latin American and Caribbean Information Center (LACIC) (2004) "Latin America's oldest guerrilla group celebrates 40th anniversary," May 26 [online] http://lacic.fiu.edu/new/lanews_view.cfm?article_id=500 (accessed May 27, 2004).

Latin American Press (2004) "How much the war costs," November 25 [online] http://www.lapress.org/ArticlePrint.asp?IssCode=0&lanCode=1&artCode=4033 (accessed November 26, 2004).

Latin American Working Group (LAWG) (2003) *The Numbers Game: Coca cultivation in Colombia*. Washington, DC: LAWG.

Latorre, Quintero and Julio César (1988) *Qué Pasó con la Tierra Prometida?* Bogotá: CINEP.

Lazzaretti, Fabrizio (2003) *Justice in a Time of War*. Documentary film.

Le Blanc, Paul (1996) *From Marx to Gramsci: A reader in revolutionary Marxist politics* (historical overview and selection by Paul Le Blanc). Atlantic Highlands, N.J.: Humanities Press International.

Lee, Gregory D. (2003) *Global Drug Enforcement: Practical investigation techniques*. Boca Raton, Fla.: CRC Press.

Lee III, Rensselaer W. (1985) "The Latin American drug connection," *Foreign Policy*, 63: 142–59.

Lee III, Rensselaer W. (1988) "Dimensions of the South American cocaine industry," *Journal of Interamerican Studies and World Affairs*, 30(2/3): 87–103.

Lee III, Rensselaer W. (1991) *The White Labyrinth: Cocaine and political power*. London: Transaction.

Leech, Garry M. (2000a) "An interview with FARC commander Simón Trinidad," *NACLA Report on the Americas*, 34(2): 24–5.

Leech, Garry M. (2000b) "An interview with FARC commander Simón Trinidad," June 25 [online] http://www.colombiajournal.org/colombia15.htm (accessed July 21, 2003).

Leech, Garry M. (2002a) *Killing Peace: Colombia's conflict and the failure of U.S. intervention*. New York: Information Network of the Americas.

Leech, Garry M. (2002b) "Colombia court declares rehabilitation zones unconstitutional," December 9 [online] http://colombiajournal.org/colombia143.htm (accessed March 8, 2006).

Leech, Garry M. (2002c) "The spy game," July 22 [online] http://colombiajournal.org/colombia123.htm (accessed March 8, 2006).

Leech, Garry M. (2002d) *Globalization and "Free" Trade in Colombia*. New York: Information Network of the Americas.

Leech, Garry M. (2003) "Right-wing terror and drug lords," pp. 67–70 in *War in Colombia: Made in the U.S.A.*, ed. Rebecca Toledo, Teresa Gutierrez, Sara Flounders, and Andy McInerney. New York: International Action Centre.

Leech, Garry M. (2004a) "Plan Petroleum in Colombia," *Canadian Dimension*, 38(4): 42–4.

Leech, Garry M. (2004b) *The War on Terror in Colombia*. New York: Colombia Journal.

Leech, Garry M. (2004c) "Plan Petroleum in Putumayo," *NACLA Report of the Americas*, 37(6): 8–11.

Leech, Garry M. (2004d) "Washington's paramilitary game in Colombia," August 2 [online] http://www.colombiajournal.org/colombia191.htm (accessed April 16, 2006).

Leech, Garry M. (2005a) "Oil and Plan Colombia," oral presentation in Hampton, New Brunswick for Amnesty International, February 27.

Leech, Garry M. (2005b) "Blanket coverage," *Oxford Forum*, 2.

Leech, Garry M. (2005c) "The success and failures of President Uribe," November 25 [online] http://colombiajournal.org/colombia222.htm (accessed November 26, 2005).

Leech, Garry M. (2005d) "Is a redistributive political project viable in Colombia?" October 5 [online] http://colombiajournal.org/colombia218.htm (accessed October 5, 2005).

Leech, Garry M. (2006a) "Uribe's new economic reforms benefit corporations, not Colombians," July 31 [online] http://colombiajournal.org/colombia241.htm (accessed July 31, 2006).

Leech, Garry M. (2006b) "Waging war in Colombia's national parks," September 3 [online] http://www.colombiajournal.org/colombia242.htm (accessed September 4, 2006).

Leech, Garry (2006c) "The massacre at Ataquer," September 18 [online] http://colombiajournal.org/colombia243.htm (accessed September 22, 2006).

Leech, Garry. (2006d) *Crude Interventions: The United States, oil and the new world (dis)order*. London: Zed.

Leech Garry (2008a) "Propagandizing human rights in Colombia," March 31 [online] http://colombiajournal.org/colombia280.htm (accessed March 31, 2008).

Leech, Garry (2008b) "Extradition of paramilitary leaders undermines para-politics investigation," May 13 [online] http://www.colombiajournal.org/colombia282.htm (accessed May 14, 2008).

Leech, Garry (2008c) "If not Colombia, then where is the cocaine coming from?" August 1 [online] http://colombiajournal.org/colombia290.htm (accessed August 2, 2008).

LeGrand, Catherine (1986) *Frontier Expansion and Peasant Protest in Colombia, 1850–1936.* Albuquerque, N.M.: University of New Mexico Press.

LeGrand, Catherine (2003) "The Colombian crisis in historical perspective," *Canadian Journal of Latin American and Caribbean Studies*, 28(55–56): 165–209.

Lenin, V. I. (1964a) "Development of capitalism in Russia: The process of the formation of a home market of large-scale industry," pp. 35–607 in *Collected Works Vol. 3: January–July 1905.* Moscow: Progress.

Lenin, V. I. (1964b) "Capitalism in agriculture (Kautsky's book and Mr. Bulgakov's article)," pp. 105–59 in *Collected Works Vol. 4: 1898–April 1901.* Moscow: Progress.

Lenin, V. I. (1964c) "On the slogan for a United States of Europe," pp. 339–43 in *Collected Works Vol. 21: August 1914–December 1915.* Moscow: Progress.

Lenin, V. I. (1964d) "Imperialism, the highest stage of capitalism: A popular outline," pp. 185–304 in *Collected Works Vol. 22: December 1915–July 1916.* Moscow: Progress.

Lenin, V. I. (1964e) "The discussion on self-determination summed up," pp. 320–60 in *Collected Works Vol. 22: December 1915–July 1916.* Moscow: Progress.

Lenin, V. I. (1964f) "Letters from afar: Third letter – concerning a proletarian militia," pp. 320–32 in *Collected Works Vol. 23: August 1916–March 1917.* Moscow: Progress.

Lenin, V. I. (1964g) "Dual power," pp. 38–41 in *Collected Works Vol. 24: April–June 1917.* Moscow: Progress.

Lenin, V. I. (1964h) "Letters in tactics: Foreword," pp. 42–54 in *Collected Works Vol. 24: April–June 1917.* Moscow: Progress.

Lenin, V. I. (1964i) "Letter to comrades," pp. 195–215 in *Collected Works Vol. 26: September 1917–February 1918.* Moscow: Progress.

Lenin, V. I. (1965a) "Days of bloodshed in Moscow," pp. 336–41 in *Collected Works Vol. 9: June– November 1905.* Moscow: Progress.

Lenin, V. I. (1965b) "The present situation in Russia and the tactics of the Workers' Party," pp. 112–19 in *Collected Works Vol. 10: November 1905–June 1906.* Moscow: Progress.

Lenin, V. I. (1965c) "The Russian revolution and the tasks of the proletariat," pp. 135–45 in *Collected Works Vol. 10: November 1905–June 1906.* Moscow: Progress.

Lenin, V. I. (1965d) "A tactical platform for the Unity Congress of the R.S.D.L.P.: Draft resolutions for the Unity Congress of the R.S.D.L.P.," pp. 147–63 in *Collected Works Vol. 10: November 1905–June 1906.* Moscow: Progress.

Lenin, V. I. (1965e) "Lessons of the Moscow uprising," pp. 171–8 in *Collected Works Vol. 11: June 1906– January 1907.* Moscow: Progress.

Lenin, V. I. (1965f) "Guerrilla warfare," pp. 213–23 in *Collected Works Vol. 11: June 1906–January 1907.* Moscow: Progress.

Lenin, V. I. (1965g) "The question of guerrilla warfare," p. 224 in *Collected Works Vol. 11: June 1906– January 1907.* Moscow: Progress.

Lenin, V. I. (1965h) "The crisis of Menshevism," pp. 341–64 in *Collected Works Vol. 11: June 1906–January 1907.* Moscow: Progress.

Lenin V. I. (1965i) "All out for the fight against Denikin," pp. 436–55 in *Collected Works Vol. 29: March–August 1919.* Moscow: Progress.

Lenin, V. I. (1966a) "Report of the Commission on the National and the Colonial Questions, July 26," pp. 240–5 in *Collected Works Vol. 31: April–December 1920.* Moscow: Progress.

Lenin, V. I. (1966b) "The 8th All-Russia Congress of Soviets," pp. 461–533 in *Collected Works Vol. 31: April–December 1920.* Moscow: Progress.

Lenin, V. I. (1968) *V. I. Lenin Collected Works – Vol. 39: Notebooks on imperialism.* Moscow: Progress.

Lenin, V. I. (1969) "Report on the present situation and the attitude towards the Provisional Government, April 14 (27)," pp. 400–2 in *Collected Works Vol. 41: 1896–October 1917.* Moscow: Progress.

Lernoux, Penny (1982) *Cry of the People: The struggle for human rights in Latin America – the Catholic Church in conflict with U.S. policy.* New York: Penguin.

Lévy, Bernard-Henri (2004) *War, Evil, and the End of History.* Hoboken, N.J.: Melville House.

Lewis, Katie (2007) "Conflicted over Colombia," *Ottawa Citizen,* April 8, p. A6.

Lieuwen, Edwin (1961) *Arms and Politics in Latin America.* New York: Frederick A. Praeger.

Lindqvist, Sven (1979) *Land & Power in South America.* London: Penguin.

Lines, Thomas (2008) *Making Poverty: A history.* London: Zed.

Lipman, Aaron and A. Eugene Havens (1965) *The Colombian Violencia: An ex-post-facto experiment.* Madison, Wis.: University of Wisconsin.

Liss, Sheldon B. (1984) *Marxist Thought in Latin America.* Berkeley, Calif.: University of California Press.

Livingstone, Grace (2003) *Inside Colombia: Drugs, democracy and war.* London: Latin American Bureau.

Lobe, Jim. (2004) "Indigenous group along Colombia–Venezuelan border threatened by tensions, smuggling," June 18 [online] http://us.oneworld.net/article/view/88496/1/ (accessed February 11, 2005).

Locher, David A. (2002) *Collective Behavior.* Upper Saddle River, N.J.: Prentice-Hall.

Logan, Sam and Tatiana García (2006) "Paramilitary politics: A Colombian reality," March 10 [online] http://www.isn.ethz.ch/news/sw/details.cfm?id=15056 (accessed March 10, 2006).

Löwy, Michael (1992) *Marxism in Latin America from 1909 to the Present.* London: Humanities Press.

Löwy, Michael (2005a) *The Theory of Revolution in the Young Marx.* Chicago, Ill.: Haymarket.

Löwy, Michael (2005b) "To change the world we need revolutionary democracy," *Capital & Class,* 85: 22–4.

Lozano Guillén, Carlos A. (2000) *¿Cómo Hacer La Paz? Reflexiones desde una posición de IZQUIERDA.* Bogotá: Ideas y Soluciones Gráficas.

Lozano Guillén, Carlos A. (2001) *Reportajes desde El Caguan: Proceso de paz con las FARC-EP.* Bogotá: Colección Izquierda Viva/Edicones Nuestra América.

Lucas, Kintto (2008) "Colombia: French negotiators were to meet Reyes the day he was killed," March 7 [online] http://www.ipsnews.net/news.asp?idnews=41513 (accessed March 11, 2008).

Luxemburg, Rosa (2004) "The mass strike, the political party, and the trade unions," pp. 169–99 in *The Rosa Luxemburg Reader,* ed. Peter Hudis and Kevin B. Anderson. New York: Monthly Review Press.

Lydersen, Kari (2005) "Paramilitaries and palm plantations: A murderous combination in Colombia," [online] December 26 http://www.infoshop.org/inews/article.php?story=20051225225156434 (accessed December 27, 2005).

MacEoin, Gary (1971) *Revolution Next Door: Latin America in the 1970s.* New York: Holt, Rinehart & Winston.

Mandel, Ernest (1968) *Marxist Economic Theory Vol. 2.* London: Merlin.

Mandel Ernest (1994) *Revolutionary Marxism and Social Reality in the 20th century: Collected essays.* Atlantic Highlands, N.J.: Humanities Press.

Marin, Olga Lucia (2004) "Mujer y revolución," *Resistencia,* 32 (no page numbers).

Markey, Patrick (2008a) "Colombia says top FARC commander killed in combat," March

1 [online] http://www.reuters.com/article/newsMaps/idUSN0122624520080301 (accessed March 1, 2008).

Markey, Patrick (2008b) "World crisis may prompt Colombia aid cuts – US envoy," October 17 [online] http://www.reuters.com/article/homepageCrisis/ idUSN17459753._CH_.2400 (accessed October 20, 2008).

Marks, Thomas (2002) *Colombian Army Adaptation to FARC Insurgency.* Carlisle, Penn.: Strategic Studies Institute.

Marsh, Robin Ruth (1983) *Development Strategies in Rural Colombia: The case of Caquetá.* Los Angles, Calif.: UCLA Latin American Center Publications.

Martelo, Lilia and Carlos A. Lozano Guillén (2004) *El Marxismo Ideologia en Constucción: Dos entrevistas sobre temas de actualidad.* Bogotá: Ideas y Soluciones Gráficas Derechos Reservados.

Martínez, Helda (2006) "Colombia: More taxes on the poorest," July 19 [online] http://www.ipsnews.net/news.asp?idnews=34029 (accessed July 31, 2006).

Martínez, Helda (2008a) "Rights–Colombia: Displaced pay homage to victims of paramilitaries," March 5 [online] http://www.ipsnews.net/news.asp?idnews=41468 (accessed March 7, 2008).

Martínez, Helda (2008b) "Rights–Colombia: Thousands come out for anti-paramilitary," March 6 [online] http://www.ipsnews.net/news.asp?idnews=41489 (accessed March 6, 2008).

Martz, John D. (1962) *Colombia: A contemporary political survey.* Chapel Hill, N.C.: University of North Carolina Press.

Marulanda Vélez, Manuel (2000) *Cuadernos de Campana.* No publication accredited.

Marulanda Vélez, Manuel (2003) "The Origins of the FARC-EP: The birth of the armed resistance," pp. 115–22 in *War in Colombia: Made in the U.S.A.,* ed. Rebecca Toledo, Teresa Gutierrez, Sara Flounders, and Andy McInerney. New York: International Action Centre.

Marx, Karl (1975a) "Letters from the Deutsch-Französische Jahrbücher," pp. 133–45 in *Collected Works Vol. 3: 1843–1844.* New York: International Publishers.

Marx, Karl (1975b) "Contribution to the critique of Hegel's philosophy of law," pp. 175–87 in *Collected Works Vol. 3: 1843–1844.* New York: International Publishers.

Marx, Karl (1975c) "Critical marginal notes on the article "The King of Prussia and social reform. By a Prussian," pp. 189–206 in *Collected Works Vol. 3: 1843–1844.* New York: International Publishers.

Marx, Karl (1975d) "Economic and philosophical manuscripts of 1844," pp. 229–346 in *Collected Works Vol. 3: 1843–1844.* New York: International Publishers.

Marx, Karl (1976a) "Theses on Feuerbach," pp. 1–5 in *Collected Works Vol. 5: 1845–47.* New York: International Publishers.

Marx, Karl (1976b) "Marx's speech: Speeches at the International Meeting held in London on November 29, 1847 to mark the 17th anniversary of the Polish Uprising of 1830," pp. 388–9 in *Collected Works Vol. 6: 1845–1848.* New York: International Publishers.

Marx, Karl (1977) "Wage labour and capital," pp. 197–228 in *Collected Works Vol. 9: 1849.* New York: International Publishers.

Marx, Karl (1978) "The Class Struggles in France, 1848 to 1850," pp. 45–145 in *Collected Works Vol. 10: 1849– 1951.* New York: International Publishers.

Marx, Karl (1987a) "Outlines of the *Critique of Political Economy* (rough draft of 1857–58) [second installment]," pp. 5–255 in *Collected Works Vol. 29: 1857–61.* New York: International Publishers.

Marx, Karl (1987b) "[Addenda to the chapter on Money and on Capital]," pp. 162– 251 in *Collected Works Vol. 29: 1857–1861* New York: International Publishers.

Marx, Karl (1987c) "A contribution to the critique of political economy," pp. 257–532 in *Collected Works Vol. 29: 1857–61.* New York: International Publishers.

Marx, Karl (1987d) "Marx to Engels," pp. 501–2 in *Collected Works Vol. 42: 1864–68*. New York: International Publishers.

Marx, Karl (1988a) "On the Hague Congress [A correspondent's report of a speech made at a meeting in Amsterdam on September 8th, 1872]," pp. 254–6 in *Collected Works Vol. 23: 1871–74*. New York: International Publishers.

Marx, Karl (1988b) "Marx to Laura and Paul Lafargue," pp. 446–50 in *Collected Works Vol. 43: 1968–1870*. New York: International Publishers.

Marx, Karl (1989a) "[Letter to Otechestvenniye Zapiski]," pp. 196–201 in *Collected Works Vol. 24: 1874–83*. New York: International Publishers.

Marx, Karl (1989b) "[Drafts of the letter to Vera Zasulich]," pp. 346–69 in *Collected Works Vol. 24: 1874–83*. New York: International Publishers.

Marx, Karl (1989c) "[Letter to Vera Zasulich]," pp. 370–1 in *Collected Works Vol. 24: 1874–83*. New York: International Publishers.

Marx, Karl (1989d) "Notes on Bakunin's Book *Statehood and Anarchy*," pp. 485–526 in *Collected Works Vol. 24: 1874–83*. New York: International Publishers.

Marx, Karl (1992a) "Marx to Vera Zasulich," pp. 71–2 in *Collected Works Vol. 46: 1880–1883*. New York: International Publishers.

Marx, Karl (1992b) "Marx to Jenny Longuet," pp. 81–5 in *Collected Works Vol. 46: 1880–1883*. New York: International Publishers.

Marx, Karl (1996a) "Preface to the First German Edition," pp. 7–11 in *Collected Works Vol. 35: Capital, Vol. 1*. New York: International Publishers.

Marx, Karl (1996b) "Capital: A critique of political economy, Volume I," pp. 3–761 in *Collected Works Vol. 35: Capital, Vol. I*. New York: International Publishers.

Marx, Karl and Frederick Engels (1976a) "Theses on Feuerbach (edited by Engels)," pp. 6–8 in *Collected Works Vol. 5: 1845–47*. New York: International Publishers.

Marx, Karl and Frederick Engels (1976b) "The German ideology," pp. 19–539 in *Collected Works Vol. 5: 1845–47*. New York: International Publishers.

Marx, Karl and Frederick Engels (1976c) "Manifesto of the Communist Party," pp. 476–519 in *Collected Works Vol. 6: 1845–48*. New York: International Publishers.

Marx, Karl and Frederick Engels (1989) "Preface to the Second Russian Edition of the *Manifesto of the Communist Party*," pp. 425–6 in *Collected Works Vol. 24: 1874–83*. New York: International Publishers.

Marx, Karl and Frederick Engels (1998) "Capital: A critique of political economy, Volume III," pp. 1–897 in *Collected Works Vol. 37: Capital, Vol. III*. New York: International Publishers.

Matta, Luis Alberto (2008) "¡Las Víctimas de la guerra sucia y el terrorismo de Estado en Colombia claman justicia!," March 6 [online] http://www.abpnoticias.com/boletin_temporal/contenido/articulos/colombia_6m4.html (accessed March 6, 2008).

Maullin, Richard (1973) *Soldiers, Guerrillas, and Politics in Colombia*. Lexington, Mass.: Lexington.

McClintock, Cynthia (1998) *Revolutionary Movements in Latin America: El Salvador's FMLN and Peru's Shining Path*. Washington DC: US Institute for Peace Press.

McClintock, Michael (1992) *Instruments of Statecraft: U.S. guerrilla warfare, counterinsurgency, and counterterrorism, 1940–1990*. New York: Pantheon.

McInerney, Andy (2003) "The Origin and Evolution of Plan Colombia," pp. 59–66 in *War In Colombia: Made in the U.S.A.*, ed. Rebecca Toledo, Teresa Gutierrez, Sara Flounders, and Andy McInerney. New York: International Action Center.

McKay, Ian (2005) *Rebels, Reds, Radicals: Rethinking Canada's left history*. Toronto, ON: Between the Lines.

McLellan, David (1971) *The Grundrisse: Karl Marx*. New York: Harper Torchbooks.

McNeely, Jeffrey A. (2003) "Conserving forest biodiversity in times of violent conflict," *Oryx*, 37(2): 142–52.

Melotti, Umberto (1977) *Marx and the Third World*. London: Macmillan.

Mercedes Pereira, Ana (2001) *Christianity, Poverty and Wealth in Colombia*. Brussels: Aprodev.

Mercopress (2008) "Uribe's tough hand on FARC issue balloons his popularity, 82%," March 14 [online] http://www.mercopress.com/vernoticia.do?id=12901& formato=HTML (accessed March 14, 2008).

Mercopress (2009) "Colombia Requests 10.4 billion from IMF Flexible Credit Line," April 21 [online] http://en.mercopress.com/2009/04/21/colombia-requests-10.4-billion-from-imf-flexible-credit-line (accessed April 22, 2009).

Mészáros, István (2006) "The structural crisis of politics," *Monthly Review*, 58(4): 34–53.

Miami Herald (2005) "Colombia," February 1 [online] http://www.miami.com/mld/miamiherald/news/world/america/10783610.htm (accessed February 18, 2005).

Mies, Maria (1986) *Patriarchy and Accumulation on a World Scale: Women and the international division of labour*. London: Zed.

Migdal, Joel S. (1974) *Peasants, Politics, and Revolution: Pressures toward political and social change in the Third World*. Princeton, N.C.: Princeton University Press.

Millar, Catherine (2003) "Retaking land in Colombia," September 18 [online]. http://globalresearch.ca/articles/MIL309A.html (accessed September 20, 2003).

Miller, Nicola (1989) *Soviet Relations with Latin America, 1959–1987*. New York: Cambridge University Press.

Ministerio de Defensa Nacional (2000) *Los Grupos ilegales de Autodefensa en Colombia*. Bogotá: Ministerio de Defensa Nacional.

Molano, Alfredo (1992) "Violence and land colonization," pp. 195–216 in *Violence in Colombia: The contemporary crisis in historical perspective*, ed. Charles Bergquist, Ricardo Peñaranda and Gonzalo Sánchez G. Wilmington, Del.: Scholarly Resources Inc.

Molano, Alfredo (2000) "The evolution of the FARC: A guerrilla group's long history," *NACLA Report on the Americas*, 34(2): 23–31.

Molano, Alfredo (2004) *Loyal Soldiers in the Cocaine Kingdom: Tales of drugs, mules, and gunmen*. New York: Columbia University Press.

Molano, Alfredo (2005) *The Dispossessed: Chronicles of the desterrados of Colombia*. Chicago, Ill.: Haymarket.

Molina, Mauricio Aranguren (2001) *Mi Confesión: Carlos Castaño revela sus secretos*. Bogotá: Editorial La Oveja Negra.

Mondragón, Héctor (2001) "Towards 'humanitarian intervention' in Colombia?" July [online] http://www.zmag.org/crisescurevts/colombia/hemon.htm (accessed September 24, 2002).

Mondragón, Héctor (2002) "Colombia: The struggle against Uribe begins," September 22 [online] http://www.zmag.org/content/showarticle.cfm?SectionID=9&ItemID=23 68 (accessed September 24, 2002).

Mondragón, Héctor (2003) "The bubble and the fleet," February 21 [online] http://www.zmag.org/sustainers/content/2003-02/21mondragon.cfm (accessed February 24, 2003).

Mondragón, Héctor (2006) "Colombia: Agrarian reform – fake and genuine," pp. 165–76 in *Promised Land: Competing visions of agrarian reform*, ed. Peter M. Rosset, Raj Patel, and Michael Courville. Oakland, Calif.: Institute for Food and Development Policy.

Mondragón, Héctor (2007) "Democracy and Plan Colombia," *NALCA Report on the Americas*, 40(1): 42–5.

Montoya, Germán (1991) "Recent trends in Colombian economic development and the place of Canada," pp. 170–4 in *Canada and Latin America: Issues of the Year 2000 and Beyond*, ed. Mark O. Dickerson and Stephen J. Randall. Calgary, AB: International Centre of the University of Calgary.

Moore, Barbara, Marta Núñez Sarmiento, and R. James Sacouman (2004) "Crisis, consequential Marxist intellectuals, and emergent forms of socialist community development in Cuba," paper delivered in Winnipeg, Manitoba for the Society for Socialist Studies, University of Manitoba, June 4.

Morales, Luis (2005) "Colombia on the brink" [online] September 8 http://www. baltimoresun.com/news/opinion/oped/balop.colombia08sep08,1,5877873. story?coll=bal-oped-headlines&ctrack=1&cset=true (accessed September 8, 2005).

Morris, Hollman (2006) "Views of the other Colombia," November 4 [online] http:// www.zmag.org/content/showarticle.cfm?SectionID=15&ItemID=11338 (accessed November 9, 2006).

Moser, Caroline O. N. and Cathy McIlwaine (2004) Encounters with Violence in Latin America: Urban perceptions from Colombia and Guatemala. New York: Routledge.

Motta de Correa, Lilian (1980) "Transformaciones de la Unidad Doméstica y el Trabajo de la Mujer Campesina en Una Zona de Avanzado Desarrollo Capitalista," pp. 117–224 in Mujer y Capitalismo Agrario, ed. Magdalena León de Leal. Bogotá: ACEP.

Müller, Ronald (1979) "The multinational corporation and the underdevelopment of the third world," pp. 151–78 in The Political Economy of Development and Underdevelopment, ed. Charles K. Wilber. New York: Random House.

Munck, Ronaldo (1984a) Politics and Dependency in the Third World: The case of Latin America. London: Zed.

Munck, Ronaldo (1984b) Revolutionary Trends in Latin America. Montreal, QC: Centre for Developing-Area Studies, McGill University.

Munck, Ronaldo (1989) Latin America: The transition to democracy. London: Zed.

Munck, Ronaldo (2008) Contemporary Latin America, 2nd edn. New York: Palgrave Macmillan.

Murch, Fiona (2000) Cocaine War. Documentary film (BBC).

Murillo, Mario A. (2005) "Presidential re-election in Colombia good news for paramilitaries," October 24 [online] www.colombiajournal.org/colombia220.htm (accessed October 24, 2005).

Murillo, Mario A. and Jesus Rey Avirama (2004) Colombia and the United States: War, unrest and destabilization. New York: Seven Stories.

Murphy, Helen (2008) "Colombia's Uribe approval rating at record 84%, Tiempo reports," March 13 [online] http://www.bloomberg.com/apps/news?pid=20601086 &sid=ahXLyUYpg6HE&refer=lati n_america (accessed March 15, 2008).

Muse, Toby (2004) "Paying the piper: Swamped with debt and fighting a war, Colombia's Uribe feels the heat inside and out," Latin Trade, 12(1): 22–3.

Muse, Toby (2006a) "Colombian elections marked by threats," March 10 [online] http:// news.yahoo.com/s/ap/20060310/ap_on_re_la_am_ca/colombia_election_intimidati on_1;_ylt=Ah1AxYtsOxoYBAU_YGfw1lqwv7kA;_ylu=X3oDMTBiMW04NW9mB HNlY wMlJVRPUCUl (accessed March 10, 2006).

Muse, Toby (2006b) "Colombian authorities urge paramilitary commander to surrender," August 25 [online] http://www.signonsandiego.com/news/world/20060825-1153-colombia- missingparamilitary.html (accessed August 27, 2006).

NACLA (1990) "Corrections," NACLA Report on the Americas, 24(2): 11.

NACLA (1998) "Multilateral invasion force for Colombia," NACLA Report on the Americas, 31(6): 46–7.

NACLA (1999) "Wall Street chief meets with Colombian Rebels," NACLA Report on the Americas, 33(1): 2–4.

NACLA (2000) "In the battalion: A soldier speaks," NACLA Report on the Americas, 34(2):42.

NACLA (2003) "Colombia: Paramilitary group agrees to peace talks," NACLA Report on the Americas, 37(2): 1–2.

Naiman, Joanne (2004) How Society Works: Class, power, and change in a Canadian context. Toronto, ON: Nelson-Thomson.

Nash, Kate (2000) *Contemporary Political Sociology: Globalization, politics, and power*. Malden, Mass.: Blackwell.

Neild, Rachel (2005) "U.S. policy assistance and drug control policies," pp. 61–97 in *Drugs and Democracy in Latin America: The impact of U.S. policy*, ed. Coletta A. Youngers and Eileen Rosin. Boulder, Colo.: Lynne Rienner.

Neira, Mauricio Archilla (2006) "Los movimientos sociales y las paradojas de la democracia en Colombia," *Controversia*, 186: 7–32.

Nelson, Richard R., T. Paul Shultz, and Robert L. Slighton (1971) *Structural Change in a Developing Economy: Colombia's problems and prospects*. Princeton, N.J.: Princeton University Press.

Norwegian Refugee Center (2003) *Conflict Increasingly Spreading to Urban Areas Causes Intra-Urban Displacements*. Norway: IDP Project.

Noticias Aliadas (2006) "US and Colombia reach FTA," March 9 [online] http://www.latinamericapress.org/article.asp?IssCode=&lanCode=1&artCode=4596 (accessed May 2, 2006).

Novosti Press Agency (1969) *Lenin and Problems of Liberation Movement*. Moscow: Novosti.

National Union of Public and General Employees (NUPGE) (2004) *Colombia: Victims of War*. Nepean, ON: National Union Publications.

O'Donoghue, Patrick J. (2003) "UN adviser snubs USA ... "FARC is NOT a terrorist group," May 19 [online] http://www.vheadline.com/readnews.asp?id=7487 (accessed March 16, 2006).

O'Grady, Maria Anastasia (2005) "Seeking the truth about a massacre in a Colombian hamlet," *Wall Street Journal*, September 23. p. A17.

O'Shaughnessy, Hugh (2008) "More popular than Enver Hoxha," August 5 [online] http://www.newstatesman.com/south-america/2008/08/colombia-lies-cocaine (accessed August 6, 2008).

O'Shaughnessy, Hugh and Sue Branford (2005) *Chemical Warfare in Colombia: The costs of coca fumigation* London: Latin American Bureau.

Obando, Liliany (2004) "Colombia in crisis: State and paramilitary violence against the campesino population," International Studies Special Lecture for International Studies at the University of New Brunswick (St John), March 24.

Obando, Liliany (2005) "Organic class-consciousness in rural Colombia," International Development Studies Special Lecture Series for the Department of Political Science at University of New Brunswick (Fredericton), November 21.

Obando, Liliany and John Velásquez (2004) *Tras Las Huellas de la Resistencia*. Documentary film (independent).

Office of National Drug Control Policy (ONDCP) (2005) *2004 Coca and Opium Poppy Estimates for Colombia and the Andes*. Washington, DC: White House.

ONDCP (2006) *2005 Coca Estimates for Colombia*. Washington, DC: White House.

ONDCP (2007) *2006 Coca Estimates for Colombia*. Washington, DC: White House.

ONDCP (2008) "Official U.S. Colombia survey reveals sharp decline in cocaine production," September 10 http://www.whitehousedrugpolicy.gov/news/press08/091008.html [online] (accessed September 14, 2008).

Oquist, Paul (1980) *Violence, Conflict, and Politics in Colombia*. New York: Academic Press.

Organization of American States (OAS), Government of Colombia, Government of Ecuador (1995) *Physical Planning and Management Plan for the San Miguel and Putumayo River Basins: Executive Summary*. Washington, DC: Department of Regional Development and Environment Executive Secretariat and Economic Social Affairs General Secretariat of the OAS.

Ortiz, Román D. (2002) "Insurgent strategies in the post-cold war: The case of the Revolutionary Armed Forces of Colombia," *Studies in Conflict and Terrorism*, 25(2): 127–44.

Ortiz, Román D. (2006) "Renew to last: Innovation and strategy of the Revolution-ary Armed Forces of Colombia (FARC)," pp. 205–22 in *Teaching Terror: Strategic and tactical learning in the terrorist world*, ed. James J. F. Forest. Boulder, Colo.: Rowman & Littlefield.

Ortiz, Sutti Reissig (1971) "Reflections on the concept of 'peasant culture' and 'peas-ant cognitive systems'," pp. 322–36 in *Peasants and Peasant Societies*, ed. Teodor Shanin. New York: Penguin.

Ortiz, Sutti Reissig (1973) *Uncertainties in Peasant Farming: A Colombian case*. New York: University of London/Humanities Press.

Oslender, Ulrich (2008) "Another history of violence: The production of "geographies of terror" in Colombia's Pacific Coast region," *Latin American Perspectives*, 35(5): 77–102.

Osterling, Jorge P. (1989) *Democracy in Colombia: Clientalist politics and guerrilla warfare*. Oxford, UK: Transaction.

Otis, John (2004) "Rebel held" [online] http://www.chron.com/content/chronicle/special/01/farc/briceno.html (accessed September 8, 2005).

Otis, John (2008a) "Colombia airstrike kills senior rebel leader," March 1 [online] http://www.chron.com/disp/story.mpl/headline/world/5585016.html (accessed March 2, 2008).

Otis, John (2008b) "Demise of rebel hurts, but FARC may still be a threat," May 26 [online] http://www.chron.com/disp/story.mpl/world/5801599.html (accessed May 27, 2008).

Pablo Toro, Juan (2004) "Colombia says it's winning vs. rebels," November 11 [online] http://www.kansascity.com/mld/kansascity/news/10156999.htm (accessed November 11, 2004).

Padgett, Tim and Ruth Morris (2004) "The new druglords," June 13 [online] http://www.time.com/time/europe/magazine/article/0,13005,901040621-650686,00.html (accessed June 21, 2004).

Paige, Jeffrey M. (1975) *Agrarian Revolution: Social movements and export agriculture in the underdeveloped world*. New York: Free Press.

Paige, Jeffrey M. (1988) "One, two, or many Vietnams? Social theory and peasant revolution in Vietnam and Guatemala," pp. 145–79 in *Global Crises and Social Movements: Artisans, peasants, populists, and the world economy*, ed. Edmund Burke, III. London: Westview.

Paige, Jeffrey M. (2003) "Finding the revolutionary in the revolution: Social science concepts and the future of revolution," pp. 19–29 in *The Future of Revolutions: Rethinking radical change in the age of globalization*, ed. John Foran. London: Zed.

Palacios, Marco (2006) *Between Legitimacy and Violence: A history of Colombia, 1875–2002*. Durham, N.C:. Duke University Press.

Parenti, Michael (2002) *The Terrorism Trap: September 11*[th] *and beyond*. San Francisco, Calif.: City Lights.

Parrar, William (2004) "Colombian rebels say leader is alive and well," July 21 [online] http://www.alertnet.org/thenews/newsdesk/N21453844.htm (accessed July 21, 2004).

Paternostro, Silvana (2007) *My Colombian War: A journey through the country I left behind*. New York: Henry Holt.

Payne, James L. (1968) *Patterns of Conflict in Colombia*. London: Yale University Press.

Peace and Socialism (1966) *Colombia: An embattled land*. Prague: Peace and Socialism.

Pearce, Jenny (2007) "Oil and armed conflict in Casanare, Colombia: Complex contexts and contingent moments," pp. 225–73 in *Oil Wars*, ed. Mary Kaldor, Terry Lynn Karl, and Yahia Said. London: Pluto.

Pearce, Jenny (1990a) *Colombia: Inside the labyrinth*. London: Latin American Bureau.

Pearce, Jenny (1990b) *Colombia: The drug war*. New York: Aladdin.

Pearse, Andrew (1982) "The making of rural proletarians: Sugar estate workers in El Valle," pp. 63–7 in *Third World Lives of Struggles*, ed. Hazel Johnson and Henry Bernstein. New York: Heinemann Educational Books/Open University.

Peceny, Mark and Michael Durnan (2006) "The FARC's best friend: U.S. antidrug policies and the deepening of Colombia's civil war in the 1990s," *Latin American Politics & Society*, 48(2): 95–116.

Peeler, John A. (1985) *Latin American Democracies: Colombia, Costa Rica, Venezuela*. Chapel Hill, N.C.: University of North Carolina Press.

Penhaul, Karl (2000) "Colombia's rebels hit the airwaves," December 24 [online] http://archives.lists.indymedia.org/imc-houston/2001-January/000277.html (accessed May 12, 2004).

Penhaul, Karl (2001) "Colombia's communist guerrillas take on a feminine face," *Global Correspondent, Boston Globe*, January 7. p. A6.

People's Daily (2006a) "Colombian gov't plans temporary tax to raise money for military," July 7 [online] http://english.people.com.cn/200607/07/eng20060707_280962.html (accessed July 8, 2006).

People's Daily (2006b) "Colombian authorities seize rebel medial center, dismantle car bomb in capital," August 3 [online] http://english.people.com.cn/200608/03/eng20060803_289531.html (accessed August 3, 2006).

Pérez, Jerónimo (2003) "We will not stay quiet," *Peace News*, 2449 (no page nos).

Perkins, John (2008) *The Secret History of the American Empire*. London: Plume.

Petras, James (1968) "Revolution and guerrilla movements in Latin America: Venezuela, Colombia, Guatemala, and Peru," pp. 329–69 in *Latin America, Reform or Revolution? A reader*, ed. James Petras and Maurice Zeitlin. Greenwich, N.Y.: Fawcett.

Petras, James (1997a) "Imperialism and NGOs in Latin America," *Monthly Review*, 49(7): 10–26.

Petras, James (1997b) "Latin America: The resurgence of the left," *New Left Review*, 223: 17–47.

Petras, James (1999) *The Left Strikes Back: Class conflict in the age of neoliberalism*. Boulder, Colo.: Westview.

Petras, James (2001a) "Neo mercantilist empire in Latin America: Bush, ALCA and Plan Colombia," June 17 [online] http://www.rebelion.org/petras/english/bush-alca170102.htm (accessed November 23, 2002).

Petras, James (2001b) *"Dirty Money" Foundation of US Growth and Empire: Size and scope of money laundering by US banks*. Montreal, QE: Centre for Research on Globalization;

Petras, James (2002) "U.S. offensive in Latin America: Coups, retreats, and radicalization," *Monthly Review*, 54(1): 15–31.

Petras, James (2003) *The New Development Politics: The age of empire building and new social movements*. Hampshire, UK: Ashgate.

Petras, James (2004) "Prologue," . pp. 8–9 in *El Marxisno Ideologia en Constucción: Dos entrevistas sobre temas de actualidad*, ed. Lilia Martelo and Carlos A. Lozano Guillén. Bogotá: Ideas y Soluciones Gráficas Derechos Reservados

Petras, James (2008) *Homage to Manuel Marulanda*. Personal correspondence.

Petras, James and Michael M. Brescia (2000) "The FARC faces the empire," *Latin American Perspectives*, 27(5): 134–42.

Petras, James and Timothy F. Harding (2000) "Introduction," *Latin American Perspectives*, 27(5): 3–10.

Petras, James and Robert LaPorte Jr. (1971) *Cultivating Revolution: The United States and agrarian reform in Latin America*. New York: Random House.

Petras, James and Morris Morley (1990) *US Hegemony under Siege: Class, politics and development in Latin America*. New York: Verso.

Petras, James and Morris Morley (1992) *Latin America in the Time of Cholera: Electoral politics, market economics, and permanent crisis.* New York: Routledge.

Petras, James and Morris Morley (1995) *Empire and Power: American global power and domestic decay.* London: Routledge.

Petras, James and Morris Morley (2003) "The geopolitics of Plan Colombia," pp. 83–108 in *Masters of War: Militarism and blowback in the era of the American empire,* ed. Carl Boggs. New York: Routledge.

Petras, James and Henry Veltmeyer (2001) *Globalization Unmasked: Imperialism in the 21st century.* Halifax, NS: Fernwood.

Petras, James and Henry Veltmeyer (2003a) *System in Crisis: The dynamics of free market capitalism.* Halifax, NS: Fernwood.

Petras, James and Henry Veltmeyer (2003b) "The peasantry and the state in Latin America: A troubled past, an uncertain future," pp. 41–82 in *Latin American Peasants,* ed. Tom Brass. London: Frank Cass.

Petras, James and Henry Veltmeyer (2005a) *Social Movements and State Power: Argentina, Brazil, Bolivia, Ecuador.* London: Pluto.

Petras, James and Henry Veltmeyer (2005b) *Las Dos Caras del Imperialismo: Vasallos y guerreros.* Buenos Aires: Grupo Editorial Lumen.

Petras, James, Henry Veltmeyer, Luciano Vasapollo, and Maurco Casadio (2005) *Empire with Imperialism: The globalizing dynamics of neo-liberal capitalism.* Halifax, NS: Fernwood.

Pizarro Leongómez, Eduardo (1991) *Historia de La Guerrilla – Las FARC: De la auto-defensa a la combinacion de todas las formas de lucha (1949–1966)* Bogotá: Tercer Mundo Editores (Instituto de Estudios Políticos y Relaciones Internacionales de la Universidad Nacional de Colombia.

Pizarro Leongómez, Eduardo (1992) "Revolutionary guerrilla groups in Colombia," pp. 169–94 in *Violence in Colombia: The contemporary crisis in historical perspective.* ed. Charles W. Bergquist, Ricardo Peñaranda, and Gonzalo Sánchez, Wilmington, Del.: Scholarly Resources.

Pizzaro Leongómez, Eduardo (1996) *Insurgencia sin Revolución: La guerrilla en Colombia en una perspectiva Comparada.* Bogotá: Tercer Mundo Editores.

Polo Democratico Alternativo, POLO (2008a) *For the Humanitarian Accord: No to war, no to kidnappings.* Bogotá: Polo Democratico Alternativo.

Polo Democratico Alternativo, POLO (2008b) *A Humanitarian Agreement is Urgently Needed to Respect Life and Dignity Statement on 4 Feb Demonstrations against the FARC from the Colombia Solidarity Campaign.* London, UK/Bogotá: Polo Democratico Alternativo.

Pomeroy, William J. (1964) *Guerrilla and Counter-Guerrilla Warfare: Liberation and suppression in the present period.* New York: International Publishers.

Pomeroy, William J. (1968) *Guerrilla Warfare and Marxism: A collection of writings from Karl Marx to the present on armed struggles for liberation and for Socialism.* New York: International Publishers.

Poppino, Rollie (1964) *International Communism in Latin America: A history of the movement, 1917–1963.* New York: Free Press.

Posada Carbó, Eduardo (2006) *La nación soñada: Violencia, liberalismo y democracia en Colombia.* Bogotá: Editorial Norma.

Post, Ken and Phil Wright (1989) *Socialism and Underdevelopment.* London: Routledge.

Pothecary, Chris (2001) "Three months in Caquetá," April 30 [online] http://www.colombiajournal.org/colombia61.htm (accessed September 21, 2003).

Poulsen, Frank Piasecki (2005) *Guerrillera.* Documentary film (Zetropa Real).

Powelson, John P. (1964) *Latin America: Today's economic and social revolution.* New York: McGraw-Hill.

Pravda (2005) "Colombia: regional intelligence chief surrenders to authorities," November 16 [online] http://newsfromrussia.com/world/2005/11/16/67827.html (accessed November 16, 2005).

Premo, Daniel L. (1988) "Coping with insurgency: The politics of pacification in Colombia and Venezuela," pp. 219–44 in Democracy in Latin America: Colombia and Venezuela, ed. Donald L. Herman. Westport, Conn.: Praeger.

Prensa Latina (2006a) "Colombia slashes FTA victims' aid," April 25 [online] http://www.plenglish.com/article.asp?ID=%7B218171C1-50E7-4073-A019-39A644FC0AC6%7D&language=EN (accessed April 27, 2006).

Prensa Latina (2006b) "Paraguay press expose plot against FARC," June 7 [online] http://www.plenglish.com/article.asp?ID=%7BEA6DD5C1-6150-42F9-865A-F1E7FA028562%7D&language=EN (accessed June 19, 2006).

Prensa Latina (2006c) "Colombia, half of population is poor," October 16 [online] http://www.plenglish.com/article.asp?ID=%7BA84B4696-97D0-4402-8C33- D6EB5BE21BAC%7D&language=EN (accessed October 17, 2006).

Prensa Latina (2007) "Bush protests close Colombia colleges," March 9 [online] http://www.plenglish.com/article.asp?ID=%7BCEAC6000-CEB4- 11DB-8B79- 0010B58BBF92%7D)&language=EN (accessed March 10, 2007).

Prensa Latina (2008) "Peru asks OAS to mediate Colombia crisis," March 3 [online] http://www.plenglish.com/article.asp?ID=%7B3F1BD8E7-D6A8-4E81-9087- 6DC6920E3AF8%7D&language=EN (accessed March 4, 2008).

Quintanilla, Carlos (2005) "Neoliberalism and poverty," February 2 [online] http://www.anncol.org/side/1155 (accessed February 4, 2005).

Rabe, Stephen G. (1999) The Most Dangerous Area in the World in the World: John F. Kennedy confronts communist revolution in Latin America. Chapel Hill, N.C.: University of North Carolina Press.

Raby, D. L. (2006) Democracy and Revolution: Latin America and Socialism today. London: Pluto.

Ramírez, Francisco Cellular (2005) The Profits of Extermination: How U.S. corporate power is destroying Colombia. Monroe, ME: Common Courage.

Ramírez Lemus, María, Kimberly Stanton, and John Walsh (2005) "Colombia: A vicious circle of drugs and war," pp. 99–142 in Drugs and Democracy in Latin America: The impact of U.S. policy, ed. Coletta A. Youngers and Eileen Rosin. Boulder, Colo.: Lynne Rienner.

Ramírez Tobón, William. (1981) "La guerrilla rural: Una via hacia la colonización armada," Estudios Rurales Latinoamericanos, 4(2): 199–209.

Ramírez-Vallejo, Jorge (2003) "Colombian coffee: The Colombian Federation of Coffee Growers (FEDERACAFE)," ReVista: Harvard Review of Latin America, 2(3): Online article.

Randall, Stephen J. (1992) Colombia and the United States: Hegemony and interdependence. London: University of Georgia Press.

Randall, Stephen J. (2001) "US foreign policy and Colombian national security," June [online] http://www.mamacoca.org/junio2001/abs_randall_politica_exterior_en.htm (accessed May 3, 2002).

Randall, Stephen J. (2002) "Colombia: Can democracy save this troubled nation?" Calgary Herald, May 23. p. A23.

Rangel Suárez, Alfredo (1998) Colombia: Guerra en el Fin de Siglo. Bogotá: Tercer Mundo.

Rangel Suárez, Alfredo (2000) "Parasites and predators: Guerrillas and the insurrection economy of Colombia," Journal of International Economic Affairs, 53(2): 577–601.

Rangel Suárez, Alfredo (2004) (Coyuntura de Seguridad – Informe Especial) El Repliegue de Las FARC: ¿Derrota O Estrategia? Bogotá: Fundación Seguridad y Democracia.

Ratliff, William E. (1976) *Castroism and Communism in Latin America, 1959–1976: The varieties of Marxist-Leninist experience.* Washington, DC: American Enterprise Institute for Public Policy Research.

Ravallion, Martin, Shaohua Chen, and Prem Sangraula (2008) *Dollar a Day Revised.* Policy Research Working Paper 4620. Washington, DC: World Bank.

Reed, Evelyn (1969) *A Marxist Approach: Problems of women's liberation.* New York: Merit.

Registraduría Nacional del Estado Civil (2002) "Votacion a nivel nacional," June 7 [online] http://www.registraduria.gov.co/2002PRP1/e/vpresidente0.htm?1 (accessed June 8, 2006).

Registraduría Nacional del Estado Civil (2006) "Boletín nacional: escrutinios," June 21 [online] http://www.registraduria.gov.co/2002PRP1/e/vpresidente0.htm?1 (accessed January 8, 2007).

Reichel-Dolmatoff, Gerardo (1965) *Colombia: Ancient peoples and places.* New York: Frederick A. Praeger.

Reinhardt, Nola (1988) *Our Daily Bread: The peasant question and family farming in the Colombian Andes.* Berkeley, Calif.: University of California Press.

Rempe, Dennis (1995) "Guerrillas, bandits, and independent republics: U.S. counter-insurgency efforts in Colombia, 1959–1965," *Small Wars and Insurgencies,* 6(3): 304–27.

Renner, Michael (2002) *The Anatomy of Resource Wars.* Washington, DC: Worldwatch Institute.

Restrepo, Jorge and Michael Spagat (2004) *The Colombian Conflict: Uribe's first 17 months.* Discussion Paper 4570. Bogotá: CEPR.

Restrepo, Juan Camilo (2003) "Tierras sin hombres y hombres sin tierras," January 15 [online] http://www.juancamilo.com.co/articulos50.htm (accessed March 14, 2006).

Restrepo M., Luis Alberto (2003) "The equivocal dimensions of human rights in Colombia," pp. 95–126 in *Violence in Colombia 1990–2000: Waging war and negotiating peace,* ed. Charles W. Bergquist, Ricardo Peñaranda, and Gonzalo Sánchez G. Wilmington, Del.: Scholarly Resources.

Reuters (2003) "Colombia eyes meeting between U.N. and FARC rebels," September 1 [online] http://edition.cnn.com/2003/WORLD/americas/08/31/colombia.peace.talks.reut/ (accessed September 4, 2003).

Reuters (2004) "Colombian rebels say leader is alive and well," July 21 [online] http://www.alertnet.org/thenews/newsdesk/N21453844.htm (accessed July 21, 2004).

Reuters (2006a) "Colombia's Uribe wants assets tax to fund military," March 29 [online] http://today.reuters.com/investing/financeArticle.aspx?type=bondsNews&storyID =2006- 03-29T175122Z_01_N29333924_RTRIDST_0_ECONOMY-COLOMBIA- ELECTION.XML (accessed March 30, 2006).

Reuters (2006b) "US embassy warns of possible Colombia rebel attack," September 22 [online] http://www.alertnet.org/thenews/newsdesk/N22199469.htm (accessed September 22, 2006).

Reuters (2008a) "Nicaragua says Colombia is a threat to region," March 3 [online] http://www.reuters.com/article/latestCrisis/idUSN04420712 (accessed March 4, 2008).

Reuters (2008b) "Mexico criticizes Colombia's Ecuador raid," March 5 [online] http://www.reuters.com/article/topNews/idUSN0454853320080305 (accessed March 5, 2008).

Reuters (2008c) "Colombia says rebels bomb oil pipeline," May 2 [online] http://www.reuters.com/article/latestCrisis/idUSN02168489 (accessed May 5, 2008).

Reuters (2008d) "Colombia coal train bombed, exports unaffected," May 27 [online] http://www.reuters.com/article/latestCrisis/idUSN27385573 (accessed May 28, 2008).

Reuters (2008e) "Colombia coal train bombed, exports affected," May 27 [online] http://uk.reuters.com/article/oilRpt/idUKN2738075020080527 (accessed May 29, 2008).

Riaño-Alcalá, Pilar (2006) *Dwellers of Memory: Youth and violence in Medellín, Colombia*. New Brunswick, N.J.: Transaction.

Richani, Nazih (1997) "The political economy of violence: The war system in Colombia," *Journal of Interamerican Studies and World Affairs*, 39(2): 37–81.

Richani, Nazih (2000) "The paramilitary connection," *NACLA Report on the Americas*, 34(2): 38–41.

Richani, Nazih (2001) "The political economy of Colombia's protracted civil war and the crisis of the war system," *Journal of Conflict Studies*, 21(2): 50–77.

Richani, Nazih (2002a) *Systems of Violence: The political economy of war and peace in Colombia*. New York: SUNY.

Richani, Nazih (2002b) "Colombia at the crossroads: The future of the peace accords," *NACLA Report on the Americas*, 35(4): 17–20.

Richani, Nazih (2005a) "Multinational corporations, rentier capitalism, and the war system in Colombia," *Latin American Politics and Society*, 47(3): 113–44.

Richani, Nazih (2005b) "Third parties, war system's inertia and conflict termination: The doomed peace process in Colombia, 1998–2002," *Journal of Conflict Studies*, 25(2): 75–103.

Richani, Nazih (2007) "Caudillos and the crisis of the Colombian state: Fragmented sovereignty, the war system and the privatisation of the counterinsurgency in Colombia," *Third World Quarterly*, 28(2): 403–17.

Richardson, Miles (1970) *San Pedro, Colombia: Small town in a developing society*. New York: Holt, Rinehart & Winston.

Ridler, Neil B. (1978) "Government policy options for agrarian reform in Colombia," *Desarrollo Rural en las Américas*, 10(1): 37–45.

Ridler, Neil B. (1983) "Labour force and land distribution effects of agricultural technology," *World Development*, 11(7): 593–9.

Rizvi, Haider (2006) "US-backed coca spraying mostly hurts legal farmers," August 26 [online] http://www.antiwar.com/ips/rizvi.php?articleid=9611 (accessed August 29, 2006).

Rochester, Anne (1942) *Lenin on the Agrarian Question*. New York: International Publishers.

Rochlin, James F. (2003) *Vanguard Revolutionaries in Latin America: Peru, Colombia, Mexico*. London: Lynne Rienner.

Rochlin, James F. (2007) *Social Forces and the Revolution in Military Affairs: The cases of Colombia and Mexico*. New York: Palgrave Macmillan.

Rodríguez, Guillermo Hernández (1949) *De los Chibchas a la Colonia y a La República*. Bogotá: Universidad Nacional de Colombia.

Rogers, Everett M. (1969) *Modernization among Peasants: The impact of communication*. New York: Holt, Rinehart & Winston.

Röhl, Katharina (2004) "Greed or governance: Why does the FARC keep fighting?" February 9 [online] http://www.monitor.upeace.org/Colombia.pdf (accessed May 15, 2007).

Rojas, Christina (2005) "Elusive peace, elusive violence: Identity and conflict in Colombia," pp. 209–38 in *Elusive Peace: International, national, and local dimension of conflict in Colombia*, ed. Christina Rojas and Judy Meltzer, New York: Palgrave Macmillan.

Rojas, Christina (2006) *The Securitization of Citizenship under Colombia's Democratic Security Policy*. CERLAC Bulletin 5(5), Toronto, ON: CERLAC.

Rojas, Humbero and Alfredo Molano (1986) "Agrarian politics and peasant organizations in Colombia," pp. 328–41 in *Third World Peasantry: A continuing saga of deprivation*, ed. R. P. Misra and Nguyen Tri Dung. New Delhi: Sterling.

Roldán, Mary (2003) *Blood and Fire: La Violencia in Antioquia, Colombia, 1946–1953*. Durham, N.C.: Duke University Press.

Roman, Fernando (2000) "Plan Colombia means war," October [online] http://www.internationalviewpoint.org/spip.php?article743 (accessed September 4, 2003).

Romero, Mauricio (2003) *Paramilitares y Autodefensas, 1982–2003*. Bogotá, DC: Instituto de Estudios Políticos y Relaciones Internacionales.

Romero, Simon (2007) "Death-squad scandal circles closer to Colombia's president," May 16 [online] http://www.nytimes.com/2007/05/16/world/americas/16colombia.html?n=Top%2 fRefere nce%2fTimes%20Topics%2fPeople%2fR%2fRomero%2c%20Simon (accessed May 18, 2007).

Roseberry, William (1993) "Beyond the agrarian question in Latin America," pp. 318–68 in *Confronting Historical Paradigms: Peasants, labor, and the capitalist world system in Africa and Latin America*, ed. Frederica Cooper, Florencia E. Mallon, Steve J. Stern, Allen F. Isaacman, and William Roseberry. Madison, Wis.: University of Wisconsin Press.

Ross, Eric B. (2006) "Clearance as development strategy in rural Colombia," *Peace Review* 19(1): 59–65.

Rubio, Mauricio (1999) *Crimen e Impunidad: Precisiones sobre la Violencia*. Bogotá: Tercer Mundo.

Rueda, Manuel (2008) "World Report – March 7," Canadian Broadcasting Corporation Radio One (personally received from Judy Maddren via email, March 7, 2008).

Ruhl, J. Mark (1980) "The military," pp. 181–206 in *Politics of Compromise: Coalition government in Colombia*, ed. R. Albert Berry, Ronald G. Hellman, and Mauricio Solaún. New Brunswick, N.J.: Transaction.

Ruhl, J. Mark (1981) "Civil–military relations in Colombia: A societal explanation," *Journal of Interamerican Studies and World Affairs*, 23(2): 123–46.

Ruiz, Bert (2001) *The Colombian Civil War*. Jefferson, N.C.: McFarland.

Ryan, Henry Butterfield (1998) *The Fall of Che Guevara: A story of soldiers, spies, and diplomats*. New York: Oxford University Press.

Sachs, Wolfgang and Tilman Santarius (2007) *Fair Future: Resistance, conflicts, security and global justice*. London: Zed.

Sacouman, R. James (1999) *Social Theory for a Change: Vital issues in the classics*. Toronto, ON: Irwin.

Sáenz V., Jorge (2008) "Uribe prefiere más gasto público y deuda, a mayor pobreza" November 1 [online] http://www.elespectador.com/noticias/negocios/articulo87432-uribe-prefiere- mas-gasto-publico-y-deuda-mayor-pobreza (accessed November 2, 2008).

Safford, Frank and Marco Palacios (2003) *Colombia: Fragmented land, divided society*. New York: Oxford University Press.

Salmón, Gary Prado (1990) *The Defeat of Che Guevara: Military response to guerrilla challenge in Bolivia*. New York: Praeger.

Sánchez G., Gonzalo (1985) "*La Violencia* in Colombia: New research, new questions," *Hispanic American Historical Review*, 65(4): 789–807.

Sánchez G., Gonzalo (1992) "The Violence: An interpretive synthesis," pp. 75–124 in *Violence in Colombia: The contemporary crisis in historical perspective*, ed. Charles W. Bergquist, Ricardo Peñaranda, and Gonzalo Sánchez G. Wilmington, Del.: Scholarly Resources.

Sánchez G., Gonzalo (2000) "War and politics in Colombian society," *International Journal of Politics, Culture and Society*, 14(1): 19–49.

Sánchez G., Gonzalo (2003) "Problems of violence, prospects for peace," pp. 1–38 in *Violence in Colombia 1990–2000: Waging war and negotiating peace*, ed. Charles W. Bergquist, Ricardo Peñaranda, and Gonzalo Sánchez G. Wilmington, Del.: Scholarly Resources.

Sánchez G., Gonzalo and Donny Meertens (2001) *Bandits, Peasants and Politics: The case of "La Violencia" in Colombia*. Austin, Tex.: University of Texas.

Sanders, Thomas G. (1981) "Food policy and decision-making in Colombia," pp. 82–102 in *The Politics of Agrarian Change in Asia and Latin America*, ed. Howard Handelman, Bloomington, Ind.: Indiana University Press.

Sanderson, Stephen K. (2005) *Revolutions: A worldwide introduction to political and social change*. Vancouver, BC: University of British Columbia Press.

Santiso, Javier (2006) *Latin America's Political Economy of the Possible: Beyond good revolutions and free-marketeers*. Cambridge, Mass.: MIT Press.

Sargent, Lydia (1981) *Women and Revolution: A discussion of the unhappy marriage of Marxism and feminism*. Montreal, QC: Black Rose.

Satchell, Michael (1999) "Enviro-guerrillas," *U.S. New and World Report*, 126(3): 41.

Saul, John S. (2006) *Development after Globalization: Theory and practice for the embattled south in the new imperial age*. London: Zed.

Saunders, John, J. Michael Davis, Galen C. Moses, and James E. Ross (1978) *Rural Electrification and Development: Social and economic impact in Costa Rica and Colombia*. Boulder, Colo.: Westview.

Scheina, Robert L. (2003) *Latin America's Wars: The age of the professional soldier, 1900–2001 – Volume 2*. Dulles, VI: Brassey's.

Schulte-Bockholt, Alfredo (2006) *The Politics of Organized Crime and the Organized Crime of Politics: A study in criminal power*. Lanham, Md.: Lexington.

Scott, James C. (1977) "Hegemony and the peasantry," *Politics and Society*, 7(3): 267–296.

Scott, Peter Dale (2003) *Drugs, Oil, and War: The United States in Afghanistan, Colombia, and Indochina*. New York: Rowman & Littlefield.

Scott, Peter Dale and Jonathon Marshall (1998) *Cocaine Politics: Drugs, armies, and the CIA in Central America*. Berkeley, Calif.: University of California Press.

Selbin, Eric (1997) "Revolution in the real world: Bringing agency back in," pp. 123–36 in *Theorizing Revolutions*, ed. John Foran. London: Routledge.

Selsky, Andrew (2004) "Colombia DEA chief discusses targets," January 21 [online] http://archive.wn.com/2004/01/23/1400/bogota/ (accessed January 22, 2004).

Selsky, Andrew (2005) "Report: Colombia coca cultivation remains," April 1 [online] http://www.guardian.co.uk/worldlatest/story/0,1280,-4907643,00.html (accessed April 2, 2005).

Semana (2005) "Las cuentas de las FARC," January 30 [online] http://semana.terra.com.co/opencms/opencms/Semana/articulo.html?id=84475 (accessed February 18, 2005).

Semana (2007) "Petro dice que en finca 'Las Guacharacas', de propiedad del Presidente Álvaro Uribe, los 'paras' asesinaron campesinos," April 17 [online] http://www.semana.com/wf_InfoArticulo.aspx?idArt=102213 (accessed May 24, 2007).

Semana (2008a) "Julián Conrado, el hombre de confianza de 'Raúl Reyes'," March 1 [online] http://www.semana.com/wf_InfoArticulo.aspx?IdArt=109879 (accessed March 18, 2008).

Semana (2008b) "Interview with William J. Burns, Under Secretary for Political Affairs at the State Department," October 22 [online] http://www.semana.com/multimedia-english/interview- with-william-burns-under-secretary-for-political-affairs-at-the-state-department/1151.aspx (accessed October 23, 2008).

Semana (2008c) "U.S. Ambassador says economic crisis will weaken the 'Plan Colombia'," October 24 [online] http://www.semana.com/noticias-headlines/us-ambassador-says-economic-crisis-will-weaken-the-plan-colombia/116974.aspx (accessed October 25, 2008).

Semana (2008d) "Colombia's human rights challenge," November 3 [online] http://www.semana.com/noticias-print-edition/colombias-human-rights- challenge/117351.aspx (accessed November 3, 2008).

Semana (2008e) "The story behind the military shake up," November 4 [online] http://www.semana.com/noticias-print-edition/the-story-behind-the-military-shake-up/117375.aspx (accessed November 4, 2008).

Semana (2009) "'En la selva el tiempo cuenta doble': Alan Jara," February 3 [online] http://www.semana.com/noticias-conflicto-armado/selva-tiempo-cuenta-doble-alan jara/120384.aspx (accessed February 6, 2009).

Shafer, Michael D. (1994) *Winners and Losers: How sectors shape the development prospects of states.* London: Cornell University Press.

Shah, Saira (2002) *Colombia: The pipeline war.* Documentary film (Frontline World).

Shanin, Teodor (1983) *Late Marx and the Russian Road: Marx and 'the peripheries of capitalism'.* New York: Monthly Review Press.

Shannon, Elaine (1989) *Desperados.* New York: Penguin.

Sharpless, Richard E. (1978) *Gaitán of Colombia: A political biography.* Pittsburgh, Penn.: University of Pittsburgh Press.

Shaw, R. Paul (1976) *Land Tenure and the Rural Exodus in Chile, Colombia, Costa Rica, and Peru.* Gainesville, Fla.: University Presses of Florida.

Shifter, Michael (1999) "Colombia on the brink," *Foreign Affairs,* 78(4): 14–21.

Shnookal, Deborah (2003) *One Hundred Hot Years: Big moments of the 20th century.* New York: Ocean.

Shugart, Matthew Soberg (1992) "Guerrillas and elections: An intuitionalist perspective on the costs of conflict and competition," *International Studies Quarterly,* 36: 121–52.

Shultz, T. Paul (1970) *Rural–Urban Migration in Colombia.* Santa Monica, Calif.: Rand Corporation.

Simons, Geoff (2004) *Colombia: A brutal history.* London: SAQI.

SIPRI Military Expenditure Database (2005) "Colombia," February 10 [online] http://first.sipri.org/non_first/result_milex.php?send (accessed February 10, 2005).

Skidmore, Thomas E. and Peter H. Smith (2005) *Modern Latin America,* 6th edn. New York: Oxford University Press.

Sklair, Leslie (1973) *Organized Knowledge: A sociological view of science and technology.* London: Paladin.

Sklair, Leslie (2002) *Globalization: Capitalism and its Alternatives.* Oxford, UK: Oxford University Press.

Skocpol, Theda (1976) "France, Russia, and China: Structural analysis of social revolutions," *Comparative Studies of Society and History,* 18(2): 175–210.

Skocpol, Theda (1979) *States and Social Revolutions: A comparative analysis of France, Russia, and China.* Cambridge, UK: Cambridge University Press.

Skocpol, Theda (1982) "What makes peasants revolutionary?" pp. 157–79 in *Power and Protest in the Countryside: Studies of rural unrest in Asia, Europe, and Latin America,* ed. Robert P. Weller and Scott E. Guggenheim. Durham, N.C.: Duke Press Policy Studies.

Skocpol, Theda (1992) *Protecting Soldiers and Mothers: The political origins of social policy in the United States.* Cambridge, Mass.: Harvard University Press.

Skocpol, Theda and Ellen Kay Trimberger (1986) "Revolutions: A structural analysis," pp. 59–65 in *Revolutions: Theoretical, comparative, and historical studies,* ed. Jack A. Goldstone. San Diego, Calif.: Harcourt Brace Jovanovich.

Smith, T. Lynn (1967) *Colombia: Social structure and the process of development.* Gainesville, Fla.: University of Florida Press.

Smith, T. Lynn (1970) "Some major impediments to agricultural development in Latin America," pp. 157–72 in *Sociology of Underdevelopment,* ed. Carle C. Zimmerman and Richard E. Dumors. Vancouver, BC: Copp Clark.

Smith, T. Lynn, Justo Díaz Rodríguez, and Luis Roberto García (1945) *Tabio: A study in rural social organization.* Washington, DC: US Department of Agriculture.

Solaún, Mauricio (2002) *U.S. Interventions in Latin America: "Plan Colombia."* Urbana-Champaign, Ill.: Program in Arms Control, Disarmament, and International Security, University of Illinois.

Solaún, Mauricio, William L. Flinn, and Sidney Kronus (1974) "Renovation of a squatter settlement in Colombia," *Land Economics*, 50(2): 152–62.

Somocurico, Monica (2000) "Colombia conference: FARC shows world how to stop coca production," July 13 [online] http://www.workers.org/ww/2000/colombia0713. php (accessed August 26, 2000).

Steinberg, Michael K. (2000) "Generals, guerrillas, drugs, and third world war-making," *Geographical Review*, 90(2): 260–7.

Stewart, Phil (2004) "Colombia wants more U.S. aid to fight drugs, rebels," April 1 [online] http://www.reuters.com/printerFriendlyPopup.jhtml?type=worldNews&storyID=4728628 (accessed April 2, 2004).

Stokes, Doug (2002) "Perception management and the US terror war in Colombia," June 7 [online] http://www.zmag.org/content/showarticle.cfm?SectionID=15&ItemID=1448 (accessed June 10, 2002).

Stokes, Doug (2003a) *Why the End of the Cold War Doesn't Matter: The US war of terror in Colombia.* Working paper. Bristol, UK: Review of International Studies, Bristol University.

Stokes, Doug (2003b) "Worthy and unworthy victims in Colombia," March 5 [online] (accessed http://www.zmag.org/content/showarticle.cfm?ItemID=3184 March 10, 2007).

Stokes, Doug (2005) *America's Other War: Terrorizing Colombia.* London: Zed.

Stratfor (2006) "Colombia: VAT plan meets opposition," September 26 [online] http://www.stratfor.com/products/premium/read_article.php?id=276330 (accessed September 26, 2006).

Summerlin, Sam (1972) *Latin America: The land of revolution.* New York: Franklin Watts.

Sumwalt, Martha Murray (1974) *Colombia: In pictures.* New York: Sterling.

Suri, Sanjay (2004) "Rights: governments fail to act over child soldiers," November 17 [online] http://allafrica.com/stories/200411170599.html (accessed November 17, 2004).

Sweig, Julia E. (2002) "What kind of war for Colombia?" *Foreign Affairs*, 81(5): 122–41.

Sweig, Julia E. and Michael M. McCarthy (2005) "Colombia: Staving off partial collapse," pp. 11–43 in *The Andes in Focus: Security, democracy and economic reform*, ed. Russell Crandall, Guadalupe Paz, and Riordan Roett. Boulder, Colo.: Lynne Rienner.

Szulc, Tad (1959) *Twilight of the Tyrants.* New York: Henry Holt.

Szulc, Tad (1964) *The Winds of Revolution: Latin America today – and tomorrow.* New York: Frederick A. Praeger.

Tamminen, Terry (2006) *Lives per Gallon: The true cost of our oil addiction.* Washington, DC: Island Press.

Tate, Winifred (2000) "Repeating past mistakes: Aiding counterinsurgency in Colombia," *NACLA Report of the Americas*, 34(2): 16–19.

Taussig, Michael T. (1980) *The Devil and Commodity Fetishism in South America.* Chapel Hill, N.C.: University of North Carolina Press.

Taussig, Michael (2004a) *Law in a Lawless Land: Diary of limpieza in Colombia* New York: New Press.

Taussig, Michael (2004b) *My Cocaine Museum.* Chicago, Ill.: University of Chicago Press.

Taylor, Francis X. (2001) *Ambassador Taylor on Terrorism in the Western Hemisphere Says that Latin America has lengthy experience with terrorism*, October 10. Washington, DC: US Department of State.

Teeple, Gary (2005) *The Riddle of Human Rights*. Aurora, ON: Garamond.

Telecom Paper (2008) "Colombia internet base grows over 20% in H2," March 19 [online] http://www.telecom.paper.nl/news/article.aspx?id=208026&nr (accessed March 19, 2008).

Thayer, Charles W (1963) *Guerrilla*. Winnipeg, MB: Signet.

Thompson, Matthew (2008) "The secret war of Colombia," August 17 [online] http://www.smh.com.au/articles/2008/08/16/1218307322835.html (accessed August 17, 2008).

Thoumi, Francisco E. (1995) *Political Economy and Illegal Drugs in Colombia*. Boulder, Colo.: Lynne Rienner.

Thoumi, Francisco E. (2005) "Why a country produces drugs and how this determines policy effectiveness: A general model and some applications to Colombia," pp. 153–81 in *Elusive Peace: International, national, and local dimensions of conflict in Colombia*, ed. Christina Rojas and Judy Meltzer. New York: Palgrave Macmillan.

Tilly, Charles (1978) *From Mobilization to Revolution*. Reading, Mass.: Addison-Wesley.

Times of India (2008) "US intelligence helped us strike rebel leader: Colombia," March 4 [online] http://timesofindia.indiatimes.com/World/Rest_of_World/US_intelligence_helped_us_stri ke_rebel_leader_Colombia/articleshow/2835513.cms (accessed March 4, 2008).

Torres, Mario and Natasha Torres (2005) "Colombian nightmares," July 16 [online] http://www.politicalaffairs.net/article/articleview/1496/1/108/ (accessed March 10, 2007).

Trapeznikov, S. P. (1981a) *Leninism and the Agrarian and Peasant Question, Vol. I.* Moscow: Progress.

Trapeznikov, S. P. (1981b) *Leninism and the Agrarian and Peasant Question, Vol. II.* Moscow: Progress.

Trimberger, Ellen Kay (1978) *Revolution from Above: Military bureaucrats and development in Japan, Turkey, Egypt, and Peru*. New Brunswick, NJ: Transaction.

Tucker, Robert (1969) *The Marxian Revolutionary Idea*. New York: W.W. Norton.

Tucker, Robert (1978) "After the revolution: Marx debates Bakunin," pp. 542–8 in *The Marx–Engels Reader*. New York: W. W. Norton.

Ungerman, Gerard and Audrey Brohy (2003) *Plan Colombia: Cashing-in on the drug war failure*. Documentary film (Free-Will Productions).

United Nations (2005) *Report of the High Commissioner for Human Rights on the Situation of Human Rights in Colombia*. Bogotá/New York: United Nations.

United Nations Development Programme (UNDP) (2003) *El Conflicto – Callejón con Salida: Informe nacional de desarrollo humano para Colombia, 2003*. Bogotá: UNDP.

UNDP (2004) "Tale of two towns in Colombia: Bloody political conflict yields to joint development," December [online] http://www.undp.org/dpa/choices/2004/dec/colombia.html (accessed November 6, 2005).

United Nations News Centre (2005) "Chief UN advisor on Colombia to conclude term in April," January 24 [online] http://www.un.org/apps/news/printnews.asp?nid=13117 (accessed January 25, 2005).

United Nations Office on Drugs and Crimes (UNODC) (2005) *Colombia: Coca cultivation survey*. Bogotá: UNODC.

UNODC (2008) *Coca Cultivation in the Andean Region: A survey of Bolivia, Colombia and Peru*. Bogotá: UNODC.

United Press International (2005) "Kill priests, FARC leader says," September 6 [online] http://www.wpherald.com/storyview.php?StoryID=20050906-042843-6181r (accessed September 18, 2005).

US Department of State (1964) *Outgoing Telegram, May 1 1964*. Bogotá: US Embassy.

US Department of State (2000) "Text: U.S. drug policy director McCaffrey speaks on Colombia," November 28 [online] http://usinfo.org/usia/usinfo.state.gov/topical/global/drugs/00112804.htm (accessed July 3, 2002).

US Department of State (2001) *Ambassador Taylor on Terrorism in the Western Hemisphere.* October 10 [online] http://ottawa.usembassy.gov/content/textonly.asp?section=issues&subsection1=terrorism&document=terrorism_wha_101001 (accessed January 4, 2004).

US Department of State (2003) *Coca Cultivation in Colombia, 2002.* Washington, DC: Department of State.

US Embassy of Colombia (2003) "Democratic security and defense Policy" [online] http://www.colombiaemb.org/opencms/opencms/defense/ (accessed November 6, 2005_.

US Joint Chiefs of Staff (1964) *Confidential Action Report, April 1964.* Bogotá/Washington, DC: United States Embassy.

Uribe Velez, Álvaro and Luis Guillermo Plata Páez (2008) "Colombia needs 'to reelect policies, not people.'" Speech to the Americas Society and the Council of the Americas, September 24, 2008.

Urrego, Miguel Angel (2003) "Social and popular movements in a time of cholera, 1977–1999," pp. 171–8 in *Violence in Colombia 1990–2000: Waging war and negotiating peace,* ed. Charles W. Bergquist, Ricardo Peñaranda, and Gonzalo Sánchez G. Wilmington, Del.: Scholarly Resources.

Urrutia, Miguel (1969) *The Development of the Colombian Labour Movement.* London: Yale University Press.

Valenzuela, Pedro (2002) *Conflict Analysis: Colombia, Bolivia, and the Andean region.* Uppsala: Swedish International Development Cooperation Agency (SIDA)/Department of Peace and Conflict Research, Uppsala University.

Valetta, Jhony (2004) "Wayuu Indians go to war against Colombian government," May 27 [online] http://www.anncol.org/uk/site/doc.php?id=146 (accessed February 11, 2005).

Van Dongen, Rachel (2004) "A coed's path from pol-sci major to leftist guerrilla," February 10 [online] http://www.csmonitor.com/2004/0210/p01s02-woam.html (accessed February 15, 2004).

Vanden, Harry E. and Gary Prevost (2002) *The Politics of Latin America: The power game.* New York: Oxford University Press.

Vanden, Harry E. and Gary Prevost (2006) *The Politics of Latin America: The power game,* 2nd edn. New York: Oxford University Press.

Vega, Luis Mercier (1969) *Guerrillas in Latin America: The technique of counter-strike.* New York: Frederick A. Praeger.

Veltmeyer, Henry (1999) *The Labyrinth of Latin American Development.* New Delhi: APH.

Veltmeyer, Henry (2001) "Decentralization and local development," pp. 46–66 in *Transcending Neoliberalism: Community-based development in Latin America,* ed. Henry Veltmeyer and Anthony O' Malley. Bloomfield, Conn.: Kumarian.

Veltmeyer, Henry (2005) "Development and globalization as imperialism," *Canadian Journal of Development Studies,* 26(1): 89–106.

Veltmeyer, Henry and James Petras (2002) "The social dynamics of Brazil's Rural Landless Workers' Movement: Ten hypotheses on successful leadership," *Canadian Review of Sociology and Anthropology,* 39(1): 79–96.

Vertinsky, Ilan, Donald Geffner, and Sylvia Fox (1972) "A perspective on land reform law in Colombia: Choice of strategy for change," *Land Economics,* 48)(4): 367–76.

Vieira, Constanza (2004a) "US Increases Colombia involvement," June 30 [online] http://www.antiwar.com/ips/vieira.php?articleid=2915 (accessed June 30, 2004)

Vieira, Constanza (2004b) "Colombia: Decades of war over land," July 4 [online] http://www.landaction.org/display.php?article=228 (accessed October 23, 2006).

Vieira, Constanza (2006a) "Colombia: Conflict to heat up ahead of elections, says analyst," January 16 [online] http://ipsnews.net/print.asp?idnews=31716 (accessed March 15, 2006).

Vieira, Constanza (2006b) "Colombia: Latest news on the FARC," April 18 [online] http://www.ipsnews.org/news.asp?idnews=32922 (accessed April 19, 2006).

Vieira, Constanza (2006c) "Colombia: Bombs explode in government's face," September 18 [online] http://www.ipsnews.net/news.asp?idnews=34763 (accessed September 19, 2006).

Vieira, Constanza (2008a) "Rights-Colombia: Workers of the world unite – in anti-paramilitary vigil," February 21 [online] http://ipsnews.net/news.asp?idnews=41298 (accessed February 29, 2008).

Vieira, Constanza (2008b) "Colombia: Displaced to march against 'senseless war,'" February 28 [online] http://www.ipsnews.net/news.asp?idnews=41390 (accessed February 28, 2008).

Vieira, Constanza (2008c) "Colombia: "Mark him on the ballot – the one wearing glasses"," May 8 [online] http://www.ipsnews.net/news.asp?idnews=42290 (accessed May 9, 2008).

Vieira, Constanza (2008d) "Colombia: Extradition of paramilitary chiefs – a blow to truth," May 13 [online] http://www.ipsnews.net/news.asp?idnews=42356 (accessed May 14, 2008).

Vieira, Constanza (2008e) "Colombia: Interpol notes improper initial handling of FARC laptops," May 15 [online] http://www.ipsnews.net/news.asp?idnews=42391 (accessed May 26, 2008).

Vieira, Constanza (2009a) "Colombia: Paramilitary chief says he helped finance Uribe's campaign," April 22 [online] http://www.ipsnews.net/news.asp?idnews=46600 (accessed April 24, 2009).

Vieira, Constanza (2009b) "Colombia: Awá Indians hemmed in by war," February 27 [online] http://www.ipsnews.net/news.asp?idnews=45921 (accessed February 28, 2009).

Vieira, Gilberto (1963) "Growth of militarism in Colombia and the line of the Communist Party," World Marxist Review, 6(4): 17–19.

Vieira, Gilberto (1970) "Lenin, Greatest revolutionary strategist of all time," World Marxist Review, 13(5): 22.

Vilas, Carlos M. (2003) "Between market democracies and capitalist globalization: Is there any prospect for social revolution in Latin America?" pp. 95–106 in The Future of Revolutions: Rethinking radical change in the age of globalization, ed. John Foran. London: Zed.

Villalón, Carlos (2004a) "Cocaine country," National Geographic, 206(1): 34–55.

Villalón, Carlos (2004b) Cocaine Country. Documentary film (National Geographic).

Villamizar, Rodrigo (2003) "The good, the bad, the ugly, and the Colombian peace plan," Crime, Law and Social Change, 40(1): 25–31.

Vivanco, Jose Miguel and Maria McFarland Sánchez-Moreno (2006) "Rosy picture belies stark problems," June 14 [online] http://www.miami.com/mld/miamiherald/news/opinion/14812963.htm (accessed June 14, 2006).

Wagley, Charles (1964) "The peasant," pp. 21–48 in Continuity and Change in Latin America, ed. John J. Johnson. Stanford, Calif.: Stanford University Press.

Walker III, William O. (2001) "A reprise for 'nation building': Low intensity conflict spreads to the Andes," NACLA Report on the Americas, 35(1): 23–8.

Wallerstein, Immanuel (1984) "The present state of the debate on world inequality," pp. 119–32 in The Gap between Rich and Poor: Contending perspectives on the political economy of development, ed. Mitchell A. Seligson. Boulder, Colo.: Westview.

Walton, John (1984) *Reluctant Rebels: Comparative studies of revolution and under-development*. New York: Colombia University Press.

Walzer, Michael (2002) *The Company of Critics: Social criticism and political commitment in twentieth century*. New York: Basic Books.

Warren, Kay B. and Jean E. Jackson (2002) *Indigenous Movements, Self-Representation, and the State in Latin America*. Austin, Tex.: University of Texas Press.

Washington Office on Latin America (WOLA) (1989) *Colombia Besieged: Political violence and state responsibility*. Washington, DC: WOLA.

WOLA (2002) "Colombian government's controversial security measures," September 24 [online] http://www.wola.org/index.php?option=com_content&task=viewp&id= 526&Itemid=8 (accessed March 25, 2008).

Washington Post (2004) "40 killed in rebel assault on Colombian village," *Washington Post*, January 1. p. A26.

Weaver, Frederick Stirton (1980) *Class, State, and Industrial Structure: The historical process of South American industrial growth*. Westport, Conn.: Greenwood.

Webb, Jason (2004) "Warlords address Colombia Congress amid protests," [online] July 28 http://www.reuters.com/newsArticle.jhtml?type=worldNews&storyID=5803 111 (accessed July 28, 2004).

Webb-Vidal, Andy (2005) "Farc poised for new battle in long war," April 11 [online] http://news.ft.com/cms/s/634286f6-aa25-11d9-aa38-00000e2511c8.html (accessed April 11, 2005).

Weekly News Update on the Americas (2004a) "Colombia: Another paramilitary massacre," Issue 730, January 25. New York: Nicaragua Solidarity Network of Greater New York.

Weekly News Update on the Americas (2004b) "Colombia: Women's group attacked," Issue 731, February 1. New York: Nicaragua Solidarity Network of Greater New York.

Weekly News Update on the Americas (2004c) "Massacre near Ecuador border," Issue 772, November 14. New York: Nicaragua Solidarity Network of Greater New York.

Weekly News Update on the Americas (2005a) "Colombia: 28 massacred in Putu-mayo," Issue 811, August 14. New York: Nicaragua Solidarity Network of Greater New York.

Weekly News Update on the Americas (2005b) "Colombia: More attacks on indig-enous," Issue 811, August 14. New York: Nicaragua Solidarity Network of Greater New York.

Weekly News Update on the Americas (2007) "Colombia: Bush visit protested," Issue 890, March 11. New York: Nicaragua Solidarity Network of Greater New York.

Weil, Thomas E., Jan Kippers Black, Kenneth W. Martindale, David S. McMorris, Fred-erick P. Munson, and Kathryn E. Parachini (1970) *Area Handbook for Colombia*. Washington, DC: Foreign Area Studies.

Weinberg, Bill (2008a) "Uribe exploits mobilization against FARC," February 7 [online] http://www.ww4report.com/node/5055 (accessed February 7, 2008).

Weinberg, Bill (2008b) "Colombians march against state, paramilitary violence," March 6 [online] http://www.ww4report.com/node/5215 (accessed March 6, 2008).

Weinberg, Bill (2008c) "Colombia: FARC blow up oil pipeline," May 3 [online] http://ww4report.com/node/5438 (accessed May 5, 2008).

Weinstein, Jeremy M. (2007) *Inside Rebellion: The politics of insurgent violence*. London: Cambridge University Press.

Weymouth, Lally (2000) "Battling 'the bad guys': Colombia's president vs. drug lords, leftist rebels and right-wing paramilitaries," February 14 [online] http://www.keep-media.com/pubs/Newsweek/2000/02/14/317646?extID=10026 (accessed March 31, 2006).

White House (1986) *National Security Decision Directive Number 221: Narcotics and national security*. Washington, DC: Department of State.

Whiteford, Michael B. (1976) *The Forgotten Ones: Colombian countrymen in an urban setting*. Gainesville, Fla.: University Presses of Florida.

Wickham-Crowley, Timothy P. (1990) "Terror and guerrilla warfare in Latin America, 1956–1970," *Comparative Studies in Society and History*, 32(2): 201–37.

Wickham-Crowley, Timothy P. (1991) *Exploring Revolution: Essays on Latin America insurgency and revolutionary theory*. New York: M.E. Sharpe.

Wickham-Crowley, Timothy P. (1992) *Guerrillas and Revolution in Latin America: A comparative study of insurgents and regimes since 1956*. Princeton, N.J.: Princeton University Press.

Wickham-Crowley, Timothy P. (1994) "Elites, elite settlements, and revolutionary movements in Latin America, 1950–1980," *Social Science History*, 18(4): 543–74.

Wickham-Crowley, Timothy P. (1997) "Structural theories of revolutions," pp. 38–72 in *Theorizing Revolutions*, ed. John Foran. New York: Routledge.

Wilkinson, Paul (1971) *Social Movement*. London: Macmillan.

Williams, Mark Eric (2005) "U.S. policy in the Andes: Commitments and commitment traps," pp. 151–72 in *The Andes in Focus: Security, democracy & economic reform*, ed. Russell Crandall, Guadalupe Paz, and Riordan Roett. Boulder, Colo.: Lynne Rienner.

Williamson, Owen (2008) "Murder in the Andes," March 30 [online] http://www.politicalaffairs.net/article/articleview/6671/1/324/(accessed March 30, 2008).

Williamson, Robert C. (1965) "Toward a theory of political violence: The case of rural Colombia," *The Western Political Quarterly*, 18(1): 35–44.

Wilson, Scott (2003) "Colombia's rebel zone: World apart," *Washington Post Foreign Service*, October 18, p. A1.

Wilson, Suzanne and Leah A. Carroll (2007) "The Colombian contradiction: Lessons drawn from guerrilla experiments and demobilization and electoralism," pp. 81–106 in *From Revolutionary Movements to Political Parties: Cases from Latin America and Africa*, ed. Kalowatie Deonandan, David Close, and Gary Prevost. New York: Palgrave Macmillan.

Wingerter, Eric (2008) "Colombia to Chavez: See you in The Hague," March 13 [online] http://www.alternet.org/audits/79210/?page=2 (accessed March 13, 2008).

Wood, Ellen Meiksins (2003) *Empire of Capital*. London: Verso.

Wood, William (2005) *Ambassador William B. Wood's Remarks before the Prosecutor General's Course on Human Rights and International Humanitarian Law*. Delivered December 16 at the Hotel Radison, Bogotá. Bogotá: United States Embassy.

World Bank (1972) *Economic Growth of Colombia: Problems & prospects*. Washington, DC: World Bank Economic Report.

World Bank (2002) *Colombia Poverty Report: Volume 1*. Bogotá/Washington, DC: Colombia Country Management Unit/PREM Sector Management Unit Latin American and the Caribbean Region, World Bank.

World Resources Institute (2003) *Colombia: Economic indicators*. Washington, DC: World Resources Institute, Earth Trends Country Profiles.

Wynter, Coral and Jim McIlroy (2006) "Colombia: Presidential election result a 'huge fraud,'" July 5 [online] http://www.greenleft.org.au/back/2006/674/674p18.htm (accessed July 3, 2006).

Xinhua (2006) "Colombia says FARC rebels operating in Bolivia, Paraguay," June 23 [online] http://english.people.com.cn/200606/23/eng20060623_276640.html (accessed June 23, 2006).

Xinhua (2007) "Colombia says to watch students at risk of rebel recruitment," December 11 [online] http://news.xinhuanet.com/english/2007-12/12/content_7234437.htm (accessed December 12, 2007).

Xinhua (2008a) "Colombian police reject any possible US role in rebel raid," March

3 [online] http://news.xinhuanet.com/english/2008-03/04/content_7711127.htm (accessed March 4, 2008).

Xinhua (2008b) "Argentina to lodge complaint over Colombia trespass to OAS," March 3 [online] http://news.xinhuanet.com/english/2008-03/04/content_7712939. htm (accessed March 4, 2008).

Xinhua (2008c) "Brazil favors OAS committee to investigate Ecuador–Colombia incident," March 3 [online] http://news.xinhuanet.com/english/2008-03/04/content_ 7713588.htm (accessed March 4, 2008).

Xinhua (2008d) "Ecuador: Colombia used US weapons in attack on FARC camp," March 7 [online] http://news.xinhuanet.com/english/2008-03/07/content_7736713. htm (accessed March 7, 2008).

Young Pelton, Robert (2002) *The Worlds Most Dangerous Places: Colombia*. Documentary film (Discovery Communications),

Zamosc, Leon (1986) *Agrarian Question and the Peasant Movement in Colombia: Struggles of the National Peasant Association, 1967–81*. Oxford, UK: Cambridge University Press.

Zuluaga Nieto, Jaime (2007) "U.S. security policies and United States–Colombia relations," *Latin American Perspectives*, 34(1): 112–19.

INDEX

www.ingramcontent.com/pod-product-compliance
Lightning Source LLC
Chambersburg PA
CBHW022135020426
42334CB00015B/901